T0353989

How the West was Won and Lost

Athenian Democracy to the BRICS: 5th Century BCE to 2016

By

Rocky M. Mirza, Ph.D.

Order this book online at www.trafford.com
or email orders@trafford.com

Most Trafford titles are also available at major online book retailers.

Print information available on the last page.

ISBN: 978-1-4907-7192-2 (sc)
ISBN: 978-1-4907-7194-6 (hc)
ISBN: 978-1-4907-7193-9 (e)

Library of Congress Control Number: 2016904892

Trafford rev. 04/13/2016

www.trafford.com

North America & international
toll-free: 1 888 232 4444 (USA & Canada)
fax: 812 355 4082

ACKNOWLEDGMENTS

I wish to thank my friend and colleague Dr. Peter Dunnett for proofreading the manuscript and suggesting minor changes. I wish to thank my wife, Penny Mirza, for her unwavering support of the ideas I have expressed in this book.

This book is dedicated to the following people I admire:
Vladimir Putin
Julian Assange
Hugo Chavez
Edward Snowden
Mahmood Ahmadinejad
Chelsea (Bradley) Manning
Daniel Ellsberg

CONTENTS

INTRODUCTION

This book is the last of my trilogy on the West. No one is happier than myself to put this massive effort behind me. The inspiration for the first book was the re-election of George W. Bush in 2004. Like so many at the time, I foolishly thought of him as the worst American president ever. No American president had ever been called a *warmonger* publicly, and in the media, before. He was publicly vilified for invading Iraq. What I did not know at the time was that every American president was a dedicated warmonger. In many countries, the commander in chief of the armed forces is not a professional soldier. But the United States has a long history, beginning with their first president, George Washington, to promote their highest-ranking general to the position of commander in chief. That person becomes president by default more than by democratic choice. That is the origin of American presidents being dedicated to warmongering. The job of a professional soldier is to fight in wars. As the highest-ranking professional soldier, the commander in chief ensures continuing wars to occupy him and his men and women. It's his job and his duty. President George W. Bush was no aberration. He was the norm. The only difference was that by the time he was elected to office, he did not have to be a professional soldier. But he was still duty bound by the American Constitution and the history of the United States as an independent country to start sufficient wars to feed the addiction of his people to warmongering. We have explained this American obsession with warmongering in much detail in all three books.

When I began this project in 2004, I had very little idea as to what I would say. But I learned a great deal about the United States and the West and history. As those ideas ballooned, I realized that I could not fit all of them in a single book. Two of the most important lessons I learned are that the United States has never been a force for good in the world and that the history of the world has been one of empires, wars, and invasions. That has been the norm since the beginning of time. The American Empire is simply the latest of a long list of empires that have invaded and killed with absolutely no logical justification. All justifications have been fabricated by lies and propaganda. A gullible public and a subservient media have aided the invaders, generals, rulers, killers, and ruthless warmongers. It matters little whether the imperial power was democratic, republican, or monarchy. They have all followed the path of waging wars while preaching peace. Nothing had changed by 2016. If anything, warmongering and military invasions have increased. The sophistication of deadly weapons used has improved immensely.

In surveying history for this long period between the fifth century BCE and the present, I have learned that all of the following facts are constants:

1. People have deep religious beliefs not grounded in reality.
2. People preach peace but use the most flimsy of excuses to wage incessant wars.
3. People do not like being colonized but find ridiculous excuses to colonize others.
4. There are no absolutes in customs, traditions, beliefs, justice, or accepted wisdoms. They change with time. But at every point in time each society declares their customs, traditions, beliefs, justice, and accepted wisdom to be far **superior** to all others. Theirs are "civilized" and all others are "barbaric." The fact that in time what is deemed barbaric becomes civilized has absolutely no effect on current norms. We never learn from history.
5. There has never been an example in history where the dominant empire has relinquished power without being defeated in battle. The most recent example was that of the British Empire waging two global wars against Germany rather than relinquishing its hegemony peacefully. If the American Empire were to cede its current dominance peacefully, it would be a historical first.

Prior to my conversion to the views I have expressed in these books, I was full of hope for humanity. Such optimism was boosted by candidate Barack Obama during the American presidential elections in 2007. Unfortunately, President Obama delivered exactly the opposite of what he promised. The world today is far worse than it was during the presidencies of George W. Bush. America's deceitful War on Terror has unleashed terror in a steadily increasing number of countries across the globe, the latest country being Turkey. In like manner, America's long War on Drugs has brought crime and mayhem to many cities in Mexico while incarcerating ever larger numbers of poor black males at home. The "unfree" Western media is so afraid to say boo that, for example, it dares not refer to the newly created Islamic State without prefacing it with "so called." Until very recently, reporters for CNN, BBC, or CBC dared not refer to China without saying **Communist** China. Since the United States has become dependent on China to fund its addiction to warmongering, it has since given permission to the so-called free Western media to soften its name-calling by saying **mainland** China. This is a subtle reminder that for many years the American Empire portrayed its *uncolony* of Taiwan as the true *Republic of China.* Western reporters are still waiting for permission from the American Empire to use the correct name for China, which is the *People's Republic of China.* Yet we are told that it's the governments of China and North Korea that use propaganda to control its people, not the governments of the United States, Britain, and Canada. Have you ever heard the Chinese or North Korean media refer to the United States as **capitalist** America or Britain as **capitalist** Britain or Canada as **capitalist** Canada? Have you ever heard the Chinese or North Korean media use the term **mainland** America to distinguish the United States from its island *uncolony* of Hawaii? Or say **mainland** Britain to distinguish Britain from the Isle of Wight? Or say **mainland** Canada to distinguish Canada from Vancouver Island? Judge for yourself which side has the more sophisticated state propaganda machine?

It's a real shame that the one country capable of leading the world out of its current miserable state of wars, injustice, poverty, extreme income and wealth inequalities, creation of millions of refugees, obesity, and planetary degradation caused by excessive Western consumption of junk food, electronic junk, and every other form of junk, **the United States,** is so totally leaderless. The United States appointed itself as the "leader of the free world," only to lead the world down the path of self-destruction, warmongering, internal and external conflicts settled with guns, massive use of propaganda, lies, and deceit. It then uses its enormous military, financial, and economic powers to force all others to follow this destructive path. How can we ever hope for change if the United States does not lead that change or at least stop its bullying of others who want to lead that change?

Western democracies thrive on vote buying; severely restricted choice by the electorate, such as two or three parties with no substantive difference in platforms; misinformation; religious dogma; dumbed-down leadership; sheep-like following; a subservient media and education system; negative criticisms of other political systems; a culture of fearmongering and national superiority; great reluctance to think outside the box; severe punishments of whistleblowers, such as Julian Assange, Edward Snowden, and Bradley Manning; lies about human rights abuses in countries like China, which never stole the lands of the First Nations or enslaved millions of Africans like the United States, Canada, and Australia; economic embargoes to punish the people of Cuba, North Korea, and Iran; military destruction of countries such as Afghanistan, Iraq, Libya, Syria, and Yemen; allowing a country like Israel to steal the Palestinian lands and commit war crimes by bombing the Palestinians; and generally portraying evil as good such as the nuking of Hiroshima and Nagasaki.

On December 4, 2015, I listened to an American couple interviewed by CNN, responding to the latest "terrorist" shooting on December 2, 2015, in San Bernardino, California. Their response genuinely implied that neither of them truly ever expected this to happen in their city. This is a perfect example of the great disconnect between the majority of Americans and the incessant warmongering of their government. The United States had, by December 4, 2015, been dropping megaton bombs for fourteen long years on millions of people in Afghanistan, Pakistan, Iraq, Libya, Yemen, Syria, and elsewhere. These "civilized" bombs have killed or wounded over a million people, destroyed the homes and livelihoods of many millions, and created over 60 million refugees. Yet the majority of Americans expect no retaliation by the families and friends of the people bombed, killed, wounded, and lives destroyed. It's no different in Britain, France, or Canada. This is one of the reasons why these Western governments get away with mass murder and genocide and why no Western leader has any incentive to reverse course. Every one of these countless tragedies is met with a Western response, which guarantees further and worse tragedies. Not a single Western leader has even suggested a reversal of this disastrous foreign policy.

Just like the French response to the "terrorist" attack of November 13, 2015, in Paris, the response by the West is always more aggression, more warmongering, more invasions, more killing of innocent women and children, more refugees, more murder and mayhem, more destruction of homes and livelihoods, more poverty and hunger, more diseases and malnutrition, more inhumanity.

The Western media also indicates its disconnect with reality, but of a different kind. Whenever these shootings occur, the media never ever suggest that the friends or families of the millions bombed, killed, and maimed by the West have even a tiny legitimate grievance against such senseless and evil killings and wanton destruction. Instead they portray the shooters as insane or radicalized or jihadists or religious fanatics. In this way the Western media contributes to the ever-increasing senseless warmongering by Western leaders.

On December 4, 2015, I also listened to a BBC interview of Britain's ex–prime minister Tony Blair. A decade after he, more than any other Western leader, other than George W. Bush, should be held responsible for the genocide the West committed in Iraq, he was instead being interviewed about the "terrorist" attacks in California and Paris, as if he was still a credible leader, rather than the "mad-dog Englishman" he is. More idiotic was the BBC reporter calmly listening to his silly notion that the West now had a better opportunity to defeat ISIS than he had to defeat Iraq because regional players were now more willing to join the Western coalition than in 2003. He pontificated that in 2003 the regional leaders saw the invasion of Iraq as a Western problem but today they have to deal with terrorism as well. As usual, the lame BBC reporter failed to point out to him that it was his invasion of Iraq that singlehandedly brought terrorism to the entire Middle East.

The West is confused by its own rhetoric, pretend ideals and propaganda. It chastises a Donald Trump for saying what is of its essence and innate nature. And that is why I came to the conclusion that a President Obama is far more dangerous that a President George W. Bush. In like manner, a President Hilary Clinton will be far more dangerous than a President Donald Trump. Democratic presidents get a free ride for warmongering and military invasions because the left will excuse them by pointing out that Republicans are worse. Far from criticizing their warmongering and invasions, Republicans will goad them on to do even more. But Republican warmongers will be called out by the left. This will restrain them somewhat. At the end of the day it's never about peace but more or less warmongering. Democrats will preach less warmongering but end up doing more because there is no one to constrain them. Republicans will preach more warmongering but end up doing less because the left will be more vocal in their protests. Under the Western democratic system there is very little choice between the two parties. Pretending that there is a choice makes Western democracies worse than one-party states like China. A genuine choice would result in many parties and the emergence of leaders. Those selected to "lead" the two parties in Western democracies are followers not leaders. They are told by their handlers what to say and do based on what the system will tolerate. Talk show hosts in the United States have more leadership opportunities than presidents. That is one reason why Donald Trump resonated with many American voters.

Many smart, intelligent, brave, and good people have tried and sacrificed to change the world from its long history of warmongering, imperialism, injustices and stupidity. All have failed. I do not expect to succeed where so many have failed. But think how much worse the world would be if no one tried. I never expected to continue what I began in 2004 to present day 2016. But here I am repeating what so many do not want to hear as controversial, at best, or want to denounce, as treasonous, at worst. I console myself with the notion that writing only what is controversial precisely because it questions accepted wisdom justifies the free giving of my scarce and valuable time. Any other writing would be a total waste of my valuable and limited time on this planet.

I will throw modesty to the winds and tell you that I have a gift. When I tell you what it is it will not seem like much. The people we have called great, such as Alexander the Great, have typically been warmongers. That should never be a valued characteristic of any civilized race. Likewise, those we admire as prophets, such as Jesus Christ, excel at fiction rather than fact. Again, we should never celebrate fiction over fact. My gift is the innate ability to think objectively and logically. As I said, you may not think much of this because you do not know that the vast majority of the human race is incapable of either objective or logical thinking. That is why religious beliefs are so dominant in their lives and why they can so easily be swayed by propaganda. If humanity is to evolve we must embrace the Age of Reason.

One of the most challenging academic disciplines is *Economics.* It's challenging for many precisely because it requires objective and rigorously logical analyses. My successes in this challenging discipline is sufficient proof to me that I have this very special gift. It would be a shame to not use this gift to benefit humanity.

CHAPTER 1

The Birth of the Christian West: Greece, Rome, and Christianity: 332 BCE to 635 CE

Religion has been and continues to be the most enduring and powerful propaganda tool used by conquerors, leaders, prophets, wise men, scoundrels, countries, and empires to stifle logical and rational dissent and discussion. In this regard Islam and Christianity are no different from all religions. All based on irrational beliefs and dedication to some seen or unseen holy Supreme Being or beings, religion has been used to suppress the questioning of dictatorial rule, imperial subjugation, inhumane sacrifices, and abuses as well as the removal of freedom of speech, individual rights, true democracy, and objective discourse. Beliefs are personal and subjective. They are based on faith and Dogma not facts and logic. They have no place in the governance of a civilized society and must be relegated to what is private and personal.

Since our goal is to explain the demise of what has been erroneously called Western "civilization," we need to explain the birth and rebirth of that civilization. This chapter addresses the birth. In the next chapter I will address the rebirth that I am suggesting as coinciding with the rise of Portugal and Spain in the fifteenth century, following the decline of the "Muslim Empire." Prior to the birth of the Greek Empire, the world was dominated by the East. What we have foolishly call civilization began over six thousand years ago in Mesopotamia in the Near East (today's Middle East) which is also called the *Fertile Crescent* because fertile land fed by the waters of great rivers such as the Tigris, Nile and Euphrates, was essential to feed an increasing population. The countries we know today as Iraq, Iran, Turkey, Palestine and Syria were all part of this *Fertile Crescent.* Next in time came the civilizations of Egypt, India and China. These are all countries very east of the Western European empires of Portugal, Spain, Holland, France, Britain and Germany, where the rebirth of our current Western civilization began. It would be more appropriate to refer to these countries as "imperialist" rather than "civilized." The notion that you must be an empire to be civilized is another Western distortion of language. Imperialism has been the worst form of human exploitation. It is **barbaric** not civilized. The people labeled as *barbarians* have typically been people using primitive weaponry to defend their freedoms against the barbaric imperialists. Historians have distorted logic and Western imperialists have used massive propaganda to capitalize on that distortion of logic.

The current Western civilization is claimed to have its roots in ancient Greece, the supposed birthplace of democracy. In this regard the current East/West conflict between Muslims and Christians can be said to originate with the wars between the Greek city states and the Persian Empire even though neither Christianity nor Islam had yet been born. This pre-Christian/Islamic origin can be justified by the fact that the Persian Empire converted to Islam while the Greeks converted to Christianity. As with all empires, religion played a central role in the Greek and Persian empires. Initially, it was the Persian Empire that attempted to expand westward into Europe by conquering the Greek city states. King Cyrus the Great of Persia founded an empire during the sixth century BCE that included all of the Middle East and more. But in the end it was the Greeks under Alexander the Great that expanded eastward into the Middle East. The Greek/Macedonian Empire led by Alexander the Great conquered the Near East in 332 BCE. This would be an appropriate date to identify the beginning of the continuing invasions of the Middle East by the West to colonize the region. In this chapter we trace the East/West conflict up to the fall of the Western Roman Empire and prior to the birth of the Muslim Empire in 635.

The history of Ancient Greece is intimately tied to the history of the Persian Empire, the Greco-Persian wars and the ultimate conquest of the Persian Empire by Alexander the Great. Ancient Greece was made up of several hundred "city states" among which the dominant "city states" were Athens, Sparta, Thebes and Corinth. During the sixth century BCE there was an explosion of economic development, population, trade, culture, literature, philosophy, art, science, **slavery, piracy,** and **wars,** within the geographical region governed by the Greek "city states." These growth indices are the hallmarks used by the West to measure the rise of a civilization. The period has therefore been identified as the beginning of the classical era of Greek civilization. Greek language and culture penetrated the Middle Eastern countries mixing Greek with Persian and Arab cultures, traditions, religion, governance and language. It was truly a two-way exchange of Western and Eastern ideas. The world experienced three centuries of "Hellenization" during and immediately following the conquests of Alexander the Great. In many ways the Middle East became very "Western." But the later Western civilization dominated by Western Europe and the United States was determined to stigmatize the Middle East as "Eastern" since Western was now civilized and **Christian** while Eastern was now barbaric and **Muslim.**

More importantly, the "Hellenization" of the world by Alexander and his successors, imperialistic and militaristic as it was, incorporated and glorified as much of what was sacred to Easterners, as it enforced on its conquered subjects what was Western and Greek. By contrast the Western Europeans and Americans totally wiped out First Nations and Aboriginal cultures and civilizations and engaged in massive ethnic cleansing. It condemned the **red** race to that of the permanent "Naked Savage" and the **black** race to temporary slavery and permanent racial inferiority. It preached "democracy" while planting and supporting the most brutal and vicious dictators to ensure that their colonies would not rebel against their imperial rule. It raped the resources of its worldwide colonies to enrich a tiny **white** aristocratic class and a growing **white** middle class in the imperial centers. It developed the most sophisticated weapons of mass destruction, WMDs, to conquer, bully, threaten, kill and maim.

The Greek invasion of the Middle East was followed by the Roman invasion. The Roman Empire dominated the world after Rome's defeat of Carthage in 211 BCE. Western writers attribute the origin of Western civilization both to the Greek and Roman empires. While Greece had a greater influence on the Western European empires the Roman Empire had a greater influence on the American Empire. The American notion that a republic has a more civilized governing structure than monarchy came from the Roman Republic. But the Roman Empire was ruled by democrats as well as dictators. We will highlight the fact that what the West copied from both Greece and Rome was **aristocracy, slavery,**

imperialism, piracy, religion, and warmongering. These characteristics of a nation are **barbaric** not civilized.

After the fall of the Western Roman Empire the West sent the Christian Crusades beginning in 1096. The Crusades were followed by incursions into the region by the Western European empires of Italy, France, Britain and Germany. Finally, the American Empire invaded the region beginning in 1801, with its invasion of Libya, and has continued the invasion to this day. In 1801, the excuse for the American invasion of Libya was to stamp out *piracy.* In 2011 the excuse for the American invasion of Libya was that *Muammar Gaddafi* was "killing his own people." This latest Western bastardization of logic implies that it's perfectly okay to kill people as long as it's not "your own people." It also implies that during the American Civil War the American government only killed *Martians,* never their own people. It's also perfectly okay for the West to use the most sophisticated weapons and unmanned drones to kill defenseless people in Vietnam, Iraq and Afghanistan but not for a leader like Gadhafi to use superior weapons against rebels armed and brainwashed by the West.

The current conflict between Israel and the Palestinians is a small part of the larger conflict between Western imperialism and the defense of the Middle East against Western colonization. The West has shown a stubborn and ruthless determination to use wars, religion, propaganda and superior weaponry to conquer and colonize the Middle East and surrounding areas such as North Africa, the Mediterranean and Central Asia. These are the countries where the majority of Muslims live. Western imperialism in every part of the globe has been fully supported by the Christian church. It is therefore no surprise that Western imperialism in the Middle East and the surrounding region is also a religious conflict between Christianity and Islam.

The Greek Invasion and Conquest of the Middle East by Alexander the Great Marks the Beginning of Western Imperialism in the Region

What is referred to as civilization gradually spread westward from the Near East through Asia Minor to the Aegean Sea, the island of

Crete, the mainland of Greece and the lands bordering the waters of the Mediterranean Sea. By the sixth century BCE the Near East was conquered by the Persian Empire, the largest empire to that point in time. As the Persian Empire expanded westward from Asia Minor it colonized the lands west of the Near East as far as many of the city states of Greece. The Greek city states or *poleis* emerged in the tenth century BCE when economic growth led to the conversion of Greek villages into semi-independent urban states. A *polis* was an urban center militarily strong enough to defend its territory and its independence. That territory included the villages surrounding the urban center. By the eighth century BCE these "city states" had become the most common political unit within Central and Northern Greece, the Peloponnese, the Aegean and Crete. In pursuit of the riches of **colonies,** trade, and commerce the Greek city states expanded outward from the Aegean Sea into Asia Minor, North Africa, Sicily, Naples and Southern Italy, and the lands surrounding the Black Sea.

Greek city states on the mainland of Greece began to **colonize** lands outside of Greece in the eighth century BCE. Most of the lands colonized by the Greek city states had indigenous populations like the colonies conquered by the Western European states in America and the Caribbean. In many ways these independent Greek city states, Athens, Sparta, Corinth, Megara, Thebes, Samos, Miletus, Ephesus, Argos, Olympia and Delphi, were the prequels to the independent Western European states of Portugal, Spain, Holland, England, France, Denmark, Sweden and Germany. Greek city states colonization spread from Asia Minor, Cyprus, Sicily and Southern Italy to North Africa, Ukraine, Spain and France. Like the Western European colonization after the fifteenth century, which conquered the lands in the New World along the coastlines of the Atlantic and Pacific oceans and the Caribbean Sea, the colonies of the Greek city states hugged the shores of the Mediterranean Sea and the Black Sea. Both of these examples of Western imperialism looked for colonies easily accessible by ships.

The Greek cities transferred their **politics,** language, culture, customs, and **religion** to their colonial conquests much like the West transferred its **politics,** language, culture, customs, and **religion** to its colonial conquests. Religious colonization made Delphi and Olympia important cities for all Greeks. The Greek God, *Apollo,* in Delphi, and the Greek God, *Zeus,* in Olympia, were used in the same way as the Christian pope, to sanctify the crimes committed by Greek and Western European imperialists, and justify the theft of indigenous lands. It was this transfer of Greek politics, language, culture, customs and religion that historians seized on to identify what they erroneously called Greek civilization. In like manner it was the transfer of Western European politics, language, culture, customs and religion that historians seized on to identify what they erroneously called Western civilization. The single common theme that runs through this long historical period from the eighth century BCE to 2016, by the unified voice of Western politicians, priests, historians and journalists, is the **insane** and **idiotic** notion that this colonization and subjugation of people less militarily equipped than the Western conquerors somehow benefitted and civilized the conquered peoples. That is the endemic **disease** of the West. I hope that my books will begin the much needed discussion to find a cure.

The westward expansion of the Persian Empire began a conflict between the Persian Empire and Greece, which culminated with the conquest of the Persian Empire by Alexander the Great. This was the first time that a European country, Greece, had established an empire. Given the Western notion that to be civilized you must have an empire, the Greek Empire under Alexander the Great represents the entry of Europe into the civilized world. Adding insult to injury, prior to the empire created by Alexander the Great, Alexander's birthplace, *Macedon,* was regarded as *barbaric* by the civilized Greeks to the south. This Western fallacy that imperial conquests are a necessary requirement to become civilized, therefore, had its origin in the very first Western empire, the Greek Macedonian Empire.

The Persian, Greek, Roman and Arab empires had easy access to the same important body of water, the *Mediterranean.* The regions surrounding the Mediterranean became the center of the world from the sixth century BCE, if not before, until the fifteenth or sixteenth century. Until the voyage of Columbus to the New World, and Vasco da Gama to India, toward the end of the fifteenth century, the regions bordering the Mediterranean were at the center of the East/West wars for imperial dominance. In the East were the Persian and Arab empires. In the north were Greece, Rome and Italy. In the West were Spain and France, and in the south were the North African states. The winners would be characterized by all Western writers as civilized and the losers would be characterized by all Western writers as barbaric. Any empire that expanded with brutal invasions, slavery, piracy, and religious extremism was civilized. Any empire that contracted was ruled by barbarians. This upside-down view of the world is the essence of the longevity of Western civilization. While we strongly disagree with historians that conquests and imperial dominance are what makes a nation civilized, by their own definition the Middle East civilization of over twenty-one centuries compares rather favorably with the less than four centuries of Western European dominance and single century of American dominance.

Warmongering, Imperialism, Slavery, Piracy, Religion, Civilization, Democracy, and Propaganda

Greece is considered to be the cradle of Western civilization both because it was the first Western empire and because of another common Western distortion. In addition to imperialism the West regards its democracy as the other most important pillar of its self-proclaimed civilization. This democratic culture is said to have originated in the Greek city states during the time of the Persian Empire. This is one of the most clever pieces of Western propaganda. To be civilized you must have an empire. But you must also be a democracy. The West could claim that Eastern empires were not civilized because they did not embrace democracy while the most uncivilized and barbaric empire, the *American Empire,* would be promoted loudly as civilized because it had embraced this democracy. As an example of this false logic, Western writers claim that the Athenian defeat of Persia at Marathon in 490 BCE and the failure of the Persian invasion by King Xerxes I are proofs of Greek civilization. Western writers do not criticize warmongering or imperialism as barbaric, which they most certainly are. In their view the rise of the Athenian Empire, following the Athenian/Greek defeats of the Persian Empire, are proofs of Greek civilization. Military victories are used as proofs of the Greeks being civilized and military defeats are used as proofs of the Persians being barbaric. No wonder that these same Western writers claim that the

American Empire is the greatest democracy the world has ever produced. They implicitly measure democracy by successful warmongering and imperial expansion.

In their view Greek democracy is a superior governing system because it produced military victories and imperial expansion. A key reason for Greek military victories over the Persians was the supposed military prowess of the *hoplites*. The *hoplites* were not professional soldiers. They were more like the English/American settlers and colonial militias who engaged in incessant wars with the First Nations, and other European empires, to steal the land and the culture and religion of the First Nations. Since the Greek city states were at constant war with their neighbors, and the Persian Empire, the *hoplites* were both military and political leaders, much like the military/political leaders of the English/American colonies, and the independent USA. As in the English/American colonies and the USA, political power in the Greek city states was based on the ownership of land and military service. In both the Greek city states, and the English/American colonies and USA, these military/political leaders had time to govern and fight wars because they used **slaves, serfs, noncitizens,** and **second-class** citizens, to farm their large land holdings as well as doing other manual labor. Both the Greek city states, and the English/American colonies and USA, were *oligarchies* not democracies. *Virginia* became the leading English/American colony, and state of the Union, for much the same reason as *Sparta* became the leading city state of Greece, *military superiority.* In *Virginia* the military/political leaders had the largest plantations using **slave** labor. These leaders had the most time to devote to wars and governance. In Sparta, the *hoplites* ruled and made wars while the *helots* did the work. Sparta, more than any other city state, perfected the roles of *masters and slaves* for military hegemony. The *Hoplites* were the equivalent of the very powerful military/political elite of Virginia. *Helots* were the equivalent of the African **slaves** in Virginia.

In our view, the Greek Empire represents not the birth of Western *civilization* but the birth of Western *propaganda.* In addition to the Christian church, a highly developed and efficient *propaganda* machine has been the most important complement to the West's superior military-industrial complex, in maintaining imperial hegemony ever since the fall of the Arab/Islamic Empire. The roots of what is called Western civilization are an obsession with warmongering, endless acquisition of colonies, commitment to slavery and piracy, limited democracy, outrageous propaganda, and religious dogma. Since the dawn of what the West calls "civilization" the "civilized" became civilized by using slaves, pirates, gods, and wars to conquer and subjugate others. The West added propaganda to the list. This is the antithesis of civilized.

Our criticism of Western civilization will be fourfold. First, we deny completely that imperialism can ever be civilized. Far from having an empire being a prerequisite for being considered civilized we will argue that imperialism is inherently inconsistent with being civilized. Second, we will argue that all wars are barbaric. Wars can never be justified by civilized societies. There are no exceptions and never any "good" wars. Third, religious beliefs are inconsistent with logical analysis. The governance of a state must be founded on logical and objective reasoning that cannot be circumscribed by religious dogma. Religious beliefs must be private affairs and never have any influence on governance of a civilized state. Finally, we will argue that the Western democracy originating with the Greek city states, and propagandized by the West since that birth, is an extremely limited and constrained democracy. We will argue, for example, that **slavery,** a cornerstone of Greek democracy, and boldly imitated by early American democracy, is inconsistent with democracy. We will further argue that the "freedoms" claimed to be the foundation of Western democracy are more propaganda than truth, and that laws are often created and enforced to maintain this very limited and constrained democracy, rather than to serve justice. The more limited the democracy the greater the need for propaganda. That is why the United States has the most efficient propaganda machine in the world.

American propaganda penetrates every aspect of American society both in the United States and in its many *uncolonies,* as well as every corner of the globe. When the democracies of the West are limited in so many ways, democracy should not be used as the standard by which the East, and Third World countries, is judged by the West. To admonish those countries that do not foolishly copy Western democracies is equivalent to condoning warmongering, slavery, imperialism, piracy, religious extremism, inequality, and limited freedoms, as the highest human achievements. This is ridiculous, immoral and barbaric, and those who lead the West are cognizant of that. They uphold such barbarism only to dominate and exploit the resources and people of the Third World. Since this exploitation benefits the citizens of the West, by increasing their income and consumption, even for the lower classes in the West, it is in the self-interest of the citizens in the Western democracies to accept, and also promote, the propaganda that the West is civilized and humane.

Athenian Democracy and Slavery

Greek democracy was born in the "city state" of Athens in the fifth century BCE when Athenian citizens were asked to revolt against the colonization of Athens by Sparta. Athens, like Sparta and other city states, embraced the *hoplites* as a warrior governing class. But Athens was less devoted to military dominance compared with Sparta. As a result of this Athenian revolt against Sparta, Athens emerged both as the dominant "city state" of the fifth century BCE, and as the model for what the West would call democracy. If we fast forward more than two thousand years to the American revolution of the eighteenth century, we see an ominous parallel. The American colonists were asked to revolt against British colonization in return for sharing political power in a new independent republic. But like the Athenian democracy of the fifth century BCE, the American democracy enhanced slavery, imperialism, piracy, religious dogma, and various forms of inequality. Slaves in Athens outnumbered citizens. Foreign residents were not allowed to participate, and intermarriage between citizens and foreign residents, made the children of such unions noncitizens. Athenian democracy was really an *oligarchy*.

The Athenian democracy limited the sharing of political power to Athenian adult male citizens who had completed military training. The Athenian citizen-soldier, the *hoplite,* was the equivalent of the white American settler, who was first and foremost an *Indian fighter,* who became a citizen-soldier of the original thirteen English colonies, which became the United States in 1783, and used the same model as Athens to steal all of the lands of the First Nations across the American continent to the Pacific Ocean. This quintessential American birthright of militarism became so addictive that the American Empire has waged endless wars and invasions across the globe.

While Sparta used the *helots* as serfs, Athens used *slaves.* In this sense the American democracy was much more *Athenian* than *Spartan.* Athens also had the largest number of slaves of any Greek city state. One estimate suggested that slaves outnumbered Athenian citizens as much as 20:1. The Greek Empire, like the Roman and American empires, has been deemed civilized by the West despite its sanction of **slavery.** Slavery alone makes these empires *barbaric,* never mind their commitments to warmongering, piracy, and imperialism. In most cases, slavery in Greece, much like slavery in the Western European and American empires, was intimately tied to warmongering, piracy, and the acquisition of colonies. Most of the slaves in Greece were acquired as prisoners of wars or piracy. In the Western European empires of Britain, France and Holland, the lucrative West African slave trade was combined with piracy to expand their empires at the expense of the Spanish empire. Slavery in Greece was also tied to the same American/Western sanctity of private property. Slaves were private property in Greece, as in the English/American colonies and the USA. In Greece, as in the English/American colonies and USA, slaves worked on the farms, in the mines, in households, as craftsmen and tradesmen, and in many other economic activities. In Greece, as in the English/American colonies and USA, the more slaves you owned the more political, economic and military influence you enjoyed, and the higher was your rank and privilege in society.

The American democracy imitated both the emphasis of the Athenian democracy on **military service** and **ownership of slaves.** Without the huge numbers of slaves, and second class nonparticipating residents, such as women and foreign residents, in both of these democracies, the adult male citizens would not have had the time to govern and fight the wars necessary for imperial expansion. Without the use of religion and piracy, imperial expansion would have been more limited. Without imperial expansion, neither the British nor the American empires, would have ever been recognized as civilized by Western writers. The privilege and leisure of Athenian citizenship mirrored the privilege and leisure of the landed gentry in both England

and the new independent United States. This privileged leisure class in what the West falsely call democracies controlled both the political and military institutions with which they forced **slaves, serfs, noncitizens,** and **colonists,** to provide the manual labor to feed, clothe, and serve their every whim and desire, as well as build their monuments to the gods whom they claimed to be serving. As usual, this Western association of civilization with imperialism, turns logic on its head, especially when these same Western writers trumpet the right to "self-determination." What was copied in the West from Athens, as the greatest form of government, was a relatively minor improvement on the historical pyramid-like governance of all empires, where a few citizens at the top of the pyramid govern. At the base of the pyramid are large numbers of slaves, and above that group are several layers of serfs and second and third class citizens, with limited political power. The small elite who govern are also the military leaders who wage the endless wars to expand the empire. They also administer the colonies. Above all are the spiritual leaders who speak directly to the gods and sanction and condone the warmongering and imperial expansion.

While many Western democracies have expanded the governing base by abolishing slavery and piracy as well as including women, they have simultaneously increased the use of propaganda, religious dogma, and biased media, to limit freedoms, maintain inequalities, and enrich their citizens by colonizing and exploiting the people and resources of the Third World. The people of the Third World pay for the time required by the citizens of the First World to govern the false democracy, to man the propaganda machine, to administer the colonies, to produce the war materials, to provide the spiritual leadership, and to fight the many wars to acquire and control colonies. Western imperialism today differs in only one important way from the imperialism of Rome, of Alexander the Great, of the Persians, Egyptians, Mongols, Chinese, Indians and others, that came before. That single important difference is *propaganda.* The West has honed and perfected its propaganda skills and propaganda machine.

By the sixth century BCE, when the classical period of Greece began, the Persian Empire had colonized the entire Middle East and today's Muslim countries, from Pakistan in the east to Libya in the west. In its expansion westward it began to colonize the Greek city states. In 546 BCE *Lydia,* led by King Croesus, foolishly attacked the Persian Empire, led by King Cyrus II, and was easily defeated. This Persian victory made many of the Greek city states, colonies of the Persian Empire, while expanding opportunities for Greek merchants. In 490 BCE the Persian Empire, now led by King Darius I, attacked Athens and was defeated at the *Battle of Marathon.* This Athenian defeat of the most powerful empire the world had seen was not unlike the defeat of the American Empire by Vietnam in the 1960s. Like the American Empire after the Vietnam disaster, Persian defeat by a relatively puny Greek city state, only strengthened the resolve of the Persian Empire to increase its dedication to warmongering. On the other hand the Athenian victory inspired Athens to use the propaganda of spreading democracy to become an imperial power over the Greek city states, much like the defeat of the British Empire by the thirteen American colonies in 1783, inspired the newly created United States to use the propaganda of "republican values" to become an imperial power over the First Nations and European colonies on the American mainland.

Athenian Imperialism and Greek Civil Wars

The *Greco-Persian* wars, which began in 546 BCE, did not end with the *Battle of Marathon* in 490 BCE. The Persian defeat in 490 BCE simply provided an opportunity for Athens to colonize an increasing number of previously independent Greek city states by using the fear tactic that they would be colonized by Persia. It was exactly the tactic used by the independent United States in the nineteenth century to colonize territory by pretending to be defending the inhabitants from Spanish colonialism. The Athenians, like the Americans in the nineteenth century, strutted their new found power and "superiority" like peacocks. This expansion of Athenian imperialism did not sit well with Sparta, which had been the dominant Greek city state prior to the Athenian military victory against Persia in 490 BCE. Athenian ascendancy within classical Greece was comparable to the economic ascendancy of the Northern states in the United States during the nineteenth century. The initial American union had been dominated by the Southern states, much like classical Greece had been dominated by Sparta. The rise of democratic Athens was seen as a threat to Sparta, much like the rise of the "slave-free" Northern states was seen as a threat to the South, in nineteenth century United States. Both led to civil war.

Another important parallel between classical Greece and the United States of the nineteenth century, is that Athens convinced Greece to build a strong navy, to complement its army, to defend against Persian imperialism, but used it both to expand its own imperialism and win the inevitable Greek civil war. In like manner the Northern states in the United States convinced the United States to build a strong navy, to complement its army, to defend against European imperialism, but used it to expand its own imperialism and win the inevitable American civil war. Initially, Athens joined forces with Sparta to defend Greece against the Persian Empire led by King Xerxes I after 485 BCE. This was no different from the Southern states combining forces with the Northern states to steal First Nations land and European colonies on the American mainland. Greek unity defeated the Persian invasion of King Xerxes I just as American unity enabled the steady expansion of colonial conquests by the American Empire. While Athens had defeated Persia at the Battle of Marathon, Sparta was still the dominant military city state. When the Greek city states formed a union against the Persian invasion by King Xerxes I it was Sparta that was chosen to lead. The Persians were defeated at sea off the island of *Salamis* in September 480 BCE and on land at the *Battles of Plataea* and *Mycale* in August 479 BCE. Persian **military** defeat by Greece, more than any other factor, made Greece, as documented by Western writers, civilized and Persia barbaric. Just as Greece is used as the founding father of Western democracy, **military** victories is the quintessential evidence of Western civilization. After the *Battles of Plataea* and *Mycale,* every war waged by the West, including the Second World War, was a war for imperial expansion. The United States became the leader of Western civilization only because it had made the most imperial conquests. Empire, **not** democracy, is what the West uses as its primary criterion for being civilized. Only when you call a spade a spade do you understand that the West is *barbaric* not civilized. The limited democracy of the West is the icing on the cake if the colonies adopt it. But it's the number of colonies, democratic or not, which makes the Western imperial power civilized.

Athens had played the key role in the Persian defeat at sea since it had the dominant Greek navy. But Sparta had played the key role in the *Battle of Plataea* since it had the dominant Greek army. The Greek military victories against Persia led to a rivalry between Athens and Sparta for leadership of Greece as did American military victories against First Nations and European colonies led to a rivalry between the Northern and Southern states in the United States in the nineteenth century. In the United States the northern states won the Civil War and effectively kept the Southern states as "colonies" of an ever-expanding American Empire. In Greece the conflict between Athens and Sparta led to civil wars with other Greek city states and the eventual dominance of Macedonia, and the expansion of the Greek Empire, by Alexander the Great. This rather unexpected outcome was never heeded by the Western European states. Their continued warmongering among themselves led to the dominance of the United States, and the expansion of the American Empire.

The inevitable civil wars in Greece are often called the *Peloponnesian Wars* because they began as wars between the *Peloponnesian League* led by Sparta and the *Delian League* led by Athens. Sparta was by far the most powerful Greek city state in the Peloponnese, the large peninsula in Southern Greece. Its allies in the *Peloponnesian League* included other powerful Greek city states such as Argos, Corinth, Tegea, and Elis. The Delian League was founded in 477 BCE and made up of almost two hundred Greek city states. Unlike the American civil war where the pro-imperialist slave-free northern states prevailed, in the Greek civil war Sparta's "southern states" equivalent, regained its prior hegemony over pro-imperial democratic Athens. During the Greco-Persian wars Athens had wrested hegemony from Sparta. Its dominance relied on its superior navy. Athens had used its modern navy and its leadership of the Delian League to become an imperial power in the Mediterranean. Sparta justifiably saw Athenian imperialism as a greater threat to its independence than Persian imperialism, just as American imperialism in the nineteenth century was a far greater threat to the First Nations, the Southern slave states, Mexico, Canada, Hawaii, Cuba, and the

Philippines, than European imperialism. In my prequels, *Rise and Fall of the American Empire* and *American Invasions,* I explained at length how "home advantage" made American imperialism far more dangerous in the New World compared with European imperialism. It was the same in classical Greece with Athenian imperialism.

The Peloponnesian Wars

The wars and alliances among the Greek city states resembled the wars and alliances among the Western empires of Spain, Portugal, France, Britain, United States, Canada and the First Nations. These numerous alliances and incessant warmongering led to what has been called the *First Peloponnesian War* in 460 BCE. It was the continuation of a fight for hegemony between Sparta and Athens, which began with the rise of Athens as an imperial power based on naval superiority. In many ways the wars between Sparta and Athens resembled the later eighteenth century battle between France and Britain for hegemony. France was the dominant military power before British naval superiority. Sparta's military dominance had forced the Greeks to move toward the coast and the islands off the coast. Athens honed its naval skills by aggressive attacks on the Persian Empire much like the British would later hone its naval skills by aggressive attacks on the Spanish Empire. While the naval superiority of Athens gave it an advantage over Sparta the ultimate outcome of this warmongering was the rise of Macedonia. In like manner, while the naval superiority of Britain gave it an advantage over France the ultimate outcome of that warmongering was the rise of the USA. Even though France and Britain joined forces against Germany, the *First World War* was Europe's equivalent of the First Peloponnesian War.

The *First Peloponnesian War* ended in 445 BCE but did not settle the question of Greek hegemony, much like the eighteenth century wars between Britain and France did not settle the question of European hegemony. The *Second Peloponnesian War* began in 431 BCE and ended with the defeat and occupation of Athens by Sparta. Unlike the Anglo-French wars where British naval superiority prevailed, Athenian naval dominance failed to defeat Sparta. Athenian strategy had been to build a wall to keep the Spartan army out while using its navy to bring in supplies by sea. But this self-imposed land blockade proved to be disastrous because of the persistence and determination of the superior Spartan army. The military prowess of the Spartan *hoplites* far exceeded that of the Athenian *hoplites.* In addition, the size of the *hoplite* army of Sparta and her allies far exceeded the *hoplite* army of the Athenian Empire.

During the self-imposed land blockade Sparta attacked the lands immediately outside the Athenian wall forcing the population to seek refuge within the Athenian wall. This led to overcrowding within the walled area, which may have created the conditions for the *plague* that broke out in 430 BCE. Some estimates suggest that this *plague* wiped out half of the population. Athens continued the war against Sparta and her allies for another twenty-six years but finally surrendered in 404 BCE. But Spartan victory did not bring lasting hegemony to Sparta much like British victories over France did not bring lasting European hegemony to Britain. While Sparta and Athens were battling for Greek hegemony, *Thebes* emerged as a new rival for Greek hegemony much like Germany emerged as the new rival for European hegemony.

Shortly after the Athenian surrender in 404 BCE three important allies of Sparta, *Thebes, Corinth* and *Argos,* formed an alliance with Athens and began the *Corinthian War* against Sparta in 394–395 BCE. This continued civil war among Greek city states enabled the Persian Empire to recuperate some of the losses it had suffered during the expansion of the Athenian Empire. The *Corinthian War* ended in 387 BCE only to be followed by a war between Sparta and *Thebes* in 378 BCE. Thebes had a decisive victory over Sparta in 371 BCE at the *Battle of Leuctra.* With the collapse of Sparta's "military invincibility" Thebes became the dominant city state much to the dismay of both Athens and Sparta. Athens formed an alliance with Sparta much like the Anglo-French alliance against Germany during the *First World War.* The Spartan/Athenian alliance was unable to defeat Thebes. In the important *Battle of Mantinea* in 362 BCE the Greek city states caused so much destruction on themselves that the barbarian kingdom of *Macedonia* in Northern Greece was able to conquer Greece much like the Second World War enabled the barbarian Americans to conquer Western Europe.

Macedonia (Macedon) Replaced the Hegemony of the City-States in Greece, Much Like the American Empire (United States of America) Replaced European Hegemony in the West

We have always contended in our *prequels* that the First and Second World Wars were a continuation of the wars for imperial expansion by the West. In the period from 1491 to 1917 this Western Empire was led by the Western European states of Spain, Portugal, France, Holland, Britain and Germany. In like manner the wars among the Greek city states were wars for an earlier Western Empire led by the Greek city states of Sparta, Athens and Thebes. Just as an upstart outsider, considered barbaric by Western European standards, the *United States,* wrested hegemony of the current Western Empire because of incessant warmongering among the Western European states of Spain, Portugal, France, Holland, Britain, and Germany, an upstart outsider, considered barbaric by classical Greek standards, *Macedonia,* wrested hegemony for the earlier Western Empire, centered in Greece, because of the endemic warmongering among the Greek city states of Sparta, Athens, and Thebes.

The root of American/Western imperialism is **not** the limited democracy of Athens but the "Blood and Gore" of Alexander the Great. Macedonia, not Athens, inspired the American Empire. The Greek city states were the equivalent of the Western European states, squabbling with each other over the same colonies. Macedonia united the Greeks to dominate the world much like the United States united the West to dominate the world. The Greek city states were ruthless in their pursuit of imperial hegemony. But none were as ruthless and blood thirsty as Macedonia under Alexander the Great. In like manner the Western European states were ruthless in their quest for imperial hegemony. But none were as ruthless and warmongering as the American Empire.

Macedonians were not thought of as real Greeks in much the same way that Americans were not thought of as real Europeans. Macedonians were not considered civilized by Greeks in much the same way that Americans in the nineteenth century were not considered civilized by Western Europeans. But like the vast geographical area of the United States compared to a Western European state, Macedonia had a large geographical area compared to that of a city state. Macedonia was also threatened by neighbors on its western and northern borders considered even more barbaric much like nineteenth-century United States was threatened by the First Nations. Macedonia was also divided between its more progressive lowland coastal region and its "backward" mountainous hinterland region much as the United States was divided between its more progressive Northern **pro-imperial** states and "backward" Southern **slave** states.

While the Greek city states fought for empires but protected their individual historical sovereignty Macedonia expanded territory under a single government. This was exactly what the United States did. We have argued in our *prequels* that invading and colonizing territory in the way that the United States did in no way negated the colonization. The Western European states governed their colonies in the traditional way all empires have governed colonies. But the United States colonized territory outside the original thirteen English colonies that became the United States in 1783, and then governed them within an ever-expanding United States. Western writers have foolishly concluded that such conquests were not imperial. This "American" form of imperialism was in fact begun by Macedonia. The "Macedonian" imperialism was more successful than the Greek city states imperialism of Athens, Sparta and Thebes for the same reason that the "American" imperialism was more successful than the Western European states imperialism of Spain, Portugal, France, Britain, Germany and Holland. It is for this reason that we concluded in our *prequels* that American imperialism was far worse that Western European imperialism, for those colonized in the New World, especially the First Nations.

Today the West faces an ominous parallel in the form of the newly created *Islamic State.* The West fabricated a "War on Terror" to provide a post-Communist excuse for continued colonization of the Middle East and other Muslim territory. Opposition to that Western colonization came from nonstate groups such as al-Qaeda, al-Nusra Front, al-Qaeda in Iraq, and al-Qaeda in the Arabian Peninsula. The West had little to fear from these lightly armed nonstate oppositions, and the West knew that. It hyped the fear among its people by making the leaders of these groups, such as the late Osama bin Laden, America's most wanted. In reality, leaders like bin Laden were in hiding with no security from even a small scale attack by a single U.S. helicopter crew. But a state with arms stolen from America's foot soldiers is reason for some fear. Imagine if that state were to expand territory in the Middle East as Israel has done? The West knows this but is reluctant to face this threat head on. It had used its powerful propaganda machine to project the image of its **cowardly** pilots, safely ensconced in its fighter jets high above the heavens, as heroes and the **brave** suicide-bombers, willing to sacrifice their lives to defend their countries from Western invasions, as cowards. As a result the Western public had treated the Western bombing as video games with no real casualties. Trapped by this propaganda, the West is now at a loss how to deal with a real threat, which cannot be defeated simply by **cowardly** bombing. It requires Western casualties.

In a rather ironic twist of fate, it may be the Russians that will once again save the West from its self-inflicted disasters. Russia had previously saved the West from both Napoleon and Hitler. ISIS expansion into Syrian territory was caused by the Western attempt to recolonize Syria. Today Russia's defense of Syria's embattled leader, Bashar al-Assad, will likely not be sufficient to defeat ISIS but will likely stop ISIS from conquering all of Syria. Stalin's opposition to Western imperialism had led to his demonization by Western propaganda. But when Stalin saved the West he was miraculously converted by the powerful Western propaganda machine to "Uncle Joe." I have no doubt that if Vladimir Putin saves the West from ISIS taking all of Syria, he too will be magically converted by the powerful Western propaganda machine from being a despised dictator, for opposing Western imperialism, to "Uncle Vladimir."

Macedonia first rose to prominence in Greece when King Philip II expanded his territory in the barbarian north and west and then southward into *Thessaly*. This expansion into the south threatened the sovereignty of city states including Thebes and Athens. Athens formed an alliance with Thebes to stop the Macedonian juggernaut. But it was an alliance like that of France and Britain trying to stop the German juggernaut in the twentieth century. Just as Germany had become too powerful for the combined power of France and Britain, Macedonia had become too powerful for the combined power of Athens and Thebes.

In 338 BCE a somewhat smaller *Macedonian* army defeated the allied *Greek* army at the *Battle of Chaeronea.* Macedon was not yet sufficiently civilized to be Greek. It became Greek, by Western historians, after its warmongering prowess had made it civilized. In the West you cannot be civilized unless you can win wars, especially wars that add colonies to your empire. The fact that this new leader of Greek Western civilization, *Macedonia,* was not even the limited Athenian democracy the West claims to be its Greek inheritance, but a *monarchy,* has been willfully lost by Western historians interested more in propaganda than truth.

The true nature of American/Western imperialism and addiction to warmongering has its origins in the *monarchy* of the son of King Philip II, Alexander III. King Philip II had risen to a leadership position in Greece very much like that of the French and English monarchs of eighteenth-century Western Europe. But monarchs can be assassinated just like American presidents. Alexander III became the king of Macedonia at the young age of twenty when his father, King Philip II, was assassinated in 336 BCE. Like King George III of England who ascended the English throne in 1760 at the young age of twenty-two, Alexander III was destined to rule over a worldwide Western Empire much like King George III. Alexander III's empire began very much like that of the American Empire. First invade and conquer the Greek city states then expand the Greek Empire outside Greece. In like manner the American Empire began by invading and conquering First Nations lands on the American continent before expanding across the Pacific to Hawaii, Philippines, Japan, and China, as well as eastward into the Caribbean and North Africa.

In the eyes of Western historians the conquests of Alexander III made him both civilized and "Great" as in *Alexander the Great,* in the same way that the conquests of the American Empire made it civilized and "leader of the free world." That both Alexander III and the American Empire used the most barbaric forms of warmongering, genocide, torture, destruction and **uncivilized** methods to conquer and steal the land, resources and culture of the conquered, has been dismissed by these Western historians for the glory of Western domination. Alexander III began his quest for Western *civilization* by butchering all potential rivals for the Macedonian kingdom and destroying the Greek city state of *Thebes,* the dominant city state at the time, much like the scorched earth policy of Tecumseh Sherman against the southern states during the American Civil War. As Alexander III went on from Greece to conquests in the Middle East and Central Asia so has the unified *North American Empire* of the United States and Canada, gone on to invasions in Iraq, Afghanistan, Pakistan, Yemen, Egypt, Syria, Somalia and Libya, in the first two decades of the twenty-first century. But unlike the Greek city states and the Middle East and Central Asia, which surrendered to Alexander the Great after his destruction of Thebes, the North American Empire and its allies will fail to colonize the Middle East and Central Asia.

The Empire of Alexander the Great: The First Western Empire

The West is proud of its Greek roots not so much because of Athenian democracy or Greek civilization, but because of Greek **imperialism.** Empire, not civilized behavior or learning, is what the West idolizes. Until the empire created by Alexander the Great the world's empires had all been *Eastern* empires. The West felt inferior much like the way it has made the *East* and the Third World feel inferior after the eighteenth century. The West continues to use a very sophisticated and effective propaganda machine to convince humanity that *military* superiority is a prerequisite for *civilized* behavior. A *civilized* nation such as the United States must conquer and acquire more and more *uncolonies* for it to maintain its *civilized* status of "leader of the free world." Canada, under the leadership of Steven Harper, has been only too eager to become civilized by aspiring to the notion of transforming the American Empire into a unified *North American Empire.* Canada, under Harper, led the charge for ever more **warmongering** by the West in the Middle East and more recently in Ukraine. Canada, under Harper, out did the United States in protecting the warmongering of Israel, and in condemning Vladimir Putin for Putin's justifiable and brave opposition to the ever-expanding Western imperialism.

Once Alexander III had colonized all of Greece, he moved against the Persian Empire. As we have explained above the Persian Empire had been competing with the Greek city states for imperial dominance in the lands bordering the Mediterranean. This would be the equivalent of the competition between Western European empires and the Japanese Empire after the *Meiji Restoration* in 1867. While the disunited Greek city states failed to defeat the Persian Empire and colonize the Middle East a united Greece led by Alexander the Great did just that. In like manner, a disunited Western Europe was unable to defeat the Japanese Empire but a united American Empire succeeded. American colonization of Japan, South Korea, Taiwan and Pacific islands, as well as its attempt to colonize China, including Tibet, and North Korea, during WW II, is proof positive that the Second World War was a war for empire.

Alexander's defeat of King Darius III of Persia at the *Battle of Issus* in November of 333 BCE marked the conquest of the Persian Empire by the West. The following year Alexander the Great expanded this first Western empire into Syria, Egypt, and *Jerusalem.* Iraq was conquered in 331 BCE. Alexander's empire expanded eastward into Central Asia, Pakistan and India up to the *Hyphasis River.* By the time of his death in 323 BCE, Alexander had given the West an empire, which included all of the Middle East as well as parts of Central Asia. Alexander had colonized Pakistan, Afghanistan, Iraq, Iran, Turkey, Saudi Arabia, Lebanon, Egypt, Syria, Jordan, the Gulf States, and Yemen. The city he created in Egypt, *Alexandria,* became the most famous city in the world. This first Western empire is the origin of the determination of the West to continue its colonization of the Middle East, North Africa and Central Asia, and explains the current American led Western invasions in Iraq, Afghanistan, Pakistan, Yemen, Libya, Syria, Egypt and Somalia.

Alexander's brutality and inhumane slaughter of those militarily weaker but who dared to resist conquest is truly legendary. Alexander began his reign as king of Macedon by murdering all potential rivals to his succession, including his cousin *Amyntas IV,* and General *Attalus,* the uncle of his father's last wife, Cleopatra Eurydice. Cleopatra and her daughter, by his father Phillip II, Europa, were burnt alive. Alexander III instilled fear into the civilized Greeks of the Greek city states by totally destroying the Greek city state of Thebes and selling the Thebans into slavery. That would be the equivalent of the barbaric American Empire enslaving the civilized English after destroying England, to send a message to Western Europe to accept American dominance. Alexander's conquests of *Tyre* and *Gaza* were celebrated by selling their women and children into **slavery** after his crucifixion of the men of Tyre and murder of the men of Gaza. During his invasion of India he captured the forts of *Massaga* and *Aornos* after bloody battles. Far from content with the blood he had so callously spilled against those defending their territory and freedom against a distant **Western** invader, Alexander proceeded to slaughter all of the inhabitants of Massaga and *Ora* and reduced their entire cities to rubble.

I find it ironic that Western historians continue to claim that the planting of Greek culture, religion, politics and customs by Alexander in his colonies in the East, symbolizes his desire to civilize those he conquered. Military conquests are the anathema of civilized behavior. It is wholly barbaric. It has no redeeming feature. Alexander was first and foremost a barbaric invader who used his military genius for evil purposes. Alexander, more than any Western leader, set the example for twenty-five centuries of Western warmongering and denial of freedoms to people who prefer peace to war. Why the West continues to think today that East and West can meet under such conditions of implicit conqueror and conquered is simply a Western fantasy first attempted by Alexander III in 326 BCE.

The Roots of American Democratic Imperialism

A kindergarten child knows that imperialism is inconsistent with democracy. However, Western propaganda has become so outlandish that since the American invasion of Iraq in 2003, the West has justified American imperialism by suggesting that it is necessary to spread democracy. Ridiculous as this latest outlandish Western propaganda is, we can trace it back to the original Western empire, which the West claims to be the birthplace of Western democracy, the Athenian Empire. The Athenian Empire, like the later British and American empires, was founded on naval superiority. It was the discovery of silver at the Athenian mine at Lavrion in 483 BCE that initially provided the money to Athens to begin its quest for naval dominance. The exclusive use of **slave labor** to maximize this Western democratic state's revenues from the silver mine, was an important precedent for the new U.S. republic of 1783, to claim that **slavery** was the birthright of all Western *democratic* republics based on liberty and freedom.

Working conditions for the **slaves** in the silver mine in Lavrion were as inhumane as for the **slaves** on the American cotton and sugar plantations in the American deep-south. American founding fathers like George Washington, would never have been so revered by Western historians had they not been large **slave** owners in the new "freedom loving" republic of the United States. The more First Nations an American leader killed in battle, to steal their land, and the more **slaves** they owned, the more civilized and freedom loving they were. When the Persian Empire under King Xerxes I invaded in 480 BCE, it was the Athenian navy that was responsible for the first Greek victory at the naval *Battle of Salamis.* After 479 BCE, following the Persian defeats at *Plataea* and *Mycale,* the growing Athenian Empire was in offensive rather than defensive mode, against the Persian Empire. It expanded its own empire by conquering Persian colonies in addition to increasing its colonization of Greek city states and colonies in the Mediterranean. In like manner the American victory over the British Empire in 1783 made the American Empire the most aggressive empire in the New World.

The Delian League and Athenian Democratic Imperialism

The *Delian League* was founded by Athens in 477 BCE, only two years after the Persian defeat. It required all members to pay tribute in cash or ships. Athens determined how much tribute was to be paid by each member and controlled how the money was spent. In 454 BCE Athens moved the treasury of the Delian League from the island of *Delos* to Athens, to increase its control of the tribute from its colonies. Its primary significance to Athens was its contribution to Athenian naval supremacy. But cash tributes were also used to finance a very expensive public building program to transform Athens into a center befitting that of an empire with the usual monuments, temples, marble architecture and infrastructure. Athens had to be transformed into the center for Greek art, culture and religion. The *Parthenon,* constructed between 447 and 438 BCE, was only the most famous of these "imperial" buildings. Built in the Acropolis in Athens, as a dedication to the Greek goddess Athena, it combined the twin pillars of *religion* and *imperialism,* with which the Christian West civilized the world after 1492. The Christian monarchs of Spain and Portugal would be blessed by the pope and they would send out "Christ-bearing" Columbus, and Vasco da Gama, from Western Europe, to steal the world for Christ and empire. The thirty-five-foot gold and ivory statue of Athena bears an uncanny goddess resemblance to the American Statue of Liberty.

With the rise of Athenian naval dominance, members of the Delian League became more and more colonies of an ever-expanding Athenian Empire. Member states were not free to leave much like the southern states in the United States were not free to leave the Union. Many city states were often coerced to provide military support for Athens' imperial wars much like America's forced "coalitions of the willing" in its imperial wars in Iraq and Afghanistan. Adding insult to injury, Western writers credit Athens with waging imperial wars to spread democracy much like the American invasions of Iraq and Afghanistan were intended to spread American and Canadian democracy. The notion that warmongers like Canada and the United States, can ever have the decency to transfer any good to countries they invade, only to flaunt their military superiority and to kill and maim innocent men, women and children, shows the depths to which Western hypocrisy and barbarity has sunk. The United States and Canada wage these brutal wars and invasions only to perpetuate the centuries of human rights abuses begun with their slaughter of the First Nations in North America. Having committed **genocide** in North America they now do the same in Iraq and Afghanistan. While committing war crimes and human rights abuses across the globe, they loudly preach to others about their supposed human rights abuses, which are a thousandfold less than those committed by the United States, Canada, and other Western states.

The Roman Empire: The Second Western Empire

Empires rise and fall. The fall of the Greek Empire built by Alexander was expected. What mattered for our thesis is whether the Greek Empire would be replaced by an Eastern or a Western empire. As we have pointed out the Greek Empire was the first Western empire. Had it been replaced by another Eastern empire that may very well have been the end of the East/West divide. But the Geek Empire was replaced by another Western empire, the *Roman Empire.* More importantly, this new Western empire converted to *Christianity.* The new Eastern empires that rose after the fall of the Persian Empire converted to *Islam.* As a result the future East/West divide, became a *religious* divide as well, between Islam and Christianity.

As we dig into the history of the rise and fall of the Roman Empire we cannot help but see how closely the rise and fall of the American Empire mirrors that of the Roman Empire. As we mentioned earlier, while the Western European states of the later period mirrored the history of the Greek city states the American Empire copied much more closely Rome rather than Greece. We have observed in our *prequels* that Western historians implicitly colluded with the propaganda of the American Empire by falsely claiming that the conquest and occupation of First Nations lands outside the boundaries of the initial thirteen English colonies, which became the independent USA in 1783, were not *imperial* conquests. Between 1783 and 1912, the United States of thirteen tiny states in 1783 had conquered most of North America. It was these continued wars and conquests of First Nations lands that created the American addiction to warmongering. In like fashion, between 500 BCE and 275 BCE, what had been the city state of Rome conquered most of Italy. It was in this conquest of Italy that the Roman addiction to warmongering was created. The same historians who call Rome an empire when the city state of Rome conquered and occupied Italy, condone the expansion of the United States as if it were some kind of godlike emancipation of the First Nations.

We have argued that the colonies acquired in the New World by the Western European empires were far less destructive of the independence and wealth of the First Nations than the subsequent colonization and subjugation by the American Empire, much like the Roman Empire was more destructive of the freedom and independence of those colonized by the prior Greek Empire. The American Empire, like the Roman Empire, was also determined to use propaganda to project a false image of invasions and warmongering as intended to protect the freedom of those conquered, when in fact it was replacing whatever freedom they still had with total subjugation, bordering on slavery. While both Rome and the United States used the rhetoric of peace they were feeding their addictions to wars with both failed and successful invasions. As the Roman Empire continued to feed its addiction to wars by expanding out of Italy into the Mediterranean and the Middle East, so did the American Empire feed its addiction to war by expanding out of the American continent into the Pacific and Asia and into the Atlantic and the Caribbean.

Today, two millenniums after the fall of the Roman Empire, Western historians belatedly write of the evils of Roman conquests. But these same historians show no equal desire to write of the same evils of continuing American conquests. On the contrary, they continue to spout the same lies and propaganda they have been peddling for two centuries. While all imperialism is inconsistent with freedom, these Western historians continue to portray American imperialism as some kind of *good* imperialism much like many today still falsely think that some wars can be *good* wars. There are no good wars and no good empires. Two millenniums from now historians will openly write that the American Empire was far more evil than the Roman Empire. President Obama's Nobel Peace Prize will be recognized by all as the first Nobel *War* Prize.

The city state of Rome, like the Greek city states, had imperial ambitions. It was natural for Rome to begin to satisfy its imperial ambitions by colonizing the land close to its home base in exactly the way the American Empire began its quest for colonies by invading the First Nations lands bordering the independent USA created in 1783. Rome's expansion into southern Italy and Sicily brought it into conflict with Greece for exactly the same reason that American expansion into Canada brought it into conflict with England. Anglo-American conflicts in Canada were *imperial* conflicts with no difference from prior Anglo-French conflicts in Canada. Yet Western historians refused to brand the USA with the same imperial ambitions as France and England because of American propaganda. In like manner, Rome used propaganda to hide its imperial intentions in the Greek colonies in southern Italy and Sicily. While these Western historians now admit that Rome was no less imperial than Greece or Persia they still make excuses for American imperialism. While historians are now willing to condemn the barbarity of Roman imperialism they still cling to the **idiocy** that American "nonimperialism" and warmongering benefits humanity.

The city state of Rome was founded in 753 BCE and became a republic in 510 BCE. While we have argued that the American Republic founded in 1783 was no more democratic than the monarchies of Western Europe it was this "Republic of Rome" with its innate propaganda value of "freedoms" for the masses, which appealed to the American Empire. This propaganda value used by Rome to camouflage its oligarchic nature and its warmongering for empire, rather than the professed liberation of people, was honed and perfected by the American Empire. By the time the Roman Empire had conquered the Mediterranean in the second century BCE, the Roman oligarchy of aristocratic families had consolidated its political, economic and military control of the Roman Empire. It was this oligarchy of wealthy families that the American Empire emulated. Romans also invoked the help of the gods as much as the Greeks in their warmongering and imperial conquests much like the American Empire called on the same Christian God as the Western European empires had done.

Roman conflicts with Greece began in the **third** century BCE in Italy much like American conflicts with the Western European empires began in the late eighteenth century on the American mainland. But by the **second** century BCE, Rome had expanded eastward outside Italy into Asia Minor, much like the American Empire had expanded westward in the **nineteenth** century across the Pacific to Hawaii, the Philippines, China and Japan, as well as eastward into the Caribbean, and northward into Alaska. The major obstacle to Roman expansion into the Mediterranean and Asia Minor was *Carthage.* In like fashion, the major obstacle to American expansion in the Pacific was *Japan.* The Roman defeat of Carthage has left us with the legend of Hannibal crossing the Alps with his war elephants in 218 BCE. Despite many early victories, Carthage was defeated and destroyed by the Roman Empire. The American defeat of Japan has left us with the infamy of Pearl Harbor, Hiroshima, and Nagasaki. Despite many early victories, Japan was defeated and nuked by the American Empire. The American Empire was as savage with the Japanese as the Roman Empire had been with the Carthaginians. The *Punic Wars* between Rome and Carthage, lasting from 264 BCE to 146 CE, are as famous as the Second World War between the United States and Japan. The Second World War was no less a war for imperial dominance than the Punic wars.

The American Empire flourished from the spoils of its victory over Japan just as the Roman Empire flourished from the spoils of its victory over Carthage. Rome became the undisputed leader of the world after its defeat of Carthage, just as the United States became the undisputed leader of the world after its defeat of Japan. In the century following its defeat of Carthage, Rome became the largest empire in the world. Rome copied and emulated Greek culture just as the Americans copied and emulated Western European culture. In the half century following its defeat of Japan the American Empire became the largest empire in the world. Western historians continue to peddle the idiotic notion that the Second World War was a *good* war. The American use of nuclear weapons, far from bringing forth the wrath of the entire human race, as it should have, on the American Empire, has set the ridiculous precedent that only the United States has the God-given right to use nuclear weapons against its enemies. Other nations are either banned from possessing nuclear weapons or must acquire nuclear weapons only as a nuclear deterrent.

Rome copied Greek civilized culture and behavior much like the Americans copied Western European civilized culture and behavior. By the **first** century BCE the Roman Empire had replaced the Greek Empire much like the American Empire replaced the Western European empires in the **twentieth** century. Athens remained a cultural and intellectual capital city under the Roman Empire much like London and Paris maintained their cultural and intellectual "superiority" under the American Empire. In general, Greek city states were treated much better than non-Greek conquests by the Roman Empire much like Western states are treated much better by the American Empire than non-Western conquests. Both Rome and the American Empire used the same justification for preferential treatment. Non-Greek inhabitants were barbarians unworthy of civilized treatment by Roman conquerors just as **nonwhites** are unworthy of civilized treatment by American conquerors.

Military Power, Wars, Conquests, and Subjugation

Despite rhetoric to the contrary, every empire, without exception, has an insatiable appetite for warmongering, conquests and the subjugation of those defeated by its superior military force and brutality. Its obsession with military dominance is never for defensive purposes. It pursues military dominance because it knows that people will never believe its propaganda that it invades for the benefit of those invaded. It needs to defeat those invaded on the battlefield before it can sell its propaganda to its allies and supporters, never to those invaded. It needs military superiority to suppress revolts against its colonial rule and suppression of freedom.

Rome became the dominant empire by the first century BCE and the United States became the dominant empire by the twentieth century because of military superiority. This dedication to wars, military victories and superior Weapons of Mass Destruction, WMDs, is misleadingly used by historians to measure how civilized the warmonger is. The greater the military victories, the more civilized the warmongering imperial behemoth. This upside-down definition of Western civilization is the key to understanding why the West can never lead humanity into a future to become free, moral, just and humane. Like the Roman Empire before, the American Empire must fall before the human race can ever have a chance to progress from the barbarity of wars, invasions, imperialism, slavery, injustices, greed, dictatorships, false democracies, inequalities, hunger, ethnic cleansing, and human rights abuses.

While this application of military superiority by the West began with Alexander the Great it was first perfected by the Romans and copied by the Americans. If we use a little imagination we can see that the westward expansion of the civilized Western empire of Greece across the Adriatic and Ionian Seas to Sicily and Southern Italy as very similar to the later westward expansion of the civilized Western European empires across the Atlantic Ocean to the Caribbean and American continent. Greek influence in Italy could be viewed in the same light as Western European influence in America. Just as a tiny city state, Rome, first dominated Italy before becoming the world's most powerful empire, the tiny strip of land that became the United States first dominated America before becoming the world's most powerful empire. After its conquest of Italy Rome expanded into the Mediterranean much like the United States expanded into the Caribbean and Pacific. The key to understanding both is to recognize their obsession with military prowess and warmongering. For example, Rome's conquest of *Veii* and defeat by the *Gauls* very early in its bid for empire is reminiscent of America's conquest of First Nations lands and defeat in Canada early in its bid for empire.

Greek city states were involved in wars like any country. But Sparta was more obsessed with military prowess than any other country. In like manner Rome and the United States followed Sparta more than any country or empire in obsessing over military prowess. Sparta, Rome and the United States were different from empires like Persia or Greece or Western European empires in that participation and respect for the military was not limited to a small aristocratic group but percolated down to the entire population. In my *American Invasions* I explained how American settlers became "Indian fighters" and how America's military permeates every facet of American society from the commander in chief, to the military families spread across the United States, to the military-industrial complex, to young men eager to get an education or a career, or to simply kick ass or kill nonwhites, propagandized by the Western media as *gooks, Communists, Islamists, or cowardly terrorists.* Rome, like the United States, fought wars continuously. A single year without a war would be an anomaly. Roman generals, like American generals, had enormous political influence. With an insatiable appetite for imperial expansion there is always some new country to invade or some old conquest to defend against rebellion. The generals and the military are always fully employed.

The governance of Rome transitioned from monarchy to republic to dictatorship. But its form of government is irrelevant to assessing its influence in history just as American republicanism, after shedding its colonial attachment to the English monarchy, made no difference to America's influence in history. Rome and the United States became imperial monsters. Whether they were governed by dictators or false democracies would not have changed their imperial domination, which destroyed the freedoms of so many. Rome, like the United States, began with established aristocracies, which kept their influential positions under both monarchies and republicanism. In the case of the United States a domestic aristocracy replaced the English aristocracy. In both Rome and the United States the aristocracy used religion to their advantage. Separation of church and state was more propaganda than reality.

The Importance of the Military in Rome and in the United States

We cannot understand the true nature of Roman or American imperialism if we do not recognize the paramount position of the military in both Rome and the United States. In both countries the military was initially served by the peasantry who took time off from farming to do their duty as soldiers when called upon by the state. At this early stage of evolution there were few professional full-time soldiers. In both Rome and the United States these "volunteers" were called a citizen militia. The first standing army was created in the United States during its War of Independence. In both Rome and the United States an ever-expanding empire required more and more full-time professional soldiers to invade and acquire the empire and to protect it from rebellion. Both empires realized that a navy must be added to the army to expand the empire.

In both empires ascendancy in the military was the key to high political office. Both empires developed and honed a military machine that thrived on wars, invasions, and protecting the empire from rebels. The military became sacred and not subject to criticism or questioning. A culture of condemnation of any, who would dare to question the sanctity of the military, as unpatriotic, was nurtured by both empires. The military in effect was made to act and behave as if it were above the law, above criticism, above budgetary constraints, above abuses of human rights, above control by the people, the media, the political institutions or the false democracy. The one major difference between Rome and the United States is that Rome increased the number of men (both empires used relatively few women) much more because there was relatively little improvement in military technology. In the case of the United States the number of service men increased relatively less as the United States improved its technological military superiority with WMDs and unmanned drones. The average **kill** per military personnel by the

American Empire increased significantly compared to that of the Roman Empire. As the American Empire expands its current warmongering in Iraq, Afghanistan, Pakistan, Libya, Syria, Somalia, Egypt and Yemen, it is shifting increasingly to using unmanned drones and robotics to economize on scarce military personnel and increase the **kill rate** of those personnel. As the leading **terrorist empire** in the world, this will reduce deaths and injuries of its own military personnel by increasing deaths and injuries to innocent Third World civilians, mostly **women and children**. By its own definition that a terrorist is someone who targets civilians the United States has become the leading terrorist nation. The American Empire began targeting civilians when it dropped the nuclear bombs on Nagasaki and Hiroshima.

It's ironic but expected that Western writers are willing to admit the destructive force and civilian casualties inflicted by the Roman Empire but ignore the much greater destructive force and civilian casualties inflicted by the American Empire. An average American, British or Canadian soldier today kills far more people than an average Roman soldier did. Public reaction to the death of a single Canadian, British or American soldier bemoans the fact that the soldier had not achieved a higher **kill** rate before being taken out by an insurgent whose country he had invaded, only because of his superior military technology and desire for an ever-expanding empire. The Western public today pushes their governments for ever more advanced military hardware and WMDs to enhance the **kill** rate of their military men. Many use their personal finances to complement the enormous expenditures of their governments to boost the **kill** rate of their "boys in uniform" who deserve the best equipment to do their killing of innocent men, women and children in far off distant lands.

I find it inconsistent and offensive that Western writers today can readily point to the integration of the military with society in Rome compared with the Western European empires, but not see the identical integration of the military with society in the United States. The following quote from Wikipedia about Rome applies exactly to the United States. "Josephus describes the Roman people being as if they were born ready armed and the Romans were for long periods prepared to engage in almost continuous warfare, absorbing massive losses. For a large part of Rome's history, the Roman state existed as an entity almost solely to support and finance the Roman military." See *en.wikipedia.org/wiki/Military of ancient Rome.*

The Roman soldier fought for land, colonies and plunder much like the American soldier would later do. In both the Roman and American empires the plunder and wealth from new colonies initially exceeded the cost of an ever-expanding military up to an optimal size. Once that optimal size was surpassed both empires experienced an increase in military cost outpacing the plunder from colonial expansion. By the fifth century, Rome found it increasingly difficult to finance its military from taxes just like the American Empire by the twenty-first century. The American Empire today is forced to fund its military with an increasing foreign debt burden. The Roman Empire collapsed under the weight of its overexpansion in 476. The American Empire will collapse under the weight of its overexpansion by 2025.

Another similarity between the Roman Empire and the American Empire was the forging of a common language as one of many ways of building cohesion throughout the empire. In the case of Rome it was the *Latin* language dominating over the Greek language. In the United States it is the *English* language dominating over the Spanish and French languages. Rome's defeat of *Carthage* enabling it to dominate the Mediterranean was not unlike the English speaking Anglo/American defeat of Spain and France to dominate the New World. Of course, the most important commonality between the Roman Empire and the American Empire is *Christianity.*

The Birth of a Religious Western Christian Empire

In 313, the Roman emperor, *Constantine the Great,* issued a decree, the *Edict of Milan*, to cease the persecution of Christians by the Roman Empire, which had begun after the crucifixion of Christ. Rome was plagued by civil wars and loss of territory in the East and the West during the *third century.* In addition, persecution of Christians only seemed to increase the numbers who defied the empire and embraced Christianity. When people are dirt-poor or enslaved, as most were under the civilized Roman Empire, the appeal of a religion promising a "heavenly" life after death for these unfortunate souls, is like winning the lottery. The more you persecute and impoverish them the more they are likely to seek salvation through Christ. By the imperium of Constantine the Great, Christianity had converted many Jews and pagans, especially in the Eastern half of the Roman Empire, despite the efforts of emperors such as Diocletian to punish severely those who converted to Christianity. Had Constantine not embraced Christianity it would likely have survived but not have the worldwide influence it has today. It's a bit like the English language. Had it not been embraced by the Americans it would likely have had less worldwide influence than it has today.

In the twenty-first century it's the Muslims who are the equivalent of the dirt-poor or enslaved Christians of pre-Constantine Rome. The more the American Empire persecutes them the more they rebel and convert to Islam. We never learn from history because those who write our history fall prey to the same powerful propaganda machine as the politicians and voters. Education is a means of spreading the lies and propaganda rather than educating. Academic historians peddle what the establishment wants to hear. I am not suggesting that the West should embrace Islam as the Roman Empire embraced Christianity. That embrace of Christianity by the Roman Empire was a disaster for the human race, since it empowered the Roman Empire to expand its colonization and domination of the world. What I am suggesting is that the West should cease its equivalent persecution of Muslims as pre-Constantine Rome did to Christians, to end the warmongering. Otherwise the West will kill and slaughter many more before it self-destructs.

As I have explained in comparing the Roman and American empires, military prowess as a general was the key to becoming emperor of Rome and president of the United States. It was therefore no surprise that Constantine would rise from humble beginnings to become the sole emperor of Rome because he was the greatest military general of his time. The Roman Empire was built on military prowess and the generals who controlled the military ruled the empire. The Roman Empire was a military dictatorship. It was that military dictatorship that was at the heart and soul of what the American Empire copied and emulated. But Constantine the Great added the sanctity of the Christian church to the arsenal of tools that the West would use to expand its empire. All else is propaganda and window dressing.

Constantine's father, *Constantius,* served the Roman Empire as a military commander in the western fringe of the Roman Empire, *Britain,* at a time when military commanders in every corner of the empire conspired for political opportunity to rule as emperor in some part of a very divided Roman Empire. During the reign of *Gaius Diocletian,* 284–305, the Roman Empire was ruled by a *tetrarchy* made up of two *Augusti* and two *Caesars.* One of those aspiring to rule the Roman Empire was *Gaius Galerius,* made Caesar by Diocletian. Constantine was seen as a political threat to Galerius. Political threats were unceremoniously murdered by those in power who felt threatened. Constantine had to be rescued from his certain fate of death, by his father. The Roman Empire had lost its colony of *Britain* to rebels. In 296, Britain was retaken as a colony by Constantius who was promoted to Caesar for his military successes in Britain and Gaul.

In 305, Constantius, recently promoted from Caesar to *Augustus of the West,* by Diocletian, asked for his son to join him in Britain to help him subdue the rebels in this remote western outpost of the Roman Empire. Galerius was naturally opposed to this request since he had been conspiring to end the young man's life while he was still in his court in Greece, the home of the Caesar of the East. Constantine seized the opportunity of a night of heavy drinking by Galerius to get permission to leave and escaped that same night before Galerius could execute a plot to kill him. He succeeded in outwitting his pursuers and joined his father in Gaul. They crossed the English Channel together to the relatively safe haven of distant Britain. Diocletian abdicated that same year as Augustus of the East because of his deteriorating health. Galerius became Augustus of the East. A year later, Constantius died and Galerius promoted *Flavius Severus* from Caesar to the new Augustus of the West. Severus had been the general that Galerius had assigned the task of killing Constantine. Galerius was reluctantly forced to grant the title of *Caesar* to Constantine to avoid a military confrontation with him and his father's soldiers who were now loyal to Constantine. As Caesar, Constantine ruled over Gaul, Britain, and Spain, the western front of the Roman Empire. The Roman capital for this Western region was *Trier* in Gaul. Constantine had inherited from his father one of the most powerful military forces in the Roman Empire. Diocletian's tetrarchy, designed to end civil wars, was now the source of intense rivalry among the four rulers for dominance.

In the civil wars that followed Constantine's confirmation as Caesar in 306, he defeated other generals, such as *Maximian, Maxentius*, and *Licinius,* who had also fought to rule the Roman Empire. In October of 306 the Senate in Rome acclaimed *Maxentius* as the Augustus of the West. This led to military conflict between Maxentius and Severus, the Augustus appointed by Galerius. Defeated in battle by Maxentius, Severus killed himself in 307. *Marcus Maximian,* the father of Maxentius, had been Augustus of the West until he was forced to retire at the same time as Diocletian in 305. Maximian now wanted to seize the title of Augustus of the West from his son. Maximian fought both his son and Constantine but was defeated in Gaul by Constantine in 310 and hanged himself. Constantine had hoped to succeed his father as Augustus of the West but would have to fight Maxentius, as he had fought Maximian, to get it. Maxentius also wanted to avenge his father's defeat by Constantine. Constantine had been declared as Augustus of the West by his soldiers since his father's death in 306. But Galerius had rejected that claim. While Constantine ruled his fourth of the empire from Trier between 306 and 312 Maxentius held on the title of Augustus of the West and ruled the Western half of the empire from Rome. In the meantime Galerius ruled the Eastern half of the empire.

In 312 Constantine made his move. Leaving most of his army to defend his fourth of the Roman Empire he led a quarter of his men to do battle with Maxentius. He crossed the Alps and marched into Italy defeating three armies sent against him by Maxentius. In October 312 he finally defeated Maxentius in the famous battle at *Milvian Bridge,* just outside the city of Rome. It was this battle more than any other that supposedly converted Constantine to Christianity. His forces outnumbered by more than two to one by that of Maxentius, it is claimed that just before the battle commenced he had a vision of the Christian cross with an inscription that said he will conquer. Maxentius was killed and his forces retreated in disarray. Many drowned in the Tiber River trying to escape. After entering Rome in October 312 he was acclaimed as the greatest "Augustus" by the Senate in Rome. By 312

Constantine had solidified his claim as Augustus of the West through military victories over his many rivals. He had also begun his personal transformation from pagan to Christian. In 312 the Roman Empire was still largely a pagan empire.

In the East *Valerius Licinius,* a friend of Galerius, had fought and manipulated his way to succeed Galerius, who died in 311. Constantine formed an uneasy alliance with Licinius, as Augustus of the East, by getting his eighteen-year-old half sister to marry the fifty-year-old Licinius in February 313. Marriage has been one of the most common methods used by Western rulers to form alliances. The wedding took place in Milan, Italy and the famous *Edict of Milan* was issued jointly by Constantine and Licinius. In addition to ending the persecution of Christians the Edict restored previously confiscated Christian church property. Licinius went on to defeat in battle his primary contender to the title of Augustus of the East, *Maximinus Daia,* in May of 313. Daia committed suicide and Licinius executed all of Daia's allies. Licinius settled into the Eastern imperial city of Nicomedia in Turkey while Constantine had returned to the Western imperial city of Trier in Gaul. But the alliance was a very difficult one because the ultimate goal of all of the generals during the tetrarchy was unifying power into a single emperor. We witness a struggle between Constantine and Licinius that would benefit Christians much like the American Civil War benefitted black Americans.

In our prequels we argued that President Lincoln used *slavery* to win his war with the Southern states and unify the American Empire. In like manner many historians claim that Constantine used the Christians to win his war with Licinius and unify the Roman Empire under his single leadership. While the evidence that Lincoln was no *abolitionist* is overwhelming the historical evidence on whether Constantine was a genuine convert to Christianity or a power hungry opportunist is less clear. In both cases what mattered was the outcome. African American slaves got their freedom because Lincoln was willing to pay that price to secure a larger empire. Christians got an increase in privileges and influence either because Constantine was convinced that the Christian God was the true God or was willing to abandon his pagan god to secure his goal of becoming the single emperor of the Roman Empire.

In the Eastern Roman Empire where the majority of Christians lived they prayed for Constantine, not Licinius. The increased popularity of Constantine with the Christians in the Eastern Roman Empire led to Licinius plotting to assassinate Constantine, while stirring up pagan resentment, both by the majority pagan population and pagan senators in Rome, at Constantine's preferential treatment of Christians. It seemed to many pagan senators that Constantine was misusing the empire's tax revenues to build grandiose Christian churches and that Christian bishops were being given too much administrative powers.

Much like Prime Minister *Pierre Trudeau* making the ability to speak French a huge advantage in getting an administrative position in Canada it seemed to the pagans that Constantine was making conversion to Christianity a huge privilege in the Roman Empire. The majority pagan population resented this change as much as the majority English speaking Canadians resented Trudeau's forced bilingualism. Constantine's support of religious freedom was disguised favoritism for Christians just as Trudeau's bilingualism was disguised favoritism for French Canadians. Pagans converted to Christianity because of these privileges rather than religious conviction just as many English Canadians forced their children to attend French immersion schools. Constantine got wind of the plot by Licinius to assassinate him and caught the assassin. Constantine used the failed assassination plot as grounds for a full blown civil war against Licinius.

Armed conflicts between the two Augusti broke out in the Balkans in 316. Licinius lost both the Balkans and Greece to Constantine. Licinius became increasingly concerned about the influence of Christians in his remaining part of the Eastern Roman Empire. To counter Constantine's increasing support for Christians, Licinius began to increase his persecution of Christians and reducing their privileges. In 323, Licinius took advantage of an invasion by the Goths to declare war on Constantine. It would result in the first of many Christian "holy wars" against heathens and savages, white and red. Constantine rallied his holy Christian warriors against those who dared to worship pagan gods. The armies met near the Hebrus River in Greece on July 3, 324. The Christian warriors crossed the Hebrus River and massacred the enemy at the *Battle of Adrianople.* Licinius' navy was next destroyed by

Constantine's son at the Battle of Hellespont. The decisive battle was fought in Turkey on September 18, 324. Licinius' army was destroyed at the *Battle of Chrysopolis.* Constantine became the sole emperor of the Roman Empire in 324. In recognition of the Eastern half of the Roman Empire being the senior partner Constantine built a new capital city in Turkey in 330. This new capital city, *Constantinople,* was built on the grounds of the ancient city of Byzantium on the border between Europe and Asia. By straddling the two continents it provided a symbolic geographical bridge between East and West. The Eastern region would maintain its long historical dominance of the world in terms of culture and civilization until the eighteenth century.

Constantine had ended the *tetrarchy,* an important legacy of Emperor Diocletian. While the tetrarchy of Diocletian was an admission that the Roman Empire was too large to be governed by a single emperor, from a single imperial center, Constantine became *Constantine the Great* because he proved Diocletian to be wrong. While the single emperor did not survive the death of Constantine, it has survived in the copycat Roman Empire, the *American Empire.* The American Empire has a single emperor and a single imperial center in Washington DC. Of course, the American emperor has the title of commander in chief since the American Empire insists that it is not an empire. When the American Empire wants to deny its addiction to warmongering it uses the more peaceful title of Mr. President.

Throughout history, rulers, and generals called on the gods to bring them victory in wars. Victory was proof that your God was the true divine one. Those who lost wars worshipped false gods. By implication, true gods loved those who won wars. True gods do not abhor wars. They only abhor losing wars. Constantine called on the God of the Christians to help him win his civil wars against competing emperors, *Maxentius* and *Licinius,* as well as expand the Roman Empire with wars against the *Sarmatians*, *Franks*, and *Goths.* The *Franks* invaded Gaul in 306–307 and Constantine defeated them. In 309–310 Constantine successfully defended the Western Roman Empire along the Rhine from attacks by the Franks and other Germanic tribes such as the Bructeri and Alamanni. In 322–323 Constantine waged successful wars on the Sarmatians and Goths.

By invoking the God of the Christians and by winning his many wars with the help of the God of the Christians, Constantine was instrumental in making the Christian God the one true God, the civilized God, the God who will bring you victory in your many wars to expand the empire and the God who will make you the supreme **warmonger.** Constantine also observed how the Disciples of Christ were using religious propaganda, rather than military victories, to convert many to their cause. If he could combine the missionary zeal of the Christians with the military prowess of the Romans he had the most winning combination to expand his empire. After becoming sole emperor Constantine was able to expand the privileges granted to Christians in the Eastern half of the Roman Empire. Since the majority of Christians lived in the Eastern half of the Roman Empire at that time this was a significant boost to the influence of Christianity. Emperor Diocletian is remembered not only for creating the tetrarchy but also for his extreme persecution of Christians. During his rule Christians represented about 10 percent of the population of the empire. Diocletian was determined to kill, enslave, torture and persecute Christians and burn and destroy their churches. This reversal of policy by Constantine is what really made him "Constantine the Great" to Christians. But in embracing Christianity Constantine also began the process of making Western states and Western empires less secular and more religious.

All future emperors of Rome, with the single exception of Emperor Julian, 355–363, were Christians. Likewise all presidents of the American Empire have been Christians. Emperor Julian's efforts to return the Roman Empire to its more secular "pagan" traditions failed and earned him the derogatory title of "Julian the Apostate." President Obama was obliged to forcefully and continuously deny his Muslim heritage and was always challenged by Americans to prove his belief in Christianity while supporting the propaganda that the West has successfully separated church and state. President Obama was even ridiculed by the media for attending a Christian church led by a **black** preacher. The black preacher had not been as supportive of American warmongering as is to be expected of a Christian priest in the American Empire. President Obama and his family were forced to attend a Christian church where the priest was more supportive of the important role of the Christian church in furthering Western imperialism.

It is not surprising that historians provide two opposing views of the legacy of Constantine the Great. Those who opposed his conversion to Christianity and ending the persecution of Christians emphasize his barbaric side. Those who recognized his importance in making Christianity the lasting religion of the West portray him as divine. The reality is that all imperialism is evil and barbaric. But religion condones and enhances that evil and barbarity to increase its converts. Christianity is only different in that it has honed this skill more than any other religion. Since Constantine, the Christian religion has been one of the most important tools used by the West to colonize and exploit the people of the world. The Christian church has absolutely no qualms in combing religion with the military brutality used by every empire to conquer and subjugate the human race. Constantine was the typical ruthless Roman general who gave Christianity the chance to combine evangelism with insatiable warmongering for the complementary goals of empire and converts. Every Western leader since Constantine has used the Christian religion to support their invasions, warmongering, conquests, and colonizations. The Christian church has been a very willing accomplice since it was the best way to increase the number of Christians across the globe.

In 380 Christianity became the official religion of the Roman Empire. Rather than being persecuted by the Roman Empire, as Christians were before 313, Christians, the Christian church and leaders of the Christian church, archbishops, and bishops exerted immense influence on the state. In many ways the political leaders, emperors, kings, dukes and princes, became subservient to the spiritual leaders of the Christian church. The Roman Empire was transformed into the *Holy Roman Empire.* Henceforth, Western imperialism would be sanctioned by the Christian God and the Christian church. That unity between Western states and the Christian religion that began in 380 continues to this day. Despite the many historical conflicts among Christians they are united when it comes to supporting Western imperialism, the wholesale conquest and subjugation of the First Nations and people of the Third World, and Western domination of the world. While many Muslim states today are pro-Western, there is not a single Christian state that is pro-Eastern.

The central role of Christianity in Western domination gained renewed vitality when the United Sates replaced Western Europe as the leader of the West. By the eighteenth century, Western European intellectuals were increasingly questioning the right of religious dogma to play such an important role in the governance of "people's democracy." Not so in the United States. If anything, the role of religious dogma in the governance of the United Sates increased. Once the United States became the leader of the West the central historical role of the Christian religion in Western imperialism, and Western domination of the world, was guaranteed to continue. The so-called *religious right* in the United States has increased its popularity and influence on the governance of the United States in the twenty-first century.

Many in the West have tried to separate "church from state," but have never succeeded. With the American Empire taking away leadership of the West from Western Europe the unity of church and state in the West is greater today than it was in the century before American dominance. American *Christianites* in the United States have more influence on the political process today than ever before. President Obama had great difficulty convincing American *Christianites* that he was sufficiently religious and Christian to be the leader of America and the West. President Obama went to great lengths to hide his *Muslim* heritage. God forbid that the leader of a country professing to have separated church from state should be a **Muslim.** It's somewhat ironic that the West accuses Muslim states of not separating state and religion without recognizing that they have not either. It's another example of Western hypocrisy, propaganda and double talk much like their professed belief in democracy, freedom and equality

Religion and Imperialism

Religion has always been a force in imperialism. But it was the embrace of *Christianity* by the Roman Empire that led to religion playing such a central role in imperial expansion. Rome's embrace of Christianity made imperialism a crusade to Christianize the "heathens" of the world.

Imperialism was no longer only a civilizing force. It was doing God's work. These twin propagandas, civilizing and conversion to the one true religion, gave imperialism such a powerful "moral" justification that it could colonize, subjugate, conquer, terrorize, exploit and plunder at will. The twinning of these two propagandas is so awesome that the West will never separate church from state despite all its rhetoric to the contrary. The *Christian church* has been, and will continue to be, a key weapon in the West achieving its goal of dominating and subjugating mankind and the world. This explains why it is so fearful of *Islam* today. Islam is the only other religion that, like *Christianity,* uses religion as an integral part of its governance and political structure and is opposed to Western domination. Judaism, of course, was the first religion to integrate religion and governance. The West co-opted the Jews by planting and arming the Western colony of Israel in the heartland of the Muslim Middle East.

The Christian religion originated in the *first* century in the Jewish kingdom of Judea. At the time Judea was a Roman colony. It was not until the *second* century that Christians were fully differentiated from Jews in Judea. The Muslim religion, *Islam,* originated in the *seventh* century in the Arab kingdom of Arabia. Both Christianity and Islam have historical roots in *Judaism.* Many coverts to Christianity and Islam were Jews. Christianity and Islam therefore converted both people who were previously religious as well as people who had no previous religion. In many cases the Christians and Muslims used force to get both religious and nonreligious people to convert to their faith and their God. This use of military force to convert "heathens" was especially true in the New World invaded and conquered by the Christian West after 1492.

In 395 the Roman Empire was split into a Greek language Eastern Empire and a Latin language Western Empire. This split had begun much earlier once it became impossible to rule such a large empire by a single unified administration. As we saw earlier, Diocletian had also followed the East/West divide by appointing a second Augustus to rule the Western half. After the death of Constantine his three sons squabbled over the empire but further consolidated the East/West divide. *Theodosius I* was the last emperor to rule a unified Roman Empire. His rule ended in 395. Constantine was also responsible for creating a tradition of *dynastic rule* for the Roman Empire. The history of an East/West division and the tradition of dynastic inheritance enabled the sons of Theodosius I to rule as joint emperors with *Arcadius* in the East, and *Honorius* in the West. Constantinople became the capital of the Eastern half and Milano became the capital of the Western half. The Eastern half continued to be the senior part of this relationship as it had been from the very beginning. This was implicitly recognized by Diocletian when he created the tetrarchy. Diocletian elected *Maximian* as coemperor but remained Augustus of the Eastern Roman Empire. The senior position of the Eastern Roman Empire was also implicitly recognized by Constantine who had been Augustus of the Western Roman Empire prior to becoming sole emperor. Constantine implicitly recognized the senior position of the Eastern Roman Empire by promoting the ancient city of *Byzantium* in the heart of the Near East into the dominant city, the New Rome, of the entire Roman Empire, and renaming it *Constantinople.* It is for this reason that the Eastern half of the Roman Empire is also known as the *Byzantine Empire*

As we have explained before, the Middle East had been the center of the civilized world since the beginning of what we call civilization. It remained the center of the civilized world under the dominance of two Western empires, Greece and Rome. The Eastern Roman Empire continued to be more urban and the center of culture. The Western Roman Empire continued to be more rural and barbaric. What has been called the barbarian invasions destroyed the Western Roman Empire. In 402 the *Goths,* led by Alaric, invaded Italy. In 406 the *Goths* invaded Italy again, this time led by Radagaisus. That same year the *Vandals* attacked the Roman capital city of Trier in Gaul. In 408 Alaric invaded Italy again. In November of 408 the Goths reached Rome and were reinforced by Huns and escaped slaves. They laid siege to the city. Inside the besieged city Romans died from hunger and diseases. Once inside the city gates the Goths did not destroy Rome in the way Rome had destroyed Carthage. This was another example that those the West claim to be civilized are barbarians and those the West claim to be barbarians are civilized. Many historians claim that it was Rome's destruction of Carthage, which had removed a moral check on its unbridled penchant for barbaric behavior, much like the fall of the Soviet Union removed a moral restraint on the penchant for warmongering by the American Empire.

Alaric died in 410 and under the leadership of Alaric's brother, Athaulf, the Goths settled in Gaul. The Western Roman Empire was rescued from the Gothic sack of Rome by the Roman general *Flavius Constantius.* Emperor *Honorius,* the younger son of Emperor *Theodosius I,* made emperor of the Western Roman Empire in 395 by his father when he was only ten years old, seized an opportunity to regain his empire after the disastrous sacking of Rome by the Goths. During the siege of Rome, the sister of Emperor Honorius, Galla Placidia, was taken hostage. Galla Placidia was rescued from the Goths by General Flavius Constantius. She was forced by her brother to marry the general. General Constantius first defeated the Goths in Gaul then used an alliance with them to defeat the Vandals. In return for his services he was made coemperor with Honorius. His son with Galla Placidia, *Valentinian III,* became emperor after the death of Honorius. Like his father's alliance with a successful Roman general, Emperor Valentinian III formed a strong alliance with the Roman general *Flavius Aetius,* who succeeded Constantius as commander in chief.

The Vandals struck again in 429 capturing Morocco and Algeria. Rome faced a new barbarian invasion during the 430s. Rome lost its important grain supplies from North Africa. Carthage, the city that had made Rome the undisputed leader of the world, was lost to the Vandals in 439. The Huns, now led by *Attila the Hun,* attacked the Eastern Roman Empire in the 440s. This made it impossible for the forces of the Eastern Roman Empire to assist the West against the renewed barbarian invasion. In 451 Attila turned his attention to the West but was defeated in Gaul by General Aetius. Attila was more successful when he invaded Italy the following year. He laid siege to the capital city of Milan forcing Valentinian III to flee to Rome. Rome was saved when Attila died suddenly that same year but North Africa was not recaptured. Emperor Valentinian III became envious of his famous general, Aetius, and assassinated him in 454. The following year two soldiers loyal to the general succeeded in killing the emperor. In that same year, May 455, the Vandals sacked Rome and killed the emperor who succeeded Valentinian III. The next emperor, *Avitus,* died in 457. In 468 the Eastern Roman

Empire attempted to recapture North Africa from the sea only to have its navy destroyed by the Vandals.

The rivalry for the title of emperor of the Western Roman Empire only intensified after the death of Valentinian III. Between the murder of Valentinian III and the fall of the Western Roman Empire in 476, there were as many as eight emperors, *Petronius Maximus, Avitus, Majorian, Libius Severus, Anthemius, Glycerius, Julius Nepos,* and *Romulus Augustus.* The end came when a Roman general, *Flavius Odovacar,* decided to overthrow the emperor, Romulus Augustus, but not make himself the new emperor. He chose instead the title *king of Italy.* Generals overthrowing Roman emperors were an almost every day affair in the history of the Roman Empire. In fact, Romulus Augustus had become emperor because his father, Flavius Orestes, was commander in chief of the Roman forces, and overthrew the emperor. Orestes was made commander in chief by Emperor Julius Nepos in 475. Orestes needed to combine his forces with those led by General Odovacar to overthrow Emperor Julius Nepos. Generals became emperors or were promoted by emperors who needed their military prowess to conquer new lands, protect old conquests, and defeat the numerous contenders for the title of emperor. What was different about the overthrow of Romulus Augustus in 476 was the decision not to replace him with a new emperor. After the overthrow of Emperor Julius Nepos, the alliance between Orestes and Odovacar fell apart. Odovacar defeated Orestes in battle and executed Orestes. On September 4, 476, Odovacar overthrew the teenage son of Orestes, Romulus Augustus. By choosing the title of *king of Italy,* instead of emperor of the Western Roman Empire, Odovacar officially ended the Western Roman Empire.

The Roman Empire had begun by first conquering Italy and expanding outward to the North and East. When it defeated its primary rival for world domination, Carthage, it felt secure as the only superpower. But in the end it was defeated not by another superpower but by attacks from many small insurgencies. In like manner the American Empire felt secured when it became the only superpower after the fall of the Soviet Union. In the end the American Empire will not be defeated by another superpower but by many small insurgencies. History has a habit of repeating itself.

The period of 313–1400 saw the rise and fall of both the Christian and Muslim empires, prior to the second rise of the Christian Empire after 1400. During the period after 1400 the conflict between Christians and Muslims, which began in the seventh century, continued. But the Christian Empire became the dominant empire after 1400. The Muslim Empire was mostly an Eastern Empire while the Christian Empire after 1400 was largely a Western-based empire, even though it dominated the entire world during the nineteenth and twentieth centuries. The religious difference between Christians and Muslims is therefore one of the important reasons for the modern conflict between East and West. The East/West division goes back to the division of the Roman Empire in 395 and before. This East/West conflict is much more than a religious conflict but religion is a fundamental weapon used by both sides.

With the rise of Portugal and Spain after 1400 the reborn Western Latin language *Christian* Roman Empire expanded westward and northward from Portugal and Spain to the New World and Holland, England, France, Italy, Germany and Scandinavia. The Muslim Empire, which was born after 635, largely held on to its conquest of the Eastern Greek-language *Christian* Roman Empire centered on *Constantinople*—now *Istanbul.* That East/West division of the world that began with the split of the Roman Empire in the late fourth century only widened after the rebirth of the Western Empire under Portugal and Spain and the birth of the Dutch, French, British, Italian, German and American empires. One example of the continuing conflict between the Christian and Muslim empires is that the new capital for the *Christian* Roman Empire created by Constantine, *Constantinople,* is today the capital of the *Muslim* state of Turkey, *Istanbul.* Today Turkey finds itself divided between its desire to be both Eastern and Western.

Since 2011 mass protests erupted in the Muslim states of Egypt, Libya, Tunisia, Syria, and Turkey as Muslims in the Middle East foolishly sought American and Western arms and propaganda, to depose autocratic governments that had been imposed by the West, or had been supported militarily by the West. The best example of this was Egypt where the protestors sought help from the West and the Western media to overthrow the Western imposed military government led by Hosni Mubarak and the Egyptian military. The United States and the West have had a field day stirring up civil unrest, civil wars and Sunni/Shia conflicts in the region. Muslims are more divided than ever, and the growing internal strife and dissention compensates for the weakening economic and military clout of the West. The long historical conflicts among Arabs, Persians and Turks, once resolved by their conversion to Islam, have been cleverly stirred up by Western propaganda about freedom and democracy. When once Islam was a uniting force its now divisive since the West has cleverly pitted Shia Iran against Sunni Saudi Arabia, adding fuel to the historical fire of Arab/Persian/Turk warmongering.

Adding insult to injury the West has used their instigated civil wars in Muslim countries to coin one of the dumbest of propaganda slogans. The fact that such a dumb slogan has any traction is yet another indicator of the dismal failure of Western education. A kindergarten child without Western brainwashing would know that in civil wars your own people are those who are killed. Yet the West has been able to make Western educated adults believe that President Lincoln never "killed his own people" during the American Civil War. Only "dictators" like Gadhafi or Bashar al-Assad, opposed to Western imperialism, "kill their own people" in Civil wars. In all other civil wars, dictators who support Western imperialism and American presidents like Abraham Lincoln kill only "aliens from outer space," never their own people.

Jerusalem and the Jewish Connection with Christianity and Islam

It is useful to understand the history of the present day struggle between the Muslim East and the Christian West in the Middle East. As late as the seventh century BCE, the Eastern *Semitic* race, Arabs, Phoenicians, Babylonians, Assyrians, Jews and others, dominated the world. Up to that time the Western *Aryan* race was considered barbaric. The Jews, a *Semitic* race, had settled in Judea before the seventh century BCE. Their capital city was Jerusalem. Judea was a tiny state surrounded by powerful empires such as Persia, Babylon and Egypt. The Roman Empire colonized this region after the Greeks. Christianity came to the region shortly after the birth of Jesus Christ but the Romans lost its colony to the Persian Empire in 226, before conversion of the West to Christianity by the Roman Empire.

Islam came to the region when it was conquered from the Persian Empire by the Arab Empire in the seventh century. Arabs share the *Semitic* race and language with Jews. The Semitic language, *Aramaic,* widely spoken throughout the ancient Middle East, came from the Arabs. Since the Persians converted to Islam, Muslim control of the region can be dated to the Persian conquest of 226. The Christian West has launched numerous unsuccessful invasions in the region ever since the Roman Empire lost it to the Persian Empire. All of these Western invasions, including the current Invasions of Afghanistan and Iraq dating back to 2001, are imperialist. The West, currently led by the American Empire, has been at war with Muslims in the Middle East for over two thousand years, for the single purpose of colonizing all of the countries in the region, including Saudi Arabia, Egypt, Iran, Iraq, Lebanon, Syria, Kuwait, Afghanistan and the Persian Gulf states. Since the relative decline in the Arab Empire, the Muslims have fought a defensive war against the Western aggressors, beginning with the Crusades. Up until Israel was planted as an American *uncolony* in the region after World War II, the West fought both the Muslims and the Jews. The Anglo/American ploy to pretend to help the Jews by giving them a home in the Middle East co-opted the Jews to the Western imperialist cause.

We know of the history of the Jews from their Bible, the *Old Testament* or *Hebrew Bible.* In this Bible we learn of creation, Adam and Eve, and prophets such as Moses and Abraham. We also learn of their kings such as Saul, David and Solomon. Their belief in a single invisible God has been adopted by both Christians and Muslims. The notion of a single God originated in Egypt during the fourteenth century BCE. The Pharaoh, *Amenhotep IV,* became famous mostly because of his beautiful queen, *Nefertiti,* but is also remembered for being the first ruler to embrace the idea of a single God. We learn from the Hebrew Bible that the "land of Canaan," present day Palestine/Israel, and much of the land of the states surrounding Palestine/Israel such as Lebanon, Jordan, Syria and Egypt, was promised to Abraham and his offspring by God as early as 1,850 BCE. The *Canaanites* had lived in the area for thousands of years. They were not a single race but a mixture of many races, including

Arabs. Basically God told the Hebrews to forcefully take the land from the Canaanites much as the American Empire told the Jews to forcefully take the same land again from the Palestinians. According to this version of history all Jews, Christians and Muslims have a historic claim to this area of the Middle East by virtue of their direct lineage to the one father, Abraham.

Abraham and his people left *Ur* in *Sumer,* to settle in Canaan. Sumer was located in what is present day Iraq, then called Mesopotamia. The Sumerians were one of the most ancient civilizations. Ur was the capital and center of power for the Sumerians who exercised imperial power over the many city states of Mesopotamia after 2,750 BCE. Arab claim to this land predates the arrival of Abraham since their ancestors built the city of *Jericho,* which is located in present day Palestine. Jericho was built some six thousand years before Abraham and is considered to be the first city that has been continuously inhabited. Today, Jericho is occupied by the American *uncolony* of Israel.

One view of the centuries of wars between Jews, Christians and Muslims is that of a family dispute over inheritance. The notion of a single God, so treasured by Jews, Christians and Muslims, has the very dangerous implication that the descendants of Abraham have the divine right to inherit the entire world. When we add the sad reality that all religions preach peace but make wars we get one important explanation of the continuing wars between Jews, Christians and Muslims. The reasons for these continuing wars are many and complex but the religious connection cannot be ignored. It's a good place to begin our explanation of why the West never became civilized and why the last six centuries of Western dominance prevented the rest of the world from becoming civilized. Western leadership was imposed on the world by military force. In the last six centuries, only the West had the choice to civilize the human race. It failed to do so and must be held accountable for that failure. The East was never given a choice during the last six centuries of Western dominance.

The Jews were a persecuted people from time immemorial. Canaan did not prove to be the "Land of milk and honey" promised to Abraham by God. In fact, the Hebrew God, *Yahweh,* may have played a sick joke on the Jews because oil was later found in Iraq, which their God told them to leave, not in Palestine, where their God sent them. It was the God of the Christians who later told President George W. Bush to invade Iraq and take the oil. Abraham's people had to eke out a living by becoming shepherds in the wilds of Canaan. They eventually immigrated to Egypt to escape their miserable life and famine in Canaan. At the time Egypt was a thriving empire built on the fertile Nile River. One of the descendants of Abraham, Joseph, had previously migrated to Egypt. He welcomed his family and helped them to settle in Egypt. Sometime after the death of Joseph the family was enslaved under the Pharaoh, Ramses II. To escape slavery Moses and Joshua led them out of Egypt back to "the land of Canaan," around 1,200 BCE. But Canaan was inhabited and the people were understandably unwilling to donate their land to the Hebrews even if God was on their side. The Jews, then as now, would have to use military force to steal the land from its rightful owners. On their return they honed their military skills and engaged in a long and brutal holy war, against those who dared to inhabit the lands promised to them by their God. That war continues today against the Palestinians.

The ten-thousand-year-old "Arab" city of Jericho was their first conquest. In two centuries of warfare the Jews exterminated all who had lived in the "land of Canaan" before 1,200 BCE—men, women, children, and animals. It was one of the earliest examples of ethnic cleansing based on religious "superiority." It's not unlike the Europeans using the excuse of their Christian God to steal the lands of the First Nations by military force and committing genocide and ethnic cleansing based on religious and racial "superiority."

Shortly after their conquest of Canaan the *Philistines* invaded Canaan. Two invaders, Hebrews and Philistines battled for Canaan much like the later wars between England and France in North America. The Philistines had the better of this conflict until the young David slew Goliath with his slingshot during the reign of the first king of the Hebrews, *Saul.* What followed was a battle between Saul and David for the Jewish kingdom. David was crowned as the new king by the tribe of *Judah,* one of the twelve tribes of Israel resulting from the twelve sons of Jacob, the grandson of Abraham, who had changed his name to *Israel.* Among the Canaanites was a group living in a hilly area called *Jebus* since 1,800 BCE. By 1,000 BCE the Israelites had wiped out all opposition and reconquered the Holy Land, as well as the Jebusite city of Jebus, which became the city we know as *Jerusalem.* Under King David, Jerusalem replaced Hebron as the capital of the Jewish kingdom. Like the American Empire's many token payments for lands stolen from the First Nations, King David made a token payment of six hundred gold shekels to the conquered Canaanites, for Jebus. Jerusalem was a militarily strategic choice by King David as well as one of godly significance. Jerusalem is located on Mount Moriah, which is the mountain where Abraham was told by God to sacrifice his son, Isaac.

This Jewish kingdom expanded its territory under David's son, King Solomon. Solomon killed his bother to seize his father's kingdom. King Solomon used **slave** labor to build the temple in Jerusalem as well as **military** bases to protect the much enlarged Jewish state. It was the slave-built temple of Jerusalem, more than its connection with Abraham, which endowed Jerusalem with holy significance for the Jews. God had told Solomon's father, David, to build a temple on Mount Moriah to house the Ark of the Covenant containing the Ten Commandments. This was the temple built by Solomon. It was 50 feet high with a length of 180 feet and width of 90 feet. It survives today only as part of the base of the holy *Western Wall.* Implicitly, the God of the Jews condoned the use of slaves to build his temple.

Jewish hegemony then, as now, was temporary. Military superiority then, as now, will not keep those you evict and conquer outside your gates forever. Even in the United States, the most powerful country in history, Mexicans are returning today to take back the lands stolen from them by earlier U.S. warmongering. The Jews were wise to conquer and make Jerusalem their capital city because of its strategic military advantage as well as its supposedly godly protection. But the twelve sons of Abraham's grandson, Jacob (Israel), who became the leaders of the twelve tribes of Israel continued their historical feuding. This family feud had begun with Joseph feeling alienated from the other brothers and fleeing to Egypt. Then we saw the tribe of Judah plotting against King Saul to give the throne to David. Under King Solomon the tribes living in the North were subjugated by those in the South. After Solomon's death the Northern tribes refused to recognize his son, *Rehoboam,* as king. A civil war in the Jewish kingdom led to the division of the kingdom into the northern

Kingdom of *Israel* and the southern Kingdom of *Judah* in 926 BCE. Ten of the twelve tribes settled in Israel and only two tribes, those led by Jacob's sons, Judah and Benjamin, settled in Judah. Jerusalem became the capital of Judah and the Jewish religion became *Judaism.*

In 722 BCE the northern Jewish Kingdom of Israel was conquered by the Assyrians. The Assyrians had conquered Mesopotamia in 1,200 BCE and expanded their empire to include Palestine and Syria. They built a new capital city in Mesopotamia called *Nineveh.* The Assyrian king *Sargon II* forced the Jews to leave the northern Kingdom of Israel. Subsequent Jewish history is based on the descendants of the two tribes in Judah since there is no record of what happened to the "Ten lost tribes" of Israel. A rebirth of Israel as the "land of the Jews" would have to be **manufactured** by the British and Americans in the twentieth century. Western imperialism takes every opportunity to reinvigorate its colonialism. As Britain and France in 2011 used the Libyan civil war to reinvigorate its colonialism in North Africa so did Britain and the United States seize the opportunity of persecuted Jews in the twentieth century to reinvigorate their colonialism in the Middle East by planting the *uncolony* of Israel on Palestinian land.

The Mesopotamian city state of *Babylon* revolted against Assyrian rule and overthrew the Assyrians in 612 BCE. Under King Nebuchadnezzar II a new empire centered on Babylon flourished. In 587 BCE the southern Jewish Kingdom of Judah was conquered by Babylon and the temple built by Solomon destroyed. God had not intervened to protect Jerusalem or the temple. Many Jews were taken as captives to Babylon after the Babylonians invaded Judah and burnt Jerusalem. But unlike the original Kingdom of Israel the Kingdom of Judah would survive and would be transformed by the twentieth-century Western empires into the militarized and nuclear armed "state" of Israel.

In Babylon the Jews were rescued by the **Persian** king, Cyrus, after Persia conquered Babylon in 539 BCE. The Persian Empire eventually expanded from Mesopotamia to India. The Persians were Zoroastrians and were tolerant of other religions. Under Cyrus the Jews were free to return to Judah and many did. By 515 BCE the temple built by Solomon had been rebuilt on the original site. This rebuilt temple is referred to as "The Second Temple." Judah was now a colony of the Persian Empire but with a lot of autonomy. It was not allowed to have a king but a "High Priest" who acted as the local ruler. Aramaic became the official language of Palestine. It was the language spoken by Jesus Christ. The Jews had moved back and forth between Iraq and Palestine during this period. Many would have remained in Iraq and many would have moved out of both Iraq and Palestine. In Palestine the Jews would never regain full independence. Even today, Israel, revered as it is by the West, survives only because it is in reality an *uncolony* of the American Empire. Take away its American protection and it would disintegrate and wither away. Many Jews would remain but there would be no Jewish state.

Exile in Egypt and Babylon had not taught Jews how to be tolerant and how to live peacefully with their neighbors. On their return to Judah after 539 BCE they wanted all of the land just as they had when they had returned from Egypt. They would wage another holy war with the inhabitants just as they are doing currently against the Palestinians. When the West expanded under Alexander the Great, Jerusalem was conquered in 313 BCE. This marked the beginning of Western claims to Jerusalem and Judah. But Alexander was no protector of Jews or the temple. He did his best to replace the God of the Jews with Greek religious beliefs and pagan worship. During the *Hellenistic* period, Judah, like all of the lands conquered by Alexander, became "Hellenized." Jerusalem became less religious and more interested in commerce and economic development. Jews traveled, emigrated, and engaged in business throughout the Greek Empire. Greek language, culture and influence replaced the Hebrew language and Jewish culture and religious practices.

Alexander died in the Iraqi city state of Babylon in 323 BCE. With the death of Alexander the Great the lands he conquered were divided up into three empires ruled by three of the generals who had served Alexander. Antigonus took Greece, Ptolemy took Egypt and Palestine and Seleucus took Iraq, Syria and Persia. Initially Judah was ruled from Egypt by *Ptolemy* but by 200 BCE Judah became part of the *Seleucid Empire* based in Syria and its capital of *Antioch*. By the time *Antiochus IV* became the ruler of the Seleucid Empire in 175 BCE, the Jews of Jerusalem and Judah were divided between those holding on to tradition and religion and those who had become secular and modern. With the support of the Hellenized urban Jews Antiochus replaced the Jewish High Priest *Onias*

III with his more secular brother, Jason. Antiochus IV, his new High Priest and the Hellenized Jews, converted Jerusalem from a Jewish holy city to a modern Greek city.

The Second Temple built after the Jews returned from Babylon was desecrated and practice of the Jewish faith was discouraged. Once again Jews were persecuted. The Jews who wanted a more traditional Jerusalem and Judah revolted against the Seleucid reforms. As with all examples of militarily weaker rebels taking on a militarily more powerful empire, the rebels resorted to guerrilla warfare. The revolt was led by Mattathias and his five sons who came to be known as the *Maccabees.* A year after the death of Mattathias his son *Judas Maccabee* led a successful rebellion defeating the Seleucid forces in 166 BCE and returned Judah to its traditional Jewish state. This military victory and subsequent purification of the Jewish temple in Jerusalem is still celebrated as the Jewish festival of lights, the *Hanukkah.*

Once again the Jews did not learn how to live with their non-Jewish neighbors. With the death of Antiochus IV there was no attempt by the Seleucid Empire to recolonize Judah. But the Maccabee brothers, Judas, Jonathan and Simon, began to conquer and expand the Jewish state much like current day Israel is doing. When the Maccabees refused to return conquered territory it was retaken by force by the Seleucid Empire. Antiochus VII reconquered Judah but independence returned with the death of Antiochus VII in 129 BCE. Judah's independence lasted until the Roman general, *Pompey the Great,* the general who defeated the most famous slave rebellion led by *Spartacus,* conquered both Syria and Judah. Like the Seleucid conquest, Pompey was helped by internal squabbling among the Jews. During the three-month battle for the temple mount, Jews were fighting both the Romans and fellow Jews. With the fall of Jerusalem, Judah became the Roman colony of *Judea* in 64 BCE.

That colonization of Judah by Rome began a period of peaceful coexistence between Jews and Romans. Pompey did not destroy or desecrate the Jewish temple in Jerusalem. In 40 BCE the Romans selected an *Arab,* who had converted to Judaism, *Herod,* to administer Judea as "king of the Jews." Herod's province was a much expanded Judah. Herod kept the peace by catering as much as possible to the religious demands of the Jews without offending his Roman masters. Herod also rebuilt the Second Temple on the temple mount, expanded the temple mount, and reinforced it with four retaining walls. The *Western Wall* is today a very sacred place for Jews. Peaceful coexistence ended with the death of Herod. Roman conquest of Jerusalem morphed the struggle between the *Semitic* and *Aryan* races into a struggle between Jews and gentiles. During the Roman occupation the struggle between Jews and gentiles became very confused after the Jew, Jesus Christ, began to preach a new religion to both Jews and gentiles in the Roman colony of Judea. Jesus Christ was born in Judea, but north of Jerusalem in Nazareth, during the reign of Augustus Caesar. At first he was rejected by both the Jewish religious leaders and the Roman imperialists. This led to his crucifixion during the reign of Tiberius Caesar.

Jesus was charged with sedition against the Roman Empire and his crucifixion was ordered by the Roman Prefect of Judea, Pontius Pilate. Pontius Pilate served as Roman Prefect of Judea during the years 26–36 CE. The crucifixion of Jesus was followed by the persecution and execution of Christians in Rome and throughout the Roman Empire. One of the important Jewish leaders who had supported the persecution of Jesus and his disciples was *Saul.* Saul was one of many Jews who converted to Christianity after the death of Jesus and preached the Christian doctrine as *St. Paul.* St. Paul used his Roman citizenship to request trial in Rome. He was convicted, imprisoned and beheaded in 67 CE.

As with the Greek colonization, under the Roman occupation the Jews were divided between those wanting to preserve the old religious ways and those favoring change and Roman ways. The traditional Jews rebelled against Roman rule in 66 CE. The rebellion was a disaster. At the time of the revolt Judea was a relatively small Roman province. The Roman administrator was a *procurator.* He had a small administrative staff and a small Roman garrison. The Roman administrator relied heavily on the pro-Roman segment of the Jewish elite. By comparison, a larger Roman province like Syria would be governed by a *legate* with a much larger Roman garrison and administrative staff. Given the relatively small Roman garrison stationed in Judea it was no surprise that the rebellion had initial successes. The success of the rebellion in Jerusalem quickly spread through the province of Judea.

The Roman Empire was forced to send reinforcements from its larger province of Syria. Like the First Nations in the American Empire an isolated victory invariably means facing a much larger imperial force. In October 66 CE the Roman legate of Syria, *Gaius Gallus,* marched from Antioch to Jerusalem at the head of thirty thousand Roman troops to crush the Jewish rebellion. When the Jewish rebels defeated Gallus, they experienced the same short-lived euphoria that Sitting Bull and his First Nations warriors experienced at the Battle of the *Little Big Horn,* 1,810 years later. Their faith in their God had once again been restored. Religion had triumphed over materialism. Defeating the power of Rome could only be proof of divine intervention. Imbued with this reaffirmation of faith the Jews prepared for a war of independence against the mighty Roman Empire. David would once again confront Goliath.

The Roman Empire predictably reacted to the defeat of Gallus by rebels in the tiny province of Judea much like the American Empire has reacted to its many defeats in Iraq and Afghanistan. A single defeat would mean rebellion throughout the Middle East and beyond. Rather than attempting to deal with the root cause of the rebellion the Roman Empire, like President Obama, used this rebellion to justify even more warmongering and military imperialism. Emperor Nero called on General *Flavius Vespasian* to take three Roman legions from Syria and Egypt to destroy the rebels. The Jewish rebels of 66 CE were the equivalent of President Obama's *Islamists* of 2011. Only Romans and Americans have the right to religious fundamentalism as exemplified by American *Christianites.* The Romans divided the Jews as much as the Americans later divided the Muslims by playing on their fears of religious fanaticism. Just as the American Empire branded Muslims who opposed American imperialism, *Islamists,* Jews opposed to Roman Imperialism were branded as *Zealots.* The Roman legions also used standard terror tactics by killing, maiming and destroying all in their path much like the Americans did in Vietnam. As with the Americans in Iraq and Afghanistan, the Romans had no way of distinguishing pro-Roman Jews from rebellious Jews. The safe response was to kill them all. Faced with certain death many of the rebels resorted to mass suicide rather than death by the sword of the Romans. To the Romans the Jews of 66 CE were no better than the *kongs* and *gooks* of Vietnam or the *al-Qaeda* or the *communists* or the *naked red savages.* The American Empire not merely imitated Roman propaganda language, it enhanced it a hundredfold.

Despite the fierce and determined resistance of the Jewish rebellion it was gradually worn down by increasing numbers of Roman legions and divisions in the Jewish resistance. At the high point of the Jewish rebellion as much as a quarter of the empire's army was sent to Judea. The Jewish rebellion was the Roman equivalent of America's Vietnam and Afghanistan. The resistance lasted four years before it was defeated. During this revolt the Roman Empire was being torn apart by civil wars, which led to Emperor Nero committing suicide in June 68 CE, before General *Vespasian* and his son *Titus* had crushed the rebellion. With the Jewish rebellion engaging more and more of the troops of the Roman Empire and civil wars still destabilizing the empire, the Roman legions fighting the rebels in Judea declared General *Vespasian* the new emperor of the Roman Empire in June 69 CE. As in the American Empire, the road to commander in chief and supreme leadership lay in a dedication to warmongering and suppression of freedom. But like the American Empire, only successful generals become heroes and Vespasian had not yet defeated the rebels. Their defeat and total annihilation were essential to consolidating his quest to rule the Roman Empire. In pursuit of this urgent goal he made his son, Titus, the new commander in Judea with the task of ending the rebellion.

Titus moved his forces for a determined assault on Jerusalem in March 70 CE. Where Gallus had failed in 66 CE Titus would succeed in 70 CE. In this final battle the Romans slaughtered Jews indiscriminately. The old and the sick were killed. The strong were enslaved. Titus had delivered the Roman Empire to his father. The failure of the so-called Great Revolt led to the destruction of the Second Temple by the Romans. The Roman soldiers looted and burnt the temple. Jewish resistance to Roman colonization led to the destruction of the Jewish temple in Jerusalem. Once again the Jews were without a dedicated place of worship. The continued attempts by some of the Jews to defy Roman rule led to most of the Jews being driven out of Judea, and forbidden to live in Jerusalem after 135 CE, when Emperor Hadrian defeated the **last** Jewish revolt. Christian Jews had not joined the Jewish rebellions, which began in 66 CE and ended in 135 CE. The expulsion of Jews from

Judea led to Christian Jews transforming from a distinct Jewish sect to a distinct new religion. Under Emperor Hadrian, Jerusalem became a Roman city and Judea became *Palestine.* Jews became a tiny minority of the population of Palestine, mostly in the area of Galilee. The Jews had basically abandoned their desire to pursue what many must now have believed was a false promise by their God, Yahweh, to make the land of Canaan their promised land.

With Emperor Constantine's conversion to Christianity, Jerusalem became a holy city for *Christians* rather than Jews. While ruling the unified Roman Empire from Constantinople, Constantine sent his mother to oversee the building of a Christian church in Jerusalem on the site where Jesus was crucified and buried. The building was completed in 335 CE, two years before Constantine's death. It was rebuilt by the Crusaders in 1144 and we know it today as the *Church of the Holy Sepulchre.* The church is located in the *Christian Quarter* of the Old City of Jerusalem. This Christian conquest of the Jewish holy city marked the beginning of a religious feud between Jews and Christians. As Constantinople replaced Rome as the center of the Roman Empire, the Middle East, including Palestine, became more and more Christian while in the West the un-Christian barbarians were destroying the Western Roman Empire.

This long historical persecution of Jews and forceful evacuations from their historical homeland of Judah and Jerusalem had a rather ironic outcome as far as Western Christian domination is concerned. The Jews moved to the lands that became the modern Western empires taking their Bible with them and maintaining their steadfast belief in the teachings and practices of their faith. They built synagogues to meet and pray. As "outsiders" they engaged in commercial practices forbidden by both Christianity and Islam, such as money lending for interest. They became relatively wealthy and influential second class citizens in Western and Eastern states alike. Their religious ideas based on the Hebrew Bible coalesced with much of Christian and Islamic religious dogma. Both Christianity and Islam accept much of what is told in the Hebrew Bible.

Christianity became the dominant religion of the entire Holy Roman Empire as far East as the border of China, between 380 CE and 635 CE. After 635 CE, Christian dominance was challenged by Islam. Muslim conquests expanded from Arabia eastward into India and westward into Spain. The Western expansion of the Muslim Empire was stopped at the border of the *Frankish kingdom,* present day France. Charles Martel defeated the Muslims at Poitiers in 732 CE. The rising military power of the Frankish kingdom, after its defeat of the Muslims at Poitiers, increased its influence in what eventually became the *Holy Roman Empire* in Western Europe. Martel's grandson, *Charlemagne,* consolidated Western rule over what had become the Latin language Western half of the Roman Empire, after 395 CE.

An interesting development arising out of this decision of the Roman Empire to co-opt the Christians rather than persecute them is the role of the pope as supreme spiritual leader of the Holy Roman *Christian* Empire. With the military decline of the Western Roman Empire the Christian church was able to secure the independence of the City of Rome. It's somewhat ironic that the shift from Rome to Constantinople as the capital of the Roman Empire by Constantine the Great enabled the *bishop of Rome,* later referred to as the *pope,* to acquire much more power and influence in the Western Christian Empire than the Christian bishops had in the Eastern Roman Empire. In the Eastern Roman Empire, the emperor continued to be the supreme leader, but in the Western Roman Empire, the privileged position of Rome, the pope, the bishops, and the *Christian* church placed religion above every Western state and Western leader, king, or emperor. This exalted position of the pope and the Christian church in the West, was consolidated under Pope *Gregory,* 590–604. Prior to Pope Gregory, the emperor of the Eastern Roman Empire, continued to dominate the election or approval of the election of the pope. Pope Gregory not only increased the independence of the papacy from the Eastern Roman emperor, but consolidated the supreme position of the Christian church in the West, and expanded the missionary expeditions of the Christian church into the lands of the "pagans and barbarians." At the time Britain was regarded as one of those barbaric pagan lands. Pope Gregory sent out the famous *Gregorian mission* to Britain in 596 to convert the Anglo-Saxon "heathens" to Christianity. History repeated itself when the English sent out Christian missionaries after 1600 to convert the First Nation "heathens" in North

America and steal their land and resources for the benefit of the Western Christian Empire.

The power of the papacy, and its independence from the Eastern Roman Empire, was further strengthened when the Frankish king *Pepin III* invaded Northern Italy between 754 and 756 on behalf of Pope Steven II, defeated the powerful *Lombards* and transferred valuable Italian real estate to Pope Steven II, for the benefit of the papacy. These lands were not returned to Italy until 1870. The popular uprising in the streets of Rome against Pope Leo III in 799, forced the pope to ask for military intervention by another Frankish king, *Charlemagne.* The supremacy of the pope and the Christian church in the West was cemented by *Charlemagne,* when he accepted the crown as emperor of the Holy Roman Empire, from Pope Leo III in 800. All temporal leaders, including temporal emperors like Charlemagne, were subservient to the pope in Rome. The Western states and empires, as well as the leaders of Western states and empires, must bow down to the dictates of the pope and the church. In future the pope would make the final decision as to which Western king or prince would be chosen as emperor of the Holy Roman Empire. The goals of the Western states and the Christian church became one and the same. But the church and the pope were the supreme leaders. No temporal Western leader dared disobey the Christian church or the pope. Many kings fought this control by the papacy, the most famous being Henry VIII of England. But the great majority of the kings of the Western European states determined that much more was to be gained by cooperating with and supporting the supremacy of the papacy in the Christian West. In many ways, that is still true today, though Western intellectuals will fallaciously deny that to be so. This new deeply *religious* Christian Empire would be challenged by an equally *religious* empire, the Muslim Empire. It was the beginning of a conflict between Christians and Muslims that continues to this day.

CHAPTER 2

Islam vs. Christianity: The Birth of the Modern Religious Conflict between East and West: 635–1300

While the Western Roman Empire officially ended in 476 the Eastern Roman Empire survived despite continuing conflict with the older Persian Empire. The Persian Empire had transformed itself into the *Parthian* Empire after invading Iraq from Iran and defeating the Seleucids in 170 BCE. The Seleucids had ruled Iraq, Iran, Syria, and somewhat later, Palestine, after the death of Alexander the Great. The Parthians created a new capital city in Iraq called *Ctesiphon.* It was located on the other side of the Tigris River from the Seleucid capital of Seleucia. This Persian defeat of the Seleucids marked a return from Greek to Persian influence in the Middle East. The Parthians were replaced by another Persian dynasty, the *Sassanids.* The Sassanian dynasty ruled the Persian Empire between 224 and 651 from the capital city of *Ctesiphon* in Iraq.

The Eastern Roman Empire was also transformed into the *Byzantine Empire.* While still Christian, and ruling over the lands where the majority of Christians lived, it began to distance itself from Western Christianity centered in Rome and the religious and political supremacy of the pope. In Constantinople the emperor, not the pope, was the supreme authority. The language and culture were predominantly Greek rather than Latin or Roman. Its Christian heritage was distinguished from that of Rome by identifying itself as the *Eastern Orthodox Church.* The countries it ruled—Egypt, Syria, Greece, Anatolia, North Africa, and Southern Italy—were the civilized part of the Roman Empire compared with barbarian Britain, France, Germany, and Northern Italy. But it was the barbarian Western portion of the Roman Empire that transformed itself into the *Europeans* and dominated the world after 1450. It wrested the banner of "Christianity" from the Eastern Orthodox

Church, abandoned the lands that had been the historical center of the civilized world for centuries, and forged a new modern civilization west of the Mediterranean and into the New World and across the Pacific. Anchored by "independent" nation-states with separate empires beginning with Portugal and Spain, it was the Papacy, not an emperor, which unified this modern **Christian** empire.

The increasingly distinct Eastern half of the old Roman Empire, along with the Sassanid Empire, dominated the Middle East until the birth of the *Muslim Empire.* The Sassanid Empire even briefly recaptured Egypt, Jerusalem and Damascus from the Eastern Roman Empire, during the rule of Emperor *Heraclius.* The Sassanid defeat of the Eastern Roman Empire, and removal of the important Christian symbol, the *True Cross to Ctesiphon,* led to a holy *Christian* war against the Persians. The Sassanids were defeated by Heraclius in 627 at the *Battle of Nineveh* and Christianity restored in the Middle East. Greek replaced Latin in official documents during the rule of Heraclius. While the West traces its roots back to both the Greek and Roman empires, especially with reference to the birth of democracy in the Greek city states, the Eastern Greek Roman Empire, *Eastern Orthodox Christian,* was never fully reconquered by the West after the decline of the "West" between 670 and 1400. After 670 the barbarians ruled the world. In the East the barbarians emerged from the desert of Saudi Arabia with a new religion, *Islam.* In the West the barbarians emerged out of France, Britain, and Germany, embracing the Western version of Christianity based in Rome and the pope. The old centers of civilization became increasingly Islamic and Arabic, replacing Greek and Christianity. But it proved to be no match for the modern Christian Empire founded by the Europeans. Nevertheless, **Islam** continues to be the only religion that has a worldwide following that can challenge the worldwide following of **Christianity.**

The Rise and Fall of the Muslim Empire: 635–1095

Out of the barren wasteland of the Arabian Desert came a new religion, *Islam,* which dominated the world after the fall of the Roman Empire. While the Christian West reclaimed its hegemony of the West after the voyages of Columbus and da Gama, it failed to reconquer the Middle

East where civilization began. What had been called the *Fertile Crescent* is today a sea of Muslim states whose populations embrace the religion of Islam. As we explained earlier, empires developed from small beginnings where the imperial power had easy access to the Sea. This was true of the empires originating from the Fertile Crescent, from Greece, from Rome, from Britain and from the United States. Not so with the Muslim Empire. It came out of the sands of the relatively uninhabitable Arabian Desert and from a nomadic tribal people who, like the Jews, were of the *Semitic* race. Legendary descendants of *Ishmael,* Abraham's first son with his maid, *Hagar,* the Arabs had tamed the *camel* to provide an efficient mode of transportation in the desert. A few hardy souls had lived in the Arabian Peninsula for ten thousand years. As population expanded in the Fertile Crescent many were pushed further and further afield. Many of these hardy souls moved as far as the desert of Arabia where they survived by embracing a nomadic lifestyle, the *Bedouin,* moving from oasis to oasis on the backs of camels. They developed a tribal political system where each family was protected by the group and by his clan, a subgroup of the larger tribe. Like the First Nations of the New World and the misunderstood communists of the modern "Cold War" period, the Bedouin Arabs believed in communal property. In time these Bedouin Arabs prospered by engaging in a very lucrative camel caravan trade. Some settled in small towns surrounding an oasis.

The unexpected origin of the Muslim Empire shocked the world, and the speed with which it replaced the Roman Empire as the dominant empire, took the West by surprise. The Sassanid Empire had expanded its reach into parts of Arabia during its confrontation with the Eastern Roman Empire. Arabs moved into countries such as Iraq and Syria, which were being fought for by the two empires. This movement of Arabs, combined with the growing camel caravan trade, made Arabs increasingly aware of the outside civilized world of the Greeks, Romans, and Persians. They also became increasingly aware of religious practices by Jews and Christians, which were different from theirs. It was this growing awareness of new religions, the belief in one God by Jews and Christians, and nonworship of idols, more than any other foreign influence, which would provide a leader for the Arabs, comparable to

Alexander the Great for the disunited Greek city states, or Genghis Khan for the nomadic Mongol tribes of Asia.

Unlike the Jews, who have accepted the second class status bestowed on them by the Christian West, the Muslims continue to oppose Christian dominance. Today, Islam is the second largest religion after Christianity and growing faster than Christianity. By contrast, Judaism has a powerful political lobby in the American Empire and a nuclear protected American *uncolony,* Israel, in the Middle East, but numbers that pale by comparison—15 million Jews compared with 1.6 billion Muslims and 2.2 billion Christians.

While Islam, like Christianity, expanded outward from the Middle East to Asia, Europe, Africa and America, its heart and soul is still centered in Saudi Arabia, Iraq, Egypt, Jerusalem and other parts of the Middle East, North Africa and Central Asia. During the nineteenth and twentieth centuries the European and American empires colonized much of the Muslim countries in Asia and Africa but failed to completely colonize the Middle East. With the relative decline of the European and American empires in the twenty-first century, the Muslim heartland of the Middle East is expanding outward today, much like the Arab Empire of the seventh century erupted out of the desert of Saudi Arabia. Today Arabs account for only twenty percent of the Muslim population, and over fifty countries around the globe have populations where the dominant religion is Islam. In the heartland of Christianity, Europe, Islam is the second largest religion after Christianity.

The birth of Islam, which means "submission to Allah," is rightly associated with the Arab, *Muhammad,* who claims to be the last of a long line of prophets going back to those in the Hebrew Bible such as Moses and Abraham as well as Jesus Christ. Muslims believe that Jesus Christ is a prophet like Moses and Muhammad, not the son of God. Muhammad came into contact with Jews and Christians as a caravan trader and merchant. Born in the *Hashemite* clan of the ruling *Quraysh* tribe of Mecca and orphaned at six years old, Muhammad was raised by his uncle, Abu Talib, a caravan trader and leader of the Hashimite clan. He married the widow *Khadija,* a wealthy caravan trader and his employer, when he was twenty-five years old. This marriage and the strategic location of Mecca, gave Muhammad the opportunity to prosper from the increasingly lucrative camel-caravan trade between Syria and Yemen, and become a leader in his community. This leadership quality, which was honed before Muhammad received his revelations from God, is important because it made Muhammad different from Jesus Christ. While Christ was only a religious leader, Muhammad was both a religious and secular leader. Muhammad used his secular leadership qualities and opportunities to preach his new religion while simultaneously uniting the Arab tribes.

From the very beginning, Islam was a unifying political force where the secular and religious were intertwined into an inseparable social, political, communal, legal, local, national, and international governing institution that saw no distinction between church and state. On the other hand, Jesus Christ had no opportunity to organize his converts into any kind of political force. Christianity became a political force only after it was adopted by an existing political force, the Roman Empire. From the very beginning of that adoption the relative dominance of the political and secular over the religious, has been debated and argued. The Western Christian empires use this important difference between Islam and Christianity to score propaganda points. First, Christians overemphasize their separation of church and state, to claim that this makes them more civilized. Second, they conveniently ignore the fact that there was never any intension in Islam to separate church and state, to chastise Muslim countries for not providing the same degree of "religious freedoms," as the West provides to its citizens.

In reality, both the Christian West and the Muslim East provides **different** but **comparable** degrees of religious freedoms and constraints on those freedoms. For example, the West criticizes the use of *Sharia laws* in Muslim countries, while conveniently ignoring that their laws and legal systems are designed to enforce **rules** and **obligations** on their citizens, many of which are patently unjust, coercive and discriminatory, rather than designed to promote justice and fair and equal treatment. Judges and lawyers have so much discretionary power in the Western legal systems that justice is rarely served. The huge monetary incentives to complicate even the simplest of procedures such as divorces, are another reason why justice is rarely served in the Western legal systems. You can pay a lawyer and a judge to tie up, in court, the most ridiculous and frivolous of cases. Just look at the fact that after four centuries of legal battles something as simple as the inalienable land claims of the First Nations in North America, have not been resolved by the legal systems of the United States or Canada, two of the supposedly shining examples of civilized Western states.

The Muslim holy book is the *Quran.* Muslims believe that the teachings in the Quran were revealed to Muhammad by the angel *Gabriel,* beginning in 610 when Muhammad was forty years old. Muhammad began to preach the new religion of *Islam* in his city of birth, *Mecca,* around 613. While Muhammad attracted a band of loyal followers, including some from the ruling Quraysh tribe, the majority of residents of Mecca, and his own ruling Quraysh tribe, opposed his teachings. He was expelled from his clan after the death of his wife, Khadija, and his uncle, Abu Talib. As guardians of the ancient shrine, the *Ka'ba,* the Quraysh tribe prospered both from the growth of trade and the pilgrims coming to worship at the Ka'ba. The continued conflict between the Eastern Roman Empire and the Persian Empire, diverted more and more trade through Arabia, and Mecca became one of the most thriving trade centers in Arabia. Muhammad's new religion was seen as a threat to the economic prosperity of Mecca. The rich merchants were understandably the most opposed to Muhammad's new religion.

Without the protection of his tribe the threat to Muhammad and his followers increased, and Muhammad was forced to flee to the city of *Medina,* two hundred miles north of Mecca, in 622. This flight to Medina is used to mark the beginning of the religion of Islam and is called the *Hijrah.* In Medina, Muhammad quickly became a respected leader of the community as he had been invited by caravan traders and others, who had made the pilgrimage to Mecca from Medina, to come to Medina and help them resolve a long standing squabble between the two Arab tribes of Medina. Muhammad used this opportunity to begin a campaign to unite all of the tribes of the Arabian Peninsula while converting them to Islam. The Medina Arabs who had invited Muhammad to Medina were aware that he had been preaching a new religion but still respected his leadership qualities. Jews and Christians in Medina were also friendly to Muhammad since his religious views were closer to theirs than the traditional religion of the Arabs. At the time Arabs were considered to be pagans and worshipped many gods and idols. Muhammad preached belief in a single god, *Allah.* This common monotheism temporarily united Muslims, Christians and Jews in Medina. Combining some of the teachings and practices of the Jews and Christians, Muhammad found many converts to his new religion of Islam and used it to unite the Arab tribes.

Muhammad eventually parted ways with the Jews in Medina, since the Jews could not accept him as a prophet of God, in the same way that they had accepted Abraham and Moses. In addition, the Jews plotted with the Arabs of Mecca to kill Muhammad. Muhammad marked this parting of the ways with Judaism by changing the direction faced during prayers from Jerusalem to Mecca. However, the Jewish threat to the Arabs of Medina, which had inspired the Arabs to invite Muhammad to Medina, had been resolved by the unity of the Arab tribes under the leadership of Muhammad. Muhammad had killed two birds with one stone, as it were. He had removed the Jewish threat by uniting the Arab tribes of Medina, thereby fulfilling his obligation to the Arabs of Medina, and he had used that same mission to spread his new religion of Islam as a distinct religion from Judaism. The Jews were expelled from Medina, for plotting with and fighting alongside the Arabs of Mecca, against Muhammad and the Arabs of Medina.

The rise of Islam in Medina, as well as competition over control of lucrative trade routes, led to military conflicts between Medina and Mecca. In 624 Muhammad defeated a much larger force sent from Mecca by the Quraysh tribe at the *Battle of Badr.* This military victory enhanced Muhammad's stature and popularity. But the Quraysh tribe found a formidable general in *Khalid ibn Walid* and defeated Muhammad the next year at the *Battle of Uhud.* The Meccans invaded Medina in 627 but failed to conquer the city. In 629 Muhammad invaded Mecca with a force of ten thousand and conquered Mecca. His relatively easy military victory over the powerful *Quraysh* tribe convinced many of the inhabitants of Mecca that Muhammad's new religion was indeed blessed by his God. Every religion prays to its God before battle and every religion use victory in battle to reinforce its claim that it's God is the one true God. The Meccans converted to Islam and Khalid Ibn Walid became a famous military general for Islam. Mecca became the most religious city for Muslims and the destination for annual pilgrimage by Muslims from the entire world.

By the time of his death in 632, Muhammad had created a united and organized Arab-Muslim political, military, and religious force that soon conquered the entire Arabian Peninsula, the largest peninsula in the world. With an area of 1.25 million square miles the Arabian Peninsula is made up not only of Saudi Arabia, the largest country, but the other Gulf States of Qatar, Kuwait, Oman, Bahrain and the United Arab Emirates, as well as other Muslim countries such as Iraq, Syria, Jordan, Yemen, Palestine and Lebanon. On the other side of the Persian Gulf is the important Muslim country of Iran. The peninsula is surrounded by other Muslim countries such as Egypt, Turkey, Sudan, Ethiopia, Somalia, Afghanistan, Pakistan and Turkmenistan.

Muhammad was succeeded by his friend and early convert to Islam, *Abu Bakr.* His successors came to be called *Caliphs.* Under the Caliphs the Islamic Empire expanded beyond anything Muhammad could have imagined. The Arab/Muslim Empire eventually reached Spain and France in the West, and the border of China in the East. Arab cities such as Baghdad, Damascus, Cairo and Cordoba, became the dominant cities of the world in terms of wealth, culture and the arts. The historical center of civilization, which had long been the area bordering the Mediterranean in the Middle East, North Africa and central Asia, was reinvigorated by this Arab-Islamic hegemony. Western Europe was doomed to maintain its historical backward "uncivilized" state for at least another millennium.

The Persian Gulf became the most important waterway for the transportation of oil. Today, the Gulf, the Arabian Peninsula, and the surrounding region, contains the world's largest proven traditional oil reserves, as well as large reserves of natural gas. The world's largest offshore oilfield, the *Safaniya Oil Field,* is located in the Persian Gulf. Iran controls the narrow *Strait of Hormuz,* strategically located in its territorial waters between the end of the Persian Gulf and the Gulf of Oman. Iran is not bluffing when it says that it will close this strategic waterway, which carries 20 percent of the world's oil shipments, if it is attacked by the American Empire or its *uncolony* of Israel. The current upheaval in the region is a continuation of the struggle for Muslim control of these lands, which began with Muhammad and his Caliphs in the seventh century.

After thirty years of autocratic rule by the Western imposed dictatorship of *Hosni Mubarak,* Egyptians are finally attempting to reassert their historic role in leading the Muslims in the Middle East. What began as a relatively quiet revolution in Tunisia in December 2010 has spread across the region. Dubbed the *Jasmine Revolution* by the West, it forced President *Zine Ben Ali* to flee Tunisia on January 15, 2011. Massive popular protests and uprisings followed in Egypt, Yemen, Jordan, Algeria, Libya and other Muslim countries in the Middle East, held hostage to American imposed puppet regimes after the decline of the Soviet Union. Bogged down in Afghanistan, and with its limited CIA spy and covert resources spread thinly across the globe, the United States was caught flat footed by the massive insurrections in the Middle East. Publicly supporting democracy while privately imposing dictatorships, the West was caught with its pants down in the Middle East of 2010–2011.

In the past the American Empire usually got rid of its imposed dictator when he became sufficiently unpopular by simply replacing him with another dictator. That is exactly what it did in Egypt, replacing the democratically elected government led by *Mohamed* Morsi with the new military dictatorship led by *Abdel Fattah el-Sisi.* So much for its propaganda claim that its warmongering is fueled by its desire to remove dictators and install democracy. However, with its relative decline in imperial power, it is very doubtful if the American Empire will still be able to replace some other unpopular dictators like Colonel Moammar Gadhafi of Libya, and Bashar al-Assad of Syria, with its own "SOB" pro-American dictators. It is not surprising that Britain, France and Italy are taking more of a leadership position over the United States in attempting to secure political, military and economic advantages from the 2010/11 uprisings in the Middle East. They hope to wrest from the United States their earlier imperial leadership in the Middle East, taken from them by the United States after the Second World War. Once again the West has been successful in using its well-honed divide-and-rule tactic. It has deepened the Sunni/Shia religious division by co-opting Saudi Arabia and its Sunni Muslim allies against Iran and its Shia Muslim allies. Muslims in the Middle East never learn despite numerous betrayals by the West.

They are in dire need of a modern day *Saladin* to lead them. Russia was fortunate to find Vladimir Putin.

By the time the Roman Empire became the Holy Roman *Christian* Empire in 380, it had been in decline for at least a century. But the Roman Empire had proved to be very resilient, bouncing back from each crisis, and internal dissentions, as well as from external threats. Emperor Constantine's decision to empower Christians with a leadership role in the Roman Empire, rather than opposing and persecuting them, gave the Roman Empire a new lease on life. Rather than opposing Roman imperialism, Christians now embraced it and worked toward a common goal of expanding the Roman Empire. The cementing of the East/West division after 395 also breathed new life into a Christian Eastern Roman Empire centered in the Middle East, also replacing the once dominant Persian Empire. Under Emperor Heraclius, Pope John IV sent Christian missionaries to convert those living in the newly conquered lands in the Eastern Roman Empire. While weakened by continued wars against the Sassanid Empire, as well as plagues, it had emerged as the dominant empire after its victory over the Sassanids in 627. In 629 Heraclius restored the "True Cross to Ctesiphon" in Jerusalem. Claimed to be the cross on which Jesus was crucified, it had become an important symbol of Christian claims to Jerusalem. The Sassanids had taken the True Cross to their capital city, Ctesiphon, after their conquest of Palestine, following their decisive military victories against Heraclius during the period 611–621.

The Muslim Arabs Expand out of Arabia

As the *Muslim* Arabs expanded their conquests outside the Arabian Peninsula following the death of Muhammad, both the remaining Sassanid Empire and Heraclius's expanded Roman-Christian Empire, fell before their military genius. Most of the Greek language Eastern half of the Roman Empire fell to the expanding Muslim Empire under the Arabs. I use the term *Muslim* Arabs because at this time there were many Arabs who had not yet converted to Islam living in the Persian and Eastern Roman empires now being invaded by Arabia. Many of these non-Muslim Arabs fought in the armies of the Sassanid and Byzantine empires. The Muslims first targeted the wealthiest country in the Persian Empire, *Iraq,* where its capital city, Ctesiphon, located on the bank of the Tigris, had become the largest city in the world. The Roman Empire had conquered and lost Ctesiphon at least five times before Heraclius victory in 627. Under the leadership of the Meccan general, Khalid Ibn Walid, who had defeated Muhammad at the Battle of Uhud, Iraq would be the first of many conquests outside Arabia.

Abu Bakr was the first Caliph to succeed Muhammad after his death on June 8, 632. Abu Bakr's first task was to crush all rebellions against his unified authority over the whole of Arabia. Much like the Greeks, Romans and Americans, once the homeland was secured it was time to expand the empire outside the solid home base. Border skirmishes between Arabia and Persian Iraq began after Muslim tribes conducted deeper and deeper raids into Iraq, which were very lucrative in terms of booty. The Arab raiders had the advantage of disappearing into the desert with their camels out of reach of the Persian army. Abu Bakr condoned and encouraged these raids. By early 633, Abu Bakr felt that his leadership in Arabia was solid enough to begin a full scale conquest of Iraq from the Persian Empire. He sent his best general, Khalid Ibn Walid, with ten thousand **Muslim** volunteers to wage war on the Persian Empire via an invasion of Iraq.

It's instructive to compare the **Muslim** attack on Iraq in 633 with the **Christian** invasion of 2003. Imagine how the Iraqis felt in the first decade of the twenty-first century when President George W. Bush sent a **Christian** army to invade it as part of the American imperial goal of conquering Persia (Iran). The irony of the twenty-first century invasion was that the possession by the United States of the most advanced military the world had ever known, had led President Bush to brag that his invasion of Iraq would be a "quick slam dunk" en-route to his invasions of Iran and North Korea. See my *Rise and Fall of the American Empire.* As it turned out the most powerful empire the world has ever known, the American Empire, was still having its ass "royally whupped" by the poorly armed Iraqis more than a decade after the U.S. invasion began in 2003. Having created *al-Qaeda in Iraq* as a direct result of its 2003 invasion, al-Qaeda in Iraq morphed into *ISIS,* the Islamic State of Iraq and Syria, in 2014, expanding territory and defeating the American

Empire in 2016. President Obama has resorted to praying for a miracle from his Christian God.

The Muslim invasion of Iraq in 633 was in stark contrast to the American invasion of 2003. In 633 it was the Persians who had the superior military force and the Muslims who achieved the "quick slam dunk" victory. Religious minds would definitely score this comparison in favor of the Muslim God over the Christian God. How else can a weaker Muslim force defeat a well-armed Iraqi resistance when the strongest Christian force ever, failed so miserably against a much weaker armed Iraqi resistance? In 633 the Muslims were about to do battle against the more powerful and far better equipped Persian army, including their **Christian** Arab allies, when the Persian commander, *Hormuz,* challenged the Muslim commander, Khalid, to a *mano a mano.* Despite the disastrous outcome of this for Hormuz, in the twenty-first century **Christian** invasion, Saddam Hussein issued an equivalent *mano a mano* to George W. who wisely, some would say **cowardly,** declined. George W. had previously called out his own dad to a *mano a mano*, which his dad had declined. According to George W.'s mother, George would have lost that one-on-one as well had his father taken him on.

Khalid not only survived his one-on-one with Hormuz, but also the planned treachery of Hormuz to have his best men kill Khalid, in the event that he lost the one-on-one. People who have deep religious convictions naturally ascribe outcomes to the will of god. The Muslim warriors were understandably energized by Khalid's seemingly miraculous survival. Hormuz's treachery had backfired, much like George W.'s 2003 treachery to falsely accuse Saddam Hussein of possessing WMDs, backfired by creating al-Qaeda in Iraq. George W. was so convinced that he could colonize the Middle East with minimal military costs because of his technologically advanced military-industrial complex, that he manufactured an excuse for his invasion of Iraq. As a deeply religious person he also firmly believed that his Christian God was the one and only true god. His conquest of the Middle East would enrich his empire materially and spiritually. But it was the Muslim God, *Allah,* which prevailed both in 633 and 2003. The Muslims conquered Iraq and the Middle East after their invasion of 633. The American Empire failed to conquer it in the twenty-first century, for the Christians.

At the battle in *Kazima* in April 633, the so-called *Battle of Chains,* Khalid's Muslim volunteers won the first of many battles against the far more powerful Persian forces. Persian defeats followed at the *Battle of River* and the *Battle of Walaja.* Some historians claim that the Persians had assembled a force that was over three times the size of the Muslim force, for the Battle of Walaja.

Another irony of the comparison of the 633 Muslim invasion of Iraq with the 2003 Christian invasion is this. Unlike George W., who saw his invasion of Iraq as an easy prelude to his planned invasions of Iran and North Korea, the Muslims never planned to use Iraq as a stepping stone to further conquests inside or outside the Persian Empire. Rather than Iraq being an expected easy conquest, the Muslims must have anticipated the possibility of failure in Iraq and an end to imperial expansion outside Arabia. Where George W. anticipated an easy victory and failed, the Muslims anticipated, at best, an unlikely victory and succeeded. Where George W. anticipated further victories in Iran and North Korea and was stymied by failure in Iraq, the astounding Muslim victory at the *Battle of Walaja* in May 633, led the Muslims to attack the Romans by invading Syria and Palestine in 634. The Muslims were emboldened by their unexpected victories against the Persians to take on the other dominant empire in the Middle East, the Eastern Roman Empire. In response to the Muslim advance, the Persian Empire even formed an alliance with the Eastern Christian Roman Empire in 635, to defeat the Arabs. By 635 many of the people of the Persian Empire had converted to Christianity.

In the twentieth century the fall of the Soviet Union had left the American Empire as the lone superpower. The 2003 invasion of Iraq was intended to be the beginning of a worldwide expansion of the American Empire using preemptive strikes, regime changes, and unilateralism. See my prequel, *Rise and Fall of the American Empire.* Failure in Iraq ended this American dream. By contrast, the Muslims had been surprised by their conquest of Arabia and had not dreamed of superpower status because of the existence of two long standing superpowers, Persia and Rome. Where America's failure in Iraq ended American expansion, Muslim success in Iraq began Muslim expansion.

Roman emperor Heraclius sent a massive army, which engaged the Muslims in August 636, at the *Battle of Yarmouk,* on the border between Jordan, Israel and Syria. In this original *Six-Day War* it was the Muslims who defeated a much larger Roman army on the plains of Yarmuk, just forty miles from the Golan Heights. The Muslims next defeated Heraclius Persian ally, *Yazdegerd III,* the last of the Sassanid rulers, in November 636, at the *Battle of al-Qādisiyyah,* just outside Baghdad. By 637 the Muslims had conquered the capital city, Ctesiphon, and the remnants of the Persian Empire. Iraq's present day capital city of Baghdad is located about twenty miles from Ctesiphon. Baghdad became the capital city of the Arab/Muslim Empire in 762, under the *Abbasid* dynasty. As an international capital it combined Arab with Greek and Persian culture. Iraq continued to be one of the primary centers of civilization. Baghdad was added to historic cities such as Babylon, Ctesiphon, Seleucia, Nineveh and Ur. By 800 Baghdad had grown in size to match the city of Constantinople, built by Constantine the Great. With a population of half a million, the Muslim Empire had a capital city as rich in every respect as the Christian capital.

Jerusalem surrendered to the Muslims in 638. By 640 the Muslims had not only conquered the Christian holy city of Jerusalem, but present day Muslim states such as Palestine, Persia (Iran), Egypt, Iraq and Syria. The Persian army was finally destroyed in 642 at the *Battle of Nahavand.* The capital of the Muslim world was moved from Arabia to Iraq, and later to Damascus in Syria, under the *Umayyad* dynasty. The Umayyads were a powerful Meccan family that seized the leadership of Islam from the descendants of the Prophet Muhammad, creating the split in Islam between *Sunnis* and *Shias.* Shia Muslims cling to the family descendants of the Prophet and represent a significant minority of about 10 percent. In Iran, which converted to Islam after the fall of the Persian Empire, Shias represent the majority of the population. Baghdad remained the cultural capital and became the richest city in the world as Ctesiphon had been. In 750 the *Abbasid* dynasty from Iran, overthrew the Umayyads, and returned the capital of the Muslim Empire to Baghdad. The Umayyads held on to power in Spain, *Al-Andalus,* causing a permanent fracture in the Arab Empire, which would later make it easier for Christian Europe to retake Muslim conquests in Southern Europe. With Baghdad as its center, the Muslim Empire expanded from Arabia to the Middle East to Central Asia, South East Asia, Indonesia, Pakistan,

North Africa, Spain and France. The Middle East, North Africa, Central Asia, and parts of Europe and India, became an Arab Empire stretching East to India and West to Spain. Arabic became the language of this expanding Muslim Empire even though Arabs represented a smaller and smaller percent of the population. The willingness of the Arabs to admit Persians, Kurds, Turks, Mongols, Tatars and Berbers into its military and bureaucracy, made it easier to expand and govern an expanding empire. But it also sowed the seeds of future dissentions and internal conflicts.

While this new Muslim Empire totally replaced the Persian Empire and dominated the world, it had not fully conquered the lands of the Roman Empire either in the Eastern half or Western half. The Christian capital of Constantinople was attacked but not captured by the Muslim Empire. The location of its center in Baghdad was symbolic of its Eastern focus even though Arab culture, language and civilization penetrated East and West out of Saudi Arabia. The Muslims held on to their eighth century conquest of Spain until 1491 but Western Europe was never a prime target for conquest by the Muslim Empire. This is extremely important to remember when we address the current **Western** invented "War **on** terror."

The Muslims never invaded the current centers of Western imperialism, the United States, Britain, France, Germany and Canada. But the current Western Empire has continuously invaded Muslim lands in the Middle East, Central Asia and North Africa. If there is a "War **of** terror" it's a war waged by the Christian West against the Muslim East, not the other way round. Neither Iraq nor Afghanistan, for example, has ever invaded Canada, the United States or Britain, but these countries have continually invaded and bombed Iraq and Afghanistan in the last two decades, killing thousands with their WMDs, and destroying the livelihoods of millions. That Western waged "War **of** terror" has expanded from Iraq and Afghanistan to Pakistan, Yemen, Libya and Syria. Killing Muslims in far off lands by engaging in military adventures, using the most technologically advanced weapons, and relatively few soldiers, has become a way of life for Americans, Brits, Canadians and Aussies, much like playing harmless video games. Teach your kids to play video games so that when they grow up they can fly supersonic fighter jets and drop bombs on Muslims, seems to be the lesson of this generation of Americans, Brits, Canadians and Aussies.

Jerusalem had become a holy city for the Jews after 1,000 BCE, and a holy city for the Christians after the Roman Empire embraced Christianity, under Constantine the Great. That Jesus was born in Nazareth, not Jerusalem, seems not to matter to Christians. Muhammad had developed friendly relations with Jews in Medina but was later hostile to the Jews of that city. In 638 the Jews had allied with Muslims to defeat the Persians and conquer Jerusalem. Once again Muslims and Jews lived peacefully, now in the city of Jerusalem. What has been called the "Golden Age" for Islam was very beneficial to Jews in Jerusalem, as well as Jews in other Muslim cities, throughout the Muslim Empire. There were large Jewish populations in many of the dominant Muslim cities. In governing an ever-expanding empire, the Muslims were willing to embrace the Jewish religion and culture, as well as Persian and Greek cultures. But Muslims, like Christians before, were determined to transform Jerusalem into a holy city for Muslims.

The traditional way of expressing religious dominance was to build a temple, church, or mosque. The Umayyad dynasty was determined to build a permanent mosque to replace the symbols of Jewish and Christian dominance in Jerusalem. It was natural that the Muslims would choose the same location of the destroyed Jewish temple built by Solomon, the temple mount on Mount Moriah. Mount Moriah's connection with Abraham is sacred to Jews, Christians and Muslims. Construction of this permanent Muslim shrine, the *Dome of the Rock,* began in 689, and was completed two years later. Adding the *Al-Aqsa Mosque,* completed in 705, on the same site was simply doubling up on this determination to make the historic temple mount *Muslim* rather than Jewish or Christian. It's like creating the original "Twin Towers" in Jerusalem rather than in New York. The area occupied by these "Twin Muslim Shrines" is called the *Sacred Noble Sanctuary.*

As Jewish military power waned, Jerusalem became a key battleground between Christians and Muslims from the Arab conquest in 638 to this day. The two Islamic shrines built on the revered temple mount signaled that control of Jerusalem would become the symbol of whether Muslims or Christians would rule the Middle East. In the fourteen centuries since 638, control of the Middle East has swung back and forth between Christians and Muslims. The Crusades failed in their bid to permanently recapture Jerusalem for the Christians.

Western control of the Middle East got a big boost during the First World War when the Arabs foolishly allied with Great Britain in their attempt to gain independence from the Ottoman Empire. With the help of the Arabs, led by the Arab, Sharif Hussein of Arabia, and the Englishman, Lawrence of Arabia, the English general Sir Edmund Allenby captured Jerusalem on December 9, 1917, and Damascus on October 1, 1918. American President George W. Bush's military invasion of Iraq in 2003 gave an equally big boost to Eastern control of the Middle East. Muslims across the region, as well as Muslims across the globe, rallied to the defense of the brutal American-led Western invasion of Iraq. Today the West is engaged in a long and difficult war in the region with intense propaganda that it is winning that war. The facts suggest otherwise. When the West finally loses the current war in Afghanistan, and it most certainly will, just as it lost in Vietnam, it will also lose the bordering states of Pakistan, Iran, Syria, Iraq, Lebanon, Yemen, Egypt, Somalia, Algeria, Libya, Ethiopia, and Sudan. Muslim control will return to the Middle East.

The Arabs Pay the Final Price for Foolishly ignoring the Western European Barbarians, the Rise of the Western Holy Roman Empire, and the Shift of the Center of Civilization from the Fertile Crescent to Western Europe, the American Empire, and the Pacific

The fall of the Roman Empire and the rise of the Muslim Arab Empire led to a relative decline of the West and a return to the historical dominance of the East over the West. Prior to the Greek and Roman empires, the dominant empires had been in the Middle East, Central Asia, China and India. The East had dominated the world. There are many reasons why one empire dies and another takes its place. The only single continuity in all of history so far is that people aspire to imperial expansions using military force to achieve that goal. Despite all of the rhetoric by what has been misleadingly called the civilized West, there has been absolutely no change in the single overriding goal of all of history to conquer and dominate by using military force and offensive wars and invasions.

The single most important mistake that the Arabs made after conquering the Persian and Byzantine empires, was to assume that the heartland of civilization would remain in the Middle East, where it had existed for almost all of history. This was an understandable but deadly error. As we saw above, the Roman Empire had co-opted Christianity in a smart move to forestall the empire's inevitable decline. We also explained the supreme power given to the pope in the Western barbaric half of the Roman Empire, which led it to morph into the *Holy Roman Empire,* after it severed its ties to the Eastern Roman emperor in Constantinople. It was a Frankish warrior, *Charles Martel,* not the Roman emperor in Constantinople, who had stopped the Western advance of the Muslim Arabs, between the cities of Poitiers and Tours in France in 732. Historically, the defeat of the Muslims in France by Charles Martel has not been given its due significance. That is largely due to the fact that the civilized world up to 732 lay to the South and East of France. The Frankish kingdom to the North, covering most of Western Europe, was viewed by everyone as uncivilized, primitive, barbaric, underdeveloped, poor, heathen, uneducated, uncultured, and generally of little economic, commercial, military, or strategic value. Just as the West initially saw Africa only as a source for slaves, the view of the civilized Middle East in 732 was that Western Europe was only of interest, if at all, as a source of slaves.

The general presumption that Western Europe had so little value was what saved it from conquest by the Muslim empires of the Arabs, Turks and Persians. Empires fail to see the changes taking place around them. Just as the American Empire today fails to recognize the "global shift" to Asia and the "emerging" economies, the Muslim empires, as did China later, failed to see the economic and military developments in Western Europe, after the creation of the Holy Roman Empire, and the rise of the *Carolingian* Empire under *Charlemagne.* The Frankish defeat of the Arab Muslims at the Battle of Tours in 732 was not in itself a turning point for the expansion of the Muslim Arab Empire. However, we have argued that the Western definitions of who are civilized and who are barbaric are erroneous definitions founded on military prowess, camouflaged as superior intelligence. How could the barbarians of Western Europe ever challenge an Arab Empire, which had defeated two civilized empires, Byzantium and Persia, to dominate the lands that everyone, up to that point in time, agreed was the cradle of civilization? In 732 who could have had the foresight to envisage a new modern empire rooted in barbaric Western Europe, and expanding westward across the Atlantic ocean to America and beyond? Certainly not the Arabs, not even the Christians.

In like manner, who could have had the foresight in the twentieth century to predict that poverty stricken overpopulated China and India would be the countries challenging the West for hegemony in the twenty-first century? But empires never learn. So they die and new ones emerge to dominate the world as they had done. This never ending cycle of expansion and contraction by nations shows no sign of ending at the dawn of the twenty-first century. And historians will continue to foolishly deem the conqueror to be civilized and the conquered to be barbarians, terrorists, heathens, savages, Islamists, gooks, congs, or guerrillas, simply for fighting for their right to govern themselves, and make their own mistakes, or develop their skills, wisdom, and desire to be different.

After the defeat of the Arabs in 732, the Franks increased their influence in the lands that had been the Western Roman Empire. The Frankish kings formed a lasting union with the pope to create what became the *Holy Roman Empire.* Historians date the end of the Western Roman Empire to be September 4, 476, when the **German** general, *Flavius Odoacer,* forced Emperor *Romulus Augustus* to abdicate. But subsequent history has shown that the 476 date was premature. What happened after 476 was the growing independence of the Western Roman Empire from its civilized Eastern ruler in Constantinople, and a growing dependence on its Western Germanic barbarian protector.

The irony of the origin of Islam as a new religion that helped create a new Arab Empire was its unintended aid in the independence movement of the Western Roman Empire. This rather ironic result has never been identified by Western historians. However, some basic research would convince you that Byzantium lost its grip on the Western Roman Empire because it had its hands full fighting both its old rival, the Persian Empire, and a new stronger rival, the Arab/Turkish Muslim Empire. The Western Roman Empire seized this opportunity to assert its independence and morph itself into the Holy Roman Empire, with the help and connivance of the expanding Western Frankish Empire. This union of the pope and the barbarians of Western Europe was of mutual benefit. The pope was able to sever his subservience to the Eastern Roman emperor, and the Frankish kings could rely on Christian support for an expanding "empire of barbarians," safe from colonial status to the former Roman Empire. Recall also that one of the ways of converting from barbarian status to civilized status is to embrace Christianity. Of course, civilized is assumed to be more intelligent than barbaric, because an unswerving belief in virgin births and resurrections from the dead somehow makes you more intelligent. That's Western logic for you.

This original empire of barbarians was destined to become what Western historians have deemed the civilized race, with the right to conquer, kill and subjugate at will. For example, U.S. forces targeted and killed Osama bin Laden on May 1, 2011, and these Western historians celebrated it as if it was the most civilized act in history. President Obama acted as judge, jury and executioner and the Western world cheered. Only Western logic would conclude that *Osama* was the greater terrorist threat than *Obama.* Western logic is based on the fallacious notion that those with the most sophisticated WMDs are **civilized,** while those who have only primitive weapons to defend against the WMDs, are **barbarians, naked savages, communists, gooks and terrorists.** From the nuking of Nagasaki and Hiroshima to countless thousands slaughtered in Vietnam, Cambodia, Laos, Korea, Latin America, Iraq, Afghanistan and the Middle East, the United States and its allies such as Australia, Canada and Britain, are deemed to be civilized because they rid the world of people who supposedly challenge their civilized way of life with slingshots, rocks, IED's, and other primitive weapons. "One day an Afghan may fly his magic carpet and command his genie to destroy Canada with his bare hands, after rubbing his Aladdin lamp. We need to kill all Afghans without mercy before they do that." Western propaganda would be laughable if it were not so deadly.

What became the *Frankish Empire* in the eighth century under the Carolingian Dynasty of Charles Martel, Martel's son, Pepin the Short, and Pepin's son, Charlemagne, had begun in the third century in the region of today's France and Germany. The *Franks* were a German tribe that began to conquer parts of the Western Roman Empire. With the fall of the Western Roman Empire after 476, this Frankish Empire expanded across Western and Central Europe. It effectively replaced the Western Roman Empire by the end of the fifth century. Between the fifth and tenth centuries, a new distinctive Western Latin-Christian Europe was allowed to develop because the civilized empires—Greek Orthodox-Christian, Persian, and Arab—were fighting for hegemony in the historical region of civilization, the Middle East and North Africa.

When the Arab Empire expanded into Europe by conquering Spain and Southern Italy, it was the Frankish Empire that prevented their expansion into France and Germany. Martel's defeat of the Muslims at the Battle of Tours in 732 was significant because the dominant Eastern Orthodox-Christian Roman Empire had failed to defend Christianity against the Muslim onslaught. It was the barbarian Franks who had defeated the Muslims. He should be rightly hailed as the new *Constantine.* In the logic of Western historians, military victories transform barbarians into civilized conquerors. Charles "the Hammer" Martel had the added advantage of defeating the despised *Saracens.* In the West, all Muslims, Arabs, Persians, Kurds, Turks, Mongols, Tatars, and Berbers became *Saracens.* In the Muslim world, all Europeans, Germans, English, French, Italian became *Franks.*

The Roman Empire was born in the city of Rome and had begun with its conquest of Italy. But Rome had lost its preeminent position to Constantinople, and in the sixth century, most of Italy was wrested from the Roman Empire by the *Lombards,* to become the Lombard kingdom. The removal of Byzantium rule of Italy by the Lombards gave the pope the opportunity to invite the Frankish king, Pepin the Short, to overthrow the Lombards, in exchange for his recognition of the Franks as the new defenders of Christian Europe. It was, after all, Pepin's father, Charles Martel, who had defeated the Muslims and saved Christianity. Pepin not only defeated the Lombards, but handed over to Pope Steven II in 756, the conquered territory in Central Italy. This territory became the *Papal States,* which were ruled by the pope until they were incorporated into the new Kingdom of Italy in 1870. This so-called Donation of

Pepin is significant for three reasons. First, it enhanced the position of the Carolingian Dynasty as the new defenders of Christianity over the Byzantine emperor. Second, it enriched the papacy materially since land was the prime source of wealth throughout the Middle Ages. Third, it was an explicit recognition that the weakened Eastern Roman emperor could do nothing about it.

In 799 Pope Leo III was under attack in Rome and called on Martel's grandson, *Charlemagne.* Charlemagne was the oldest son of Pepin the Short who had both expanded the Frankish Empire and promoted Christianity within his empire. In return for his help Pope Leo III crowned Charlemagne as Roman emperor, on Christmas Day in 800. This act simultaneously cemented the alliance between the Carolingian Dynasty and the papacy and consolidated the severance of the lands of the Western Roman Empire from Constantinople. It marked the end of the old **Roman**-Christian West and the dawn of the new **German**-Christian West or *Holy Roman Empire.* The name was even changed to *Holy Roman Empire of the German Nation* in 1512. This new Western Roman Empire was first called "holy" by Otto the Great, king of Germany. Otto the Great became the first to have held the title of **holy** Roman emperor after he was made Roman emperor by Pope John XII in 962, for rescuing the pope again from his Italian enemies. The Western European civilization that would take Christianity to the New World and to Asia, after the voyages of Columbus and da Gama, was born with the Carolingian Dynasty of Martel, Pepin and Charlemagne. The Muslims lost the war with the Christians because the Muslims inherited a world that had identified the lands Southeast of France, in the areas surrounding the Mediterranean, as the civilized world. The Muslims conquered those lands from the dominant Christian power, the Eastern Roman Empire. But civilization would shift from the historical heartland of the Middle East to the West. In those new lands the Christians had the decisive advantage in every measure of what is deemed to be civilized, arms, economy, governance, propaganda, culture, language and religion.

This relationship between the Christian church led by the pope, and the secular leaders of Western empires and nation-states, which began with the Carolingian Dynasty, has lasted to this day. It has, of course, been a rocky relationship as each side has competed for dominance. At times strong popes dominated the relationship. At other times strong kings and emperors dominated. But the relationship was never severed. In the West, despite rhetoric to the contrary, the Christian church has been, and continues to be, a central force in its culture and governance and in its conviction to use military force to conquer and subdue the heathens and the "inferior" races of the planet. The rise of the Christian West originating with the defeat of the Arabs at Tours in 732 was aided by other factors, which we examine briefly below. These include the wealth of the Christian church and its control of public education, the rise of the military and sea-faring prowess of the Vikings, and the willingness of the West to learn from the Arabs and Greeks.

Feudalism, Private Property Rights, Church Property and Church Schools, Vikings, and Commerce

An important factor in the power of the Christian church was the ownership of land. During the Middle Ages land ownership was a significant determinant of the structure of the society and the social and economic order. Land was owned by a tiny percent of the population and by the Christian church. Those who owned land were the rulers and the masses were poor landless peasants in a state of semislavery. Agriculture was the primary means of eking out a miserable subsistence. By comparison, the First Nations in the New World had a much higher standard of living and greater economic and political freedoms than the mass of the population of Western Europe, throughout the Middle Ages. First Nations societies were far more civilized than Western European societies.

In the New World land was relatively plentiful, communally owned, and there were vast opportunities for hunting and fishing. The West inherited from the Carolingian Dynasty the *feudal* system, which gave so much power to landlords. The Frankish Empire was a *feudal* empire. It was Charles Martel, the savior of the Christians at Tours in 732, who was primarily responsible for entrenching *feudalism* within the expanding Frankish Empire of Western Europe. Martel insisted on providing titles to land in exchange for loyalty to him. These titles were effectively, private property rights. France, Britain, Germany, Russia, Scandinavia,

Spain and Italy became feudal societies with landlords and serfs during the Middle Ages.

The sanctity of private property, implicit in a feudal society, did not die with the end of feudalism. If anything it became even more entrenched, with private property rights expanding from the ownership of land to the ownership of capital, slaves, and entrepreneurship. The Christian church, by virtue of its ownership of land, became an inherent part of this feudal society. The Lords of the Manor were blessed by the Christian church and the church leaders had spiritual influence over both the Lords and their serfs. In the New World and colonies of the post-fifteenth-century Western European empires, the Christian church cooperated with the imperial power in subjugating the native populations in return for land, privilege, influence and converts to Christianity. The combination of conquests with religious conversions, made the Christian church an integral part of Western imperialism. While the Christian church enriched itself with material possessions, it preached the importance of spiritual over material possessions to the native populations in its efforts to assist the imperial powers to **steal** the lands and mineral wealth of the native populations. The Western sanctity of private property was a tool to steal lands and resources from communal owners, nothing more.

The Christian church had no qualms about benefitting materially from these thefts of native resources. In fact, the acquisition of material wealth by the Christian church was often a condition for its implicit and explicit aid and connivance with the imperial conquerors. Western European imperialism and the expansion of the Christian church, materially and spiritually, were never in conflict. They worked hand in glove to achieve the same goal. That goal was to conquer, enrich the Christian West, and subjugate, enslave, demonize, and impoverish those conquered by military force.

The ownership of property, which in the Middle Ages meant land, by the Christian church, began with the restoration of property rights to the Christian church by Constantine the Great. Constantine also began the first of many donations of property to the Christian church. One of the largest donations was by Pepin the Short. These donations from the wealthy made the Christian church one of the most wealthy property owners. Until the industrial revolution, land was the primary factor of production, conferring wealth, power, privilege and prestige to its owner. The Christian church used its ever-increasing wealth to control and influence the ruling class, to convert the poor and to indoctrinate. Church schools were often the only schools for the majority of the people and the Christian priests were often the only "educators."

The sanctity of *private property* and its implication that inequalities of wealth and income were not simply acceptable in the civilized West, but celebrated as superior and more godly than *communal property, Communism,* is one more example of the upside-down logic of the West. Private property and wealth inequality caters to the selfish side of humanity. How can it ever be more civilized or godly than communism? Christianity celebrated the idea that it was admirable to profit from the ownership of land, capital, slaves and entrepreneurship, and to accumulate vast amounts of wealth, and even exploit the advantages of that ownership, at the expense of other human beings. This implicit promotion of selfish struggle to become materially rich, and to have the law and society protect individual ownership rights, over communal or societal rights, was fundamental to the advances made economically and militarily in the Christian West. The Christian church could indeed serve God and Mammon at the same time. This sanctity of private property was later used to wage aggressive wars against societies such as Russia and China, which attempted to deny both the religious and human blessing of private property and income inequality.

Despite the widespread suffering of the poor caused by private property rights, the West and its Christian church, has continued to defend its sacred nature. Income inequality has had to be addressed through methods other than abandonment of private property rights. There is much evidence to show that this insistence on the sanctity of private property and the admiration for private profit has helped the West expand economically at a much faster pace than societies that have emphasized equality of income and wealth, communal efforts, and communal property rights. But this economic advantage has been exploited by appealing to the selfish side of human nature rather than nurturing its social and communal nature. What is dastardly about this Western admiration for private property rights, is the ridiculous notion that it is civilized and that communism is evil. I am willing to concede that private property rights and private incentives may enhance economic development, by appealing to the selfish nature of human beings, but to suggest that it is civilized or even a prerequisite for freedom, as many in the West argue, is preposterous.

The Christian church had a near monopoly on literacy and "education." The Christian church was the center of learning before there were universities and government funded schools. The Christian priests were the writers, scholars and teachers. The church used that power and privilege to impart a culture of Christian religious values and indoctrinate the subjects of an ever-expanding Holy Roman Empire in the West, and later in the far flung colonies of the Western European empires. This power to indoctrinate Christian values as superior and civilized, together with the doctrine that "private property" was sacred, while "communal property" was evil, is one of the keys to understanding why the "freedoms" boasted by the West, as a foundation of their open and democratic governance, is totally flawed.

The Christian subjects are brainwashed into supporting a system of government based on unchanging and sterile values of dominance, racism, religion, false notions of freedoms and democracies, warmongering, military invasions and imperial expansions. The media, the education, the values, the institutions, the choices and the distinctions between right and wrong are so manipulated that the subjects live in the cocoon without even being aware of how tightly controlled and limited are their ability to think objectively and make rational choices. Good versus evil is inherited from birth, parenting, education, media, language, limited options, unchanging dogmas, restricted debates, consumerism, employment, militarism, nationalism, politics, ignorance, punishment and ostracism. The Christian church has worked together with the political rulers in this modern Western civilization since its birth, to create a manipulated society of servile and docile people, who are happy not to have the courage or capacity to question the crimes of their governments.

The Vikings and Arab/Greek Influences on Western Europe

As Roman Europe transitioned from its colonial status under the Roman Empire to its feudal Christian nature under the pope and the Frankish kings and holy Roman emperors, a new group of barbarians from the northernmost part of Europe began to invade, ravage and conquer parts of this new Christian Europe. The single most important advantage of these barbarians was their seafaring prowess. The Vikings were the original explorers and adventurers of the modern European period of exploration. As we will see later it was their command of the high seas and naval superiority that helped the Western Europeans defeat the Arabs and other Muslims after the fourteenth century. This command of the high seas began with the Vikings who became part of the new civilized Western Europe. The Viking sailor/warriors originated from Scandinavia, which was not a part of the Christian Europe ruled by the Franks. They built a new kind of sailing vessel called the *Knorr* in the ninth century, and used it to expand out of Scandinavia. First they explored the relatively uninhabited lands nearest to their shores such as Iceland and Greenland. Then they moved south sailing to and raiding Britain. Next they sailed along the coastline into what were Frankish Europe, Muslim Spain, and North Africa, eventually reaching Russia. But the Scandinavians converted to Christianity in the eleventh century and became an integral part of the new Western Europe. For four centuries beginning in the eighth century, the Vikings expanded their conquests and trade outward from Scandinavia. They began the conquests, colonization, settlements, trade, plunder, piracy, and brutality that would be the hallmarks of later Western European civilization.

While the Vikings were making their mark on Western Europe, the Normans conquered Southern Italy and Sicily from the Muslims. The pope's support of this conquest further severed the papacy from Constantinople. At the same time Western Europeans were gradually emerging from their dependence on subsistence agriculture by increasing agricultural productivity and engaging in increasing trade with the civilized Muslims. The growth of towns provided new economic opportunities for the poor and reduced the power and influence of the church and the feudal landlords. It was natural that the West would be more willing to learn from their more civilized neighbors to the East and South than the more developed Muslim Mediterranean and Middle East would be willing to learn from the barbarians.

It was also very common for Christians to travel eastward as pilgrims to Jerusalem than for Muslims to travel to the West. In fact Muslim travel to the West was discouraged both by Muslims and by Christians alike. Islam discouraged Muslims travelling to non-Muslim lands and Christian states were far more hostile to Muslim visitors that Muslim states were to Christian visitors. These Christian travelers would be far more aware of Muslim advances and learn and copy from the Muslims. Muslims would not even be aware of advances made in the West. There was also very little interest by Muslims in trade between the advanced Muslim Empire and "backward" Western Europe. The West was also more interested in Eastern languages than the Muslims were in Western languages.

As the West emerged from the Dark Middle Ages their progress was hardly noticed by the Muslims. More importantly, it would be the coastal cities of Spain, Portugal, France and Britain, which were able to take advantage of the Atlantic Ocean to enable a westward expansion of a new European Empire that would not, initially, impinge on the Muslim Empire, centered in the Mediterranean, and looking eastward for trade opportunities with China and India, overland and via the Indian Ocean. The West would be able to explore the coast of West Africa and the islands in the Atlantic, the Azores, the Canaries, the Madeiras, without being noticed by the civilized world. They would hone their seafaring skills as the Vikings had done, for the time when the world would expand across the Atlantic, Indian and Pacific oceans, and the center of civilization would no longer be the Fertile Crescent. This larger world will be dominated first by the Western Europeans, largely because of their superior naval power, and later by the Americans, largely because of their control of the skies. With Islam secure in the historical center of the world, the Middle East, and its conquests and trade stretching eastward to India and westward to Italy, Spain and Portugal, it felt invincible. How could barbarian Western Europe ever be a threat when the far more civilized Byzantine Empire was not? To Muslims, Christian power resided in the Byzantine Empire, and that empire was puny and weak, compared to the Muslim Empire. Compared with Western Europe, Islam was more advanced in military and economic power, as well as in technology, arts, culture, medicine, mathematics, governance and science. Islam made the fatal mistake thinking that it had nothing to learn from the West.

The Christian Crusades Mark the Beginning of a Holy War between the Christian West and the Muslim East

While the emergence of the West from the Dark Ages was largely unnoticed by the Muslim Middle East, the West decided to confront the Muslims in a holy war or Crusade. There were several significant facts about the series of Crusades launched by the Christian West beginning in 1096. First, it was launched by the Western Roman Empire, which had transformed itself into the Holy Roman Empire and later became Roman Catholic Europe. This was one more attempt for this transformed Western Roman Empire to assert its independence from the Eastern Roman or Byzantine Empire. The Byzantine Empire had launched holy wars against the Persians, and had collaborated with the Persians, to wage holy wars against the Arab Muslims. But the Arab Muslims had defeated both the Persians and Byzantium. The Byzantine emperor was far too weak militarily to deal with the Muslim menace. Second, it indicated that the Middle East was still regarded in 1096 by both the Christians and Muslims as the center of civilization and therefore worth fighting over. Third, it was a brilliant effort by Pope Urban II to unite the still disparate Christian states of Western Europe into a single Holy Roman Empire, with the papacy as the center of its power. In the Western half of the Roman Empire, the church always had more political clout. Pope Urban's leadership in calling for the Crusade would enhance the political power of the church over the secular leaders, laying the lasting foundation for the inseparability of church and state, in the West. Fourth, it began two centuries of almost continuous warfare between Christians and Muslims, which started all over again during the First World War and shows no signs of letting up a century later.

At a time when these disunited Western European nation-states were far less advanced than the Arab Empire, and the remnants of the Byzantine Empire, centered in Constantinople, it was a surprising but brilliant move by Pope Urban II. At this time the lands occupied by Muslims were still regarded as the civilized centers of the world, while the lands occupied by the Holy Roman Empire were inhabited by barbarians. Pope Urban called on the military aristocracy of Europe to wage a *holy war* on the Muslim Empire in the Middle East. The call to arms was issued on November 27, 1095, at the Council of Clermont. More surprising than the call to arms was the overwhelming response by the people and leaders of Western Christendom. The most able Christian generals signed up for the task. Aristocrats were attracted both by their natural instinct for warmongering and their desire for land and booty. Serving both God and Mammon would become the lasting characteristic instilled into Christians by the Crusades. The call to arms united Western Europeans from the Northern most part of Western Europe to the southernmost part of Western Europe. This alliance is unbroken to this day.

By the time of the First Crusade the Christian West identified Jerusalem as the city to be conquered for the West to reassert its dominance over the Middle East. With the known world including only Asia, Africa and Europe at the time, Jerusalem, the Middle East and the Mediterranean, represented the center of the world. Conquest of Jerusalem, Palestine, Syria, Egypt, and the Middle East would simultaneously reassert dominance of West over East and destroy *Islam*, which had claimed to be the rightful successor to Judaism over Christianity. It was the Arab Islamic Empire that had expanded westward from the Middle East to Spain. Reconquest of this region would expand European dominance as far as the Middle East, placing Christian Europe on a solid footing to expand eastward into Central Asia, India and China. This historical call to imperial expansion by Pope Urban II in 1095, for religious purpose, laid the foundation for all future imperial conquests by the West to be inseparable from religious purpose. Church and state were unified. Those heeding the papal call would get both material possessions and spiritual salvation. The Christian church and its millions of followers worked selfishly and selflessly to ensure that all of the lands conquered by the West would be governed by those committed to religion and in most cases, the Christian religion. Despite its rhetoric to the contrary, the West has never separated church from state. Marriage by both church and state is only one of many examples of the unity of church and state in the West.

Another important historical fact was that by the time of the First Crusade, Jerusalem had become a holy city for Muslims as well. King David's choice of Jerusalem as the capital city for the Jewish kingdom had made it the holy city for the Jews. Judaism first offspring, Christianity, made Jerusalem a holy city for Christians and Judaism second offspring, Islam, made Jerusalem a holy city for Muslims. Like the Christian West, Muslims had also unified church and state for governance and imperial expansion. The Christian Crusades were simultaneously a war for empire and religion and a war against *Islam.* Islam was an obstacle to Western imperialism because Western imperialism relied on converts to Christianity who would use the Christian church and commitment to the Christian faith to colonize the world. Islam competed for those converts and those colonies. The Christian Crusades were not a historical anomaly in terms of them representing a holy war between Christians and Muslims. Rather it is the foundation of six centuries of Western dominance based on a unity of church and state and the continued use of Christianity as the explicit and implicit religion for political and military leaders in the West.

During the period of the Arab conquests preceding the First Crusade, Europe had declined in status and power. Since imperial expansion is the primary factor that Western writers universally use to determine who are civilized, by this rather ridiculous measure, Christian Europe had become barbaric, while the center of civilization had become the Muslim Middle East. Pope Urban II's call to the Christian princes and military leaders of a disunited and barbaric Europe, to wage war on the Middle East, was therefore a call for Europe to return to the civilized status it had achieved under the Roman Empire. By Western standards you cannot become civilized unless you conquer an ever-expanding empire and enforce your laws, governance, culture, language, and way of life by military force, on those you conquer and subjugate. That is why the West still pretends to invade countries like Iraq and Afghanistan to promote democracy and freedom even though their own citizens have very limited freedom and democracy.

Another ironic hallmark of this notion of civilized, is the type of military weapons used to colonize. The more sophisticated the WMDs used to colonize the more civilized the conquering imperial power. On the other side of the coin, the more primitive the weapons used by the colonists to defend their right to be independent, the more barbaric they are represented by Western writers. To conquer and expand is civilized. To defend against conquest is barbaric. The West calls this "self-determination." For example, the use of bunker busting bombs, unmanned drones and precision bombing by sophisticated fighter jets to pummel and kill millions of men, women and children in Iraq, Afghanistan, Pakistan, Vietnam, Laos, and Cambodia is civilized. Primitive weapons used by Iraqis, Afghans, and Vietnamese to defend their homeland are barbaric. In this beginning of both holy wars and civilized weaponry, the Christian Crusaders were promoted to legendary status as *chivalrous knights* waging wars by certain civilized codes of behavior, and using the new weapon of the lance. The *Knights Templar,* King Arthur's *Knights of the Round Table,* the *Teutonic Knights,* the *Knights of St. John,* and the Spanish *Knights of Calatrava and Santiago* are a few examples of the creation of these new "civilized orders" for religious warmongering. These knights killed to save their Christian souls as much as President Obama killed Osama bin Laden to save his Christian soul.

This special type of warmongering was promoted by Christianity as both noble and civilized. Those who used other methods of warfare were barbarians. This is the origin of the United States today fooling the world that precision bombing, by technologically advanced aircrafts, is civilized warfare, while suicide bombers are barbaric. The fact that the West kills at least a thousand with its civilized weapons for every one person killed by the methods the West deems terrorist is totally lost on an inhumane and barbaric Western civilization. President Obama could boast that Osama bin Laden had been killed by the most advanced and civilized military machine the world had ever known. Civilized killing by the West, such as the killing of Osama bin Laden, is cause for celebration. The highly trained and equipped *Navy Seals* are God's warriors. Osama bin Laden's freedom fighters are cowards and terrorists. The reality is that the key difference between the two is that Obama's men are Christians and Osama's men are Muslims. The West is the aggressor because it has the more advanced weapons. It's that simple.

Today a *knighthood* by the Queen of England is still regarded as conferring the highest status on a "commoner of the realm," promoting the glory of the kingdom and its colonies. While it is no longer confined exclusively to military achievements, the military is still at the apex of this kind of glorification. One example of the exalted position of the military is the continued promotion of the idea that military careers for members of the Royal family are still the favored choice. This is consistent with the ridiculous notion that continued global warmongering by the United Kingdom, and a strong and technologically advanced military, is the best way of achieving and securing peace. Princes William and Harry, for example, see no contradiction with military careers for themselves and worshipping their mother, Princess Diana, for working tirelessly to ban landmines and the use of cluster bombs. Prince Harry felt that it was important that he personally had a tour of duty in Afghanistan, to show his unquestioned support for Prime Minister Tony Blair's decision to continue the *holy war* began by Pope Urban II in 1095, against the Muslims. Since every public opinion survey of the electorate of the United Kingdom opposed the UK's invasion of Afghanistan, it was even more important that the Queen and the Royal family gave their blessing to Tony Blair for promoting democracy in Afghanistan, since democracy was out of the question for British *subjects.*

The fact that the Crusader *knights* committed the worst massacres recorded in history was never condemned. It was for that reason that their unjustified hero worship led to their civilized codes of warmongering to be later copied by the Spanish Conquistadors, who outdid their religious brutality in exterminating the First Nations in the New World. In fact, Pope Urban II call to arms was motivated by the possibility of personal riches from looting and confiscating the spoils of war from the barbarians. That same combination of simultaneously serving God and Mammon, was transferred to the European conquests in the New World, in Australia and New Zealand, and in the Western colonies in Asia and Africa. That quintessential *Christian* need for the most savage and blood thirsty of killings and genocide of "heathens" and "pagans," combined with the theft of their land and resources, originating with Pope Urban

II call to *holy war* in 1095, saw fulfillment on the battlefields of the New World, in Hiroshima and Nagasaki, and in the *killing fields* of Vietnam, Cambodia, Laos, Iraq, and Afghanistan.

Far from these crimes against humanity being condemned by the West, they are glorified in the name of the church, and of Western fantasies, such as spreading civilization, democracy or freedom. In reality, the West continues to use sophisticated weaponry and propaganda to simultaneously steal the resources of the Third World and spread its Christian Westernization, which is a uniquely *Eurocentric,* and largely primitive, and constraining view, of the human potential. Its preference for private property over communal property, its definition of democracy as having two parties that both defends the status quo, its tolerance for extremes of wealth and poverty, its identification of free markets with freedom, its intolerance of all non-Western ideas and cultures, and its continued hero worship of wars and the military are but a few examples of its primitive vision of the human potential.

Christian Crusades beginning in 1096 were a rather desperate attempt by the West to use religion to regain some semblance of the influence it previously had during the Roman Empire. Pope Urban II's call for a *holy war* against the Muslim Empire would unite Christian Europe. Instead of fighting each other they would unite to fight a common enemy. That enemy was robbing Europe both of its imperial destiny to be civilized, and the destiny of Christianity to be the one true religion of the entire world. Pope Urban II made the call for a *holy war* to "liberate" Jerusalem on November 25, 1095. In doing so he invented the modern version of *holy war*, which the West falsely accuses Muslims of inventing as *Jihad.* Just as *terrorism* was invented by Jews in Israel, and later copied by Muslims, *holy war* was invented by Christians and later copied by Muslims. Every atrocity the West accuses its enemies of using was invented and used by the West. The Crusaders set out from all parts of Western Europe beginning in September 1096. With some help from the Greek Christians of the Byzantine Empire, they captured Antioch and massacred the Muslim inhabitants, destroyed their mosques, and laid waste the land. They proceeded along the Syrian coast toward Jerusalem. They reached the gates of Jerusalem on June 7, 1099. By July

17, 1099, they had butchered every inhabitant of the city, men, women, and children. Blood flowed like a river in the streets of Jerusalem.

Pope Urban II had issued the call to arms by using the standard Western propaganda that the enemy was a savage and brutal barbarian. Such propaganda prepares a naïve world for justifying the incomparable savagery and brutality of the West. It's always the West, not those invaded and colonized by the West, which is capable of the most heinous crimes against humanity, and commits those crimes over and over again with impunity. The Western media is the instrument by which Western atrocities are covered up, and also the mouthpiece by which opponents of Western imperialism, are demonized. Western conquests, brutality and theft are never unconscionable since Western soldiers are the servants of the Christian God, who has commissioned them with the mission to decimate the heathens, and steal their land and resources. By enriching yourself with the booty of the heathens you are serving your Christian God by impoverishing the heathens. You have enriched both body and soul. There is no shame or inconsistency. The West never feels any guilt from the fact that its wealth is based on its exploitation and impoverishing of millions in the Third World. Western materialism is inseparable from Western spiritualism. That was the lasting effect of the Crusades.

The brutality of the First Crusade made Western atrocities not only acceptable but an essential ingredient of Western imperial expansion. Since those who oppose a civilized Western empire are always "barbarians, heathens, pagans, savages, guerrillas, congs, communists, terrorists, or Islamists," the West has the moral right and moral obligation to destroy them with brute force and without remorse or conscience. To kill, maim, dehumanize, torture, subjugate, terrorize, decapitate, destroy, humiliate, and victimize is justified in the name of freedom, democracy, religion, God, and preservation of civilization. Those who dare resist the civilizing force of Western imperialism are less than human and must be exorcised from the human race. The more brutal and vicious the exorcism, the greater the glory.

Thus it was written that the cruel and bloody massacres with which Jerusalem was reconquered in 1099 by the First Crusade led the victorious Christians to kneel in prayer "sobbing from excess of joy."

The killing was done in the name of the Christian God. Muslims, Jews and all other inhabitants of Jerusalem were brutally exterminated by the civilized Christian West. This laid the foundation for the West to exterminate the First Nations and the indigenous people of the New World, Australia and New Zealand, nuke Hiroshima and Nagasaki, bomb Vietnam, Cambodia, Laos, Iraq and Afghanistan back to the Stone Age, all in the name of civilized behavior. Both President George W. Bush and prime minister of the United Kingdom Tony Blair claimed to be inspired by their Christian God to invade Iraq in 2003. The West has never admitted its crimes against humanity much less apologize for them. That is why they continue to commit these crimes with impunity after six centuries.

The Christian Crusades failed to reconquer the Middle East for the West and for Christianity. But it did begin the process of creating a Western Christian Empire, which was eventually led by the United States some nine centuries later. At the same time as Christianity spread outward from Western Europe to the New World, Australia and New Zealand, Islam expanded eastward from Arabia and its Arab roots to the Persian and Ottoman Turkish empires and to Central Asia and India. Just as the Holy Roman Empire shared its leadership of Christianity with countries such as Spain, France, England, Germany and the United States so did the Arab Empire share its leadership of Islam with countries such as Iran, Turkey, Pakistan, Indonesia, Central Asian and African states. Christianity and Islam, both products of Judaism, expanded outward from their birthplace in the Middle East. But Christianity found its bedrock in the West while Islam found its bedrock in the East. The East was economically and politically more powerful than the West until the last three centuries. Since all historians consistently, though foolishly, claim that the more economically and politically advanced is civilized, while the less economically and politically advanced is barbaric, the implication is that until the last three centuries Westerners were barbarians and Easterners were civilized. By the same token Eastern culture was civilized while Westerners had no culture.

The spread of Islam to the East gave it a decided advantage over Christianity until the last three centuries when the West wrested dominance from the East. The Christian Crusades marked the beginning of a long but persistent struggle by the West to dominate the world. By the eighteenth century it had succeeded. With the discovery of the New World, Europe, not the Middle East, became the center of the world. Western Europe used its maritime advantage of easy access to the Atlantic to expand by sea westward. The relatively land-locked Arab/Islamic Empire was at a decided disadvantage as the importance of the Atlantic surpassed that of the Mediterranean and Western Europe developed faster and cheaper water transportation both southward around the Cape of Good Hope and westward across the Atlantic and Pacific oceans. The expansion of the Arab Empire westward to Spain was a temporary conquest. It enabled the transfer of Arab advances in cartography, mathematics, science, astronomy, philosophy, art, and medicine to Western Europe, which was of great benefit to the future technological superiority of the West. The expansion of the Arab Empire eastward also enabled the transfer of Chinese and Indian advances to Western Europe via the western part of the Arab Empire. The East and Islam have been on the defensive ever since the West dominated the world with its sea power following the industrial revolution. In the twenty-first century the balance of power is gradually shifting eastward. Western dominance will very likely end by 2025. What comes after cannot be fully anticipated. However, there is absolutely no doubt in my mind that it will be more civilized than what has been falsely claimed by the West as civilized.

The Origin of Western Anti-Semitism and the Creation of the State of Israel

The Christian Crusades against Islam coincided with the birth of Western persecution of Jews throughout the Jewish Diaspora and anti-Semitism as an innate cultural disease of the so-called civilized West. With Pope Urban II's call for the First Crusade, Christians in Europe felt it their religious duty to begin a persecution of Jews. As we saw above Jews had moved out of Judah before and after the Roman conquest. Many Christians blamed the Jews for the crucifixion of Jesus Christ. Pope Urban II's call to holy war led to the beginning of an ongoing discrimination, persecution and racial animosity by Christians in the West of Jews, both in Jerusalem and in Europe. We saw that when the First Crusade entered the gates of Jerusalem they slaughtered both Jews and Muslims. At home in Europe the religious arousal caused by the call to holy war used the Jews as their targets. Many Christians, unable to undertake the arduous military march to Jerusalem, saw their contribution to the holy war as one of making war on the Jews in Europe. These so-called Crusader mobs roamed Europe massacring Jews at will.

The Second Crusade of 1147–1149 began with the Christian massacre of Jews in the Rhineland. These attacks on the Jewish population in Europe continued through the later Crusades and led to a permanent dislike of Jews by Christians. Anti-Semitism, like white racism against all nonwhites, became ingrained cultural traits of Western societies. As we will explain later this dislike of Jews born out of the call to holy war against Muslims was one reason for the West to create the state of Israel as a "homeland" for Jews in the Middle East rather than in the West. The West could fulfil its penchant for hypocrisy by preaching a desire to assist Jews while hiding its inability to cure its innate anti-Semitism. As we will see throughout this book Western hypocrisy and double-talk is one of the most ingrained characteristic of its false civilization.

The Second Crusade: Franks vs. Turks: 1147–1149

The First Crusade, 1096–1099, succeeded in its intended goal of recapturing Jerusalem from the Muslim Arab Empire. Its conquest of Jerusalem was followed by the creation of four small **Latin,** Western Roman-Christian or *Frankish* states on the Eastern coast of the Mediterranean, in Palestine and Syria. These were Antioch, Edessa and Tripoli, in addition to what they called the *Kingdom of Jerusalem,* the largest of the four states. This was the beginning of a very determined post-Roman West to colonize the Middle East. This emphasis on "Latin" was another attempt to distinguish its conquest from the Greek Orthodox Eastern-Christian or Byzantine Empire. But these newly created "Crusader states" ultimately failed because the Christian conquerors had no desire to share the Holy Land with Muslims or Jews. In like manner the reconquest of Jerusalem by the Jews after World War I would also fail because of the refusal of the Jews to share Palestine with the Palestinians.

Pope Paschal II, who succeeded Pope Urban II after his death, fully embraced the *holy war* by Christians against Muslims. In like manner President Obama fully embraced the holy war of George W. Bush and Tony Blair against the Muslims in Iraq and Afghanistan during the first decade of the twenty-first century. This renewed holy war by the West is destined to fail as the first *holy war* began by Pope Urban II ultimately failed.

The success of the First Crusade emboldened the Christians to envisage the conquest of Muslim lands in Egypt, Africa and Asia. In like manner the victory of the Bush/Blair 2001 invasion of Afghanistan emboldened the Christians to invade Iraq in 2003. The twelfth century was the century when Christians would roll back the Arab/Muslim Empire by rallying the new civilized warrior class, the *chivalrous knights,* to serve God while finding fame and fortune in distant and exotic lands populated by heathens. The Second Crusade began in 1147 and lasted until 1149. One of the four "Crusader states," Edessa, had been reconquered by the Muslims in 1144. A Seljuk Turk, *Zengi,* had launched a successful invasion on December 24, 1144. France and Germany responded to the loss of the Crusader state by calling for a second Crusade. King Louis VII of France and Emperor Conrad III of Germany united with King Baldwin III of Jerusalem to defend Jerusalem, the Crusader states, and expand territorial conquests in Palestine and Syria. Continued rivalry between Byzantium and the Western Latin Christians was partially responsible for failure of the Second Crusade to recapture Edessa, much less expand on the territorial gains of the First Crusade. In addition, the Seljuk Turks, like the Mongols, were among the best mounted archers in any army. The Crusaders were attacked from all sides by the Seljuks both inside and outside Byzantine territory. It was a war between barbarians, Turks vs. Franks.

By the criterion of the West the Arabs had become civilized by winning wars against the Byzantine Christians and the Persians. It was now the turn of the Seljuk Turks to pass the Western test and become civilized. The Seljuks had conquered Syria from the *Fatimid* Dynasty after 1071. The Fatimid Dynasty had conquered both Syria and Egypt after the decline of the Abbasid Dynasty. The Seljuk Turks had a formidable leader in *Nur-al Din,* the son of Zengi. In November of 1146

Nur-al Din defeated an earlier attempt by the Franks to recapture Edessa. By thrashing the Franks the Seljuks were not only becoming civilized they were preventing the Franks from becoming civilized. In July of 1148 the combined forces of France, Germany and Jerusalem invaded Seljuk Syria by attacking the Muslim city of Damascus. The Muslim Prince of Damascus called on Nur-al Din for military assistance and the Franks retreated. Germany's emperor, Conrad III, departed the Holy Land in September of 1148 and Louis VII of France left the following year. In May of 1149 Nur-al Din successfully invaded the Crusader state of *Antioch,* adjacent to Edessa. The two remaining Crusaders states, Tripoli and Jerusalem, united under the leadership of King Baldwin III of Jerusalem. But all Baldwin III could do was lead a retreat of the Christians out of the Holy Land. The Christians held on to a strip of land on the Syrian coast. The Second Crusade also captured the city of Lisbon from the Arabs. While the Crusades ultimately failed in their quest to roll back the Muslim Empire they were the inspiration for the *Spanish Conquistadors* who succeeded four centuries later. That later success in the sixteenth century laid the foundation for a Western Empire strong enough to recapture Jerusalem and the Middle East in the twentieth century.

Two centuries of crusading zeal had lasting effects on the West. Western colonization was sanctioned and blessed by a Christian God. Muslims will forever be enemies of Christianity to be demonized and exterminated with religious fervour. The Christian God was the only true God. Muslims were unbelievers. It was the duty of every Christian to invoke the wrath of God on the Muslim devils. Wars must be waged on the unbelievers and their property must be confiscated for the benefit of the Christian warrior or the Christian church. Christians must become "Soldiers of the Lord." Salvation lay not only in prayers and belief but in killing, stealing and converting. Body and soul must be enriched. Christians and the Christian church must be enriched spiritually and materially with the plunder.

This demonization of Muslims by the Crusades was carried over to all non-Christians as the West moved from plundering the Muslim Empire to plundering the New World and other non-Christian lands. The pinnacle of this primitive invocation of religion by Christians was the enslaving of Africans for profit while converting them to Christianity. This is why the West saw no inconsistency between claiming to be civilized while condoning ownership of African slaves. All of the civilized fathers of the American Revolution, for example, were devout and proud Christian slave owners. As a devoutly Christian state the leaders of the new United States of America had to be leaders of the Christian church. As political leaders they had to be large land owners. As large land owners they had to be large slave owners. This simultaneous service of God and Mammon is an important reason for the United States being accepted by Christianity as the rightful successor to what Pope Urban II began with the Crusades in 1095.

Egypt, Saladin, and Richard the Lionheart: The Third Crusade

By the end of the Second Crusade in 1149, both the Muslim and Christian worlds were fragmented and disunited. The two Sunni Arab dynasties, Umayyad and Abbasid, as well as the Shia Fatimid and *Buyid* dynasties, had failed to create a lasting unified Arab/Persian Empire. The Buyid Dynasty had expanded Persian influence and culture within the Arab Empire after capturing Baghdad in 945. The Fatimid Dynasty had expanded out of Tunisia into Egypt, capturing Syria and Palestine. In like manner the Latin Christians of the Western European states of Germany, France, Italy and Britain had failed to unite with Greek Christians of the Byzantine Empire.

At the time when the barbarian Vikings were plundering Christian Europe the barbarian Turks were plundering the Muslim Empire. The Seljuk Turks conquered Baghdad from the Buyid Dynasty and Syria from the Fatimid Dynasty, adding a significant third racial element into the Arab/Persian Muslim Empire. It was the Seljuk Turks who defended Syria from the Crusaders. Having done so convincingly, it was natural that they would attempt to conquer Egypt from the declining Fatimid Dynasty. But it was a *Kurd, Saladin,* who would unite Syria and Egypt again under the *Ayyubid* Dynasty, adding another racial element to the Arab/Persian/Turkish Muslim Empire.

Under the Fatimid Dynasty, Egypt and Shia Islam had prospered relative to Sunni Iraq, Syria and Spain. During their dominance in the eleventh and twelfth centuries, Egypt became the center of the Muslim world and Cairo rivaled Baghdad and Damascus. But the Arabs and Persians were losing ground to the Turks. After the Second Crusade the Seljuk Turks were determined to unite the kingdoms of Syria and Egypt. It was the Turkish Syrian ruler, *Zengi,* who had reconquered Edessa from the Christians and prevented the Second Crusade from capturing Damascus. Zengi was succeeded by his son, *Nur al-din,* and in 1163 Nur al-Din sent the Kurdish general, Shirkuh, and his young nephew, Saladin, to conquer Egypt from the declining Fatimid Dynasty. Egypt's sultan, Shawar, formed an alliance with the Christians to defend Egypt from the Syrian invaders. But the Christians turned on their ally and tried to conquer Egypt for themselves. The Christians were defeated by the Syrian forces and Egypt was united with Syria.

This is a lesson that the American Empire has never learned. Time and time again the American Empire has befriended a country fighting for its independence with the ulterior motive of colonizing that country itself, only to fail. Afghanistan is only the latest of such failed American/ Canadian treachery. Christian treachery against their Muslim Egyptian allies provided the circumstances for the emergence of a formidable Muslim general, Saladin, to roll back the Christian invasions. With the defeat of the Christian forces by General Shirkuh and Saladin, Egypt's sultan was executed for "sleeping with the enemy." The Fatimid Dynasty's attempt to rule the Muslim world from its center of Cairo in Egypt and North Africa ended when General Shirkuh made his entry into Cairo in January of 1169. Egypt was once again united with Syria under the Seljuk Turk, Nur al-Din. Nur-al-din returned Egypt to its Sunni roots. But Saladin's uncle, General Shirkuh, the Sunni Kurd, was the effective ruler of Egypt. When he suddenly died in March of the same year Saladin succeeded his uncle as ruler of Egypt.

Saladin was thirty-one years old and destined to be another great Muslim general. The Turks had defeated the Persians and Arabs to rule over Muslim Mongols, Berbers, Tatars, Persians and Arabs only to see a Kurd rise up to lead Islam. With the increasing racial mix of the Islamic Empire the common unifying force was religion. In like manner, it was religion that was the common factor uniting Greeks, Italians, Germans, French, Spanish, British, Irish, Scandinavians, and Russians against Islam. The conquest of Egypt by the Seljuk Turks was crucial in preventing the Christians from conquering Egypt from the declining Fatimid Dynasty. Had the Christians conquered Egypt they would have used its immense wealth to bolster their presence in the Middle East. Egypt would become the key to controlling the Middle East and the Christians and Muslims would continue to fight for it. The Christian/Muslim wars for Egypt began with the Third Crusade and have continued to this day. In 2011 they were still fighting for Egypt in what was dubbed the *Jasmine* revolution.

Saladin became the sultan of a united Egypt and Syria after the death of Nur al-Din in 1174, beginning the Ayyubid Dynasty. A primary reason for his promotion to this position over the young son of Nur al-Din was his military ability to roll back the Christian Crusaders and retake Jerusalem and the Crusader states in Palestine and Syria. Nur-al-Din's young son, Malik al-Salih, had attempted to form an alliance with the Christian Franks to prevent Saladin from conquering Syria. But Saladin invaded the Syrian cities of Damascus, Homs, Hama and Aleppo, winning every battle against King Salih and his Christian allies between November of 1174 and July of 1176. Saladin was able to return to Egypt in September of 1176 as the sultan of a unified Syria and Egypt. But his battles against the Christian Crusaders had only just begun. He became the most famous Muslim (Saracen) general in the West. His battles with the English king *Richard the Lionheart* became legendary, thanks to their portrayal in many Hollywood movies. Richard's abandonment of England to his "evil" brother, John, to lead the Third Crusade against the Muslims and Saladin, gave rise to the legend of Robin Hood and Sherwood Forest, portrayed in even more Hollywood movies. Saladin's first attack on the Christians in Jerusalem, November of 1177, was a dismal failure. His Muslim army proved no match for that of King Baldwin IV of Jerusalem. Saladin was defeated at Tel al-Jazzar and forced to return to Egypt.

Saladin continued to engage the Frankish armies after his defeat in 1177, but it took a full decade before he was able to score a decisive victory. In June of 1187 Saladin once again invaded the Kingdom of

Jerusalem and captured Tiberius on the Sea of Galilee on July 2, 1187. The Frankish armies were concentrated fifteen miles west of Tiberius at Saffuriya, where King Guy of Jerusalem called a council of war. On July 3, 1187, the Christian armies marched from Saffuriya toward Tiberius and camped at Lubya on the night of July 3, 1187. They engaged the Muslims at the *Battle of Hattin* on July 4, 1187. Saladin struck the decisive blow against the Christians on the "Horns of Hattin" beside the Sea of Galilee. King Guy was taken prisoner. Saladin marched his army west from Hattin toward the Mediterranean Sea. There he captured the important port city of Acre. At the same time Saladin's brother captured Jaffa to the south of Acre while Saladin advanced north from Acre to capture Sidon and Beirut. Only the port city of Tyre remained in Christian hands. Saladin began his siege of Jerusalem on September 20, 1187. The Christians surrendered and Saladin entered Jerusalem on October 2, 1187.

The fall of Jerusalem was the inspiration for the Third Crusade of 1189–1192, led by the holy Roman emperor Frederick Barbarossa and the king of France Philip II, in addition to Richard the Lionheart, king of England. Saladin had anticipated such a response. Since the Crusaders would arrive by sea Saladin attempted to capture the port cities in the Mediterranean. He had captured Jaffa, Acre, Sidon and Beirut before his conquest of Jerusalem. After conquering Jerusalem, Saladin captured the port cities of Tortosa, Jabala, and Lataqiya. But Saladin tried and failed to capture the port city of Tyre. It was in Tyre that the first Christians of the Third Crusade arrived in April of 1189. The Franks also held the port city of Tripoli. Guy de Lusignan, the king of Jerusalem imprisoned by Saladin, had been released by Saladin in 1188, and he had made his way to Tripoli. With the arrival of the Third Crusade in Tyre, Guy joined forces with them from Tripoli and together attacked Acre. They were reinforced by Christian Crusaders arriving directly at Acre in September of 1189. Emperor Barbarossa led an army of one hundred thousand but drowned in the Saleph River in June 1190 on his way to the Holy Land. The German army panicked after the death of Barbarossa and only a smaller contingent arrived at Acre. The Christians dug themselves in at Acre for a protracted period of trench warfare.

The French king Philip II arrived in Acre in April of 1191. King Richard of England arrived in June of 1191. The Muslims surrendered Acre on July 11, 1191. The French and English kings quarreled over sharing the spoils of the Crusade. As a result Richard was abandoned by many of the French, German and other European troops and left to fight Saladin with a reduced Christian army. In August of 1191, King Richard ordered that the captured men, women and children of Acre be slaughtered. This act of barbarity by King Richard is another example of Western Europeans in the twelfth century continuing to be the barbaric race compared to their more civilized Muslim adversaries.

After the slaughter of the Muslim prisoners Richard led his forces from Acre toward Jaffa. On the march to Jaffa the Muslims attacked but were unable to prevent the Lionheart from conquering and holding Jaffa. From Jaffa, Richard would attempt his march to Jerusalem. By December of 1191 Richard had advanced from Jaffa to Bayt Nuba on the road to Jerusalem. In the meantime Saladin had sent out his own call for holy war, to the Muslims. Reinforcements arrived to defend Jerusalem. Fearing an easy defeat by the Muslims, Richard retreated from Bayt Nuba to Jaffa in January of 1192. He then marched south along the coast to capture Asqalon. This gave the Christians control of the Mediterranean coast from Asqalon in the south to Sidon in the north. But Richard failed to recapture Jerusalem and was forced to make peace with Saladin, signing the Treaty of Ramla in September 1192. The Muslims kept control of Jerusalem in return for allowing Christian pilgrimage to the Holy Land. Richard departed from the Holy Land in October of 1192 to return to England and rescue his kingdom from King John. His return was not an easy one. His European allies imprisoned him and asked for a ransom of 150,000 marks. He reached England in 1194. Saladin had died the year before of yellow fever.

Several Christian Crusades followed King Richard's failure to recapture Jerusalem. They not only failed to recapture Jerusalem but failed to prevent the Muslim Empire from forcing the Christians out of every city in the Middle East. Innocent III became the new pope in January 1198 and immediately called for a Fourth Crusade to recapture Jerusalem. No king or emperor responded to Innocent's call. It was agreed that Boniface de Montferrat would lead the Crusade. Boniface was the brother of Conrad and uncle of Baldwin, both of whom had served as kings of Jerusalem. By this time the Ayyubid Dynasty began by Saladin was firmly in control of the Muslim Empire and Egypt was now the center of that empire. The Fourth Crusade therefore decided to recapture Jerusalem after invading Egypt. Transportation to Egypt was arranged with the thriving Italian city state of Venice. Venice would provide both the ships and the sailors. Venice had sacrificed some of its profitable commerce to build the ships and was rightfully angry when the Crusaders squabbled over the agreed payment of eighty-five thousand silver marks. The problem arose because many of the Crusaders had chosen to leave from ports other than Venice with the result that those departing from Venice did not need all of the ships they had asked the Venetians to build and did not have sufficient funds to pay the full amount. This rather unfortunate squabbling between the Crusaders and the Venetians had the unintended effect of solidifying the split between the Latin Western-Christians and the Greek Eastern-Christians when the Fourth Crusade conquered Constantinople in 1204 and attempted to push the Latin-Christian frontier eastward.

The invasion of Constantinople by the Venetians is reminiscent of the invasion of Kuwait by Saddam Hussein. The American Empire had promised monetary payments to Saddam Hussein to invade Iran. When those payments were not forthcoming the American Empire initially agreed to let Saddam Hussein invade Kuwait and take its oil in lieu of the failed American payment. In like manner the Crusaders agreed to aid the Venetians in settling a grievance with the Byzantine Empire in lieu of their failure to meet the full payment for the ships the Venetians had built for them. The Venetians had lost their colony of Zara on the Adriatic Sea to a rebellion aided by the Byzantine Empire. The Crusaders agreed to help Venice invade and recapture Zara as payment for what was outstanding for the ships. Constantinople protested the connivance of the Crusaders with the Venetians as much as Saudi Arabia protested the connivance of the American Empire with Saddam Hussein. But while President George Herbert Bush retreated from supporting Saddam Hussein in the face of Saudi opposition Pope Innocent III did not retreat in the face of opposition from the Eastern Orthodox Church. For Innocent III the Crusade was more important than a breach with

Constantinople. While the American Empire could not afford to anger the Saudis, Innocent III welcomed the opportunity to increase the independence of the papacy from Constantinople and the Eastern Roman emperor. The world did not know it at the time but this incident was one more unplanned contribution to the rise of a Christian West that would dominate the world independent of the more advanced Eastern Roman Empire.

There was a very surprising turn of events after the Venetians reconquered the port of Zara in November 1202 with the aid of the Crusaders. We have documented at length the incessant competition among rival military leaders for the position of emperor or coemperor throughout the life of the Roman Empire, both before and after its split into an Eastern and Western Empire. This rivalry had not ended in 1202. A rival faction in Constantinople, led by *Alexios Angelos,* the son of the recently deposed emperor, Isaac II, took advantage of the conflict between Constantinople and the Holy Roman Empire caused by the Venetian invasion of Zara, to invite the Crusaders to invade Constantinople and replace the emperor, Alexios III, with Alexios Angelos. That invitation turned out to be a disaster for both Alexios III and Alexios Angelos and, more importantly, for Constantinople. The city created by Constantine the Great had become the envy of the world. The Muslim Empire had tried but failed to conquer it. The irony of all ironies was its conquest and pillage by fellow Christians.

The Crusaders arrived in Constantinople and captured the city in April 1204. The Crusaders did not disappoint those who expected nothing less than massacres and wanton destruction of artifacts. The prior massacres in Jerusalem and Acre had become hallmarks of Crusader conquests to be excused by those pointing to their occupation by the Muslim Empire. But Zara had not been spared by the Crusaders even though it had been a Christian port and Innocent III had specifically instructed Boniface not to harm Christians. Constantinople was the foremost Christian city. The rather savage sacking and burning of Constantinople by the Crusaders is a lasting testimony to the brutality of **Latin Christian** invaders even to other Christians. Christian churches and monasteries in Constantinople were not spared from looting and desecration. The murder, rape, looting, massacres and wanton destruction of Constantinople by civilized Christians far surpassed any acts of brutality inflicted by barbarians. The Spanish conquistadors would inflict similar pain and suffering on the indigenous peoples of the Americas in the name of their Christian God.

The conquest and rape of Constantinople by Latin Christians initially expanded the Latin-Christian Empire eastward. The count of Flanders, *Baldwin,* was made the first Latin emperor of Constantinople. Boniface de Montferrat was rewarded with Macedonia. The Venetians were also rewarded with Byzantine territory for aiding the Crusaders. The Crusaders established a number of "Crusader states" on what had been territory governed by the Greek Byzantine Empire. The Greek Christians were forced to establish a new capital city about sixty miles from Constantinople at Nicaea. By weakening the Greek Christians it aided the dominance of the East by the Muslim Empire. Until the rise of the West after the fourteenth century it helped the Muslims and hindered the Christians. If the center of the world had remained the Middle East this would have been significant. Latin/Greek disunity between Christians would have prolonged the dominance of the Muslim Empire. As events turned out the decline of Greek-Christian power and rise of Muslim power hastened by the wanton destruction of Constantinople by Latin Christians only forced the Christians to look westward.

With the discovery of the New World and the sea route from Western Europe to Asia the center of the world shifted from the Middle East to Western Europe. The Muslim Empire clung to the historical center of "civilization" while civilization was moving to a new modern location. The Christians, driven out of the historical center of civilization by the simultaneous rise of Muslim power and decline in Greek-Christian power had no choice but to focus their energies westward. This westward push by Muslim dominance in the Middle East could have been halted by the Atlantic Ocean. But the Atlantic Ocean instead of constraining westward expansion only gave the impetus for seafaring explorations and naval dominance. The totally unexpected discovery of the New World, which resulted from the Muslims pushing the Christians from the civilized east to the barbaric west, was the single most important factor for the modern domination of the world by the Christian West.

A Fifth Crusade to recapture the Holy Land was called by Pope Innocent III in 1213 but did not begin until 1217. As with the Fourth Crusade the plan was to conquer Egypt and overthrow the Ayyubid Dynasty before taking back Jerusalem. It was led by Jean de Brienne. From Acre the Crusaders reached the Egyptian port of Damietta in June of 1218 and looted it. The Muslims blocked the Nile to prevent the Crusaders from reaching Cairo by sea. The Muslim army, led by *Al Kamil,* the nephew of Saladin, camped south of Damietta at Mansoura, to prevent the Crusaders reaching Cairo by land. This delayed the invasion of Cairo until July of 1221. The Crusaders advanced toward Mansoora on July 24, 1221, only to be drowned by the Muslims in the Nile. The Christians were forced to surrender Damietta and Jean de Brien signed an eight year truce with Al Kamil. The Fifth Crusade was another failure.

The Sixth Crusade of 1228–1229 changed its tactics by first recapturing Jerusalem before invading Egypt. While it failed to conquer Egypt it secured a peace treaty with Egypt giving the Christians control of Jerusalem. Christian control of Jerusalem lasted for more than a decade before it was overthrown by the Muslims in 1244. The Seventh Crusade of 1248–1254 failed to recapture Jerusalem. There were two more crusades between 1271 and 1272 which also failed to recapture Jerusalem. By 1291 all of the "Crusader states" created after the success of the First Crusade, Edessa, Jerusalem, Antioch and Tripoli, as well as Acre, had returned to Muslim rule. The Christians had been pushed out of the entire Middle East.

The Christian West had failed to colonize the Middle East. But Christian imperialism from Western Europe was not dead. It had just begun. The militancy and religious vigor of the Crusades gave birth to the search by the West for every conceivable weapon with which to invade, conquer and steal or decimate the resources of those too militarily weak to defend their homelands. They would find it in sea power, the slave trade, piracy and the industrial revolution. Western European imperialism lay dormant for the next two centuries until Portugal began its colonization of West Africa, the Madeiras, the Azores, the Canary Islands and the Cape Verde islands, and Spain began its colonization of the New World. Until the First World War the West gave up on the Middle East to expand its empire across the Atlantic, Indian and Pacific oceans. God and Mammon were better served by simultaneously exploiting and converting the heathens outside the Middle East. The Middle East was no longer the center of the universe and until oil was discovered in Iran in 1908 it had little in the way of "mammon" to be able to satisfy the crusader search for God and Mammon.

Post–Arab Muslim Empires

There was another similarity between the rise of Christianity and Islam. Christianity, as a political force for imperial expansion, was born when the Roman Empire under Constantine the Great embraced it as its official religion. But Christianity, as a political force for imperial expansion, outlived the Roman Empire. It was adopted by Western Europe under the Holy Roman Empire and by the American Empire. Islam, as a political force for imperial expansion, was born with the origin of the Arab Empire. Like Christianity, Islam outlived its original founding empire. In this section we trace how Islam expanded its empire under the Turks and the Persians up to the fourteenth century. The Persian Empire predated the Arab Empire. But it declined after it was conquered by Alexander the Great. After it converted to Islam during its conquest by the Arabs it experienced a revival after 750 when the Persian Abbasid-Dynasty ruled the Arab Empire from its center in Iraq. Under the Abbasids the Arabs lost their monopoly as the rulers of the Arab Empire. Leadership was open to Persians and later to Turks, Berbers and Kurds. The Arab Empire was transformed into a **Muslim** Empire. Persians had maintained their identity as Persians after conversion to Islam. They became Muslims but not Arabs. While the two cultures mingled with each other it's possible that Persian culture had much more influence on the Arabs than the other way round. After the conquest of the Persian Empire by the Arabs, the Arab rulers adopted much of the Persian administrative structure and Persian customs.

Much more important than the revitalized Persian Empire was the rise of the Turkish Empire, which took over leadership of the Muslim world from the Arabs and subsequently declined to become the country we now know as Turkey. While the Persians had been civilized long before the Greeks, Romans, Christians and Arabs, the Turks were the equivalent of the Western barbarians, the Franks and Vikings. The Turks were part of the "Mongol hordes" who plundered and ravaged the lands from the Middle East to China, while the Vikings plundered and ravaged the lands from the North to Western Europe and Russia. As the "barbarian" Christians ruled the West after the decline of the Byzantine Empire so would the "barbarian" Muslims rule the Middle East after the decline of the Arab/Persian Empire. While the Latin Christians were launching their holy wars against the Muslims to seize control of the Middle East the Arabs were losing their dominance over others they had converted to Islam, including the Turks, Mongols, Berbers and Persians.

The Turks expanded their empire by conquering lands controlled by the dying Byzantine Empire as well as lands conquered from Byzantium and the Persian Empire by the Arabs. The Persians reconquered some of the territory it had lost to the Arabs. The Arabs, Turks and Persians shared the common religion of Islam. Islam had become a force that was bigger than the Arabs. This unification of Arabs, Persians, Berbers, Mongols and Turks under the same religion enabled Islam to continue to dominate the historical center of civilization, the Middle East, long after the Crusades. But the center of civilization was shifting westward to Western Europe and eastward to Russia. In the end the Muslims would be squeezed between these two emerging civilizations and their relative power in the world eroded. While Russia and the West would unite during the First World War the Muslims would self-destruct by an alliance of the Arabs against the Turks. As the 2011 uprisings in the Middle East show, the Arabs still foolishly trust Western propaganda about freedom, democracy and the right to self-determination.

Muslim Turks: Ghaznavids and Seljuks

Turks, Mongols and Vikings were making their mark on history while the Arabs and Christians were battling for control of the Holy Land. Unlike the Vikings and Mongols whose imperial conquests in Europe and the Middle East were lost well before the rise of Portugal and Spain in the fifteenth century, the Turks converted to Islam and both competed with and complemented the Arab/Persian Muslim Empire into the twenty-first century. The Turks, like their Mongol cousins, trace their origin to Mongolia, a vast area in Central Asia stretching for thousands of miles. They were nomadic tribes like the Arabs.

Turks and Mongols had a long history of internal warmongering, which made them good candidates for recruitment into the armies of the Arabs and Persians. Their prowess with the bow and arrow while mounted on horseback gave them a decisive military advantage. The first Turkish Empire, *Gokturk,* dates back to the sixth century. It therefore predated the Arab Empire. Its sphere of influence stretched from Mongolia to Ukraine. During this period the Turks came into contact with both China and India in the East, and Persia and Byzantium in the West. As the Arab nomads expanded their movements out of the Arabian Peninsula the Turks and Mongols expanded out of Mongolia. While the Vikings raided and plundered the lands under the Holy Roman Empire in the West, the Turks and Mongols raided and plundered the lands of the Byzantine Empire in the East. The Turks encroached on the lands of the Byzantine Empire and allied with as well as competed with the Arabs for *Anatolia.* Just as a single religion, *Christianity,* was the force that bound the Greeks, Romans, Franks, Goths, and Vikings in the West, so it was that a single religion, *Islam,* was the force that would bind the Persians, Egyptians, Turks, Mongols, Tatars, Berbers, Kurds, and Arabs in the Middle East.

Two religions, both of which came from very humble beginnings, would divide the world into two opposing blocs, which would continue the history of mankind as a race addicted to warmongering as its preferred means of settling disputes. Religion is not the cause of this obsession with wars and aggression. It's only the excuse and one of the instruments for galvanizing each side to develop more and more sophisticated weapons and feed its innate addiction to wars and conflicts. Every Western country's Ministry of Defense is truly a Ministry of aggressive and offensive warmongering. Poor people in the developed West give their political support to wars and expenditures on wars even when their governments use the excuse of lack of funds to provide them economic opportunities such as subsidized education, training, health care or food and housing. Warmongering, under the guise of "defense," is a sacred cow, supported by every political party in Western countries. As the 2008–2011 financial crisis and economic recession increased the numbers of unemployed and destitute in the United States, UK, France, and Canada, for example, there was still no limit to the increased expenditures on warmongering or popular support for such warmongering. In fact, the so-called Arab Spring of 2011 has led to these countries expanding their warmongering from Iraq, Afghanistan, Pakistan, and Yemen to Libya and Syria.

As Turks came into contact with Arabs and Persians they began to convert to Islam and became members of the armed forces and governments of the expanding Arab Empire. They learned the language and customs of both the Arabs and the Persians. This conversion of Turks to Islam and members of the ruling class was similar to the conversion of Persians to Islam and members of the ruling class in this Arab Empire. As the Arab Empire expanded, Turks and Persians became semi-independent rulers in parts of the Arab Empire. The expanding Arab Empire had to deal with conflicts among the Arab factions as well as challenges from the Persians and Turks.

One of the more outstanding Turkish Warrior Class to serve the expanding Arab Empire was the *Ghaznavids.* We saw above that Persian influence in the Arab Empire increased after 750 when the *Abbasid* Dynasty replaced the *Umayyad* Dynasty and even more after 945 when the Shia Buyid-Dynasty captured Baghdad from the Sunni Abbasid Dynasty. Under the Abbasids the number of Turks in the armed forces and administration increased significantly. As Turks moved up the ranks of the Persian/Arab armed forces they began to demand greater freedom and independence for Turks within the Arab/Persian Empire. As Persian dominance in the Arab Empire began to decline after 975 the Ghaznavid-Turks carved out a semi-independent empire stretching outward from their original city of *Ghazna* in Afghanistan to include all of Afghanistan and Pakistan as well as parts of Iran and India. These Turks, like the Arabs, had absorbed much of Persian culture and governance by the time they carved out their own empire. The Ghaznavids were primarily responsible for spreading the religion of Islam to India, from which Pakistan was later carved out.

By the time the Ghaznavids were replacing the Persians as rulers of the Arab Empire, Turks were moving from Central Asia into the Middle

East in increasingly large numbers. As the power and influence of the Ghaznavid-Turks declined, another group of Turks, the *Seljuks,* increased their power and influence in the Muslim Empire. The Seljuks took their name from a tribal chief, Seljuk, who had become a Muslim and led his tribe as members of the Muslim armed forces. Seljuk's grandson, Togrul Beg, made the Seljuk-Turks famous when he allied with other Turkic tribes to defeat the Ghaznavids in 1040. While the Ghaznavids were busy expanding their empire in India, the Seljuks successfully attacked their base in Afghanistan and expanded westward into the heart of the old Persian Empire, conquering Baghdad. The Persians under the *Abbasid* dynasty had been responsible for returning the capital of the Muslim Empire to Baghdad. In 1055 the Seljuk-Turks were welcomed into Baghdad by the Abbasids and their leader, Togrel Beg, became the new sultan. As sultans for the Abbasids the Seljuks expanded their rule from Iraq to Syria, Palestine, Azerbaijan and Armenia. The Seljuk Empire expanded both eastward to Central Asia and westward into Anatolia. But the Fatimid Dynasty in Egypt broke with Muslim solidarity to ally with the Byzantine Christians to oppose the Seljuks.

Togrel Beg died in 1063 and his nephew, *Alp Arslan,* succeeded him as sultan. Arslan scored an overwhelming Seljuk victory over the Byzantine army at Manzikert in 1071. Alliance with the Fatimid Muslims had not saved them. Arslan's son, *Malik Shah,* became the new Seljuk sultan in 1072. In 1075 the Seljuks captured the important Byzantine cities of Nicaea and Nicomedia. The Seljuks proceeded to conquer all of Asia Minor up to the Bosphorus. This marked the beginning of Turkish-Muslim control of Anatolia and the beginning of the end of the Christian Byzantine Empire. The old Eastern Roman Empire, known as *Rum* by the Arabs and Turks, became the *sultanate of Rum* under the Seljuk-Turks and in 1099 *Konya,* in the center of Anatolia, became its capital city. Anatolia would see an influx of Turks who would transform it into the country we know today as Turkey.

The Seljuk-Turks put the final nail in the coffin of what was the heart of the old Christian Roman Empire. The Roman Empire was born in the West, in Italy, but had become famous by conquering the civilized world, which was the Middle East. By the end of the eleventh century it had been driven out by people who had chosen Islam over Christianity.

But the Muslims had little knowledge or interest in the Western Roman Empire, which had transformed itself into the Holy Roman Empire. The Byzantines appealed for help from the Holy Roman Empire. Help came in the form of the Crusades beginning in 1095. The Crusades postponed the invasion of Europe across the Bosphorus but failed to restore Christian power in the Middle East. Forced out of the Middle East and Anatolia, the Holy Roman Empire would build an empire in the West, which would surpass the power of the Persian, Greek, Roman, Arab, and Turkish empires. The Persian Empire would be reduced to the state of Iran. The Turkish Empire would be reduced to the state of Turkey. The Arab Empire would be reduced to a number of independent states, including Saudi Arabia, Egypt, Iraq, and Syria.

The Birth of the Ottoman Empire

The Seljuk-Turks were defeated by the Mongols in 1243 at the *Battle of Kose Dag*. The Mongols had followed their Turkish cousins from Central Asia into the Muslim Empire. In the late twelfth century the Mongols united under a fearsome leader, *Genghis Khan*. Under Genghis Khan they raided, conquered and plundered the Muslim lands from Central Asia to Anatolia. Their brutal slaughter of the inhabitants made them more feared than the Christian Crusaders. The Mongol incursion into Anatolia continued after the death of Genghis Khan in 1227. Their defeat of the Seljuk-Turks in 1243 led to the breakup of the old Byzantine Empire into small semi-independent principalities, called *beyliks,* controlled by different Turkish tribes. These Turkic beyliks had existed to some extent before the Mongol invasion but prospered after. It was from one of these beyliks that the Ottoman Empire would emerge.

While the Mongols struck hard but disappeared into history, much like the Vikings, the Turks had staying power. It was, in fact, another group of Turks, the *Mamluks,* who helped to rid the Muslim Empire of the Mongol menace. The Mamluk-Turks had seized control of Egypt in 1250 from the *Ayyubid* Dynasty created by Saladin. In the meantime the Mongols, led by the grandson of Genghis Khan, *Hulegu,* continued to harass and plunder the Muslim lands. In February 1258 Hulegu destroyed Baghdad and committed the most horrible atrocities on the inhabitants. In September of 1259 Hulegu advanced on Egypt from his base in Tabriz. On his way to Egypt, Hulegu destroyed Aleppo in January 1260 and conquered Syria in March 1260.

There was a fortunate turn of events for the Muslims when Hulegu received news of the death of his brother and decided to return home to Mongolia with most of his men. The Mamluks took advantage of Hulegu's absence and marched its army out of Egypt on July 26, 1260, into Palestine, reaching the port city of Acre. The remaining Mongol army marched out to meet the Egyptians. The two armies engaged on September 3, 1260, at the *Battle of Ayn Jalut* in Palestine. The Mongols were outnumbered and defeated by the Mamluks. The Mongols eventually converted to Islam and disappeared from history much as the Vikings converted to Christianity and disappeared from history. It was during this period of rivalry between the Mongols and the Mamluk-Turks that another Turkish tribe made the most lasting mark on Turkish/ Muslim power in the world. We know this Turkish tribe as the *Ottoman-*Turks. The Ottomans would also have to fight the Mongols but would prevail. Their empire would prevail for six centuries, far longer than the American or British empires.

The history of the Ottomans began in one of those Turkic beyliks in Anatolia in the thirteenth century. The tribal chief was *Ertuğrul* who was succeeded after his death in 1281 by his son, *Osman.* Osman conquered the city of *Sogut* in Anatolia and declared himself a sultan. Osman was destined to become the first sultan of the very powerful Ottoman Empire in 1299 as Osman I. The Ottomans took advantage of the declining power of the Seljuk-Turks after their defeat by the Mongols, the failure of the Holy Roman Empire to rescue the ailing Byzantine Empire, and the continuing disunity among the Arabs. The first important conquest by Osman I was the city of *Bursa* in 1326. Osman's son, *Orhan I,* made Bursa the capital of the Ottoman Empire and went on to capture the important cities of Nicaea in 1331 and Nicomedia in 1337. In 1354 Orhan I crossed into Europe and captured *Gallipoli.* Orhan I cemented the Muslim/Christian union of the Ottoman Empire by marrying the daughter of a Byzantine prince. With the continued influx of Turks into Anatolia and their conversion to Islam, Constantine's dream of making

Anatolia the center of the Christian Empire was dead. Christian Anatolia was destined to become Muslim Turkey.

While the Europeans were pushing back the first Muslim invasion of Europe, which the Arabs had executed in the South, in Italy and Spain, the second Muslim invasion of Europe was executed by the Ottomans via Turkey across the Dardanelles. This second Muslim expansion into Europe began when Orhan I expanded his conquests into Thrace and forced the Byzantine emperor, John V, to recognize these conquests by treaty in 1356. The Ottomans were led by Murad I after Orhan's death in 1360. Murad I continued his father's expansion of the Ottoman Empire into Thrace and westward into the Balkans, conquering Serbia and Bulgaria before the end of the fourteenth century. Murad's defeat of the Byzantine Empire at the *Battle of Adrianople,* in 1365, signaled the opening of a new front in Europe for the Muslims. Adrianople was the center of Byzantine power in Thrace. Murad I moved the Ottoman capital from Bursa in Asia to Adrianople in Europe, renaming it *Edirne.* It was from this central fortified position in Europe that Murad launched his conquest of Greek cities and his Balkan conquests of Bulgaria and Serbia. Murad's forces defeated the seventy thousand strong army of Greeks and Serbs at the *Battle of Maritsa* in 1371.

Greece and Macedonia became part of the expanding Ottoman Empire. By 1371 the Ottoman Muslims had conquered both the remnants of the Roman Empire in Anatolia and the birthplace of Alexander's Greek Empire in Macedonia. The last Christian Greek city in Western Asia Minor, *Philadelphia,* came under Ottoman control in 1378. Murad I fought his final battle, the *Battle of Kosovo,* in 1389. He led the largest Ottoman force against a coalition of Serb, Greek, Bosnian, Hungarian and Albanian troops. He was killed in action but not before he had inflicted losses on the forces of the Serbian alliance from which it could not recover. Murad's son, *Beyazid I,* who succeeded him, quickly brought Serbia under Ottoman rule. By 1393 Bulgaria was conquered. In 1396 a Hungarian army was soundly defeated.

The Arabs had established the Muslim presence in Europe by conquering the lands on both sides of the Mediterranean, North Africa, Italy and Spain. Their push northward into Europe from Spain was halted in France by Charles Martel in 732. But they had achieved naval superiority in the Mediterranean and taken control of the cradle of civilization by subduing both the Persian and Byzantine empires. In the early fifteenth century the Mediterranean was still the center of the civilized world. In the period following the Golden Age of Arab power, Islam and Christianity had suffered from the devastation caused by invaders who were deemed to be barbarians by historians. This included the Mongols and Turks from Asia and the Vikings, Franks and Goths from Europe. While the Vikings, Franks and Goths had made Christian Europe stronger the Turks and Mongols had destroyed Christian power in what had been perceived as the center of the civilized world. In the meantime the Arab/Muslim Empire had suffered from internal dissentions and ceased to be a single unified empire. In addition to the struggle for power by three Arab dynasties, Umayyad, Abbasid and Fatimid, the Persians, Berbers, Turks and Mongols, who had been converted to Islam by the Arabs, wanted greater independence or leadership in the empire.

With the decline of the Byzantine Empire, between the Arab conquests of the eighth century and the birth of the Ottoman Empire in the fourteenth century, it became easier for the Muslims to attack Europe from the Balkans. That is what the Ottomans did. The Ottoman expansion into Europe across the Dardanelles into the Balkans was temporarily halted by defeats inflicted on them by the Mongols. But after this setback the Ottomans recovered and expanded the empire from the Balkans to Greece. Muslim losses in Sicily, Italy, North Africa and Spain were more than offset by gains in Anatolia and the Balkans. In this way the Muslims continued to dominate the civilized Mediterranean. But this new Muslim power was Turkic rather than Arab, Persian, Mongol or Berber. As Turkic/Muslim power penetrated Europe from Anatolia, Greece and the Balkans, two European powers in Southern Europe, Spain and Portugal, would push the Muslims out of Southern Europe and expand the Christian Empire by sea to Africa, Asia and America. The Muslims would continue to control the Mediterranean but the Mediterranean would cease to be the center of the civilized world.

CHAPTER 3

The Ottoman Empire Cemented Islamic Dominance East of the Aegean Sea: 1300–1700

Islam survived the decline of the Arab Empire much like Christianity survived the decline of the Roman Empire. Christianity survived the decline of the Roman Empire because the Western Europeans, North Americans and Australians are Christian powers. In like manner Islam survived the decline of the Arab Empire because the Persians, Turks, Mongols, Tatars and many of the people in North Africa, the Middle East, Central Asia and Asia are Muslims. In the previous chapter we saw that Muslims got the better of the Muslim/Christian conflict in what were the civilized parts of the world. Muslim dominance would decline, not because Christians succeeded in reconquering the old civilized world from the Muslims, but by forging a new civilized world across the oceans. That began with the Portuguese and Spanish empires, which we will turn to in the next chapter. But the post-Arab Muslim empires, *Ottoman, Mughal, Safavid Persian, and Uzbek,* predated the Portuguese and Spanish empires.

The post-Arab Muslim Empire that presented the greatest challenge to the Christian West was the *Ottoman Empire.* We, therefore, document here the rise of the Ottoman Empire and its importance in expanding the Muslim Empire into the Balkans and southern Russia and prolonging Muslim dominance in the ancient civilized world. By the time Western Europe and the United States came to dominate the world, the four post-Arab Muslim empires, along with the original Arab Empire, had spread the religion of Islam across Asia, Europe and Africa. During the nineteenth and twentieth centuries the Christian West colonized much of these Muslim dominated territories but failed to convert the majority of the population to Christianity. That is why the Muslim/Christian conflict is alive to this day.

The Turks played an increasingly important role as soldiers and administrators alongside Arabs and Persians during the expansion of the Arab Empire. The Turkish language was merged with Arabic and Persian to provide somewhat of a common language for the post-Arab Muslim Empire. Turkic dominance of the Muslim Empire, in some ways, resembles the wresting of Christian leadership by the Americans from the Western Europeans. Just as the Turks had been junior partners to the Arabs and Persians the Americans had been junior partners to the Western Europeans until the First World War. Excessive warmongering by the Western Europeans had weakened them to the point that the USA could seize the leadership from them. While the Western Europeans fell in line and acquiesced to the American leadership, the Arabs made the deadly mistake of allying with the Christian West against Turkic leadership. Arab disunity continues to divide the Muslim world and make it a much easier prey to Christian domination. In this chapter we will explain how the Turks, Mongols and Tatars wrested leadership of the Muslim world from the Arabs and Persians.

In the vast grass lands and forests of Mongolia and Siberia, to the east of the Middle East and west of China, dwelled the nomadic Turkic, Mongol and Tatar tribes. The Turks dominated the western half of this region while the Mongols and Tatars dominated the eastern half. The Turks were therefore located geographically closer to the civilized world centered in the Middle East and the Mediterranean. It was therefore natural that they would make contact with this civilized world before their Mongol and Tatar cousins. But the Mongols and Tatars interacted with and married into Turkish tribes. Mamluk soldiers imported as young boys into the Arab/Persian Muslim-Empire were Mongols and Tatars as well as Turks. The first great Mongol conqueror, *Genghis Khan,* was respected by Mongols, Tatars and Turks. By 1300, Turks, Mongols, and Tatars had converted to Islam. The nomadic tribes of Central Asia would join forces with the nomadic tribes of Arabia to make the ancient civilized Persian Empire, a Muslim Empire, which would expand eastward to India and China, westward into the Balkans, southward into Africa and Spain, and northward into Turkestan and Russia.

Christians would be forced out of the civilized world into Western Europe. A modern civilized world would be created by the Christians in Western Europe and North America. These two civilized worlds continue to wage barbaric wars on each other. In the previous chapter we traced the evolution of Turkic-Mongol influence in the Muslim Empire created by the Arabs up to the 1300. This chapter will continue that evolution up to the First World War. Empires rise and fall. The Turkic Ottoman-Empire was no exception. But Turkey, like Arabia, Persia (Iran), Afghanistan and Pakistan, continues to play its part in preserving a Muslim Empire stretching from the Aegean Sea past the borders of India and China, and defending that empire from its Christian adversary.

The Ottoman Empire Begins

In the thirteenth century, the Mongols, under the leadership of Genghis Khan, and his grandson, Hulegu, had successfully invaded China, southern Russia, the Muslim empire in the Middle East and the shrinking Byzantine Empire. The Mongols divided up the lands of the declining Byzantine Empire in Asia Minor into semi-independent *beyliks,* administered by their Turkic cousins. One of these beyliks was destined to give birth to the Ottoman Empire. Ottoman is the Western derivation of the Turkic prince, *Osman,* who ruled this beylik as Osman I at the end of the thirteenth century and into the fourteenth century. Mongols and Tatars would compete with Turks for Asia Minor into the fifteenth century, but the Ottoman Turks would dominate. The Ottoman Turks would also compete with other Turks, such as the Mamluks, as well as the Persians and Arabs, for the leadership of Islam. At the same time they would defend Islam both against the Christian West and a rising Russian Empire advancing from the east.

While the Muslim Empire would splinter into several independent states and four competing empires, Ottoman-Turk, Mughal, Uzbek and Safavid Persian, the Ottoman Empire would become the most powerful and long lasting. With the rise of a new civilized West centered on the Atlantic, the Ottoman Empire would also be the Muslim Empire that straddled both East and West. Even today, the remnant of that empire, Turkey, continues to struggle with its eastern and western heritage. With Western Europe and the United States plagued by debt and stagnant economic growth in the second decade of the twenty-first century, Turkey is once again looking for a leadership role in the Middle East. In 2014 it's at the center of the new war between the West and ISIS, the Islamic State of Iraq and Syria. It's under immense pressure from the West to ally with the West against Islam.

Ottoman power began when Western Europe wrested Christian leadership from the dying Byzantine Empire. The Latin occupation of Constantinople by the fourth crusade led to a further decline of the Eastern Roman Empire. The Holy Roman Empire had little interest in defending the Byzantine Empire against the threat from Islam since it was in competition with Byzantium for the leadership of Christianity. Its focus, instead, was to push back the Muslim presence in Spain and southern Europe and incorporate those lands into the Holy Roman Empire. In the period after 1300 the Christians were as divided as the Muslims. Christian squabbling would make it easier for the Ottoman-Turks to conquer Byzantium while Muslim squabbling would make it easier for the Christians to conquer all of Western and Southern Europe.

The irony of this is that the desire of the Holy Roman Empire to wrest Christian leadership from Byzantium led to the Christians sacrificing to the Muslims the more civilized portion of the world at the time. But with the future dominance of sea power this sacrifice of the Christians turned out to be a blessing in disguise. The more barbaric Western-European Christians were much better located to access the seas both to Asia around the Cape of Good Hope, and to the New World, than Byzantium. The Muslims would continue to dominate the civilized world under the Ottoman Empire only to see that dominance taken away by the naval superiority of the nations on both sides of the Atlantic Ocean. World domination shifted from the nations controlling the Mediterranean Sea to the nations controlling the Atlantic Ocean and the Caribbean Sea.

Ottoman Conquests in Anatolia (Asia Minor): 1300–1354

Ottoman conquests in Asia Minor simultaneously advanced the Muslim Empire into Western Europe while enhancing the Ottoman-Turk leadership of the Muslim world at the expense of the Mongols, Tatars, Arabs and Persians. Ottoman rule began rather modestly in 1281 when

Osman's father died and he declared himself the *bey* of the principality of *Sogut* in Asia Minor. At the time this region was known as the *sultanate of Rum* and was ruled by the Seljuk-Turks and the Mongol Khans. But it was divided into several semi-independent principalities or *beyliks* with a *bey* or warrior prince as the local ruler. The Byzantine Empire had long been in decline having been attacked by the Persians, Arabs, Seljuk-Turks, Western-European Christians and Mongols. As Ghazi warriors and other Turks moved from Central Asia into the lands previously governed by the Byzantine Empire many settled in Osman's principality.

By 1299 Osman's population, territory, and armed forces had expanded sufficiently for Osman to declare his principality independent of the sultanate of Rum. Under attack by the Mongols, the Seljuk-Turks were too weak to continue their subjugation of the Ottoman-Turks led by Osman. At the same time the Byzantine Empire was too weak to contain Osman's territorial expansion westward into Byzantium, Anatolia and the Balkans. Osman's expansion into Byzantine territory began almost immediately after his declaration of independence from the sultanate of Rum.

Osman expanded the territory of his principality in all directions but mostly westward into territory still controlled by the Byzantine Empire. This implied that most of the conquered territory was Greek Orthodox Christian territory. We see in this an interesting coincidence. Western Latin Christians were expanding territorial gains in Muslim lands in Italy and Spain while Ottoman–Turk Muslims were making territorial gains in Christian lands in Asia Minor and the Balkans. This coincidence led to Latin Christians wresting Christian leadership from the Greek Christians and Ottoman-Turks wresting Muslim leadership from Arab Muslims. Osman's first important military victory against Byzantium came at the dawn of the fourteenth century on July 27, 1302, at the *Battle of Bapheus.* Osman's successful invasion of Christian lands attracted Muslim fighters to his expanding military force from all over the Muslim Middle East as well as from Central Asia. At the same time the 1302 defeat suffered by Emperor Michael IX (1294–1320) led to Christians fleeing the area and further reducing the population of Christians relative to Muslims. Under the Seljuk rule many Anatolians had converted to Islam. Osman's major conquest of the city of *Bursa,* just before his death, paved the way for his son, *Orhan I,* to make Bursa the capital city of this nascent

Ottoman Empire. Orhan I went on to conquer the neighboring cities of *Nicaea* and *Nicomedia.* These cities just outside the European border were strategically located for the Ottomans to launch their invasion of Europe from the east while the Muslims were losing their southern European possessions. Just as no one saw these early Ottoman victories as leading to a new powerful Ottoman-Turk Muslim-Empire no one saw the Muslim loss of Southern Europe as leading to the emergence of the Portuguese and Spanish Christian empires.

The conquest of Constantinople by the Latin Christians in 1204 had forced the Greek Christians to flee to the new capital city of Nicaea. They ruled over an empire referred to as the *Empire of Nicaea,* located mostly in Anatolia. The Greek-Christian emperors returned to Constantinople in 1261 after a Byzantine force reconquered the city and forced the Latin emperor, Baldwin II, to flee. Unfortunately, the internal squabbling for the position of emperor, which was endemic to the Roman Empire, continued into the fourteenth century invasions by Osman I and his son Orhan I. The Byzantine Empire was engaged in another of their many civil wars from 1341 to 1347. During the reign of Orhan I (1326–1361), the first bey to take on the title of *sultan* and have coins minted in his name, the Byzantine emperors invited the Ottomans to help them settle their internal squabbles for leadership.

Just as so many Arab states invited the West to help them fight for their independence from the Ottoman Empire only to become colonies of the West so did the invitations of the Ottomans by the Byzantine emperors to help them settle internal disputes led to their colonization by the Ottomans. In 1346, for example, Orhan I used his forces to help the Christians overthrow Emperor John V only to install his *Christian* father-in-law, John VI, as coemperor. During the coimperium of John VI (1347–1354) the son of Orhan I, *Suleiman Pasha,* captured the Ottoman's first European city, *Gallipoli.* Ottoman Turks immediately began to settle in Gallipoli.

European Conquests by the Ottoman Empire: 1352–1683

Constantine the Great had transformed the ancient city of Byzantium, founded in the seventh century BCE, into his namesake, *Constantinople,* so that the Roman Empire could rule the civilized peoples of the Middle East rather than the barbarians of Europe. The Romans had followed the Greeks in pushing their empires eastward into what had long been the civilized world instead of northward and westward into what was considered the lands of the barbarians. As the power of the Roman Empire shifted back to its European origins in Italy and expanded across southern, western and northern Europe, its Byzantium base in Constantinople and Eastern Europe was under threat from another barbaric nomadic race, the Ottoman-Turks, which had roamed far from their origins in Central Asia. In 1345 Orhan I became an ally of the Byzantine emperor, John Cantacuzenus, and provided him with military assistance against the Serbs. Orhan I provided military assistance to Cantacuzenus again in 1353 and used that opportunity to establish a European base of operations for the Ottoman Empire at Gallipoli. By 1354 the Ottomans had conquered Asia Minor from the Seljuk-Turks, Mongols and Greek Christians. Under their second sultan, *Murad I (1361–1389)*, they were about to conquer the European lands of the Byzantine Empire from the base established in Gallipoli by the first sultan, Orhan I.

While the Greek Christians squabbled over who should rule their dying empire, the Ottomans produced a long line of efficient sultans who possessed both the military abilities needed to conquer new territory from other Turks, other Muslims, and, most importantly, from the Greek Christians, as well as the administrative skills to govern this expanding empire. Murad I succeeded his father after his death in March of 1361 and lost no time expanding his father's empire. Murad's older brother, *Suleiman Pasha,* had crossed the Hellespont, modern day, Dardanelles, in 1354 to occupy Gallipoli. Murad I inherited his father's empire, including the European foothold in the Gallipoli peninsula, after Suleiman fell from his horse and died from a sporting accident. The Dardanelles is a very important narrow strait, only 1.2 kilometers wide in parts, separating Asia from Europe. It was of immense strategic significance in defending the Christian capital of Constantinople. It also links two important bodies of water, the Aegean Sea in the west with the Sea of Marmara in the east.

The Aegean Sea provides access by water to the Mediterranean Sea, the most important waterway in the historical civilized world. On the eastern side of the Sea of Marmara is the other important narrow straight separating Asia from Europe, the Bosporus. The Bosporus links the Sea of Marmara with the Black Sea farther to the northeast. The Black Sea provides easy access by water from Asia Minor to Thrace, the Balkans and Russia. Murad I launched a successful military campaign against Thrace conquering Edirne and forcing the Byzantine emperor John Palaeologus to become an "Ottoman vassal." In 1366 he moved the Ottoman capital from Bursa, south of Constantinople, to Edirne, north of Constantinople. Fortress Constantinople was being surrounded by Ottoman conquests.

Fall of Constantinople

Constantinople was the symbol of Roman-Christian rule over the civilized world. This was recognized by the Persian Empire, the Arab Empire and the Western Holy Roman Empire of the Latin Christians. The Arab Empire had attempted to conquer it, but had failed. It was to be the Ottoman Empire led by its sixth sultan, *Mehmet II* (1452–1481), that would put the final nail in the coffin of Constantine's Roman Empire by conquering Constantinople in 1453. The Ottoman-Turks had expanded and surrounded the city fortress of Constantinople. Isolating Constantinople from the Christian world had begun when Murad I moved the Ottoman capital to Edirne in 1366. But Constantinople's high walls made it difficult to successfully bombard the city.

The third Ottoman sultan, Beyazid I, nicknamed the *Thunderbolt,* had invaded in 1402 but retreated to defend his realm against the onslaught of the Mongol/Turk led by Timur Lenk (Tamerlane). Timur defeated the Ottoman army near Ankara and captured the sultan. Christian Constantinople was saved temporarily by this Turko-Mongol leader whose military prowess rivaled that of Genghis Khan and his grandson, Hulegu, and who claimed to be the rightful successor to Genghis Khan. Timur temporarily reestablished Mongol hegemony in Anatolia over the Ottoman Turks. But Timur died in 1405 and Bayezid's son, *Mehmet I,* reigned as the fourth Ottoman sultan. The fifth Ottoman sultan, Murad II, made another attempt to conquer Constantinople in 1423 and failed.

Mehmet II succeeded his father in 1452 and in preparation for his siege of Constantinople he built a fortress, *Rumeli Hisari,* on the European side of the Bosporus. This gave him strategic control of the Bosporus and the Black Sea. The Byzantine emperor, Constantine XI, protested but could do nothing about it. The Holy Roman Empire took advantage of the situation to offer union between the remnants of the Byzantine Empire with the Holy Roman Empire. This symbolic union took place in December of 1452 but only strengthened the determination of Mehmet II to conquer Constantinople before the Eastern and Western Christians could unite their forces against him. In March of 1453 Mehmet II began to build a fleet large enough to take on Christian navies. In addition, Mehmet had some of the largest cannons ever, constructed for him by a Hungarian engineer, with which he would bombard the formidable walls of Constantinople.

The Turkish siege of the Christian city began on Easter Monday of 1453. The Christian emperor, Constantine XI, was given the chance to surrender, but refused. The Christian navies, including ships from the Holy Roman Empire, attacked Mehmet's newly constructed fleet. Mehmet was forced to transport his ships overland to enforce an effective blockade of Constantinople and continue his siege. Heavy bombardment began toward the end of May and the city fell on May 29, 1453. The Christian church of St. Sophia was converted to a Muslim mosque. More than a thousand years of Christian rule had ended. Constantinople became the capital city of the Muslim Ottoman-Empire. Under the Ottomans the city flourished and reversed years of steady decline. Christians were given the freedom to practice their faith within the Muslim Empire. This ensured the survival of the Greek Orthodox Church as well as its independence from Rome. The Ottoman sultans attempted to straddle a fine line between preserving the old Eastern Roman-Greek Empire of Alexander and Constantine while expanding Muslim rule. This implicit Muslim/Orthodox-Christian partnership increased the isolation of Western/Latin Christians from the historical civilized world.

Constantinople had been an important Christian city for overland trade between Western Europe and the orient. Its conquest by Muslims was another factor that led to the search for sea routes to the orient by the emerging Christian powers of Portugal and Spain. The Turks had secured the ancient civilized world centered on the Mediterranean for Muslims only to help usher in a modern civilized world centered on the Atlantic. The modern Christian Empire centered on the Atlantic would deny both their own historical relationship with Byzantium as well as the influence of the Arabs, Persians, Mongols and Turks on their modern civilization. They would only acknowledge a historical link to ancient Greece and Rome. But the fall of Constantinople was only the beginning of the expansion of the Ottoman Empire into Europe. By the end of the fifteenth century the Ottomans would conquer Greece, Macedonia, Bulgaria, Albania, Bosnia and Herzegovina.

Ottoman Conquest of Greece

The Ottoman conquest of Constantinople positioned it strategically to expand westward into Europe. Rome had expanded the boundary of the civilized world westward to Italy. Any post-Roman Empire had to dominate both the ancient civilized world centered in the Middle East as well as Eastern and Southern Europe at least as far as Italy, if it were to be the new superpower. For the Ottoman Empire of 1453 this meant conquering Greece and the Balkans. Greece had long been incorporated into what was deemed civilized by historians. This incorporation into the civilized world had begun with the Persian invasions into Greece in the sixth century BCE and continued under Alexander the Great and the Roman Empire. As the Romans had recognized that they must conquer Greece as well as the Middle East to gain superpower status so did the Ottomans understand the need to conquer Greece. It should therefore come as no surprise that Mehmet II would view his conquest of Constantinople only as a stepping stone to conquering Greece and replacing its Roman heritage. Mehmet II portrayed himself both as the sultan of the Muslims and the successor Roman emperor to the Greek Christians of the Eastern Roman Empire. By allowing the Orthodox-Greek Christians to continue to freely practice their religion Mehmet

II both safeguarded his conquest against Christian rebellion while preventing the Western Latin Christians from conquering Greece. It's ironic that an Islamic state would show more tolerance for the Greek Orthodox Christians than the Latin Christians of the Holy Roman Empire with the pope as its supreme leader.

When the Roman Empire had conquered Greece the Romans had given preferential treatment to Greeks within its empire much like Britain later gave preferential treatment to its American colonists in its empire. When the Roman Empire splintered into two halves the Greeks improved their dominant position in the Eastern half of the Roman Empire much as the American colonists improved their dominant position in the "New World" portion of the British Empire after the American War of Independence. The Byzantine Empire was more Greek than Roman just as the New World became more American than British. When the Ottomans conquered Constantinople in 1453 they were in many ways completing the process whereby the centuries of Roman/Latin influence and culture in this region had been in decline ever since Constantine moved the capital of the Roman Empire from Rome to Constantinople. The Ottomans would complete the process of returning Greece to its Eastern roots, albeit as a colony of the Ottoman Empire, but safe from conquest by the Holy Roman Empire centered in Western Europe. The initial threat to Ottoman rule would come not from the Latin Christians in the West but from Russia, where the Greek Orthodox Church had flourished. Russia was forever doomed to be the outsider who would save the West from the Ottomans, Napoleon and the Germans, but never accepted by the West as equal partners. Greece would eventually fall prey to the charms and hypocrisies of the West and choose semicolonial status under Anglo/American hegemony.

Macedonia had already been conquered by Murad I after he had moved the Ottoman capital to Edirne. Athens was conquered in 1458 and the Peloponnese in 1460. The Ottomans moved south from Constantinople to conquer the island of Rhodes in the Aegean Sea in 1522. Murad's son, Beyazid I, had conquered most of Greece after he had consolidated and expanded his father's conquests in the Balkans. The island of Cyprus was conquered in 1570. The island of Crete was conquered in 1669 after a lengthy war against the Republic of Venice and her allies. At the time Crete was the richest colony of the Republic of Venice. Under the Roman Empire a Greek aristocracy or "landed gentry" had emerged much like the American slave-based aristocracy under the British Empire.

The Ottomans relieved these privileged Greeks of their "landed gentry" status. The land was transferred to Ottoman aristocrats thereby maintaining the feudal system. Greece was divided into six regions for administrative purposes. The power and influence of the Greek Orthodox Church was enhanced under Ottoman colonization. The Orthodox Church was expected to work hand in glove with the Ottoman rulers much like the Catholic church in the New World vis-à-vis the Spanish Crown. Both were encouraged to recruit new members, non-Greeks in the case of the Ottoman Empire and First Nations in the case of the Spanish Empire. This arrangement between the Ottomans and the Greek Orthodox Church enhanced the power and influence of religion in this expanding Ottoman Empire. Both Muslims and Orthodox Christians were subjected to rules and governance based on religious convictions. All Muslims were identified as *Turks* by Christians and all Christians were identified as *Greeks* by Muslims.

Initially treated as subject people the Greeks were eventually incorporated into administrative positions in the Ottoman Empire. By the second half of the eighteenth century Greeks were pulled in three conflicting directions. One was to improve their status within the Ottoman Empire. The second was to form an alliance with Russia against the Ottoman Empire. The third was to ally with the Western **Latin** Christians. In the end the Greeks decided to ally with the West and begun a "War of Independence" with Anglo/American and French support. Naval support from Britain and France, as well as Russia, was crucial in winning its "War of Independence" from the Ottoman Empire in 1832. The West and Russia imposed a monarchy on Greece with Prince Otto of Bavaria as its first king. As in many future instances of Russia cooperating with the West to promote its claim for equal treatment, its military assistance to the cause of Greek independence was ignored by the West and Greece became a purely Western colony.

Conquest of the Balkans by the Ottoman Empire

The Balkans is a historically significant region in South-Eastern Europe adjacent to the historical center of civilization, the Middle East. Its eastern border is the Black Sea, which provided easy access by water from Asia Minor to Eastern Europe. Its southern border is the Ionian Sea, which gave it easy access by water to the Mediterranean Sea, which was the dominant body of water for the original civilized world. Today the Balkans includes all or portions of Eastern European countries such as Macedonia, Montenegro, Slovenia, Albania, Bulgaria, Romania, Bosnia, Serbia and Croatia. The close geographical proximity of the Balkans to the Fertile Crescent enabled early economic development in farming and domestication of livestock to reach this part of Europe long before those practices reached Western Europe. Its close geographical proximity to Greece enabled it to benefit from Greek civilization as well. The Roman Empire arrived in the Balkans via its conquest of Greece, enhancing Greek culture while adding Latin culture to the region. By the time of the Ottoman conquest the Balkans had been influenced by both Greek Orthodox Christianity and Latin Roman Catholic Christianity. The Ottoman Empire added Islam to the religious mix. The Ottoman Empire expanded from Asia Minor into the Balkans via its conquests in Thrace and Greece. The Balkans would become the dominant region where the Ottoman Empire would engage both Russia and the West for world domination in the centuries leading up to the First World War.

Ottoman conquests in the Balkans were long piecemeal efforts with many successes and failures. The process was complex, confusing and fragmented. Resistance to Ottoman rule was never fully extinguished. But the Ottoman Empire was the most powerful force in this region after Constantinople fell to the Ottoman Empire in 1453. It conquered the Balkan states of Bulgaria, Albania, Bosnia and Herzegovina, in addition to Macedonia and Greece. The first Ottoman sultan, Orhan I, had crossed into the Balkans in 1345 as an ally of Byzantine emperor Cantacuzenus, against the Serbs. Orhan I invaded and began to settle Bulgaria as early as 1352. In 1371, Murat I defeated the Serbs, the Ottoman most formidable foe in the Balkans, and their allies at the *Battle of Maritsa.* After conquering Thrace and moving the Ottoman capital to Edirne, Murad I conquered Bulgaria in 1379 forcing "vassal status" on King Sisman. Next, Murad I conquered Sofia and Albania in 1385 and began the conquest of Serbia after defeating the Balkan Slavs at the Battle of Kosovo in 1389. Murad's son, Beyazid I, completed his father's conquests of Bulgaria, Serbia and Albania. Ottoman expansion in Europe was temporarily halted by the defeat and capture of Beyazid I by the Turko-Mongol leader, Timur. Bayezid's son, Mehmet I, restored Ottoman rule over Anatolia, Greece and the Balkans. He was succeeded by Murat II in 1421, who faced opposition from the combined forces of Hungary, Serbia, Bosnia, Poland, and Wallachia. This allied force under John Hunyadi of Hungary, defeated Murat II in the first war but was in turn defeated in 1448, in the second Battle of Kosovo.

The conquest of Constantinople by Mehmet II marks the beginning of Western recognition of the Ottoman Empire. The people of the Balkans settled into and acquiesced to Ottoman rule over the Balkans. Catholic Europe had distanced itself from the Orthodox-Greek Christians of Greece and the Balkans. Mehmet II took on the titles of both sultan and caesar to placate both his Muslim and Orthodox Christian subjects. Most of the people of the Balkans showed a preference for Ottoman rule over that of the Western Holy Roman Empire. When Mehmet II invaded Bosnia in 1453, the Bosnian nobility refused to support their Roman Catholic king Stephen, opting for Ottoman rule instead.

The Ottomans, under Mehmet II, moved on to conquer Herzegovina in 1454 and completed the conquest of Bosnia by 1463. Despite the strong military resistance of the Albanians, Albania was conquered in 1468–1478. Wallachia was conquered in 1476. The whole of the Balkan Peninsula south of Hungary was now part of the Ottoman Empire. The Ottoman Empire also controlled trade in the Black Sea and had expanded north of the Black Sea into the Crimea. The important European trading city of Venice was invaded by the Ottomans in 1463 and conquered by 1503. At the time the Republic of Venice was an imperial power in its own right and the Venetians continued to resist Ottoman rule. It was after the fifth war against Venice in 1645–1649 that the Ottomans conquered the rich Venetian colony of Crete. The southern Italian port, Otranto, was temporarily occupied by the Ottomans in 1480–1481. Hungary and Belgrade resisted Ottoman invasions for more than a century but Belgrade was finally conquered in 1521 and Hungary was incorporated into the Ottoman Empire after the *Battle of Mohacs* in 1526.

These European conquests by the Muslims only served to motivate the Latin Christians to find a sea route to compete with the Muslim controlled overland spice trade with the Indies. Western Europe, led by Spain and Portugal, was looking for riches outside the Ottoman controlled lands of the Balkans, Greece and the Middle East. Rather than confront the militarily powerful Ottomans for the lucrative spice trade with the Orient the Western Europeans used their naval skills to find a sea route to the Indies. Portuguese naval skills and the support of Prince Henry the Navigator would give Portugal an edge in the lucrative spice trade with the Indies. Good luck, more than naval advantage, would lead to Spain's rediscovery of the New World. It was this accidental discovery of the New World by Columbus that explains why the Christian West seized hegemony from the Muslim East in the last two centuries, rather than any of the "killer apps" touted by Niall Ferguson for explaining the rise of the West, in his 2011 TV documentary *Civilization: Is the West History?*

The Golden Age of the Ottoman Empire: Beyazid II, Selim I, and Suleiman the Magnificent: 1481–1566

Beyazid II was the eldest son of Mehmet II and the first of three sultans widely acclaimed as rulers of the "Golden Age" of Ottoman supremacy. Mehmet II, known as "Mehmet the Conqueror," died in May 1481 after subduing internal dissentions and consolidating the expansion of the Ottoman Empire from Anatolia into Greece and the Balkans. Beyazid II took over the reins of the Ottoman Empire in 1481 at a time when the Muslim Moors of the Iberian Peninsula were fighting their final battles against Christian Europe. The Christian reconquest of the Iberian Peninsula from the Muslims took more than five centuries and ended in 1492 when Spain inflicted the final defeat on the last Muslim ruler of the rich Moor Kingdom of Granada, *Muhammad XII.* The unification of the Spanish kingdoms of Castile and Aragon in 1469 provided the military muscle to overwhelm the Kingdom of Granada. Many Muslims and Jews fled to North Africa. Islam continued to dominate North Africa and expanded into East Africa as well. As the Europeans began to conquer the

Eastern seaboard of the American continent before penetrating inland the Muslims were doing the same in the African continent. In time the Muslim/Christian wars for hegemony expanded from the historical center of civilization to Africa as well.

While the Ottoman Empire under Beyazid II, Selim I and Suleiman I, would consolidate Muslim conquests in Eastern Europe and Greece, two powerful Iberian European states, Portugal and Spain, would begin a transformation of the epicenter of the civilized world. Western historians understandably focused their attention on the domination of the Middle East and the Mediterranean by the Ottoman Empire. I say understandably, because this had been the center of the civilized world for thousands of years. But in doing so they took their eyes off the true prize. Historians even continued to focus their attention on the Ottoman Empire after it became the "sick man of Europe," so misled were they of where the center of civilization lay. Once Portugal and Spain had unleashed the Western European expansion westward across the oceans even the rise of Russia and Germany could not restore the historical center of civilization to its original glory. But we need to document this obsession of Western historians with the Ottoman supremacy before turning to the true prize.

Sultan Beyazid II: 1481–1512

Beyazid II began the so-called Golden Age of the Ottoman Empire by continuing the empire's expansion into the Balkans and the Black Sea. In 1482 Bosnia, which had been conquered by the Ottomans in1463, was fully incorporated into the Ottoman Empire. In 1484 Beyazid II secured the overland road to the Crimea. After several wars Moldavia was fully subjugated in 1486. In 1493 Beyazid II defeated the Croatian army at the *Battle of Krbava*. At the time the Kingdom of Croatia was part of the larger Kingdom of Hungary. With the defeat of the Croatian army Beyazid II was able to begin the capture of Croatia from the Kingdom of Hungary. Hungarian rule of Croatia ended in 1526. In time Hungary would fall to the Ottoman Empire at the hands of Bayezid's grandfather, Suleiman the Magnificent.

Beyazid II understood the importance of naval superiority and built a powerful Ottoman navy. Naval power had transformed the Republic of Venice from a rich city state into a powerful empire controlling the maritime trade with the Balkans and much of the territory in the Balkans. In 1423 the Ottoman Empire had launched a seven year war against the Republic of Venice for maritime supremacy in the Aegean and Adriatic Seas. The Republic of Venice had aided the defense of Constantinople against Bayezid's father, Mehmet II. After the fall of Constantinople Mehmet II had resumed what would become a very long and bitter struggle with the Republic of Venice for the Balkans, Greece and Cyprus. Mehmet's war with the Republic of Venice began in 1463 and halted temporarily in 1479 when Mehmet II signed a peace treaty. Beyazid II resumed the war against the Republic of Venice in 1499. The *Ottoman-Venetian War* of 1499–1503 was primarily a naval war for control of the Aegean, Adriatic and Ionian Seas. Beyazid II inflicted his first naval defeat of the Republic of Venice at the *Battle of Zonchio* in August 1499. Under the command of *Kemal Reis* the Ottoman fleet defeated the Venetian fleet commanded by *Antonio Grimani.* This defeat led to the surrender of several strategic military bases—Navarino, Lepanto, Modon, Coron, and Durazzo—by the Republic of Venice. In an effort to regain lost bases the Venetians attacked Lepanto in December 1499. The Venetian navy suffered its second defeat by Kemal Reis at the *Battle of Modon* in August 1500. With these naval defeats the Venetian Republic surrendered its possessions in Greece to the Ottoman Empire.

Cyprus was annexed by the Republic of Venice in February of 1489 and Beyazid II began another long struggle against the Venetians that same year for the island of Cyprus. He launched an attack on the Karpasia Peninsula. Ottoman wars against Venetian control of Cyprus continued under Selim I and Suleiman I. In 1492 Beyazid II sent his ships to Spain to rescue both Muslims and Jews from the Spanish Inquisition following the Spanish defeat of the Moor Kingdom of Granada. His welcome of the expelled Spanish Moors and Jews was a humanitarian gesture that brought many talented people into the Ottoman Empire. This is only one of many examples of Muslims being far more tolerant and respectful of Jews than Christians.

Sultan Selim I: 1512–1520

Selim I wrested the leadership of the Ottoman Empire from his brother, Ahmed, in 1512, a month before his father's death. Known as "Selim the Grim" he expanded the Ottoman Empire into both Muslim and Christian lands. His Muslim conquests in Syria, Egypt, North Africa and Arabia, made the Ottoman sultan the leader or *Caliph* of Islam and protector of the holy cities of Mecca and Medina in Arabia, as well as Jerusalem. The Ottoman Empire had surpassed all others for leadership of the Muslim world. The Arabs, Persians, Mamluks, Moors and Mongols had been subjugated by the Ottoman Turks. It was the sixteenth-century equivalent of the American Empire's subjugation of Britain, France, Germany, Italy and Canada for leadership of the Christian world in the twentieth century. The important difference was that Britain, France, Germany, Italy and Canada never wavered in their support for American leadership and even glorified that leadership. The Muslims, especially the Persians and the Arabs, continued to oppose Ottoman leadership. For example, Selim I fought several wars against Iran. Wars against the Persian Empire intensified after his son's death. Muslims are disunited to this day.

Sultan Suleiman I: Suleiman the Magnificent: 1520–1566

Selim's son, known as "Suleiman the Magnificent," maintained the hegemony of the Ottoman Empire over all other empires, Muslim or Christian. He saw himself as a worthy successor to King Solomon who was revered by Jews, Christians and Muslims. He made sure that the site of King Solomon's original temple at the Dome of the Rock in Jerusalem got as "magnificent" a facelift as the splendors of his court for which he was admired. The most famous of Suleiman's construction legacies is the *Topkapi Palace*, which became the official residence of the Ottoman sultans in 1465.

Construction of this lasting monument to Ottoman supremacy was begun by Suleiman's great grandfather, Mehmet the Conqueror, in 1459. But it was Suleiman the Magnificent who was responsible for most of the changes and expansions that added to its grandeur and status. Suleiman

I had inherited a very powerful empire but he expanded the empire both into the Muslim East and the Christian West as well as in North Africa. He was also responsible for wresting naval dominance in the Red Sea from Portugal. He was regarded by both Christians and Muslims as the greatest of the Ottoman sultans. Despite strong competition from the Habsburg rulers, such as *Charles V,* the holy Roman emperor, Suleiman I was the dominant ruler of the sixteenth century. The expanded Topkapi Palace in Constantinople was a reflection of the sultan's expanded power in the world. In 1985 the Topkapi Palace was designated a UNESCO World Heritage Site and is now a major attraction for tourists in Istanbul.

During Suleiman's reign the Christians were divided in the West. France and Spain were at war for leadership of the Holy Roman Empire. This Christian rivalry gave Suleiman I the opportunity to form an alliance with France and conquer Spain's ally, Hungary. We saw earlier that his grandfather, Beyazid II, began the conquest of Croatia from the Hungarian Empire after the Battle of Krbava in 1493. After several failed attempts beginning in 1521, when Belgrade was captured, Suleiman I conquered Hungary in his final military campaign before his death in 1566. Under Suleiman I, the Ottoman navy continued to be strong while that of the Republic of Venice continued to decline. In 1538 Suleiman's navy was able to defeat a combined Venetian-Spanish fleet at the *Battle of Preveza.* But after Suleiman's death the Ottoman navy lost half of its ships in a later battle, 1571, against the combined Venetian-Spanish fleet. After that disaster the Ottoman navy lost its supremacy in the Mediterranean, still regarded at the time as the center of the world.

Decline of the Ottoman Empire: 1566–1700

After the death of Suleiman I the Ottoman Empire declined in size and stature. Western historians have focused on its relative decline in the Mediterranean and the traditional center of civilization. For us this decline was unimportant. But we will address it. Western historians generally neglect the more important fact that hegemony in the traditional center of civilization had become almost irrelevant after the shift of the center of civilization from the Mediterranean to the Atlantic Ocean. In the remainder of this chapter we document the relative decline of the Ottoman Empire in the historical center of civilization. In the next chapter we document the shift of the center of civilization to the Atlantic Ocean.

The decline of the Ottoman Empire in the historical center of civilization was a natural result of its expansion over too large a territory. The reasons for its decline are similar to those explaining the decline of the Persian, Greek, Roman and Arab empires in this same geographical area. Imperial expansion and domination is evil and cancerous. People naturally resist colonization and imperial exploitation. In addition, every nation in history has been afflicted by this cancerous disease. Nations instinctively compete for empires. The dominant empire has to fight both internal rebellions and competing empires. Every empire must use military force to subjugate those it colonize. As it spreads outward from its original base it has to acquire ever more military force both to continue its expansion and to put down internal rebellions. In time it spreads its military force too thinly and will suffer increasing defeats from rebellions and competing empires. More importantly, the economic gains from stealing the resources of the colonies will begin to fall short of the military cost of maintaining and holding an expanding empire. Imperial decline is as natural as imperial expansion is unnatural. The imperial expansion is akin to injecting a slow but deadly poison into your body. The poison makes you physically stronger and materially richer for a while. But it also makes you morally weaker and hypocritical. Death is inevitable.

The relative decline of the Ottoman Empire in the historical center of civilization can be divided into three parts. First, we will deal with its failure to expand westward into Europe after its failure to conquer Vienna. The Ottomans would lose territory to the powerful Habsburgs rulers of Europe rather than gain more. Second, we will deal with the threat from an expanding Russia. Once again the Ottomans lost territory to the expanding Russian Empire. Finally we will deal with Muslim opposition from the Persians and the loss of territory to the Safavid Persians.

Background to the Ottoman/Habsburg Rivalry for Europe

Decline of the Ottoman Empire in Europe is usually associated with its failure to conquer Vienna, capital of the Habsburg Austrian Empire, as well as its failure to expand its naval dominance in the Mediterranean. In chapter I we traced the transformation of the Western half of the Roman Empire into the Holy Roman Empire up to 800 CE when the Frankish king Charlemagne was crowned holy Roman emperor by Pope Leo III. Western Europeans had partially reclaimed their independence as nation-states after the decline of the Roman Empire. As the barbaric half of the Roman Empire, they had never been as integrated into the civilized world as the Middle East, Anatolia, Greece, or North Africa. But Western Europe did not fully escape the innate nature of rulers to conquer, colonize and expand their empires. After the collapse of the Western Roman Empire several Germanic tribes attempted to carve out empires in Western Europe and North Africa. The most successful was the Franks, beginning with the defeat of the Roman governor of Gaul in 486 by *Clovis I.* Clovis I expanded the Frankish Empire into the south-western parts of today's Germany and France.

In 534 the Franks expanded their empire by conquering the Kingdom of Burgundy, centered on today's Geneva and Lyons. The Burgundians had previously been allies of the Franks. It was the Franks who ended Arab expansion into Western Europe and removed the Lombards from Northern Italy. However, the Frankish Empire was divided into East and West in 843, as well as a portion in the middle, by the grandson of Charlemagne. The Eastern half became what is Germany today and the Western half became what is France today. Western Europe was more divided than ever. The last *Carolingian* king in the Eastern Frankish Empire died in 911. The *Ottonian* dynasty came to power in the Eastern Frankish or German Empire with the election of the duke of Saxony as King Henry I in 919. The German Empire expanded into Bohemia, Hungary and Italy under *Otto the Great* (Otto I). In 962 Otto I became the first of several holy Roman emperors from the Eastern Frankish Empire. Under Otto I the Holy Roman Empire became synonymous with the German Empire and effectively the successor of the empire created by Charlemagne and the Carolingians. Some historians date the beginning of the Holy Roman Empire with the coronation of Otto I as the holy Roman emperor in 962 despite the coronation of Charlemagne as holy Roman emperor in 800.

Consolidation of Western Europe under the Ottonian *Saxon* dynasty did not last. In 1024 the Ottonian dynasty was replaced by the Salian *Frankish* dynasty. There began a period of intense rivalry between the power of the pope and that of the German kings, referred to as the "Investiture Controversy." Ever since the Western Roman Empire morphed into the Holy Roman Empire the popes and kings competed for political and spiritual leadership of the Western European states and empires. This power struggle was intensified by the conflict over the right of emperors to appoint, "invest," bishops and abbots. The power to appoint these church leaders is an important example of the *hypocrisy* underlying Western democracy and separation of church and state. The kings and emperors wanted the power to appoint bishops and abbots primarily because of the monetary benefit from "selling" these positions to the land owning aristocratic class. Selling the rights to govern in Western democracies has exploded today as politicians compete for votes by promising "free" health care, education, pensions, roads, housing and other goodies. Western European countries today are sinking into the abyss of "sovereign" debt because of the same hypocrisy of pretending to appoint rulers on the basis of merit instead of bribery. In the United States, the bastion of Western democracy, political lobbying for all types of "goodies" is at its most extreme.

The church took advantage of the Investiture Controversy after Henry IV became the German king in 1056 when he was only six years old. The church in Rome declared that secular leaders would not have any role in the selection of the pope. With the church selecting the pope the church would also control the appointment of bishops and abbots. Matters came to a head in 1075 when Pope Gregory VII declared that the pope had the sole authority to appoint church leaders. When Henry IV opposed the pope he was excommunicated. The pope has been able to exploit the endemic problem of secular leaders competing with each other for the titles of kings and emperors since the days of the Roman Empire. The *Saxons* revolted against Henry IV and elected Rudolf von Rheinfelden as king. This led to civil war and Rudolf was killed by

Henry IV in 1081. Pope Gregory VII then called on the *Normans* to defend him against Henry IV. Henry IV marched on Rome and replaced Pope Gregory VII with Pope Clement III.

Gregory VII was forced to flee from Rome with his Norman allies but future popes continued to foment rebellions in Germany so as to prevent the German kings from having sufficient power to challenge the right of the church to appoint church leaders. The political unity of the German Empire disintegrated. Henry V forced his father to abdicate in 1106 only to lose vast parts of the German Empire in Bohemia, Poland and Hungary. This conflict between pope and emperor continued after the *Salian* dynasty was replaced by the *Hohenstaufen* dynasty in 1138. The German Empire was severely weakened by political strife despite the efforts of Emperor Frederick I, *Barbarossa,* to keep Italy united within the German Empire. Barbarossa drowned in 1190 on his way to Jerusalem while leading the Third Crusade leaving the German crown to his son, Henry VI. The death of Henry VI in 1197 led to another civil war over which prince would rule the German Empire.

Two rival kings, the *Hohenstaufen* Philip of Swabia and the *Welf* Otto IV, were elected in 1198, but the son of Henry VI, Frederick II, regained the crown and became emperor in 1212. Conflicts between pope and emperor continued and Frederick II was excommunicated in 1247. *William of Holland* was made king of Germany. When Frederick II died in 1250 the German Empire was once again divided between William of Holland and the son of Frederick II, *Conrad IV.* The period known as the "Great Interregnum" began with the death of Conrad IV in 1254. Christendom was in crisis.

Ottoman/Habsburg Rivalry for Europe

Among the many Western European rulers seeking to expand their base in Western Europe, the most successful and powerful was the *House of Habsburg.* It was this "House" which produced Western Europe's most accomplished sixteenth-century ruler, *Charles V,* who simultaneously forged Europe's transformation of the center of the civilized world from the Mediterranean to the Atlantic and opposed Suleiman the Magnificent in Europe. Charles V became known as "world emperor." This important

"House" dates back to the eleventh century fortress, *Habsburg Castle,* built in Switzerland by Count Radbot. Its Austrian connection dates back to the thirteenth century when a descendant of the count, *Rudolph von Habsburg,* acquired lands in the Duchy of Austria and the neighboring Duchy of Styria. The Habsburgs expanded their family property in Swabia and Alsace through marriages.

William of Holland died in 1256, two years after the death of Conrad IV. The political squabbling for the German Empire continued after the deaths of William and Conrad. This provided the opportunity for the House of Habsburg. Rudolph von Habsburg, at the time a relatively minor Swabian prince, but relatively large family land owner, became the king of Germany in 1273, Rudolph I. In 1282 the Habsburgs became rulers of the Duchy of Austria and ruled Austria for six centuries. Rudolph's sons, Rudolph II and Albert inherited the Duchies of Austria and Styria. The Habsburgs supported their rule from their own property, which made them less dependent on the sale of church positions to the nobility. It also meant that they were more inclined to increase their own family property. An ever-expanding family estate can support the political power of the family. The Habsburgs expanded their family estates into Hungary, Bohemia, Burgundy and Spain using the age-old traditions of conquests and royalty marrying other royalty. The Habsburgs were fast becoming the most powerful family dynasty in the German Empire.

The Great Interregnum ended in 1273 since the election of Rudolph I as king of Germany was supported by all the rival factions. But the first holy Roman emperor after Frederick II was Henry VII of the House of *Luxembourg,* crowned emperor in 1312. Using the marriage weapon again, in 1422, the Habsburg, Duke Albert V of Austria, married the daughter of the king of Hungary, the Luxembourg, *Sigismund,* who was also the holy Roman emperor. This convenient marriage not only united the wealth of the Habsburg and Luxembourg families but made the Habsburgs temporary rulers of Hungary. Albert became king of Hungary after his father-in-law died in 1437. In 1438 Duke Albert V also became king of the Romans and holy Roman emperor as Albert II. When Albert II died the next year defending Hungary against invasion by the Ottoman Empire, his cousin, Frederick III became holy Roman emperor in 1440 and held the title until 1493. This important title was held continuously by the House of Habsburg until 1740.

With the marriage of Frederick III to Eleanor, daughter of the king of *Portugal,* the Habsburgs reached into Southern Europe. Continuing to use the marriage weapon, Frederick III forced the duke of Burgundy, Charles the Bold, to marry his daughter, *Mary,* to his son, *Maximilian,* after defeating Charles at the Siege of Neuss during the "Burgundian Wars." Charles was killed in 1477 at the Battle of Nancy, and Mary inherited the *Flemish Netherlands,* which became Habsburg property through her marriage to Maximilian. However, Frederick III sold Luxembourg to France and was unable to keep Hungary under his rule. In 1458 *Matthias Corvinus* was elected as king of Hungary. He waged several wars against both Frederick III and the Ottoman Empire to keep Hungary independent. In1485 Matthias made a triumphal entry into Vienna and made Vienna his capital city. The next year Frederick III was forced by the German nobility to transfer power to his son, *Maximilian I.* Maximilian I took the title of king of the Romans in 1486 and the title of holy Roman emperor in 1493, after his father's death. Maximilian I began a war with the king of France, *Louis XI,* over the lands that had been owned by his father-in-law, Charles the Bold, as ruler of the Duchy of Burgundy. The lands had been divided between France and Maximilian's wife, Mary, after the military defeats suffered by Charles the Bold during the "Burgundian Wars." The war ended in 1493 with the lands still divided between France and the Habsburg family.

Family feuds between the House of Habsburg and the French ruling family, the *Valois,* began after the death of the king of Naples, Ferdinand I, in January 1494. The Valois, King Charles VIII of France, invaded Italy in 1494 to claim the Kingdom of Naples. His army of twenty-five thousand reached Naples in February 1495. Charles VIII seized the crown from the son of Ferdinand I, *Alfonso II,* to become king of Naples. When Charles VIII laid claims to the Duchy of Milan, the duke of Milan, *Ludovico,* sought an alliance with Emperor Maximilian I by offering his niece, *Bianca,* in marriage. Maximilian's first wife, Mary, had died in 1482, and the Habsburgs were always keen on expanding their domain through marriage. Maximilian I joined other monarchs to form an alliance, the *League of Venice,* to oppose Charles VIII. This marked the beginning of the *Habsburg-Valois* wars, which lasted until 1559. The alliance defeated Charles VIII at the *Battle of Fornovo,* in July 1495. Charles VIII was forced to abandon his claim to Naples. These incessant wars and family feuds among the Christian rulers made it easier for the Ottoman Empire to expand westward into Europe. The Ottoman sultan, Suleiman I, even formed an alliance with France during the Habsburg-Valois wars.

Louis XII succeeded Charles VIII to the French throne after the death of Charles VIII, and renewed French claims to the Duchy of Milan. Maximilian I was engaged in another war with France after Louis XII invaded Italy in 1498 and conquered the Duchy of Milan. He was unable to retake the Duchy of Milan from France. Maximilian I was also forced to cede independence to the Swiss after the empire was defeated by the Swiss at the *Battle of Dornach* in 1499. But Maximilian scored his greatest marital coup d'état when he arranged for his son, *Philip the Handsome,* to marry *Joanna,* the daughter of the Spanish monarchs, Ferdinand of Aragon and Isabella of Castile, in 1497. These were the Spanish monarchs responsible for driving the Muslims out of Granada and sending Columbus to rediscover the New World. With this marriage the House of Habsburg became the most powerful family in Europe. The eldest son of Joanna and Philip became King Charles I of Spain in 1516 and Holy Roman Emperor *Charles V* in 1519, one year before Suleiman the Magnificent became sultan of the Ottoman Empire. While Suleiman advanced the Ottoman Empire westward into Hungary, Charles V was creating a modern civilized world centered on the Atlantic Ocean. The Ottoman Empire and the Muslims would dominate the ancient center of the civilized world for another two centuries while the Christians, led by Spain, would create the future civilized world inherited by the American Empire. We will address this significant change in the next chapter.

In 1521, the House of Habsburg was divided into a *senior* Spanish branch led by King Charles I of Spain and a *junior* Austrian branch led by Ferdinand I, the younger brother of Charles I. Ferdinand I inherited the Kingdom of Hungary by marriage to Princess Anna of Hungary and Bohemia. The Austrian branch led the Austro-Hungarian Empire and took the title of Holy Roman Empire after the death of Charles I in 1558. The Spanish branch ruled the Habsburgs lands in Spain, Italy, Portugal, the Netherlands, and their colonies in the New World. As Holy Roman Emperor Charles V, King Charles I of Spain ruled an empire larger than that of Charlemagne. The wealth from his colonies in the New World helped to fund the wars against the Ottoman Empire in Europe. But the two halves of the Habsburg family were divided by both geography and the growing religious conflict between Catholics and Protestants. The Spanish branch continued under Philip II, son of Charles I, but eventually died out in 1700 after the death of Charles II, as a result of intermarriage and inbreeding, within the family.

During the reign of Charles V an old family conflict between the Habsburgs and the French *Valois* dynasty erupted because the Valois ruler, *Francis I,* contested Charles V for the position of Holy Roman Empire. Charles V had succeeded his grandfather, Maximilian I, because Maximilian's son, the father of Charles V, Philip the handsome, had died in 1506. War between the two European families broke out in 1521 and Suleiman the Magnificent took advantage of the Christian conflict to conquer Belgrade from the Kingdom of Hungary that same year. Francis I suffered a major military defeat at the *Battle of Pavia* in 1525, which forced him to renounce French claims to Italian possessions in Milan, Naples, and Genoa as well as claims to the Duchy of Burgundy. The Habsburg-Valois wars continued until 1559 with the Habsburg family keeping control of Italy.

In the meantime Suleiman I expanded into Hungary and Austria after capturing Belgrade in August of 1521. He defeated King Louis II of Hungary at the Battle of Mohacs in 1526, and King Louis II was killed. With the victory at Mohacs the Ottoman Empire gained control of South-Eastern Hungary. In May of 1529 Suleiman I attempted to conquer all of Hungary. On his long march to the imperial capital of Vienna he was plagued by bad weather but proceeded to lay siege to the imperial capital in late September of 1529. His wary and depleted army, with limited supplies, was defeated by the Austrians and Suleiman I began a disastrous retreat as the winter weather worsened. A second attempt by Suleiman I in 1532 also failed, mostly due to bad weather. But the Ottoman-Habsburg war for control of Hungary and Austria continued until the *Battle of Vienna* in 1683.

In 1541, Ferdinand I of Austria sent an army to capture the city of Buda in Central Hungary. Suleiman I attacked Ferdinand's army and defeated it. The Ottomans occupied the city. The next year Ferdinand I laid siege to the city of Pest. Once again his army was defeated and the Ottomans occupied the city. In the following year, 1543, Suleiman I captured the Hungarian cities of Esztergom, Szekesfehervar, Szeged, and Siklos. These military defeats led to Ferdinand's brother, Charles V of Spain, the senior Habsburg ruler, agreeing to a peace treaty with the Ottomans in 1547. Under the *Truce of Adrianople,* both Ferdinand I and Charles V agreed to recognize Ottoman control over all of Hungary. In 1566 Suleiman I made his last attempt to capture the Habsburg capital of Vienna. He began his march from Constantinople with an impressive force on the first of May 1566. He reached Belgrade on June 27, 1566. In the meantime the leader of the Habsburg force, Count Nicholas Zrinsky, had marched on the city of Siklos. Suleiman I decided to attack Zrinsky at the fortress of Szigetvar in August of 1566. The siege of Szigetvar turned out to be the sultan's last battle. It took over a month for the powerful Ottoman artillery to successfully bombard the formidable castle. Suleiman I died in his tent of natural causes on September 6, 1566, at the ripe old age of seventy-two, shortly before the Ottoman victory at Szigetvar. Zrinsky was killed in battle, defending his Croatian homeland and saving the Habsburg capital of Vienna from another attack.

Most historians agree that the forty-six-year rule of the Ottoman Empire by Suleiman the Magnificent marked the high point of Ottoman expansion and growth. Suleiman's closest rival for leading statesman of the period, Emperor Charles V of Spain, had died almost a decade earlier in 1558 and his younger brother, Ferdinand I of Austria, had taken over as holy Roman emperor in 1556. Ferdinand I was succeeded by his son, Maximilian II in 1564. Suleiman I was succeeded by Selim II. Maximilian II signed a peace treaty with Selim II in February 1568, giving the Ottoman Empire control of Wallachia and Moldavia.

In the Mediterranean the Ottomans engaged the Republic of Venice in a fourth war in 1570–1573. During this war Selim II took on both the Republic of Venice and the *Holy League,* a coalition of Christian states, including Spain. The Ottomans had conducted military raids into

Cyprus ever since Cyprus became a colony of the Venetian Republic in 1489. The Ottomans finally conquered Cyprus in August 1571. On October 7, 1571, the Ottoman navy suffered a decisive defeat at Lepanto by the Christian naval forces of the Holy League, led by the Austrian, Don John. A peace treaty was signed in March 1573. Cyprus remained Ottoman territory until World War I. Peace lasted until the Fifth Ottoman–Venetian War of 1645–1669 was fought over the island of Crete, the richest colony of the Republic of Venice. Venice lost Crete to the Ottoman Empire. During the Morean War of 1684–1699 the Venetians captured Morea from the Ottoman Empire. Morea, the Peloponnese peninsula in Southern Greece, had been conquered from the Byzantine Empire by the Ottoman Empire, since 1460.

The Ottomans recaptured Morea during the last Ottoman-Venetian war, which began in December 1714. While the Ottomans remained a significant naval force and dominated the Eastern Mediterranean for another century they never established naval dominance in the Western Mediterranean. Their loss at Lepanto made it impossible for the Ottoman Empire to conquer the states in Southern Europe, Italy, Spain and Portugal. The Ottoman navy was eventually surpassed by those of the British and French. But it was Spain and Portugal that would forge the new Western Empire centered on the Atlantic. While Western historians point to the failure of the Ottoman Empire to conquer Vienna as its key failure to conquer Europe, its naval defeat at Lepanto was more important because naval superiority was the key to imperial dominance after the voyages of Columbus and da Gama.

In August 1574, a few months before the death of Selim II in December, the Ottomans recaptured Tunisia from Spain. Selim's successor, Murad III, expanded the Ottoman Empire into Azerbaijan and the Caucasus. Murad III also tried to form an alliance with England against Spain. At the time Queen Elizabeth I of England was supporting the plunder of Spanish galleons laden with the treasures of the American colonies by the English privateers. During the sixteenth century the only civilized Western occupation more lucrative than piracy was the slave trade. The civilized English dominated both. In 1581 Murad III signed a trade agreement with England that gave preferential treatment to English merchants in the Ottoman Empire. War between England and

Spain was inevitable and England contemplated military assistance from Murad III against Spain. The fact that England was the implicit leader of the Protestant Christians while Spain was the leader of the Catholic Christians was not lost on the Ottomans who had their own religious conflicts with the Shia Muslims of Safavid Persia.

Murad III was succeeded by his son, Mehmet III, in 1595. Another Ottoman/Habsburg war had begun in 1593. The Habsburg wanted to reclaim Hungary while the Ottomans wanted another shot at conquering Vienna. Mehmet III scored an important military victory at the *Battle of Keresztes,* in Hungary, October 24–26, 1596. But at the end of what has been called the "Long War," in 1606, both sides had failed in their respective objective. The next and final major Ottoman/ Habsburg war was the "Great Turkish War," under Sultan Mehmet IV. In 1683 the Ottomans invaded with an army of 140,000 and laid siege to Vienna. Another Holy League was formed to back the Habsburgs but the Ottomans failed to conquer Vienna this time primarily because of superior European arms. After several other military defeats by the Habsburgs, the Ottoman Empire signed the *Treaty of Karlowitz* in 1699, ceding control of Hungary to the Habsburgs.

At the dawn of the eighteenth century the Ottoman Empire was largely irrelevant even as a great power much less the dominant empire. In the Middle East it had been squeezed by the Austro-Hungarian Empire, the Russian Empire and the Safavid Persian Empire. But more importantly, the senior branch of the Habsburg Empire, Spain, had conquered an empire largely outside Europe. This new empire would be fought over by the Western European states of Portugal, Holland, France and Britain. The center of the world would shift from the Mediterranean and Middle East to where it is today. This post-Ottoman **Christian** Empire is the core of our book. Chapters 1–3 simply provide some important background to the rise and fall of the West.

The Role of the Persians in the Decline of the Ottoman Empire

The Muslims were as divided as the Christians during the struggle for imperial domination in the period from the sixteenth to the eighteenth centuries. In this part we will focus only on the role of the Safavid Persians in helping to destroy the Ottoman Empire. The Ottoman/Persian conflict among Muslims was similar to the Greek Orthodox/Roman Catholic conflict among Christians. In the end, just as the Roman Catholics of the Western Roman Empire won the imperial battle among Christians, the *Sunni* Muslims won the imperial battle with the *Shias* among Muslims. But both the Christian and the Muslim internal religious disagreement continue to haunt both religions to this day. Today the much reduced Ottoman Empire, represented by the unified state of Turkey, is very uncertain about its desire to lead Islam or simply become a Westernized member of the European Union. On the other hand the much reduced Persian Empire, represented by the unified state of Iran, is ever more convinced of its destiny to lead the Islamic world centered in the Middle East, despite the fact that Shias represent only 10 percent of Muslims.

The original people of Iran are Persians, descendants of Aryans, who migrated out of Central Asia. Iran has struggled to combine its historic Persian roots with its conversion to Islam after its conquest by the Arabs. As we saw earlier the Persian Empire converted to Islam but never totally surrendered its Persian heritage. In fact, the Arab Empire was as much Persian as it was Arabic. The Arabs were wise to adopt the far more civilized Persian culture in governing an ever-expanding empire after the seventh century. During the Arab conquest the Persians were determined to maintain a distinct identity while accepting the religion of the Arabs. It's not unlike the determination of Francophones in Canada to keep their French culture while accepting conquest by English Canada. Just as the French in Canada held on to the French language to bolster their distinct status in Canada the Persians embraced the *Shia* sect of Islam to bolster their distinct status from the majority *Sunni* Arabs and Turks. In Canada, the province of Quebec, not only guards the rights of its French majority in that province, but attempts to fight for the rights of Francophones in every province of Canada. In like manner, Shia Iran not only safeguards its distinct Persian heritage in Iran but seeks to speak for Shia Muslims throughout the Middle East. In 1501 the *Safavid* dynasty, 1501–1736, declared that Persia would be a **Shia** Muslim state.

Safavid power began in *Azerbaijan* and *Anatolia* and threatened the *Sunni* Ottoman control of Anatolia in the fifteenth century. In the late fifteenth century the *Shia* Safavids were led by *Ismail,* who claimed to be a descendant of *Ali,* the cousin and son-in-law of the Prophet Muhammad, and the true successor of Muhammad according to Shia Muslims. In July of 1501, thirteen-year-old Ismail and his *kizilbash* fighters captured Tabriz. Ishmael took the title of *Shah* and made Tabriz the capital of his kingdom. Despite the majority Sunni population of Tabriz, Shah Ismail I declared his kingdom to be Shia, effectively declaring war on the Sunni Ottoman Empire. Within eight years the Safavids reconquered Persia from the Ottoman Empire early in the sixteenth century. The Safavids controlled the cities of Tabriz, Hamadan, Kerman, Shiraz, Isfahan, Qazvin, Hormuz, Baghdad, and Herat. But the new independent Shia kingdom of Iran had to be defended against continued attempts by the more powerful Ottoman Empire to reconquer it. This ongoing military conflict between Shia Iran and the Sunni Ottomans weakened the Muslim struggle against Christian Europe. Two centuries of wars between Safavid Persia and the Ottoman Empire made it easier for Western Europe to create the new center of civilization west of the Mediterranean. In 1514 the Ottoman Empire led by Sultan Selim I invaded Safavid Persia and reconquered some territory. Shah Ismail I lost the important *Battle of Chaldiran* in August of 1514. The Ottomans took control of Iraq and Eastern Anatolia. The Safavids and Ottomans fought for control of Iraq for more than a century.

Just as the Ottomans took advantage of internal Christian squabbling the Christians took advantage of the Persian/Ottoman squabbling. During the reign of *Shah Abbas I,* 1587–1629, the Western European leaders supported Persia's independence from the Ottoman Empire. Abbas successfully reconquered the territory lost by Ismail during the 1514 Ottoman invasion. He moved the capital of Persia to Isfahan. Abbas encouraged the expansion of trade between Iran and the West, especially with England via the English East India Company. The Christian West courted Safavid Persia in their efforts to destroy the Ottoman Empire. But Persian expansion, like Ottoman expansion, was constrained by the rise of the West and Russia. Tsar Peter the Great of Russia invaded Persia in 1722.

The Safavid dynasty ended in 1736 when Shah Abbas III was deposed by a very successful army general, Nadir Beg, who claimed the title of

Nadir Shah. Nadir Shah forced both the Russians and the Ottomans to retreat but in the end the Persian Empire was left with the state of Iran and the Ottoman Empire was left with the state of Turkey. Even today the Christian West continues to exploit the historical rift between Iran and Turkey. The new civilized world would be dominated by Western Europe and the United States with modest opposition from Russia. Today it's Turkey that the Christian West befriends more than Iran while Russia is more friendly to Iran than to Turkey. In the next chapter we look at the rise of the West beginning with Portugal and Spain.

The Very Important Russian Role in the Decline of the Ottoman Empire

Russia has never been given the credit it deserves for saving the so-called Western civilization from the Turks, Napoleon, or Hitler. But in each of these three cases its contribution was decisive. Russia took its name from the Swedish Vikings, who were called "Rus," who invaded the Novgorod Republic in the ninth century and moved the capital city from Novgorod to *Kiev.* Hence the name, "Kievan Rus." The state of Kievan Rus reached its high point during the eleventh century when it embraced Christianity. It had begun to decline and disintegrate by the time of the Mongol invasion of the 1230s. After the Mongol invasion Russia was ruled by the *Tatar/Mongol Golden Horde,* who had converted to Islam. The Tatars converted to Islam in the tenth century. In the thirteenth century they were subjugated by the Mongol Empire and became part of the *Golden Horde* led by the grandson of Genghis Khan, *Batu Khan.* When the Mongols invaded and burnt Moscow in 1238, Moscow was only a tiny trading post. But its strategic location gave it access to both the Black Sea and the Baltic. Beginning with *Daniel I,* the local rulers of Moscow collaborated with their Mongol Overlords. Daniel's son *Yuriy* married the sister of the ruling Khan of the Golden Horde, *Uzbeg Khan.* Uzbeg Khan was the most powerful of the Khans of the Golden Horde, ruling Russia from 1313 to 1341. After converting to Islam he made Islam the state religion of Russia. This marriage created the grand Duchy of Moscow with Yuriy taking the title of grand duke. *Ivan I* succeeded Yuriy in 1325 as grand duke of Moscow and continued the collaboration between an ever-expanding Duchy of Moscow with the Khans of the Golden Horde. The grand Duchy of Moscow expanded its territory from twenty thousand square kilometers in 1300 to 5.4 million by 1584.

The power of the Golden Horde suffered from the Black Death in the 1350s, internal political strife and the invasion of *Tamerlane* in 1396. Ivan III, 1462–1505, expanded and consolidated the power of the grand Duchy of Moscow. In 1470 Ivan III invaded the Republic of Novgorod. Novgorod had been the capital city of Russia until 882 when Oleg, the Viking ruler between 882 and 912, transferred the capital to Kiev and Novgorod became a part of Kievan Russia. By the time of Ivan III both Novgorod and Moscow had expanded their territory and political power. Ivan III scored military victories against Novgorod in 1471 and captured most of their territory.

By 1476, Ivan III felt strong enough to refuse payment of tribute to the Khan of the Golden Horde, *Akhmat Khan*. At the time Akhmat was at war with the powerful Crimean Khanate. Annual tribute had been paid to the Khans beginning with Batu Khan in the thirteenth century. In 1480 Ivan III formed an alliance with the Crimean Khanate against his overlord, Akhmat Khan. Ivan III scored a decisive military victory against the Khan at the Ugra River in 1480, ending what has been called the "Tatar Yoke." The grand Duchy of Moscow had secured its independence from the Golden Horde in 1480 under the rule of Ivan III, who took on the title of Tsar, "Ruler of all Rus." Ivan III had expanded the territory of the Duchy of Moscow to three times its original size at the beginning of his reign. Ivan's conquest of *Novgorod* and independence of Moscow from the Golden Horde is used by some historians to date the beginning of the Russian Empire. Ivan III began diplomatic relations with the Ottoman Empire with a Russian embassy in Istanbul in 1495. Russia was preparing to challenge the Ottoman Empire for the Orthodox Christian lands and people of the Eastern Roman Empire, Byzantium. It was setting itself up as the third Rome. The Ottoman Empire would be squeezed between the Greek Orthodox Christians led by Russia and the Catholic Christians of Western Europe.

Ivan III went to war with the Grand Duchy of Lithuania in an effort to reconquer Russian territory previously lost to Lithuania during the fourteenth and fifteenth centuries. The first of many future wars against Lithuania began in 1492 and continued intermittently until 1503. Lithuania lost a third of its territory to Ivan III. At the time when Spain and Portugal were initiating the shift of the center of civilization from the Mediterranean to the Atlantic, Russia, led by Ivan III, was initiating the rise of the Russian Empire as the new dominant power in the old center of civilization. Ivan III died in 1505 and was succeeded by his son *Vasili III.* Vasili III continued his father's efforts to conquer territory from Lithuania by going to war in 1507–1508 and 1512–1522. He succeeded in capturing the important trading city of *Smolensk.* But it was his son, Ivan IV, also known as *Ivan the Terrible,* who made Russia an imperial power feared by both the Ottoman Empire and the rising Catholic West. Ivan IV was the first grand duke of Moscow to be crowned "Tsar of all of the Russias" in 1547. The title of Tsar was intended to be the equivalent of the sultan of the Ottoman Empire and of the emperor of the Byzantine Empire, which the Ottoman Empire had replaced. The sultans of the Ottoman Empire had fought many wars to conquer the Greek Christians of the Eastern Roman Empire, the Arabs and the Persians, to rule a vast empire stretching east into Egypt and west into the Balkans. It would now face a new challenger, Russia.

The Catholic West had failed to protect Byzantium and its Greek Orthodox Christian inhabitants from the Muslims, despite their many Crusades. It would be left to Mother Russia to reclaim the power of Rome from the Muslim invaders. During his rule Ivan the Terrible invaded and conquered the important *Khanates* of Kazan, Astrakhan and Siberia, expanding the territory of Russia to over 1.5 million square miles. The first of many wars between the emerging Russian Empire and the Ottoman Empire was fought over the Khanate of Astrakhan. At the time the Ottoman Empire had just passed its peak following the end of its rule by Suleiman the Magnificent. Sultan Selim II had begun his rule in 1566, the year in which Ivan IV conquered and annexed Astrakhan. The war began in 1568 with the Ottomans invading by land and sea. The Ottoman fleet was destroyed by a storm and its army failed to conquer Astrakhan. A peace treaty was signed in 1570. War broke out again in 1571 over control of the Crimea. The Ottoman army, supported by the Tatars in the Crimea, invaded and burnt Moscow. But the Russians scored a decisive victory at the *Battle of Molodi,* in August of 1572.

As the Ottoman Empire began its decline with the death of Suleiman the Magnificent the Russian Empire expanded under Ivan the Terrible and the future Tsars. During the Great Turkish War between the Ottomans and the Habsburgs, the Russians engaged the Ottomans and their Crimean ally in a **third** war of their own, 1676–1681. Russia, the Ottoman Empire and the Crimean Khanate signed the *Treaty of Bakhchisaray* in January 1681. But the Great Turkish War was a joint effort by the Christian powers of Europe, which now included Russia, to roll back the European territory held by the Ottoman Empire. War with Russia resumed after Russia joined the Holy League in 1686. The Russians signed the *Treaty of Constantinople* in 1700, a year after the Ottomans and Habsburgs signed the Treaty of Karlowitz.

Under the rule of Tsar *Peter the Great,* 1682–1725, the emerging Russian Empire, centered on Moscow, began a long struggle against the Ottoman Empire for control of the Black Sea. In 1712 the Russian capital was moved to St. Petersburg. In 1721 Russia declared itself an empire with Tsar Peter I as its first emperor. Peter I had just successfully concluded the *Great Northern War* against Sweden, which had again expanded the territory of Russia while giving Russia access to the Baltic. Tsar Peter built a Russian navy to take on the Ottomans and the Crimean Khanate. After a failed attempt to capture the Ottoman fortress of *Azov,* near to the Don River, in 1695, Peter succeeded with his second attempt in July 1696. The 1700 Treaty of Constantinople allowed Russia to keep Azov. During the **fifth** war with the Ottomans, 1710–1711, the Ottoman Empire recaptured the Black Sea ports lost in the previous war. During the **sixth** war with the Ottomans, 1735–1739, the Russians recaptured Azov. But the Russians signed a peace treaty in which they agreed not to build a fleet in the Black Sea. The **seventh** war against the Ottomans, 1768–1774, was even more disastrous for the Ottomans. In 1771 the Russians, now led by Tsarina *Catherine the Great,* 1762–1796, conquered the Crimea. The Russians annexed the Crimea in 1783 and expanded the Russian Empire along the coast of the Black Sea. But it was not until the nineteenth century that the Russian Empire took control of the Black Sea from the Ottomans. Russian control of the Bosporus and Dardanelles gave the Russian Empire access to the Aegean and the Mediterranean, the historical center of the civilized world.

An **eighth** war was fought in 1787–1792 when the Ottoman Empire made a futile attempt to reconquer lost territory. Somewhat ironic, Austria joined the war as a junior ally to the Russian Empire signifying the decline of both the Ottomans and Habsburgs relative to the rise of the Russian Empire. Russia would replace both the Habsburgs and Ottomans in Central Europe just as Britain and France had replaced the Habsburgs and Arabs of Spain and Portugal, as the dominant powers in Western Europe. The Ottomans were at war with the Russians for control of the ancient center of civilization while Britain and France were at war over the modern center of civilization. Under Catherine the Great the Russians had the upper hand. The *Treaty of Jassy,* signed in January 1792 confirmed Russia's annexation of the Crimea and dominance in the Black Sea. In the West the British had the upper hand because naval power was the key to ruling a worldwide empire.

The Treaty of *Kuchuk Kainarji,* signed in 1774, gave the Russian Empire the right to protect Greek Orthodox Christians living in the Ottoman Empire. Catherine the Great's defeat of the Ottomans in the war of 1768–1774 was a humiliating blow to the Ottoman sultans and another mark of the continued decline of the Ottoman Empire and the simultaneous rise of the Russian Empire. By the end of Catherine the Great's rule in 1796 Russia saw itself as the successor of the Greek Orthodox Eastern Roman Empire since Greek Orthodox Christianity in Byzantium had been replaced by the Islamic Ottoman Empire. It was a Muscovite prince who had married the niece of the last Byzantine emperor. The Russians saw an opportunity to use its claim as the legitimate new leader of the Greek Orthodox Christians to reconquer *Christian* Byzantium from the *Muslim* Ottomans and liberate the Christian inhabitants. This implied attempts to conquer the old Roman capital of Constantinople, which the Ottomans had renamed Istanbul, as well.

But Russian aspirations for imperial expansion and Greek Orthodox Christian liberation renewed the old contest between Greek Orthodox and Roman Catholic Christians as to which sect would rule the Christian Empire. This conflict had begun with the division of the Roman Empire between an Eastern and a Western half. Up until this time the Eastern Greek half was regarded as the advanced civilized half while the Western Latin half was regarded as the primitive barbaric half. But the rise of the new maritime empires of Portugal, Spain, Holland, France, and Britain had begun the shift of public opinion, which eventually succeeded in claiming that it was the West that was the new civilized ruler of the world. After all, the only requirement to be civilized is to win wars. With the advent of naval dominance over armies in winning wars the new maritime powers had the decisive advantage. It was therefore not surprising that while Catherine the Great got the support of the holy Roman emperor, *Joseph II,* in her quest to replace Ottoman supremacy with Russian power the two dominant maritime empires of the day, Britain and France not only opposed the Russians but supported the Ottoman Empire. The Russians, like the Ottomans, were unaware that the center of the world was shifting from the Mediterranean to the Atlantic. Even so, the Western European empires were not willing to allow Russia to dominate even the old center of the civilized world.

Despite numerous examples of Russia aiding the West in its struggle for world domination the West has never been willing to embrace Russia as part of the Western family. Russia was forever doomed to be part of the backward, dying, primitive, East. Even Napoleon's failure to defeat Russia, while scoring military victories in Western Europe, only served to confirm Russia's claim to be the dominant Eastern power to have replaced the Muslims, never to be accepted as a civilized Western power. However, the issue we are addressing here is not the divisions within Christianity but Russia's crucial role in aiding the decline of the Ottoman Empire.

Russia continued its expansion into the Ottoman Empire during the nineteenth century with conflicts in the Balkans in 1806–1812 and the Greek independence struggle in the 1820s. The **ninth** war with Russia, 1806–1812, took place while France under Napoleon was conquering much of Europe. Not only had France been Britain's primary rival to replace Spain as the dominant empire throughout the eighteenth century, France had overthrown its monarchy in favor of a republic, as the Americans had done. The English were determined to defeat France to save both its imperial dominance and its preference for rule by kings. The British monarchy is revered to this day. In the past kings and queens were paid to fight wars and administer the country. The British monarch is paid to do nothing. As long as the British monarch agrees not to govern the British are very happy to maintain the institution at tax-payers' expense. It's another one of those Western symbols of civilization that it's a very enlightened notion to pay someone a princely sum to do nothing. During the ninth war the Russians destroyed the Ottoman navy. Russia added to its territorial gains when it signed the *Treaty of Bucharest* with the Ottoman Empire in May of 1812. A month later Napoleon's ill-fated invasion of Russia began. Russia's defeat of Napoleon saved the British Empire and the British Crown. Britain would lead the Christian West until the Second World War when the Western European states would self-destruct and the American Empire would have no Western power to challenge it.

During the **tenth** war of 1828–1829 the Russians intervened to support Greek independence. Once again Russia used its self-declared right to protect Greek Orthodox Christians as the primary reason to defend the Greeks from the Ottoman Muslims. The Greeks had been opposed to Ottoman rule since the fall of the Byzantine Empire in 1453. But Greece was militarily too weak to secure independence from the Ottomans without the help of Russia just as the Americans needed the help of France to secure independence from the British. When Russia participated in the destruction of the Ottoman fleet at the *Battle of Navarino* on October 20, 1827, the Ottomans closed the Dardanelles to Russian ships. When peace came with the *Treaty of Edirne* in September 1829, the Ottomans lost more territory again to the Russian Empire. Greece gained its independence in 1832. Russia's control of Eastern Europe increased at the expense of the Ottoman Empire as well as Austria. The Russian Empire would be the ultimate winner in the long conflict between the Austrian Habsburgs and the Ottomans just as the American Empire was the ultimate winner in the long conflict among Britain, France and Germany.

More far reaching conflicts with the Ottomans took place in the second half of the nineteenth century during the Crimean War of 1853–1856 and the Russo-Turkish War of 1877–1878. By the time of the Crimean War the Western European powers had become more anti-Russian than anti-Ottoman since the Russian Empire had replaced the Ottoman Empire as the dominant power in Central/Eastern Europe. It was the Russian Tsar, *Nicholas I,* who had first referred to the Ottoman Empire as the "Sick Man" of Europe, in 1853. During the Crimean War,

Britain and France allied with the **Muslim** Ottoman Empire instead of the **Christian** Russian Empire. The Peace Treaty of 1856 provided for equal rights for Christians and Muslims in the Ottoman Empire. But Western and Central Europe was undergoing an important change as the power and influence of Austria and France weakened while that of Prussia grew in stature. Prussia defeated Austria in 1866 and France in 1870. While Austria and France had become increasingly anti-Russian, Prussia, the emerging power in Western and Central Europe, was friendly to Russia.

The Balkan crisis of 1875–1876 provided the opportunity for Russia to regain the right to have a fleet in the Black Sea, a right it had lost by the peace treaty ending the Crimean war. Rebellions against Ottoman rule broke out in many parts of the Balkans beginning in 1875. Russia condemned Ottoman efforts to suppress the rebellions. In 1876 Serbia and Montenegro declared war on the Ottoman Empire. Russia declared war on the Ottoman Empire on April 24, 1877. In the 1877–1878 War, Russia formed a coalition with the Balkan states against the Ottoman Empire. Russia had its mind set on conquering Constantinople, the original capital of the Byzantine Empire. But the British intervened to prevent that. A Peace Treaty was signed on March 3, 1878. Russia's expansion into the Balkans undermined efforts by the Austrian Habsburgs to regain territory conquered by the Ottoman Empire. Russian/Habsburg competition for Ottoman lands in the Balkans, such as Austria's annexation of Bosnia and Herzegovina, was an important cause of World War I. The Communist Revolution of 1917 was the final straw that placed the Russian Empire squarely into the anti-Western, anti-Christian, anti-civilized camp that dominated the modern civilized world of the twentieth century. Under the capable leadership of Vladimir Putin, today Russia defends the Muslims of the Middle East against the tyranny of the Christian West and the genocide committed against the Palestinians by Israel. Canada's prime minister Stephen Harper and American president Barack Obama, not only provide the military weapons and moral support for the slaughter of women and children in Gaza by Israel, but also use their control of the world's media to demonize Vladimir Putin. Another glaring example of the upside-down logic of Western civilization.

CHAPTER 4

Portugal and Spain: The Unsung Heroes of the Rise of the West: Colonies, Genocide of the Indigenous People, Slavery, Racism, Warmongering, Religious Intolerance, Piracy, Propaganda, and Hypocrisy: The Foundations of the Myth of Western Civilization

We cannot emphasize sufficiently that the evidence is overwhelming to support the view that there is absolutely nothing civilized about Western civilization. What is called Western civilization is in fact the determined and sustained suppression and repression of civilized behavior by militarily powerful Western states for the economic, political, cultural and religious benefit of a tiny percent of the world's population. We began this book by going back before the birth of Western civilization to show that imperialism and the suppression of freedoms by imperial powers did not begin with the rise of the West but has been the norm of human existence. There has never been a period in human history where states have not used military force to invade, conquer and subjugate their militarily weaker inhabitants of the planet. This unfortunate human experience in no way excuses the primitive behavior of the West. If we are to have any hope of changing this age old primitive behavior we must begin by acknowledging it. Unfortunately, the most important difference between Western imperialism and previous imperialism is the extent to which the West has perfected the skill of propaganda.

The West is still able to use its powerful propaganda tools to convince many people throughout the world that it is a force for good when its actions show undoubtedly that it is a force for evil. Moreover, American leadership of the West, or rather the lack of even the most primitive of leadership skills, has been the single most important factor in killing any chance of the West ever becoming civilized or democratic. It's not that the United States is incapable of producing capable leaders. It's the fact that those Americans who show good judgment or common sense are marginalized by a system that promotes mediocrity, warmongering, hypocrisy, and downright stupidity.

A good example of this was the 2012 race for the Republican nominee for president. Ron Paul was the only candidate who continued to speak out about the insanity of continued American warmongering across the globe. By 2012, President Obama had been totally transformed from 2008 pro-peace Candidate Obama to **warmongering** second-term Candidate Obama. As a result the United States began another of its countless wars, this time in Syria, during this election campaign. Once again it used typical Western upside-down logic. It claimed that the war was caused by an evil dictator, Bashar al-Assad, when the evidence was clear that it was caused by continued Western imperialism in the Middle East. The president of Syria was told by the West that it was evil to use force to suppress a **Western instigated** revolt against his government while it's okay for the West to use one hundred times more powerful military force to kill women and children in Iraq, Afghanistan, Pakistan, Yemen, Libya and the most remote corners of the globe, only for the purpose of acquiring more colonies. Of course, the Western propaganda is that these insane killings of poor helpless people are to make the world safe from *al-Qaeda*. To quote an insightful comedian, "Are you confused by what is going on in the Middle East?

Let me explain.
We support the Iraqi government in the fight against ISIS.
The Iraqi government is mainly Shia.
We don't like ISIS, but ISIS is Sunni and is supported by Saudi Arabia who we think is on our side.
We don't like Assad in Syria. He is also Sunni but a different Sunni to ISIS or Saudi. We support the fight against him, but ISIS is also fighting against him.
We don't like Iran, they are Shia, but Iran supports the Iraqi government in its fight against ISIS but they also support Assad.
So some of our friends support our enemies, some enemies are now our friends,

and some of our enemies are fighting against our other enemies, who we want to lose,
but we don't want our enemies who are fighting our enemies to win because if the people we want to defeat are defeated, they could be replaced by people we like even less.
And all this was started by us invading a country to drive out terrorists who were not actually there until we went in to drive them out.
It's quite simple, really! Do you understand now that I've made it perfectly clear?"

Leaders of Libya and Syria are told that it's evil to kill "your own people" with great emphasis on "your own people." One implication is that it's okay for the West to slaughter thousands of Iraqi and Afghan women and children with their far superior military hardware because they are **not** "your own people." Another implication is that the U.S. government did not kill "its own people" during its civil war. It only killed *Martians.* That could explain why the United States still refer to illegal immigrants as illegal *Aliens.* Quite apart from the moral insanity of wars and its devastating effect on the American economy, Ron Paul correctly pointed out that the U.S. military expenditure exceeding that of the rest of the world combined was not sustainable with the United States having an ever declining share of the world's GDP. But Paul was demonized by his own GOP colleagues for being naïve when the evidence was overwhelming that it was the other candidates who were naïve. Meanwhile the economy supporting the American Empire is self-destructing during the term of America's first *token* "half black" president.

Western European Nation-States: Prelude to Western Imperialism

We begin our history of Western imperialism with the two countries, Portugal and Spain, which both inhabited the Iberian Peninsula. Western imperialism originated with the birth of the independent nation-states that inherited the lands of the former Western Roman Empire. While the nation-states in France, Germany, Austria, Italy, the Netherlands, and Britain were initially more powerful and influential than Portugal and Spain, in the immediate post-Roman era, it was these two Iberian nation-states that had the foresight to look outside the historic civilized Mediterranean for a new modern civilization. Portugal began its imperial conquests during the fifteenth century and was the first of the Western European empires to make the *African slave trade* one of the signature hallmarks of so-called Western civilization. The other Western European nation-states were too focused on *crusades* against the Muslims to regain territory of the former Eastern and Western Roman empires. When Constantinople fell to the Ottoman Empire in 1453 the Iberian states were better positioned to cash in on the lucrative spice trade with the East. With the disruption of the overland spice trade, Western Europe was forced to look for a sea route to the East. Portugal and Spain led the way. The Venetian merchants lost their lucrative control of the Western end of the overland spice trade controlled by the Arabs. Many moved to Iberia after the fall of Constantinople.

The Iberian Peninsula became a part of the Roman Empire after 200 BC, following the defeat of Carthage by Rome during the *Punic* wars. The Roman name for the peninsula was *Hispania.* At the time, the Iberian Peninsula would be as remote from the center of civilization as the Canadian North is today. However, as we have explained in our earlier chapters, the center of civilization shifted with the current Western civilization. This shift from the Mediterranean to the Atlantic, began with the explorations and colonizations of Portugal and Spain. When the Roman Empire splintered into the Eastern Greek Orthodox and the Western Latin-Catholic empires, it was the Eastern Byzantine Empire that was regarded as the civilized half. The Western barbaric half of the Roman Empire disintegrated into independent and semi-independent states, held together by the spiritual leadership of the pope. The Iberian Peninsula was part of this barbaric half. It was conquered by the barbarian *Visigoths,* one of the Germanic successor states of the Western half of the Roman Empire. The Visigoth kingdom ruled both the Iberian Peninsula and South-western France between the fifth and eighth centuries.

As we have explained before, being **Christian** became one of the many essential ingredients of becoming civilized once the Roman Empire had converted to Christianity. Fortunately for Portugal and Spain the Romans introduced Christianity to the Iberian Peninsula during the fourth century long before the Muslims conquered the Iberian Peninsula between 711 and 718, beginning with their decisive military victory at the *Battle of Guadalete,* on July 19, 711. The Muslims called this part of their empire *Al-Andalus.* Under Muslim rule the population of the Iberian Peninsula increased with the influx of Muslims, Jews **and Christians.** It practiced a much greater degree of religious tolerance than the Christian states of Europe. Many Christians in Iberia converted to Islam. Jews, in particular, representing about 5 percent of the total population, enjoyed what has been called the "Golden Age of Jewish culture." The Peninsula grew not only in population but also in wealth, culture and military power. But the Muslims and Christians were in a continual state of war after the Muslim Moors of North Africa crossed the Strait of Gibraltar in July 710 and began their conquest of Iberia. Iberia opened up a new front in the long war between Christians and Muslims, which shows no sign of letting up to this day. The old front in the Middle East never ended but the new front beginning in Iberia would in time cross the Atlantic to America and round the Cape of Good Hope to Asia. Today the Christian/Muslim war is truly a global phenomenon.

While Christians were divided between Greek Orthodox and Catholics the Muslims were divided among Arabs, Persians, Turks, Mongols and Berbers. It was the Berbers of North Africa who had initially conquered Iberia for the Muslims. They came to be known as "Moors" because they were a mixture of Arabs, Berbers, and black Africans. The Arab Empire had expanded into North Africa and the Berbers were defeated and converted to Islam by the end of the seventh century. The Berber, *Tariq ibn Malik,* first raided Iberia in 710. With four small ships, he sailed from *Ceuta* and landed a force of less than a thousand in Iberia. The raid was an overwhelming success. The following year the Berber governor of Tangier, *Tariq ibn Ziyad,* landed a force exceeding seven thousand in Iberia. The Visigoth king, *Roderick,* was defeated and killed in battle. This gave the Muslims a foothold in the southern tip of the Iberian Peninsula. Tariq moved inland to capture the city of *Cordoba* and the Visigoth capital of *Toledo* by the winter of 711. In June of 712, Tariq's commander, *Musa bin Nusayr,* crossed over from North Africa and landed a much larger mixed force of Arabs and Berbers in Iberia to continue and consolidate the conquest. By 718 the Muslims had completed their conquest of Iberia. Henceforth, Christian *Iberia* came to be Muslim, *Al-Andalus.*

The Arab advance into Western Europe had been stopped at Tours in 732 by Charles Martel. The Christian kingdoms that battled each other for territory and dominance following the fall of the Western Roman Empire were simultaneously pushing back the Muslim conquests in Europe. In the East the Christians were stopped by the powerful Ottoman Empire. But in the West, including Al-Andalus, Muslim power was relatively weak and fragmented. Al-Andalus initially became part of the powerful *Umayyad* Caliphate that ruled the Arab Empire from Damascus. The rulers of Al-Andalus were granted the rank of *Emir* by the Umayyad Caliph, *Al-Walid I.* This created the *Emirate of Cordoba.* The capital city of Cordoba became the political, cultural, intellectual and religious center of Muslim Iberia. In time it became the richest city in the West, rivaling the cities of Baghdad and Constantinople in grandeur and opulence. But the Umayyads were overthrown by the *Abbasid* dynasty in 750. One of the Umayyad leaders, *Abd al-Rahman I,* fled to Al-Andalus via North Africa and seized power in 756 to become the Emir of Cordoba. While the *Umayyads* held on to power in Al-Andalus it meant that they would face the Christian opposition alone and simultaneously defend against threats from the more powerful *Abbasids.* In addition, the majority Berber Muslims of Al-Andalus resented being ruled by the minority Arab Muslims. Berber revolts were common.

The *Emirate* of Al-Andalus became the *Caliphate of Cordoba* after 929 when Emir *Abd-Al-Rahman III,* severed all ties with Damascus and declared himself to be the independent *Caliph.* Rahman III had become the Emir of Cordoba in 912 and expanded Cordoba's rule into North Africa. Rahman III ushered in what has been called "the Golden Age" of the Caliphate of Cordoba. Under his rule the *Umayyad* Caliphate of Cordoba rivaled the *Abbasid* Caliphate in Baghdad. The Umayyad family ruled the caliphate until 1031, except for a brief period between 1017 and 1022. After the fall of the Umayyad family, Al-Andalus disintegrated into several semi-independent principalities, called *taifas.* This made the Muslims much more vulnerable to the continuous wars with the

Christians. In 1086 the Muslims of Al-Andalus reached out to a Berber dynasty in North Africa, the *Almoravids,* to come to their aid against the attacks by the Christian kingdoms. As a result Muslim Al-Andalus became a part of the Almoravid Empire centered in the North African city of Marrakesh. But in 1147, the Almoravid ruler, *Ishaq ibn Ali,* was killed by rebels in Marrakesh. As a result the *Almoravid* dynasty was replaced by another Berber dynasty, the *Almohads.* The Almohad dynasty, in turn, ruled Muslim Al-Andalus as part of its empire until 1228. The Almohads moved the capital of Al-Andalus from Cordoba to Seville. This incessant internal strife among the Muslims of Al-Andalus, North Africa and the Middle East led to the Christian reconquest of Iberia.

The Reconquista

The Christian reconquest of Iberia, known as the *Reconquista,* is, in our view, the most important turning point leading to Christian domination of the world after the seventeenth century. The importance of the *Reconquista* has been given relatively short shrift by Western historians. Western historians have given greater importance to the **failed** *Crusades* compared with the **successful** *Reconquista.* The Christian Crusades, which we have documented, were an attempt by the Western Christian states to reconquer from the Muslims the ancient civilized world centered in Iraq, Iran, Palestine, Syria, Egypt and the Mediterranean. Its failure, in our view, was a blessing in disguise. That failure, combined with the overthrow of the Eastern Roman Empire by the Ottomans, and the expansion of the Ottoman Empire to the gates of Vienna, was what forced these same Western-Christian states to use the successful *Reconquista* to look outward by sea along the coast of Africa and across the Atlantic Ocean. By contrast, the Muslim successes in the Middle East, Eastern Europe, and overland to Afghanistan, India and China, put the Muslims at a disadvantage in challenging the West for naval superiority and dominance in the Atlantic.

Civil wars during and after the eleventh century weakened and disintegrated the Muslim *Caliphate of Cordoba* making it easier for a Christian reconquest. The Christian reconquest of Iberia really began as soon as the Muslims first invaded in 711 from their North African base in Tangier. But it lasted almost eight centuries, culminating with the fall of *Granada* in 1492. The rise of the Franks was one of the many important factors that enabled the success of the *Reconquista*. The Frankish general, Charles Martel, prevented the Muslims from expanding from Iberia into the more powerful nation-states in Western Europe. More importantly, as we will see below, the Muslims in Iberia were isolated from the much larger Muslim conquests advancing westward from the Middle East through Eastern Europe to the gates of Vienna. It was this isolation from the rest of the Muslim world, more than anything else, which guaranteed the success of the Reconquista.

Among the many Christian states and kingdoms competing for land and power in what had been the Western Roman Empire, the most powerful by far was the kingdom/empire of the *Franks*. The Franks were becoming so successful in their wars and conquests that they were transitioning from barbarians to civilized. As we have observed, one of the implicit hallmarks of civilized, as defined by Western historians, is to be successful in war. Successful warmongering also implied that your God was superior. With God and successful military conquests on your side you could no longer be deemed to be barbaric. The Frankish Empire dominated Western Europe after 500. But it was not the powerful Frankish Empire that drove the Muslims out of Iberia but two tiny barbaric states, *Portugal and Spain*. These tiny barbaric states, like *England* and the USA of 1776, would grow to become massive world empires after the Reconquista.

After the Muslims had completed their conquest of Iberia in 718, they had naturally attempted to expand their empire into territory that had been captured by the expanding Frankish Empire. But as every so-called civilized empire has done they underestimated the military power of the barbaric Franks. The civilized Muslims had failed to recognize that the Franks were in the process of transitioning from one of the many barbarian hordes of Western Europe to a civilized Christian empire. When you kill a few with your primitive weapons because they invade your land you are *naked savages, barbarians, guerrillas, communists, terrorists* or *Islamists*. When you kill millions by using advanced weapons like the American Empire does, you are civilized and God and public opinion are on your side. The Franks were becoming the new civilized

Christians who would replace the Western Roman Empire with the blessing of the Catholic pope.

We have already documented the rise of the Franks in previous chapters. In this chapter we will review their important contribution to the successful *Reconquista.* One of the earliest conquests of the Franks was *Gaul.* The Franks had conquered Gaul from the Western Roman Empire in 486 after *Clovis I* defeated the Roman governor of Gaul. In 534 the Franks had conquered the Kingdom of Burgundy. After 718 Frankish control of Southern France was threatened by the Emirate of Cordoba following its successful conquest of Iberia. From Iberia the Muslims crossed the Pyrenees and expanded into the territory of the Franks in Southern France, including Gaul and Burgundy. But as the Muslims pushed north to conquer *Aquitaine,* they suffered their first military defeat in 721 at the *Battle of Toulouse.* The Duchy of *Aquitaine* was a semi-independent duchy of the Frankish empire ruled by Duke Odo. When the Muslims attacked his most important city, *Toulouse,* the duke fled. Confident of victory, the Muslim invaders were caught by surprise when Odo returned three months later and defeated them. The Muslims were to suffer their second military defeat only a year later at the *Battle of Covadonga,* this time inside the Iberian Peninsula. It was this combination of the isolation of Cordoba from the larger Muslim Empire, defeats from rebellions inside Iberia, and external defeats by the Franks and other Christian states, which led to the eventual success of the long and painful *Reconquista.*

The first of many Christian rebellions against Muslim occupation was that of the Visigoth nobles who had fled to the Cantabrian Mountains in North-Western Iberia after the defeat of their king, *Roderick,* in 711. They founded the small "kingdom" of *Asturias* in North-Western Iberia following their defeat by the Moors. In 718 the nobles elected *Pelagius* to be their king. Even though it attracted a growing number of Christian rebels from the south it posed no great threat to the Muslim Emirate of Cordoba. The emirate made several halfhearted attempts at reconquest but was more focused on expanding its empire outside Iberia into the empire of the Franks than in recapturing the relatively sparsely populated and desolate Kingdom of Asturias. However, after the humiliating defeat of the Muslim army at the Battle of Toulouse in 721 the Muslims were understandably reluctant to return to Cordoba empty handed. On their retreat from Toulouse they decided to reconquer the Kingdom of Asturias for the emirate. In addition, the Muslim governor of Asturias, *Munuza,* who had previously been forcibly expelled by the Visigoths, saw an opportunity to regain his governorship. He joined forces with the Muslim force retreating from Toulouse. The Muslims thought Asturias would be an easy consolation prize. They could not have been more wrong.

The Visigoths had the advantage of a relatively inaccessible mountainous region with caves to hide in as well as an able military leader in King Pelagius. Pelagius led his forces out of the mountainous caves and attacked the Muslim forces. First, Al Qama fell to the Visigoths and his forces were decimated by the villagers as they fled the battle. Next Munuza faced off against Pelagius. He fared no better and was killed in battle. While this was a major defeat for the Muslim conquerors it was rightfully dismissed as no major threat to the military superiority of the civilized Muslims. It was a relatively remote localized rebellion. The failure to recapture Asturias was no more significant than the failure of the American Empire to subdue Afghanistan in the first decade of the twenty-first century. It did not threaten the military might of the Emirate of Cordoba any more than an independent Afghanistan threatened the military might of the American Empire. In fact, the Muslims downplayed their defeat in the mountains of Asturias as much as the American Empire downplayed its defeat in the mountains of Afghanistan. Both empires would learn that those defeats signaled the beginning of their decline.

The Emirate of Cordoba saw the Franks, not the "primitive" rebels in the mountains of Asturias, as their primary rival. In much the same way, during the first decades of the twenty-first century, the American Empire view China, not the rebels of Afghanistan or Iraq, as its primary rival. In the eighth century the Emirate of Cordoba was the civilized power with God and history on its side, much like the American Empire in the twenty-first century. The Franks were the barbarians attempting to emulate the civilized Muslims but had a lot of catching up to do much like barbarian China attempting to emulate and catch up to the West in the early twenty-first century. Replace the word "barbarian" with "communist." "Communist," as applied to the Chinese, had the same connotation as "barbarian" applied to Western Europeans in the eighth century. The civilized Muslims confronted the barbarian Franks and lost. We have to wait and see how the American Empire will fare once it confronts China.

The Franks vs. the Emirate of Cordoba

Many Western historians have claimed firmly that the victory of Charles "the Hammer" Martel over the emirate of Cordoba at the *Battle of Tours* in 732 was the decisive military victory that marked the return of Christian dominance of the world following the fall of the Roman Empire. This is a misrepresentation of the facts. The Battle of Tours was a conflict between one of many Christian leaders, the Franks, and one of many Muslim leaders, the Emirate of Cordoba. It was a much smaller Christian/Muslim confrontation than either the Crusades or the wars between the Ottomans and the Habsburgs. Another misrepresentation by Western historians is the notion that the victory of the Franks was a surprise because the Muslims were the superior military power. While it's true that in 732 Muslim power in the Middle East and the center of the civilized world was far superior to that of the Christians, the Muslims confronting the Christians at the Battle of Tours were a recently established and **isolated** emirate. It had only completed its conquest of Iberia in 718 and had failed to crush the first rebellion as late as 722, only a decade before the Battle of Tours. The Franks, on the other hand, had been the single most important rising Christian power in Western Europe since 486 when they defeated the Roman governor of Gaul.

The importance of Martel's victory at Tours, in our view, is that it helped the emergence of Portugal and Spain, the two European powers that would begin the creation of a new civilized center outside the Middle East and the Mediterranean. This was certainly not what the victory at Tours intended. Martel's dream was an expanded Frankish Empire within the territory of the Western portion of the old Roman Empire **not** an overseas empire centered on the Atlantic Ocean. In addition, while Tours was significant in halting the expansion of the Umayyad dynasty into France and Germany, it was the internal overthrow of the Umayyad dynasty by the Abbasid dynasty **after** Tours, in 750, that sufficiently **weakened and isolated** Muslim power in Iberia to the point that the puny states of Portugal and Spain could wrest their independence and become important Christian powers. Martel's victory prevented Muslim conquest of Frankish territory but it did not expand the Frankish Empire into Iberia. The surprising result of Martel's victory over the Muslims was the emergence of two empires, the Portuguese and Spanish empires, which became more powerful than the Frankish Empire.

The Muslims had begun to cross the Pyrenees shortly after completing their conquest of Iberia in 718. They conquered *Septimania* from the Visigoths in 719 and established a base of operations at *Narbonne,* from where they could bring in supplies from Iberia by sea. Despite their defeat at the Battle of Toulouse in 721 they continued their military incursions into the Frankish Empire. By all accounts, the leader of the Franks, Charles Martel, was a military genius. He had been preparing for battle against the Emirate of Cordoba ever since the Muslims crossed the Pyrenees in 719. He built and trained a full-time army, seizing church property to pay for it. At the time most armies depended on part-time soldiers who returned to their farms when crops had to be planted or harvested.

The Muslims were at a disadvantage because they had marched far north from their base at Narbonne. Prior to facing Martel they had easily conquered Aquitaine and Bordeaux. But as they advanced North of Bordeaux toward Tours their army had splintered into several raiding parties and supplies had been stretched thin over such a long distance. By comparison, Martel had a compact force on home ground with good cover from the forest and on high ground. Martel's defeat of the Muslim army at the Battle of Tours was so decisive that it earned him the nickname of "the Hammer." The Muslim general, *Abdul Rahman,* was killed and his army retreated to Narbonne. The Muslims continued their attacks on Frankish territory from their base in Narbonne. Abdul Rahman's son attempted an invasion by sea in 736. He landed forces in Narbonne and moved inland against Martel. During 736–737 Martel scored several victories against the Muslim invaders.

The Muslims were isolated and surrounded at Narbonne but held on to their base. It was left to Martel's son, *Pepin the Short,* to reconquer

Narbonne from the Muslims in 759. In 778, Martel's grandson, *Charlemagne,* crossed the Pyrenees to attack the Muslims in Iberia. He was defeated at Zaragoza and forced to retreat. Charlemagne proceeded to create a buffer zone, the *Spanish March,* between Muslim Iberia and the Frankish Empire. It began with the conquest of Gerona in 785. The Franks expanded from Gerona to Cardona, Ausona, and Urgel by 795. Charlemagne also created the Kingdom of Aquitaine in 781 with his son, *Louis the Pious,* as king. King Louis expanded into Muslim Iberia by conquering Barcelona in 801, Tarragona in 809 and Tortosa in 811. King Louis became emperor of the Franks after his father's death in 814. He was crowned by Pope Steven IV in 816 to succeed his father as the second holy Roman emperor.

The Birth of the Portuguese Empire Marks the Birth of the West

What we call the "West" today began in the fifteenth century when Portugal and Spain became the first two of many Western European empires. Western Europe formed a partnership across the Atlantic with the United States, which has dominated and controlled the world to this day. Unlike the previous Western empires of Rome and Greece, the new West looked outward to Asia and the New World. Portugal and Spain became independent kingdoms in the Iberian Peninsula after the *Reconquista.* Portugal secured its independence from the Muslims before Spain. While Spain became the more powerful of the two Iberian empires we begin our history of Spain and Portugal's role in ushering in the current Western civilization with Portugal. Not only did Portugal secure its independence from the Muslim power in Al-Andalus before Spain, it began its overseas empire before Spain. It can therefore rightly claim to be the original Western European power to have begun the shift of civilization from its cradle in the Middle East to Western Europe and America. The key military weapon of this shift was **naval power.**

Portugal was ideally located to expand by sea both westward across the Atlantic Ocean and southward around the coast of Africa. Portugal is the most south-westerly country in Europe with its entire coastline along the Atlantic Ocean. Portugal was also ideally located to push back the dominant Berber Muslim presence in North Africa. Its conquests in Africa would provide both gold and slaves to fund its overseas empire. This global empire began in North Africa but expanded along the west coast of Africa, across the Indian Ocean to Asia, into the Atlantic Ocean and Across the Atlantic Ocean to the New World. At its height it covered seven percent of the land area of the world.

Birth of the Independent Nation-State of Portugal

Prior to Portugal becoming an empire, it had to secure its independence as a nation-state both from the Muslim empires and from competing Christian rulers. It is important to digress somewhat from our primary goal to describe briefly the events leading up to Portugal's independence. When the Muslims conquered Iberia they divided it into five administrative areas. Two of these areas were *Portugal and Galicia* and *Castile and Leon.* The birth of Portugal as an independent state is linked to these two administrative regions of Muslim Iberia and the county of Portugal. The first Visigoth king of Asturias died in 737 and his son, *Favila,* was killed by a bear in 739. *Alfonso I* ruled the kingdom from 739 to 757. During his rule he reconquered both *Galicia* and *Leon* from the Muslims. This was the beginning of the *Reconquista.* By the end of his rule he had reconquered about 25 percent of Muslim Iberia. His son, *Fruela I,* and grandson, *Alfonso II,* continued to push the Muslims further and further south. *Alfonso III,* 866–909, continued to rule Asturias, Galicia and Leon but was forced by three of his sons to divide the kingdom. The Kingdom of Asturias went to *Fruela.* The Kingdom of Galicia went to *Ordono.* The Kingdom of Leon went to *Garcia.*

The Kingdom of Leon expanded and became the most important of the Christian kingdoms in Iberia. The county of Portugal became a semi-independent county within the Kingdom of Leon. As the Kingdom of Leon expanded to the south and east it came into conflict with *Castile.* **Christian** Castile was so afraid of **Christian** Leon that the count of Castile allied with the **Muslim** Caliphate of Cordoba against Leon but was still defeated by King Sancho I of Leon in 966. But Leon and Castile were united under *Ferdinand the Great,* count of Castile, after he became the king of Leon in 1037.

Henry of Burgundy fought the Muslims on behalf of King Alfonso VI of Leon, Castile and Galicia. He was made *count of Portugal* in 1093 for his military services and as a dowry for marrying *Theresa,* the daughter of King Alfonso VI. Portugal became a direct dependency of the Kingdom of Leon in 1097. Henry's son, *Afonso Henriques,* became the count of Portugal in 1112. Portugal took advantage of a civil war between Leon and Castile and on June 24, 1128, Afonso Henriques defeated the Kingdom of Leon at the *Battle of Sao Mamede.* Portugal declared itself an independent country. Afonso Henriques became the first king of Portugal on July 25, 1139, as Afonso I. The capital city was *Coimbra.* Leon recognized Portugal's independence in 1143 with the *Treaty of Zamora.* Afonso I was confirmed as king of Portugal by Pope Alexander III in 1179. This recognition of Portugal with the papal bull *Manifestis Probatum* marked the beginning of a long and important relationship between Portugal and the Papacy, which was beneficial to both. In return for increasing Christian converts, the pope would sanction Portuguese enslavement of Africans and indigenous people along with the other horrors of Western imperialism.

Portugal's desire for independence from Leon would give rise to military conflicts between Portugal and other Christian states in Northern Iberia. Rivalry between King Afonso I of Portugal and his cousin, King Alfonso VII of Leon, was especially bitter. But the rise of Portugal as a Christian military power was instrumental in pushing the Muslims out of Northern Iberia. The Frankish Empire had pushed the Muslims out of Narbonne. Portugal was now leading the Christian push back of the Muslims from Northern Iberia to the southern portion of the Iberian Peninsula. This leadership role against the Muslims further endeared Portugal to the Papacy. During his rule from 1139 to 1185, King Afonso I doubled the size of the Kingdom of Portugal by reconquering territory from the Muslims. His conquest of *Lisbon* in 1147 was significant as Portugal was now penetrating the southern portion of Iberia, which had been the stronghold of the Muslims. Lisbon became the new capital of Portugal in 1260.

King Afonso I was succeeded by his son, *Sancho I.* Sancho continued his father's policy of simultaneously expanding Portugal into Southern Iberia and championing the *Reconquista.* In 1189 he conquered the important southern city of *Silves* on the banks of the Arade River in the Algarve. While he lost the city two years later it marked the beginning of the conquest of the Algarve by Portugal. Sancho I was succeeded by his son, Afonso II in 1212. The "Afonsine Dynasty," or *House of Burgundy,* continued to rule Portugal until 1385. Afonso III, 1248–1279, was the first king to take the title *king of Portugal and the Algarve.* He conquered the Algarve shortly after removing his brother, King Sancho II, from the throne in December 1247. He moved the capital of Portugal to **Lisbon,** at the mouth of the Tagus River, in 1260. The Algarve gave Portugal clear and easy access to the Atlantic Ocean with important ports in Lisbon, Lagos and Faro. It was from these ports that Portugal would launch the conquest of its overseas empire.

With the conquest of the Algarve Portugal had removed all threats to its independence, from the Muslims. But its border with the Christian state of *Castile* was still in doubt. After several wars with Castile, the Portuguese border was agreed to in 1267 by the *Treaty of Badajoz.* This treaty was signed by Afonso III of Portugal and King Alfonso X of Castile. Portugal's southern border was set west of the Guadiana River in 1267 and is the border to this day. Portugal surrendered some territory to the east of this boundary. However, wars with Castile continued to haunt Portugal's efforts to be an independent Christian state in Iberia.

King Afonso III was succeeded by his son, *Denis I,* in 1279. After another war with Castile, Denis I signed another peace treaty with King Ferdinand IV of Castile in 1297. Denis I was succeeded by his son, *Afonso IV,* in 1325. Rivalry between Portugal and Castile continued during the reign of Afonso IV. Another war was followed by another peace treaty in 1339. The Burgundian Dynasty continued to rule an independent Portugal until 1383. Afonso IV was succeeded by his son, *Peter I,* in 1357. His reign was relatively peaceful. Peter's son, *Ferdinand I,* was the last Burgundian king of Portugal. When Ferdinand I died without a **male** heir, Castile made another attempt to colonize Portugal. King Juan I of Castile tried to colonize Portugal by marrying the daughter of Ferdinand I, in May 1383. But once again Castile was unable to secure the necessary military victory against those opposed to the union of Castile and Portugal. The two Christian Iberian powers went to war again. At the *Battle of Aljubarrota* in August 1385 Portugal defeated Castile and the half-brother of Ferdinand I, *John I,* of the House of Aviz, became the new king of Portugal. The House of Aviz continued to rule Portugal until 1495. It was during this period that Portugal began to build an empire outside the Iberian Peninsula.

Portugal's African Conquests

It was natural for Portugal to look across the narrow strait of Gibraltar to the riches of North Africa. After all, it was from North Africa that the Berber Muslims had expanded their empire into Al-Andalus. The Muslims had launched their invasion of the Iberian Peninsula from Ceuta. Portugal determined that Ceuta would be a good place to launch its imperial dream after driving these same Muslim invaders from the Algarve. Portugal's conquest of Ceuta in **1415** marks the beginning of the Portuguese Empire, which became the first Western European Empire of the modern era. At the time Ceuta was a rich and thriving Muslim city. As the final destination for the camel caravans it benefitted from the lucrative overland spice trade with the Orient. Control of Ceuta took on new significance after the Christians lost Constantinople in 1453. In 1471 Portugal conquered another important North African city, *Tangier.*

Conquest of Ceuta cemented Portugal's special relationship with the Papacy as it was recognized as an important crusade against the Muslims and the conversion of new souls to Catholic Europe. King John I personally led his three sons in the crusade against the Muslims of North Africa to conquer the Moroccan city in August 1415. Some of the wealth generated from the civilized, **slave trade,** along with gold **discoveries/ thefts** was used by Portugal to fund other crusades against the Muslims, fanatically promoted by the Papacy. Portugal was on a mission from the pope to **enslave** the unbelievers while enriching itself with military thefts. Serving both *God and Mammon* would be its unspoken rallying cry. In 1452 and 1455 Pope Nicholas V issued a Papal Bull granting King Afonso V of Portugal the right to **enslave** Muslims and other non-Christians. Western civilization had truly begun. Is it not ironic that Western historians claim that the abolition of the **slave trade** is proof of how civilized we have become. Yet we think of the **slave owners** who created the American Empire as both civilized and "enlightened." Today Western historians point out how civilized the West is in bombing and destroying the homes and livelihoods of **60 million refugees.** It's civilized because it proves that we are taking the fight to the "terrorists" who had the audacity to publicly behead an American journalist. Of course, countries like Canada, whose prime minister, **Steven Harper,** leads the call for the creation of this civilized refugee disaster makes sure that the millions of refugees find their way to Pakistan, Jordan, Turkey and Lebanon, **not** Canada. That way we are doubly civilized. We create the problem and use it to ensure we impoverish further, **poor** countries, so that we can show the world how Canadians are so lucky and fortunate to live in paradise.

Portugal's successful conquest was greatly facilitated by the continuing disunity of the Muslims, which was the major cause of its military defeats in Al-Andalus. That same Muslim disunity today is the primary cause of the continued success of the West in engineering civil wars in Syria, Libya, Egypt and Yemen after the failure of the West to conquer Afghanistan, Iraq and Pakistan. The connivance of Saudi Arabia and Turkey with the West, to destabilize the governments of Syria, Libya, Lebanon and Iran, shows that Muslims and Arabs learned nothing from their monumental betrayal by the West during the First and Second World Wars. The West is still able to use the same divide-and-rule tactic perfected by the British.

Portugal established the common ingredients that all of the Western empires used to dominate the world. These common ingredients are **religious dogma, slavery, hypocrisy, military brutality, theft of land and resources, genocide, and indoctrination.** Ceuta was just the beginning of the second **Christian** domination of the world after the fall of the Roman Empire. This **Christian** domination continues to this day. The invasion of Ceuta by King John I was encouraged by his third son, Prince Henry, who became famous as *Henry the Navigator.* His mother was the sister of King Henry IV of England. Prince **Henry** was twenty-one years old when he joined his father and two older brothers in the military conquest of Ceuta. Personal participation in warmongering was then and now one of the qualifications for "knightly honor." This may explain why the children of Princess Diana, William and Harry, feel the need to participate personally in the killing of Afghans during the British invasion of Afghanistan in the first and second decades of the twenty-first century. Prince Henry's personal participation in the conquest of Ceuta gave him the opportunity to promote religious fanaticism, warmongering, slavery, colonialism and the subjugation of non-Christians, many of the hallmarks of this second Christian domination of the world.

In September of 2012 Prince **Harry** returned to Afghanistan for his second tour of duty. This time he was armed with an Apache helicopter. His job description was "copilot gunner." One could argue that flying a helicopter was slightly more dangerous than flying the Western jets dropping their deadly payloads on the Afghans. Even so, an Apache helicopter is a far more effective killing machine than a roadside bomb set by a relatively poorly armed Afghan insurgent fighting a brutal and totally unwarranted invasion of his country. Prince Harry was very determined to score as many kills as possible before returning to more playboy displays of nudity in Las Vegas. On this second tour of duty he flew his attack **killer** copter on the frontline of the Western invasion.

In 1419 Prince **Henry** became governor of the Algarve and in 1420 he was appointed as the governor of the *Order of Christ,* the Portuguese successor to the famous *Knights Templar* who led the Christian Crusades against the Arabs. But the post-1415 Christian Crusades would not be against the Muslims of the Middle East but against poorly armed Africans and First Nations. The rallying Western hypocrisy will be, "enslave their bodies to enrich us and to save their souls." After the conquest of Ceuta, Prince Henry sent ships to explore the Western coast of Africa, beginning in 1418. The port of Lagos in the Algarve was ideally located for these explorations by sea. It was from Lagos that King John I and his sons had launched their naval conquest of Ceuta. But North Africa proved to be too formidable a foe for the newly independent **puny** state of Portugal. Muslim presence was too entrenched. By contrast the Western coast of Africa was a much easier military target. Prince Henry would launch from the port of Lagos, his so-called Age of Discovery, along the west coast of Africa, with Portugal's famous *caravels.*

The caravel was a revolutionary sailing ship designed under the sponsorship of Prince Henry to explore both the West African coast and the Atlantic. Its shallow keel allowed it to sail into shallow coastal waters. But it was also fast, easy to maneuver and could sail into the wind. The *Nina* and the *Pinta,* used by Columbus in his 1492 voyage to the New

World, were caravels. Lagos became the center of Portugal's ambition to be the first European nation to build an empire outside the historic civilized world, centered in the Mediterranean and the Middle East. Prince Henry pushed his explorers to sail further south along the West African coast past *Cape Bojador.* European sailors had never sailed past the strong currents and frequent storms encountered at Cape Bojador. But in 1434 *Gil Eanes* sailed from Lagos along the west coast of Africa past the dreaded Cape Bojador. In 1441 Prince Henry's explorers reached *Cape Blanc* and returned to Portugal with their first cargo of **African slaves.** Prince Henry was only too happy to collect his fifth of the price paid for the African slaves sold in Lagos. Portugal had no qualms about using this very **evil** and inhumane subjugation of the human race to promote its pretend civilization of the world in the name of Christianity. The African slave trade simultaneously enriched both the Western European empires and the Christian church. The Christian church was doubly enriched with the money from the slave trade and the conversion of the slaves to Christianity.

Portugal, like all previous empires, was in search of colonies with valuable resources to steal by using superior military and brutal force, while simultaneously preaching that it was civilizing the natives. The hallmark of modern Western colonization was the obsession with committing the most heinous crimes against powerless people while glorifying such crimes with hypocrisy, lies, double-talk and brainwashing. Portugal's exploitation of the native landowners in Africa, Asia and America was combined with religious zeal and religious dogma to the point that it justified the killing, maiming, enslaving and exploiting of millions in the name of bringing Christian civilization to them. To this day the West continues this masquerade in all corners of the globe, most obviously in Syria, Afghanistan, Libya, Iraq and Palestine. President Obama, for example, has secretly assassinated more people with unmanned drones than any other Western leader. Western atrocities caused by the desire to colonize the world show no signs of abating in the twenty-first century.

Portugal found traces of gold in Africa as early as 1441. But **African slaves** turned out to be the most valuable resource for the imperial power. Slaves, gold and ivory soon became valuable imports by Imperial

Portugal. The slaves were either caught by the Portuguese themselves or by Africans working for or trading with the Portuguese. Another constant trait of Western imperialists is the use of locals willing to connive with the imperial power against their own people. This is not only useful in supplying the imperial power with much needed additional manpower but a key ingredient in their use of propaganda. The West is always gung ho about pointing to locals working with the empire as evidence that the colonists support their grand scheme to bring civilization to "primitive" colonists. The fact that locals are always bribed or coerced into serving their imperial masters is always hidden by a subservient Western media.

The Portuguese explorers pushed slowly but steadily further and further south along the West African coast. The Gulf of Guinea and the islands in the Gulf were extensively explored by Fernao Gomes. The Portuguese reached the Gold Coast, present day Ghana, in 1471. As trade increased, trading posts were set up and in 1482 Portugal built an armed fort in the Gulf of Guinea, *Elmina Castle,* to protect its trading/stealing rights. The Gold Coast became an important Portuguese colony. The fort provided a secure harbor for Portuguese ships and security to expand the African slave trade. It became the mainstay for developing the "Guinea trade." The Portuguese explorers pushed inland crossing the equator and reaching the Congo River. After the rediscovery of the New World, Elmina Castle, also known as *Fort Sao Jorge da Mina,* became the primary "trading post" for the Atlantic slave trade. In addition, the Gold Coast produced one tenth of the total world production of gold by the early sixteenth century.

Portugal's conquest of the West African coastline was significant in itself since it provided valuable **slaves,** gold and ivory. But it had an even greater value to Portugal and to the modern West. By exploring the entire west coast of Africa it provided the opportunity of finding a sea route to the spices, silks and other valuable products of Asia. This sea route to Asia and the African slave trade were the two major contributions of Portugal to the founding of modern Western domination. The Portuguese explorer, *Bartolomeu Dias,* reached the Cape of Good Hope in 1487 paving the way for Vasco da Gama's historic voyage to India in 1498. After reaching India, Portugal conquered several Muslim states in East Africa. Christians had lost the original center of civilization to the

Muslims. This was itself a major blow to Christian hegemony. But loss of Eastern Europe and the Middle East also meant a loss of any opportunity to push eastward overland to the riches of Asia. None of this mattered after Portugal discovered the sea route to Asia. Worse still, Muslim conquest of the original center of civilization made it complacent. It was unable to see that the future domination of the world would lie with **naval** military power and **enslaving Africans.** In the fifteenth century the maritime states of Western Europe had the decisive advantage because of their easy access to the Atlantic. For the first time in history control of the Atlantic became more strategic than control of the Mediterranean.

The two hallmarks of measuring how civilized an empire is, are the number of humans it **enslaves** and the sophistication of its military weapons used to kill, conquer and steal, destroy and impoverish. Today, those impoverished by such civilized weapons are called **refugees.** The latest UN count is **60 million** refugees. By this measure alone, Western empires like the United States and Canada are the most civilized. The latest excuse for this civilized creation of the staggering numbers of refugees is **ISIS,** the Islamic State in Iraq and Syria**.** The civilized West responds to the beheading of one Western person by ISIS, by creating another million refugees with its infinite supply of bombs. Why? Beheading is primitive but bombing is civilized. Why is beheading primitive and bombing civilized? Beheading kills only one. Bombing is capable of killing or impoverishing a million. The more refugees the West creates the more it claims to be degrading ISIS.

The Confirmation of Hypocrisy in Western Democracy: Slavery, Racism, and Nuking Japan

In previous chapters we have explained how the West has been very proud of tracing their civilization back to both Greece and Rome. Since both Greece and Rome condoned slavery the West has implicitly accepted that slavery is not inconsistent with its rather ridiculous notion of what freedom and democracy really mean or what the notion of being civilized should entail. It's therefore not surprising that all of the modern Western empires, beginning with Portugal, would use slaves to enhance their wealth while using hypocrisy to preach that slavery was consistent with freedom, democracy and other pretense at being civilized.

Lagos was the Portuguese port from which Portugal launched its imperial conquests. Lagos also became famous for being the center of a booming Western European market for African slaves. Prince Henry was one of the chief architects of the beginning of the lucrative trade in African slaves. He profited immensely from his sponsorship of the trade since he received a fifth of the price of every African slave sold in Lagos. Prince Henry "the Navigator" was also Prince Henry **"the Slave Trader."** Prince Henry's navigators were eager slavers supplying a growing European market for African slaves. Portugal monopolized the African slave trade for two centuries, 1440–1640. The other European empires, far from criticizing Portugal for enriching itself from enslaving Africans, eagerly participated in the African slave trade. In 1637 the Dutch captured the valuable Portuguese slave trading post of Elmina Castle to gain control of the lucrative trans-Atlantic African slave trade based in the Gold Coast. The worst hypocrite, of course, was the United States. Promoting itself as the republic for freedom and equality all of its founding fathers were slave owners.

Another evil characteristic of Western imperialism is **racism.** The birth of white racism against nonwhites owes much to the enslavement of Africans. The West was quick to demonize the black race as inferior in order to justify their enslavement. Africans were not enslaved because they were blacks. They were enslaved because they added enormous value to Western colonization. However, since the West was obsessed with providing ridiculous justifications for their evil deeds, it naturally latched on to using color as a powerful propaganda tool to justify the enslavement of Africans. In the New World this same promotion of white superiority was used to justify enslaving the **red** First Nations. It was not long before the **yellow** Chinese and the **brown** Indian were also deemed inferior races. This promotion of the superiority of the white race continues to this day and colors the way that the white leaders of the West think of the nonwhite leaders of the emerging Third World nations. This is one reason why President Obama tries so hard for both him and his family to be treated as white. Hitler was no aberration in his promotion of the pure white race. He was only the one to be vilified by his own Western coimperial racists. Finding a scapegoat for your own evil deeds is also a very useful propaganda tool to convince the naïve into thinking you are different.

What is critical in understanding Western hypocrisy is how the West turns the most evil of deeds into a measure of what it calls civilized. Slavery is an excellent example of this convoluted propaganda. One of the key measures of wealth, importance and influence in Rome was the number of slaves you owned. The more slaves you owned the more important and civilized you were as a leader. No wonder the West so easily dismissed slave ownership by the founders of the United States as not being inconsistent with their claims to be the foremost defenders of freedom and inequality. In fact, the leaders of this new republic were deemed to be more important and influential, and therefore, more civilized, the more slaves they owned. It's not unlike American hypocrisy about nuclear weapons. The Americans both invented and used nuclear weapons. By nuking Japan it committed the most heinous crime in the history of humanity. Yet its propaganda is so powerful that it is able to convince the world that this most heinous of crimes was a good and civilized deed. Unlike the Germans who have long since apologized for the crimes of Hitler, the United States is so worshipped by the West for nuking Japan, that it is not only never expected to apologize for its crime, it cajoles the world to join its ridiculous call for embargoes and military threats to states like Iran for developing nuclear capability. The fact that a leader like President Obama, the most warmongering of all Western leaders, has any credibility when he calls for attacks on North Korea, Libya, Iran, Syria or ISIS, is only more evidence of the upside-down nature of what the West calls civilized.

While President Obama holds the record for "most warmongering," it has to be President Bill Clinton, the "I never had sex with that woman" president, who holds the record for "master of spin." In a September 2012 CNN interview with Piers Morgan he explained with the conviction of a spin God why the United States was not making the same mistake by claiming that Iran was developing a nuclear weapon as it had done with Iraq, in regards to the totally false claim by the United States that Saddam Hussein had WMDs. The difference, according to Dr. Spin himself, was that President Ahmadinejad admitted to refining uranium while Saddam had not made such an admission. That is the key to knowing that Saddam was telling the truth while Ahmadinejad is lying about not developing a nuclear weapon. So why did President George W. Bush not know that Saddam was telling the truth? Unfortunately Piers Morgan either did not ask Dr. Spin that obvious question or edited it out so that Clinton will not look like the total idiot he is.

The Portuguese Empire up to 1580 and the Birth of Christian Domination

The Portuguese empire began in the fifteenth century with its conquests in North Africa and the west coast of Africa. It expanded with conquests of nearby islands in the Atlantic and with colonies in Asia and the New World. For a while it dominated almost half of the world with its colonies spread across the globe from islands in the Atlantic and colonies along the West African coastline to the interior of Africa, to the Middle East, to India, Ceylon, the spice rich Moluccas, China, Japan and other parts of Asia, to the Far East and to the Americas. Throughout the period from Portugal's fight for independence from Muslim Iberia to its dominant imperial status, Portugal competed fiercely with its Christian Iberian neighbor, Spain. In 1580 Spain finally succeeded in conquering Portugal after centuries of military rivalry. Philip II of Spain became king of Portugal in 1580 after his successful invasion. The world's two largest empires were ruled by the same king. In the next chapter we will look at the post-1580 Portuguese Empire after dealing with the rise of the Spanish Empire to 1580.

Prince Henry began this vast Portuguese Empire by sending his explorers both along the West African coast and into the Atlantic. One of the first groups of the many groups of islands in the Atlantic to be colonized by Portugal was the *Madeiras.* Portugal began its colonization and settlement of the Madeiras immediately after the island of *Porto Santo* was accidentally discovered by two of Prince Henry's explorers in 1419. While exploring the west coast of Africa for Prince Henry, Captains Zarco and Teixeira were forced to seek shelter from a storm on Porto Santo. Prince Henry introduced sugarcane production to the islands in the 1450s. This valuable crop attracted settlers from Portugal and Genoa.

Just as the Portuguese exploration and colonization of the West African coast led to the discovery of the sea route to Asia, the Portuguese exploration and settlement of the Atlantic islands led to the discovery of the sea route to the New World. The first Portuguese administrator of Porto Santo was Bartolomeu Perestrelo. Christopher Columbus married Perestrelo's daughter and joined his father-in-law on Porto Santo before making his historic crossing of the Atlantic in 1492. Columbus had also sailed to the Portuguese Gold Coast in December 1481 onboard one of the Portuguese ships taking materials to build Fort Elmina.

Another important group of islands colonized by Portugal in the fifteenth century was the *Azores.* This was a group of nine islands. Portuguese settlement of the Azores began in 1433. Sugarcane was cultivated in the Azores. Most of the settlers were from Portugal and Flanders. At the time Flanders was ruled by the duke of Burgundy who was married to the sister of Prince Henry. Some colonists moved from the Madeiras to the Azores. Both the Madeiras and the Azores produced wheat for export to Portugal.

A third group of islands in the Atlantic colonized by Portugal in the fifteenth century was the *Cape Verde islands.* This group is made up of ten islands. Its location in the Atlantic Ocean much further south of both the Azores and the Madeiras made it invaluable for explorations along the West African coast. It's not surprising that Vasco da Gama made a stop-over in Cape Verde during his voyage to India. Cape Verde was also conveniently located for explorations in South America. Columbus made a stop-over in Cape Verde during his third voyage to the New World. At this time and at least for another two centuries, South America was much more valuable than North America. Portuguese settlement of the Cape Verde islands began in 1462. The city of *Cidade Velha* in the Cape Verde islands became the new center for Portugal's control of the African slave trade. African slaves from the west coast of Africa were sold by the Portuguese to Brazilian and Caribbean plantation owners in the slave market in Cidade Velha.

Portugal's colonization of these three groups of islands in the Atlantic was recognized by the *Treaty of Alcacovas* signed in 1479 by Portugal and its primary colonial rival in the Atlantic, Castile. Portugal and Castile had fought many wars for territory in Iberia. This rivalry continued after

Castile became a part of the independent nation-state of Spain. As both Portugal and Spain competed for empires outside Iberia they looked to the pope for support. The infamous Papal Bull of Pope Alexander VI, which divided the world between Portugal and Spain in 1493, not merely promoted peaceful competition between Portugal and Spain but marked the beginning of the domination of the world by the **Christian** West. It's important that we recognize that what is called Western civilization is simply world domination and one of the many parts to that domination is **religious.** Furthermore, the only religion permitted to be considered civilized enough to dominate the world was the **Western Christian** religion. By Western Christian I mean the Roman Catholics and Protestants. Both Portugal and Spain were Roman Catholic nations. They founded the new Western empires, not the Eastern Greek Orthodox Christians. As a result, to be civilized you had to be a Roman Catholic Christian not a Greek Orthodox Christian. The adoption of the Greek Orthodox Church by Russia only served to further demean that original half of Christianity since Russia was never admitted to the civilized Western club.

The conversion of England by King Henry VIII to Protestantism led to Protestant Christians becoming even more civilized than their Catholic brothers and sisters. This enhanced position of Protestants was given a big boost when the American Empire took over the Western leadership of the world from the British. Not until President Kennedy were Americans allowed to elect a Catholic Christian as their president. With the pope recognized as the spiritual leader of the billions of Catholic Christians around the world the Protestant Christian nations grudgingly accord civilized second class status to Catholic Christians in their countries. The Jewish religion is also given civilized second class status in the West because of the strategic location of the American *uncolony* of Israel in the Middle East. Other religions are tolerated because it helps the Western propaganda related to religious freedom. This need to use religious freedom as one of its propaganda tools forces the West to tolerate Islam but rank it lowest on the Totem Pole. As you may expect, I cannot subscribe to the notion that a belief in any religion, much less one specific religion, has any role, much less such an integral and sacred role, in creating a civilization. To be civilized is to be free of religious dogma and even religious beliefs.

The process of transforming humanity from a primitive state to a civilized state must include replacing religious beliefs with objective and rational thoughts and ideas. Western promotion of "religious freedom" as an integral part of becoming civilized is nonsensical. First, religion has been an important force since the dawn of history. To continue to make religion an integral force in a civilized or modern society is inconsistent since there is no change from past practice and behavior. A change that would both modernize and civilize is to sever religion from progress and development of humanity. What the West calls "religious freedom" is simply the toleration of other faiths, which many states and empires have done in the past. The West, like those previous empires, implicitly or explicitly, insist that its "state" religion, Western Christianity in the case of the West, is superior, but that other religions, must be tolerated to varying degrees. This is no different from what the Muslims did when they ruled Al-Andalus. Of course, such toleration of other religions is far superior to the kind of religious persecution practiced by the Spanish Inquisition or by Adolf Hitler. But there are more examples from history of the kind of religious toleration practiced by the West today than of religious persecution. We have therefore, made no progress in this area just as we have made no progress with warmongering and imperial conquests.

In fact, Western "religious freedom" is often an excuse to promote the state religion. Recent examples include President Barack Obama's determined efforts to hide and downplay his Muslim roots and President Obama's decision to reinsert "God" in his platform for re-election, after it had been deleted by his staff. It is also a useful tool of imperialism. For example, in the past, Christians persecuted Jews more than any other religion. But once the United States recognized that it could use the state of Israel as a beachhead for its desire to colonize the Middle East, Judaism was ranked second only to its state religion, Christianity, on its Totem Pole of ranking religions. Since the West must blindly follow the U.S. leadership, the Jews became second cousins to the Christians. Since the Palestinians are Muslims and Israel stole the land from the Palestinians the reason for moving Judaism to the top of the second class Totem Pole is the same reason for moving Islam to the bottom of the second class Totem Pole.

An even more recent example occurred during the 2015 U.S. presidential campaign. Republican front-runner Donald Trump was outed by the American media for not being sufficiently religious. The media did not have to explain that it meant the **Christian** religion since that is understood by all Americans and non-Americans. In the case of President Obama he was questioned on his **Christian** faith because his father was a **Muslim.** In the case of Donald Trump there was no question of the fact that he was Christian. The concern was that he was too materialistic to be sufficiently **Christian** for the job of "High Priest" of the realm. I have explained that Christianity, especially Protestant Christianity, had no qualms about serving both God and Mammon. But in Trump's case the media was arguing that he had leaned too far toward Mammon to be able to serve God as much as the Constitution of the United States required. Trump had devoted too much of his time and energy to becoming such a successful businessman to have the required percent of Christian faith to serve the United States as president, commander in chief, and high priest.

Another fall out of Western "religious freedom" is that it is often used by the West to coerce non-Western states, especially Muslim states, to grant religious freedom to Christians. This is often used by the West to plant Christian missionaries to convert non-Christians and aid Western colonization. The Christian church has been an important force for Western colonization since the beginning of this modern Western domination of the world started by Portugal in the fifteenth century. I have explained how many countries have tried to keep out the Christian church precisely because it is always a prelude to colonization by the West. That role of the Christian church is alive and well today. Using the example of North Korea today, the regime has caught several American spies posing as **Christian** missionaries. The American media is forced to portray these charges of spying by the North Korean government as another example of demented leadership by the Kim dynasty. Yet in 2015 it was found out that the United States secretly used a **Christian** NGO, Humanitarian International Services Group, **HISG,** since 2004, to spy on North Korea. The only reason we found out about this example was that this program ended in January 2013 after it was determined that it had not gathered sufficiently useful intelligence. In other words, the Kim leaders were not as stupid as the American media portrayed them.

Finally, "religious freedom" is a dangerous tool in the West's double standard tool kit. A recent example of the use of this double standard by the West, is comparing how the United States dealt with the cases of Julian Assange and Bradley Manning compared with the U-tube video of the anti-Muslim film, *Innocence of Muslims.* The United States, in connivance with Britain and Sweden, went to great lengths to stifle free speech and freedom of the press in the Assange/Manning case but claimed that it was not even aware initially of the anti-Muslim film, Innocence of Muslims, despite its immense spy apparatus. Once admitting to becoming aware, it used the same ridiculous line about protecting the freedom of people in the United States to express their views.

Another example is how Britain and the West went to great lengths to protect the relatively unknown idiot, *Salmon Rushdie,* compared with their total lack of defense of Assange. People in Canada and the United States are free to express their views so long as those views are pro–United States, pro-Canada, pro-West, anti-Muslim, anti-China, anti-Russian, etc. That is why, for example, a celebrated pop singer like Madonna would defend the *Pussy Riot* Russian pop group but not dare to defend Assange.

There are two separate points being made here. The first is that there is absolutely no freedom of the press, free speech or freedom of religion, in the West. Such freedoms are not only highly restricted, but used as a propaganda tool to coerce these freedoms from non-Western states. Second, and more important, even if such freedoms existed in the West, it is absolutely no reason to demand that non-Western countries follow the West. The West has no God-given right to determine what is best for every country. Its record of inhumanity, wars, slavery, genocide, etc., is so disgusting that no state should copy, much less be coerced into copying it. If Muslim states decide that even a tiny hint of blasphemy against their prophet should not be tolerated it's their right, and only theirs, to make that determination. The supposedly free Western media is not only biased, it's ignorant, uneducated and illogical. But most importantly, it is protected by the military and financial power of the West. Non-pro-Western reporters have no such protection, as both Julian Assange and Bradley Manning found out.

Portugal's Colonization of Asia Begins Five Centuries of Eastern Decline

Portugal's discovery of a sea route to Asia was responsible for half of the domination of the world by the modern West. The other half was Spain's rediscovery of the New World. While Spain's rediscovery was a fortuitous accident, Portugal's was not. In fact, both Portugal and Spain were searching for the same prize, a sea route to the riches of Asia, when Columbus stumbled on the New World. Initially seen as an obstacle to finding Asia and a great loss to Spain, this accidental rediscovery of the New World turned out to complement Portugal's prize by a full 50 percent, if not more. The conquest of Asia by the West, following da Gama's voyage on behalf of Portugal, gave the modern West a big boost over Muslim control of the Middle East and the overland route to Asia. But it was the complement of this boost to Western Europe with the military and economic resources of America that cemented the fate of the East to five centuries of Western domination.

Once Dias had rounded the Cape of Good Hope it was simply a matter of time before Portuguese explorers would find a way to cross the Indian Ocean to find the riches of Asia. The West was well aware of the value of the spices, silks and exotic exports of Asia. But overland imports were limited and control of the trade was dominated by their adversary, the Muslims. A sea route controlled by Portugal would simultaneously give control to the Christians and enrich Portugal. Less than a decade after Dias rounded the Cape of Good Hope, Vasco da Gama set sail from Lisbon, crossed the Indian Ocean and reached India in May 1498. This in itself was a most remarkable feat. As late as 1434, Cape Bojador had been accepted by all Europeans to be the ultimate limit for European explorers to be able to return. Europeans had never thought it possible to reach the Indian Ocean much less cross it and find India. But what proved to be even more remarkable was that this relatively small newly emerging nation-state, Portugal, would soon control access to the

Indian Ocean by defeating the Arabs who had dominated this ocean for centuries. Portugal's colonization of India marked the beginning of six centuries of Western invasions and colonization of Asia that will very likely end in this century. Ironically, Western rhetoric used to justify those six centuries of brutal invasions and conquests has remained exactly the same. The West supposedly went to Africa, Asia and America to civilize the natives. Today, Western invasions in Afghanistan, Libya, Syria, Iraq, Lebanon, Yemen, Pakistan, Egypt, Palestine, etc., are justified with exactly the same ridiculous rhetoric.

Canadians, for example, who forcefully justify Canada's invasion of Afghanistan by pointing to ridiculous notions of civilizing the Afghans, by using self-righteous slogans such as promoting women's rights, are deliberately ignoring Canada's role in committing genocide and other crimes against our First Nations. We civilized our First Nations by exterminating most of them with our diseases and superior firepower. The remainder we imprisoned in reserves, which today still have poor housing without basic amenities such as heat and running water. We forced their children to attend Residential Schools so that our priests could abuse them and destroy their culture and language. We stole their land and fight their justified land claims in the courts to this day. We observe the Canadian media showing how the children on these reserves sniff gas because it's the cheapest drug. Then we relieve our guilt and shame by telling the world loudly and incessantly how China should improve its human rights. We condemn the use of child soldiers in Africa while condemning our child soldier, *Omar Khadr,* to torture in Bagram prison and Guantanamo.

The West today is civilizing the Muslim inhabitants of the world. Why? I do not have to repeat my skepticism of all religious beliefs. But the West believes in Jesus and the Muslims believe in Mohammad. Jesus was a carpenter who died nailed to a cross by the Romans. Of course the West claims that he walked on water and healed the sick with miracles. He is the son of God but his father forsook him when the Romans nailed him to a cross. His mother was still a virgin when she gave birth to Jesus. After he was buried he escaped from his grave and flew into the sky to join his father who had forsaken him. By contrast Mohammad was a caravan trader who dictated a book he claimed was revealed to him, united the tribes of a barren desert who had been ignored by all of the great ancient empires, and produced military leaders who conquered the Persian and Roman empires? That those who believe in Jesus, a simple carpenter, born in a manger because of poverty and crucified by the Romans and Jews can claim to be more civilized than those who believe in Mohammad, a military genius whose followers conquered the world, is yet another example of the upside-down logic of Western civilization. This is even more illogical when you add the fact that it's the West that deems a people to be more civilized the greater their military prowess and imperial conquests.

Da Gama's Historic Voyages to India

Despite the tragic colonization and exploitation of Asia, which followed da Gama's discovery of the sea route to Asia, and his many **crimes against humanity,** it has to be recognized that his first voyage in 1497–1498 was historic. King John II of Portugal ascended the throne in 1481 and set about expanding Portugal's trade in **slaves** and gold. He was also determined to capture as much as possible of the very lucrative spice trade from the Arabs. To do so he had to find an alternative to the historical overland trade route. In 1487 King John II sent out both an overland expedition and a sea expedition to find a route that would be less confrontational with the Muslims. This two-pronged approach indicated how determined the new king was. It should be noted that finding a sea route to Asia was the ultimate goal. But these explorations by land and sea would also enhance trade and colonies in Africa. In May of 1487, the king sent the explorers, *Pero da Covilha* and Arabic speaking *Afonso de Paiva,* on the overland mission across Africa with the objective of expanding trade and colonies in Africa and finding how the Arabs got to India across the Indian Ocean. The overland explorers penetrated Africa to reach Ethiopia. They also gathered important information on how to reach India from the East African coast and the island of Madagascar, just east of the African coast, in the Indian Ocean. It's very likely that Covilha traveled on an Arab ship to *Calicut*, the "City of Spices," and landed in November of 1488. He sent valuable information to King John II on how to reach India by sea around Africa and the location in India of the spice trade with the Arabs. This information was very likely used by Vasco da Gama to reach Calicut.

In October of 1487, the king sent the sea expedition under the command of Bartolomeu Dias to sail around Africa. This expedition, like many before, hugged the west coast of Africa to the Portuguese fortress on the Gold Coast. After picking up supplies the expedition continued along the coast to Angola, rounded Africa and continued up the east coast reaching Mossel Bay on February 3, 1488. Since the inhabitants of Mossel Bay were not welcoming, Dias continued along the East Coast to reach Kwaaihoek, located in the Eastern province of South Africa, in March of 1488. There Dias planted a stone cross to mark the furthest point of his expedition. In returning from Kwaaihoek, Dias encountered the storms of the Cape in May of 1488 and named it the Cape of Storms. King John II was so thrilled by Dias rounding the Cape that he renamed it the *Cape of Good Hope.* At the time it was assumed that the Cape was the southern tip of Africa. While the southern tip is located a little further southeast at Cape Agulhas, the fact remains that Dias had reached further along the African coast than any prior Portuguese explorer. King John II was presented with the immediate opportunity of further colonies and trade up the East Coast of Africa and the even more exciting possibility of seizing a good portion of the spice trade from the Muslims. Nothing excites a Western king more than riches combined with doing God's work.

Da Gama's First Voyage: 1497–1498

It was July of 1497 that King Manuel I dispatched Vasco da Gama to find the sea route from the Cape of Good Hope to Calicut. Da Gama had served King John II faithfully when he had been sent by the king in 1492 to destroy French attacks on Portuguese ships. Da Gama was given four ships and a crew of 170 men, including his brother, *Paulo.* Some of the most experienced Portuguese navigators, including the brother of Bartolomeu Dias, *Diogo,* were recruited for the voyage. In addition, Bartolomeu Dias accompanied da Gama until the Cape Verde islands.

The expedition departed from Lisbon on July 8, 1497. After Cape Verde it hugged the African West Coast to Sierra Leone before venturing into the open ocean. By mid-December it reached as far as the end of the 1488 journey of Bartolomeu Dias. Da Gama pushed further up the East African Coast reaching Mozambique. After Mozambique, da Gama engaged in one of the many ironic activities that Western historians deem to be civilized, **piracy,** taking advantage of lightly armed ships.

It was no coincidence that da Gama landed at the port of *Malindi* to seek help in finding the way to Calicut since there is evidence that *da Covilha* would have sent word to the king of Portugal that he had sailed to Calicut from Malindi. In any case, da Gama got a friendlier reception in Malindi compared with Mozambique and Mombasa. He was able to find and hire a local navigator to guide him from Malindi to Calicut. He landed in *Calicut* on May 20, 1498, and was able to secure a meeting with the ruler or *Zamorin* of Calicut. He was also allowed to do some genuine trade, not theft or colonization. Unfortunately, his gifts from King Manuel I did not impress the Zamorin. Moreover, the Arabs were opposed to Portugal encroaching on their monopoly of the spice trade.

While the Zamorins and their subjects were Hindus they had established long-term trade relations with the Muslims. The Muslims had also been allowed to build mosques in their sector of the city. At the time the city-state of Calicut was the center of the lucrative spice trade of the state of Kerala in Southern India. It was also the dominant city on the Malabar Coast of India. The Zamorin of Calicut also exercised control over his semi-independent "vassal" rulers in the other ports along the Malabar Coast.

Da Gama responded to the Zamorin's objections to a trade agreement between Calicut and Portugal with the arrogance and military force that would become the hallmark of Western colonization. It's important to understand that trade is a voluntary exchange between two partners. Once force is used it is no longer trade but colonization. The West has never been interested in pure international trade though it has used that term in its dealings with those it colonized. Colonization is **not** trade. International trade is a voluntary relationship based on mutual benefits to both trading partners. Imperialism is the military theft of the resources of colonies by the imperial power. It benefits one party at the expense of the other. The imperial power reaps positive benefits at the expense of the colonies. The West engages in trade, or other lofty platitudes such as civilizing the natives, only if it's too weak militarily to colonize. Lately, the lofty platitude has been "bringing democracy." Trade is often a necessary first step until sufficient military force is acquired to colonize. Colonization is always the ultimate goal.

This is the pattern that da Gama set, beginning with Calicut, when he forcibly captured Indians because the Zamorin refused a voluntary trade agreement. Despite offending the Zamorin and taking some locals by force da Gama had succeeded in his mission from King Manuel to find the route from South Africa to India. He was also able to do some very profitable trading before departing on August 29, 1498. Limited use of force was sensible since this was the first encounter. The next expedition would be better prepared militarily to force a "commercial treaty," the term preferred by Western historians instead of the correct term, Western colonization. The East did not know it at the time but this was the beginning of the fall of the East and the rise of the West.

Da Gama encountered some personal problems on his return. He was down to two ships when his ship, the *Sao Gabriel,* got separated from the only other ship, the *Berrio,* captained by *Nicolau Coelho.* Da Gama's brother, Paulo, became ill and da Gama stayed with him in Portugal's Cape Verde colony. As a result it was Coelho who first returned to Lisbon on July 10, 1499, with the great news for King Manuel I. Da Gama did not return to Lisbon until August 29, 1499. Nevertheless he returned a hero and was rewarded accordingly. Da Gama was awarded a substantial royal pension and the overbearing title of Admiral of "the Seas of Arabia, Persia, India and the Orient." The East and the Muslims would have rightly snickered at such a bombastic title but the West would eventually conquer Arabia, Persia, India and the Orient. It was not until 1519 that da Gama would receive a more realistic title, and full admission to Portugal's exclusive nobility, as count of Vidigueira.

Portugal's Second Expedition to India: Pedro Alvares Cabral: 1500

King Manuel I lost no time in pursuing his opportunity to colonize India. On February 15, 1500, he appointed *Pedro Alvares Cabral* as commander in chief of a squadron of thirteen ships to launch Portugal's colonization of India and simultaneously attack the Arab monopoly of the spice trade. Once again enrich your Crown while waging a crusade against the Muslims. Spices, not oil, were the spoils of the time. Pedro Alvares Cabral was of noble birth, educated, a knight of the *Order of Christ,* and more qualified as a military commander than a navigator. There were seven hundred soldiers in addition to the crew of seven hundred. This was more of a military mission than a trade mission. Trade if you must but colonize whenever you can. The Zamorin of Calicut had proved that he could not be easily seduced with Western trinkets. Among experienced navigators included in this expedition were Bartolomeu Dias and two who had accompanied da Gama, Diogo Dias and Nicolau Coelho. In addition, the expedition was briefed by da Gama himself on the route to Calicut taken by him.

The Portuguese fleet departed from Lisbon on March 9, 1500. It sailed past the Canaries and Cape Verde islands. By taking a more western route than da Gama the fleet landed in Brazil on April 22, 1500. This seemingly accidental landing in the New World had very important new colonization prospects for Portugal in Brazil, which we explain below. Water and supplies were picked up in Brazil. Four ships were lost in a storm as the expedition turned eastward towards the African coast. Bartolomeu Dias was among those who lost their lives. The ship commanded by his brother, Diogo, also got separated from the main fleet, but managed to return to Lisbon. The main fleet reached Malindi on August 2, 1500. Cabral recruited pilots for the last leg of the journey to Calicut, arriving on September 13. The Portuguese set about building a trading post on Indian land. It was attacked, forcing the Portuguese to retreat to their ships. Cabral then bombarded Calicut from his ships.

It has been written that the Portuguese were outraged by this attack, calling it a massacre. What amazes me is how Western historians and the Western media never tire of the same identical rhetoric after six centuries, beginning with this incident in India in 1500. The West invades some new land. The people defend their land and the West calls such defense barbaric. The West then vows to bring the barbarians to "justice." Of course, the West has absolutely no interest in justice only in conquests. In fact, the West has engaged in so much lie, deception and hypocrisy, it would have no idea what justice was, even if it had a remote interest in it. So it responds with greater military force. It then acts surprised and amazed that the colonists rebel and respond in like manner. It denounces even more the reasonable response of those defending their homes against increased Western aggression and proceeds to develop and use even more vicious weapons against those who are now totally defenseless or relatively lightly armed. It calls its invasion, civilized and the response of the colonists, "primitive and barbaric." In reality, the only thing civilized is the superior weapons of the Western aggressor and the only thing "primitive" is the weapons used by the defenders from Western aggression.

So the Portuguese again set the pattern of how the West would do business with the rest of the world in Asia, Africa and America. As we saw earlier, it would pretend to want trade but colonize. It would use slavery, Christianity and piracy as weapons. And now we see it would demonize those who resisted Western military invasion as barbarians, heathens, red savages, terrorists, cowards, communists, gooks, and Islamists. After six centuries you may have thought that this would have become tiresome but it has not. Now they add "killing his own people," to the list. They start civil wars in Libya, Yemen, Syria and other countries to remove an anti-Western ruler and demonize the ruler by saying that he is "killing his own people." In the U.S. civil war President Lincoln only killed aliens, not "his own people." And it's okay to kill other people, just bad to kill your own. Their convoluted logic always escapes me.

Cabral did not have sufficient firepower to defeat the Zamorin and colonize Calicut. However, he was aware that another port city, *Cochin,* a vassal city of the Zamorin, might welcome an alliance with him in return for his support for its independence. This divide-and-rule tactic was another weapon of Western colonization passed down from the Portuguese to the British and Americans, among others. Cabral sailed for Cochin in December of 1500, signed an alliance with the local ruler and set up a "trading post." As usual, it begins as a "trading post" but escalates into a military fortress capable of defending the invaders from punishment by the local landowners whose lands and resources the invaders steal. After loading his ships with spices Cabral began his return voyage on January 16, 1501. He lost more of his ships on the return voyage. A total of six ships were lost. But five ships returned fully loaded with spices. It had been a profitable voyage both in terms of money and, more importantly, in expanding Portugal's colonization of India.

Da Gama's Second Voyage: 1502

It was time for da Gama to make his second voyage to India. It was da Gama who had set the example of using military force to steal whatever you could. Naturally he could hardly wait to return with sufficient military force to punish the Zamorin for being so insolent as to question the right of the civilized West to **steal** his land. Cabral was also dying to command what was called the "Revenge Fleet." But he lost out to da Gama. King Manuel I could hardly wait to wage war on Calicut. According to Western historians, warmongering is an important mark of civilized behavior, especially when it's waged by a Christian king. This is why the American Empire has been the most civilized empire. It has waged more wars than any other. The "Revenge Fleet" consisting of fifteen fully armed ships left Lisbon on February 12, 1502. An additional five ships were scheduled to depart later and join the main fleet. It departed on April 1, 1502.

As I indicated earlier, Portugal was interested in colonies both in Africa as well as in India. Cabral's fleet had made landfall at *Sofala,* a gold trading port on the Southeast African Coast, on his return voyage. However, Cabral did not have the firepower to colonize Sofala. The Portuguese explorer, Pero da Covilha, had also visited Sofala in 1489 and identified its wealth from trading gold. Da Gama determined that he had sufficient firepower to colonize Sofala and steal as much gold as possible before proceeding to Calicut. He did just that on his second outbound voyage to India. Next da Gama landed in *Kilwa,* the dominant city-state in East Africa. He threatened the sultan and forced him to hand over some gold. Happy to have established his civilized credentials as a head thief and bully he sailed to Malindi.

In 1505 the Portuguese built a fortress in Sofala to protect their East African colonies. In 1507 the Portuguese colonized the island of Mozambique just north of Sofala. Cabral's fleet had also made landfall on the island of Mozambique on his return voyage. Da Gama had also made landfall on the island on his first outbound voyage to India in 1498. He had been well received by the locals but still plundered and bombarded the island on that occasion. Since these territories were ruled by Muslims at the time he was simply doing his civilized Christian duty. The island of Mozambique became the capital city for all of the Portuguese colonies in East Africa.

Da Gama landed on the southern coast of India just south of *Goa.* As he sailed south along the Indian coast toward Calicut he attacked and plundered the coastal city of *Onor.* Ships in the harbor were burnt. Next he threatened the city of *Batecala* with the same fate. The raja of Batecala saved his people by signing a piece of paper agreeing to cease trade with Arabs and pay an annual ransom to Portugal. But these crimes against the Indians pale in comparison to da Gama's next **massacre.** As da Gama continued along the southern coast of India toward Calicut he spotted a merchant ship, the *Miri,* carrying Muslim pilgrims returning from the Hajj in Mecca. Da Gama plundered the ship and set it on fire burning the pilgrims, men, women and children, alive. He had his crew circle the burning ship and kill any survivor trying to swim to safety. They circled the ship until it sank and everyone perished. Such a dastardly act by the civilized West, if committed today, would surely have garnered da Gama the same Nobel "War" prize awarded to President Obama for his wars against the Muslims in Iraq, Afghanistan, Pakistan, Yemen, Somalia, Libya and Syria. Nevertheless, da Gama's weapons, while civilized relative to the "primitive" weapons of the Indians and Arabs, pale in comparison to the weapons of the British and American empires. The Portuguese killed in the hundreds, three hundred on the Miri, but the British became more civilized by developing weapons that killed in the thousands. Now the Americans, the most civilized of all empires, kill in the **millions.** Da Gama would have had great difficulty competing with the likes of President Barack Obama who holds the record for the greatest numbers killed, maimed, homes and livelihoods destroyed. His legacy as the most civilized killing machine in history will be difficult to challenge even by a George W. Bush.

Da Gama proceeded to nearby *Cannanore* after the Miri massacre. There he forced the raja to agree to what Western historians hypocritically call a "commercial treaty." He next sailed further south to *Cochin.* Cochin had been secured by Cabral in 1500. Once again

Western historians refer to a "commercial treaty" with the ruler of Cochin. In reality it was an expansion of Portugal's colonization of the ports and cities along the Malabar Coast. The Portuguese had found a local traitor in the king of Cochin as an ally against the Zamorin of Calicut. Cochin had therefore been selected as their primary base for expanding their conquests in India. Alliance with a local ruler against a more formidable local opposition would be used over and over again by all of the European empires to pursue their ultimate goal of total domination. Once the local alliance had served its purpose it would be severed and its territory confiscated. Should the local puppet ruler raise any objections he would be demonized by the West as a vicious dictator who "kills his own people."

The English, French, Americans and Canadians made such temporary alliances with the First Nations in North America only to help them steal every inch of their land. While the British became infamous for their extensive use of this divide-and-rule strategic military tactic it was the Americans who perfected its use. The Americans would install a local puppet, usually a vicious local dictator, before or during an invasion. It would then claim to be invited by the people to liberate their country while giving minor governing duties to its local puppet. If the invasion was successful the Americans would stay and govern with the help of local puppets. If the invasion failed, as it did in China, North Korea, Vietnam, Iraq and Afghanistan, the United States would claim that the people no longer wanted its liberating efforts. Canada eagerly signed on as little brother to the U.S. invasion of Afghanistan when the United States used this same ploy in Afghanistan.

The Portuguese effectively colonized the Indian ports along the Malabar Coast by force. Henceforth, Portugal would dictate which nation would engage in the lucrative spice trade. Nations would either pay Portugal for the privilege of trading with its colonies or fight the Portuguese. Cannanore and Cochin were both trading hubs for the spice trade. The Portuguese used whatever superior military force they had to secure "trade concessions" in Cochin and Cannanore. With the Portuguese wresting control of the lucrative spice trade from the Arabs it was not surprising that the ruler of *Quilon* would want to get on board with the new boss. Quilon was another trading hub for the spice trade just south of Cochin. The ruler of Quilon invited da Gama to do business in Quilon. In response da Gama sent two ships to Quilon to load up on spices.

Early Battles for Calicut

What is surprising to me was the audacity of the Portuguese. The Arabs and Chinese had been trading with the spice ports along the Malabar Coast for centuries. Portugal was a relatively tiny Southern European state that had only recently secured its independence from the Moors and the Spanish. It had colonized some territory in areas on the African West Coast and in the Atlantic Ocean far removed from what was then the center of civilization. It had been very fortunate to get help from Muslim pilots to find its way to Calicut. Once it got there you would have thought that it would have been extremely happy to steal from the Arabs a small slice of what was a very large trade in spices. To have the audacity to oust the Arabs and all others was truly amazing. But that was its intention from the very beginning. We have already explained prior failed attempts by da Gama and Cabral to succeed in securing this monopoly.

A third attempt had been made by *Joao da Nova* who had commanded the third expedition sent to India by Portugal, a year before da Gama's second voyage. It had departed from Lisbon in March of 1501 and had landed on the Malabar Coast in August of 1501 in the same vicinity of Onor and Batecala where da Gama had landed on his second voyage the year after. As Da Nova sailed south toward Calicut he attacked and captured two merchant ships from Calicut. In Calicut's harbor he attacked and stole the cargoes of another three merchant ships. At least one of those ships belonged to the Zamorin. He burnt the ships in the harbor, an act clearly intended to publicly humiliate the Zamorin. This aggressive resort to piracy of merchant ships by the Portuguese led to the first *Battle of Cannanore.* As da Nova attempted to depart India with his ill-gotten booty the Zamorin launched a naval attack on December 31, 1501. Unfortunately, the Indian cannons were no match for those of the Portuguese. The battle raged on for two full days with the Portuguese doing most of the damage.

Da Gama was determined to try for a fourth time to conquer and colonize Calicut. He had effectively conquered all of the important spice cities that had been vassal states of the Zamorin of Calicut. He had acquired more than enough spices to fill all of his ships. If all he wanted was trade he would have departed India after completing his "trade" with Cannanore, Cochin and Quilon. But his goal was **colonization** not trade. The Zamorin of Calicut had not surrendered his territory as a colony of Portugal. Da Gama would have to invade and conquer it from the Zamorin. He was ready to attempt just that.

Da Gama's fully armed Armada arrived in Calicut on October 29, 1502. Da Gama set another precedent for the West, *ridiculous conditions,* before "negotiating." Once again, Western historians use the misleading term, "negotiation," when they mean colonization. That is why the preconditions set by the West are always ridiculous. The West never negotiates unless it is first whipped by military force. Da Gama's precondition for "negotiating" a commercial treaty with the Zamorin was the exclusion of Muslim traders. Such a ridiculous precondition was just another way of signaling da Gama's intension to **colonize** not trade. He reinforced this signal with another barbaric act. He captured fifty defenseless fishermen and strung them up by their necks to the masts of his ships for easy viewing by all along the Calicut beach. He was clearly intimidating and shaming the Zamorin by behaving as the typical civilized Westerner. As the Indians watched the civilized Western atrocity da Gama opened fire from his ships. He destroyed the houses along the beach. But the atrocity got even more civilized when the Zamorin refused to surrender. Da Gama cut off the hands and feet of the strung up fishermen and sent them by boat to the beach. He continued to bombard the city with his powerful cannons, destroying as many homes as he could.

Da Gama got a lucky opportunity to increase even further his civilized Western penchant for atrocities. A merchant fleet arrived in Calicut, unaware of da Gama's invasion. The fleet was quickly captured and relieved of its cargo by da Gama. The unlucky crew had their hands and noses cut off and their teeth pulled out. The Zamorin had sent an emissary to speak with da Gama. His emissary was sent packing with a bag filled with the body parts of the merchant crew. Da Gama blockaded the port of Calicut and patrolled the Malabar Coast to proceed with his colonization plans.

Another emissary sent by the Zamorin of Calicut to da Gama got the same civilized Western treatment. Da Gama not only cut off his ears but sewed on **dog ears** before sending him back to the Zamorin. Such brutal torture is always explained away by Western historians as anomalies rather than typical Western penchant for unique inventions of bestiality. It became clear to the Zamorin that da Gama was intent on colonizing his city by force. This led to the *Battle of Calicut* on January 5–6, 1503. Despite assistance from Arab pirates the Zamorin lost the battle. Da Gama won the Battle of Calicut but this victory did not enable him to colonize Calicut. It enabled him to hold, at least temporarily, his conquests in Cannanore, Cochin, Batecala and Onor. With his ships fully loaded with spices it was time for him to return to Portugal. Further conquests could safely wait for a future invasion. On his return to Portugal in September 1503 he advised King Manuel I of the need for greater military force to colonize Calicut.

Once da Gama had departed for Portugal, the Zamorin saw his opportunity to reclaim his losses. He set about reclaiming Cochin since it was his vassal raja of Cochin who had been the primary traitor in helping the Portuguese. He attacked Cochin in March of 1503. The raja of Cochin defended the Portuguese and engaged in a war with Calicut. He lost the war and the Portuguese fled the city of Cochin to a nearby island. Unfortunately for the Zamorin, Portugal's **fifth** expedition to India arrived in time to save Cochin from a complete reconquest. This fifth expedition had departed Portugal in April of 1503 before the return of da Gama from his second voyage. It was commanded by *Afonso de Albuquerque.* Albuquerque was a seasoned military commander who had fought the Muslims in both North Africa and the Mediterranean. Albuquerque rescued the raja of Cochin and erected the fortress of Fort Manuel in Cochin to defend it from reconquest by Calicut. He left an armed guard of 150 men in Fort Manuel. A Catholic church was added to aid in the colonization of Cochin. All of the European empires used the Christian religion to further their imperial conquests. This is yet another precedent set by Portugal.

Albuquerque, like da Gama, had failed to conquer Calicut but held on to the Portuguese conquests of the vassal spice hubs of Cochin and Cannanore. He also expanded the Portuguese presence in Quilon, the spice hub south of Cochin where da Gama had sent two of his ships for spices. Albuquerque established a "trading post" in Quilon and left an armed guard of twenty men.

The rise and fall of the Portuguese Empire provides a great example of our analyses of the rise and our predicted fall of the West. Portugal used many of the same weapons used by all of the Western empires to achieve dominance. These weapons included slavery, military victories, naval superiority, the Christian religion, hypocrisy, deceit and pretend democracy. With these weapons, this newly independent state from outside the center of the civilized world, Iberia, defeated the Indians, Egyptians, Ottomans, Mughals, and many more to carve out the first of the modern global European empires. Today Portugal begs its European partners for a bailout because it is buried under a mountain of debt and threatened with a return to Third World economic status. It is ranked as the world's forty-fourth's largest economy as measured by GDP. Its accidental colony, Brazil, by contrast, is ranked as the world's seventh largest economy today. Long before its current desperate plight the Western Europeans relegated it to **inferior** Southern European status. Portugal's demise can be traced back to its unwillingness to share power with the locals it colonized and its reliance on wars, deceit, hypocrisy and lies. Its overwhelming greed and desire to dominate led to its downfall. We predict that the West will experience the same fate as Portugal before the end of this century if it continues its six century old striving for continued world domination. It will self-destruct under the weight of its lies, hypocrisy and military expenditures. Its advanced military weapons will not save it from its fall.

Portugal Begins the Dominance of Sea Power

At the beginning of the sixteenth century the Muslim Ottomans were fighting the Christian Habsburgs for control of the historical center of civilization. We covered this at length in the previous chapter. While there were naval battles in the Mediterranean, it was typically the empire with the superior army that won the day. Portugal would change that by making sea power the more strategic military weapon. In addition, naval reinforcement arrived much faster by sea from a distant home base. This enabled a truly global empire across many oceans. One way of thinking of this major change is to compare the geographical area accessible from three mighty oceans, the Indian, the Atlantic and the Pacific, with the relatively small geographical area accessible from the Mediterranean Sea. My reading as a nonhistorian finds that both the Muslims and Christians were mostly unaware of this rise of Portugal to dominant imperial status. My reasoning is that the Muslims and Christians were so focused on what had for so long been the center of civilization that they were unable to think outside that box. Portugal wrested hegemony from both the Ottomans and the Christians fighting the Ottomans, mostly the Christians of Venice, France, Germany, Austria and Hungary. They were fighting for the control of the Mediterranean, the Middle East and the overland spice trade. In the meantime Portugal was fighting the Muslims in the Indian Ocean, in East Africa and in the spice ports along the Malabar Coast of India. It was not unlike the United States wresting hegemony from both Britain and Germany when superior air power replaced superior sea power after World War II.

The first five expeditions sent to India by Portugal had been more successful than anyone in Europe could have imagined. But Portugal was greedy for more and greater conquests. It saw an opportunity to get a monopoly of the lucrative spice trade, expand colonies in Africa and control traffic in the Indian Ocean. That opportunity was presented to it because the primary Muslim and Christian powers of the day were still fighting for control of the Mediterranean. They had failed to notice the global center of the world shifting from the Mediterranean Sea to the Indian Ocean. Portugal was determined to seize this opportunity before the great powers realized what was happening.

King Manuel I heeded da Gama's advice and sent the **sixth** expedition to squash the Zamorin's power and colonize Calicut. He was also intent on controlling the Indian Ocean. He had previously sent *Vincente Sodre* in 1503 to pirate and capture booty from Arab ships in the Indian Ocean. In typical Western fashion, Sodre's official title was Captain-major of the first Portuguese *Naval Patrol* of the Indian Ocean.

In practice Sodre was a "privateer," the term used by Western historians for pirates who were appointed by a Western state. Maritime powers, beginning with Portugal, were very willing to use the naval skills of pirates as a weapon of colonization. Portugal set the precedent for all of the modern Western European empires to sanction and encourage piracy. The Portuguese expeditions to India engaged in various degrees of piracy beginning with da Gama's first voyage. Sodre was the uncle of da Gama and just as **demented.** He is credited with capturing a wealthy Egyptian merchant, tying him naked to a post, forcing him to eat pork and beating him half to death before sending him back to Cairo.

In April of 1504 the sixth expedition departed with thirteen ships and 1,200 men, including soldiers, under the command of *Lopo de Albergaria.* De Albergaria's chief mission was to destroy the Zamorin of Calicut. He arrived in Calicut in September of 1504 and bombarded the city with the powerful cannons of his ships. Next he attacked the Zamorin's forces in *Cranganore* and destroyed it. His men sacked, looted and burnt the ancient city of Cranganore. A naval force sent by the Zamorin to defend Cranganore was defeated by the Portuguese. Another city, *Tanur,* was captured by the Portuguese after defeating a force sent by the Zamorin to defend Tanur. De Albergaria departed India loaded with spices after weakening and humiliating, but not destroying, the Zamorin, capturing two more vassal cities of the Zamorin and pirating other merchant ships. On his way out from Cochin north along the Malabar Coast he attacked and looted an Egyptian fleet, killing two thousand family members being evacuated from Calicut.

Portugal Formally Colonizes India in 1505: Seventh Portuguese Expedition to India

Portugal's formal colonization of India barely **six years** after da Gama first limped into Calicut in 1498 was truly an amazing feat. It rivaled the Spanish conquests of Mexico by Cortez in 1519 and of Peru by Pizarro in 1531 (see Mirza, *Rise and Fall of the American Empire,* chapter 1). In 1505 King Manuel I appointed his first "Viceroy of India." In fact, King Manuel had decided that a **Viceroy for India** was needed the year before when he nominated *Tristao da Cunha.* As it happened, da Cunha was stricken with temporary blindness and could not assume this most important colonial position. This was a lucky break for *Francisco de Almeida* who was appointed instead. The audacity of King Manuel I was later matched by the thirteen tiny English colonies in North America that called themselves the United States of America. Portugal had barely colonized a few spice ports along the Malabar Coast when it implicitly claimed India as its colony. In like fashion the thirteen tiny English colonies had taken from England a small portion of the thin Western coastline of the American continent when it named itself *America.*

Western historians have claimed that the founding fathers of the United States were "visionaries." They were indeed visionaries but very **evil** visionaries. As I have explained in *American Invasions* their evil vision was to steal by brutal military force as much of the prime real estate they could from the First Nations. King Manuel I of Portugal must have had the same evil vision for India. In 1505 he sent de Almeida to India with twenty-one ships to reinforce and expand both his Indian and East African conquests. De Almeida was given the lofty title of *Viceroy of India* before he had made those conquests just as the thirteen tiny English colonies took the name of *America* before they had conquered the First Nations lands across the continent.

We explained earlier how Portugal had impressed the pope by defeating the Muslims, first in Iberia and then in North Africa. King Manuel I was now expanding Portugal's crusade against the Muslims in East Africa, the Indian Ocean and in India itself. While the Christians of France, Germany, Venice, Austria, Hungary and England were still fighting the old battles against the Muslims via the Mediterranean, Portugal saw an opportunity to attack from the opposite side of the world. First it would conquer the Indian Ocean then invade Egypt and the Middle East. The Christians and Muslims must have both thought that the Portuguese king was insane. But it was precisely the audacity of King Manuel I, much like the audacity of the thirteen tiny English colonies that had become the United Sates, that helped both succeed. Britain had called the emerging American Empire a "puny" empire. The same could be said of the Portuguese Empire of 1505. Both the Portuguese Empire and the American Empire succeeded partly because the rest of the world ignored their conquests and treated them as inconsequential.

Portugal recognized that to conquer India it had to secure military bases along its sea route to India. This included islands in the Atlantic Ocean such as the Cape Verde islands, bases along the west coast of Africa to the Cape of Good Hope, and bases along the East Coast of Africa after rounding the Cape of Good Hope. This was exactly what the American Empire did in the Pacific Ocean to defeat Japan and conquer the Pacific. It's also the reason why the Japanese attacked the American *uncolony* of Hawaii and its military base in Pearl Harbor. See *Rise and Fall of the American Empire.* Prior to da Gama's voyage, Portugal had already secured sufficient military bases both on the West African Coast and in the Atlantic Ocean. By 1505 it had attempted to, but not yet secured, sufficient military bases on the East African Coast. It was for this reason that Viceroy de Almeida was commissioned with the task of securing sufficient military bases in East Africa before proceeding to India.

The most secured Portuguese military base in East Africa was *Malindi.* Portugal had also colonized *Sofala.* If the Portuguese were only interested in trade, the secure and friendly port of Malindi would have been sufficient. It was the port from which the Portuguese ships crossed the Indian Ocean, beginning with da Gama. Malindi had befriended the Portuguese from the very beginning of its spice trade with India. But like the American Empire later the Portuguese Empire was after world domination not trade. To secure its intent to monopolize the spice trade and remove the Arab traders Portugal had to destroy all opposition from the East African coastal city states. Portugal had already destroyed opposition from the city state of Sofala but the primary opposition to Portuguese domination came from the city state of *Kilwa.* In 1502 da Gama had used military force against Kilwa on his outward voyage and forced it to pay tribute. No one is happy to pay tribute. Kilwa would rebel if it had the opportunity and Portugal knew that. De Almeida's first military task was to conquer and colonize Kilwa.

De Almeida arrived in Kilwa on July 23, 1505, and attacked the city. The ruler of Kilwa fled the city and de Almeida found a local puppet to rule Portugal's new colony. A fortress was built in Kilwa and a garrison of eighty men was left to defeat any rebellion. Imbued by his easy conquest of Kilwa, de Almeida sailed north to *Mombasa* and attacked the city. Unlike Kilwa, Mombasa defended itself. While de Almeida won the battles he was unable to fully colonize Mombasa. He burnt the city and consoled himself with plunder and two hundred slaves, many of the slaves being children and women. Happy with his conquest of Kilwa and looting of Mombasa he crossed the Indian Ocean in late August. He landed on the island of *Angediva* and immediately constructed the two requisites of Western colonization, a fortress and a church.

Angediva was a strategic addition to the Portuguese colonies of Cannanore, Cochin and Quilon on the Malabar Coast. Angediva was slightly north of the two ports, Onor and Batecala, which da Gama had attacked, plundered and demanded ransom, during his second voyage. While Batecala had capitulated to da Gama, Onor had resisted and the port city had been looted and burnt. De Almeida burnt and looted Onor again to ensure no future resistance. With the conquests of Angediva, Onor, Batecala and Cannanore north of Calicut, and the conquests of Cochin and Quilon south of Calicut, the Portuguese were squeezing the Zamorin of Calicut from both sides. Like the British and French later, with regard to the North American East Coast, the Portuguese were conquering the spice rich Indian Coast as a prelude to conquering a "continent." When you invade a continent by sea your first goal must be to conquer the land along the coast.

In Cannanore de Almeida built another fortress before sailing to Cochin, where he strengthened Fort Manuel and took up residence. He sent six of his ships under the command of his son, Lourenco, to destroy the ships of the Zamorin of Calicut, anchored in Quilon. Lourenco destroyed twenty-seven ships and secured the Portuguese colony of Quilon. The Zamorin of Calicut attempted a naval response to the Portuguese aggression but lost the *Battle of Cannanore* to Lourenco in March of 1506. The Battle of Cannanore marks the beginning of small maritime nations like Portugal, Holland and England dominating the globe with naval power. This domination only ended with the advent of air power after the Second World War. England became the largest global empire before the Americans, because sea power was more far reaching than land armies. The Americans became the largest global empire because air power can reach even further.

The Portuguese Dominate the World in the Sixteenth Century

The immediate mission of the Portuguese was the destruction of the Zamorin's rule in Calicut. But the Portuguese, like any invader, faced new local opposition from the rulers of Cannanore and Gujarat. The Indian rulers also asked for naval assistance from Muslim Egypt and the Ottoman Empire as well as Christian Venice. The Muslim rulers of Egypt and the Ottoman Empire had a dual reason for supporting India. Portuguese aggression was cutting deeply into their profits from the overland spice trade and the Portuguese were simultaneously waging a new religious crusade against Muslims. The Venetians were the prime Christian beneficiaries of the overland spice trade. The Arabs sold their spices to the Venetians who then retailed it to the Europeans. The Venetian Christians had an important commercial reason to support the Arabs and their suppliers on the Malabar Coast. As a result Venice broke off diplomatic relations with Portugal and allied with the Muslims and Indians.

The problem for this unified opposition to the Portuguese was that the Portuguese control of the spice trade had occurred with such speed that it totally surprised both the Muslims and the Christians. Once again we see a parallel with the birth of the American Empire. When the thirteen tiny English colonies secured their independence from England both England and France largely ignored as ridiculous the notion that this "puny" emerging nation could ever be a threat to the powerful British or French empires. France helped the Americans get their independence from Britain as a strategy to weaken the British and increase French power in North America. In like manner the British supported the rebellious Americans at the peace treaty as a strategy to weaken France and increase British power and influence in North America. The Americans outfoxed both Britain and France just as the relatively "puny" nation of Portugal outfoxed the more powerful Ottomans, Venetians and Egyptians.

In 1507, the Zamorin of Calicut received military support from both the Arabs and the ruler of Cannanore. Portugal's puppet ruler of Cannanore had died in 1506. The new *raja* of Cannanore restored the historical relationship between Calicut and Cannanore, which had existed for centuries prior to the Portuguese invasion. His people were offended by the continued barbarity of the Portuguese. The most recent incident was when the Portuguese had brutally drowned the sailors of an Indian ship by stitching them into the sails of the ship so they could not escape when dumped into the ocean. Unfortunately for the Zamorin the previous puppet raja had allowed the enemy to build a fortress, *Fort St. Angelo,* in Cannanore before he died.

In April of 1507 the Zamorin and his allies laid siege to Cannanore. The siege lasted until August when Portuguese reinforcements arrived with Portugal's **eighth** expedition to India. Da Cunha, who had been unable to command the seventh expedition because of temporary blindness, arrived with eleven ships and saved Cannanore. On his outward voyage to India, da Cunha had expanded the Portuguese conquests in East Africa by conquering the island of *Socotra* and attacking the Arabs in *Mozambique.* The Portuguese had clearly enhanced their goal of ruling the waterway from the west coast of Southern Europe to the Malabar Coast of India.

The next year the Zamorin received naval support from Egypt, Venice and the Ottoman Empire. A combined Indian and Egyptian/ Venetian/Ottoman fleet defeated the Portuguese at the *Battle of Chaul,* March 1508, and the Viceroy's son, Lourenco was killed. Francisco de Almeida vowed to avenge the death of his son and expand the Portuguese Empire. He avenged his son's death at the *Battle of Diu,* February 1509. Once again the Portuguese took on a combined Indian and Egyptian/ Venetian/Ottoman fleet. But the Portuguese had received reinforcements from Portugal. The Viceroy had a much larger fleet than his son had had for the Battle of Chaul, consisting of eighteen ships. Francisco de Almeida was also very determined to simultaneously capture the important Indian port of *Diu* and avenge his son's death. He personally commanded the Portuguese fleet that launched the attack on Diu. Despite a defensive force made up of the local Indian rulers of both Calicut and Gujarat and supported by naval assistance from Egypt, Venice and the Ottoman Empire, the Portuguese won the *Battle of Diu.* Portugal had established that it had the superior navy and that sea power would now dominate the world.

The Ottoman Empire should have taken notice of this naval victory by the Portuguese. It did not and the reason was understandable but disastrous. No empire before had reached India by sea. The Persians, Alexander the Great, the Muslims, had all reached India by first dominating the Mediterranean, the Middle East and advancing slowly and painfully overland to India. The Ottomans had conquered Constantinople, the heart of the powerful Eastern Roman / Byzantine Empire. It had replaced the Christian Roman Empire with an equal Muslim Empire. It felt safe and saw no threat from an upstart barbarian state, Portugal, which had only recently secured its independence from Muslim Iberia.

What the Ottomans did not realize was that the Portuguese Empire had revolutionized warfare. It was the precursor of the American Empire. Like the American Empire today the Portuguese Empire could use its ships with large cannons to kill thousands while suffering few casualties. The Portuguese Empire was the sixteenth century **killing machine** equivalent of the American Empire. With its high tech planes and unmanned drones the American Empire killed **millions** in Vietnam, Cambodia, Laos, Iraq, Afghanistan, Pakistan, Yemen, Somalia, Libya and elsewhere, while suffering very few casualties.

The Indians handed over the Portuguese prisoners taken at the Battle of Chaul. They had been treated with respect and were well fed and clothed. The Portuguese showed how cruel and barbaric they were by burning alive many prisoners, blowing up their bodies with their cannons and hanging others. Portugal had set the standard for what the West would call civilization. Every barbaric act by Portugal was copied by Spain, Holland, France, Britain the United States and Canada. Western imperial powers share a rather eerie commonality of calling the most inhumane actions civilized. Just think of the speeches made in 2012 by Canada's prime minister, Steven Harper, and those of Israel's prime minister, Benjamin Netanyahu, with regard to the genocide committed against the Palestinians and you will get the picture.

The Zamorin of Calicut was on the defensive after the Battle of Diu. But *Afonso de Albuquerque,* who replaced de Almeida in 1509, was unable to fully destroy the Zamorin, despite continued reinforcements of ships from Portugal. In 1510 the Portuguese invaded, conquered and began their colonization of **Goa,** an important Indian port on the Arabian Sea, just north of the island of Angediva. The Portuguese transferred their colonial government of colonies in India and Asia to Goa. They began to mint their own coins in Goa. From Goa the Portuguese expanded northward into India settling in Madras, Bombay, Daman, Salsette, Diu, and Bassein. In addition to their conquests the Portuguese converted the Indians to Christianity. The Catholic church was combined with military muscle to colonize Asia. Hindus, Muslims and Jews were converted to Christianity. The *Goa Inquisition* used the barbarian tactics of the Spanish Inquisition to punish those who were accused of not being as faithful to the Catholic church as they should have been and to steal their property and wealth. This brutality to non-Christians increased the Portuguese control of the population but sowed the seeds for popular revolts.

The Portuguese also conquered territory outside East Africa and India. Many of the spices traded in India were imported from other countries in Asia. This was one of the many reasons for the Portuguese Empire to expand their conquests to other countries in Asia.

Ceylon was invaded in 1505 and Madagascar in 1506. On his second voyage to India, de Albuquerque conquered *Hormuz* in the Persian Gulf, in 1507. Together with da Cunha's conquest of Socotra the Portuguese controlled the entrance to the Red Sea. This blocked the old sea route to India via the Mediterranean. Malacca in Malaysia was invaded in 1509 and Thailand in 1511. The rich spice islands of the Moluccas, as well as Indonesia and Mauritius, were invaded in 1512. China was invaded in 1513 and Timor in 1514. Japan was invaded in 1542. The Chinese island of Macau was occupied by the Portuguese in 1557. In the Persian Gulf the Portuguese added Bahrain to their conquests. These global conquests established the Portuguese Empire as the dominant empire controlling the East-West trade during the sixteenth century.

Attempts by the powerful Ottoman Empire to challenge Portuguese hegemony failed, but only because the Ottomans were myopic. After winning the Battle of Dui the Portuguese built a formidable fort in Diu in 1535. In 1538 the Ottoman Empire allied with the sultan of Gujarat to attack the Portuguese stronghold in Diu. The attack failed. The Ottoman Empire continued to form other alliances in Asia to launch naval attacks on the Portuguese for most of the sixteenth century, but they were halfhearted. One of the more important of these alliances was that with the sultan of Aceh. Located in Indonesia, the sultanate of Aceh waged war on the Portuguese for control of the trade through the Strait of Malacca in the Malay Peninsula. Ottoman opposition, combined with attacks by Ottoman allies such as the sultan of Aceh, threatened Portuguese hegemony but did not displace it.

The clearest example of Ottoman myopia was its wars against the Venetian Republic in the sixteenth century. As we said earlier the Venetians were implicit commercial allies of the Muslims because of the spice trade. Prior to the Portuguese conquests in East Africa, India and the Persian Gulf, it may have made some sense for the Ottomans to wage wars on the Venetians to control the Mediterranean. But to have continued to do so after the Portuguese conquests and threats to the lucrative spice trade was stupid and childish. Since both the Muslims and the Venetians suffered from the Portuguese aggression, it made strategic sense for the Ottomans to ally with the Venetians against the Portuguese. This was even more sensible given the Portuguese advance of naval warfare and the fact that the Venetians were also an advanced naval power. The Ottoman Empire squandered its opportunity to form an alliance with the Venetians against the Portuguese by waging **three** expensive and disastrous wars against the Venetians in 1499–1503, 1537–1540 and 1570–1573. It won most, though not all, of these wars. But it was fighting for the control of the Mediterranean that was the ancient and dying waterway of the civilized world. While wasting its costly warmongering resources for control of the Mediterranean it allowed the Portuguese to control the modern waterway, the Indian Ocean, of the future civilized world.

Portugal's Empire in the New World: Brazil

We began our history of the two Iberian empires with Portugal rather than Spain because the Portuguese Empire predated the Spanish Empire from a global perspective. However, with regard to imperial conquests in the New World, Portugal followed Spain. While Portugal's empire outside the New World was planned, its rediscovery of Brazil was as much an accident as Spain's rediscovery of the New World. The other coincidence is that both Spain and Portugal stumbled on their New World discoveries while searching for Asia. In Portugal's case, Spain had already stumbled on parts of the New World, without fully understanding what it had found, before Portugal stumbled on Brazil.

After finding the sea route to India in 1498 it was only natural that Portugal would pursue this commercially lucrative find with great vigor. Portugal selected *Pedro Alvares Cabral* to captain a second and much larger voyage to India within months of da Gama's return. Da Gama returned to Lisbon at the end of August 1499 and Cabral departed Lisbon in early March of 1500. Da Gama had four ships and a crew of 170 men. Cabral had thirteen ships with 1,400 men, half of whom were soldiers.

Cabral's journey from Lisbon to the Cape Verde islands was to be expected since all previous Portuguese expeditions had taken that route. What no one has been able to explain is why he sailed so far West after the Cape Verde islands instead of the route taken by da Gama and Dias. One possibility was that Cabral was looking for more islands in the Atlantic especially since Columbus had claimed to have found new land to the West. In any case, Cabral accidentally or willfully landed on the American continent on April 22, 1500, south of where Columbus had explored. This was fortunate since the landing on the North-eastern coast of Brazil was just within the Portuguese half of the world established by the *Treaty of Tordesillas* of 1494. This was the treaty that divided the entire world between Portugal and Spain, with the implicit blessing of the pope.

Prior to Cabral's landing in Brazil the Portuguese had explored Newfoundland and Labrador but had not colonized them. Cabral exchanged gifts with the inhabitants of Brazil and picked up provisions for his journey to India. Despite the fact that the land was inhabited, Cabral claimed it for Portugal signaling his intention to have Portugal **steal** the land by military force. The people had inhabited this land for thirty thousand years. Yet Western historians referred to them as "indigenous" as if to say that they were somehow peripheral. At least that is what terms like *indigenous, First Nations, aborigines* have come to mean both with regard to the original owners of the lands and resources in the

New World and in Australia. The entire premise of this brutal Western colonization and **theft** of resources from the inhabitants of the New World was, and still is, implicitly justified by using the term "indigenous" to marginalize those who had lived and owned the land and its resources for thousands of years.

Theft is theft and it should be called that. It was theft by Europeans, Americans, Canadians and Australians, using superior military force, from the people of the Americas and Australia. It was theft in 1500 and its still theft today. The people of the New World and Australia must be paid in full for the land and resources stolen from them by Portugal, Spain, France, England, the USA, Mexico, Canada, and Australia. "Indigenous" is not some kind of inferior minority that should be regarded as another charity cause for the West. The West has absolutely no moral right to criticize a single other nation for the worst human rights abuses until it repents for its genocide of the people of the New World and Australia, and fully compensate them for the land and resources it stole from them. The Western strutting of its supposed morality is nothing more than a cover for its innate immorality.

Cabral explored the east coast of Brazil to find a safe harbor and get an idea of how much land was available for Portugal to **steal.** He found his safe harbor at *Porto Seguro* and planted a wooden cross, twenty-three feet in height, to signal the collusion of the Catholic church in the theft of the land of the inhabitants. Cabral hastily sent one of his ships with the news of his discovery to King Manuel rather than wait for his return from India. The new land should be stolen by force as quickly as possible before some other thief took it. With the inhabitants being so friendly and hospitable to the potential robbers, Cabral was convinced that conquest would not be difficult. In fact, finding owners of the land was a clear benefit since they could be forced into slavery to provide the labor to work on their own land after it was stolen from them by Portugal. It was a double win for the thief.

The immediate resource to be **stolen** from Brazil, in addition to the land of the inhabitants, was not spices, but a red dye. The dye was used as a stain for expensive textiles. While less lucrative than the spices of Asia, Portugal was the typical greedy European empire. It had to steal as much as it had the military power to. In fact some of the riches from the spice trade could be used to finance expeditions to Brazil. While concentrating its theft on the land and spices of Asia it simultaneously colonized Brazil.

King Manuel sent a second expedition to Brazil in 1501 and a third in 1503. As usual, the Portuguese initially pretended to be friendly traders paying the inhabitants to provide them with the *brazilwood* from which the dye was extracted. But once it was confident of its military superiority colonization began and the inhabitants who had befriended the Portuguese were **enslaved.** Resistance by the inhabitants was no match for the military brutality of the conquerors. The inhabitants were mostly hunter gatherers without civilized weapons.

Portugal's first large scale military expedition was sent in 1530. Its first colonial settlement of *Sao Vicente* was in 1532. Between 1534 and 1536 there were fifteen colonial settlements. These were united under a single colonial administration in 1549. The *Jesuits* landed in Brazil that same year to ensure that the Christian church would get its fair share of the colonial spoils. The Catholic church worked hand in glove with the military brutality of the invaders to enslave and rob the Brazilian people. The Jesuits were good at learning the language of the Brazilian people, which helped the Portuguese to convert some to Christianity. Once an inhabitant was converted to Christianity he would help rather than resist the theft of their land and resources. The West would call this theft of land "civilizing the natives." In this context, civilizing meant **stealing** with minimal use of force.

Sugar was the Brazilian colonial product that rivaled the wealth from the spices of Asia. The wealth came partly from the high price of sugar in Europe and partly from the riches of the African "slave trade" which the production of sugar fueled. Prince Henry the Navigator had enriched Portugal from both the gold of Africa and the African "slave trade." Portugal did the same in Brazil but with sugar instead of gold. The slave trading forts that the Portuguese had built on the West African Coast proved invaluable for capturing Africans to sell as slaves to the Portuguese sugar barons in Brazil.

In 1549 the Portuguese king, *John III,* sent his first governor-general, *Tome de Sousa,* with a massive military reinforcement, to centralize the colonial administration. The capital city was established at *Salvador da Bahia.* Wars with the inhabitants whose land had been stolen were inevitable. But Portugal used the same divide-and-rule tactic it began in India. The inhabitants of the land stolen by the Portuguese were divided along tribal lines and manipulated or intimidated by the Portuguese. The Brazilian people's fierce resistance to the Christian church was evidenced by the fact that they killed and ate Portugal's first bishop of Brazil to prove their point. Unfortunately, they had little natural immunity to European diseases and were easily infected by the Jesuit priests. Thousands died of smallpox, typhoid, dysentery, tuberculosis, measles and the flu. While sugar was the most profitable product the Portuguese also stole land to produce tobacco, cotton and other products. These were all valuable exports to Europe. The city of Sao Paulo was created in 1554. Rio de Janeiro was founded in 1565.

The Confusion of Westernization with Civilization

This final section of this chapter may seem repetitive and redundant. Many who read my book will dismiss it as a continuation of my unjustified rant against the West. From my standpoint I see it as the only reason to donate my time to this worthy cause. I have not studied the Western European empires in the same depth that I have studied the American Empire. However, I have concluded that Western European colonization outside the New World made some effort to co-opt the leadership and culture that they found in the East. During the five centuries of Western European imperialism from 1450 to 1950 the Western European imperial powers of Spain, Portugal, France and Britain, were governed primarily by the wealthy and educated aristocracy. This governing class was very conscious and protective of its privileged and "cultured" birthright. Rather than empower the masses in its own countries it was more willing to forge links with the equally privileged and "cultured" ruling class of its colonies in India, Asia, North Africa and the Middle East. It was somewhat torn between its desire to conquer and subjugate and its desire to enlighten and civilize, even though the desire to conquer and subjugate was always more dominant than the desire to enlighten and civilize.

Its civilizing instinct or mission must also be interpreted in the context of its own privileged class at home and its view that the masses in its own country were "uncivilized" and uneducated. In this context it was somewhat willing and eager to learn the culture and civilized behaviors of the equally privileged ruling class of the Eastern countries it colonized. While I have no desire to downplay the evils of any form of colonization I am attempting to distinguish the five centuries of Western European imperialism outside the New World to be able to demonstrate why American leadership of the West, after the Second World War, killed any chance of the West making the world either civilized or democratic. Had Western Europe continued to lead Western imperialism in the East and Middle East there was always a small chance that the West would have been somewhat willing to learn from the East and gradually develop and share fundamental human rights and genuine freedoms.

Control of the world by the American Empire after the destruction of Western Europe by the Second World War caused Western Europe to regress from some of its more progressive beliefs. One example of this is how Western Europe came to join with the American Empire in demonizing *communism* even though communism, and its superior moral vision of communal property over private property, was born in Western Europe. Another example is the American led Western control of institutions, intended to be international, such as the United Nations, the World Bank, the IMF and the WTO. Another example is the use of the $US as the world's dominant reserve currency and the control of the world's media by the United States. Western European intellectuals went into hiding after the rise of the American Empire. Western European statesmen disappeared off the face of the earth and Western Europeans more and more dumbed down their political leaders to the level of the American political leaders.

The West may always have deprived itself of being led by the most gifted, wise and civilizing of its people. But I see much evidence of Western leadership becoming even more stupid, unwise, callous, hypocritical and inhumane since the American Empire became the "leader of the free world." The most obvious example of this is the use by the West of bigger and bigger bombs to kill more and more innocent people and destroy more and more of the world's resources. At least earlier Western colonization stole the resources for the benefit of a small minority of people. Now the United States and its Western allies just destroy, kill and maim, to the benefit of no one. It has become a **video game** since Western casualties are relatively few compared to non-Western casualties. It also seems to me that the institutions for peace are marginalized by the public giving them very little traction. People in the West are more easily galvanized to save animals and the environment or provide charity for those who are very poor both in the West and outside the West. These are great causes but why is it increasingly difficult for a peace movement to get to anything like a critical mass when it's so obvious that what is saved from warmongering can do so much more than any amount of charity.

Poor Americans have suffered greatly from the expensive and totally unnecessary warmongering of President Obama. But either the poor do not complain about this or if they do the American and Western media refuse to show it. People in Libya, Egypt, Syria and elsewhere suffer immensely from the civil wars begun by the West. Yet we see from the Western media only those who seem to enjoy being uprooted to become refugees. We never see those who must blame the West for destroying their livelihood and killing their children and women. We also never hear from the thousands of migrant workers of Asia who fled the Middle East because of the Western instigated civil wars. There is no purpose to these civil wars since it was the West that installed and supported the leaders who are now vilified as dictators. Is it just another insane divide-and-rule tactic of the West pitting the Saudis and Turks against the Persians?

CHAPTER 5

The Spanish and Dutch Empires Continue the Myth of Western Civilization with More Religious Persecution, Warmongering, Genocide of First Nations, Slavery, Piracy, and Theft of the Land and Resources of Those Colonized by Military Force and the Christian Church

We continue our history of the birth of Western domination by documenting the rise of the two Western European empires to follow the Portuguese Empire. As we explained earlier, an important difference between previous empires and the modern Western empire was the transformation of the post-Roman nation-states of Western Europe into several competing Western European empires. This began with the empires of Portugal, Spain and Holland. It later expanded to France, Britain, Germany, Italy, Sweden, Belgium and others. While they competed with each other they presented a "united" expansion of the West, relative to both the East and the Middle-East.

This "united" front was not always deliberate but derived from geographical commonality in Western Europe, commonality of Christianity, commonality of the rise of sea power, commonality of **white racism,** commonality of enslaving Africans and First Nations, **blacks, and reds,** commonality of an increasing sense of the superiority of Western culture and governance, commonality of theft of land and resources from those militarily unable to defend against colonization, commonality of the use of piracy, commonality of the use of propaganda, and commonality of warmongering. Most important of all was the delusion that their behavior was **civilized.** In reality nothing could be more barbaric than the firm belief in slavery, piracy, racism, warmongering, religion, especially religious persecution as exemplified by the *Spanish Inquisition,* limited freedom of the press, limited reduction of poverty and the replacement of leadership by the dumbing down of democracy to the point that votes had to be bought with gross lies and deception.

Spain was the first of the Western European empires to follow Portugal. While Spain had competed with Portugal for lands in Iberia that were taken from the Muslims, its empire mostly complemented that of Portugal. This was different from Holland, which mostly competed with Portugal, and, to a lesser extent, Spain. A second difference was that Portugal and Spain initially began as independent nation-states and empires but later united in 1580 under King Philip II, forming the powerful Iberian Union. Holland, on the other hand, began as a colony of Spain and became an imperial power while fighting for its independence from Spain. That independence came shortly after the Iberian Union between Portugal and Spain. The relatively tiny nation-state of Holland quickly developed a navy that would compete successfully with the unified Iberian empire for world domination in both Asia and the New World. In addition to superior sea power its other civilized weapons were the **slave trade** and **piracy.**

A third difference was that Portugal and Spain were both Catholic-Christian states while Holland was a Protestant-Christian state. Being Christians was a unifying feature but the Protestant/Catholic division added another dimension to their competition for imperial domination. Christianity had already splintered into Greek Orthodox and Roman Catholic after the division of the Roman Empire into East and West. Now the Western half was dividing into Catholics and Protestants. Divisions into different sects within Christianity helped the Muslims. But the Muslims were even more divided. Today Christians are much more unified while the Muslims are even more divided.

These three empires, together, laid the foundation for the subsequent rise of the West. During their heyday in the sixteenth and seventeenth centuries the West did not rule the world. The Middle East, China and India were still powerful entities yet to be penetrated by the West. But the riches that they acquired from trade and colonization were imitated by France, Britain and others. The Ottoman Empire had conquered Constantinople to dominate the world and monopolize the spice trade. The Mongols had invaded and conquered both China and India. While

Portugal, Spain and Holland were carving out the thin coastal strips of India, Indonesia, Japan and the Americas, the Ottomans, China and the Mughal Empire in India, still felt secure. Sea power could not penetrate into the hinterland, or so it may have seemed. The powerful cannons of the navy could level the defenses of coastal areas but had limited reach into the interior cities and rural areas. The non-Christian empires, both in the old and the new worlds, would soon pay a heavy price for their complacency. More on that in the next chapter.

Birth of the Independent Nation-State of Spain

In this chapter we begin with Spain since it predated the Dutch Empire. As with Portugal, we begin with the creation of the nation-state of Spain. Much of what we documented in the previous chapter for Portugal overlaps with the origins of Spain, as a nation-state, since both states were carved out simultaneously from the Iberian Peninsula by the *Reconquista.* In the previous chapter we traced the *Reconquista* to the birth of the independent state of Portugal out of the "county of Portugal" which was part of the *Kingdom of Leon.* The independent state of Spain would also be born out of the Kingdom of Leon.

The Kingdom of Leon originated from the small Northern Christian holdout, *Asturias,* during the rule of Iberia by the Muslims. It took its name from the city of Leon, which was founded by the Roman Empire. The Kingdom of Leon was born in 910 when the capital of Asturias was moved to the city of Leon. It merged with Castile in 1037 under the rule of Ferdinand I. King Alfonso VI, who ruled Leon, Castile and Galicia, was crowned *emperor of Spain.* His conquest of the Muslim city of Toledo in 1085 was an important milestone in the Reconquista. King Alfonso VII of Leon, Castile and Galicia, 1111–1157, also took the title of emperor of Spain.

King Alfonso VIII, 1158–1214, defeated the *Almohad Dynasty* at the Battle of *Las Navas de Tolosa,* in July 1212. This marked the beginning of the end of Muslim rule in Iberia. King Ferdinand III, 1217–1252, conquered the important cities of Cordoba and Seville. Cordoba was conquered in 1236 and Seville in 1248. Other cities captured by King Ferdinand III included Badajoz, Merida, Cartagena, Huelva, Lucena, and

Alicante. The only remaining Muslim holdout in Iberia was the Emirate of Granada.

The Kingdom of Castile was united with the Kingdom of Aragon in 1479. King Ferdinand of Aragon had married Queen Isabella of Castile in 1469. This unification of two powerful Christian kingdoms doomed the fate of the disunited Muslim rulers of Grenada. Isabella and Ferdinand quickly became known as the *Catholic monarchs* who would launch the final crusade against the Muslims in Iberia. They began the conquest of Grenada in1482. Unlike the Christian rulers, the Muslim rulers continued to squabble with each other making Granada a relatively easy target. After ten years of intermittent warfare the Emir of Grenada, Muhammad XII, surrendered his emirate to Castile on January 2, 1492. This final conquest of Muslim Iberia marked not only the end of Muslim expansion against Christian Europe but the beginning of the domination of the world by the Christian West. That domination would last until the present century. For the first time in six centuries the West is under threat from Muslims and ancient empires such as China and India.

Religious Persecution and the Spanish Inquisition

The most important fact that we take from the Spanish Empire to illustrate the primitive behavior of the West is the extreme forms of religious persecution under the terror of the *Spanish Inquisition.* The West has a habit of glossing over its innate barbarity and using language and propaganda to trumpet a false sense of civilized behavior and cultural superiority. But persecution of the Jews was not an invention of Adolf Hitler. It was an innate characteristic of the Christian West and best exemplified by Spain both before and after its conquest of Iberia from the Muslims. Under the first of the modern Western empires, Portugal, the West had honed its innate primitive nature by engaging in warmongering, military invasions and conquests, enslavement of nonwhites, racism, piracy, theft of the land and resources of those militarily weaker, and use of propaganda. The second of the modern Western empires, Spain, added religious persecution to this ever-growing list of actions that support our contention that the West has never been civilized but always primitive and barbaric.

Religious persecution is timeless but we begin with the Roman Empire since our goal is to show that the West has not made us any more civilized. The Roman Empire persecuted the Christians beginning with the crucifixion of Jesus Christ. But once the Roman Empire embraced Christianity after Emperor Constantine it was the Christians who began persecuting others. Christians were given political power to persecute non-Christians by the powerful Roman Empire. In our view that makes the Roman Empire barbaric not civilized. It is somewhat ironic that it was the Jews who lived among the Christians and bore the brunt of Christian religious persecution. It is even more ironic that today the primary example of religious persecution is carried out by Jews against Palestinians in the same Holy Land where the Jews conspired with the Romans against Jesus Christ. Today the Jews conspire with the Christian West against the Muslims of Palestine and the Middle East. The Jews today have been given the political and military power to persecute Palestinians by the American Empire and its closest ally, Canada. In our view this makes the American Empire and Canada barbaric, not civilized.

These three religious groups, Jews, Christians and Muslims, have been at war with each other since the birth of Islam. In the beginning, Islam was much kinder to the Jews than Christianity. Since the planting of Israel as an "uncolony" of the United States in the Middle East, Christianity has bonded with the Jews in a joint effort to conquer the Middle East from the Muslims. We have explained this at length in our prequels, *Rise and Fall of the American Empire* and *American Invasions.* But before we get to the present century where Jews and Christians are common brothers in arms against Muslims, we begin here with the persecution meted out to both Jews and Muslims by the rising Iberian empire of Spain.

We begin with the Spanish persecution of Jews since that predated its persecution of Muslims. This was simply a matter of political power. You need political power to persecute. That is why the Jews today persecute the Muslims in Palestine. The Jews have the political power because of military support from the Christian West. When the Muslims controlled most of Iberia, the Spanish could only persecute the Jews, and only in the parts of Iberia that they had conquered from the Muslims. But once all of Iberia was conquered the Spanish were able to persecute both Jews and Muslims. Persecution of the Jews in Iberia began after the Visigoth rulers converted to Christianity in the sixth century. During the seventh century Jews were forced to convert to Christianity or be expelled from Iberia by Christian rulers. Is it not ironic that since 2014 it's the Christians who are being forced to convert to Islam by ISIS?

Most Jews welcomed the Muslim conquest of Iberia because they had been so persecuted by the Christian rulers. Under Muslim rule, far from being persecuted, they were given a great degree of freedom to practice their religion. The Jews of Iberia experienced what has been called a "Golden Age" following the Muslim conquest in the eighth century. With better economic opportunities under Muslim rule many Jews immigrated into Iberia.

Birth of Inquisitions, Segregation, Ghettos, and Race Riots

The Reconquista was a disaster for the Jews in Iberia, much as the Crusades were a disaster for Jews throughout Christian Europe. When the Christian West fought Islam it simultaneously persecuted Jews. Inquisitions began with the papal bull, *Ad abolendam,* issued by Pope Lucius III in November 1184. It was intended to be used by Catholics to deter and punish those who dared to question the orthodox teachings of the Catholic church. These "Papal Inquisitions" began in France and later spread to other European states. Western historians singled out the Spanish Inquisition for special attention for much the same reason that Western historians have singled out the persecution of Jews by Adolf Hitler for special attention. Only when barbaric acts committed regularly by the West take on extreme forms does the West condemn them.

The West thinks of many barbaric acts such as racism, warmongering, religious persecution, piracy, torture, imperialism, genocide, etcetera, as normal and acceptable. How else would they dominate others? The West is outraged only if these acts are committed by non-Western countries or becomes extreme in the West. Every Western country persecuted Jews at the time Hitler was persecuting them. Hitler's only crime, according to the West, was to be so extreme. In like manner, the Catholic church used "Papal Inquisitions" to commit numerous crimes, including torture, against humanity. The Spanish Inquisition made the mistake of being too extreme. Every American president has committed numerous crimes against humanity. President George W. Bush made the mistake of being too honest about his crimes. At the other extreme, President Barack Obama is a master at fooling his supporters with regard to his many crimes against humanity.

Massacres of Jews in Iberia began after the Christians lost the *Battle of Ucles,* against the Muslims, in 1108. These massacres or **race riots** led to the killing of Jews and the burning of their synagogues and homes. Jews were forced to wear a yellow badge on their clothing so that they could be easily identified. Crusaders invited into Toledo by the Archbishop in 1212 massacred many of the Jews living in that city. In April of 1250 Pope Innocent IV issued a papal bull that imposed a high degree of **segregation** between Jews and Christians as well as making it difficult for Jews to build new synagogues. This was yet another barbaric trait copied by the United States when it segregated blacks and whites. Far from being hallmarks of civilized behavior they are characteristics of primitive and inhumane behavior. Jews in Spain were forced into *Ghettos,* called, *Juderias,* much like blacks later in the United States. In addition, laws were passed to place severe restrictions on Jews, which would limit their participation in the economy and in the professions and, in general, impoverish them. The Jews of Iberia were treated much like First Nations and blacks were treated by the civilized West in the New World.

Anti-Semitism in Spain increased in the fourteenth century along with the expanding conquests by Spain in the Iberian Peninsula. This led to frequent *massacres* of Jews, the most bloody being those of 1366 and 1391, much like the frequent race riots experienced later by blacks in the United States. Race riots, massacres of minorities, segregation, and ghettos became cherished characteristics of every civilized Western state. England, France, and the United States were very proud to copy what was being done to the Jews by civilized Spain.

Conversos, Ethnic Cleansing, and the Unique Role of the Spanish Inquisition

Christianity is always looking for new converts. Jews in Iberia were easy targets. Having been discriminated against, segregated into ghettos, subjected to massacres, race riots and mob violence, impoverished by legal restrictions on their economic activities and the destruction of their homes and properties, and having their synagogues burnt, Jews were encouraged to convert to what they were told was the only true religion, Christianity. Many chose to convert rather than suffer the brutality and inhumanity of the civilized West. But many Jews held on to their faith and were threatened with expulsion from Iberia. Expulsions of Jews by most of the civilized Christian states of Europe were quite common and had been done by France and England, two stalwarts of Western civilization. Jews were expelled from England in 1290 and from France in 1321. Expulsions were not only popular but also lucrative since the wealth and property of the Jews were confiscated by the civilized Christian rulers. Convert to Christianity or be forcibly expelled from Iberia in poverty. Two stark choices! Many chose to convert and became known as *Conversos.* But this created a problem for the civilized Christian rulers.

Jews who were forced to convert to Christianity were very likely to continue to practice their faith in secret. But Christianity could not tolerate false conversions. In addition these false converts took advantage of the economic and political opportunities open to them as Christians. They became both rich and powerful. In many ways the forced conversions had back-fired on the naive Christians. The "Papal" Inquisitions were given the task of ensuring that Conversos ceased practicing Judaism and practiced Christianity. If a Converso was suspected of secretly engaging in Jewish religious practices he/she would be charged, tried and punished by the Inquisition. But the rulers of Spain were not content with having the "Papal" Inquisitions punish, threaten and torture Conversos. It wanted this power in its own hands. In previous chapters we have explained the continuing conflicts between the pope and the national rulers of the independent nation-states that occupied the territory of the Western Roman Empire. This is one more example of that continuing conflict for power.

In 1478 the Catholic monarchs Ferdinand II of Aragon and Queen Isabella of Castile asked the pope to permit the establishment of an Inquisition in Castile to investigate these false Jewish converts known as *Crypto-Jews.* Ferdinand II further threatened to withdraw his military support against the Turks unless Pope Sixtus IV granted him and Queen

Isabella independent control of the Inquisitions and the right to appoint their own Inquisitors. In 1478 the pope issued a Papal Bull to grant such powers to the Catholic monarchs Ferdinand II and Queen Isabella. This enabled the creation of what came to be known as the *Spanish Inquisition.* In reality this was not a single Inquisition in Castile but Inquisitions in each of the major cities in the Kingdom of Castile. The first civilized act of the Spanish Inquisition was to order the burning of six convicts alive.

In 1483 *Tomas de Torquemada* became the inquisitor-general. In that year most Jews who had not converted were forcibly expelled from Spain. By 1492 the Spanish Inquisition was active in eight cities in the Kingdom of Castile. Torture was used to extract confessions from those charged. During de Torquemada's fifteen-year tenure he ordered at least two thousand public executions. Other convicts were sentenced to life imprisonment. Those who confessed being guilty of the charges and/or accused others, were given lighter sentences.

The Infamous Alhambra Decree of 1492

When Granada was conquered from the Muslims by Spain it presented another "Jewish problem" for Spain. As we said Jews were treated much better by Muslim rulers than by civilized Christian rulers. In Muslim Granada they had prospered. Now they would be persecuted as all other Jews in Spain. But persecution had not been sufficient to force them to convert. And when they had converted they had continued to secretly practice their faith. Civilized Christian Spain could not permit such religious toleration. One of the hallmarks of what the West deems to be civilized is intolerance for any religion except Christianity. So it was that the Catholic monarchs issued the *Alhambra decree* on March 31, 1492. Under this decree all Jews had to convert to Christianity or leave Spain within four months. If they chose to stay without converting they would be executed without trial. But conversion was no guarantee from prosecution and conviction by the powerful Spanish Inquisition. Estimates suggest that the great majority of Jews chose forcible expulsion over conversion. Spain was intent on being a *Christian state* with no religious minorities. This was one of the prime examples of **ethnic cleansing**, which would be practiced by most of the Western empires.

But Spain was not the only European Nation persecuting the Jews. Many Jews who fled Spain to other European countries found only temporary relief. Portugal, for example, was only too willing to imitate the crimes of its Iberian neighbor. In 1497 Portugal forced its Jews to convert or be expelled. In 1536 Portugal established its own Inquisition, the somewhat less famous *Portuguese Inquisition.* Many Jews who had moved to Portugal to escape the wrath of the Spanish Inquisition were targeted by the Portuguese Inquisition. The civilized nation-states of Europe found common cause in their crimes against humanity.

The Spanish Inquisition expanded its powers throughout Spain and into all of the colonies of the Spanish Empire. In like manner the Portuguese Inquisition expanded its persecution to its many overseas colonies. Once again we need to emphasize that all Western states are *Christian states.* The Alhambra decree is only singled out by Western historians because of its extreme nature. Most Christian states tolerate other religions in varying degrees. Such toleration not only helps to feed their propaganda about separation of state and religion but allows them to pressure non-Christian states to grant privileges to Christians.

Persecution and Expulsion of Muslims from Spain

Since Spain was determined to be a Christian state without religious minorities it could not tolerate Muslims any more than Jews. Jews were initially the easier target because of their lesser political and military power. But once all of Iberia had been conquered by the Christian states of Portugal and Spain the Muslims became equally vulnerable. Christian states will tolerate religious minorities if it helps their ambition to dominate the world. Today Jews are tolerated in most Christian states because they help to develop the economy, support specific political parties and are dependable allies in fighting Muslims.

As we explained above, the last remaining Muslim territory, the Emirate of Granada, was conquered by Spain in January 1492. Despite the protection of Muslims agreed to by Spain in the *Treaty of Granada,* Muslims, like Jews before, were forced to convert or be expelled. The Treaty of Granada had several clauses intended to protect the rights and religious practices of the Muslims of Granada. But typical of Western

Nations, Spain reneged on the pledges as soon as it had the military power to do so. Western Nations have a nasty habit of promising the moon if such promises help them to steal territory and resources from those fooled into surrendering. Converted Muslims were called *Moriscos.* Moriscos, like Conversos, continued to practice their faith secretly. The Spanish Inquisition therefore investigated, tortured and persecuted Muslims for the same reasons it persecuted Jews. Civilized Christian Spain did not restrict its ethnic cleansing to Jews. Despite the choice of many Muslims to convert rather than leave Spain the Moriscos were expelled from Spain in 1609, without trial, regardless of whether they were genuine or false converts. It was another popular as well as profitable move by King Philip III since the Moriscos had to leave behind most of their property and wealth.

The Spanish conquest of Granada was significant not only because it marked the beginning of the Christian domination of the modern world but because of the mistreatment of Muslims by Spain. Prior to the conquest of Granada there was an implicit agreement that the best way to guarantee freedom from religious persecution of Christians living in Muslim states was for Christian states to offer the same protection to Muslims living in Christian states. Christians and Muslims had been at war for six centuries before the fall of Granada. But they had a kind of respect for each other similar to European nation-states at war with each other. This Christian respect for Muslims came to an end with the fall of Granada. The Western imperial powers of Portugal, Spain, Holland, Britain, France and the United States will never again ever respect Muslims. The West will use its powerful propaganda machine as well as its growing military and economic power to persecute, denigrate, torture, ethnically cleanse and demean Muslims while stealing their land and resources, including their oil. Until the West ends its barbaric behavior toward Muslims and become civilized, rather than using propaganda to say that it is civilized and the Muslims are barbaric, there can be no peace between Christians and Muslims. The classic example of this is Israel and Palestine. There are no two sides to this conflict. Israel is the criminal and Palestine is the victim. Using propaganda to say otherwise does not change the facts.

The Spanish Empire Begins

The Spanish Empire grew from very modest beginnings in the Atlantic to become the largest global empire of its time. It conquered 13.5 percent of the land area of the world. Together with the Portuguese Empire after the union in 1580 it ruled over 20 percent of the world. The Spanish Empire maintained its dominant size for three centuries. In the previous chapter we referred to the Portuguese and Spanish empires as the "unsung" heroes of Western domination because they have not received sufficient credit for Western domination compared with the British, Americans or French. The reason is that the Spanish stumbled into the rediscovery of the New World by accident. At the time this New World was more of a curse than an asset in the fight with the Ottoman Empire for the lucrative spice trade with Asia. But without the United States, which this accident produced, it's very doubtful that the West would have ever dominated the world.

Up until the leadership of the West by the United States, after the Second World War, the West had no unity that was sufficient to dominate the world. The European powers were very conscious of a "balance of power," which would not allow any unification of European empires to dominate even Europe much less the entire world. They were quite content to live and let live with several Western European empires as well as the Ottoman, Russian, Japanese and American empires. In fact, they were very determined not to let anyone get too strong and would wage wars on each other, if needed, to prevent any one empire or alliance of empires getting too powerful. This was the primary reasons for the many wars fought among them up until the Second World War. Two World Wars to prevent Germany from becoming too powerful finally weakened them to the point that the American Empire was able to dominate.

The Americans, unlike the Europeans, permitted zero competition. You either did the bidding of the American Empire or you were squashed like a bug. The Western European empires, Japan, Canada, Australia, South Africa, Mexico, Latin America, and many more agreed to do the bidding of the United States so that they would not be invaded and bombed back to the stone age like Cuba, Vietnam, China, Korea,

Cambodia, Laos, Chile, Panama, Nicaragua, Lebanon, Grenada, Iraq, Somalia, Afghanistan, Pakistan, Yemen, Libya, Syria, and many more, large or small. The Americans used threats, excuses, propaganda, economic blackmail, financial blackmail, bribes, dictators, torture, ethnic cleansing, but mostly military destruction and devastation to intimidate everyone. They dominated the skies with superior air power and dropped bombs, large and small, on anything and everything. Land mines, atomic bombs, bunker busting bombs, cluster bombs, drones, tanks, chemical weapons, etc. They kill and maim by the millions and respect no law or institution. They see themselves above all laws, customs, civilized behavior, sanity, common sense, principle, morality or disagreements. They kill for no other reason than having the power to do so. Killing and warmongering are embedded in their DNA. Worst of all, they use the most powerful propaganda to justify the most heinous crimes.

Spain's Colonization of the Canary Islands

It was quite natural for Spain to begin its maritime conquests with the Canary Islands because of their close geographical proximity to its Atlantic coastline. Spain began its policy of ethnic cleansing of the inhabitants of its colonies with the Canary Islands. It waged wars with the inhabitants to conquer and steal territory. This was not trade but colonization using superior military force. Military conquest of the islands began in 1402. The islanders fought the Spanish imperialists for almost a century before they were fully conquered by 1495. Spain, like Portugal, had the superior firepower, and was not reluctant to use it to steal land and resources as well as kill, enslave and destroy the inhabitants.

In 1479 Spain and Portugal divided up imperial control of the islands conquered in the Atlantic with the *Treaty of Alcacovas.* Spain kept the Canary Islands as its colony while Portugal kept the Cape Verde Islands, the Madeiras and the Azores. This treaty marked the beginning of European Christian empires dividing up stolen land and resources among themselves without any regard to the people who had owned those lands and resources for many centuries.

Spain used the stolen land to produce export crops such as wine and sugar. What turned out to be much more important was the use of these islands as valuable stops for Spanish ships en-route to the New World and beyond. This enriched the European settlers benefitting from the stolen land and resources, thereby encouraging even more Europeans to immigrate to the islands.

Europeans absolutely knew how to play up the **race card.** Since the owners whose land and resources were stolen were **nonwhites,** the Europeans used this as propaganda to portray nonwhites as barbaric and whites as civilized. The more powerful your guns the more civilized you were. Nonwhites deserved to have their land and resources stolen by whites because they were primitive and wasteful or incompetent in using the land and resources. Whites were entitled to steal the land and resources so that they could be better used, managed and developed for the good of all mankind. Only more whites from Europe were good enough to take ownership of the stolen land and resources. The original nonwhite owners were only good as slaves, docile converts to Christianity, servants to the superior white race or dwellers in the very remote unconquered lands. Should such "primitives" resist by force they should be mercilessly destroyed by the civilized weaponry of the white "gods."

This use of race propaganda to justify theft and all manner of evil was practiced to the extreme in the British colonies of Canada, the United States and Australia where the indigenous populations were largely exterminated and the few who survived were imprisoned on "Reserves" where they remain to this day. Canada, the worst of these violators of First Nations, incessantly preaches to the nonwhite world of their supposed human rights violations, to this day. A Reserve was a prison where First Nations too old, feeble and weak to fight the theft of their land, were forced to live. As prisoners they were fed and cared for. They were deliberately made dependent on their white captures. They were humiliated and deprived of their language and customs. Their children were taken away by force and educated by white priests who abused them physically, sexually and emotionally.

White Canadians today justify what was done by saying that it was not done by them but by their forefathers. The current generation of whites use new propaganda that First Nations are lazy, drunken, dependent, and a drain on their taxes. How ironic that they ignore the fact that it was their forefathers who made them that way by imprisoning them in the reserves to make them too docile to resist the theft of their lands and resources? The *Idle No More* Movement of 2013 is just one of countless efforts by First Nations in Canada to get from their white conquerors humane and decent treatment. Canada continues to focus on excuses and propaganda to justify to a very naive world that Canada is not one of the worst human rights abusers in history. It gets a free ride from the international community to continue its historical abuse of its First Nations whose land and resources it stole. At the same time its uneducated media and public chastises other countries for far less human rights abuses.

Spain's Colonization of the New World and Asia

Spain's **accidental** rediscovery of the Caribbean islands and the American continent is the key to understanding how the West has come to dominate the modern world for the last five centuries. We have documented in much greater detail than we will do here the voyages of Columbus and the conquests of the Spanish conquistadors in our *Rise and Fall of the American Empire.* Here we focus on the evils of that conquest and its implication for Western world domination. It's important to understand that imperialism, unlike trade, is always a zero sum game. The bigger the gain by the imperial power the greater the loss to the original inhabitants of the colonies. The bigger the haul thieves steal from you the greater your loss. Worse still is the use of propaganda such as civilizing the natives. It's the imperial power that is the **barbarian** not those colonized with their brutal military weapons and their Christianizing tomfoolery. If the West had traded instead of conquered and stolen, only then would both parties have gained.

In the fifteenth century Spain found itself in a race with its Iberian neighbor, Portugal, for the lucrative spice trade. This opportunity had arisen because of the conquest of Constantinople by the Ottoman Empire. Prior to this conquest Venetian merchants bought the spices from the Muslims to resell to Europeans. A sea route from Spain or Portugal would not only replace what had been lost but increase quantities. Portugal and Spain were ideally located geographically to use the Atlantic as the springboard to finding that sea route directly from Europe. We have documented in the previous chapter the successes of the Portuguese and their use of superior naval power, piracy and enslavement of Africans to dominate the new sea route around South Africa. Spain sought a competing sea route directly West from Spain across the Atlantic Ocean.

Initially this westward route was blocked by the Caribbean islands and the American continent. Spain was very disappointed both because it had lost a valuable opportunity and because its Iberian neighbor would have a monopoly to make itself more powerful than Spain. However, Spain, like Portugal, was interested both in colonies and the spice trade. We explained in the previous chapter how Portugal secured many colonies in the Atlantic and in Africa and elsewhere while simultaneously pursuing the spice trade. In fact, as we pointed out before, to colonize and steal resources and land was the preference of all of the Western empires. Trade was done only if there was insufficient military power to colonize and steal.

Spain's interest in colonization is evidenced by its pressure on the pope to grant it the same rights to **stolen** lands as it had granted to Portugal. Portugal had received papal blessing to **all** stolen lands in papal bulls issued in 1452, 1455, and 1456. Under these bulls Portugal naturally claimed the land discovered by Columbus in 1492. But the unwritten intent of the papal bulls was recognition of lands **stolen** from heathens, not from another Christian Empire, which had already **stolen** the lands from the **heathens.** Spain was fortunate that the pope at that time, *Pope Alexander VI,* was a Spaniard and very friendly to the "Catholic monarchs," Queen Isabella and King Ferdinand of Spain. Since both Portugal and Spain were Catholic countries, it mattered little to the pope which one stole the land from the non-Christian inhabitants since both would use the same propaganda that the land was stolen to save their heathen souls. In fact two militarily powerful **thieves** are much more likely to steal more land and convert more heathens than a single militarily powerful **thief.** For those reasons Spain convinced the pope, despite objections by Portugal, to pass the papal bull *Inter caetera* on May 4, 1493.

This gave the pope's blessing to the lands in the New World **stolen** by Spain, to Spain instead of Portugal. Portugal was forced to recognize the pope's decision and signed the *Treaty of Tordesillas* with Spain on June 7, 1494. This audacious treaty effectively divided the world inhabited by the millions of **nonwhites** between two white Christian countries, Portugal and Spain, with absolutely no consideration for the age old rights of the original inhabitants. These **inhabitants** were the rightful **owners** of the land and resources stolen from them. They were not some kind of Indians or red savages or Eskimos or aborigines or indigenous or natives or refugees or coolies or gooks or barbarians or other exotic or lesser people or subhuman species or tribes. They were people just like the whites, no less, and in many ways far more civilized since they were not thieves like the whites. The only identifiable difference was skin color.

These invented names for the nonwhite **people** whose land and resources were stolen and livelihoods destroyed only serve to continue the evil meted out to them ever since Portugal and Spain began their imperial conquests in the fifteenth century. The Christian powers justified their theft by implying that the theft was based on a moral obligation to civilize the heathens, another ridiculous invented designation for people. It led to ethnic cleansing on a scale that dwarfs what Hitler did to the Jews. Estimates suggest that 95 percent of the **inhabitants** of the New World were killed off by their white conquerors. It's the failure of the world to chastise the West for its many historic crimes against humanity that allows it to continue its ethnic cleansing to this day so that by 2016, its **cowardly** bombing of **Muslim** countries has created over 65 million refugees. Flying supersonic jets high above those who have zero defense and dropping bombs on them is the most **cowardly** of acts ever committed by the human race. It's even more **cowardly** than the American nuking of Hiroshima and Nagasaki, which was certainly the most **cowardly** act at that time in history.

Canada's Truth and Reconciliation Commission reported in 2015. Among its many findings was the fact that the papal bulls of 1452–1493 gave the Catholic church and the Portuguese and Spanish invaders free rein to convert the heathens to Christianity and steal their lands. A 2009 UN report concluded that these papal bulls were "at the root of the violations of Indigenous Peoples' human rights and the mass appropriation of the lands, territories, and resources of the Indigenous Peoples." As a result of the findings of Canada's Truth and Reconciliation Commission, some Canadians would like to have these papal bulls repealed by the Vatican. Imagine that after six centuries of injustice against our First Nations in Canada the majority of Canadians still need to be convinced to put an end to such injustice. Yet, very few Canadians are unwilling to demonize China for far fewer human rights abuses. That's the power of Western propaganda.

The Western colonization of the New World, Australia and New Zealand was different in one very important way from Western colonization in Africa and Asia. While both colonizations involved the same degree of Western crimes against humanity the greater degree of ethnic cleansing in the New World, Australia and New Zealand enabled Europe to populate these colonies with sufficient numbers of white immigrants to create white majorities in these colonies. They could then justify their continued theft of these lands by using their very convenient brand of *democracy.* Unlike South Africa, for example, Canada, the United States, Australia, Mexico, New Zealand, and the countries in the Caribbean and South America can continue to deny the moral and legal claims of the original inhabitants by pretending that they have free and fair democratic elections, which give the governments legitimacy. The fact that it is a governing class rooted in theft by military force and democratized by killing off 95 percent of the original inhabitants, and replacing them initially by a **whites**-only immigration policy, is conveniently lost by the Western historians, the Western media, and Western public opinion.

Worse still, the West continues its use of similar propaganda to make its continued colonizations and ethnic cleansing in Korea, Vietnam, Laos, Cambodia, Palestine, Lebanon, Iraq, Afghanistan, Pakistan, Libya, Syria, Yemen, Somalia, Mali, Algeria, etc., seem self-righteous. The most ridiculous justification used today is that the people asked the West to invade and kill their leaders. In 2013, for example, France invaded Mali claiming that the people of Mali asked for its military assistance. The French president implied that France had no poverty at home and that the French people had so much excess money over their needs, all of which had been met, that they felt morally obliged to squander the excess funds on military aid to the people of Mali.

In like manner, the millions of Syrian refugees, cold and hungry in the refugee camps in Turkey, Jordan and Lebanon, had asked the West to move them from their homes, jobs, family and friends to the disastrous refugee camps, like the First Nations had begged to be imprisoned in reserves. The poor foreign workers who lost their jobs in Libya, the Libyan refugees and the Libyan people are now very happy that the West killed their leader and created chaos, poverty and destruction of their livelihoods. The Libyan people became even happier after France invaded Mali to take back the same Western weapons sold to the people of Mali, as a result of the chaos created by the Western invasion of Libya. In 2014 we are told that the West has a moral obligation to fight ISIS. Why? Because the West invaded Iraq to remove Saddam Hussein but created Al-Qaeda in Iraq. Unfortunately, Al-Qaeda in Iraq has now morphed into ISIS because the West subsequently invaded Syria to remove Bashar al-Assad. By fighting ISIS we kill two birds with one stone. We kill both Iraqis and Syrians at the same time. Most importantly, we do it like **cowards.** We use high flying planes totally out of reach of those we **kill** and rain down bombs on them safely ensconced in our cockpits. Since 1980 the American Empire has used this **cowardly** method of warfare to rain down bombs on at least fourteen **Muslim** countries. That so many support such utter brutality and **cowardice** as the mark of civilized behavior is a testimony to how uncivilized we are as a human race.

Christopher Columbus Begins the Genocide by Spain in the New World

Columbus landed on the Caribbean island of *Guanahani* in the Bahamas in October 1492, and renamed the island *San Salvador,* meaning Holy Savior. He immediately took advantage of the generous and friendly welcome he received from the inhabitants to terrorize, rape, enslave, kill, maim, and force them to denounce their religion and customs. Columbus kidnapped nine of the inhabitants to take back to Spain. Initially, Columbus may have thought that he had reached Japan. Nevertheless, he still opted for conquest and colonization rather than trade. The simple reason was that he had the military muscle to do so. Columbus wrote that he was greeted by the inhabitants with no weapons except small spears. He further wrote that the inhabitants could be conquered by fifty Spaniards. As I have said the West will trade only it does not have the superior military force needed to conquer, enslave and steal. It matters little whether the inhabitants of the land are peaceful or resist by force. As long as the West has the superior force it will always opt for conquest and theft rather than trade. The genocide of **70 million** inhabitants of the New World had begun. This was a far greater crime against humanity than Hitler's genocide of **six million** Jews. First Nations are no lesser people than Jews.

Columbus began Spanish colonization of the New World rather modestly much like the Portuguese in India. His largest ship, the Santa Maria, ran aground on the jagged northern coast of the island of Santo Domingo, which Columbus called *Hispaniola.* The first Spanish fort, *La Navidad,* was constructed in today's Haiti, from the wreckage of the Santa Maria, where Columbus left thirty-nine of his men before returning to Spain. He returned to Spain with his nine captives, some gold, and a sample of products, such as tobacco and pineapples, which could be profitably grown if the land was stolen and the owners enslaved. Spaniards could be enticed to go for the profits as well as the opportunity to rape the young women. Propaganda could be used to justify the theft, rape and enslavement by converting the original land owners to Christianity thereby saving their heathen souls. It was a win-win for the explorers, the Spanish Crown and the pope.

Like the Portuguese in India, Columbus returned with a much larger contingent of Spaniards to conquer and enslave the inhabitants of the New World. His second voyage consisted of seventeen ships compared with only three on the first voyage. His conquistadors were relatively heavily armed compared with the inhabitants. Columbus had both cavalry and foot soldiers. His soldiers were protected with heavy steel armor and carried swords, lances, muskets, bows and arrows. Spanish armor and swords were the best in the world. Columbus also had hunting dogs and even a small cannon. The first fortified settlement did not survive but Columbus began a new settlement, *La Isabella,* in the same northern part of Santo Domingo, during his second voyage. Some gold had been found at this location during the first voyage. Portugal had enriched itself with slaves, gold and ivory from Africa before it reached India. Spain would do the same while searching for Asia. It mattered little to the conquerors whether the slaves were black or red.

Columbus used his military power to force the inhabitants to find gold for him. Those inhabitants who failed to find gold in sufficient quantities had their hands cut off and bled to death. This is one of numerous examples of how the West civilized the people whose land they colonized and stole. Today the West just flies their civilized planes and drop bombs like **cowards.** Columbus and his men also kidnapped and shipped some of the New World inhabitants to Spain to be sold into slavery. Many died on the voyage to Spain. The genocide of the inhabitants of the New World begun by Columbus was limited to the islands of the Caribbean such as Hispaniola, Cuba, Puerto Rico, Dominica, Guadeloupe, Trinidad and others, because Columbus did not reach the mainland until his third voyage. Some estimates suggest that over **eight million** inhabitants of the Caribbean were killed, more than the **six million** Jews killed by Hitler.

The genocide of the inhabitants of the mainland American continent fell to the Spanish conquistadors such as *Hernando Cortez, Francisco Pizarro, Pedro de Alvarado, Pedro de Valdivia,* and many more. Gold, silver, slaves and land were the prizes for killing off the millions of original owners, enslaving the survivors, turning them into docile church going Christians or chasing them off into the remotest parts of the continent. The Spaniards used the Caribbean islands discovered by Columbus as their initial home base to colonize the much richer Aztec, Mayan and Inca empires in the southern half of the American continent. The richest prize was silver, found in large quantities in Peru and Columbia. The owners were not simply deprived of their land, resources and livelihoods but enslaved to work the gold and silver mines for the benefit of their conquerors. In the mines of the city of *Potosi* in Bolivia alone, at least another **eight million** enslaved New World inhabitants died, more than the **six million** Jews killed by Hitler. Many New World inhabitants were also sold as slaves in Europe. New World inhabitants were also enslaved to grow export crops such as sugar, cattle, coffee, bananas, grapes, wheat, etc.

The conquerors came armed with their civilized weapons and religious propaganda. But they were helped immensely by a fortuitous weapon, European diseases such as smallpox and measles, to which the original inhabitants had no immunity. More of the New World inhabitants were killed by European diseases than by the weapons and brutality of the imperial powers. Superior weapons was combined with enslavement, forced religious conversions, starvation, malnutrition, poverty, biological warfare using blankets infected with the smallpox virus, theft of agricultural land, induced suicides, and every form of brutality to kill off the majority of the inhabitants. The relatively small remaining minority could be easily induced by the conquerors to do manual and menial work for the further benefit of those who had stolen their land, resources, religions, customs and self-respect. To this day the descendants of surviving original inhabitants of the New World live in poverty relative to the descendants of the conquerors.

Vice Royalties of New Spain and Peru

Between the first voyage of Columbus and 1650 the Spanish conquered most of the Caribbean and Central and South America. Their most important colony was Mexico. The Spanish Empire in 1600 was the largest empire in the world. It had united with the Portuguese Empire in 1580. In Europe it was still challenged by the Ottoman Empire and in the New World and Asia it was facing increasing competition from the Dutch Empire. By 1600 it had also found a sea route to Asia across the Pacific Ocean, which had been its original goal since the first voyage of Columbus. It had conquered the Philippines and the rich Spice Islands in the Moluccas. But Asia was no longer its primary target of colonization. Having stumbled on the riches of the Caribbean and American colonies it had no intention of giving them up. The large inflow of silver from the New World far surpassed the riches of the spice trade. It is fair to say that while the Portuguese were obsessed with spices the Spanish were obsessed with silver and gold.

The population that replaced the original inhabitants of the New World by 1600 was a very mixed bag. It included the descendants of the surviving original owners of the land, the descendants of the Spanish and

Portuguese invaders and other Europeans who continued the conquest, theft and settlement of the lands of the original owners. But there were also a growing number of mixed race inhabitants, the offspring of unions between the Europeans and the original inhabitants. Africans were also added to the mix as African slaves were added to the declining numbers of enslaved New World people. This led to two other mixed race population. Africans mixed with Europeans and Africans mixed with New World people. A political/economic hierarchy was created with whites at the top and the descendants of the original land owners, called **indigenous,** to marginalize them as inferior, at the bottom.

Administration of this vast empire was divided between two vice-royalties, *New Spain,* created in 1535 and *Peru,* created in 1542. We will deal with New Spain first. The creation of the vice-royalty of New Spain owed much to a daring conquistador, *Hernando Cortez.* Cortez almost single-handedly defeated the mighty *Aztec Empire* capturing Mexico for Spain. The capital of the Aztec Empire, *Tenochtitlan,* was renamed Mexico City, and became the capital of New Spain. The vice-royalty of New Spain governed the Spanish colonies in the Caribbean, North and Central America and the Spanish East Indies. It covered a land area far greater than Spain. As in the case of Portugal, Spain capitalized on its naval power to conquer and govern large parts of the globe.

The global colonies of both Portugal and Spain were controlled respectively, by a distant and relatively tiny European power, through its control of the High Seas. The Spanish Caribbean colonies included present day Cuba, Haiti, Dominican Republic, Puerto Rico, Jamaica, Trinidad and the Cayman islands. The North American and Central American colonies included present day Mexico, more than half of present day United States, Guatemala, Nicaragua, Belize, Costa Rica, El Salvador and Honduras. The Asian colonies included the Philippines, the Moluccas, the Mariana Islands, Taiwan and the Caroline islands. In 1571 *Manila* became the capital of the Spanish colonies in Asia. After Magellan crossed the Pacific to the Philippines in 1521 the Spanish East Indies was linked to the Spanish colonies in the New World via the Mexican port of *Acapulco.* In addition to the gold, silver, spices and silks, Asians could now be enslaved to add to the enslaved New World people to enrich the civilized Europeans.

The creation of the vice-royalty of Peru owed much to another daring conquistador, *Francisco Pizarro.* Pizarro defeated and conquered the Inca Empire for Spain in 1532. His principal weapon was the smallpox virus. The Inca Empire was even more wealthy than the Aztec Empire. It provided even more gold and silver for Spain than the colonies governed by the vice-royalty of New Spain. Pizarro cunningly captured the Inca emperor, *Atahualpa,* and bargained for a room full of gold and silver as ransom for his release. A room was filled with some twelve tons of gold and twenty-four tons of silver. The civilized European took the ransom but killed his prisoner, after converting him to Christianity, of course. The Spanish monarch was very pleased by the very civilized behavior of his most daring and cunning conquistador since he received 20 percent of the ransom. Pizarro's men were ecstatic since they shared the other 80 percent of the ransom with Pizarro.

Most importantly, their Christian God was happy to have received another converted Christian soul. Dead or alive makes no difference to their Christian God. According to Western historians the people of the Inca Empire would also sing the praises of their Spanish liberators for saving their heathen souls in return for stealing their land and resources. They would even be happy to become the slaves of the very civilized European rulers. You have to admire the audacity of Western historians who continue to perpetuate the myth that the nonwhite people of the New World benefitted from being enslaved and robbed by the civilized white Christians. In reality, Peru was conquered with even greater barbarity than the other parts of the Spanish American colonies. After taking the ransom Pizarro looted the Inca capital of *Cuzco.*

Pizarro's conquest led to the creation of the vice-royalty of Peru in 1542 with its capital in *Lima.* Spanish colonies south of Costa Rica were governed by the viceroyalty of Peru. The territory included present day Peru, Panama, Chile, Columbia, Ecuador, Argentina, Paraguay, Bolivia and Uruguay. As with the land area governed by the viceroyalty of New Spain the area governed by the viceroyalty of Peru was larger than Spain. Gold and silver from the conquered Incan Empire poured into Spain throughout the sixteenth century. In 1545 the silver and tin mines in the city of Potosi in Columbia were discovered. New discoveries in both viceroyalties led to the enslavement of more of the original owners to work the mines stolen from them by their civilized European thieves. There were as many as five thousand mines in Potosi alone.

The Dutch Empire to 1800

We begin our analyses of the Dutch Empire as the third of the modern European empires that created the Western hegemony. The Portuguese, Spanish and Dutch empires had very strong original connections. Portugal and Spain fought together as Christians to oust the Muslims from Iberia and both began their major quest for empire by searching for a sea route to the East Indies. Holland began as a colony of Spain and used the African **slave trade** and **piracy** to challenge the post 1580 unified Portuguese/Spanish Empire.

While Spain was busy colonizing the New World its European colony, Holland, was fighting for its independence. There are a number of similarities between the rise of the Dutch and American empires. Just as the Anglo-American colonies in the New World fought for their independence from Britain only to challenge the British Empire for hegemony so too did the colony of Spain, Holland, fight Spain for its independence only to go on to challenge the Spanish Empire for hegemony. In both cases taxation and an unpopular king were cited as grievances. The American colonies rebelled against the king of England, *George III,* and taxation by Britain, to become the American Republic. In like manner the Netherland provinces rebelled against the king of Spain, *Philip II,* and taxation by Spain, to become the Dutch Republic. Another important similarity was that the thirteen American colonies that united and successfully won independence from Britain by military force were "puny" compared to the mighty British Empire. In like manner, the seven Dutch provinces that united and successfully won independence from Spain by military force were "puny" compared with the mighty Spanish Empire. Spain dismissed the possibility of Holland ever becoming a competitor just as Britain dismissed the United States as ever becoming a competitor. They both paid dearly for those dismissals.

Holland, like Belgium and Luxembourg, are independent countries that were part of the geographical area in Europe called the *Low Countries.* This area fell under the rule of the holy Roman emperor. In

1519, Charles V, the grandson of the holy Roman emperor Maximilian I and reigning king of Spain since 1516, became the holy Roman emperor. This brought the entire area of the Low Countries, including Holland, under the rule of the Spanish Empire. As we said in chapter 3, Charles V and his primary rival, Suleiman the Magnificent, were the two most powerful rulers in the world during that period. Maximilian I had married his son to the daughter of the Catholic monarchs Isabella and Ferdinand of Spain. Their eldest son was Charles V. That is how the grandson of Maximilian I inherited not only the worldwide Spanish Empire but the powerful House of the Habsburgs and the lands of the Holy Roman Empire in Central and Western Europe. His rule covered a land area of some four million square kilometers.

As the grandson of the Catholic monarchs Isabella and Ferdinand, Charles V saw himself as the protector of the Catholic faith against the rising tide of Protestant Christians. Christian Europe was splitting along sectarian lines just as the Roman Empire had done previously. The Roman Empire had split into Eastern Greek Orthodox and Western Roman Catholic. Now the Western Roman Catholic half was splitting again into Catholic and Protestant Christians. It fell to Charles V, and his son Philip II, to lead the fight against that. One of their "puny" European colonies, *Holland,* would prove to be a very surprising but formidable foe.

Charles V was born in the Low Countries, which he inherited from his father in 1506 when he was only six years old. At the time the Low Countries were divided into seventeen semi-independent provinces. In 1549 Charles V declared the region to be a unified entity. The son of Charles V, Philip II, inherited the Low Countries in October 1555. Philip II became king of Spain in January 1556. The seven Northern provinces that would eventually unite to become Holland began to rebel against Spanish rule in August of 1566. Spanish persecution of Protestants and high taxes were among the grievances claimed by the rebels. Religious freedom is the oldest and most powerful rallying cry for rebellion. When you combine religious freedom with the distaste of taxation of any kind by the subjects of any kingdom you have a very powerful weapon to stir the masses into revolt. Add to this the fact that King Philip II, unlike his father, Charles V, was viewed by his Dutch subjects much more as a *foreign* ruler because he was not born in the Low Countries and spoke no Dutch.

Protestantism had become a divisive force in the Low Countries during the sixteenth century. While the Southern provinces continued to be Catholic the Northern provinces were increasingly Protestant. Think of Ireland. Since King Philip II saw himself as the primary defender of the Catholic faith it was natural for him to favor the south and deal harshly with the north. He had also inherited the demonic Spanish Inquisition, which he could use to terrorize and punish heretics. As in the American colonies later, a mob began the Dutch revolt against Spanish rule when it stormed a church in Flanders in August 1566. The mob was led by a preacher, *Sebastian Matte.* Likewise, in the United States later, a mob attacked English soldiers in Boston. The U.S. mob was led by Crispus Attucks, but instigated by *Samuel Adams,* a cousin of the second president, John Adams.

Calvinists in the Northern provinces of the Low Countries stormed churches and destroyed Catholic holy symbols. As in the United States, where the mobs were supported by the American aristocracy, the Dutch nobility in the Northern provinces supported the attacks on Catholicism. Just as the American aristocracy wanted to steal the English colonies to enrich themselves so did the Dutch nobility want to steal the Northern provinces of the Low Countries from Spain to enrich themselves. In both cases there was a very powerful economic motivation for the rebellion. This explanation is consistent with the fact that in both Holland and the United States this powerful economic motive for the rebellion led to both Holland and the United States quickly transforming themselves from puny servile colonies to powerful wealthy empires dominated by a small aristocratic merchant class.

The Dutch War of Independence, 1568–1648, was not unlike the later American War of Independence, 1775–1783, except that it was much longer. The independent Dutch Republic predated the independent American Republic by almost two centuries. But Republican governments in Holland and the United States were no more liberal, free or egalitarian than the monarchies they replaced. Both Holland and the United States enriched their republics with the evil institution of **slavery,** for example. Like the thirteen American colonies the seventeen provinces in the Low Countries had a high degree of political autonomy from the mother country. Like the American colonies there was a North/

South divide. In the Low Countries the division was religious, Catholics versus protestants. In the United States the division was slavery versus nonslavery. But in both cases there was unity in opposing taxes and imperial rule.

One difference in outcome was that in the case of Holland only the seven Northern provinces unified to fight for independence. In the case of the United States it was the Southern colonies that led the revolt since their slave plantations produced more wealth than the Northern slave-free colonies. But the Northern states joined the Southern rebels. Rather ironic, as the wealth generated from manufacturing and theft of more and more First Nations lands enriched the Northern states of the Union the South felt increasingly colonized by the North. They wanted out from the Union but were militarily too weak to fight the North for it. The South had helped the North to win its independence with military force only to be dominated within the Union by military force. The seventeen provinces in the Low Countries were wise to have avoided the mistake made later in the American Revolution. By not joining the Northern provinces in rebelling against Spain, today there are three independent countries in this region, Holland, Belgium and Luxembourg. The American experience shows that it's much more difficult to separate from a Union than to join it. Quebec feels much the same way about the Canadian union.

Another commonality between the Dutch and American experience was the military help provided by other powerful empires. The American rebels were helped by France. In like manner the Dutch rebels were helped by England. In both cases help was based on national self-interest. During the Dutch revolt the British was competing with the Spanish Empire for colonies. During the American revolt the French were competing with the British for colonies.

Finally, during both revolts the mother countries were heavily engaged in other major wars. During the Anglo-American War of 1812–1814 the British were hampered not only because of French support for the rebels but by the British involvement in the Napoleonic Wars in Europe. In like manner Spain was hampered not only by English support for the rebels but by Spanish involvement in the wars against the Ottoman Empire. The Ottoman Empire even offered some support to the Dutch rebels on the grounds that Protestant Christianity was closer to Islam than Catholic Christianity. During the Dutch revolt, Spain saw itself as the leader of the Christian war against the Muslims. In like manner, during the American revolt Britain saw itself as the leader of the war against Napoleon.

Spain responded to the attacks on Catholic churches much like the British responded to the dumping of English tea in the Boston Harbor. Both empires sent troops to reinforce imperial forces in the colonies. The Dutch rebels found a military leader in William I of Orange much like the American rebels found George Washington. William converted to Calvinism in 1573. Most of the population of the seven Northern provinces converted to Calvinism during the revolt. William is still celebrated as the father of Dutch independence just as Washington is still celebrated as the father of the American Revolution.

The first victory for the Dutch rebels came with the *Battle of Heiligerlee,* in May of 1568. In 1579 the seven provinces signed the *Treaty of Utrecht* to formalize their Union. The seven provinces were *Utrecht, Holland, Zealand, Flanders, Groningen, Guelders,* and *Brabant.* In 1581 they declared independence from Spain. Spain responded as all empires do when colonies declare independence. But just like the British and the American revolt, Spain could not focus all of its resources in defeating the Dutch rebellion. Spain, like Britain later, had a worldwide empire to govern and control militarily. The very nature of colonization is that colonies will rebel on a continuous basis. No people enjoy being colonized despite Western propaganda to the contrary. Spain had to choose where to put its limited military resources just as Britain had to later. This is the primary reason for the long drawn out Dutch rebellion.

A Spanish military victory against the Dutch rebels would require Spain transferring military resources from defending other rebellions or preventing the British or French from stealing some of its colonies. But without totally crushing the Dutch rebellion the rebels would return once the Spanish had withdrawn forces. This is why the Dutch rebellion lasted eighty years. The British defeat of the Spanish Armada in 1588 was especially disastrous for Spain. The independent Dutch Republic is dated as beginning in 1581 but Spain's acceptance of this independence did not come until 1648 when the *Treaty of Munster* was signed.

The Dutch rebellion was largely financed by an elite class of nobles and merchants who had enriched themselves from the international trade generated within the Spanish Empire. During the eighty years of war against the mother country these nobles and merchants took full advantage of the war to plunder and steal the wealth of the mother country. In addition, during the rebellion, many Protestants, including rich merchants and nobles, fled from the Catholic southern provinces to the United Protestant North.

Portugal and Spain had both used piracy and the slave trade to enrich themselves. But the Dutch would carry these two **evils** of Western civilization to new heights. The Dutch *Sea Beggars* became the most feared pirates and the Dutch *slavers* became the most feared "slave traders." The Dutch did not distinguish between the West and the rest. They went for the richest. That meant mostly the Portuguese colonies, Portuguese shipping and Portuguese slave forts in West Africa. While Spain was losing its naval dominance because of attacks from the British and French the Dutch rebels were building a very formidable Dutch navy. The Iberian Union of Spain and Portugal turned out to be a disaster for Portugal because of the Dutch rebellion. With Spain unable to fully protect even the Spanish Empire from military attacks by the Ottoman Empire, England and France, it had very few resources to protect the Portuguese Empire. It had stolen the Portuguese Empire in 1580 only to see it plundered by its Dutch colonial rebels.

The Dutch Empire replaced both Portugal and Spain as the dominant naval power. King Philip II of Spain had foolishly over extended his military capability when he had invaded and conquered Portugal in 1580. The fall of most empires has been caused by overexpansion because of insatiable greed. Spain was no exception to this insatiable desire to conquer beyond the limits to control and govern. Today the American Empire is suffering from this same disease. Its foolish invasion of Iraq in 2003 will prove to be the final nail in its coffin. It had learned no lessons from its failed invasion of Vietnam.

The Dutch East India and Dutch West India Companies

Merchants had always played an important role in financing Western explorations and conquests since they benefitted immensely from selling the products stolen from the colonies. But it was the Dutch who first made free enterprise the controlling partners with the state in colonization. Up until 1800 Dutch colonization was done primarily by two private enterprises, the Dutch East India and Dutch West India corporations. This is not surprising since Dutch merchants had largely funded the Dutch rebellion against Spain and felt that the wealth and resources of the colonies of the unified Spanish-Portuguese Empire were fair game for them to steal. The world outside Europe had been divvied up between Spain and Portugal by the Catholic pope. Since the Iberian Union of 1580 it was all stolen by King Phillip II of Spain.

Holland was a Protestant Nation, owing no allegiance to the pope. In addition, Protestants, by nature and religion, were more interested in material goods than the spiritual concerns of their Catholic cousins. Catholics were brainwashed into thinking that they must enrich the church more than themselves to save their souls. Protestants had no such qualms about their ill-gotten gains from the people they colonized and robbed. What has come to be called "the Protestant work ethic" really began with the Dutch, but later perfected by the *Brits* and *Yanks,* working their butts off to steal the land and resources of the world for their personal fortunes. The Protestants made *private property* sacred and *communal property* evil and used propaganda to justify that it was moral to permit one percent of the world to have **legal** rights to 99 percent of the world's resources. The Yanks even went so far as to claim that stealing all of the land of the First Nations was morally justified because the First Nations had foolishly not divvied up the land to selfish individuals. It was not simply illegal to recognize the communal property rights of First Nations but morally reprehensible to do so. A Protestant God would simply not tolerate such immoral behavior. Let the greedy one percent inherit the earth and be blessed by the Protestant God.

The Dutch East India Company: 1602–1800

While the English East India Company and the Hudson Bay Company became more famous, one of the first of these *joint-stock* **monopolies** to legally steal the land and resources of those colonized by the West, was the *Dutch East India Company,* created in 1602, less than two years after the founding of the English East India Company. Its shareholders were initially given twenty-one years of monopoly rights by the Dutch government to steal from the East Indies. Its shares were sold to the wealthy on the Amsterdam stock exchange. These shareholders did not simply condone piracy, the African slave trade and theft of land and resources from those unable to defend their property with military force, but demanded that the management used these **evil** means to the fullest extent to provide them with the highest returns to their investment in the company. Piracy and the "slave trade" were legally sanctioned by the Dutch state.

These private monopolies not only stole land and resources from the owners by force but set up institutions to govern those they had robbed. The Dutch East India Company, for example, was empowered by the Dutch state to create its own military force, wage wars, sign treaties with Asian rulers, convict, execute and punish those who disobeyed its rules, and even mint its own coins. The *governor general* was the CEO of the company in Asia. It was both a political and entrepreneurial position. It was free enterprise with the legal and military powers normally entrusted to the state, all rolled into one. This is how Western democracies began in the United States, Canada, Australia, India, Pakistan, the Caribbean, Africa, and elsewhere. In countries like the United States, Canada, Australia, and New Zealand, the majority of the nonwhite owners whose land had been stolen, were killed off or imprisoned in "Reservations." Whites were brought from Europe to ensure a white majority in elections where votes had to be largely bought with false promises and propaganda. In colonies that had nonwhite majorities other creative ways were used to ensure continued power in the hands of a white governing elite. The most infamous of these was *Apartheid,* used by the Dutch in South Africa.

We explained in the previous chapter how the Portuguese had taken away the lucrative spice trade from the Muslims. The Portuguese began its base of operations in India, which had a majority Hindu population. The Dutch began its base of operations in Indonesia, which had a majority Muslim population. The Dutch first reached Indonesia in 1596. The Dutch implicitly formed an alliance with Muslims against Portuguese expansion into Indonesia. The Dutch obtained an exclusive agreement to buy spices from the *Hitu* Muslims, giving the Dutch control of *Ambon Island.* Ambon Island is located in the Maluku Islands of Indonesia. Ambon Island had been reached by the Portuguese in 1513. But by 1605 the Portuguese had been forced out by the Dutch. In 1610 the headquarters of the Dutch East India Company was located on Ambon Island. This alliance of a colony with one European imperial power against another European imperial power became quite common and exists to this day.

The first permanent "trading" fort of the Dutch was established in 1603, in *Banten,* where the first Dutch ships had landed in 1596. Banten was an important spice port in West Java. Java is the most populated island of Indonesia accounting for 60 percent of its total population today. The Indonesian capital city of *Jakarta* is located in West Java. The Dutch built a fort in Jakarta in 1611. The headquarters of the Dutch East India Company was moved from Ambon Island to Jakarta in 1619. The Dutch proceeded to kill off the entire population of the Banda Islands, a group of ten small volcanic islands in the Banda Sea, so as to steal their land for clove and nutmeg plantations. This is yet another typical example of what Western historians call civilizing the natives. The most important conquest of the Dutch was the *Moluccas.* The Moluccas were referred to as the Spice Islands because they produced the most valuable spice of the time, *cloves.* The Dutch were able to monopolize this trade by forcing out both the Portuguese and the British.

The Dutch East India Company expanded its Asian "trade" from Indonesia to Malaya, India/Pakistan, China, Japan, Ceylon, Taiwan, Thailand, Australia, Iran and Africa. The Dutch were the only people to secure a "trading post" in Japan. The Dutch East India Company established the "trading post" on the island of *Dejima* in 1640 and was able to hold this monopoly "trade" with Japan until 1854. As the Dutch stole more and more of the resources of Asia from the Portuguese it faced increased competition from the English. But the Dutch East India

Company dominated the spice "trade" between Europe and Asia until it was forced to declare bankruptcy in 1800. Its debt and colonies were taken over by the Dutch government.

Apartheid: Western Democracy in South Africa

Southern Africa had become an important port for the West ever since Portugal began the search for a sea route to India around the southern tip of Africa. We documented the African colonies captured by Portugal both before and after reaching India by sea. But it was the Dutch who were instrumental in creating the colony of what became the independent country of the *Republic of South Africa* after centuries of genocide committed by the West on the African population whose land and resources were stolen. To this day most blacks in South Africa live in dire poverty compared to the descendants of the whites who stole their land and resources. Many blacks today live on less than one dollar United States per day and most are unemployed. Like the treatment of First Nations in Canada the descendants of the thieves find all kinds of excuses to keep the stolen land and resources.

In 1652 the Dutch East India Company created the colony of *Cape Town* in South Africa. Its initial purpose was to provide fresh supplies to the Dutch ships engaged in the spice "trade" with Asia. Columbus called the owners of the land he stole "Naked savages." The Dutch called the owners of the land they stole "Bushmen." These primitive names for the rightful owners were deliberate efforts by the civilized West to justify their evil deeds. The stolen land was given to European settlers. Just as the Spanish imported **African** slaves into their colonies the Dutch imported **Asian** slaves into their African colony. By this time the Dutch West India Company had been an active participant in the lucrative African "slave trade." The Dutch East India Company owned both **Asian slaves** and **African slaves** it had captured on the island of Madagascar. The Cape Town colony was used as another base for the Dutch to profit from the African "slave trade" as well as adding slaves from Indonesia, Ceylon, India, Mauritius and Madagascar. The Dutch used both African and Asian slaves in their colonies in Asia and Africa. In its Cape Town colony slaves were the primary source of labor. Whites were too civilized to do their own manual labor. The "inferior" nonwhite races were enslaved because the whites had the military muscle to do so. This makes whites even more civilized. The more nonwhite slaves a white person owned the more civilized he was as measured by Western standards and Western historians. Within a century of the initial settlement of Cape Town by the Dutch the Europeans were outnumbered by **slaves.** The more slaves you owned the more civilized you were.

Western Democracies

One political invention by the West to enhance their claim to be both superior and civilized was what they called *democracy.* Some inhabitants will be allowed to form parties and vote for a party of their choice. There must be at least two parties. The party with a plurality of votes will govern. It was, of course, extremely important that the winning party had **white** leaders. In the United States this was guaranteed by killing off most of the First Nations, enslaving the blacks and generally ensuring that the vast majority of voters were white. In Canada this was guaranteed by killing off most of the First Nations and ensuring that the vast majority of immigrants were white. In Israel the Jews used guns provided by the Western imperial powers to kill off most of the Palestinians, force the remainder into refugee camps and allowed massive numbers of Jews to immigrate into Israel to ensure a Jewish majority government for their civilized democracy. In South Africa the Dutch protected their false claim to be civilized democrats with a system that came to be known as *Apartheid.*

When *Apartheid* was formally legislated in South Africa in 1948 South Africa was an **English** colony. The British captured the Dutch colony in 1795 after France had invaded Holland. We explain British imperialism in the next chapter. However, the roots of this policy of **segregating** the races so that **whites** can be the dominant racial, political, religious, economic, educated and legal group dated back to the Dutch theft of the land and resources and Dutch enslavement of blacks and Asians. The same policy had been implemented by the English in the United States. Just as the **white** Americans continued the English policy of enslaving and segregating nonwhites from whites in the United States so did the English in South Africa continue the Dutch policy of enslaving and segregating nonwhites from whites. The difference, of course, was that by 1948 the white Americans in the Northern states had enlisted the help of the blacks to prevent the Southern states from separating and forming their own independent country. As a result efforts were made in the United States to reduce racial segregation rather than entrench it in legislation as South Africa did. The West, led by the United States, supported the policy of apartheid in South Africa, by labeling African opposition to this vile policy, *communism.* It was the much maligned Soviet Union, not the West, which provided aid to the black struggle to end apartheid in South Africa.

In the United States the Americans could afford to be more democratic since nonwhites in the United States in 1948 were a much smaller percent of voters than would be the case in South Africa if there was the same degree of integration as in the United States. In South Africa nonwhites were 90 percent of the population. In addition the United States deliberately and forcibly prevented and discouraged voting by nonwhites, kept the races as segregated as it legally and morally could while disadvantaging blacks in education, housing, politics, and economics. First Nations who had not been killed off by genocide, wars and diseases, were still mostly imprisoned in *Indian Reserves.* They had even fewer rights and economic opportunities than blacks. English policies in Canada and Australia were not much different. Ultimately, the goal of **segregation,** whether you call it Apartheid or not, was the continued rule of the stolen land and resources by the whites. To nonwhites it mattered little whether the white rulers were Dutch, English, Americans, Canadians, or Australians. White rulers of colonies were equal in their brutality, evil deeds, warmongering, genocide, torture, and racism.

The Dutch West India Company: 1621–1800

The Dutch were not content with theft, piracy and slave ownership in the Eastern half of the world given to Portugal by the pope. It wanted to engage in theft, piracy and the slave trade in the other half of the world given to Spain by the pope. In fact, the Dutch began theft of land and resources in the New World before venturing into Asia. As early as

1590 the Dutch explored the Amazon and founded the colony of *Guyana* on the Essequibo River. Guyana was supposed to be the legendary city of gold known as "Eldorado," which attracted famous explorers such as Sir Walter Raleigh. In 1600 a Dutch pirate briefly conquered a city in Chile. In 1609 Henry Hudson was sent by the Dutch East India Company to explore for the famous Northwest Passage. As a result of this expedition the Dutch laid claim to lands in North America. In 1615 the Dutch founded a settlement near present day *Albany.* In 1623 *New Amsterdam* was founded on Manhattan Island. These initial settlements were populated by immigrants from many European countries and became the Dutch colony of *New Netherland.* The Dutch were extremely brutal in their attacks on the original inhabitants, the *River Indians.* The Swedish colony of *New Sweden* was stolen by the Dutch and added to New Netherland in 1655. In 1657 the Dutch attacked and decimated the *Esopus Indians.* But the Dutch suffered the same fate when the land they had stolen from the First Nations was in turn stolen by England from the Dutch in 1664 and renamed *New York.*

Dutch colonization in the Caribbean began in 1620. The Dutch colonized Tobago, St. Martin, Curacao, Aruba, Bonaire, Saba and St. Eustatius. Many of these tiny Caribbean islands were rich in salt, which was an extremely valuable commodity at the time. The Dutch West India Company was given a monopoly by the Dutch government on June 2, 1621. It would compete with Spain and Portugal for the Western half of the world just as the Dutch East India Company was competing with Portugal and Spain for the Eastern half of the world. This Western half included the lucrative "slave trade" between West Africa and the New World, the Spanish colonies in the Caribbean and South and Central America and the Portuguese colony of Brazil. The Dutch were on a mission to seize dominance of the world from their imperial master, Spain. Two centuries later the thirteen English colonies in the United States would seize dominance of the world from their imperial master, Britain. Empires come and go and nothing is learned.

The initial intent of the Dutch West India Company was to steal the profits from what was called the "trade" in slaves and sugar. Sugar was the most profitable crop. It was grown in plantations in Brazil and the Caribbean using African slaves from the west coast of Africa. Huge profits could be made growing sugar with slave labor, selling slaves and pirating the ships carrying sugar and slaves. The Dutch West India Company engaged in all three. The Dutch attacked the Portuguese capital in Brazil in 1624. The Dutch West India Company began stealing land from the Portuguese along the Brazilin coast to grow sugar after 1630. They used both First Nations and African **slaves** while also modernizing the sugar plantations. Holland held on to the stolen land until 1654 when it was returned, not to the original inhabitants, but to Portugal. The Dutch expanded its sugar cultivation to the Caribbean, beginning in Barbados. Rather than selling the African slaves to other European colonies it would use them on its own plantations in Brazil, Guyana, Suriname (Dutch Guiana) and the Caribbean. But the Dutch used its Caribbean conquests mostly as slave "markets" for its import of African slaves.

Since the average life of a slave on the sugar plantation was barely **six years** there was an insatiable demand for the human cargo of the civilized West. In 1662 the Dutch received permission, the *asiento,* from Spain to supply African slaves to the colonies of the Spanish Empire. The Dutch supplied most of the African slaves to the Spanish colonies up until the 1690s. On the supply side the Dutch conquest of the Portuguese fortress, *Elmina,* in 1637 enabled the Dutch to have unlimited supplies of African slaves. As we saw in the previous chapter the Portuguese had consolidated their African slave "monopoly" by stealing the African land on the west coast of Africa known as the *Gold Coast.* Initially the Portuguese concentrated on stealing gold, ivory and pepper. When you use guns to get products its theft, not trade. The Dutch, in turn, stole the Portuguese colonies in Africa, including the Gold Coast. The Dutch began its colonization of the Gold Coast in 1598. Like the Portuguese before them, the Dutch stole products such as gold, ivory and pepper, in addition to African slaves.

Theft of African slaves became more valuable than theft of gold after the Dutch stole land in Brazil to grow sugar. This was one reason for the Dutch to capture the Portuguese fortress of Elmina. In 1641 the Dutch captured the Portuguese colony of Angola as well but lost it in 1648. It was a Dutch ship that had brought the first twenty African slaves to the English colony of Virginia in 1619. The Dutch began landing

African slaves in their North American colony of New Netherland in 1625. By 1650 the Dutch were the largest **slave** trading nation in the world. In that year, the Dutch sent 30,000 African slaves to Brazil alone. When the Dutch were forced to return Brazil to Portugal in 1654 it increased shipments of African slaves to its North American colony, New Netherland. Of the estimated 550,000 African slaves the Dutch shipped to the New World some 75,000 died during their miserable voyage across the Atlantic. The central position of the Gold Coast to the African "slave trade" declined after the British abolished the slave trade in 1807. However, while the British abolished slavery in its colonies in 1833 the Dutch did not abolish slavery in its colonies until 1863.

Dutch piracy also profited from capturing Spanish ships carrying the silver and gold from the mines in South America. In 1628, for example, the Dutch captain, *Piet Heyn,* captured one of the largest Spanish silver fleets in the Caribbean. The Dutch West India Company also competed with the British and French for the fur "trade" in North America. The Dutch briefly captured two of the French forts in Acadia. It's possible that the company was far too greedy since it was forced to declare bankruptcy in 1636, just fifteen years after receiving its monopoly from the Dutch government. There were several partially successful attempts to restart the company, and it limped along as a private company until 1791 when its charter was not renewed by the Dutch government, and its remaining assets were bought by the Dutch government.

CHAPTER 6

The British and French Empires to 1785

I will begin this chapter by confessing that I am not the typical avid reader that writers are supposed to be. My primary reason is that much of what Western historians write is utter nonsense. It's not easy to separate the wheat from the chaff to find the very few who use some basic common sense such as recognizing, for example, that there is an obvious inconsistency to claim that **slave owners** such as George Washington can be fighting for freedom. One of these many acclaimed Western historians who has been "in my face" is *Niall Ferguson.* If I Google my book, *Rise and Fall of the American Empire* without the first three letters of my subtitle, "A Reinterpretation…" his book invariably comes up instead of mine. In addition he seems to be constantly on TV peddling his views of history, such as in the PBS documentary, *The West and the Rest.*

Niall Ferguson is the prototype Westerner, much like President Obama or British prime minister Tony Blair or any CNN or BBC reporter, who captures the audience, Western and non-Western, by cunningly pretending to give both sides of a story but very subtly giving the standard Western propaganda. They are the Western experts who will convince you, for example, that there are two sides to the Palestinian question while simultaneously chastising, correctly, those who dare suggest that there are two sides to Hitler's treatment of the Jews. They are the experts who will convince you that every current military invasion by the West is justified while simultaneously chastising every past invasion, such as the invasion of Vietnam. The difference between these pro-Westerners and a President George W. Bush, for example, is that President Bush was lacking in this very gifted Western ability at double talk. That is why it was easy for so many to hate President Bush but not President Obama. President Obama is as much a warmonger as President Bush and all of the Western leaders over the last six centuries. But the Tony Blairs, Barack Obamas, and Niall Fergusons have the gift of fooling their audience without seeming to be trying to. They are far more dangerous than the President Bushes or conservative Republicans in the United States.

In one of his many acclaimed books, *Empire,* Ferguson asks the question, "Can you have globalization without gunboats?" (page xxii). Ferguson and many of his contemporaries, show their deliberate Western bias regarding inherent inconsistencies by asking questions like these. It's the same nonsensical question as asking if the United States could ever have fought for freedom without its founding fathers having been **slave owners?** Imperialism and free trade are inherently inconsistent just as owning slaves and fighting for freedom are inherently inconsistent. To ask if you can have free trade without imperialism is a **stupid** question because it's impossible to have free trade with imperialism. In like manner the United States could never have founded a freedom-loving republic when its founding fathers were **slave owners.** Imperialism requires military force only because it is **theft.** Free trade implies no use of military force. Globalization is only possible if we do **not** use gunboats. If we ever use gunboats it is colonization not globalization. Acclaimed historians like Ferguson get away with such dumb questions because of centuries of Western propaganda intended to claim that Western imperialism, British or other, somehow benefitted those colonized, that it was not a zero sum game, when in fact it always is. Let me say emphatically here that imperialism is as **evil** as slavery and genocide and has absolutely not even one single redeeming feature.

The British and French empires imitated the attacks on the unified Spanish/Portuguese Empire by the Dutch Empire using the same tools of piracy, the slave trade and naval superiority. The Catholic pope had given his blessing to Portugal and Spain to steal the world outside Western Europe. The Dutch had both added to the thefts by Spain and Portugal as well as stealing some of the land and resources previously stolen by Portugal and Spain. The British and French would steal some of what Portugal, Spain and Holland had previously stolen as well as stealing what these three earlier Christian empires had not yet stolen. The empire that was able to steal the most land and resources would dominate the world. That was the British Empire. We begin with the British Empire in this chapter.

The British Empire: Rule Britannia: Britannia Rule the Waves

Once again a relatively tiny Western European nation-state would use superior naval forces to steal much of the land and resources of the world. Britain, like Holland, was a Protestant Nation. The Catholic pope had given the world to two Catholic nations, Portugal and Spain. Two Protestant nations, Holland and Britain, would take a big chunk of that world. Portugal and Spain had used superior weaponry and naval skills to conquer and steal. Now they faced the even more superior naval skills of the Dutch and British. The British and Dutch would also compete with each other in addition to competing with Spain and Portugal. One of the important differences between Western European imperialism and American imperialism is that Western Europe never colonized the world as a single imperial power the way the United States has done. Western European states have competed with each other ever since the fall of the Western half of the Roman Empire. That competition continues to this day.

The English had observed how the tiny nation-state of Holland had used piracy, the slave trade, Protestant free enterprise and naval skills to steal from the Portuguese and Spanish. England was determined to both copy and compete with the Dutch. As a result the British fought four wars with the Dutch between 1652 and 1784. At the end of the day Britain emerged as the dominant slave trading nation responsible for transporting one third of the total African slaves across the Atlantic. British *privateers* became far more successful pirates than the Dutch *sea beggars.* The English East India Company became more successful than the Dutch East India Company. Most importantly, the British stole far more land and resources than the Dutch. We document here the rise of the British Empire by looking at the initial cooperation between the two Protestant nations and their four wars for dominance.

Prelude to Anglo-Dutch Rivalry

England had aided the Dutch in their fight for independence from Spain. In August of 1585 the English Queen, Elizabeth I, signed the treaty of *Nonsuch* with Holland. Queen Elizabeth sent both financial aid and cavalry and foot soldiers under the command of the Earl of Leicester, Robert Dudley, to assist the rebels. The rebels were further helped when King Philip II of Spain responded to the English support by diverting financial and military resources from fighting the rebels to invading England in 1588. Spain's invasion of England turned out to be a disaster for Spain and the English renewed the treaty of Nonsuch in 1598. The Anglo/Dutch Protestant alliance was further aided by the war between the two Catholic nations, France and Spain, in 1595–1598.

At the outbreak of the Dutch rebellion in 1568 England was a relatively powerful European state much like France at the outbreak of the American rebellion in 1776. Just as the French help to the American rebels turned out to be disastrous for the French Empire the English support for the Dutch rebels turned out to be a disaster for the English Empire. The English had been stealing from the Spanish Empire long before the Dutch rebellion. Their primary reason for helping the Dutch rebels was to weaken Spain and aid its own theft of Spanish gold, silver and colonies. Never in her wildest dreams did England ever contemplate these seven tiny Dutch provinces becoming an imperial rival. In like manner the French would later assist the American rebels only to weaken England and aid its competition with England for imperial dominance. Never in her wildest dreams did France ever contemplate the thirteen tiny English North American colonies becoming an imperial rival. See *American Invasions: Canada to Afghanistan.*

English competition with Spain can be dated to the voyage of discovery by *John Cabot* in 1497. News of Columbus reaching land by sailing West in 1492 provided the incentive for other Western European states to chase the myth of reaching the spices and silk of the Orient by sailing west. King Henry VII, the first of the Tudor kings of England, commissioned Cabot for the voyage. Unfortunately for Henry VII, Cabot landed too far north in Newfoundland. As it turned out Columbus had not found a sea route to the Orient. But Spain found gold and silver in its American colonies. The English determined that it was much more lucrative to pirate Spanish galleons transporting ill-gotten loot from the people of the Americas and selling African slaves to the Portuguese empire than to engage in voyages of discovery. The Tudor Queen, *Elizabeth I,* encouraged both English piracy and English participation in the evil African "slave trade." The so-called enlightened British Empire, lauded by acclaimed historians like Niall Ferguson, began its life as nothing more than an evil **slave trader** and **pirate.** Like the American Empire, which began with slave plantations and genocide of First Nations, there is absolutely nothing enlightened or civilized about the British or American empires. Moreover, the atrocities inflicted on the human race by these two empires only multiplied as they became more powerful, more greedy, more technologically armed, more addicted to senseless warmongering, more hypocritical, more immoral, more adept at the use of propaganda and more immune to criticism.

The English had honed their skills at killing, and exterminating those they colonized, in Ireland. Norman England had invaded Ireland in 1169. Since then the Irish have fought the English to regain their independence. That struggle continues to this day much like the continuing struggles of First Nations in North America. One of the dastardly ways in which the West continues to justify its use of force against rebels is to label them as terrorists. The moral right of people to rebel against continued Western bombing and destruction of their land and resources is turned on its head by proclaiming the idiotic slogan that the West is intervening to spread democracy and that killing the millions of women and children is just collateral damage. Millions killed by WMDs by the West is simply collateral damage. A single person killed by a rebel defending his land makes him a terrorist. Acceptance of the evil deeds committed by the West as somehow necessary for human progress is the hallmark of Western propaganda. In 2015, for example, how any Canadian can think that a cowardly Canadian pilot, safely ensconced in his fighter jet flying high above the heavens, dropping massive bombs on Libyans, Iraqis and Syrians to kill and maim them and to destroy their livelihoods and homes and adding to the 60 million refugees, is good for the human race, simply boggles my mind. Adding insult to injury, the civilized Canadian government cooperates with the United States to ensure that the refugee camps are set up in relatively poor countries like Jordan, Lebanon, and Turkey rather than in Canada or the United States. There is simply no limit to the evil of Western propaganda.

By 2015 a few of these refugees have dared to risk their lives to cross the waters of the Mediterranean separating them from Italy and

Western Europe. Rather ironically, this desperate attempt to reach Western Europe is facilitated by the Canadian/Western destruction of Libya. By destroying the government of Libya the West inadvertently created a "safe haven" in Libya for a few of the 60 million refuges created by the incessant and totally insane Western bombing of Afghanistan, Iraq, Syria, Yemen and other parts of the Middle East and North Africa. From Libya these few daring refugees used make-shift boats, facilitated in part by ruthless and Western impoverished businessmen, to cross the narrow waters separating Libya from Italy. Italy's colonial past in Libya has returned to haunt it with a vengeance. Western Europe is at a loss to deal with the relatively small influx of refugees from the massive refugee problem it helped the Americans and Canadians to create.

Canada, on the other hand, is safe from the reach of these 60 million refuges it has so deliberately helped to create simply to show that it has the military planes to do so. Canada's prime minister, Steven Harper, can win the votes of a gullible electorate by pretending to be tough on terrorism. Canada's military, like Prince Harry, boasts how tough it is when it is killing defenseless men, women, and children, with advanced fighter jets—or killer copters, as used by Prince Harry. Now that these people have gotten their hands on some American weapons, after the U.S./Canadian-trained Iraqi soldiers dropped them and ran for their lives, there is no more talk of Canadian soldiers or Prince Harry being brave. Now the West pretends that it does not want to put boots or killer copters on the ground rather than admitting cowardice. But they have no qualms about pestering Arab countries to put their soldiers in harm's way. The new reality is that the citizens of the countries invaded by the West have better weapons than before. It's easy for Canadian an American soldiers to boast of their bravery when they have high tech weapons and those they are invading to colonize have only sling shots. But when those they are invading have been able to get their hands on some of these high tech Western weapons the tune changes to that of not putting boots on the ground but only bombing from the safety of the heavens out of reach of the weapons of those being bombed senselessly. It's now up to Arabs to display bravery with boots on the ground not our "cowardly" military or Prince Harry.

No people have fought this ridiculous immorality of the West than Irish rebels. Like the First Nations, the Irish were also robbed of their religion by the English invaders. Catholicism had arrived in Ireland in the fifth century. The English forcibly replaced Catholicism with Protestantism as one of its tools to colonize Ireland. The Irish have shown great determination to resist both the English and their religion. Gaelic resistance during the thirteenth century weakened the English "lordship" of Ireland. King Henry VIII decided to reconquer Ireland rather than engage in the voyages of discovery began by his father with John Cabot. In 1541 Henry VIII was proclaimed king of Ireland. Henry's primary claim to fame was to convince the entire English nation that they must convert to Protestantism so that he could have many wives and continue the Western tradition that sons must be preferred to daughters. Nevertheless it was Henry's daughter, Queen Elizabeth I, who continued his reconquest of Ireland.

Irish land was stolen so that English thieves could establish plantations similar to the slave plantations of the New World. Irish Catholic landowners were replaced by English Protestant landowners who became the rulers of the English colony of Ireland. The Irish rebellions were met with the same cruelty and brute force of the English imperial power as the First Nations rebellions in North America. As much as one-third of the original Irish owners of the land were killed off by civilized English thieves. The English added to their wealth from selling African slaves, by selling **Irish slaves.** Both were sold to the European plantations in the Caribbean and America. In the eyes of Western historians selling both black and white slaves made the seller even more civilized providing that the whites sold into slavery were deemed to be inferior whites, as the Irish were at that time in history. Western propaganda is so powerful that it can convince the world that your race is inferior even when it's the same color as the civilized race. Like the First Nations, the Irish were called *savages* since the word *terrorists,* had not yet been invented by the West as the best term to use to dehumanize those fighting Western imperialism. Irish slaves, like African slaves, were sold to plantation owners in the New World. Many were tortured and executed. Today the descendants of these English thieves in Ireland, just like the descendants of the English thieves in the other English colonies such as the *Malvinas* (Falkland Islands), hold Western-style democratic votes to continue as English colonies. New Boss man in 2013, Prime Minister David Cameron, told the world to respect the votes of the descendants of thieves since that is what Western democracy is all about.

English Colonization in the New World before the Anglo-Dutch Wars

After colonizing the Irish the English continued to hone their penchant for genocide and mass murder on the inhabitants of the New World and in Asia and Africa. Since the English would compete with the Dutch both in the New World and in Asia and Africa it was inevitable that they would end up fighting each other. The Dutch had been the first imperial power to steal from the Spanish/Portuguese Empire. The Portuguese and Spanish had used superior naval power to steal the world outside Europe. The Dutch and English navies became more powerful than the Portuguese and Spanish. Once the English had defeated the Spanish Armada in 1588 it was just a matter of time before the English would become the bigger thief and slave trader compared with the Dutch.

In the New World the English stole the land of the First Nations along the Atlantic coast easily accessible by ships and protected by the superior cannons of the English navy. As with Columbus, the First Nations were initially friendly to the English. Without assistance from the First Nations the first English settlement in *Jamestown,* Virginia, in 1607 would not have survived. Like the Spanish before them, once the English had the upper hand in terms of military superiority, they killed off most of the First Nations and stole their land. Between 1607 and the first Anglo-Dutch war of 1652–1654 the English had stolen enough land from the First Nations to claim **seven** colonies along the Atlantic seaboard. These were the colonies of Virginia, Plymouth, Massachusetts, Maryland, Rhode Island, Connecticut and New Haven.

In the Caribbean the English stole First Nations lands to colonize the islands of St. Kitts, Barbados and Nevis, between 1624 and 1628. The English also stole land in Bermuda, Montserrat, Antigua and the Bahamas. These tiny islands were ideally suited for growing sugar, which was the most valuable crop at the time. The English could now provide African slaves, as well as Irish slaves, to their own Caribbean slave plantations in addition to selling African and Irish slaves to the Spanish and Portuguese. Their mainland colonies benefitted from the specialization of their Caribbean colonies on sugar since they could supply the Caribbean colonies with food products such as fish and corn, lumber and other supplies, which enabled the Caribbean colonies to specialize almost exclusively on sugar. The North American colonies also imported sugar and molasses from the Caribbean colonies to manufacture rum.

While colonies are always obtained by theft rather than trade they are only profitable if their value exceed the military cost of stealing them. This is why Columbus and the Spaniards were so obsessed with finding gold. It also explains why the Vikings left North America after finding nothing of value to steal. The English had found a valuable export crop in tobacco. It was grown both on the mainland and in the Caribbean. But it was sugar that made theft of the First Nations land so valuable. The English colonies in the Caribbean were valuable enough to steal because sugar was a high value crop and African slave labor was cheap. The English colonies on the Atlantic seaboard were, in turn, valuable enough to steal partly because they could supply the needs of the sugar producing Caribbean colonies.

English Colonization in Asia and Africa before the Anglo-Dutch Wars

While the English East India Company was established in 1600, two years before the Dutch East India Company, the Dutch had stolen a significant portion of the lucrative spice "trade" from the Portuguese long before the English were able to steal as much. An English warship, the *Edward Bonaventure,* had reached Asia in 1593, three years before the Dutch first sailed to Asia. The English East India Company set up its first "trading" fort in the city of *Banten,* in 1602, a year before the Dutch.

Since the Portuguese Empire had established its military dominance in Asia, the English, like the Dutch, would have to fight the Portuguese to get any part of Asia. The English scored a naval victory against the Portuguese at the *Battle of Swally* in 1612. Swally was located in the important port city of *Surat* in Gujarat, India. This victory over the Portuguese enabled the English to secure permission from the Mughal emperor of India, *Nuruddin Jahangir,* to "trade" in India. The English allied with the Dutch to attack the Portuguese and Spanish ships off the coast of China. The English East India Company established a "trading" fort in *Madras* in 1639. Prior to the Anglo-Dutch wars the English East India Company had over twenty "trading" forts in India. Products exported from India by the English included silk, cotton, tea, indigo dye, and saltpeter.

Anglo-Dutch competition for world domination was certainly not restricted to piracy of the wealth of the Spanish and Portuguese empires or theft of land and resources in the New World and Asia but centered most tellingly on capturing, transporting and selling Africans as **slaves.** Prince Henry the Navigator and African "slave trader" had seen it fit to do his Christian duty by using the profits from the vile African "slave trade" to fund the Christian wars against Islam. England would join Holland as the leading Protestant Nations to pretend that their Christian God saw no evil in enslaving Africans to profit both the church and the state.

The English **pirate,** Sir John Hawkins, is credited by Western historians as the Englishman clever enough to have made England the dominant empire after the Dutch by selling Africans as **slaves.** That Western historians would glorify such a dastardly "trade" is the most compelling evidence of the hypocrisy of Western civilization. As for the enlightened English who carried the "white man's burden" for so long before the Americans obliged, Sir John was knighted by the Queen for his skills as a **pirate** and a **slave trader.** Combine two evil deeds and you are doubly heroic in the eyes of Western historians.

Sir John made three voyages for African slaves during the 1560s. His African "slave-trading" business was supported by Queen Elizabeth I and wealthy English merchants. It is estimated that he captured some 1,200 Africans and sold them into slavery in the New World. The "enlightened" English followed the lead of Sir John with over ten thousand voyages to Africa for slaves. Of the 6 million Africans sold into slavery by the West during the eighteenth century the English accounted for almost half.

No nation can ever be called civilized if it condones slavery. But African slavery imposed by the West was more evil than most because it involved the grossly inhuman transatlantic voyage where Africans were packed into the holds of the ships and chained together for weeks. Many died during capture, during the wait at the slave warehouse prior to the transatlantic voyage, and during the voyage. Many books have been written about the inhumane treatment of the Africans by the West. But the West is still glorified as civilized despite these many and continuing uncivilized and barbaric behavior. The West simply moves on from one barbaric behavior, such as slavery, to another and another. Examples include genocide of the inhabitants of its colonies, piracy, warmongering, WMDs such as nuking Japan, carpet bombing, land mines, bunker busting bombs, drones, etc. Yet all of these barbaric acts are the same acts that Western historians use to deem the West to be civilized and worthy of Nobel Peace Prizes. Furthermore, the West pressures those conquered by these same barbaric actions to emulate what Western historians deem to be the civilized behaviors of the West. It's depravity gone wild.

The Anglo-Dutch Wars for Imperial Dominance: 1652–1674

While the Dutch would come from well behind and surpass the English during the first half of the seventeenth century the English navy would not only prove superior to the Dutch but also to the French who challenged it after the Dutch were defeated. The English had helped the Dutch gain their independence from Spain. But as the Dutch Empire grew at the expense of the Spanish Empire, England began to ally with Spain against the Dutch. The English challenge to Dutch naval supremacy was postponed temporarily by the English Civil War of 1642–1651.

The Dutch ended its war with Spain in January of 1648 with the *Peace of Munster.* The Dutch navy was less funded after the Dutch had made peace with its former ruler, Spain. The Dutch even sold many of their ships. By the outbreak of the first Anglo-Dutch war in 1652 the English navy was in much better shape than the Dutch. Under the rule of Oliver Cromwell, 1653–1658, England further upgraded its navy. At the same time English **pirates** preyed on Dutch ships. Between October

1651 and the outbreak of war in July 1652, English pirates had captured over a hundred Dutch ships. The Dutch had been the first to make piracy civilized when used by the West. The English had quickly seen the profit of copying this civilized Dutch practice against the Spanish and Portuguese. Now it was the turn of the English to use this civilized Western weapon against the Dutch. The Dutch responded to English piracy by increasing and better arming their ships. When the Dutch retaliated against English piracy, England declared war on the Dutch on July 10, 1652. Thus began the first of four wars for imperial dominance between the English and Dutch empires.

In the first war the Dutch and English tested the strength of their respective navies. During the war the Dutch resumed funding of its navy. English pirates continued to attack and capture Dutch ships. Both sides had victories and defeats and the economies of both countries suffered as trade was interrupted. The English disrupted Dutch trade in the Baltic and Dutch fishing in the North Sea. The Dutch, in turn, defeated the English fleet in the Mediterranean. There were several battles but none were sufficiently decisive. The only winner was Portugal who took advantage of the Dutch war with England to drive the Dutch out of its colony of Brazil. As a result the Dutch lost their lucrative sugar producing colony on the North coast of Brazil. In fact, this war between these two Protestant nations, benefited the Catholic empires of both Portugal and Spain.

As early as February of 1653 both sides sent out signals that they were interested in peace talks. But the war continued and in May of 1654 Oliver Cromwell decided that it was time to negotiate seriously with the Dutch. The Dutch responded favorably because the English naval blockade of the Dutch coast following the English victory at the *Battle of the Gabbard,* June 2–3, 1653, was making it difficult for the Dutch to feed their people. After another battle proved extremely costly to both sides, the *Battle of Scheveningen,* August 8–10, 1653, both sides were more than ready for peace. Peace negotiations began and the *Treaty of Westminster,* April 5, 1654, put an end to the first war.

The Second Anglo-Dutch War for Imperial Domination: 1665–1667

The Dutch continued the upgrade of their navy after the first war ended. Sixty new heavier ships were added. Once war broke out again the Dutch added seven ships to its fleet for every ship added to the English navy. The Dutch had no illusions of the intention of the English to continue to pirate its ships and steal the African "slave trade." The English placed their faith in the weapon of **piracy,** which is deemed a very civilized weapon of war only when used by a Western imperial power. English pirates captured more than two hundred Dutch ships. The English also fought the Dutch in West Africa to dominate that other very civilized Western tradition of selling **African slaves.** By the outbreak of the second Anglo-Dutch war in 1664 England had restored her monarchy. Charles II became the king of England in 1660. The king's brother, James, was the duke of York, Lord High Admiral of the English navy and head of the *Royal African Company,* the English company specializing in "trading" **African slaves.**

The Royal African Company was originally called the *Company of Royal Adventurers Trading to Africa* when it was first granted a royal charter in 1660 to monopolize the "trade" in gold, silver and **African slaves.** The slaves were branded with the letters "DY" for duke of York. In return for granting monopoly rights, the king received half of the profits. Trade is the Western historian term for theft by colonization. Since it was theft rather than trade the company built or captured military fortresses along the West African coast. The Dutch had followed the Portuguese in enslaving the Africans and the English followed the Dutch. As the West increased their colonies in the New World there was more and more profits to be made supplying the civilized slave plantation owners, including those who would found the "freedom loving" republic of the United States of America. The company captured and sold over one hundred thousand African slaves.

In addition to competing with the Dutch for the African slave "trade," the king's brother, James, also stole New York and New Jersey from the Dutch, who had previously stolen them from the First Nations. The English invaded and captured the Dutch colony of New Netherland in June 1664. The land was given to the duke of York by King Charles II. The duke gave a piece of New Netherland to two of his friends. That piece of stolen First Nations land became the American state of *New Jersey.* The remainder of New Netherland became the American state of *New York.* The Dutch responded to the English attacks in West Africa and North America. They recaptured the fortresses in West Africa taken by the English and captured some of the English fortresses. In response England declared war on Holland on March 4, 1665.

This second Anglo-Dutch war battered the economies of both countries and resolved very little. King Charles II of England was on the verge of bankruptcy. It was ended on July 31, 1667, by the *Treaty of Breda.* The English kept their conquest of New Netherland. The Dutch were able to secure some softening of the English *Navigation Act.* The English Navigation Acts, beginning with the first Act in 1651, were intended to prevent the Dutch from trading with English colonies. As a result of the Treaty of Breda the Dutch secured some guarantees from harassment and search of Dutch ships on the high seas by the English navy. This made it more difficult for the English to prevent Dutch trade with her colonies.

The Third Anglo-Dutch War for Imperial Hegemony: 1672–1674

King Charles II had felt personal humiliation at not being able to defeat the Dutch during the 1665–1667 war. As we said above, the war had driven him to the verge of bankruptcy and that was his primary reason for seeking peace. As a result of this personal humiliation and desperate financial situation King Charles II signed a secret alliance with King Louis XIV of France whereby the French king subsidized Charles II to the tune of 225,000 pounds per year. In addition to this subsidy Charles II repudiated a debt of 1.3 million pounds in January 1672. Charles was now in a better financial situation to start a new war. The opportunity was provided when the French declared war on Holland on April 6, 1672. As a result of the Anglo-French alliance, England declared war on Holland the following day.

The French invaded Holland by land while the English continued their Anglo-Dutch wars at sea. The Dutch increased their budget for their navy and sent their hero from the previous war, Admiral-General Michael de Ruyter, to destroy the combined Anglo-French fleet anchored off the east coast of England in Solebay. At the *Battle of Solebay,* June 7, 1672, the allied fleet was only saved by a sudden turn of the wind. But the damage inflicted by de Ruyter was severe. The Dutch engaged the allied fleet again, this time off the Dutch coast. At the first *Battle of Schooneveld,* June 7, 1673, de Ruyter managed to divide the allied fleet into four confused parts and there was no decisive result.

At the second Battle of Schooneveld, June 14, 1673, de Ruyter used fresh crews and an addition of four ships to his fleet, to attack the allied fleet out at sea. The allied fleet had been afraid to engage the Dutch inland because of their disarray in the first battle. They had kept their distance from the Dutch coast forcing de Ruyter to come to them. When de Ruyter obliged the allies, by attacking out at sea, the allied fleet, rather surprisingly, was thrown into even more confusion than in the June 7 battle and forced to flee the battle and into the Thames. De Ruyter returned the Dutch fleet safely to Holland. The allied fleet was damaged and it was another victory for the Dutch navy. After repairs to their damaged ships the allied fleet once more sailed out to sea to tempt de Ruyter to come out of his defensive advantage in Schooneveld.

Fearing for the safety of the Dutch spice fleet returning from Asia, de Ruyter was ordered by the Dutch *Stadholder* (the term for the head of state in Holland), William III, to engage the enemy at sea. On August 21, 1673, de Ruyter engaged the allied fleet at the final *Battle of Texel.* Despite being as outnumbered again as in the previous battles, de Ruyter's exceptional naval ability scored another victory for the Dutch. The war became increasingly unpopular in England and the English parliament forced King Charles II to make peace with the Dutch by refusing a war budget for 1674. A second *Treaty of Westminster* was signed on February 19, 1674.

Anglo-Dutch Unity and the Challenge of France

Empires emerge because a country invents or copy a superior military weapon. That weapon for the Vikings, the Portuguese, the Spanish, and the Dutch, was naval prowess. The English challenged the Dutch for naval hegemony with four wars. At the end of the first three wars the Dutch remained the dominant naval power. The fourth and final war was postponed because of the temporary unification of England and Holland by William III and his wife Mary in 1689. In the third war the French had joined the competition by forming an alliance with the English. The Dutch defeated that Anglo-French alliance at the naval battles of Solebay, Schooneveld and Texel.

The secret Anglo-French alliance between the king of England, Charles II, and the king of France, Louis XIV, turned out to be a golden opportunity for the ambitious and able Stadholder of Holland, William III of Orange, nephew of King Charles II. The rivalry between Louis XIV and William III would dominate the period following the third Anglo-Dutch war. William III would use the Catholic/Protestant rift in Christianity to seize the English throne and unite Holland with England to enable England to seize naval hegemony from Holland and simultaneously defeat a challenge from France.

Background to the Rise of the French Empire

Portugal, Spain, Holland and England were not major continental powers. They were maritime powers on the fringes of the European continent, which had used naval superiority to conquer vast colonies outside Europe. France, like Germany later, was different. France was first and foremost a European power. The union of England and Holland under William III in 1689 effectively ended the rivalry between England and Holland and the future competition for both European and world domination would be between England and France. It's therefore important that we continue to trace the rise of France under the Frankish Empire, which we began in chapter 3.

In 843 the Western half of the Frankish Empire became France. The Western half of the old Roman Empire was dominated by the German

Empire after Otto I became holy Roman emperor in 962. But the power struggle between the pope and that of the kings and emperors in Western Europe continued. The pope encouraged rebellions by independent minded princes in Germany to enhance his power. In chapter 3 we also traced the rise of the House of Habsburg with Rudolph von Habsburg becoming king of Germany in 1273. In 1438 a Habsburg, Albert V of Austria, became holy Roman emperor.

The Habsburg emperors were in a state of continuing conflicts and wars with the French ruling family, the Valois. The Habsburg-Valois wars lasted from 1494 to 1559. At a time when the Christian West was under constant threat from the expanding Ottoman Empire the French typically allied with the Ottomans against their Christian brothers. But the unification of the Habsburg family with the Spanish monarchs by marriage in 1497 made the Habsburg family once again the most powerful family in Western Europe. King Charles I of Spain became holy Roman emperor in 1519 and ruled both Christian Europe and most of Europe's overseas empire. The Valois family opposed the rule of Charles I as Emperor Charles V and this led to continued wars with France.

King Francis I of France seemed to have had an intense personal hatred for Charles V. He had contested Charles V for the title of holy Roman emperor. He felt that France was encircled on every side by the lands of the Habsburgs. After failing to form an alliance with King Henry VIII of England he allied with Suleiman the Magnificent of the Ottoman Empire against Charles V. During the Italian War of 1521–1526 he lost the *Battle of Pavia* in 1525 and was captured by Charles V and held as a prisoner in Madrid. Pressure from the Ottoman emperor helped to get his release in March of 1526. But war broke out again later that same year. Francis I allied with England, the Republic of Florence, and Pope Clement VII against Charles V. This time it was Pope Clement VII who was captured by Charles V, forcing Francis I to renounce his claims to Italy.

With the death of the duke of Milan, Francis I invaded Italy, again with the aid of his Ottoman ally, in 1536. He captured Turin but failed to capture Milan. Peace came in 1538 and France kept Turin. During the next Italian War of 1542–1546 a Franco-Ottoman fleet captured Nice. King Henry VIII of England allied with Charles V against Francis I.

Francis I made peace with Charles V in 1544 but continued to fight the English until 1546. Both Francis I and Henry VIII died the next year. Charles V continued to be the most powerful Christian ruler until his abdication in 1556 and death in 1558.

Henry II became the king of France in 1547 after the death of his father Francis I. He continued his father's efforts to replace Habsburg domination of Europe with the Valois family of France. He maintained the Franco-Ottoman alliance and began the eighth Italian War against Charles V in 1551. After some initial victories he lost the crucial *Battle of Marciano* in 1553. Henry II was forced to renounce French claims to Italy by the 1559 treaty of *Cateau-Cambresis.*

Spain had triumphed in the wars with France but the division of the Habsburg family between the Spanish and Austrian branches weakened the Habsburgs. The Austrian branch led the Austro-Hungarian Empire and the Holy Roman Empire after 1556 when Ferdinand I succeeded Charles V as holy Roman emperor. It was under constant threat from the Ottoman Muslims, the French Catholics and the Protestant Christians. Philip II became the new king of Spain and ruled the Spanish overseas empire. France had its own problems. Henry II died in a jousting match in 1559 and his son King Francis II died the next year. The ten-year-old Charles IX became the new king of France on December 5, 1560. France, like the Habsburgs, had to deal with the rising tide of Protestantism sweeping through Europe. These so-called religious wars beginning in 1562 and lasting until 1598 kept France from effectively continuing her efforts to dominate continental Europe.

The House of Valois ended after King Henry III of France died in 1589 without an heir. France was led thereafter by the equally powerful *House of Bourbon.* The House of Bourbon would have greater success compared with the Valois family in making France the dominant continental power in Europe. During Bourbon rule the powerful Habsburg family would suffer many setbacks. Somewhat ironically, the first of the Bourbon kings of France, *Henry IV,* was a Protestant who had fought for the Protestants against the Valois kings in the "wars of religion" between the Catholics and Protestants. In 1572 he only narrowly escaped death during the St. Bartholomew day's massacre of Protestants in Paris. He had to fight a four year war against the Catholic League and convert to Catholicism to secure his position as king of France. He was opposed by Catholic Spain and aided by Protestant England. He continued the quest of the Valois rulers to replace the Habsburgs with France as the dominant power in Europe. Under his rule France continued its alliance with the Ottoman Empire. He ended the religious wars with the 1598 *Edict of Nantes.* The Edict granted political and civil rights to Protestants. He was distrusted by Catholics and assassinated in 1610.

The French Empire Takes on the British

Louis XIII became king of France in 1610 when he was nine years old. During the seventeenth century, France would fight many wars with Britain for imperial hegemony. Until the American Empire no Western empire was able to unify the West after the fall of the Roman Empire. We saw that the Portuguese Empire was defeated and absorbed by another Western European empire, Spain, and that the Spanish Empire, in turn, was reduced by another Western European empire, Holland. Holland, in turn, was challenged by yet another Western European empire, England. When England merged with Holland it was yet another Western European empire, France that would challenge it. This desire for the sovereignty of the nation-state after the fall of the Roman Empire prevented the unification of Europe just as it has prevented the unification of Africa and Asia. But until the rise of the American Empire these Western European empires, based on small nation-states such as Portugal, Spain, Holland, Britain and France, were powerful enough to dominate the world. Far from wanting a single unified world power they fought for what was called a "balance of power."

France, like Holland and Britain, began its quest for imperial dominance by using the two civilized tools of the West, the **African "slave trade"** and **Piracy. Justice and injustice** are defined by the West, not by morality or humanity, but by Western vs. non-Western usage. Torture, slavery, piracy, nuclear weapons, warmongering, unmanned drone kills and propaganda are **just** if used by the West but unjust if used by others. The United States is entitled to have an abundance of nuclear weapons but North Korea and Iran are entitled to none. The United

States is entitled to steal Cuban land to imprison and torture to such an inhumane level that **Guantanamo** has become the most infamous torture chamber the world has ever known, surpassing Abu Ghraib and the "black sites" created by the United States in Thailand, Poland, Lithuania and other parts of the U.S.-dominated globe. President Obama is entitled to kill anyone he dislikes, even receiving the Nobel "war" prize to do so. Canada is entitled to imprison First Nations in reserves without housing and running water. So it was with the 1494 *Treaty of Tordesillas.* This was a **just** treaty since it empowered the civilized West to steal the lands and resources of the non-Western peoples. It was equally **unjust** to the civilized Western states of Holland, England and France. They were therefore justified in enslaving Africans and using state sanctioned piracy to offset the injustice inflicted on them by this treaty.

France began her capture and sale of African slaves after she secured a port in Senegal on the West African coast in 1659. Some French ships had participated in this inhumane, but legal, activity earlier. It has been estimated that more than 1.3 million Africans were enslaved and transported in French ships from Africa to the New World. Nantes, on the west coast of France, was the leading French slave port from which the French ships departed to West Africa. The French government imposed taxes on what Western historians call the slave "trade." The so-called Black Code or Code Noir was passed by the French government in 1685 to both regulate and encourage this crime against humanity. Only five French ports were permitted by the French government to engage in this crime so that the French government could more easily manage and tax it. The French ships were "baptized" with Christian names to make one of the most inhumane and sadistic activity a civilized Christian act. The captured slaves made the horrendous voyage across the Atlantic packed like sardines in the lower holds of the ships and bound in pairs with leg irons. Those who were unfortunate enough to survive this miserable voyage were sold in the New World to the slave plantation owners who had stolen the lands of the First Nations. The brutality and inhumanity of the African slave trade made the French feel racially superior and so very civilized. They now joined the ranks of the other civilized Europeans, the Portuguese, Spanish, Dutch and English. Since the slave "trade" was the most lucrative form of "trade" during the seventeenth century any Western nation not participating in such a profitable business could not be civilized. Of course, if you were **not** a Western nation, participation would be deemed barbaric by western historians.

Western historians often claim that the African slave "trade" was crucial in spurring the massive increase in international trade during the seventeenth and eighteenth centuries. The reality is that what these Western historians call **trade** was mostly criminal activities. Colonization is the theft of lands and resources, not trade. Capturing and selling African slaves is not trade. Piracy is not trade. Such criminal activities are only called **trade** when they are done by the West. The greater the crimes committed by the West the more civilized the West is deemed to be. Their degree of civilization is measured not by their crimes but by their wealth. The more wealthy and prosperous they become the more civilized they are deemed to be. The crimes committed are not hidden but twisted by propaganda to be viewed as civilized by using words such as **trade** or **commerce.** A few may be willing to refer to this **crime** as "forced migration." But it's not trade, or commerce, or migration. It's a **crime,** and the most evil of crimes ever committed by people and by nation-states. Such a crime makes those who commit it evil, not civilized.

The French Corsairs Compete with the Dutch Sea Beggars and the English Privateers to make France As Civilized as the Dutch and English

The Portuguese and Spanish had ventured across the seas to find the silks and spices of the Orient. But the richest prizes for the nascent empires of Holland, England and France were African slaves and pirating Spanish treasure ships loaded with gold and silver from the New World. French pirates attacked the Spanish ships on their way from Peru and Mexico to their Caribbean ports in Cuba and Santo Domingo. The French state had no qualms about legalizing this crime and collecting her share of the booty. Piracy, like slavery, was a state sanctioned activity that enabled France to join the Western club of civilized nations and compete as the equal of Holland and England. Since these three Maritime powers, Holland, England and France, depended heavily on naval warfare, their state sanctioned pirates were indispensable allies in these wars. This was a period where the navies of the countries were supported by merchant ships and pirates in the fight for imperial dominance. The accepted hypocrisy of the time was that a pirate attacking any ship of another nation was a hero worthy of protection by his king. In France he was a **corsair** not a pirate. He was a pirate only if he attacked a ship of his own country and was to be hanged for such a vile crime.

State-sanctioned piracy began in France prior to the rise of the Spanish Empire. It dates back to 1144 when the port of St. Malo provided refuge to French corsairs. The French state, like Holland and England before, encouraged the growth of piracy as an imperial weapon after the pope had divided the world between Portugal and Spain. This division was sealed by the 1494 Treaty of Tordesillas. Piracy, like enslaving Africans, was justified by France as opposition to the unjust Treaty of Tordesillas. The reality was that Western states were engaged in theft and all manner of crimes against humanity to get rich. This sanctioning of theft had begun with the Viking raids and has continued to this day. Today these raids are conducted mostly by air rather than by sea and led by the American Empire rather than the states of Western Europe. The Western European states still play an important supporting role, much like Canada and Australia. The latest victims of these raids are Syria, Libya, Mali, Pakistan, Yemen, Afghanistan and Iraq.

In addition to selling African slaves and engaging in piracy the French copied the Dutch and English by colonizing lands and stealing their resources. This was done both in the New World and in Asia and Africa. Colonies, African slaves and piracy were the three important weapons against the Spanish Empire and were used by Holland, England and France. In time they used these same weapons against each other. We documented the three wars between Holland and England. We will now turn to the wars between England and France.

Wars between the nation-states of Western Europe date back to the break-up of the Roman Empire. What was new was that naval battles had moved from the Mediterranean to the Atlantic and the Far East. These same nation-states of Western Europe expanded their wars for territory outside their homes in Western Europe. Portugal, Spain, Holland and England were fighting mostly for power outside Western Europe. France was fighting to be both the dominant continental power as well as for colonies and power in the New World and in Asia and Africa.

The Anglo-French Wars for Imperial Dominance: 1688–1785

France and England had engaged in wars with each other ever since the Norman invasion of England in 1066. However, we begin with 1688 after the unification of England with Holland, because Holland ceased to be the primary rival to England's quest for imperial hegemony and was replaced by France. French colonization in the New World and Asia began well before 1688 and was the primary reason for the wars between England and France after 1688. French colonization began during the reign of King Francis I. In 1517 Francis I built the deep water port of *Le Havre* to launch French voyages of exploration. As with the Portuguese, Spanish, Dutch, and English, these so-called French "voyages of exploration" were really naval expeditions intended to prospect for land and resources, which could be stolen by military force. Giovanni da Verrazano was sent by Francis I to North America in 1524 to find the Northwest Passage to the spices in the Indies. He failed to find the passage but claimed Newfoundland on behalf of France. French fishermen had been fishing off Newfoundland since 1504. The French fishermen began drying their catch on the Newfoundland coast and made contacts with the First Nations. French corsairs attacked Portuguese ships fishing the Grand Banks. Despite the fact that John Cabot had discovered Newfoundland for England in 1497 the French began selling some of their Newfoundland catch to England as early as 1529.

In 1534 Francis I sent Jacques Cartier to explore for gold and find the Northwest Passage through the St. Lawrence River. Cartier made three voyages to North America between 1534 and 1541. He attempted to steal some First Nations land for France but the Huron Nation was militarily superior. Francis I next used the services of the French Corsair, Jean-Francois de Roberval. He sent Roberval with two ships and two hundred colonists to complement the five ships and five hundred colonists of Cartier. Cartier left France in May of 1541 and Roberval left a year later. Roberval's attempts to steal First Nations lands were no more successful than that of Cartier. But France would persist and eventually defeat the

First Nations with superior weapons as the Portuguese, Spanish, Dutch and English had done. Since the French competed mostly for the First Nations lands in North America they were opposed primarily by the English. The Portuguese and Spanish had stolen First Nations lands mostly in South and Central America while the Dutch had merged with the English after 1688.

With regard to French competition for Asia, Francis I sent the first French ship to India in 1527. Other ships followed but it was not until the reign of Henry IV that French colonization in Asia began. The first French company set up to "trade" with Asia was formed in 1600. It sent two ships in 1601, one of which reached Ceylon but was captured by the Dutch on its return voyage. In 1604 Henry IV gave his permission to French merchants to create a French East India company to compete with the Dutch and English East India companies. The company of the Moluccas was formed in 1615. French ships continued to meet fierce resistance from the Dutch. In 1619 the French ships were armed to fight the Dutch. But the Dutch had the naval superiority. It was not until the reign of Louis XIV that the French were more successful against the Dutch.

The French East India Company was finally formed in 1664 by combining the resources of three earlier companies. It knew that it would face fierce resistance from the Dutch and English. The French established their presence in Asia from a base set up in Pondicherry, India, in 1673. The French established a naval presence in the Indian Ocean as well. This was another reason for the wars with England after 1688. England and France would fight each other for colonies in both North America and Asia. The unification of Holland and England gave the English the edge. In the end both England and France would be forced to return the stolen lands in Asia. But in North America the lands stolen from the First Nations would go to the United States, Canada and Mexico. The First Nations who survived the genocide would end up permanently imprisoned on reserves.

The First Post-1688 Anglo-French War: The Nine Year's War: 1689–1697

The English king Henry VIII became infamous because of his six or seven wives. But his more important legacy was changing England from a Catholic Nation to a Protestant Nation. While Protestants rebelled against every Western European monarch they were only successful in changing the official state religion in England and Holland. It was the desire of English Protestants to prevent a return to Catholic rule in England that provided the Stadholder of Holland, William III, the opportunity to become king of England. It was also England's colonization of North America that led to the United States and Canada becoming Protestant Nations. With the dominance of the British and American empires, Protestants took over leadership of the world from Catholics.

In the Third Anglo-Dutch War of 1672–1674 France had allied with England against the Dutch. This was an obvious choice for King Louis XIV of France. Ever since Holland had won its independence from Spain, France saw an opportunity to conquer the Spanish Netherlands. France was first and foremost a continental power. As such it wanted territorial expansion on the continent. The Spanish Netherlands was a relatively easy target. Holland opposed this conquest because Holland saw the Spanish Netherlands as an important military buffer between itself and France. The second reason for the Anglo-French alliance was that France was competing for colonies in the New World and Asia. It saw Holland as the more powerful naval competitor. An alliance with England would likely defeat Holland. King Charles II of England had signed the Treaty of Dover with France in 1670.

King Louis XIV personally led a French force of 130,000 in the French invasion of the Spanish Netherlands in 1672. Holland was saved only by deliberately flooding it to halt the French advance. The two most important outcomes of this war were that King Louis XIV emerged as the most powerful ruler in Western Europe and William III became the Stadholder of Holland. When the war began William was only a captain-general in the Dutch army. It was the success of the French invasion that forced Holland to make William the Stadholder. William III was the nephew of King Charles II of England. Following the war William III married Mary, the niece of King Charles II of England, in November 1677. Mary was the daughter of the king's brother, James, duke of York. James became the king of England, James II, after the death of Charles II on February 2, 1685. William's marriage to Mary enhanced his claim to the throne of England. Marriage and invasions were the two most common tools used by monarchs to expand territory.

William III, like Louis XIV, was a very ambitious man. To compete with Louis XIV, William III needed the English throne. His relationship to Charles II and his marriage to Mary were not sufficient to get him the English crown. But England had inherited a religious conflict after King Henry VIII had severed England's ties to the Catholic faith and the pope to satisfy his need for a **male** heir to the English throne. William III exploited this religious conflict by helping those opposed to the Catholic convictions of King James II. In what came to be known as the *Glorious Revolution* William III invaded England in November 1688 after he had been assured of English support by Protestant leaders. King James II was forced to flee England and William III, along with his wife Mary, became joint monarchs of England in February 1689. This united the Protestant Kingdom of England with the Protestant Dutch republic of Holland.

In April of 1689 a naval treaty was signed between England and Holland to unite the world's two most powerful navies. This gave William III the military muscle he needed to challenge King Louis XIV of France for leadership of Europe and the world. In the process Holland would suffer relative decline as a naval and imperial power while England would gain in relative stature and military power. William III declared war on France on May 18, 1689. This war proved to be financially exhausting to Holland. Holland was mired in debt and never able to fund a large navy again. Many Dutch merchants moved their businesses to England and London replaced Amsterdam as the leading financial center of the world. The Glorious Revolution was good for Britain but disastrous for Holland. Britain emerged from this first post-1688 war with France as the dominant naval power eclipsing both Holland and France.

This first post-1688 Anglo-French war was mostly a continental war for European leadership. France had been challenging the Holy Roman

Empire for the leadership of Western Europe long before this war. This is why the holy Roman emperor *Leopold I* was able to form an alliance with Habsburg Spain led by King Charles II and German princes of the Holy Roman Empire against King Louis XIV of France. William III joined this coalition because he wanted to protect Holland against French territorial expansion as well as challenge Louis XIV for leadership of Western Europe. Most of the fighting took place in the lands adjoining France such as the Spanish Netherland and the Rhineland. But France was also competing with Holland and Britain for overseas colonies. The war therefore spread to North America and the Caribbean as well as Asia. The war exhausted the resources of both sides without either side being victorious. Peace came in 1697 with the *Treaty of Ryswick.*

The coalition of Catholic powers with Protestant Holland and England turned out to be disastrous for Catholic Europe and the power of the pope. The war did not resolve the leadership dispute between the holy Roman emperor, Leopold I, and the French king, Louis XIV. But it had the unintended consequence of making Protestant Britain more powerful than Catholic France. While France concentrated its financial resources on the army to fight the continental war Britain devoted most of its financial resources in improving its naval dominance. While a strong army kept France as a leading continental power, Britain's naval dominance made it the leading world power. It would then lead to the rise of the Protestant American Empire dominating the world.

The Second Post-1688 Anglo-French War: War of the Spanish Succession: 1701–1714

France attempted to do what Holland had done. It attempted a unification of France with Spain to counter the unification of Holland with England. This made sense not only to counter the rise of English power but the rise of Protestant opposition to Catholic Christians. Holland and England were Protestant powers while France and Spain were both Catholic powers. In addition, Spain had the worldwide empire to complement the continental power that France possessed. On the other side of the coin it was important to England and Holland to prevent the unification of France and Spain. Nations go to war for the tiniest of excuses. The history of the world is not one of a quest for peace. It is the addiction to constant warmongering. Peace treaties are never intended to be permanent but only a respite from the exhaustion of wars. The peace is simply a period to rest and prepare for the next war. During the war, military and financial resources are stretched to the limit. During the peace, the military becomes restless for action in battle. Leaders need to prove their worth as military commanders and subjects need to be distracted by another conflict.

This second post-1688 Anglo-French war was also fought mostly on continental Europe. French claims to the crown of Spain resulted from the death of King Charles II without an heir. Charles II had married when he was eighteen years old but was likely impotent as he had no children after ten years of marriage to Marie Louis and a second marriage to twenty-three-year-old Maria Anna. In his last will Charles II named his grand-nephew, Philip, duke of Anjou, as heir to the Spanish throne. The will clearly indicated that Philip was named as heir to "all our Realms and all our Domains without any exception whatever." Philip was the grandson of King Louis XIV of France. The grandmother of Louis XIV was also the sister of the father of Charles II, King Philip IV of Spain. Such blood relationships among the rulers of Western Europe were quite common. It was this history of family "inbreeding" that led to the physical and mental disabilities of Charles II.

Philip, duke of Anjou, was named the new king of Spain, Philip V, on November 24, 1700, following the death of Charles II. This ended Habsburg rule of the powerful Spanish Empire and replaced it with the House of Bourbon. This increase in Bourbon power did not sit well with William III. But William III died on March 8, 1702. Like Charles II, William III had no children with his wife Mary. His death ended the rule of England by the House of Orange. It also ended the short-lived unification of England and Holland. That unification had been good for England but disastrous for Holland. By the time of the fourth and final Anglo-Dutch war of 1780–1784 the Dutch navy was but a shadow of its glory days.

William's successor to the throne of England was his wife's younger sister, Queen Anne, daughter of the deposed King James II. She distanced herself from her Dutch brother-in-law, King William III, but joined the second Grand Alliance intended to contain France and Louis XIV. She declared war against France on May 4, 1702. She appointed her husband as Lord High Admiral of the Royal Navy. The war spread from Europe to the North American colonies where it was called *Queen Anne's War.* The war ended in April 1713 with the *Treaty of Utrecht.* The grandson of Louis XIV kept the throne of Spain and the Spanish Empire. But the treaty prevented a unification of the two Bourbon kingdoms of Spain and France. The notion of a *balance of power,* first mentioned in 1701, became part of the negotiations leading up to the treaty. It became a cornerstone of European politics until the Second World War.

Louis XIV died on September 1, 1715. The wars against England and the Grand Alliance had been extremely costly to France. But France continued to be a strong continental power. During the reign of Queen Anne, England united with Scotland to become Great Britain on May 1, 1707. Great Britain ruled the British Empire, which dominated the world until the American Empire. But Britain, unlike France, was never fully committed to being a continental power. France continued to compete with Britain for world hegemony until the rise of Germany.

The Third Post-1688 Anglo-French War: War of the Austrian Succession: 1739–1748

It's no surprise that the deaths of King William III and King Louis XIV did not end the wars between Britain and France. Wars are not caused by leaders such as William III and Louis XIV. Wars feed a human addiction. Wars are a curse of mankind, since the beginning of time. For example, the more wars President Obama starts the more wars the American people beg him to start. Their appetite for wars is insatiable. So it was with the people of Western Europe before and after William III and Louis XIV.

The excuse for this third post-1688 Anglo-French war was the conflict between a rising Prussia and a declining Austria. During the first two post-1688 Anglo-French wars Austria had allied with Britain. It was therefore natural for France to ally with Prussia against Austria. It was also natural for Britain to use the defense of its ally, Austria, as the excuse to wage another war on France. At this time the Dutch continued their alliance with Britain despite the death of William III. Likewise Spain continued its alliance with France, which began after Louis XIV's grandson became King Philip V of Spain.

Britain initially declared war on Spain on October 23, 1739. This began the *War of Jenkins' Ear*, which morphed into the European war of the Spanish succession. The two notable civilized features of the War of Jenkins' Ear were the **slave trade** and **piracy.** Britain was determined to fight for its civilized duty to steal and sell **African slaves** and uphold its civilized right to protect **privateers.** One of the civilized awards Britain had won from the Treaty of Utrecht in 1713 was the infamous *asiento,* the civilized right to sell unlimited numbers of **African slaves** to Spain's colonies in the New World for the next thirty years. Britain's pirates, smugglers and privateers took advantage of the *asiento* to smuggle goods into the Spanish colonies. At this time the prevailing economic doctrine for international trade was *Mercantilism.* This view of international trade was that Imperial powers should restrain other empires from trading with their colonies. It was therefore natural that Spain would object to this illegal trade by Britain's pirates, smugglers and privateers. When Britain sent its navy to the Caribbean to protect these illegal British traders, King Philip V annulled the *asiento* award. This was the excuse for Britain to declare war on Spain. The British navy was heavily supported by English pirates and privateers. The Spanish and French pirates happily joined in the fray to take booty from the British ships.

The War of the Austrian succession began when Prussia invaded the Austrian territory of *Silesia.* The Austrian branch of the Habsburg Empire had been declining because of attacks from both the Ottoman Empire and France. King Frederick II of Prussia saw an opportunity to steal some of the territory of the declining Austrian Empire. Theft by military force was another common civilized practice of the West. That is how the United States and Canada acquired the vast lands from the First Nations. Both Canada and the United States are held up as among the most civilized countries in the world. Israel is viewed as the most civilized state in the Middle East even though it stole Palestinian land by military force.

France was not going to stand idly by and let the Prussians steal territory they had been after for many years. Britain was not going to miss an opportunity to feed its addiction to warmongering. So it was that Spain and France allied with Prussia against Britain, Austria and Holland for the third post-1688 Anglo-French war. As with previous wars this war spread to the colonies. In North America it was called *King George's War.* King George I had inherited the English throne after the death of his cousin, Queen Anne, in 1714. As usual the war provided another opportunity for Britain and France to steal more resources and land from the First Nations. More important was the fight between Britain and France for the control of India, viewed later as the *Jewel of the Crown* in the British Empire, after Britain lost its thirteen American colonies.

During the War of the Austrian Succession the French captured the British colonial settlement in *Madras,* India, in September 1746. The English East India Company had begun operations in Madras in February 1640 and had built Fort St. George to **militarize** its operations. The English East India Company had expanded its colonization of India from its original base in *Surat* to Madras, *Bombay* and *Calcutta.* Each settlement was protected by military forts. These English **military** settlements were in competition with the French **military** settlements. The French East India Company was founded in 1664. The French had arrived in India more than half a century after the English. The English began their colonization of India with their first factory in Surat in 1612. The French had also begun their colonization of India with their first factory in Surat, but much later in 1668. *Pondicherry* was acquired by France in 1673 and *Chandernagar* in 1692. Pondicherry is located south of Madras along the coast of the Bay of Bengal. After the Glorious Revolution of 1688 unified England and Holland the French East India Company became the primary competitor of the English East India Company.

This competition heated up after *Joseph Francois Dupleix* became governor general of French India in 1742. Dupleix had joined the French East India Company in Pondicherry in 1720. After securing the position of governor general, he formed alliances with local Indian rulers and recruited large numbers of Indian soldiers, *sepoys,* to wage war on the English East India Company. Hyder Ali, who fought the British with his son Tipu Sultan, during the later Anglo-Mysore wars, trained as a sepoy with the French at this time. This led to the later French military alliance with Mysore, after Hyder Ali became sultan in 1761. Dupleix, as governor of Pondicherry, ordered the attack on Madras. The English governor of Madras, *Nicholas Morse,* surrendered on September 9, 1746.

A rather innocent incident in the French capture of Madras which became significant to the future of the British colonization of India was the escape of a clerical employee of the English East India Company, *Robert Clive.* Clive began his career with the English East India Company in 1744. Conquests and adventures in Asia and the Orient were the dream of every Englishman and Scot at this time. Clive had the good fortune of being born in a family with the right political connections. He began working at Fort St. George in Madras in June 1744. Madras, renamed Chennai, is the capital city of the Indian state of Tamil Nadu and the fourth largest city in India today.

After the surrender of Madras to the French, Clive was imprisoned but managed to escape and make his way to the safety of another English fort, *Fort St. David,* some fifty miles south of Madras. The French attacked Fort St. David in December 1746 and again in March 1747 but failed to capture it because the British fleet had arrived from Bengal, and the Nawab of the Carnatic, *Anwaruddin Khan,* switched sides temporarily, aiding the British instead of the French. This is where Clive's escape from Madras in 1746 became significant. On his arrival at Fort St. David he participated in its defense against the subsequent French attack and changed careers from being a clerk to becoming a soldier. In the defense of Fort St. David, Clive proved his worth as a soldier. In August 1748 the British laid siege to the French fort of Pondicherry. Clive distinguished himself again as a very competent soldier during this English attack on the French fort. He was given a commission in the English army and soon promoted to lieutenant. The siege ended in October because of the monsoon rain. The war ended shortly thereafter with the *Treaty of Aix-la-Chapelle,* October 18, 1748. More on Clive later.

Much to the disappointment of Dupleix, Madras was returned to Britain. It was exchanged for the French fortress of *Louisbourg* in North America which the English had captured from the French during the same war. But the Treaty of Aix-la-Chapelle did not stop the fighting for India between Britain and France. Clive became the key Englishman to oppose French aspirations in India led by Governor General Dupleix.

Clive distinguished himself again as a soldier during the British conquest of Fort Devikotah in *Tanjore.* In April 1749 an English East India force under the command of Major Stringer Lawrence sailed along the coast from Fort St. David and launched an attack on Fort Devikotah. Lieutenant Clive was a member of that invasion force and played a key part in the capture of Fort Devikotah from the raja of Tanjore, Pratap Singh. Major Lawrence returned to England in 1750 and Clive was promoted to Captain.

War between Britain and France continued in India. It was called the second *Carnatic War* because Madras was located in the coastal Carnatic region of India. The Anglo-French fighting during the War of the Austrian succession is called the first Carnatic War. The second Carnatic War between Britain and France was part of an Indian **civil war** between French and English backed Indian contenders for the position of *Nawab of Arcot.* Arcot was the capital city in the Carnatic region. The French initially succeeded in getting their Indian contender, *Chanda Sahib,* appointed as the Nawab of Arcot.

In August 1751 Captain Clive led an English attack on Arcot and took the fort. He defended it successfully against the French backed forces of Chanda Sahib. The French surrendered in June 1752. Chanda Sahib was replaced by the Anglo friendly Nawab, *Mohammed Ali Khan,* son of Anwaruddin Khan. During the first Carnatic War, Anwaruddin Khan was the Nawab and he had initially supported the French, switched his support from France to Britain, and then back to France. In 1753 Clive returned to England as a hero and was honored both by the English East India Company and Prime Minister William Pitt. France recalled Dupleix in 1754 and replaced him with *Charles Godeheu.* The 1754 *Treaty of Pondicherry* ended the second Carnatic War.

The Fourth Post-1688 Anglo-French War: The Seven Years' War: 1756–1763

Most historians say that the Seven Years' War made Britain the dominant Imperial power. France lost the war to Britain. But France remained the dominant continental power since Britain was never fully committed to being a continental power. It was really Germany, not Britain, which replaced France as the dominant continental power, after the First World War. The Seven Years' War was nothing but a continuation of previous Anglo-French wars. As we said above, warmongering is the normal state of affairs for what Western historians call civilized nations. But there must be periods of rest and recuperation. That is the reason for the endless temporary peace treaties. In this case the war never really stopped since it was continued in India except for the brief two years of peace between the Treaty of Pondicherry in 1754, and the outbreak of the Seven Years' War in 1756. In India this renewed war between England and France was called the **Third Carnatic War.**

In Europe Britain saw the advantage of ending its alliance with a declining Habsburg Holy Roman/Austrian Empire and forging a new alliance with a rising European powerhouse, *Prussia,* against Bourbon France and Spain. At the time, the Prussians had an extremely efficient army, led by the military genius of Frederick the Great, which nicely complemented the powerful British navy. In addition it was a member of the **German** royal dynasty, the *House of Hanover,* which was now ruling Britain. As usual, the British were more interested in imperial rather than continental dominance. They devoted their powerful navy to defending and expanding their worldwide colonization. The French were still fighting primarily for continental dominance. France devoted her army mostly to defending and expanding her territory on the continent. This left her colonies relatively easy prey for the British. The Austrians had little choice but to ally with France. The Russians and Swedes joined the alliance against Prussia. The Dutch had finally realized that the so-called *Glorious Revolution* of 1688 had brought glory to Britain at their expense. Britain was unable to persuade the Dutch to continue their post-1688 "war alliance" and Holland declared her neutrality during the Seven Years' War. In fact, Holland made an attempt to reinforce her old presence in Bengal, during the Seven Years' War, by sending seven warships to India in 1759, while the English were engaged in consolidating their victories over the French.

The formal declaration of war between France and Britain took place on May 18, 1756. But there had been earlier fighting between France and Britain in North America while Anglo-French fighting in India was almost continuous between 1746 and 1763. In August 1756, the

Prussians invaded and occupied Saxony, an ally of Austria. The next year the Prussians invaded Bohemia but encountered stiff resistance from the Austrian forces. At the same time the Russians invaded East Prussia. Despite the military genius of Frederick the Great, the Prussians were surrounded by the Russians from the east, the French from the West, the Austrians from the south and the Swedes from the North. By 1763 the warmongering had taken its usual military and financial toll on all of the participants. It was time to negotiate a respite from warmongering to rest and recuperate before the next outbreak of war. The *Treaty of Paris* was signed by Britain and France on February 10, 1763. Nothing changed on the continent. But Prussia had survived the assault from Russia, France, Austria and Sweden. It marked the rise of Germany and the demise of Austria. In time Germany would also replace France as the dominant continental power.

By focusing on the continent France had enabled Britain to make significant colonial gains in North America, the Caribbean and India. British policy of colonies first and Europe second had paid off for now. The Treaty of Paris ending the Seven Years' War in 1763 made Britain the primary imperial power in India. In North America, Britain took all of the land which eventually became Canada, from France and the First Nations. She also took Florida and the eastern half of the massive Louisiana territory from Spain, France, and the First Nations. But it did not end Anglo-French rivalry in Asia, North America or continental Europe. The greatest military challenge to Britain by France was yet to come. The ultimate losers were the First Nations. Lands stolen in India were eventually returned to India and Pakistan. But the lands stolen from the First Nations were never returned. The implanted nation-states of Canada, the United States and Mexico, not only inherited the lands stolen from the First Nations by Britain and Spain but stole almost all of the remaining First Nations lands in North America.

The Seven Years' War in India

In India both the English and French had Indian allies just as in North America they both had First Nations allies. During the War of the Austrian Succession both the British and French had received military aid from the Nawab of the Carnatic, Anwaruddin Khan. In the Indian state of Tamil Nadu, the English colony was in Madras and the French colony was in Pondicherry. Both were located along the Carnatic coast. In the state of West Bengal, the English colony was in Calcutta while the French colony was in *Chandernagar.* During the Seven Years' War of 1756–1763, between England and France, the Anglo-French competition in India shifted from Madras/Pondicherry in Tamil Nadu to Calcutta in the state of West Bengal. The Calcutta English settlement was protected by Fort William. In 1634 the English East India Company had obtained permission from the Mughal emperor, *Shah Jahan,* to establish a factory in Bengal. Calcutta became the center of operations for the English East India Company. The French had established the settlement of *Chandernagar* in Bengal in 1692 after receiving permission from the Nawab of Bengal. The Nawab is the local ruler appointed by the Mughal emperor. Pondicherry in Tamil Nadu and Chandernagar in Bengal were the two most important footholds in India for the French Empire.

Ever since the English East India Company had received permission from the Mughal emperor to do business in Bengal there were conflicts between the *Nawab of Bengal,* the local ruler, and the English company. This is to be expected since the European Empires begin by asking for trade concessions and start to steal as soon as they have the military muscle to do so. When the British began to increase their military fortifications in Bengal the Nawab, *Siraj ud-Daula,* became alarmed and asked them to cease. The British naturally refused since it cannot steal if it does not have the military fortifications to protect what it steals.

The British excuse for her increased militarization of her colony was that she needed to defend against a French attack. While there was some truth to this, the Nawab knew that once the French were defeated the British would use their military improvements to steal more land and resources in Bengal from the Nawab. Empires are never satisfied with what they have stolen in the past and by nature wage wars to steal more and more. It's a common addiction of all thieves. With some encouragement and support from the French, the Nawab launched a preemptive military attack on the English to stop their military improvements. The Nawab first attacked and captured the British fort of Cossimbazar on June 3, 1756. Next he attacked Fort William and captured *Calcutta* on June 20, 1756.

Clive Rescues the English East India Company at the Battle of Plassey

Clive had returned to India in July 1755 as deputy governor of Fort St. David, the fort he had escaped to after he had been imprisoned in Madras by the French. He was promoted to the rank of lieutenant-colonel in the English army. Clive learned of the capture of Calcutta while he was stationed at Fort St. David and was determined to recapture it. He launched a joint army/navy attack on the Nawab of Bengal and his French allies. Clive led the English army while Admiral Watson was in command of the British navy. This joint attack was successful and the Nawab was forced to return *Calcutta* to the English East India Company in February 1757. The British then proceeded with their original plan to improve the military fortifications at Fort William. Together with Admiral Watson, Clive next launched an attack on the French settlement of Chandernagar, twenty miles north of Calcutta, in March 1757. His army plundered the city of Chandernagar before moving to the town of *Hooghly,* three miles north of Chandernagar. The British had captured Hooghly in January 1757.

The British also made plans to remove the ruling Nawab, Siraj ud-Daula and replace him with a *puppet.* Siraj ud-Daula had gained a reputation for fighting Western colonization and reducing Western theft of Indian land and resources. The British could no longer seduce him into an alliance against his people. The British used the Nawab's uncle, *Mir Jafar,* who was the paymaster of the Nawab's army at the time, to overthrow his nephew in return for British military protection as the "puppet" Nawab of Bengal. After the British had signed a treaty with Mir Jafar on June 4, 1757, she was ready to launch an all-out attack on the ruling Nawab, Siraj ud-Daula. The English army in Calcutta joined forces with Clive on June 12, 1757. A declaration of war was sent to the Nawab on June 14, 1757. In response the Nawab moved most of his forces to the island of Cossimbazar. On June 22, 1757, the English forces and their Indian allies crossed the river to the island. The two armies met at the village of *Plassey* on the island. The *Battle of Plassey* began on June 23, 1757. The British defeated the forces of the Nawab of Bengal, *Siraj ud-Daula,* and his French allies at the *Battle of Plassey.* He was replaced as the Nawab of Bengal by the British puppet, Mir Jafar. French competition with the English in Bengal was virtually destroyed by Clive's victory at the Battle of Plassey. This was a significant victory for the British leading to its eventual colonization of India. The French had lost in India as much as they had lost in North America.

The English East India Company was rescued almost singlehandedly by Clive from future defeat by the French. Clive even defeated a Dutch attempt in 1759 to reinforce her old Bengal colony of *Chinsura.* Chinsura was located in the district of Hooghly which the English had captured in 1757. The Portuguese had colonized it in 1536 but were removed by the Mughal emperor, Shah Jahan. The area was later colonized by the Dutch. Since Clive's rescue of the English East India Company from both the French and the Dutch led to the British colonization of India, Clive is referred to as "Clive of India." He returned to England in 1760 with a fortune stolen from the people of India. His victory at the Battle of Plassey had made the wealth of Bengal easy picking for Clive and those who worked for the English East India Company. In 1764 he was rewarded for his theft of Indian land and resources with a knighthood from a grateful King George III. Thieves like Clive make sure that they enrich both themselves and their sovereign.

After Clive returned to England there was one more important battle between the English and the French in India during the Seven Years' War. This was the *Battle of Buxar* in 1764. As it turned out, Mir Jafar was not quite the subservient puppet the English expected him to be. He played the role of puppet initially. But when the Dutch showed up with a naval force in 1759 Mir Jafar tried to increase his independence by playing off the Dutch with the English. The English replaced him with his son-in-law, *Mir Qasim,* in 1760. Mir Qasim soon found out that his lavish bribes to the English only served to increase their insatiable demand for booty. As with his father-in-law before he made the mistake of trying to play hardball with the English. This led to the Battle of Buxar on October 23, 1764. The British forces led by Major Hector

Munroe defeated the combined forces of the Nawab of Bengal and his overlord, the Mughal emperor, *Shah Alam II.*

Two More Civilized British Inventions: Drug Lord (Opium Monopoly) and Taxation of Colonists

Sir Robert Clive returned to India with his knighthood to steal more than the land and resources of India. He enabled the British to impose taxes on the same inhabitants whose land and resources the British were stealing in India. He also brought about the conditions which enabled Britain to become the world's largest **drug dealer.** On May 3, 1765, Sir Robert arrived in Calcutta. He negotiated the peace treaty with the Mughal emperor following the Battle of Buxar. Taking advantage of a military weak Mughal emperor, Shah Alam II, Clive stole the right to impose and collect taxes from the province of Bengal-Bihar-Odisha. With the treaty of *Allahabad,* August 16, 1765, Clive secured what has been called *Diwani rights.* This gave England the power to tax 30 million Indians living in Bengal, Bihar and Odisha. This gross injustice imposed on the people of India by military force marked the beginning of what Western historians call the *British Raj* for propaganda purposes. It was of course a criminal act almost as vile as the African slave trade and piracy. The British had found another barbaric tool to make them ever so civilized. Britain appointed its first governor-general of India, *Warren Hastings,* in 1773. Like Clive, Hastings had joined the English East India Company as a clerk, to pursue the dream of the typical poor British commoner to gain fame and fortune by stealing from the people of India. He arrived in Calcutta in August 1750. He volunteered in Clive's reconquest of Calcutta in 1757. With the help of Clive he moved up the English colonial administration of India, and in 1771 he became the English governor of Calcutta.

While Western historians have foolishly referred to the British imposition of taxes on its thirteen American colonies as "taxation without representation," they have conveniently made light of this crime imposed on the people of India. The inhabitants of the thirteen American colonies pleaded with Britain to provide military help against the First Nations, whose lands and resources they had stolen, and the French Empire which wanted to steal the same First Nations lands for French colonies. It was just that Britain should impose taxes on the American colonists to help pay for that military cost since it was the colonists, not the mother country, who were enjoying the fruits of the land and resources stolen from the First Nations. By contrast, in India the British were there to steal from the Indians for the benefit of the mother country. Colonization is **theft.** Taxing the rightful owners of the land and resources you are stealing from, to pay for the cost of administering a colony, is adding insult to injury. Only the West can justify such insults and use effective propaganda to portray **stealing** as a white man's burden.

The second heinous crime which Sir Robert enabled with the Treaty of Allahabad was the creation of a British monopoly on the production of the drug, **opium,** in Bengal. The British began to administer Bengal and one of their first acts was to control the production of opium in India. Opium was now produced on Indian land stolen by the British by their colonization of Bengal. It was smuggled into China to make the Chinese people drug addicts for the glory of the civilized British Empire. This was as **illegal** then as Mexican drugs currently sold to Americans. But unlike the U.S. and Mexican governments the British government was very proud to engage in this **illegal** drug trade. The British Empire had become the most civilized empire by becoming the world's leading **drug lord, African slave trader, pirate, warmonger** and **taxation of subjugated colonists.**

In addition to the crime of producing opium and addicting millions, the use of stolen Indian land to produce opium reduced the land used by the original inhabitants to produce food. This contributed significantly to the death from starvation of 10 million Indians in the Bengal famine of 1769–1773. This was a third of the population of the territory colonized by the English East India Company after the treaty of Allahabad. After this colonization, the English East India Company increased the land tax on agricultural produce from 10 percent to 50 percent. Agricultural land producing rice was shifted to producing opium as well as another cash crop, *indigo.* The British had also passed laws prohibiting Indians from storing rice. This meant that there were no reserves of rice to offset the decline in rice production caused by adverse weather and drought beginning in 1768. Between 1765 and 1777 the profit of the English East India Company doubled.

The Fifth Post-1688 Anglo-French War: War of the American Revolution: 1779–1783

France had been militarily humiliated by Britain during the Seven Years' War. It saw an opportunity to redeem its claim to be a civilized empire when the thirteen American colonies rebelled against the mother country. Recall that to be civilized by any acceptable norm you must win wars. It was eager to return to the battlefield. Both of the Bourbon kingdoms, France and Spain, had rebuilt their navies. France would humiliate Britain by allying with their colonial rebels in the thirteen American colonies. Despite the many military victories by Britain against France during the Seven Years' War, Britain in 1779 was in worse financial shape than France. Wars exhaust the financial resources of the combatants. However, Britain had learned from the Dutch the nasty habit of borrowing heavily to finance the Seven Years' War, rather than just printing money, as much, and increasing taxes, as much. It was short-run gain for long-term pain. Once the war was over, taxes had to be increased to repay the debt with interest. After the Seven Years' War the English paid the highest taxes in the Western world. France had not incurred as much debt as the British had done to fight that war.

Another ironic outcome of the debt incurred by Britain to win the Seven Years' War was that the repayment of this debt turned out to be the primary reason for the American rebellion. It was natural that England would ask the American colonists to help with this repayment. After all most of the colonists wanted the mother country to defend them from both the French and the First Nations, whose lands and resources they had stolen. They rejoiced when England defeated the French and their First Nations allies. But when Britain imposed taxes on the colonists they used it as a rallying cry for independence. "No taxation without representation," they shouted. They were colonists for God sake. Why would any imperial power give representation to colonists? And why would they dictate to the imperial power? Their rallying cry was, of course, pure propaganda. But if there are two tools the Americans excelled at even before their independence from Britain were **warmongering** and **propaganda.**

By winning the Seven Years' War against the French in North America, Britain had won from the French the equivalent of what the Americans won from their invasions of Afghanistan and Iraq. And just as the Afghans and Iraqis insisted on their independence from the American Empire the American colonists insisted on their independence from the British Empire. Both had to fight for that independence even though it would have been financially beneficial to grant independence gracefully. Britain had nothing to gain from keeping the American colonies as colonies any more than the American Empire had anything to gain from keeping Iraq and Afghanistan as American *uncolonies.* But empires never learn how to let go peacefully, let alone, gracefully. That is why French help to the American rebels during the American War of Independence was a blessing in disguise to Britain.

Imperial powers crush rebellions. That has been standard practice ever since the beginning of time. That is why Britain engaged the rebels during the American War of Independence. It's the normal instinctive response. It may not be a rational or logical response. Rebels often get help from competing imperial powers. It was therefore no surprise that the American rebels reached out to the French Empire for military aid. The Treaty of Alliance between France and the rebels was signed on February 6, 1778. The treaty was both military and commercial. It was called the "Franco-American treaty of amity and commerce." The commercial part was important to France because the major loss to France from its North American colonies was trade and commerce with the First Nations. Without the help of the French Empire the rebels had almost zero chance of succeeding. But in aiding the rebels France miscalculated badly.

First, the American colonies were desperate for an alliance with France only until they secured their independence from Britain. The French foolishly thought that the alliance would continue after the rebels had gained independence from Britain, and help France increase, or at the very least, keep its existing colonies in North America. The treaty said that the United States was obliged to guarantee the present possessions of France in America **forever.** But the rebels saw their opportunities to create their own empire through a long-term alliance with Britain. On the other side of the coin, France had hoped to punish Britain for its losses and humiliation in the Seven Years' War. But France did Britain a great favor by enabling the rebels to succeed. This may seem to be a contradiction so we need to explain this insight on our part.

Colonies are profitable only if what can be stolen from them exceed the military cost of putting down rebellions. All colonies rebel but most fail because the imperial power usually has a far superior military. That is why they are foolishly called civilized while the rebels are foolishly called "barbarians" or "naked savages" or "guerillas" or "communists" or "terrorists" or "gooks" or "Islamists" or "radicalized." In the case of the thirteen American colonies the military cost to the British Empire of defending against future rebellions and future attacks on them by the First Nations and the French Empire had now far exceeded what the British could steal. The colonists had gained "legal" ownership to most of the land and resources. A home grown **slave owning aristocracy** and a domestic merchant class, descendants of the European settlers, had inherited these rights from the original **thieves.** There were no valuable land or resources left for the British Empire to steal, nor was there gold or silver or African slaves as in Africa or South and Central America. The land and resources which the British had originally stolen from the First Nations now belonged to the American colonists. Furthermore, these same American colonists were hell bent on stealing more of the First Nations lands to the west. This meant even more wars with the First Nations in these Western lands. But the new stolen land and resources would go mostly to the American colonists rather than to the mother country. But the mother country would bear most of the military costs of these new wars.

Once the American colonists had rebelled, the British Empire quickly recognized the fact that an independent United States of America was far more valuable to the British Empire as a trading partner and military ally than as English colonies. An independent United States would bear the full military cost of their defense from attacks by the First Nations and other Western imperial powers. Both Britain and the United States would gain from trade, while continued colonization of the United States by Britain would incur a large and growing **net loss** to the British Empire.

A military alliance with the United States would help the British Empire in fighting off the continued challenge from the French Empire. At the same time such an alliance would enable the United States to begin to create its own empire since the British would have their back until it had grown up to stand on its own. Britain gave the United States a more or less free hand to expand west and south. Only the North, Canada, was out of bounds.

From the very beginning Americans were deceptive and dishonest. That trait is embedded in their DNA. The newly independent USA did not honor the implicit obligations of the alliance with France any more than the subsequent American Empire ever honored future alliances. As soon as they had used France to get independence from Britain, they reneged on the alliance with France, because they had more to gain in territorial expansion and trade by friendly relations with Britain than with a continued alliance with France. In the second Peace Treaty of Paris, the French lost to the British and Americans. The Americans negotiated independently of the French to secure favorable terms from the British. As the French said, "the English buy the peace rather than make it." The French had totally missed the fact that the American colonies were far more valuable to Britain as an independent ally and trading partner than as colonies. Far from punishing Britain by making it lose its American colonies, as the French had thought, the French had made it easy for the British Empire to sever what would have been a long and painful net loss to its worldwide imperial thefts.

The British agreed to American demands to help them steal more First Nations lands in the rich agricultural lands in the Ohio valley. The powerful *Iroquois League* had helped the British defeat France in North America. In return the British had promised to restrain the American colonists from stealing more and more First Nations lands. In particular, the lands west of the Appalachian Mountains, ceded by France to Britain in the first Treaty of Paris, were protected from theft by a *Proclamation line.* This British protection was abandoned by the second treaty of Paris. It marked the beginning of the British sanctioning the theft of the entire North American continent from the First Nations by the American Empire and its ally, Canada. The Americans were also granted fishing rights in Newfoundland by the British. As an independent nation, Britain got all the advantages of trade and commerce without the military cost of protecting them from the French or the First Nations. France had done Britain an immense favor by helping the American rebels gain independence from Britain. Furthermore, over a hundred thousand United Empire loyalists had moved from the thirteen colonies to British North America, Canada, to help the British fight the French in Canada, and secure the lucrative fur trade of the Hudson Bay Company. On the other side of the coin France gained no new territory or trading rights that justified the immense financial cost of the war.

The British Empire in India

It was no surprise that Britain would also use this new war with France to continue pursuing its goal to drive the French out of India. Indian trade and commerce were very important to France. The British became the dominant European power in India after their defeat of the French Empire during the Seven Years' War. During that war the armed forces of the English East India Company joined forces with Indian allies and the most powerful navy in the world, the British navy. But the 1763 Treaty of Paris did not transfer any French colonies in India to Britain. France still controlled her **five** different locations in India to continue her colonization of India. As we mentioned before, the French had colonized *Pondicherry* in 1673 and *Chandernagar* in 1692. In addition to these two French colonies, France had colonized *Yanam* in 1723, *Mahe* in 1724, and *Karaikal* in 1739. The French would find new Indian allies to continue their war with Britain over the colonization of India by the West. One such alliance was the 1782 formal alliance between King Louis XVI and the Maratha Empire. A more important French alliance was made with the sultan of Mysore. We address that below. The Indian rulers were accustomed to the continuous rivalry between the European imperialists, beginning with the Portuguese and the Dutch.

Even before the American War of Independence the British had shifted their prime colonial target from the New World to India and Asia. As we observed above the English had already realized that the thirteen American colonies had become a net liability as colonies. Colonies are more profitable than trade only if the colonies have valuable resources to steal with military force. By the outbreak of the Seven Years' War in 1763 the thirteen American colonies had outgrown their profitability as colonies. The military cost to keep them colonized and to defend them from the First Nations and the French Empire had increased significantly while the resources to be stolen had decreased significantly in value. The gains from trade far outweighed the gains from colonization.

By contrast the land and resources of value to be stolen from India and other parts of Asia had increased significantly. Stealing these resources was far more profitable than trading for them. In addition, the English had devised a very effective military strategy of "Divide and conquer" which greatly minimized their military cost of colonization and theft. India was ideal for providing the opportunity for England to claim that it was there to carry out the white man's burden. Many English aristocrats gloried in the opportunity to immerse themselves in oriental customs, culture and languages. The Scots took advantage of their subjugation by the English to subjugate the Asians. Combining all of these factors made India to the British much like children finding a candy store from which they could steal rather than having to buy.

The British moved to India in droves to seek their fortunes; learn new languages; learn to govern people they believed to be inferior to them; lead Indians in military battles against other Indians; bear the white man's burden like the call to Crusade in an earlier age; find cures for common diseases so that those cured would die of **hunger and starvation** after their land and resources were stolen, rather than die of diseases; share their tales of adventure with family and friends in Britain; become heroes in the eyes of many; cover up their crimes against the people of Asia with tales of heroism, courage, deceit, and propaganda; make Britain the civilized ruler of the world, while enriching both themselves and the mother country; take English pride in enslaving the "Coolies" of Asia; and use the advanced weapons developed by the English industrial revolution to kill and maim without mercy. It launched the glorious British century of "Rule Britannia, Britannia rule the Waves."

To this day English prime ministers like Margaret Thatcher, Tony Blair and David Cameron continue the dirty deeds of British imperialism while using the same old propaganda to justify their criminal warmongering in Palestine, Ireland, Argentina, Iraq, Afghanistan, Libya,

Syria and elsewhere. The British people continue to elect these brain-dead individuals and showcase them as *leaders* when in fact they are far worse criminals than those who call themselves "leaders" of drug cartels. If these brain-dead individuals had any leadership qualities they would have quickly recognized that today more can be gained from trade than old fashioned theft by military force. That is why countries like China, India and Brazil are gaining ground on the West. For five centuries colonization and theft by the West was far more profitable than trade. Today the opposite is true. The only people who gain from continued Western imperialism are those who make and sell the ever more advanced weaponry. They gain at the expense of the larger electorate. When once the spoils of theft by colonization was so great that some of it filtered down to the wider electorate over five centuries, it's now the wider electorate which pays for the very expensive advanced weapons used by the military.

The most glaring examples of this change are Iraq and Vietnam. The French had pounded Vietnam for more than a decade when the American Empire was sure that it could walk in and easily steal its rice fields. We know the outcome of that. It spent billions of dollars on the invasion and came away with zilch. Today it is trading with Vietnam. Since those elected to govern the American Empire are brain-dead they committed exactly the same mistake in Iraq. Those elected are followers not leaders. They get their inspiration from dumbed-down talk show hosts like Oprah Winfrey. Like Vietnam, Iraq had been pounded for over a decade by the high tech bombs of the American and British empires. President George W. Bush and Prime Minister Tony Blair were sure they could easily walk into Iraq and steal its oil. We know the outcome of that one as well. They spent trillions of dollars and came away with nothing. Stealing the oil of Iraq today is far more expensive than trading for it. The West needs to elect leaders, not brain-dead criminals, both for the wellbeing of their own electorate and for the advancement of the human race.

In the past it was more profitable to steal than to trade. That explains the British expansion in India and across Asia after defeating the Dutch and French empires. British colonization of Asia began in India in 1600 with the formation of the English East India Company. This joint-stock company was granted monopoly "trading" rights in India by Queen Elizabeth I. It's worth reminding readers that Western historians refer to theft by colonization as "trade." As we have clarified, trade is voluntary and benefits both trading parties. Colonization is the use of superior military force to steal, not trade. Until recently, at least 95 percent of what Western historians call "trade" was theft. The Portuguese were the first Europeans to steal from India beginning with da Gama's invasion of Calicut in May 1498. They were joined by the Dutch, English and French in the seventeenth century. At the time India had many local rulers but the Mughals had invaded and conquered India in 1526 and were the imperial rulers of India. After 1674 the Mughal Empire was in competition with the *Maratha Empire* for control of India.

Tipu Sultan, Tiger of Mysore, Defends India against British Imperialism

The French had not given up on India despite the successes of Sir Robert Clive. In India the French allied with the local Indian ruler, *Hyder Ali.* Hyder Ali was the sultan of the southern Indian Kingdom of *Mysore.* He became the ruler of Mysore in 1761 and used French advisers to train his military. He began fighting the British to prevent them from stealing his land after the outbreak of the first Anglo-Mysore war in 1767. He formed an alliance with France during the second Anglo-Mysore war of 1779–1784 after the British captured the port of *Mahe* on the Malabar Coast. Mahe was one of the five French colonies in India. In 1780 Hyder Ali invaded the Carnatic with a force of eighty-three thousand to drive the British out of their stronghold in *Madras.* With the aid of his advanced use of rockets Hyder, and his eldest son, *Tipu Sultan,* inflicted one of the worst military defeats of the British in India, during the *Battle of Pollipur,* September 10, 1780.

The British military strength was their powerful navy. This is why Hyder's alliance with France was so important. The French Empire sent Admiral *Andre de Suffren* to India in 1781. In the Bay of Bengal, Suffren worked collaboratively with the sultan of Mysore against the British. He provided much needed naval support to the sultan. Suffren engaged the British Admiral, *Sir Edward Hughes,* in the Battle of Sadras in February

1782. Suffren was able to make repairs in Pondicherry because Hyder Ali had recaptured it from Britain. Suffren provided transportation for French troops to capture the British port of Cuddalore in April 1782. Using Cuddalore as a base he captured supplies from British ships attempting to reach Madras. In August, Suffren recaptured the Dutch port of Trincomalee from the English, and used it as another base of operations. Despite several military defeats inflicted by Hyder and his French ally on the British, the British were able to use their superior navy to hold on to Madras. Hyder Ali's death from cancer in December 1782 also helped the British. France ended their war with Britain in September 1783.

The British fought a total of four wars with Hyder Ali and his son *Tipu Sultan* between 1767 and 1799. Tipu, nicknamed the *Tiger of Mysore,* because of his determined military resistance to British colonization, fought in all four wars. He was trained in warfare by French officers and barely seventeen years old when he joined his father in the first war against the British. After the *Treaty of Mangalore* ended the second war in March 1784, Tipu Sultan continued his father's efforts to prevent the British from stealing the Kingdom of Mysore by military force. He became the ruler of Mysore after his father's death. He improved the famous *Mysorean rockets* his father had developed and used successfully against the British. Tipu pleaded with the Ottoman Empire for military help to defeat the British in India. Unfortunately, the Ottoman Empire was in severe decline at this time and unable to help Tipu.

Tipu engaged the British in the third Anglo-Mysore war of 1789–1792. He attempted to get an alliance with the French against the English as his father had done in the previous war. But the French were unwilling to engage the British at this time. On the other side, the British were able to form an alliance with two other powerful rulers in southern India, the *Nizam of Hyderabad* and the *Maratha Empire.* It's unfortunate that both Tipu and his father had been fighting the Maratha Empire at the same time they were taking on the British in India. The Nizam of Hyderabad had also long opposed the claims by Hyder Ali and Tipu Sultan that they could rule Mysore independently of the Nizam's blessing. The Nizam claimed sovereignty over all Muslim-ruled territory in southern India. As a result of the alliance of these two powerful Indian leaders with the British, Tipu lost the third Anglo-Mysore war. It was in India that the British perfected the very successful Western imperial strategy of divide and rule. Tipu was forced to sign the humiliating peace treaty of *Seringapatam* on March 18, 1792, by which he surrendered half of Mysore to the British and their Indian allies.

The fourth and final war between Tipu Sultan and the British took place between 1798 and 1799. Tipu was convinced that the French, now led by Napoleon Bonaparte, would form a military alliance with him against the British. Napoleon had invaded Egypt in late June 1798 with the intention of joining forces with Tipu to oust the British from India. Napoleon captured the Egyptian city of Alexandria and led his army inland while his fleet was anchored in *Aboukir Bay.* The British had sent Admiral Horatio Nelson after Napoleon's fleet over two months earlier. Nelson had sailed from Tagus after the French but Napoleon evaded Nelson, landing in Alexandria before having to engage Nelson. Nelson caught up with the French fleet on August 1, 1798, after Napoleon had landed his army in Egypt. It took Nelson only three hours to crush the backbone of the French fleet during the *Battle of the Nile,* August 1–3, 1798.

With the defeat of his fleet in Aboukir Bay, Napoleon was unable to send military help to Tipu Sultan in India. The British invaded Mysore with their old allies, the Nizam of Hyderabad and the Maratha Empire, with a combined force exceeding fifty thousand. Tipu was outnumbered almost 2 to 1. Tipu was killed on May 4, 1799, defending his capital city, *Srirangapatna.* Mysore was stolen from the people of India and held by the British until 1947.

The Fourth and Final Anglo-Dutch War for Naval Dominance: 1781–1784

As we explained above the Dutch had received the short end of the stick from the "Glorious Revolution" of 1688. By the outbreak of the Seven Years' War the Dutch had recognized this sufficiently to stay neutral rather than ally with England against France. It was therefore understandable that by the outbreak of the fifth post-1688 Anglo-French war, the Dutch would proclaim its neutrality again, and so it did. But the British Empire was now the world's primary bully much like the American Empire later. Today you either ally with the Americans in every one of their incessant warmongering adventures across the globe or suffer their wrath. So it was with the British Empire in 1780.

The Dutch had signaled to the world their desire to be a neutral state and not compete for naval dominance with the British and French by running down their navy. The British took advantage of this and tried to bully the Dutch into helping them put down the rebellion in the thirteen American colonies. The Dutch refused to "loan" their military to the British. Dutch merchants fully expected to profit from the war by selling supplies to the belligerents. The Dutch foolishly thought that the British would honor the principle of "free ship, free goods" enshrined in the Anglo-Dutch Commercial Treaty of 1668, which the Dutch had secured following their military victories against the British during the second Anglo-Dutch war of 1665–1667. Far from honoring this treaty the British saw an opportunity to reduce the Dutch state to a British dependency. The long Anglo-Dutch alliance had always been a ploy by England to colonize Holland.

The British declared war on the Dutch in December 1780. At the time the Dutch navy had only twenty ships. The Royal navy moved quickly to capture or destroy many of the Dutch ships in the Caribbean before the Dutch captains had received news from their government that the British had declared war. In like manner the important Dutch colony of *St. Eustatius* in the Caribbean was easily captured and looted by British Admiral, George Rodney, in February 1781, mostly because the Dutch were unaware that Britain had declared war. The tiny Dutch colony of St. Eustatius was an important entrepot which the Dutch could use effectively to enable supplies to reach the American rebels. Rodney's arrival surprised the Dutch who agreed to surrender the colony. Rodney not only seized the rich cargoes of the Dutch merchant ships in the harbor but sent three British warships to seize the rich cargoes of a convoy of Dutch merchant ships which had recently departed the colony. Within a relatively short period the British had captured or disabled over five hundred Dutch merchant ships.

The British were long aware that the Dutch were the first to challenge the Portuguese for the lucrative trade and colonies brought about by Da Gama's sea voyage to India. They had fought both the Dutch and the French for this trade and colonization. During this time the British were currently engaged in another war with the French in this region which we have documented above. Once the British declared war on Holland in 1780, the British used the opportunity to steal the Dutch trade and colonies in this region. In August 1781 the British captured and looted the Dutch colony of *Padang* in Western Sumatra, Indonesia. The British governor in Madras, Lord Macartney, ordered the attacks on the Dutch possessions in India. In November 1781, the British captured the main Dutch colony in India, *Negapatnam*. Britain kept Negapatnam after the 1783 Treaty of Paris. In Ceylon the British captured the Dutch colony of *Trincomalee* in January 1782. Fortunately for the Dutch it was recaptured by the French and returned to Holland. The French had tried but failed in their attempt to recapture Negapatnam. Padang was also returned to Holland but its defenses had been destroyed during the British occupation.

The British sent Admiral George Johnstone to capture the Dutch colony in South Africa. Johnstone captured several ships of the Dutch East India Company but failed to capture the Cape Colony because the French had sent help to the colony. The Dutch Republic had lost most of its colonies in the Caribbean and Asia to the British. But most had been recaptured from the British by the French. As a result of the French victories the Dutch only lost their Indian colony of Negapatnam to the British when the Dutch made peace with Britain in 1784. But Britain secured from the Dutch the right to trade in the Dutch East Indies. During the French Revolutionary and Napoleonic wars which began in 1793, the British would take over permanently many of the Dutch colonies around the globe. The Glorious Revolution of 1688 had begun the process whereby Britain would build its empire at the expense of the Dutch.

European Empires in Other Parts of Asia

In chapter 4 we traced the beginning of Western colonization of Asia, Africa and America. We saw that the Portuguese Empire began by colonizing parts of Africa before reaching India. The Portuguese were looking for the Orient and were not focusing exclusively on India. But India is where it happened to land. As a result India became the base for colonies in other parts of Asia. Using India as the base was followed by the Dutch, English and French East India companies. This is our reason for giving so much focus to India in our historical overview of the Portuguese, Dutch, British and French empires. However, it's time to expand our overview to other parts of Asia so as not to leave the impression that the West had colonized only India and not Asia as a whole. Prior to the British colonizations in other parts of Asia, the Portuguese had colonized *Macau, China, Ceylon, Indonesia, Malaya* and *Japan,* the Spanish had colonized the *Philippines* and *China,* and the Dutch had colonized *Indonesia, Malaya* and *Ceylon.* Note that Western historians would call these colonizations trade. As I have clarified, once military force is used it is colonization not trade. The Portuguese, Spanish and Dutch used superior military force to colonize parts of these countries before the British and French. Even before these military colonizations the West went to Asia armed with another of their many tools of colonization, the *Christian church.*

The Portuguese, as the first Europeans, used their powerful naval advantage not only against the Asians but against the Arabs. The Arabs had a historical lead over Europe in getting the Asian products to Europe. The Portuguese used their navy to control the Indian Ocean. The Portuguese used that naval advantage to colonize Goa in India and used this Indian base to invade and conquer other parts of Asia. Only one year after stealing Goa from India the Portuguese stole *Malacca* from Malaya. In 1511, Afonso de Albuquerque, Portuguese Viceroy of India, sailed from Goa with eighteen ships to steal Malacca. With the conquest of Malacca the Portuguese controlled the important Straits of Malacca through which most of the trade prior to European colonization passed. There can be no question that this was colonization by force since de Albuquerque slaughtered all of the Muslims living in Malacca except for those more valuable as slaves. The Portuguese conquered parts of the richest spice islands, the Moluccas, from their base in Malacca. This began European colonization of Indonesia. Ever since the Portuguese arrived in 1512, they engaged in wars with those defending their land and resources from theft. This was **not** trade but colonization. The Portuguese were expelled from their first colony on Ternate Island, despite building a fortress to defend their thefts. In 1513 the Portuguese colonized the island of Ambon. But they continued to face fierce resistance from the local inhabitants. Their ploy to use the Christian church as a tool of colonization did not succeed.

The Portuguese were the first Europeans to use their base in India to begin European colonization of China. Albuquerque sent several of his captains to the Pearl River between 1513 and 1516 to prospect for trade and colonization. This marked the beginning of Canton's preeminent position in the subsequent Western conquests in China. From the beginning the Portuguese were met with military opposition and battles at sea. The Chinese caught and imprisoned some of the Portuguese sailors. These military confrontations clearly support our view that this was colonization not trade. The Portuguese were not deterred by these military confrontations with China. As a result of this persistence the Portuguese established their permanent colony in **Macau** in 1557. Macau was not returned to China until 1999. The Portuguese were also the first European Empire to begin European colonization of Japan.

The European empires engaged in thefts from each other. The Spanish began competing with the Portuguese for trade and colonization in the Moluccas and China after it had established its colonial base in the Philippines. The Dutch were the second European empire to steal from the Portuguese. The Dutch stole Malacca from the Portuguese in 1651 and Ceylon in 1656. The Dutch also competed with the Portuguese and Spanish in the Moluccas. The Dutch expanded European colonization of Indonesia by stealing land in Jakarta and Aceh. Other Asian thefts included Mauritius, Thailand, Taiwan, Japan and China. The British joined the Dutch in stealing from the Portuguese and Spanish in the Moluccas and Malaya.

The British joined other European empires in their mad rush to colonize China. It found a unique weapon to add to its deadly arsenal of WMDs to conquer China. After its conquest of Bengal it used the land stolen in India to produce the illegal drug, **opium,** and forced the Chinese to buy it. In most cases a land is colonized to steal its resources or to produce goods that can be sold to Western consumers. At the beginning of the eighteenth century it would have been too expensive militarily for Britain to steal the Chinese land to take the tea that was so valuable to consumers in England. It was less costly to steal land in India to produce opium and exchange it for the Chinese tea. The British found out that the people of China had a long history of using opium and could be addicted, much like many Americans today are addicted to illegal drugs. While the Chinese had used opium for medicinal purposes before Western invasions they were taught to mix opium with tobacco by the civilized West and smoke it. In 1729 China made importation of opium **illegal.** But the total import of opium into China increased from 200 chests in 1729, to 4,500 chests by 1800, and to a staggering 40,000 chests by 1840. Mexican drug lords today are opposed by both the American and Mexican governments. But Britain was a civilized Empire. That meant addicting the Chinese because they were the "primitive" counterpart.

The British devised a complex scheme to smuggle the illegal drug into China. To add insult to injury the British used their extensive diplomatic skills to get the Chinese government to make the British imports legal. Imagine today the Mexican government trying to convince the United States to make imports of illegal drugs from Mexico legal. Imagine further Mexico waging war on the United States because the United States would not change its law and allow Mexico to make many more Americans, drug addicts. Next imagine all of the emerging economies, China, India, Russia, Brazil, South Africa, Indonesia, Malaya, Vietnam, Saudi Arabia, Argentina, etc., backing the Mexicans with weapons, finance, and trade embargoes on the United States. When the British waged war on China to force the Chinese to buy ever larger quantities of its illegal drug it was backed by France, the United States, Japan, and other Western powers. These Anglo-Chinese wars have been rightly demonized as the "Opium Wars." They began in 1839 and ended with the British defeating China, forcing the Chinese to buy their opium produced on land stolen in India. The British also stole the island of Hong Kong which they were forced to return in 1997 because China had become militarily more powerful than the British Empire. I discussed the U.S. involvement in the Opium Wars in my *American Invasions, chapter 3*. France and the United States were the two empires who benefitted most, after Britain, from the British defeat of China.

Implicit in the accepted definition of civilized is the flip side of that coin which goes by the many derogatory terms invented by the West to demonize those they invade, conquer and steal from. We have listed these terms many times but they bear constant reminders. The flip side of civilized can be barbaric, guerilla, coolie, gook, naked savage, terrorist, Islamist, radicalized, communist, etc. In the case of the Chinese it would be "coolie." The British were not acting as primitives or criminals when they forced the Chinese to pay for the opium in exchange for British payment for Chinese tea. Far from it. To use superior military force to make the Chinese consume this illegal drug was a sign of how civilized the British were and how backward the "Chinese coolies" were. The power with the superior military is always the civilized power. How else could it prove its civilized nature if it did not use that superior military force to dominate and destroy the primitives. In particular it must perform many acts of wholesale slaughter and genocide to teach the primitives to show submission to the civilized power.

Once the British forced their way into China the other Western powers followed and supported the British. If you want to join the civilized club you do their dirty bidding without awkward questions. For example, at the 2013 G8 summit in Northern Ireland, Canada's prime minister, Steven Harper, was not shy about spelling out to the Russian president, Vladimir Putin, that he could not be counted as a member of the civilized G8 club so long as he questioned the West's criminal destruction of Syria and the genocide imposed by the West on the Syrian people. He should learn to follow the U.S. lead just like the willing and devoted brain-dead sheep, Steven Harper. Instead of castigating Harper for being such an idiot the Canadian media portrayed him as making a bold stand against Putin. Furthermore, the Canadian media suggested that when Harper referred to the G7 plus 1 he was subtly implying that Russia should be kicked out of the G8. At a time when countries like China, India and Brazil have far more justification than Canada to be included in the G8, it's amazing that the Canadian media can continue to live in the dark ages and be as brain-dead as their prime minister. Thank God, Canadian voters showed better judgment by replacing Steven Harper with Justin Trudeau in November 2015.

European colonization of China began in the province of Guangzhou which was called Canton at the time. Access was provided by the Pearl River. As we have said before the West begins its colonization with trade. Trade benefits both parties but theft by colonization provides all of the gains to the imperial power. During the period of trade the West had to pay China for its imports of tea, silk, porcelain and other Chinese exports. But the West is too civilized to pay people they regard as inferior. They prefer to steal and justify the gains from theft over trade by trumpeting the rights of civilized people over barbarians. The people whose goods are stolen naturally oppose. But the only thing primitive about the victims of Western theft is the military weapons of the victims. By using superior military weapons to subdue the victims and continue the theft is the unquestioned proof that the **thief** is indeed, the most civilized.

CHAPTER 7

Napoleon Bonaparte, Rise of Germany and Italy, Second French Colonial Empire, Belgium Congo, and the Scramble for Africa

In this chapter we continue the competition between Britain and France after France found a military genius in *Napoleon Bonaparte.* Napoleon provided the greatest challenge to British hegemony since King Louis XVI. Next we address the challenge to the British and French empires by the rise of Germany and Italy. We end the chapter with the Second French Colonial Empire, Western atrocities committed in the name of civilization in the Congo, and the "Scramble for Africa" by Britain, France, Germany, Italy, Belgium, Portugal, and Spain.

The Sixth Post-1688 Anglo-French War: The Revolutionary and Napoleonic Wars: 1793–1815

This sixth war between England and France after 1688 was the final battle of importance between England and France much like the third Anglo-Dutch war of 1672–1674 was the important marker for ending Anglo-Dutch rivalry. There was a difference between the Anglo-Dutch rivalry and the Anglo-French rivalry. In the case of the Anglo-Dutch rivalry both Holland and England were relatively tiny maritime states on the fringe of Western Europe fighting for worldwide colonies at the expense of Spain and Portugal. The English out-smarted the Dutch with the Glorious Revolution of 1688. France, on the other hand, had been the dominant European power long before the Glorious Revolution of 1688. It could have easily held on to that political, military and economic dominance. In like manner the British Empire had become the dominant naval power after the Glorious Revolution and could easily have held on to its worldwide colonies with that naval dominance. However, empires and their military and political leaders have insatiable appetites for warmongering and conquests. France wanted what Britain had in terms of worldwide colonies and Britain wanted what France had in terms of continental power and influence.

The sixth post-1688 Anglo-French war severely reduced French power while increasing British supremacy. But it left a power vacuum on the continent which was filled by Germany, and to a lesser extent, Italy. The British were unable to destroy German/Italian power without destroying itself. In the end only the American Empire gained from the long rivalry, first between England and France and later between England and Germany/Italy. Many historians foolishly wrote off France after the Seven Years' War. The reason was that Britain had decisively won the worldwide conflict with France during that war. It had won it with a superior navy. But by winning a vast worldwide empire Britain had even less interest in maintaining an influence in Europe than it had before. France always had a greater interest in Europe and maintains that greater interest to this day. So while Britain was busy enjoying the fruits of its victory in the Seven Years' War, France was busy maintaining and consolidating its long dominance in Europe. Had it stuck to a single goal of ruling Continental Europe it may have very well succeeded.

It took the military genius of Napoleon Bonaparte to take that French dominance to new heights. On land it's the army, not the navy, which wins wars. France had the most powerful army in Europe. The supremacy of the Royal Navy was almost irrelevant to this fight for continental domination. The French had won earlier dominance of Europe during the long reign of King Louis XIV, 1643–1715. It would win it again under Napoleon Bonaparte. Napoleon's folly would be to attempt to bring Russia into his vision of Europe. It would be Hitler's folly as well. This sixth post-1688 Anglo-French war had a number of lasting consequences, many of which have been missed by Western historians.

The first important consequence is the recognition of the false claims to *Republican values* by the newly independent United Sates of America. As we have explained at length in our *Rise and Fall of the American Empire,* the U.S. war against Britain in 1775–1783 was never about Republican values over *monarchy* or the rights of colonial people over imperial powers or taxation without representation. It was a very selfish desire by a landed gentry and a small oligarchic merchant class stealing the lands and resources of the First Nations with superior military force and propaganda. This newly independent "republic," which had seized independence only because of the military help of France, showed that it had no desire to support the French revolution against monarchy, nor honor its military alliance with France during this sixth post-1688 Anglo-French war.

Second, the newly independent United States had shown clearly that it intended to become an **imperial** power like Britain and France by its conquests of First Nations lands outside the original thirteen colonies and by its invasions of Canada in 1775 and 1812. It also showed its denial of the rights to equality enshrined in its Constitution and Bill of Rights, strictly for **propaganda** purposes only, by **not** supporting the abolition of slavery by the later French Revolution of 1789. In fact one of the key *compromises,* which are what **slave owners** like George Washington and his landed gentry like to call them, of the 1787 Constitutional Convention, was that slaves are both "100 percent *nonhuman* for ownership rights and *60* percent *human* for voting rights." Only a convoluted pretend freedom-loving republic like the warmongering American Empire could have come up with such a boldface dastardly subjugation of human rights and convince the world that it was an ingenious compromise.

The third consequence of this war was a century of British imperial rule and influence across most of the globe, much like the Roman Empire before and the American Empire after. This generation and the one before has witnessed the same kind of in your face propaganda, pretend moral superiority, racist white man's burden, warmongering, deceit, lies, theft, and gunboat diplomacy by the American Empire as those who lived during the century of *Pax Britannica.* The American Empire copied the **criminal and immoral** behavior of the British Empire down to the language of English and was able to use the media and superior propaganda to convince many that British and American subjugation, exploitation and total control of freedoms, were for their own good. The two centuries of Pax Britannica and Pax Americana have been lost centuries for the human race. Far from teaching humanity how to live peacefully with dignity, pride, truth, visionary leadership and concern and care for each other, it has reinforced the same lessons of past centuries, that of warmongering, colonization and subjugation of the military weak by the military powerful, destruction of the planet with the consumption of junk, and the development and use of weapons of mass destruction.

False Ideals of the French and American Revolutions

This sixth post-1688 war between the British and French empires took place within a context of the West struggling with demands by intellectuals and the people for greater freedoms and individual rights. Both the French Revolution, and the American Revolution which preceded it, have been held up as symbols of individual freedoms which the West embraced. In reality, there was very modest progress on this front, hardly anything one would call *revolutionary.* First and foremost these revolutions embraced rather than denounced **warmongering.** Second, they embraced rather than denounced **imperialism.** Third, they embraced rather than denounced **slavery.** Fourth, they embraced rather than denounced **racism** and the supremacy of the **white** race. While the intellectuals and leaders spoke of the rights of man, the need to abolish absolute monarchies, the need to use reason and science rather than religious dogma, the need to promote equality and justice for all, there were so many contradictions in the goals these same leaders and intellectuals aspired to that very little real progress was made toward these ideals. But pretending to espouse such ideals, while preventing their occurrence, was extremely important for their powerful propaganda war.

These revolutions remind me of the hope and euphoria surrounding the American Empire democratically electing its first "black" president in Barack Obama. Obama changed absolutely nothing about U.S. foreign or domestic policies. If anything, it made the American Empire an even more ruthless and inhumane empire by co-opting many more **black** leaders, than under white presidents, to carry out its **warmongering, military invasions** and **propaganda.** In like manner, the American Revolution, led by **slave owners** such as George Washington, prolonged slavery, and led to the theft of far more First Nations lands than would have occurred under British colonization. The British abolished slavery in all of their colonies by 1833. As we have explained in *American Invasions,* the British would never have been able to conquer so much First Nations land in the middle of the continent since they could only use firepower from the guns of the Royal Navy. The French Revolution led to many atrocities worse than those committed by the French monarchy and even more warmongering and colonizations. The revolutions may have helped the process whereby more of the people in the West got a small say in who governed them and how they were governed. But this was evolutionary not revolutionary. Most importantly, the privileged few made sure that their stranglehold on power was never diluted or challenged. But it also meant that there were more people in the West having to gain from warmongering and colonizing and raping the land and resources of the militarily weaker nations. There is absolutely no evidence that this wider western democracy had any desire to reduce western imperialism, invasions, colonizations and thefts. If anything, the evidence suggests the opposite. They demanded a share in those evil gains much like **black** leaders in the United States have, since the election of President Obama.

The *ideals* for these revolutions came from what has been called the *Enlightenment and the Age of Reason.* This was an intellectual movement preceding both the American and French revolutions. It was led by Locke, Voltaire, Rousseau, Montesquieu, Hobbes, Newton, Kant, Russell, Descartes, Paine, Jefferson, Franklin and many more. It can be traced back to 1637 when Descartes published *Discourse on Method.* It was supposed to usher in a Western leadership of the world based on reason, science, logic, objective and consistent application of rules, humanity, justice, laws, individual freedoms, equality, and rejection of propaganda, ignorance and subjective religious beliefs. Both the American and French revolutions declared certain basic rights for individuals. Ideals are great when they support leaders to govern fairly and wisely. They are **deadly** when used by leaders for propaganda purposes to hide their crimes. There was no shortage of proclamations such as the "Rights of Man." But Western leaders have consistently used these ideals and proclaimed rights to deceive and hide their crimes, appetite for warmongering, and imperial expansion. These declarations have never been observed by a single Western leader since the American and French revolutions. But many have been used to hold the leaders of countries the West invaded and plundered, to account. All of their so-called international institutions have been used to support their colonizations and exploitation of those colonized by military force. In like manner, far from religion becoming a dying force during this so-called Age of Reason, the Christian church and the pope continued to lead the charge to invade and steal the lands and resources of the people of the Third World while pretending to save their souls. Religious freedom in the west simply meant that in the countries invaded and colonized by the west Christians had the right to steal on behalf of the Christian church.

President Obama was supported my many, like myself, who were fooled into thinking that he believed in these ideals. He had the best opportunity to bring about change, and to govern with these ideals in mind, both because of wide-spread domestic and international support for change, and the end of the hated Bush era. Instead he, more than any other Western leader, used these ideals to deceive even his own supporters. While President Bush felt the wrath of his liberal opponents, President Obama was given a free ride by his liberal supporters and by **blacks**. Every crime and invasion President Obama engaged in, and there were far more than those of President Bush, his supporters and **blacks** fell for his charm and propaganda. He had to commit these crimes and start these invasions because the Republicans made him do it or because he had to protect America from those who would invade us by flying carpets and kill us with sling shots. The fallback position of **blacks** and liberals was that President Obama was at least a better alternative than a Republican president. The 2010 mid-term elections was a god-send for President Obama. He could now blame the Republicans for every heinous crime he committed since he did not control both Houses of Congress. Never mind the fact that few U.S. presidents ever controlled both Houses of Congress.

As I said above, neither of the American nor the French revolutions amounted to much, in terms of changing policies, or evolving the human race. They changed leaders but not policies and visions. Both the United States and France became republics rather than monarchies. But the visions of the Republican presidents of the United States and France were no different from the visions of the monarchies who ruled Western Europe. That vision was one of expansion by colonization, using military force, slavery, racism, propaganda, lies, criminal activities, illegal drugs such as opium, piracy, and white supremacy. The only difference between the French and the American Revolution was that the French king, Louis XVI, was French, one of their own, while the English king, George III, was English, not American. But that was a minor difference since the rebels in the American colonies were as English as the rebels in France were French. Both had grievances against their respective monarchs. Both pretended that their rebellion were not motivated by selfish desires for wealth, power and prestige, when in fact, those were exactly their motives.

Today, in both France and the United States, the rulers of these rebels still show their preference for warmongering and military expenditures over the rights of the poor and unemployed. The rebels wanted to rule to promote their own wealth, power, prestige, military skills, propaganda, criminal activities, injustices, exploitation of the weak, enrichment of their family and friends, and most important, of course, to be of the privileged ruling class rather than the underprivileged class. In both the American and French revolutions the rebels saw an opportunity to promote their own selfish interests and grabbed it with both hands. By claiming to support the ideals of the Enlightenment and Age of Reason they got the backing of many intellectuals. By blaming monarchies for the sad plight of the poor they got the support of the masses. But the new governance structure was no more democratic than the ones they replaced. In time a carefully honed and indoctrinated middle class was given some powers by the ruling elite. But there was never any challenge to the power of the elite or the military or the imperialists because any such challenge by a *Julian Assange* or a *Bradley Manning,* or an *Edward Snowden* was squashed like a bug. When not one single Western leader dare give even the tiniest support to such defenders of freedom and democracy you have the proof of what I say.

American Betrayal of the French Revolution

Those who led the French Revolution had been foolishly convinced that they would receive military, financial and moral support from the independent American Republic. They were sadly mistaken because of the reasons I explained above. The rebels in the American Revolution used the ideals of the Enlightenment only as propaganda. In time the French rebels would do exactly the same. The French Revolution against monarchy began with the "storming of the Bastille" on July 14, 1789. The use of propaganda began when the "Declaration of the Rights of Man" was passed in August 1789. France abolished the monarchy and declared itself a republic on September 21, 1792. Among its first actions was warmongering and invasions. The new French Republic with its phony ideals invaded Germany, Italy and the Low Countries much like the phony American Republic invaded Canada as one of its first acts. Western republics are no less warmongers and imperialists than Western monarchies.

It may seem ironic that it was after this French Republic showed its appetite for warmongering that it would turn to its Republican brother in the United States for support. If this American Republic was true to the ideals of peace and human progress that would be reason to deny assistance to a French Republic for being a warmonger. But that was not the case. The new American Republic was as dedicated a warmonger as the new French Republic. This was proved by its invasions of Canada to its north and First Nations lands to the west of its original borders. The reason the United States reneged on its 1778 military and economic alliance with France was the same selfish reasons for its rebellion against England. The United States had far more wealth and prosperity to gain from a postindependence alliance with Britain than with France. It had entered into a long-term military and economic alliance with France only to get French military support during its war of independence against Britain. It had absolutely no intention of honoring that long-term alliance once it had achieved its independence.

It was February 1, 1793, when the French Republic declared war on Britain fully expecting the American Republic to honor the terms of the 1778 Treaty of Alliance. The French Republic sent their Ambassador,

Edmund Charles Genet with great haste to the United States. He arrived in the United States on April 8, 1793. But honoring the alliance would have been costly to the new American Republic. By declaring its neutrality on April 22, 1793, the USA would grow its economy and power by selling supplies to the warmongers. The French Revolutionary War provided an early opportunity for the USA to work toward its goal of becoming an empire like France and Britain. Why would it resist this opportunity just to be honorable when its very foundations were dishonorable?

Reneging on the 1778 treaty by the Americans was a serious blow to the French Republic. It gave an edge to the British navy in the Atlantic and the Caribbean. The French colonies in both the Caribbean and in North America would not be defended by the United States. The United States, instead, used its neutrality to increase its own imperial opportunities in the French Caribbean at the expense of the French Empire. After the infamous *XYZ affair,* see *Rise and Fall of the American Empire, pages 215–216,* the USA began capturing French ships. The USA and the French Republic were in a state of undeclared war between 1797 and 1800. The USA settled with France by agreeing to pay $US 20 million for reneging on the 1778 treaty.

The French Revolutionary War: 1792–1802

France declared war on Austria on April 20, 1792, and invaded the Austrian Netherlands. Opposition to the French Revolution was coordinated by the holy Roman emperor *Leopold II.* Leopold II saw an opportunity to take advantage of the turmoil in France to increase the power of the Austro-Hungarian Empire. France and Austria had long competed for leadership of the territory once ruled by the Western Roman Empire. Leopold II was also the brother of the wife of King Louis XVI of France. He feared both for the life of his sister and the threat of the French Revolution spreading to his domain. As holy Roman emperor he also felt an obligation to defend the rights of kings. Leopold II appealed to all the sovereigns of Western Europe to defend the rights of monarchy. Leopold II began to form a Coalition against the French Republic by meeting with the king of Prussia, *Frederick William II,* in

August 1791. But Leopold II died suddenly in Vienna on March 1, 1792. He was succeeded by his eldest son, Francis II.

When the French invaded the Austrian Netherlands in April 1792 the Prussians were the first to support Austria. King Louis XVI was guillotined on January 21, 1793. During what has been called the *Reign of Terror* some twenty thousand French people, including Queen Marie Antoinette, were beheaded with the infamous guillotine. Spain and Portugal joined the First Coalition against the French Republic in January 1793. Britain and Holland joined in February 1793. This First Coalition also included several Italian states and the Ottoman Empire. The French were initially pushed back out of the Austrian Netherlands. But the French army counter attacked and made significant territorial conquests in the Austrian Netherlands, Germany, Italy, Holland and Switzerland. By 1795 France had scored victories over most of Western Europe. By 1798 the First Coalition had disintegrated. Peace had been made with Prussia on April 5, 1795, and with Spain on July 22, 1795, Treaty of Basel. With the Treaty of Campo Formio, France made peace with Austria on October 18, 1797. In Holland the French expelled the House of Orange and created the client *Batavian Republic* on January 19, 1795. In 1798 the French created the client *Helvetic Republic* in Switzerland. Pope Pius VI was deposed by the French and replaced by the Republic of Rome.

During the remaining period of the French Revolutionary War the French Empire was fighting only the British and Ottoman empires. France had won the war for continental dominance. But it still wanted the worldwide colonies it had fought the British for in so many previous wars. The French had found a military hero in Napoleon Bonaparte and he would be the one to steal the colonies from Britain. Napoleon would first invade Egypt, conquer the Ottoman Empire, and then steal British India. But the Egyptian invasion was a failure and France was unable to support their Indian ally, Tipu Sultan, as we explained in chapter 6. The French could not take the colonies from Britain as its navy was weak relative to the British navy. As I said above the French military advantage was on land because of its powerful army.

In 1798 the French navy controlled the Mediterranean because the British navy was fighting the Spanish in the Caribbean. Spain had switched sides in 1796 and allied with France. As a result of French naval dominance in the Mediterranean, Napoleon's army boarded the French fleet at Toulon on May 19, 1798, and captured Malta in June. Napoleon arrived in Egypt in late June and captured the city of *Alexandria.* The French navy anchored in Aboukir Bay twenty miles northeast of Alexandria because the harbor in Alexandria was too shallow. In the meantime the British had sent their most competent Admiral, Sir Horatio Nelson, to prevent the French fleet from reaching Egypt. Nelson failed to prevent Napoleon from reaching Egypt. However, after Napoleon had landed his army and was marching inland after his conquest of Alexandria, Nelson arrived and engaged the French fleet anchored in Aboukir Bay. At the *Battle of the Nile,* August 1798, Admiral Horatio Nelson annihilated the French navy in Aboukir Bay.

After Alexandria, Napoleon marched into Syria and captured *Jaffa* in March 1799. Napoleon's next target was the important port city of *Acre.* But the British navy, fresh from its victory at Aboukir Bay, was on hand to help the Ottoman Empire defend Acre. New French supplies were blocked by the British navy as well. A plague outbreak devastated Napoleon's army. Napoleon's defeat at Acre ended the French attempt to conquer the Middle East and India. Napoleon was forced to return to France leaving the remnants of his battered army in Egypt. It was defeated by the British in 1801.

While Napoleon was in Egypt, a Second Coalition of European powers had been formed in 1798 to defeat France. This Second coalition consisted of many of the members of the First Coalition, except Spain, and added Russia initially. Napoleon returned to France from Egypt on August 23, 1799, overthrew the French government and made himself the new ruler. After the Reign of Terror, France had created a new Constitution in September 1795 and was governed thereafter by the *Directory.* Napoleon overthrew the Directory and reorganized the army. With this new army he engaged the allies in Italy, Switzerland and the Rhine. Russia was defeated in Switzerland (French Helvetic Republic) and left the Second Coalition in late 1799. Austria was defeated and signed the Treaty of Luneville on February 9, 1801. After the remnants of Napoleon's army in Egypt were defeated by the British, the Ottoman Empire withdrew from the Second Coalition. Left alone, the British signed the Treaty of Amiens on March 27, 1802. This ended the first phase of the sixth post-1688 Anglo-French War.

The Napoleonic War: 1803–1815

Britain declared war on France on May 18, 1803. Several new coalitions were formed to defeat France. They included Britain, Russia, Austria, Prussia, Portugal and Sweden. After Napoleon defeated the combined forces of Russia and Austria in December 1805, the Austrians made peace with France and left the coalition. Next Napoleon defeated Prussia in October 1806. Russia signed a peace treaty in July 1807 after its army had lost several battles against Napoleon. The Swedish army was defeated in September 1807. By 1810 the French Empire dominated Western Europe. Napoleon had failed to expand the French Empire overseas because the British navy dominated the high seas. But the expanded French *Napoleonic Empire,* on the continent, was massive. It included Poland, Prussia, Italy, the Papal States, Spain, Holland and Austria. It covered an area of almost a million square miles and had a population of almost 45 million. It was the latest version of the Western Roman Empire, replacing the Holy Roman Empire. Napoleon became emperor of this new "Roman" empire in 1804 and copied the age old custom of Christian rulers of expanding and securing territory by marriages of convenience. In 1806 the Habsburg House ended the title of holy Roman emperor.

Napoleon was no different from all other conquerors and emperors. He was as addicted to warmongering and territorial expansion as every other conqueror and emperor. He wanted to destroy the British Empire. But the British Empire was protected by the English Channel and the powerful British Navy. To feed his addiction, Napoleon had no choice but to expand overland eastward into Russia. Invading Russia made no military, economic or political sense, much like the later American invasions of Iraq or Afghanistan. Both were done to feed an addiction to warmongering. French rule of Europe crashed after Napoleon's failed invasion of Russia in June 1812. Getting to Russia was the easy part since his army marched eastward across territory controlled by Napoleon and during good summer weather. Even a stupid and incompetent general knows that a long march stretches your supply line to a dangerous level. Napoleon was no stupid or incompetent general. But he was addicted, much like a heroin or crack addict. He could not help himself. Feeding an addiction is the greatest of highs. Napoleon fed his addiction all the way to Moscow, totally ignoring the coming of winter. It was September 14, 1812, when Napoleon reached Moscow.

The Russians simply had to wait for the Russian winter to destroy Napoleon's army. It would not have mattered if Napoleon had simply failed to conquer Russia. But the disaster was the destruction of his army during its long march back to France in bad winter weather. Now he had no military force to hold the Western European territories he had conquered. The cost of the failed Russian invasion was worse than Napoleon's earlier failed attempt to reconquer its colony of St. Domingue in 1802. That reconquest would have had economic value since St. Domingue was the richest colony in the world because of the high price of sugar at the time. St. Domingue produced 40 percent of the total world output of sugar when it revolted successfully from the French Empire in the 1790s. Napoleon needed the island's sugar to fund his wars. He lost St. Domingue because its hot tropical climate decimated the military forces he sent. Hostile weather in St. Domingue had cost him the money he needed to fund a larger military and hostile weather in Russia had destroyed the smaller military he was able to fund. His one consolation was that he would still be able to feed his addiction to warmongering until his "Roman" empire was taken from him in war.

The reconquest of Napoleon's empire reached the gates of Paris in March 1814 and Napoleon abdicated in April 1814. The French monarchy was restored and Louis XVII became the new king of France. The Western allies naturally missed the fact that, like them, Napoleon was addicted to warmongering. In doing so they enabled Napoleon to return to the battlefield to feed his addiction until he was defeated at the Battle of Waterloo on June 18, 1815. He abdicated for the second and last time on June 22, 1815. Napoleon had the military ability to make France the dominant continental power in Europe. But his addiction to warmongering and imperial expansion ended French chance for hegemony. It was the fall of Napoleon, not the Seven Years' War, which ended Anglo-French rivalry for European/world domination. The British

Empire would be the unchallenged "absentee" European power until the rise of Germany.

Foundation for a New German Empire

The German Empire which dominated Western Europe after the fall of the French Empire was given a big boost by the rise and fall of Napoleon and the Treaty of Versailles which ended the Napoleonic wars. It was in 1806, during the Napoleonic War, that the Holy Roman Empire ended. At the Congress of Vienna, Prussia was considered a **great power** alongside Britain, France, Austria, and Russia. At the time, Austria was still regarded as the primary German power while Prussia ranked lowest among the five great powers. But the future German Empire rose out of the rise of Prussia as the dominant German power. When the duke of Prussia, *Albert Frederick,* died in 1618 without a son, his son-in-law united Prussia with Brandenburg. Brandenburg was part of the Holy Roman Empire and had been ruled by the House of Hohenzollern since 1415. Prussia had not been a part of the Holy Roman Empire.

The Holy Roman Empire was in decline since the end of the *Thirty Years War* of 1618–1648. While there were many reasons for this war, such as the Protestant/Catholic religious conflict and the demands for regional independence, an important reason was the continued rivalry between France and Germany for European hegemony. The 1648 Peace of Westphalia weakened Habsburg power in both Germany and Spain while increasing the power of France, Prussia, Holland and Switzerland. France acquired Alsace, and Brandenburg-Prussia acquired Pomerania. Brandenburg-Prussia became the *Kingdom of Prussia in 1701.* Frederick III of the House of Hohenzollern became the first king of Prussia, *Frederick I.* Under the rule of Frederick I and his son *Frederick the Great,* Prussia became a powerful military power. Frederick the Great added Silesia to the Prussian kingdom during the War of the Austrian Succession. By adding part of Poland in 1772 the Territory of Brandenburg in the East was joined to the Duchy of Prussia in the West. More Polish territory was added to Prussia in 1793 and 1795. Prussia added further territory from the Congress of Vienna ending the

Napoleonic wars. After the Napoleonic wars the expanded Kingdom of Prussia was divided into ten provinces.

The Congress of Vienna created a German Confederation as a result of the ending of the Holy Roman Empire. While the Austrian emperor was the president of the Confederation, Prussia would challenge Austria for leadership. Most of the ten provinces of the expanded Kingdom of Prussia were included in the Confederation. One of the key obstacles to German unification was the barriers to trade. Prussia was smart to begin the economic unification of Germany with a customs union, the *Zollverein.* Prussia was also smart in promoting its hegemony over Austria by excluding Austria from the *Zollverein.* The process of economic integration began during the Napoleonic wars and continued after. It was formalized with the Zollverein treaties of 1833. At the time a custom union was a novel idea. But the number of states joining the economic union steadily increased. The birth of railroads provided the necessary cheap transportation needed to make the economic union profitable. By 1865 the major centers of this economic union were fully linked by railroads carrying both raw materials and finished products. While this economic union grew in wealth and stature, Austria's continued exclusion and protectionism reduced its economic growth. Without a growing economic base Austria began to lose its historic political dominance.

Austro-Prussian War and the Rise of the New Post-Napoleonic Germany

The Austro-Hungarian Empire had been attacked for centuries both by the Ottomans in the East and by the French in the West. But it had survived those attacks. Now it was being attacked from within since Prussia, like Austria, was located in Central Europe and both were German speaking. It was inevitable that these two German states would settle the question of who would rule Germany, by military means. Wars are the natural solutions to conflicts by nations deemed to be civilized. The more successful your warmongering the more civilized and "godly" you are. This has been implicitly accepted by all, without exception, who have written the history of civilization since the beginning of time. I would certainly like to change that view and associate warmongering with how we define **barbaric** behavior. A civilized state should never ever invade and colonize. The invaders are the barbarians not those who defend against invasions. Winning a war does not make a nation civilized. But in 1866 Prussia went to war with Austria to determine which state was the more civilized.

Ever since the fall of the Western Roman Empire the people of Central Europe fought for independence from the Holy Roman Empire and the Habsburg rulers. This innate desire for independence was boosted by the Napoleonic wars as Napoleon sought control of all Europe. In particular, many German states wanted independence from the old Austro-Hungarian Empire and saw the end of the Holy Roman Empire in 1806 as presenting them with the opportunity to do so. Unfortunately, history is replete with examples of weak states allying with a powerful state to fight for independence only to be colonized or dominated by that new ally. In this case the German states in the North allied with Prussia to fight for independence from Austria. As is usually the case with these civilized conflicts, it began with a military invasion. Prussia invaded Holstein, a duchy governed by Austria since 1864, in June 1866, and in response Austria declared war on Prussia.

Prussia and Austria had been fighting for the territory of *Schleswig-Holstein* ever since it was conquered from Denmark during the second Schleswig war of 1864. The Duchies of Schleswig and Holstein were ruled by the Danish *House of Oldenburg* for many centuries. Since the days of the Vikings, Schleswig had been a part of Denmark and became a Danish duchy in the twelfth century. In 1460 it was decided by the Treaty of Ribe that the king of Denmark should also hold the titles of duke of Schleswig and count of Holstein. Holstein was part of the Holy Roman Empire, its northernmost state, but ruled by the king of Denmark. It became a member of the post-Napoleonic German Confederation and is now part of the German state of Schleswig-Holstein. Both Schleswig and Holstein were populated by Danes and Germans but the percent of the German population in Holstein exceeded the percentage in Schleswig because of the longer historic association of Schleswig with Denmark.

The first *Schleswig War* of 1848–1851 was a conflict between Danes and Germans over the rule of these two Duchies. The peaceful solution would have been to divide the two Duchies with Schleswig kept by Denmark and Holstein going to the new Germany. Some Danes would have moved from Holstein to Schleswig and some Germans would have moved from Schleswig to Holstein. But that would have deprived the warmongers of another opportunity to feed their addiction to war. The German population of the Duchies decided to rebel against Danish rule and Prussia was forced into war with Denmark. Sweden allied with Denmark against the Germans. The Danish navy blockaded the German ports and the Prussian army occupied the Duchies. Demark won the war and prevented Prussia from gaining new territory. In this first war Austria had not participated.

During the second Schleswig War in 1864 the Prussian army once again invaded Schleswig. In this war Prussia was supported by Austria while Denmark was not supported by Sweden as it had been in the first war. Denmark was soundly defeated by the combined forces of Prussia and Austria. The territory of the two Duchies ceased to be ruled by Denmark. Prussia would rule Schleswig and Austria would rule Holstein. In total, Denmark lost some 40 percent of its territory and its population. Prussia had emerged from this war as a military superpower and would soon go to war with Austria to take Holstein and strengthen its claim to rule the new post-Napoleonic Germany. At the time the dominant political figure in all Europe was the Iron Chancellor of Prussia, *Otto von Bismarck.*

Bismarck began his political career rather modestly by obtaining a seat in the lower house of the Prussian Diet (Assembly) in 1849. In 1848 most of Western Europe experienced popular rebellions demanding more power for the people. Bismarck was opposed to these rebellions as he saw them as resulting from the efforts of a small urban middle class wanting more power than the larger and poorer peasants. One response to these rebellions in Germany was the creation of the *Frankfurt Diet,* a popular national assembly to represent all Germans. It was this Assembly which had pressed Prussia to invade Schleswig-Holstein in 1848 to help the Germans, who had rebelled against Danish rule, and established a provisional government. In 1851 King Frederick William IV of Prussia appointed Bismarck to the Frankfurt Diet as Prussia's representative. Bismarck used his eight years in the Diet to oppose Austria and get

Germans to support Prussian leadership of a new unified Germany that would exclude Austria. His ultimate goal was to have European powers recognize Prussia as an equal great power not a lesser one. Bismarck was appointed as Prussian ambassador to Russia in 1859. He became Prussian ambassador to France in May 1862 but was recalled to Prussia by King William I in September 1862. He was appointed as prime minister and Foreign minister of Prussia on September 23, 1862.

During the second Schleswig-Holstein war Bismarck cooperated with Austria. After the defeat of Denmark, Bismarck was the key figure in enabling the division of the two Duchies between Prussia and Austria with the *Gastein Convention* of August 14, 1865. It was this Convention which Bismarck used as his excuse to begin the inevitable war with Austria to determine whether Austria or Prussia would lead the post-Napoleonic Germany. When Austria asked the Frankfurt Diet to reexamine the Schleswig-Holstein issue, Bismarck charged Austria with violating the Gastein Convention and invaded Holstein on June 9, 1866. In response to this invasion the German Confederation began to mobilize its troops on June 14, 1866, and Austria declared war on Prussia on June 17. While most of the German states backed Austria, Bismarck was able to get military support from Italy as a result of the alliance with Italy signed earlier on April 8, 1866. The Italian alliance meant that Austria was attacked on two fronts.

The war ended with a decisive Prussian victory. The *Peace of Prague,* August 23, 1866, formally dissolved the post-Napoleonic German Confederation and increased the territory of Prussia. The following year Prussia created the *North German Confederation* to exclude Austria from the new Germany. The enlarged Prussian state made up 80 percent of the population and territory of the North German Federation. King William I of Prussia became the president of this federation, and Bismarck became its chancellor. Prussia made military alliances with the Southern German states to further isolate Austria.

Franco-Prussian War of 1870 Ends French Hegemony in Europe

France had waged wars against the Austro-Hungarian Empire and against Britain over several centuries, to lead Europe. With the defeat of Napoleon, Britain had emerged as the unchallenged world power. But British power lay more with its worldwide colonies than with Europe. The defeat of France had created new opportunities in Europe for Austria and Russia. In 1815 no one would have imagined that the new power which would replace France would be Prussia. Naturally, Prussia could only prove that it was more civilized than France, and therefore worthy of leading civilized Europe, by defeating France in war. Civilized warmongering with military victories using civilized WMDs is the most important implicit hallmark for leading Western civilization. Never forget that President Barack Obama was awarded the infamous Nobel Peace Prize for being the best at civilized warmongering. While many questioned whether President George W. Bush was always a civilized warmonger no one questioned President Obama. President Obama's unmanned drones are deemed to be the most civilized way of killing men, women and children. His massive destruction of the homes of men, women and children lead to the most civilized ways of starving them to death in refugee camps. These refugee camps are even more civilized than the reserves used to imprison the First Nations after their lands and resources were stolen by previous American presidents.

While Prussia was warmongering its way into equality of great power status with Britain, Russia, and Austria, France was attempting a comeback from its 1815 defeat by finding another Napoleon to lead it once again to imperial greatness. After the defeat of Napoleon in 1815 his family members were forced into exile. Napoleon's nephew, *Louis-Napoleon Bonaparte,* was living in England when the 1848 revolutions swept across most of Europe. During the February Revolution in France the French people deposed their monarch once again and returned to Republican rule. The Second Republic held elections for president on December 10, 1848, and Louis-Napoleon won by a landslide. Despite the fact that it was these popular rebellions which enabled Louis-Napoleon to return to France from exile, as president of the Second French

Republic, he sent French troops into Italy to restore the rule of Pope Pius IX in the Papal States. The rebels had overthrown the pope. French troops remained in Rome to protect the pope until the outbreak of the Franco-Prussian War in 1870. This military intervention signaled Louis-Napoleon's support for the Catholic church and French traditions over popular democracies. An attempt to impeach the president for violating the new constitution failed.

The Constitution of the Second Republic only allowed Louis-Napoleon one four-year term as president. To stay in power Louis-Napoleon staged a successful coup on December 2, 1851. The next year Louis-Napoleon became the new emperor of France, *Napoleon III.* The title of Napoleon II had been used by those who had continued to support Napoleon I, after his exile in 1815, to refer his son. Napoleon II had died in 1832. With Napoleon III the French Empire was back in business. As usual this meant a return to what the West would call civilized warmongering.

Napoleon III began his warmongering in the Crimean War of 1854–1856, barely two years after the birth of the Second French Empire. In the Crimean War a Franco-British alliance defeated the Russians. This immediately returned the French Empire to civilized great power status. As I have said repeatedly you cannot claim to be civilized unless you have the military power to win wars. Paris played host to the Congress ending the Crimean War and France added its signature to that of Britain in March 1856. The reality of the Second French Empire was accepted as legitimate and an equal to that of Britain in terms of its civilized behavior and military power.

Napoleon III was also quick to seize the opportunity presented by the Anglo-Persian war in the very next year to play the role of civilized peace maker. The Crimean War had ended in March 1856. The British needed another war to feed their addiction to warmongering. The British declared war on Persia on November 1, 1856. France had established a relationship with Persia under Napoleon I. The Franco-Persian alliance between Napoleon I and Iran, 1807–1809, was anti-British. In 1857 the Persians turned to Napoleon's nephew, Napoleon III, to help them negotiate peace with Britain. Paris once again played host to the peace process which ended the Anglo-Persian war in March 1857.

The next civilized war of Napoleon III was the Franco-Austrian War of 1859. Napoleon III used the attempted assassination of him by an Italian to join forces with the Kingdom of Piedmont-Sardinia to wage war on Austria. In addition, in secret talks between the prime minister of Sardinia and Napoleon III, France was promised the Duchy of Savoy and the county of Nice if it provided military support to the Kingdom of Piedmont-Sardinia in a war of independence from Austria. During the French Revolutionary Wars, the Kingdom of Piedmont-Sardinia had allied with Austria. As a result, the Duchy of Savoy had been annexed by France in 1792 but returned to the Kingdom of Piedmont-Sardinia in 1815. The Second French Republic had made another attempt to annex the Duchy of Savoy in 1848 but had failed.

Piedmont-Sardinia was leading a second war of Italian independence from Austria. The Kingdom of Piedmont-Sardinia was ruled by the *House of Savoy* from its capital in Turin. The House of Savoy dates back to the eleventh century. As we have explained before, France had waged many wars against Austria to determine whether Europe would be led by France or Austria. The restored French Empire was now ready to renew that long fight and simultaneously feed each other's addiction to civilized warmongering. In May 1859 Napoleon III marched into Italy with half of the total French army to fight the Austrians, led by Emperor Franz Joseph. The Austrians were defeated at Magenta on June 4 and at Solferino on June 24. Napoleon III met with Franz Joseph on July 11, 1859, at Villafranca and agreed to peace terms. The Austrians agreed to cede Lombardy to France. The French in turn ceded it to the Kingdom of Piedmont-Sardinia in return for Savoy and Nice. As a result of French support, the Kingdom of Piedmont-Sardinia controlled most of Central and Northern Italy. France received Italian territory in Nice and Savoy with the 1860 Treaty of Turin. Today Nice is populated by the world's rich and famous as part of the French Riviera.

Napoleon III's dream of restoring French hegemony in Europe received an unexpected jolt when Prussia defeated Austria in the Austro-Prussian war of 1866. Given the long history of Franco-Austrian wars it was difficult for France to form an alliance with Austria against Prussia. France remained neutral during the Austro-Prussian War. Napoleon III may have even assumed that such a war would be good for France by weakening her historical rival. But Prussia's victory was unexpected and while Austria had been weakened there was no indication that Prussia had suffered. If anything, Prussia had gained in military and political stature as a great power. The Prussian victory not only ended the Austrian dominated German Confederation but also led to the creation of the new Prussian dominated North German Confederation.

Napoleon III made a belated attempt to salvage something from his miscalculation of the expected result of the Austro-Prussian War. He made an offer to buy Luxembourg from the king of Holland, William III, in 1867. The 1815 Congress of Vienna had united Luxembourg with Holland. William III was both king of Holland and duke of Luxembourg. But the Duchy of Luxembourg had also been a member of the German Confederation which Prussia had ended after defeating Austria. Luxembourg was also a member of the Prussian dominated German Custom's Union, the *Zollverein.* William III accepted Napoleon's price of 5 million guilders. Napoleon III was shocked when Prussia opposed the sale and created what has been called the *Luxembourg crisis.* Russia intervened to prevent a war between France and Prussia. At the London Conference of May 1867 the great powers of Europe settled the dispute by reaffirming both the neutrality of Luxembourg and its union with Holland. Prussia agreed to withdraw troops it had stationed in Luxemburg since the Congress of Vienna. The London Treaty was mostly a victory for Prussia and a loss to France. War between France and Prussia was just a matter of time.

As we explained earlier, Prussia had been ruled by the House of Hohenzollern since 1415. That family was given the opportunity to rule Spain in 1870 when *Leopold,* the cousin of the king of Prussia, became a candidate for the vacant crown of Spain. Spaniards revolted against their monarch in 1868 and overthrew Queen Isabella II. The Queen escaped to France. History has a habit of repeating itself. When the Bourbon Philip V inherited the throne of Spain, Austria made war on France, the War of the Spanish Succession, to prevent the unification of France and Spain. Queen Isabella II was a direct descendant of King Philip V. In 1870 it was France which feared the unification of Prussia with Spain. It provided the opportunity for the inevitable war between Prussia and France which would feed their addiction to civilized warmongering. France declared war on Prussia on July 19, 1870.

Prussia had the military support of the entire North German Confederation as well as some of the Southern German states. More importantly, Germany was now more technologically advanced than France. It is technologically superior weapons, more than anything else, which has defined the nation or empire, throughout history, as the more civilized and deserving of victory. All you have to do is win wars to become the most "godly" as well as the most civilized. And France was most soundly defeated by the military superiority of Prussia. Napoleon III was personally humiliated by being captured and imprisoned for six months before being exiled for the second time to England.

Shortly before the German conquest of Paris the new German Empire was proclaimed in the Palace of Versailles in Paris, on January 18, 1871. The king of Prussia, William I, became the first emperor of the new German Empire. Bismarck became its first chancellor. The North German Confederation was transformed into the new German Empire. It was a federal state with the emperor being both president and head of state. Prussia was the largest kingdom in the new empire with over 60 percent of the territory and population of the empire. The empire was made up of three other kingdoms, six grand duchies, five duchies, seven principalities, three cities and one imperial territory. The war ended with the *Treaty of Frankfurt,* May 10, 1871. France lost the provinces of Alsace and Lorraine to Germany.

Germany as the New Economic Powerhouse of the World

The rapid economic growth of the new German Empire in the second half of the nineteenth century was of a speed and surprise matched only by that of Japan in the 1970s/1980s and by China today. As China challenges the United States today so did Germany in the second half of the nineteenth century, challenge Britain. During the second half of the nineteenth century, Germany industrialized rapidly. As usual, the foundation for this rapid industrialization was developing the iron, steel, coal, railroad, canal and chemical industries, advancing new technologies, and moving large numbers of workers from the countryside to cities.

This rural/urban shift was complemented by rapid population growth from 40 million in 1870 to 70 million by 1914. Cities which experienced significant population growth included Berlin, Hamburg, Munich, Breslau, Dresden and Konigsberg. With this rapid economic growth, Germany was able to support a rapidly growing army and navy. Rapidly increasing income produced a growing middle class which supported the new German Empire rather than embracing the revolutionary ideas of Karl Marx and the 1848 revolutions.

This new German Empire was both a political/military union as well as an economic one. In fact, the economic union began before the creation of the new German Empire. The economic union began with the creation of the *Zollverein* in 1834. The economic union was an important tool used by Prussia to steal the leadership of Germany from Austria. Like all economic unions the Zollverein sought both to increase trade and economic integration among its members while increasing protectionist policies against nonmembers. The new German Empire took control of the Zollverein. Railroads played a crucial role in enabling relatively cheap movement of raw materials and manufactured goods.

Italian Unification

The creation of a unified Italian state occurred at the same time that the new German state was being created. Like the new German state, Italian unification can be traced back to the 1815 Congress of Vienna and the defeat of Napoleon. Like Austria, France and Germany, Italian states were carved out of the territory that had been the Western portion of the Roman Empire. As we explained, the two dominant powers fighting for hegemony and territory were Austria and France. Most Italians saw their fight for independence as being opposed mostly by the Austrian Empire. Italians participated in the 1848 revolutions sweeping across Europe. Partly as a result of the 1848 revolutions the king of Piedmont-Sardinia, *Charles Albert,* declared war on Austria on March 24, 1848. This has been called the First Italian War of Independence. The Kingdom of Piedmont-Sardinia was supported both by the Papal States and the Kingdom of the Two Sicilies.

A prior insurrection in 1820 by the Two Sicilies against Austria had failed. Likewise a prior insurrection in Piedmont in 1821 against Austria had also failed. After the July Revolution of 1830 in France, many Italian provinces revolted against Austria but were crushed by the Austrian military. Without the aid of a great power it is almost impossible for colonial revolts to be successful. The risk of asking for the military assistance of a great power is that a colony is likely to exchange one imperial power for another. The examples of the United States aiding a Spanish colony only to replace Spanish imperialism with American imperialism are numerous. It was this risk which led to many Italians not asking for French aid against Austria in the First Italian war of Independence. But it was the lack of French military aid which enabled Austria to win the war.

The Second Italian War of Independence coincided with the Franco-Austrian War of 1859. As we explained above the Austrians were defeated by the combined forces of France and Italy. The key result for Italy was that most of Northern and Central Italy became independent of Austria. After the failure of the First Italian War of Independence, King Charles Albert of Piedmont-Sardinia, handed over the crown to his son, *Victor Emmanuel.* When Austria was defeated in the Second Italian War of Independence, King Victor Emmanuel conquered Naples with the help of *Giuseppe Garibaldi.* Garibaldi, along with *Giuseppe Mazzini,* were the two most famous revolutionary heroes of Italy. They were the Italian equivalent of Che Guevara and Fidel Castro. Garibaldi and Mazzini were members of the revolutionary *Carbonari* movement for Italian independence. The secret Carbonari movement was inspired by the French Revolution. Born in the early nineteenth century in Southern Italy it moved through the states of Italy north to the Kingdom of Piedmont-Sardinia.

It was in Piedmont that Garibaldi and Mazzini participated in the rebellion of 1834. Like Castro and Che, Mazzini had begun his efforts to liberate Italy before meeting Garibaldi much like Castro had begun his efforts to liberate Cuba before meeting Che. Mazzini joined the Carbonari in 1827 and was arrested and imprisoned. After his release he moved to Marseilles in 1831 where he founded a new secret society called *Young Italy.* Branches of Young Italy were founded in several Italian cities and its membership grew. In 1833 Mazzini was sentenced to death for plotting an insurrection even before the 1834 rebellion. Prior to the 1834 rebellion Garibaldi served two years in the Piedmont-Sardinia navy before joining Young Italy. Much like Castro and Guevara's first attempt to liberate Cuba from American imperialism in December 1956, the 1834 revolt by Mazzini and Garibaldi was a failure. Garibaldi was also sentenced to death and had to escape from Italy. He moved to South America where he honed his revolutionary skills and in 1843 created the Italian Legion known as the *Redshirts.* Mazzini was forced to move to London after he was imprisoned in Paris. The two men united again in September 1860 during the liberation of Naples. This time it was Garibaldi who led the revolt.

Garibaldi returned to Italy and participated in the liberation of Rome in 1849. He was forced to flee Rome after Napoleon III reconquered it for Pope Pius IX. After another period of exile Garibaldi returned in 1854 and began guerilla warfare against Austria. In 1859 he conquered Lombardy from Austria. On May 6, 1860, Garibaldi led a revolutionary force into Sicily to liberate the Kingdom of the Two Sicilies. By the end of May he had conquered its capital, Palermo. After conquering Sicily, Garibaldi crossed into the Italian mainland and proceeded north into Naples. In Naples, Garibaldi was joined by the forces of King Emmanuel of Piedmont-Sardinia. The king entered Naples as the king of Italy with Garibaldi riding beside him. On March 17, 1861, the First Italian Parliament proclaimed Victor Emmanuel II as king of Italy. On March 27 Rome was declared the capital of Italy but since Rome had not yet been conquered the capital was initially in Turin. The capital was moved to Florence in 1865 and to Rome in 1871. The United States officially recognized the Kingdom of Italy on April 11, 1861.

Third Italian War of Independence: 1866

With Napoleon III making peace with Austria on July 11, 1859, the Italian Independence movement lost its great power support and halted. In June 1862 Garibaldi organized a revolt against Rome with two thousand volunteers. He was joined by Mazzini. French troops were still stationed in Rome to protect the pope. But King Emmanuel II opposed the revolt this time and sent troops to attack the volunteers. Garibaldi was wounded but returned to the battlefield in 1866. In September 1864 King Emmanuel negotiated a treaty with Napoleon III to remove French troops from Rome within two years.

The Austro-Prussian War of 1866 provided another opportunity for great power support for Italian Independence. Italy formed an alliance with Prussia on April 8, 1866, and declared war on Austria on June 20, 1866, a few days after Prussia had declared war on Austria. King Emmanuel II invaded Venetia while Garibaldi invaded Tyrol. Venetia was added to Italy in October 1866. But Rome had still not been captured and the Italian capital remained in Florence. Once again Italy lost its great power support when Prussia agreed to peace with Austria in October 1866. Garibaldi continued the liberation efforts by leading another invasion of Rome in October 1867. But Napoleon III sent French troops back to Rome and Garibaldi was defeated. French troops remained in Rome until August 1870.

With the outbreak of the Franco-Prussian War in July 1870 leading to the recall of French troops from Rome, Italy seized the opportunity to capture Rome from Pope Pius IX. The Italian army invaded in September 1870. Rome was added to Italy in October 1870. The unification of Italy was complete and the capital was moved to Rome in July 1871.

Second French Colonial Empire

Napoleon III reignited French colonial expansion across the globe, focusing this time more on Asia and Africa than the New World. Despite the humiliating defeat of France by Britain in the Seven Years' War and the subsequent defeat of Napoleon Bonaparte in 1815 the French were determined to continue to challenge Britain for Western imperial hegemony. In North America the French never recovered from their defeat by the British in the Seven Years' War. Napoleon's attempt to reconquer St. Domingue had failed and he had been forced to sell the vast Louisiana Territory to the United States to fund his war.

During the American Civil War, Napoleon III attempted to seize the opportunity to colonize Mexico with the help of *Maximilian I.* Ferdinand Maximilian Joseph was a member of the powerful Austrian

Habsburg family. He was the grandson of the last holy Roman emperor, Francis II. In 1859 Maximilian I was offered the Crown of Mexico by the aristocrats of Mexico who wanted the return to monarchy in Mexico. In 1861 the French formed an alliance with Britain and Spain to invade Mexico. The excuse was Mexico's failure to continue paying interest on loans from the Western imperial powers which had stolen land and resources from Mexico. The combined fleets of France, Britain and Spain arrived in Veracruz, Mexico in December 1861. The British and Spanish subsequently withdrew their support of Napoleon III in April 1862. But the French were able to conquer Mexico singlehandedly by June 7, 1863. Mexican president *Benito Juarez* was forced to flee Mexico City on May 31, 1863. After the French conquest, Maximilian I agreed to accept the offer of the Mexican Crown which he had been made earlier in 1859. He was proclaimed emperor of Mexico on April 10, 1864, and arrived in Mexico in May 1864. He served as the puppet of Napoleon III and was not recognized either by the United States or by the deposed Mexican president and his supporters.

Once the American Civil War ended the United States could turn its attention to French intervention in Mexico. The United States wanted to colonize Mexico long before Napoleon III. It had no intention of allowing France to keep Mexico as its colony. The United States began to supply weapons to the Mexican opposition and formally asked France to withdraw their forces on February 12, 1866. The United States moved its army to the Mexican border and imposed a naval blockade to prevent the French from landing any reinforcements. Napoleon III was forced to withdraw his military support for his puppet Maximilian I. Maximilian I attempted to escape but was caught and sentenced to death. He was executed on June 19, 1867, by President Juarez with the blessing of the United States. The French had once again failed to colonize North America.

French Colonization of Algeria

The Second French colonial empire began even before Napoleon III with the French invasion of Algiers in 1830. One of the key elements of Western democracies is the popularity of invasions and conquests or colonization. Western voters can always be counted on to support any and all military conquests. Whenever a Western leader is challenged at home he can always create a popular diversion by starting a new war or military invasion of some Third World country. So it was that King Charles X of France needed a boost to his waning popularity in 1830 and found an easy target in *Algiers.* Algiers had been weakened by two U.S. invasions in 1801 and 1815. See my *American Invasions,* chapter 2.

The French king began by refusing to pay Algiers for wheat Algiers had sold to France. Fearing reprisals by the ruler or *dey* of Algiers, *Hussein Dey,* the French fortified their warehouses in Algiers. That was an implicit signal that France would rather steal with military force rather than trade. France imposed a naval blockade of the port of Algiers. When Algiers fired on one of the French ships, France invaded on June 14, 1830. France landed a force of thirty-four thousand and conquered Algiers with its technologically superior weapons, in three weeks. Hussein Dey was forced into exile and the French plundered, desecrated mosques, stole property and assets, and massacred and killed at random. The conquest of Algiers failed to satisfy French citizens and King Charles X was deposed and replaced by his cousin, *Louis-Philippe.* French colonization expanded rapidly along the North African coast. Initially referred to as French possessions in North Africa it was renamed *Algeria* in 1839. By 1848 almost all of Northern Algeria had been colonized. France had begun the new scramble for Africa by the West.

French colonization of Algeria quickly expanded as French immigrants were encouraged by grants of stolen agricultural land and French businesses saw opportunities for commerce based on stolen property. It was natural that the original population would oppose the theft of their land and resources. It was also natural that the civilized French would use the most brutal and barbaric methods to suppress rebellions. As one French Lieutenant-Colonel put it, "annihilate all who will not crawl beneath our feet like dogs." Algeria had become a French military colony where over two million **Muslim** inhabitants were brutalized, robbed and *terrorized* by the technologically superior weapons of the civilized West. Yes, it was the West which invented **terrorism** to keep those it colonized by military force from rebelling. Of course, since it was the West that was doing the terrorizing it was civilized terrorism. A suicide bomber is a "cowardly" terrorist only because his weapon is primitive. President Obama's drone strikes by the United States, for example, are civilized terrorism. Americans dropping nuclear bombs on Hiroshima and Nagasaki are all examples of civilized terrorism committed by the West. They are done to save lives. That people would believe such utter nonsense is a testimony to our inhumanity.

The Second French Republic copied one of the most remarkable pieces of propaganda invented by the American Republic. As I explained in my previous books, the United States was able to claim that its colonization and theft of First Nations land was not an act of imperialism because it made the stolen land an integral part of the United States. Never mind the fact that the original owners were killed or imprisoned in reservations and European immigrants were given the stolen land. In 1848 the French declared that Algeria was no longer a French colony but an integral part of France. Like North America, Europeans moved to Algeria to take ownership of the stolen land. Just as the First Nations in North America must have been very relieved to learn that the United States and Canada had not colonized them but simply incorporated the stolen land into their expanded state the Muslims of North Africa must have been very relieved by the fact that their stolen land was now an integral part of France. Unfortunately for the French they proved to be too militarily weak to enforce this propaganda. Algerians, like the First Nations of North America, never surrendered to European imperialism. After a bloody war between 1954 and 1962, the original inhabitants of Algeria won their independence from the French Empire on July 3, 1962, retaking the stolen land.

First Nations in Canada and the United States have not had the military power to take back their independence or stolen land from the military powerful imperial powers of Canada and the United States. Integrating stolen land into an expanded state rather than calling it a colony makes only one difference to those whose land you stole. That difference is that the original owners have a far less chance of ever getting their land back. It was a brilliant propaganda move by those who stole the lands which became countries like Australia, Canada, and the United States. Australia, Canada, and the United States became very powerful and influential civilized Western states by stealing the lands of the original inhabitants. No civilized Western state ever expects Canada, Australia, or the United States to ever grant independence to those they colonized, much less condemn their theft and colonization of the First Nations lands. Instead, these three thieves are allowed to preach to the rest of the world about human rights abuses while keeping their ill-gotten gains.

French Colonization of Indochina

French Indochina included Vietnam, Cambodia and Laos. At the time there were three French colonies in Vietnam. *Cochinchina,* the most prominent French colony in French Indochina, was in South Vietnam. *Annam* was in Central Vietnam and *Tonkin* was in North Vietnam. The capital city was *Saigon* until 1902. Together with Cambodia and Laos there were five French colonies in French Indochina.

One of the most important tools of Western imperialism is the Catholic church. In the case of the New World the Catholic church accompanied Columbus. In Asia often the Catholic church went before the military invaders to prepare the victims for the coming imperial power. So it was in what became French Indochina. It began early in the seventeenth century with the Jesuit missionary, *Alexandre de Rhodes.* A Jesuit mission had been started in Hanoi, North Vietnam, in 1615 and Rhodes arrived a few years after. He was expelled by the North Vietnamese ruler in 1630 but the damage had already been done. The Western imperial powers are very determined and persistent. The North Vietnamese rulers were under continuing threats from Christian missionaries. After Rhodes had been evicted by the Vietnamese he moved to the Portuguese colony of Macau but made his way back to Vietnam, this time to *Hue,* Central Vietnam, a decade later. After another six years trying to convert the Vietnamese he fared no better with the Central Vietnamese ruler and was sent packing again. Missionaries prepare people who are about to be colonized by the powerful military force of the West to accept God rather than resist the awesome power of technologically advanced weapons. They are given the stark choice of having their religious beliefs confiscated by Christianity or being enslaved and tortured by ruthless military invaders who practice the most sophisticated forms of brutality against nonwhites they deem to be so inferior to them that they are less than human. The invaders have the audacity to call these brutal forms of torture, theft, rape and killing, civilized.

The Catholic priests rightly inform the victims that whether they convert to Christianity or not their land and resources will be stolen since the invaders have far more powerful weapons. Better to surrender those lands and resources to the church and the invaders peacefully and turn to God for salvation. In return the church will educate your children in the language of the coming invaders and teach them civilized customs. That some of these children will be sexually and physically abused by the priests, as they were in Canada and elsewhere, is carefully omitted. Recently, the resources of these lands have been called the "Curse of wealth" because the richer the resources you have the more determined will be the Christian church and the imperial power to steal them. It is for this reason that priests and explorers exaggerate the wealth of lands they want their governments to colonize. Rhodes was one of those determined priests who exaggerated the wealth of Vietnam. In Europe he campaigned for greater funding of Catholic missions to Vietnam and inspired the founding of the *Society of Foreign Missions of Paris.*

Of course the initial involvement of the Catholic church was through the two original Western imperial powers, Portugal and Spain. But in 1658 a missionary institution not controlled by Portugal and Spain was created in France. This was the Society of Foreign Missions of Paris inspired by Rhodes. It sent over four thousand priests to the New World and Asia. Missionaries, like settlers, count on their governments to send troops to defend their missionary work and theft of land and resources when the local inhabitants oppose their religious conversions and thefts. Both the missionaries/settlers, and the imperial power, benefit from this mutual understanding. The missionaries/settlers get to keep their stolen property and missionary work and the imperial power get an excuse to invade and colonize. This was how France began its colonization of Indochina. The French government sent troops to protect the Catholic missions forced on the people of Indochina by Rhodes and his Paris Society. The most powerful Western propaganda was, and still is, the civilizing mission of the West to teach nonwhites the virtues of white people while stealing their souls and their wealth. Christianity has absolutely no problem with serving both God and Mammon with a single act of converting the heathens. In fact, Protestant Christianity eventually dominated over Catholic Christianity precisely because Protestants were furious that Catholics did not sufficiently pursue more vigorously the "Mammon" portion of colonization.

The Paris Society convinced the pope to ordain three bishops, *Francois Pallu, Pierre Lambert de la Motte* and *Ignace Cotolendi,* recruited by Rhodes, to serve in Vietnam, China and Laos. Their goal was to both convert the heathens and train locals to become Catholic priests. This "pyramid" method was far more effective in converting the maximum number of souls compared to recruiting only European priests. It was similar to the imperial powers recruiting local soldiers to fight under them. Travel to Vietnam was made very difficult by Portugal, Spain, Holland and Britain, who knew that the French priests would pave the way for French colonization. As a result two of the three bishops ended up in Thailand which became the initial base of operations for the Paris Society. Since Thailand bordered Vietnam, Laos and Cambodia it was ideally located for the subsequent French colonization of Indochina. The determination of the French priests is clearly indicated by their decision to undertake the dangerous and arduous two-year journey overland because sea travel was blocked by Portugal, Spain, Holland and England. The overland route went through Persia and India. One priest, Cotolendi, died shortly after reaching India. Lambert left France in November 1660 and reached Thailand in 1662. Pallu left in January 1662 and reached Thailand in 1664. Together they established a seminary in the capital city, Ayutthaya. Pallu attempted to sail to Vietnam but was captured and imprisoned by Spain. Lambert was able to reach Vietnam in 1670. He built a church in Tonkin.

Vietnamese Disunity

A recurring theme of how the West conquered the world was the failure of the locals to unite against the foreigner. In North America the First Nations allied with Western invaders rather than among themselves. In India it was the same. Today Muslims continue to fight each other and support the West in its colonization and subjugation. So too was

Vietnam before French colonization. In 1765 the Paris Society sent another notable priest, *Pigneau de Behaine,* to Vietnam. His specialty was not as a priest but as a leader of the divide-and-rule policy perfected by the British. Western imperial powers have all used local puppets to help them colonize and rule. This is what Pigneau did for France in Vietnam. Pigneau arrived in South Vietnam in 1767 after short stays in India and Macau. Prior to his arrival the Paris Society had established a school to teach locals to become Christian priests in the town of *Ha Tien,* on the coast of South Vietnam. Located close to the border with Cambodia it was ideal for the subsequent colonization of Indochina by France. The School had about forty students from Vietnam, Thailand and China. By this time the Paris Society had been operating in Asia for a century. Pigneau became the head priest at the school in Ha Tien but the school was burnt down by pirates two years after he arrived. Pigneau fled to the French colony of Pondicherry in India, determined to return to Vietnam. In Pondicherry he learned Vietnamese and published a Vietnamese-Latin dictionary to help other priests he hoped to recruit to go to Vietnam. He traveled to Macau to recruit students and returned to Ha Tien in 1775.

Pigneau's opportunity to play colonial ruler in Vietnam presented itself in 1777 after the ruling *Nguyen Dynasty* had been attacked by both the ruler of North Vietnam and the *Tay Son* rebellion. This is but one example of the disunity which had plagued Vietnam for centuries. The Nguyen Dynasty had ruled Southern Vietnam since 1558 beginning with Nguyen Hoang. Its capital city was *Hue.* The Dynasty's rule over Southern Vietnam was weakened by attacks from Thailand beginning in 1769. This provided the opportunity for a peasant rebellion led by Nguyen Hue and his two brothers, Nhac and Lu, the so-called Tay Son brothers. In addition, the ruler of North Vietnam, *Trinh Sam,* took the opportunity to attack and conquer South Vietnam. The Trinh Dynasty had united with the Nguyen Dynasty to overthrow the Mac Dang Dung Dynasty and rule both North and South Vietnam. But the two families were often at war between1627 and 1673 until a peace treaty was made in 1673. This peace between the rulers of North and South Vietnam was broken a century later during the Tay Son rebellion. The Trinh Dynasty seized an opportunity to rule both North and South Vietnam. The Trinh army invaded in 1774 and captured Hue. The Nguyen ruler, Nguyen

Phuc Thuan, and his family were forced to flee to Saigon. In the end they would all lose to the second French Colonial Empire because of their failure to rule together peacefully.

After defeating the Nguyen family the Trinh army had to face the Tay Son rebels. It made an uneasy truce with the rebels. Saigon was captured and most of the Nguyen family were killed. A fifteen-year-old nephew of Nguyen Phuc Thuan, Nguyen Anh, and his brother escaped. This is where the French priest, Pigneau, saw his opportunity. Nguyen Anh made his way to Pigneau's school in the city of Ha Tien on the southern coast of Vietnam. The priest hid Anh in his church and together they escaped to the island of Pulo Panjang. Vietnamese disunity only increased with the Tay Son rebels fighting both the Trinh family, that had defeated the Nguyen family, and Nguyen Anh. Nguyen Anh was able to return to Saigon with a new army recruited for him by Do Thanh *Nhon* while the Tay Son rebels were advancing north to fight the Trinh Dynasty. Pigneau was able to provide French and Portuguese military support to Anh. But disunity between Anh and Nhon led to Anh murdering Nhon and losing his supporters. As a result Anh was defeated by the Tay Son rebels and forced to flee to Thailand.

Never to be deterred by military defeats Pigneau returned to France to speak directly with the French government. He took Anh's son, Nguyen Phuc Canh, and Anh's royal seal with him to convince the French government of his personal influence over Anh. The young son, *Canh,* bonded quite well with the young son of King Louis XVI, Louis-Joseph. This led to a treaty of alliance between France and South Vietnam, French *Cochinchina,* on November 17, 1787. This 1787 Treaty of Versailles was the beginning of the end of Vietnamese independence until the successful defeat of the American Empire by Vietnam. It was the centuries of wars among Vietnamese which led Anh to invite the foreign West to Vietnam to satisfy his own selfish desire to rule all of Vietnam. These selfish local rulers are often willing to serve as puppets of the West rather than share power with their own people. French help did enable Anh to unify and rule all of Vietnam. He crowned himself Emperor *Gia Long,* named after Saigon and Hanoi, in 1802. His capital city was Hue. He was succeeded in 1820 by his son, Nguyen Phuc Dam, who ruled as Emperor *Minh Mang.* But it would simply be a matter of time before the West took it all from him and his family. Western colonization was made easier by the continuation of Vietnamese disunity after Gia Long's unification. One source of this disunity came from *Le Van Duyet,* the military commander who had defeated the Tay Son rebels in North Vietnam for Gia Long. Long had rewarded him by making him Regent of South Vietnam. But like every other Vietnamese ruler he wanted more. He stirred up rebellions against Minh Mang.

Emperor Minh Mang did his best to keep out the West and the pesky Catholic priests. He made it illegal for Christian missionaries to peddle their religion in Vietnam. But the priests and their governments were both determined to use their superior weaponry to colonize and steal Vietnam. In addition to the inherent disunity of Vietnamese, the attempt at isolationism made countries like Vietnam easy targets for the West because isolationism meant the inability to modernize their military defense. It was very much a catch-22 situation. Ban foreigners from your ports and you become militarily weaker because you have no access to modern western weaponry. Encourage foreign intervention by opening your ports and they colonize you and steal everything. Emperor Minh Mang did succeed in preventing colonization by France during his reign but only because French colonization of Vietnam was delayed by the French Revolution and Napoleon Bonaparte's inability to send forces to Vietnam because of his egotistical blunder in invading Russia. Bonaparte had intended to colonize both Egypt and Vietnam to oust the British from India. He failed to do so because of his colossal defeat in Russia. Emperor Minh Mang died in 1841 and was succeeded by his eldest son, Emperor *Thieu Tri.*

During the six-year reign of Thieu Tri both France and Britain were determined to knock down the barriers put up by Vietnam to prevent Western colonization. The Catholic priests were becoming more vocal in their calls to France to invade and conquer Vietnam before the British did. They had already succeeded in converting about three hundred thousand Vietnamese who would support French theft by military force. The British had used military force to colonize Hong Kong and get China to agree to the Unequal Treaty of Nanjing in 1842. Their goal had been to sell opium and poison the people of China. This had made both the French and Americans envious. Western empires peddle all kinds of immoral behavior under the pretext of civilizing the natives. As First Nations in North America learned, civilizing meant getting you to turn your back so it's easier for the West to steal both your land and your soul. The French and the Americans simultaneously competed and cooperated with the British to steal China. In 1844, for example, both the French and the Americans forced the military weak Qing Dynasty to grant privileges to them similar to those forced on them by the British.

Meanwhile in Vietnam, Emperor Tri was under continuous attacks by French priests and ships of the French navy. In 1843 the French government sent a fleet to Vietnam which threatened invasion unless five priests detained by the emperor, for illegally entering Vietnam to convert Vietnamese, were released. The emperor released the priests. Another Catholic priest, *Dominique Lefebvre,* was imprisoned. This time an American ship attempted but failed to get Lefebvre out of Vietnam. This provided another excuse for a French invasion. The West is capable of manufacturing excuses at a dime a dozen. The reality was that neither Lefebvre, nor the Paris Society that had sent him and other priests, wanted to get out of Vietnam. They wanted French colonization of Vietnam. In 1845 the French threatened another invasion unless Lefebvre was released. Once again the Vietnamese emperor called their bluff and released Lefebvre. Lefebvre had to escape again into Vietnam to provide France with the excuse it needed to invade and conquer Vietnam. So once Lefebvre had done that, the French sent an even stronger invasion fleet in 1847 under the pretext of rescuing missionaries.

This time the emperor's hand was forced. How many times can he back down without his subjects thinking he is a coward who cannot enforce his own laws or be seen to be catering to the tiny minority of converted Christians? But the Vietnamese navy was no match for the technologically advanced French fleet. The French fleet destroyed the entire Vietnamese fleet and all of the coastal forts built by the Vietnamese before sailing away. This "bombardment of Tourane" took place on April 15, 1847. Tourane is now called *Da Nang.* The French attack was intended both to test its naval superiority and soften up Vietnamese resistance against a full military invasion much like the Americans tested the power of their atomic bombs against the defenseless people of

Hiroshima and Nagasaki and the Americans and British softened up Iraq with a decade of vicious nonstop bombing before their invasion.

French Invasion and Colonization of Vietnam and Cambodia: 1857–1886

Emperor Tri died in November 1847 having failed in his efforts to prevent the theft of his country and the enforced Christianization of his people. His son became the new emperor, *Tu Duc.* Under his rule the long history of Vietnamese disunity continued. This time the rebellion was led by the emperor's older brother, Hong Bao. In addition, there were many smaller rebellions, some inspired by Vietnamese who had been converted to Christianity. It was normal for the West and the Christians to exploit such divisions to enhance their thefts. In 1857 the emperor executed two Spanish priests. This gave France the opportunity to mount a joint invasion of Vietnam with Spain. Napoleon III was competing with Britain for China and had forces in China. While this made it easier for France to move forces from China to Vietnam it also meant less possibility of China aiding Vietnam. The Crimean War had ended the year before so a new war would feed Napoleon III's addiction to warmongering. In November 1857 Napoleon III ordered the invasion of Vietnam. The joint invasion with Spain landed in Da Nang in September 1858. It established a base of operations in Da Nang. Next the joint Franco/Spanish invasion established a second base in Saigon in 1859. By that time Napoleon III had begun the Franco-Austrian War. His forces were needed closer to home. French forces were also tied up in its attempt to colonize China with Britain and the Americans. The French tried to trick the Vietnamese into agreeing to a peace treaty without any colonized territory, but with guarantees for allowing the conversion of their people to Christianity. The Vietnamese were well aware that these same Christian Vietnamese would be used by the French to help them colonize Vietnam at some future date. In fact the emperor was already being threatened by Vietnamese Catholics in North Vietnam led by *Le Bao Phung.*

With the French forces engaged elsewhere, the French were unable to hold both Da Nang and Saigon against the Vietnamese counter attacks.

France abandoned Da Nang to hold Saigon. But the Anglo-French War against China ended on October 18, 1860. By that time the Franco-Austrian War had already ended as well. France now had more forces to send to Vietnam. In 1861 the French sent its most formidable fleet yet to invade Vietnam. Against such overwhelming Western force the Vietnamese could only use guerilla tactics. But they continued to resist the French and Spanish invaders. It would certainly not be the last time that Vietnam would fight a guerilla war against the West. Like the Americans later, the French used the most brutal and barbarian methods to punish both the guerillas and innocent peasants. The West invents and uses the most civilized means of torture as much as they invent and use the most civilized weapons of mass destruction. The Vietnamese were forced to agree to punitive peace terms on June 5, 1862. The French had gained their first colony in what became French Indochina. This was *Cochinchina* or South Vietnam, with its capital of Saigon. It was the beginning of the end for all of Vietnam along with Cambodia and Laos. Tu Duc was the last emperor of an independent Vietnam.

Sadly, after the people of this region had fought successfully against the French for their freedom they would be invaded and colonized again by the most brutal and warmongering of the Western civilized empires, the **American Empire.** Like North America where the First Nations suffered first from European colonization only to be totally colonized by the United States and Canada the people of Indochina would have to fight the Americans, aided by their Canadian cousins. Unlike the American invasion of Afghanistan when the United States expected its allies, including Canada, to join the "military coalition" explicitly, the Americans did not force a military coalition on its allies when it invaded Vietnam. At that time it felt strong enough to conquer Vietnam on its own given that Vietnam had just fought a long war against France. But it did insist on Canada providing all and any military supplies it demanded. Canada was happy to oblige.

As expected, France would not be satisfied with only the Southern part of Vietnam. Empires keep invading until they are stopped by military defeats. They never run out of excuses to conquer more territory and subjugate more people while stealing, raping and pillaging. Any development they bring is a by-product of their need to create transportation, communication, governance and infrastructure to achieve their single minded pursuit of colonization and theft.

French expansion of its conquest from South Vietnam began with its conquest of Cambodia in 1863. As in Vietnam there was disunity in neighboring Cambodia. By the time of French colonization of Cochinchina in 1862, Cambodia's independence was threatened by both Thailand and France. France saw the colonization of Cambodia as providing a military buffer between its colony of Vietnam and the independent country of Siam, today's Thailand. In 1863 King Norodom of Cambodia decided to become a puppet ruler of France rather than continue as a vassal state of Thailand. France came to an arrangement to share Cambodia with Thailand. In 1867 France allowed Thailand to take the Cambodian province of Battambang as well as keep its control of Angkor in return for its recognition of French colonization of the rest of Cambodia. The Cambodians revolted against French rule but were defeated by the superior technology of the French military. The French kept King Norodom as a puppet head of state and in 1885 the king's brother led an insurrection against French rule. He too was defeated. It was not until the Second World War that Cambodians were able to resist French subjugation more effectively thanks to the military and moral support of Japan with the slogan "Asia for Asiatics." Since the West had no intention of granting independence to its Asian colonies, the defeat of Japan turned back the clock for Cambodia and all of French Indochina. France had to defend all of Indochina against a determined insurgency which forced France to grant independence to Cambodia on November 9, 1953. This was essentially a military defeat for France despite assistance from the American Empire. Unfortunately, Cambodia would suffer from the American War in Vietnam.

Next the French colonized North Vietnam or *Tonkin* as well as Central Vietnam or *Annam,* beginning with its invasion in 1873 and capture of the city of Hanoi. The French governor of South Vietnam sent an expedition led by Francis Garnier to Tonkin in November 1873. The Vietnamese invited the Chinese Black Flag Army to help them defeat the French imperialists. Garnier's forces were defeated and Hanoi recaptured. France was forced to abandon temporarily its colonization of North Vietnam. The French attempted another invasion of North

Vietnam almost a decade later in 1882. This second invasion was led by Henri Riviere. Once again Vietnam invited the Chinese Black Flag Army, to aid their defense from the foreign invaders. Like Garnier before, Riviere was defeated and killed by the Vietnamese and their Chinese allies. Quite apart from the interest of the Chinese Black Flag Army all of Vietnam was regarded by China as one of its "Protectorates." This explains why China supported and armed the Chinese Black Flag Army. It also explains why China sent its own forces into Tonkin in 1882 to aid both the Vietnamese and the Black Flags. The French had already stolen South Vietnam because China itself was being invaded by the British, Americans and French, and as a result was unable to provide sufficient military assistance to Vietnam. In addition the Vietnamese continued to fight among themselves. As a result China attempted to make a deal with France to share North Vietnam similar to the deal between France and Thailand to share Cambodia.

In the end France was unwilling to share North Vietnam with China and decided to take advantage of the continuing Vietnamese disunity and the weak military position of China to engage China in a war for North Vietnam. This was the Sino-French war of 1884–1885, also referred to as the *Tonkin War.* Initially, the Black Flags bore the brunt of the massive French invasion of Tonkin beginning in December 1883. French victories led to China agreeing to the *Tientsin Accord* of May 11, 1884. This Accord effectively recognized all of Vietnam as a French colony. The Accord was extremely unpopular both in China and Vietnam. As a result, the military conflict between France and China continued and spread from North Vietnam to Southeast China and Taiwan. But China was threatened by most of Europe as well as Russia and Japan. Even the Germans lent their support to France by delaying its promised delivery of two modern battleships it had built for China. The French supported the Japanese attempt to colonize Korea in return for Japanese support for French colonization of Vietnam. French military victories in Tonkin and Taiwan (Formosa) led to China signing the *Treaty of Tientsin* on June 9, 1885. This treaty confirmed the French as the new imperial power in Tonkin and Annam.

While China had surrendered, the Vietnamese continued to oppose French imperialism both in Tonkin and Annam. French forces were attacked in Hue on July 2, 1885. In Tonkin the insurgency was akin to what the Americans experienced in Iraq after the fall of Saddam Hussein. What has been called the *Tonkin Campaign* of 1883–1886 did not end until April of 1886. France consolidated its conquest of all of Vietnam by defeating both the Vietnamese and China. Vietnam and Cambodia was combined to form French Indochina in October 1887. Like the First Nations of North America who lost far more independence under the United States and Canada than under British and French colonizations the Vietnamese lost far more independence under French colonization than under China's "Protection."

Adding Laos to French Indochina after the Franco-Siamese War

It was inevitable that France would go to war with Siam (Thailand) to increase its colonies. Siam was the first country in Southeast Asia where French Catholic priests had set up shop to begin French theft of souls and wealth. The initial base of operations for the Paris Foreign Mission was the capital city of Siam, *Ayutthaya.* The first priest sent by the Paris Mission, Pierre la Motte, arrived in Ayutthaya on August 22, 1662. Together with Francois Pallu, who arrived two years later, they established the Seminary of Saint Joseph. Siam's mistake was simply one of religious tolerance. Religious tolerance is an admirable quality of any society but a **deadly** one if Western colonization is a threat. And Western colonization was a serious threat to all of Asia after da Gama's voyage of 1498. Part of the problem for Siam was that by the time the French showed an interest in Siam it was under threat of colonization by the Portuguese, British and Dutch. The Portuguese had already established a settlement in Ayutthaya. When la Motte arrived in 1662 there were already ten Portuguese priests and one Spanish priest stealing souls and wealth while paving the way for their country to colonize Siam. Caught between a rock and a hard place Siam welcomed the French partly because of its religious tolerance but partly as an offset to the Portuguese, British and Dutch threats. Siam's King Narai granted land for the seminary and his permission to the French priests to train locals as Christian priests. That the priests were primarily interested in colonization rather than saving souls explains why the Portuguese converts fought with French converts.

Since the French Empire had already made war on Vietnam and China to colonize the region, Thailand was simply next in line. At the time Laos was seen by the French as a relatively easy addition to its colonial conquests in Vietnam and Cambodia. With the conquest of Laos on the border with Siam, Siam would be ripe for French colonization. As I have said many times no empire stops its military expansion unless it is defeated by military force. France began its colonization of Laos when it invaded Northern Laos in 1888. In 1893 France demanded that Siam transfer all lands in Laos east of the Mekong River to France. When Siam refused, France effectively declared war on Siam in March 1893, when it began sending its gun boats up the famous *Chao Phraya River* to Bangkok. The goal was to colonize *Laos.* By July of 1893 the French war ships had reached Bangkok and their guns threatened the Grand Palace. This was followed by a blockade of the coast of Siam. Siam had foolishly assumed that the British would aid their defense against French aggression. But the British only wanted to colonize Siam's territory as well. Siam agreed to French colonization of Laos with the Franco-Siamese treaty of October 3, 1893. France had stolen territory from Siam in both Cambodia and Laos and continued to steal more of Siam's territory even after the 1893 treaty. Siam also gave up territory in Burma to the British just to prevent a British military alliance with France against it. Britain and France signed an accord in 1896 agreeing to the division of territory in their joint colonization of Thailand.

French conquest of Laos completed most of its territorial expansion of what came to be called French Indochina until 1954. The Kingdom of Laos became its fifth colony. Saigon in South Vietnam continued as the capital for the whole of French Indochina until 1902. In that year the capital was moved to Hanoi in North Vietnam. World War I led to intensified rebellions against French subjugation. During the reign of the Vietnamese emperor *Duy Tan,* 1907–1916, the emperor attempted to cease being a puppet of France by encouraging his subjects to rebel against French subjugation. Unfortunately, he was captured, deposed and exiled by France to join his father on Reunion Island in the Indian Ocean. France had previously deposed and exiled his father for inciting rebellion against French rule. But France continued to appoint puppet emperors from the Nguyen family. This family had ruled Vietnam since 1802 and France saw the value of keeping the peasants ignorant as to the brutal control of their country by a foreign invader and thief. Duy Tan was replaced by the more subservient French puppet, Emperor *Khai Dinh, 1916–1925.* Khai Dinh was the twelfth emperor from the Nguyen Dynasty. He was naturally very unpopular with the Vietnamese people. He was succeeded by his son, Emperor *Bao Dai* who was the last emperor of Vietnam and of the Nguyen Dynasty.

The Second World War provided the opportunity for the Vietnamese people to launch a full scale rebellion against almost two centuries of French atrocities and cultural and religious genocide in Vietnam, Cambodia and Laos. The First Indochina war began in 1941 with the formation of the *Viet Minh,* a national independence coalition, on May 19, 1941. When Japan defeated the French in Vietnam, Bao Dai continued to be the emperor until Japan surrendered in August 1945. When Bao Dai abdicated on August 25, 1945, he transferred power to the Viet Minh. World War II also provided the opportunity for the people of Siam (Thailand) to reclaim stolen territory from France. Anti-French demonstrations became common in Bangkok. The Thai air force conducted bombing raids into the French colonies and Thailand invaded both Cambodia and Laos. With the help of Japan, Thailand won the Franco-Thai War of 1940–1941 and regained some of its territory stolen by France in Cambodia and Laos. Unfortunately, Thailand had to return some of it to France after Japan was defeated.

As expected, France refused to grant independence to Vietnam until it was defeated on the battlefield. The French overthrew the *Democratic Republic of Vietnam* in October 1946. Vietnam was once again helped by China to drive the French imperialists out. As expected the phony "freedom loving" American Empire assisted rather than resisted the dastardly French recolonization of Vietnam. By providing military assistance to France it enabled the wholesale slaughter of the Vietnamese people who were rightfully rebelling against two centuries of French subjugation, theft of its lands and resources, and wholesale destruction of its religious, political and cultural freedom. French defeats by the Vietnamese people forced the French to agree to the Geneva Accords in 1954. North Vietnam secured its independence but the West, now led by the new imperial behemoth of the American Empire, continued its colonization of South Vietnam. The American Empire saw an opportunity for a relatively easy military invasion to colonize all of Vietnam since the French had pummeled the Vietnamese resistance, with American military aid, for almost a decade. At the time it was as easy for the Americans to pretend that they were invading Vietnam **not** to colonize it, but to prevent the spread of communism, as it is today for the American Empire to invade and colonize Muslim lands by pretending to fight terrorism. When Vietnam defeated and humiliated the powerful American Empire it signaled to others that American military power was not invincible.

After licking its wounds and rebuilding its shattered economy the American Empire invaded Afghanistan in 2001 and Iraq in 2003. It was defeated and humiliated again. But no lessons were learned. Warmongering is a nasty but very addictive habit. Since the Vietnam invasion, the cost to the American economy and the American people of American warmongering has far exceeded the benefits of what can be stolen from the countries invaded. Yet there is no sufficient public outcry to end this madness. There is a limit to how much debt can be used to postpone the pain of paying for these senseless wars. High taxes are needed to repay the war debt with interest and Americans hate taxes as much as they love wars. One day soon the Americans will feel the pain of years of costly warmongering.

Civilized Atrocities Committed by the West in the Congo and in Africa

What has been called the "Scramble for Africa" began long before the atrocities committed in the Belgian Congo. It began with the Portuguese under the leadership of Prince Henry the Navigator. What was unique about Africa was not the Western thefts of land and resources or the genocide the West committed on those colonized? That was done everywhere the West colonized. The unique atrocity committed by the West in Africa was the capture, enslavement and transportation of Africans to Western colonies in the New World. This so-called slave trade began with the Portuguese led by Prince Henry the Navigator. The term "trade" is once again misused. Trade is voluntary exchange. There was absolutely nothing voluntary about the "slave trade."

One of the important propaganda tools of the West is to point the finger at atrocities committed by others in order to hide their own heinous crimes against humanity. Canada, for example, endlessly points to atrocities committed in China to hide their theft of First Nations lands and their incarceration of First Nations and Japanese, among their many heinous crimes. The United States and the West point to atrocities committed by Hitler or Saddam Hussein to hide their heinous crimes against the Palestinian people, enslavement of Africans, destruction of indigenous cultures, killing their own people in civil wars, using nuclear weapons, chemical weapons, land mines and cluster bombs and bombing countries at will with their advanced tomahawk missiles, drones, B52 bombers and general control of the world's air space. It's a sure sign that whenever any Western country points to some atrocity committed by any other country it's to hide a greater atrocity committed by itself. The West is never ever shamed by being caught with using gross hypocrisy or double standards. It thrives on being shamed as it is totally shameless.

This brings us to the West pointing its finger at the atrocities committed in the Belgian Congo. Sure enough the theft of the Congo by King Leopold II of Belgium was a heinous crime against humanity. But the real story is not the finger pointing by the West but "the pot calling the kettle black." Every Western imperial power was equally guilty of crimes against humanity committed in Africa. No Western power was better or worse. Pointing the figure at King Leopold or Hitler or any other Western or domestic leader was done only to hide the crimes being committed by the figure pointers. Typically, in the case of crimes committed in Western colonies a Western imperial power would point the finger at another Western imperial power because it wanted the colony for its own empire. For example, the raging battles in Africa during the Second World War had absolutely nothing to do with Hitler or saving freedom but everything to do with the continued Western colonizing of Africa and the fighting over these colonies by Germany, Italy, France and Britain.

Once Columbus and da Gama had made their sea voyages to the New World and Asia, respectively, no corner of the globe was safe from Western imperialism. Africa, like America and Asia, was increasingly colonized as the Portuguese were followed by the Dutch, British and French. Like America and Asia only the coastal areas of Africa were colonized since most of the hinterland was inaccessible by ship. But just as two American imperialists, Lewis and Clark, became famous "explorers" in the Western history books for crossing the American continent overland, two British imperialists, David Livingstone and Henry Morton Stanley, became famous "explorers" in the Western history books for crossing the African continent overland. But none of these were primarily explorers. Like Columbus and da Gama they were imperialists looking for new lands and resources to steal for their respective empires. Once they had discovered the route into the hinterland they knew with **certainty** that Westerners would follow to steal, pillage, plunder, Christianize and destroy indigenous religions, cultures and languages in the name of Western civilization. At the time of the inland voyages of Livingstone, only about ten percent of Africa was colonized. It was the inland voyages of imperialists like Livingstone's which expanded the colonization of Africa from this ten percent to almost all of Africa just as the transfer of English colonies to the USA and Canada expanded the Western colonization of North America from a tiny percent to all of North America by killing off or imprisoning in reserves all of the First Nations.

Livingstone, like Pallu and la Motte, was initially a Christian missionary using the church to achieve his imperial goals. Just as Pallu and la Motte were sent to colonize Southeast Asia by the Christian Mission in Paris, Livingstone was sent to colonize Africa by the Christian Mission in London, the *London Missionary Society.* France and Britain were competing for colonies with guns, propaganda and **religion.** Livingstone has been idolized by the West as some kind of God because he was opposed to the slave "trade" and treated the Africans with more respect than other Europeans. But he was as much an imperialist as every other European missionary, slave "trader," "explorer," pirate or captain. His view was that British imperialism was great as long as it rejected the slave "trade." This is like stating that war is great as long as warmongers obey the Geneva Convention on torture. Our position is that all warmongering and all colonizations are equally evil. Abolishing the slave "trade" is good only if it helps to portray imperialism as an evil. If it does the opposite by helping to portray imperialism as civilized or enlightening then it does more harm than good. Just as President Lincoln abolished slavery in the United States only because it helped him to win the Civil War, Livingstone wanted to abolish the slave "trade" only to make British imperialism civilized. He was no anti-imperialist. He even had the audacity to give the *Mosi-oa-Tunya* falls he visited in Southern Africa the British imperial name of Victoria Falls, after Queen Victoria. Perhaps an African visitor to North America should pretend to be an explorer discovering Niagara Falls and rename it Sheba Falls, after the queen of Sheba.

What has been called the "Scramble for Africa" is dated as occurring during the period of renewed European imperialism during 1870 to 1914. By this time the old imperial powers of Portugal, Spain and Holland had been replaced by Britain and France who were now facing competition from Germany, Italy, the United States, and Japan. In Africa, Belgium was also a new competitor. The British colonies in Africa included Egypt, Sudan, South Africa, Rhodesia, Ghana, Nigeria, Kenya, Sierra Leone, Tanzania, Uganda, Botswana and the Cameroons. The French Empire had the African colonies of Algeria, Morocco, Tunisia, Chad, Gabon, Ivory Coast, Togo and Senegal among others. Some of these had changed hands from Portugal, Spain and Holland to Britain and France. During this new period of Western colonization in Africa the Germans, Italians and Belgians got into the act. German colonies in Africa included parts of East Africa and Southwest Africa. The Italians colonized Libya, Ethiopia, Eritrea and Somaliland.

While there was no shortage of atrocities committed by all of the European imperialists in every corner of Africa we will highlight those atrocities by focusing on the Belgian Congo. It's important to remember that all Western colonization is intended to steal land and resources rather than trade for them. The fact that these colonizations bring with them advanced modes of transportation, medicines, infrastructure, education, etcetera, should never be viewed as the reasons behind Western imperialism. They are essential improvements necessary for the imperial power to steal more than would be possible without these improvements. For example, if the imperialists are killed off by malaria the colonization would come to an end. If there are no roads or improved infrastructure it would never be possible to colonize further inland. If there is no education it would be impossible to use propaganda and destroy local languages, cultures and religions. The by-products of colonizations are like the by-products of warmongering. Many new inventions and innovations are discovered by the large investments in weapons. But just as many more innovations and inventions would be discovered if the investments were exclusively focused on inventing and innovating rather than warmongering so too would many more people be helped by medicines, education, infrastructure, etcetera, if the exclusive focus of expenditures were on these and on trade rather than theft by military force.

The Belgian Congo

The Belgian Congo was not unique because of the atrocities but only because the nature of its colonization was unique. Just as the British blamed apartheid in South Africa on the Dutch the European imperialists blamed the atrocities in the Congo on the Belgian king, Leopold II. The British practiced apartheid in all of its colonies including Canada, Rhodesia, Australia, New Zealand and India. Today, Britain, Canada, and the United States support the practice of apartheid against the Palestinians in Israel. Every European imperial power practiced apartheid in their colonies since apartheid empowered a tiny **white** minority to rule a large nonwhite majority. South Africa was different only because the West said it was unique. Sometimes the West will choose a scapegoat for propaganda purposes.

King Leopold II was rightly concerned that his Western European state seemed to be among the very few Western European states not to have colonies. He felt it his kingly duty to his subjects to remedy what seemed like a defect of the Belgian people. Since Western historians measure the degree to which you have advanced from barbarian to civilized status by your imperial conquests Belgium was under threat of losing its civilized status if it did not conquer some barbarians and colonize them. Leopold began to urge his nation to conquer colonies as early as 1855 when he was appointed to the Belgian Senate. Given all the nonsense that had been written by Western historians, he naturally concluded that Belgium would never become a great nation if it had no colonies. It was colonies which had made the Portuguese, Spanish, Dutch, French and British great civilized nations. Once he became the king of Belgium in 1865 he set about remedying the defect of Belgium being disrespected as a fully-fledged member of "great" Western European states because it had no colonies.

Leopold began his quest for colonies by attempting to take the Philippines from the Spanish Empire. When this effort failed he looked to Africa. At the time only 10 percent of Africa had been colonized. A determined imperialist like King Leopold II would be able to steal at least a small part of the remaining 90 percent. It's important that we understand the mindset of Western Europeans. Military conquests of colonies in Africa and Asia were acts of a civilized Western European state to be applauded across all of Europe. No Western European state saw them as acts of aggression or barbarity, which of course, they were. You had to play by the rules of civilized empires just as you must play by the rules for civilized warmongering. For example, civilized warmongering requires you to observe the Geneva conventions. Likewise civilized colonization requires you to publicize your intentions of carrying out the white man's burden, Christianize the heathens, provide western medicines and schools, learn the local customs, and treat the colonized people whose lands you have stolen, as good workers and servants. Keep the locals at a "respectful" distance and pretend you admire their barbaric customs. Use locals as deserving employees wherever it was to your advantage in keeping the peace while enhancing your theft. Use western propaganda to confuse the locals and divide those who are smart enough to oppose your theft, from those who you brainwash to defend you. Another acceptable ploy is to pretend that you are explorers, missionaries, journalists or scientists.

King Leopold II learned the rules of the game and set about his colonial conquest in Africa with great zeal and determination. He began by choosing the most politically correct name for his undertaking, "the International Association for the Exploration and Civilization of the Congo." Using the word "international" as the Americans always do whenever they mean "unilateral" is politically correct. Using "exploration" when you mean theft by military force is also politically correct. And stating that your purpose is to civilize is the most politically correct purpose. If you were ever truthful and stated that your intention was to steal and plunder, you would be so chastised by your peers that you would become an outcast. The key to being an acceptable warmonger like President Obama is to never be a truthful warmonger like President Bush. The same is true about civilized colonization. Steal, rape and pillage all you want but be civilized about it.

King Leopold II knew instinctively that the man to help him civilize his bid to colonize the Congo would be none other than the respected African "explorer" Henry Morton Stanley. In addition he needed the "exploring" skills of Stanley since Europeans had not yet explored this part of Africa until Stanley had done so. In 1874 Stanley had led an expedition to the Congo region financed by two leading news media, the British *Daily Telegraph* and the American *New York Herald.* Stanley was successful in mapping the Congo River Basin. After his return, Stanley was hired in 1878 by King Leopold to find his African colony in the Congo region. As expected once Stanley and Leopold had shown the way other Western Europeans followed. Leopold's attempt to colonize the Congo combined with Stanley's 1874–1877 explorations provided a big boost to what was called the "Scramble for Africa." Stanley returned to the Congo in 1878 as an envoy of King Leopold. Once France got wind of Leopold's plans she sent her own expedition into the Congo. The French flag was raised in the Congo in 1881. The Portuguese also contested the Belgian claims. It had been a Portuguese explorer, *Diogo Cao,* sent by King John II of Portugal, who was the first European to have found the mouth of the Congo River in 1482. Diogo Cao made two voyages up the Congo River reaching as far as Matadi, an important sea port of the Democratic Republic of the Congo. He erected several markers on behalf of Portugal.

Portugal convinced the influential German chancellor Otto von Bismarck to convene the Berlin Conference on November 15, 1884, to get the competing Western empires to discuss, and agree to a division of the Congo region as well as spheres of influence throughout Africa. By hosting the conference Germany was serving notice to Britain and France that Germany was the new imperial competitor. Leopold was able to keep most of the Congo, an area of almost one million square miles. France was allocated over a quarter of a million square miles. Portugal received somewhat more than France. Leopold's share of the Congo was constituted as the *Congo Free State* on May 29, 1885. This Central African state is today's Democratic Republic of the Congo. King Leopold played up the typical Western propaganda that it would be a much more civilized colonial power compared to Portugal because of Portugal's history of starting the African slave "trade" by the West.

The atrocities committed in the Congo during the personal rule of King Leopold II are well documented. Some studies claimed that half the population was killed off. But that would be comparable to what the Spanish, Portuguese, British, French, American, Mexican and Canadian empires did to the First Nations in the New World. The setting of unrealistic rubber quotas on the original inhabitants, by King Leopold, was equivalent to the setting of unrealistic gold quotas by Columbus. The semislavery conditions enforced on the people of the Congo were no different from the semislavery conditions enforced on the people of the New World. The widespread cutting off of hands in the Congo mirrored the barbarity of the Spanish conquistadors. Congolese resistance to colonization was as widespread as the resistance of the First Nations in the New World. The lesson to be learned from the atrocities committed in the Congo was that the so-called civilized West had learned nothing about the barbarity of their crimes against humanity after four centuries of imperialism. Much like today they invent all manner of excuses for their underlying addiction to warmongering, colonization and mistreatment of those they are able to kill, maim and destroy with their advanced military weapons. They kill, maim, humiliate and destroy simply because they have the military power to do so. They have no morality or goodness in their bones. They are simply evil. They point out the evil of others only to distract attention from their own innate evil characters. None is better than the other, not even the missionaries or doctors or relief workers or humanitarian workers or other so-called Western "do-gooders." This may seem harsh but the reality is that they all have the same biased Western perspective on colonization. By helping to relieve some of the pain inflicted by their governments they help to perpetuate the myth of the civilized West. They are like the American soldiers giving out chocolate bars to the children whose parents they slaughtered with the bombs they dropped from the heavens.

Western historians seemed to have breathed a sigh of relief when the Congo ceased to be the personal possession of King Leopold in 1908 and became the colony of Belgium. I doubt if many Congolese cared much whether their lands, resources, religions, cultures and languages were stolen by the king of Belgium or by the state of Belgium. Apart from the name change from the Congo Free State to the Belgian Congo, Leopold's governor-general and all of his administrators continued to rule the colony in much the same manner as if they were working for the king. Leopold had achieved his ultimate goal of making his country an imperial power so as to get the respect shown by the West to all Western empires. He was no different from the rulers of the United States or of other Western states. The West had identified colonies as an essential credential to be a civilized nation. The fact that this was the very antithesis of what is civilized is consistent with the West turning all logic on its head with its very sophisticated propaganda machine.

The Belgian Congo, like most of the colonies in Africa and Asia, eventually became independent. In this respect the Congolese did far better than the First Nations of the United States, Canada, and Mexico. But Congolese independence from Belgium was very little different from Vietnamese independence from France. The Western European empires had been militarily weakened by the Second World War but all Western colonies were now under threat of colonization by the powerful American Empire. It proved to be very easy for the West to invent civilized reasons for colonization. The American Empire invented "fighting communism" as its civilizing mission after colonizing to carry the white man's burden had fallen into disrepute. The Congo became somewhat independent from Belgium on June 30, 1960. It was renamed the Republic of the Congo. But Belgium was very reluctant to give up its colony much like France was unwilling to give up Vietnam. Both had found a willing ally with money and military power in the American Empire.

As many colonial people had done, the Congolese helped the Western allies fight the Germans and Italians in Africa hoping to shame their imperial masters into granting them independence. The American Empire stole the uranium deposits of the Congo to build its nuclear weapons used against Japan. The Congolese people founded several organizations, mostly along ethnic lines, to lobby the people and the West for independence from Belgium. The largest of these associations was *ABAKO* led by Joseph Kasa-Vubu. During the 1950s Belgium was under increasing international pressure to grant independence to its colony in the Congo. A national independence party was founded in 1958 led by Patrice Lumumba. Attempts by the Belgian government to restrict the activities of these organizations led to widespread riots in the major cities, including Leopoldville and Stanleyville, in 1959. The Belgian government responded with greater restrictions, including the arrest of the prominent leaders, Joseph Kasa-Vubu and Patrice Lumumba, which led to even more riots and the formation of many more political parties. The Belgian government was forced to convene a conference in Belgium to discuss the independence movement with the Congolese political associations. Despite the best efforts of the host to stall the independence movement, Belgium was forced to allow elections to be held on May 22, 1960. The party led by Lumumba won the most seats and formed a coalition government with him as the prime minister and Kasa-Vubu as president.

But over a hundred parties had contested the elections. Even without Western opposition a Central Revolutionary government would have needed a miracle to survive. As it was, both Belgium and the American Empire were chomping at the bits to get their hands on some, if not all, of the mineral resources of the Congo. The key mining province was *Katanga.* This province alone was over sixteen times the area of Belgium. It was rich in copper, tin, uranium, diamonds, cobalt, and radium. One of the many parties which had contested the 1960 elections was led by an American educated Congolese from Katanga, *Moise Tshombe.* Tshombe saw his opportunity to rule a rich breakaway province as a puppet of the West. Shortly after the elections he declared Katanga as an independent country becoming its president in August 1960. Belgium was only too happy to provide the military fire power to prop up his government. Naturally, the Western dominated UN refused the request of the Revolutionary government to intervene on its behalf. Worse still, the Americans plotted with the Belgians to overthrow the Revolutionary Nationalist government, led by Lumumba. Their excuse was that Lumumba had sought aid from the Soviets even though Lumumba had only asked for Soviet assistance after the UN had failed to help him. The U.S. president Dwight Eisenhower ordered the assassination of Lumumba.

The American Empire found their SOB dictator in *Mobutu Sese Seko.* Mobutu had been appointed as Chief of Staff of the army by Lumumba. With help from the CIA he organized a military coup and deposed Lumumba. Lumumba was flown to the Western client state of Katanga where he was beaten, tortured and killed in January 1961. His body was dumped by the CIA. Shortly after, Mobutu was promoted to Major-general by a subservient President Kasa-Vubu. The iconic revolutionary, *Che Guevara,* entered the Congo with Cuban fighters in 1965. But his forces were no match for the Americans. Shortly after Che left the Congo the Americans led a second successful coup on November 25, 1965. President Kasa-Vubu was deposed and Mobutu became the American SOB dictator, installed to fight communism. He renamed the country *Zaire* on October 27, 1971, and ruled it until May 17, 1997. As a typical American imposed dictator he amassed a personal fortune while his people lived in dire poverty. In June 1989 he was invited to the United States by President George H. W. Bush. In 1996 Zaire was invaded by neighboring Rwanda. This led to what has been called the First Congo War. Military forces from a coalition of African countries, including Rwanda, Uganda, Angola, Zambia, Ethiopia and Zimbabwe, joined the rebel leader, Laurent Kabila, who had opposed the Mobutu government. After suffering military defeats by this massive coalition, Mobutu fled the Congo in May 1997. Kabila became president on September 7, 1997. Zaire was renamed the Democratic Republic of the Congo, DRC.

But the problems caused by Western colonization of the Congo continue to this day. Kabila had been supported by many African countries in ousting the American imposed dictator, Mobutu. Now those African countries wanted a share of the spoils of war. In addition, there remained the many ethnic divisions which had participated in the 1960 elections. When Kabila asked foreign forces to leave it led to the Second Congo War of 1998–2003. This was a far more bloody conflict involving nine African countries and killing five million Africans. The DRC, like many ex-Western African colonies, continues to suffer from the fear of Western recolonization, ethnic conflicts, scramble for minerals, poverty and ineffective governments.

CHAPTER 8

Germany's Challenge to British Hegemony Replaces Anglo-French Warmongering with Anglo-German Warmongering While the Japanese Challenge to the American Empire in the Pacific Unites the Anglo Powers against Germany, Japan, and Italy

One of the constant themes of my books is that the West is addicted to warmongering and imperialism. While all of the Western European empires were guilty of invading and colonizing Asia, Africa and the Americas, they all cooperated and competed with each other for colonies. The British had made war on the Portuguese, Spanish, Dutch and French before the rise of Germany. It should therefore come as no surprise that the British would make war on this new imperial rival. In like manner the Americans had made war on the First Nations, Canada, Mexico and numerous countries in Latin America. After the First World War, the American Empire was ready to make war on the Japanese Empire for control of the Pacific. While the causes of a specific war are many, the underlying cause, which has remained unchanged since the birth of the Portuguese and Spanish empires, is the quest to have more colonies than your imperial rivals. That is the key reason for the First and Second World Wars. While there were many nations involved in these wars the key players were Britain, France, Germany, the United States, Japan, Russia, and Italy.

The German Colonial Empire

In the previous chapter we traced the rise of Prussia and how the new German state under Prussia replaced both Austria and France as the leading continental state. This by itself posed a threat to Britain even though British imperial hegemony was largely based on its worldwide colonies more than its leadership role in continental Europe. But when Germany decided to add colonies to its continental hegemony Britain became paranoid. While Prussia was competing with Austria for German leadership the British supported Prussia both because of family ties through the House of Hanover and because Prussian competition with Austria reduced the great power status long held by the Austro-Hungarian Empire. But the Prussian defeat of Austria in 1866, and France in 1871, made Britain take notice that its new imperial rival would very likely be a new German Empire led by Prussia. Germany's rapid industrialization provided the necessary economic base for this German challenge to British hegemony.

The acquisition of colonies by a Western European state was the natural and civilized thing to do. You did not have to be a great power. Even tiny states like Belgium, Denmark, Holland, Sweden, England, Portugal and Granada had invaded and colonized. It would have been inconceivable to think that a rising power like Germany would not play the civilized Western European game of conquering colonies with its superior military force. How could it even dare to call itself civilized if it had no colonials to civilize? Of course, the fact that it was more profitable to steal the raw materials and valuable resources to grow your industrial base using military colonization rather than trade, was just the icing on the cake. Carrying the white man's burden was just what an advanced European state must do then, just as today the American Empire must bomb countries like Vietnam, Cambodia, Laos, Iraq, Afghanistan, Libya, Syria, Lebanon, Yemen, Pakistan, etcetera to prove their civilized concern for the people of those countries. If some oil or other valuable resources can be stolen in the process, that is just a windfall.

German Participation in the Western Colonization of China, Asia, and the Pacific

China was the country which most fascinated the West beginning with the travels of Marco Polo, the Silk Road, and the Arab spice trade. A sea route to China was the key incentive for the discoveries of both Columbus and da Gama. Once the West had found the sea route to China every Western power tried to colonize China. As expected, the

German Empire was a late-comer. Germans had participated in the overland trade with China through Siberia and many Germans had traveled to China by sea since the seventeenth century. After China was defeated by the combined imperial forces of Britain, France, Russia, and the United States in the Second Opium War, the *Unequal Treaty of Tianjin* gave many colonial rights in China, to the West. As a result Prussia was able to get its own Unequal Treaty of Tianjin with China only a year after the Qing emperor had ratified this humiliating treaty with the other Western imperialists. Prussia sent three warships which reached China in May 1861. Within a few months the Qing emperor was forced to agree to add Prussia to the growing list of Western powers colonizing China with their superior military forces. Prussia had signaled to Britain and France that it had the same rights to colonies as they had.

The German Empire wanted more from China than punitive trading rights. It wanted a naval base. The Prussians had explored the *Bay of Jiaozhou* beginning in 1860 and concluded that it was suitable for a German naval base. In 1897 Germany invaded the Chinese city of Qingdao (Tsingtao) in Shandong province, with the goal of establishing a naval base in the Bay of Jiaozhou, much like the Americans had invaded Hawaii to create its naval base in Pearl Harbor. With only three warships Germany forced a military weak China to grant it what the West called a "concession," a ninety-nine-year lease similar to what the British had forced China to agree to with regard to Hong Kong. This naval base became the home base for the East Asia and Far East Squadron of the German navy. By this time German "trade" with China was second only to Britain. With this naval base the German Empire signaled its intension to compete with the United States, Britain, France, Russia, and Japan for control of both China and the Pacific. The other great powers responded by establishing their own naval bases in China.

Germany allied with the other great powers against China during the Boxer Rebellion of 1900. It also strengthened its defenses in Shandong province in response to that uprising by building trenches, batteries, other well manned fortifications and mining the harbor. Like other Western powers Germany expanded its colonization of China to other parts of Asia and the Pacific, such as New Guinea, Samoa, the Solomon Islands, the Marshall Islands, the Mariana Islands, and the Caroline Islands. New

Guinea was the first Asian colony of the German Empire after China. The island of New Guinea is located in the Pacific near to what was the British colony of Australia. The island had been explored by the Portuguese and Spanish in the early sixteenth century. In1884 the New Guinea Company was formed in Berlin to colonize New Guinea. This German colony occupied the entire north-eastern portion of the island as well some of the islands off the coast of New Guinea. The Dutch had already colonized the western half of the island in 1828. The British had colonized the south-eastern portion of the island just before the German colonization in 1884. By 1884 the island of New Guinea shared three Western colonial masters. Colonial control of the German colony was transferred to the German government in 1899. The German colony in New Guinea became a good base for the German Empire to add other islands in the Pacific to its growing colonial empire. The Northern Solomon Islands and the Marshall Islands were added in 1885. The Mariana and Caroline Islands as well as Samoa were added in 1899.

German Participation in the Western Colonization of Africa

Germany was a relatively minor player in the colonization of Africa until the 1880s. But during the 1880s the German Empire established colonies in both East Africa and West Africa. As a latecomer it had to content itself with parts of Africa not yet colonized by Portugal, France and England. By the time of the First and Second World Wars, the German Empire had become a major player in Africa. Its African colonies included Togo and *Kamerun* in West Africa, German South-West Africa and German East Africa. This explains, more than any Western concern about Hitler or freedom or democracy, why so much of these two World Wars were fought in Africa. The West African coast had been the first area of Africa to be colonized as the Portuguese sailed further and further down this coast hugging the coastline for safety. The Portuguese had found both gold and **African slaves.** The Dutch, French and English had followed the Portuguese. German colonization of West Africa followed the other Western European imperialists by establishing colonies in Ghana. As early as 1682 the Prussian king, Frederick William I, had permitted the creation of the Brandenburg African Company to colonize the West African coast. It founded two colonies in Ghana, which was then called the Gold Coast. The luxurious Brandenburg fort, *Fort Gross Fredericksburg,* erected along the coast in Princess Town in 1683, by the Brandenburg African Company, still stands today as a tourist attraction in Ghana.

A principal **slave station** established by the Portuguese along the West African coast was in the *Bight of Benin.* In 1472 Portugal began to export African slaves from its base located in the Bight of Benin which is in the Gulf of Guinea. This coastline became known as the "Slave Coast" because such a large percent of African slaves were caught and exported from this location. Prussia joined the other Western European slavers in this location in 1685. While the primary focus of the Western European empires in West Africa was their vile human cargo they were not averse to stealing other valuable products such as gold, ivory or fish. It was the abundance of fish which led Prussia to join the other Western European imperialists in colonizing the island of *Arguin.* This island is located off the western coast of Mauritania. The Portuguese discovered the island in 1443 and the infamous Prince Henry the Navigator began catching and exporting slaves to Portugal after setting up shop in 1445. Arguin became a Portuguese colony which the Dutch captured in 1633. France captured it from the Dutch in 1678 but abandoned it. This enabled Prussia to colonize it in 1685.

The German African Colonies in West Africa: 1884–1914

When Prussia became the leader of the new Germany its West African colonies could not be transferred to Germany because by the time of German unification Prussia had lost all of its West African colonies. Nevertheless, there was a history of African colonization which the new Germany would use to its advantage in the 1880s. By this time the misnamed "slave trade" had been abolished. There had to be other products of value to justify the military and administrative cost of acquiring African colonies. The Prussian prime minister Otto von Bismarck, most responsible for German unification under Prussia, was initially of the opinion that colonies were not cost effective and would therefore be a financial burden on the state. However, it was impossible to become a great power and justify a powerful navy without colonies. By the 1850s, Germans looked to overseas colonies both as sources of raw materials and markets for their industrial goods. With a population of 20 million there were many Germans who aspired to making their fortunes by immigrating to overseas German colonies. Germany therefore joined rather aggressively in what became known as the "Scramble for Africa." Most of Africa had not yet been colonized by Western Europe and offered opportunities for markets, German missionaries, settlers, administrators, military men, wild game hunters and those searching for minerals and other valuable resources.

The new German Empire acquired two colonies in West Africa, Kamerun and Togo, beginning in 1884. Both of these colonies were inland expansions just north of the infamous Slave Coast along the Bight of Benin where Prussia had established its colonial presence in the seventeenth century. Togo was the more northern colony squeezed between the English colony of Ghana and French Dahomey. Another English colony, Nigeria, separated French Dahomey from the German colony of Kamerun. Ghana, Togo, Dahomey, Nigeria, and Kamerun were all Western European colonies with borders on the infamous Slave Coast. The German colony of Kamerun included parts of Gabon and the Congo as well as what is today the Republic of Cameroon. The Hamburg trading company of Carl and Adolf Woermann began "trading" in West Africa in 1849. During this time most of German "trade" with Africa was done from the German city of Hamburg. In 1868 the Woermann Company established the first German "trading" post in the Kamerun. Others followed and in 1884, when there were at least twelve private German companies "trading" and growing crops on stolen land in West Africa, they petitioned the German state for military protection. Germany sent its first gunboat to protect the so-called traders. Bismarck had also instructed his consul to Tunisia, *Gustav Nachtigal,* to secure Togo and Kamerun as colonies for the German Empire. Tunisia became a French colony in 1881 and Nachtigal was appointed as German consul in 1882. Nachtigal was a German doctor who had explored West and Central Africa before his appointment as consul. Bismarck sent a clear signal to France and Britain that Germany would join the European competition for African colonies.

Rail and communication infrastructure were built to get the produce from the two German colonies to the coast. Let us remind our readers that trade is a voluntary activity by two parties. It does not require military protection. Once there is need for military protection it is not trade. During the five centuries of Western European colonization trade took place only where the European power was not militarily strong enough to steal rather than trade. It was the same in German West Africa. The early German companies traded with the Africans but resorted to colonization and theft after they got military protection from the German state. German plantations growing tobacco, cocoa, coffee, palm oil, rubber and bananas on stolen land in the Kamerun, began in 1885. The German colony in the Kamerun followed all of the Western European powers in forcing the defeated indigenous people to work as slaves or in semislavery conditions on the land stolen from them for the plantations. As in other Western European colonies the forced African labor in the Kamerun were poorly fed and housed and were whipped and brutalized while working as many as eighteen hours each day. Adding insult to injury, the Germans followed the Portuguese, Spanish, Dutch, French, and English in proclaiming loudly that they were teaching the "lazy African savages" how to be civilized productive workers.

The German African Colony in East Africa: 1884–1914

The "Society for German Colonization" was founded on March 28, 1884. The founder of the German colonization society, Dr. Karl Peters, began his colonizing mission in East Africa. He traveled to the island of Zanzibar and to the East African mainland in 1884. What became the German colony of "German East Africa" had an area of almost one million square kilometers. It included what is today the countries of Rwanda and Burundi as well as the mainland of Tanzania, which was the country of Tanganyika before 1964. It was Vasco da Gama who had first landed on the East African coast in 1498 before travelling to India. The Portuguese had colonized the island of Zanzibar which Dr. Peters visited in 1884. But German missionaries had explored East Africa before Dr. Peters. As we explained above, missionaries have often laid the groundwork for colonization. Two German missionaries who explored East Africa were Johannes Rebmann and Johann Krapf. Both men worked for the Church Missionary Society, CMS. CMS was founded in London, England in 1799 when it was then called the Society for Missions to Africa and the East. The famous abolitionist, William Wilberforce, was one of the founding members.

Krapf had previously worked as a missionary in Ethiopia before moving to Egypt. It was from Egypt that he traveled to Kenya in East Africa where he later met Rebmann in 1846 and together they began to explore the interior. They found both Mount Kilimanjaro and Mount Kenya. Other German explorers such as Karl von der Decken and Otto Kersten led more expeditions into East Africa during the 1860s. These German explorations and missionary work played an important role in dividing all of East Africa between the Germans and the British at the Berlin Conference of 1884. This infamous conference was hosted by the German chancellor Otto von Bismarck. It led to the division of all of Africa into colonies of the Western imperialists. In 1884 less than 20 percent of Africa had been colonized, mostly the coastal areas which were more easily accessible to the powerful navies of the West. The conference failed in its efforts to colonize Africa without wars between the Western imperial powers. In the end these Western warmongers fought two World Wars over Africa.

On March 3, 1885, the German government granted an imperial charter to a company founded by Dr. Peters and other prominent German imperialists, the *German East Africa Company.* The Germans sent five warships to East Africa to ensure that the sultan of Zanzibar did not resist military occupation of East Africa by the German company. The Arabs had expelled the Portuguese from Zanzibar and established their trade with East Africa from Zanzibar. Despite assistance from the German navy the private company was unable to defeat the resistance to colonization by the Africans. As a result the German government took over the colony in 1891. The Africans continued to resist German colonization and theft of their resources with guerilla warfare. Like all the other Western European imperialists the Germans were brutal in punishing those who resisted the theft of their land and resources. With its technologically advanced weapons a handful of Germans defeated a relatively large African population. By the outbreak of the First World

War the German population that occupied East Africa was somewhat less than five thousand. The Germans used the stolen African land to grow crops such as coffee, sisal, cotton and rubber. Gold was discovered in 1894 and stolen as well. Since the railway had already been invented by this time it was quicker for the Germans to penetrate the hinterland compared with the Americans in the United States.

The German African Colony in South-West Africa: 1884–1914

A third colony was claimed by Germany around the same time it colonized German East Africa. Once again missionaries paved the way for this other brutal Western colonization, theft of land and resources and destruction of indigenous cultures, customs and historic lifestyles. In the case of German colonization in South-West Africa it was the missionaries sent out by the German *Rhenish Missionary Society, RMS.* We explained above the part played by the London based CMS. Another prominent London based missionary society was the London Missionary Society, LMS, founded 1795, four years before the CMS. In 1840 the LMS transferred its missions in South-West Africa to the German RMS. The RMS had been founded in 1828 and had sent missionaries to South Africa, then a British colony stolen from the Dutch during the Napoleonic wars. When the German missionaries arrived in South Africa they worked closely with their English brothers in crime sent earlier by the LMS.

Not content with the land and resources stolen by the Dutch and English in South Africa the missionaries sent out by the RMS explored further north and claimed a new colony for Germany called *South-West Africa.* They first made this claim in 1880, and in 1882 they sought military protection from the German state. German state protection was granted in 1884 and the German flag was raised over its new colony on August 7, 1884. The infamous Berlin Conference confirmed Germany as the imperial master of another 835,000 square kilometers of stolen African land. This colony had a land area almost as large as that of German East Africa. In 1885 the German Colonial Society for South-West Africa was founded. The German state granted it a monopoly to steal all the minerals it could find, in addition to the land and other raw materials. Minerals found included gold, diamonds, copper and platinum. As in German East Africa the Africans resisted German colonization and theft in South-West Africa. Germany sent military reinforcements in 1888. But the private corporation was unable to defend its theft and the German state was forced to make German South-West Africa a crown colony in 1890 and send more troops. African rebellions against the theft of their land and resources continued in the two decades before World War 1. Germany sent another fourteen thousand soldiers to crush the rebellions. The German soldiers tracked down the African rebels from one water hole to another like a "wounded beast," killing them or forcing them to die from thirst. The Germans killed off over one hundred thousand Africans. Those not killed were forced to work in the mines for the German owners. They were "imprisoned" in camps much like the First Nations were "imprisoned" in reserves in Canada and the United States. Twice as many Germans immigrated to South-West Africa as had immigrated to East Africa. By the outbreak of the First World War there were almost ten thousand German settlers in South-West Africa.

World War I: First War for *Imperial Hegemony* between Britain and Germany

Britain had fought many wars for imperial hegemony with Holland and France. By the end of the Napoleonic wars in 1815 Britain had defeated both Holland and France. The British Empire ruled the world for a century after 1815 much like the American Empire ruled the world after the Second World War. But by 1914 a new imperial challenger had risen in the form of Germany. In two wars Britain and Germany destroyed each other enabling the dominance of the American Empire. After the fall of the Roman Empire, Christian hegemony was largely replaced by Muslim hegemony. Up until the rise of Portugal and Spain, hegemony was based on dominant armies. While Christians had lost hegemony to Muslims the dominant Christian powers were still the mainland European powers such as Austria, Hungary and France. But with the advent of sea power, small states on the edge of Western Europe such as

Portugal, Spain, Holland, and England became great powers by using their powerful navies to colonize lands across the oceans.

Portugal and Spain used their powerful navies to reach the coasts of lands in Africa, Asia, America and the Pacific. The Dutch built an even more powerful navy to claim imperial hegemony from Portugal and Spain. The English wrested that hegemony from the Dutch only to be challenged by France. But with the English defeat of Napoleon the English became the dominant world power because the Royal Navy was superior to any other until challenged by Germany. The American Empire replaced both Britain and Germany not only because they destroyed each other during two wars but also because air power replaced sea power as the decisive military weapon. In the previous chapter we explained how the new united Germany under Prussia had defeated both Austria and France to claim the status of dominant continental state in Europe and thereby the dominant Christian power on the European mainland. Like France before, Germany was not satisfied with continental hegemony but wanted the colonial hegemony still claimed by Britain and France. In this chapter we will trace the continued rise of Germany from where we left off in the previous chapter focusing on its wars with the British Empire.

After the creation of the German Empire in 1871 following Prussia's defeat of France, the German chancellor Bismarck formed a military alliance between Germany and Austria-Hungary, the so-called *Dual Alliance.* Germany and Austria were natural allies but had fought over whether Prussia or Austria would lead a united Austro-German Empire. After the Napoleonic wars, the German states were unified under Austrian leadership in 1815. But the economic and military power of Prussia increased after 1815 relative to that of Austria. When Austria was defeated by Prussia in 1866, Prussia was seen as the future leader of a united Germany. The Dual Alliance uniting all of the German states, including Austria, was created on October 7, 1879. The *Triple Alliance* of May 20, 1882, added Italy to the military alliance of Germany and Austria. As we explained in the previous chapter, Italian unification took place during the same time period as German unification. Like the new Germany, the new united Italy looked for colonies to boost its claim for great power status. Tunisia in Africa was an obvious choice for an

Italian colony. When France colonized Tunisia in 1881, the Italians saw it as a military threat from France and agreed to an alliance with the rising German Empire led by Prussia. Germany saw the alliance with Italy as weakening the possibility of France ever regaining the territory it captured from France, Alsace-Lorraine, after its defeat of France in 1871. Furthermore, France had sought an alliance with Russia ever since it had been defeated by Prussia. Russia was receptive to such a military alliance once Germany had concluded the Triple Alliance with Italy and Austria. A draft Franco-Russian alliance was agreed to on August 17, 1892.

The rise of Prussia at the expense of Austria and France was not the only change sweeping Europe after the Napoleonic wars. The Ottoman Empire was also in decline. The primary opposition to the Ottoman Empire had been the Austro-Hungarian Empire led by the powerful Habsburg family. But the decline in the Austro-Hungarian Empire did not benefit the Ottoman Empire. Rather it had to face a new threat from Russia. At the time of the Crimean War of 1853–1856 France and Britain were unwilling to let Russia defeat the Ottoman Empire and steal its territory. Britain and France therefore provided military support to the Ottoman Empire to defeat Russia. But that was before Prussia defeated France. That Prussian defeat led France to see Russia more as a potential ally against a rising German Empire rather than as an enemy. France was willing to let Russia carve up some of the territory of the Ottoman Empire in return for a military alliance against Germany. France therefore did not support the Ottoman Empire during the Russo-Turkish War of 1877–1878 and the Ottoman Empire was defeated. Russia expanded its territory at the expense of the Ottoman Empire. Russia also reestablished its dominant control of the Black Sea, which it had surrendered after its defeat in the Crimean War.

Russia replaced the Ottoman Empire as much as the new Germany replaced the Austro-Hungarian Empire. France had to struggle to regain great power status after its humiliating defeat by Prussia. By the time of the Russo-Turkish War, France was beginning to reassert itself as a primary player in Europe. While its new colonial acquisitions in Africa pushed Italy into an alliance with Germany it saw this as a small price to pay for regaining its worldwide imperial prestige as the only true rival to the British Empire. A military alliance with Russia would protect its territory in continental Europe against German aggression while allowing it to return to its historic competition for worldwide colonies with the British Empire. Russia would gain territory in continental Europe while France would expand its colonial empire alongside Britain. It was a win-win for the two new allies. A new continental balance of power had been reestablished with the new great powers being Germany, Russia, France, and Britain. Germany had replaced Austria and Russia had replaced the Ottomans.

Europeans, like Americans, like every previous so-called civilization, can never be at peace for long. Warmongering is an addiction. Had it not been for this addiction, the new balance of power established after the Franco-Russian alliance of 1892, would have led to permanent peace. Russia, Germany, France and Britain had all achieved their goals. Russia and Germany had more continental territory and France and Britain had more colonies. But the addiction to wars, the military and the war machine, foolishly called *defense* instead of *warmongering and imperialism,* has to be fed after only a few years of rest and recuperation. Peace treaties are always a short temporary respite from the norm, which is over ten thousand years of incessant *warmongering.* Unlike Western historians who foolishly think the so-called civilized West prefers peace to war, the question is not what caused a war, such as the First World War, but what excuse did the West invent to pretend that it preferred peace to war? The standard "excuse" given by Western historians for the First World War, for example, is that the presumptive heir to the throne of the declining Austro-Hungarian Empire, Archduke *Franz Ferdinand,* and his wife, *Sophie,* had been assassinated during their state visit to Sarajevo on June 28, 1914. That Western historians would claim that Britain declared war on Germany because of this incident, which was of no consequence to the future prosperity of the world's most powerful empire of the time, is simply ludicrous. Britain, like the United States today, was addicted to warmongering. It needed a new war to feed that addiction. Germany was a possible threat to its imperial hegemony. Kill two birds with one stone. Feed your addition to warmongering and degrade your primary imperial challenger with a single war. The German emperor Wilhelm II was correct in saying that Britain used the Austro-Serb conflict as a **pretext** for waging war on Germany.

The Economics of Imperialism

Lenin had added to Marxism the notion that Capitalism leads to imperialism. See my *Rise and Fall of the American Empire, chapter 9.* Colonies are acquired by capitalist countries both to steal their raw materials and to sell manufactured goods to them. We have claimed that the Western European powers, beginning with Portugal, colonized rather than traded whenever they had the military power to do so, because there was more to gain from theft than from trade. What has been called *Mercantilism* by economists is the system of "trade" whereby an imperial power uses its military power to prevent other nations or empires from "trading" with its colonies. We have argued that this so-called trade was largely theft by military force. We have inserted this section here because the economy played an important role in causing the First World War between Britain and Germany. In our *Rise and Fall of the American Empire* we also argued that it was the decline of the **share** of the world's economy held by the United States that would be the key reason for its ultimate loss of imperial hegemony.

Britain, like the earlier Western imperial powers, had become an economic and industrial giant, both because of its expansive colonial empire and its agricultural and industrial revolutions. During the half century following the Napoleonic wars Britain had been both the dominant industrial and imperial power. But by the second half of the nineteenth century its industrial hegemony was being challenged by both the United States and Germany. Britain viewed the German threat as the more imminent and serious. Prior to the Napoleonic wars Germany was still mostly rural. But after the Napoleonic wars it began to reform its agriculture and crafts as well as industrialize and urbanize as Britain and France had done earlier. One of the most valuable new agricultural crops it began to grow was beet sugar. Britain and France had become rich partly by stealing the tiny islands in the Caribbean to grow cane sugar. Other new high productivity farm products included potatoes and turnips. By the beginning of World War I, Germany had the most efficient agriculture in all of Europe.

In industrializing, Germany followed Britain by beginning with coal, textiles, heavy industry, steel and railways. Coal output dated back to the 1750s. By the late nineteenth century Germany became the largest producer of steel in Europe. The Zollverein created in 1834 broke down the internal barriers to trade, urbanization and economic development. The German railway boom began in the 1840s and boosted the internal expansion of trade, urbanization and economic development begun by the Zollverein. By the First World War, Germany had been transformed into a modern urban state. The government continued to support the trades and crafts as well. Organizing production through *Cartels* was largely a German invention. A cartel is a way for the firms in a single industry to work cooperatively rather than compete with each other. German banks were also allowed to form cartels to raise finance for the industrial cartels. By the First World War there were over five hundred cartels in Germany. Cartels were illegal in both Britain and the United States. Another focus of German industrialization was chemicals. By the First World War Germany had the world's most advanced chemical industry and controlled 90 percent of the global trade in chemicals. But chemicals was not Germany's only example of technological and scientific hegemony. Another measure of its scientific lead was the fact that German scientists received far more Nobel prizes in science than any other country.

A large economic base is a prerequisite for imperial hegemony. But a lot of that economic prosperity must be squandered on the military to defeat your imperial rivals. In the case of Germany, that meant building a navy powerful enough to challenge the Royal Navy. Just before the First World War, Germany compared to Britain much like China today compares to the American Empire. Britain had a long lead in economic, industrial and military development over Germany then, just as the United States today has had a long lead in those same areas compared with China. Just as China today is rapidly gaining on the United States in economic and industrial development Germany narrowed its gap with Britain in economic and industrial output. But just as China today will have to significantly improve its **air power** before going to war with the United States, Germany had to significantly improve its **naval power** before going to war with Britain. Germany was well aware of its naval inferiority compared to the British much as China today is well aware of its air force inferiority compared to the Americans. China will likely engage the Americans in an arms race in the air much like the Germans engaged the British in an arms race at sea in the years leading up to the First World War.

Germany had a lot of catching up to do. The German Empire inherited a tiny navy from Prussia in 1871. It was not until the reign of Emperor *Wilhelm II,* beginning in 1888, that Germany paid much attention to its navy. It's somewhat ironic that Wilhelm's historical family ties with the British monarchy spurred his desire to compete rather than cooperate with his grandmother, *Queen Victoria,* his uncle, *King Edward VII* and his cousin, *King George V,* of Britain. King Edward VII succeeded Wilhelm's grandmother, *Queen Victoria,* in 1901. Wilhelm referred to his uncle somewhat condescending as the *old peacock.* His first cousin, King George V, succeeded Edward VII in 1910. Under the new emperor and Admiral *von Tirpitz* the German navy expanded rapidly. By the beginning of the First World War the German Navy was second only to the Royal Navy. The trigger for the naval arms race between Germany and Britain came from offensive measures by the British much like the offensive measures being taken by the Americans today against China. In 1905 the British began plans for a naval blockade of Germany. Once the First World War began the Royal Navy immediately imposed such a blockade of Germany. In like manner, President Obama announced his intentions of encircling China by expanding American military bases in Australia and Asia. Another similarity between China and the United States today with that of Britain and Germany before World War I was the invention of a new superior weapon by the **aggressor.** In the case of Britain that new weapon was a new type of battle ship called the *dreadnought.* In the case of the United States that new weapon is *unmanned drones.* In 1906 the British launched its first dreadnought. It was seen as a warship so superior to previous warships that every great power decided to build them. By the outbreak of World War I, the British had built twenty-nine dreadnoughts, the Germans had built seventeen, France had built ten, while Russia and Austria had built four each.

But Britain was not simply planning to destroy Germany all on its own. Like the United States in the post–World War II period, where the United States allied with Britain, France, Germany, Japan, Canada, Australia and many other highly developed rich countries, Britain formed an alliance with two other great powers, France and Russia, as well as an alliance with Japan, to ensure the defeat of Germany. There was no hope of Germany winning a war on both its Eastern and Western fronts. France was eager to ally with Britain to avenge its defeat by Prussia in 1871. Russia was eager to ally with Britain to expand its territory eastward into lands previously controlled by the Ottoman Empire. Russia's defeat by Japan in 1905 spurred its interest in an alliance with Britain. This *Triple Entente,* as it was called, began with the earlier alliance between France and Russia we referred to above. That was finalized in January 1894 in response to the 1882 Triple Alliance between Germany, Austria and Italy. The British began with an alliance with Japan in January, 1902. See my *Rise and Fall of the American Empire,* chapters 7 and 8. This was followed by the 1904 *Entente Cordiale* to settle colonial disputes with France. The final alliance was the Anglo-Russian Convention of August 1907 to settle old disputes with Russia over their respective colonizations in India, Afghanistan, Iran, Central Asia and Tibet. By 1907 Britain was allied with Japan, France and Russia against Germany. Under such circumstances it's foolish to suggest that it was Germany, not Britain, which was primarily responsible for the First World War. If you seek the truth about history just assume the opposite of what is written by Western historians.

The result of the First World War was inevitable. It was started by Britain to preserve British imperial hegemony and it succeeded in doing so by Britain forming alliances with other superpowers such as Russia, Japan and France. Germany was defeated but not destroyed. The British succeeded in their propaganda to blame Emperor Wilhelm II for starting the war. Not surprisingly Western historians emphasized atrocities committed by Germany while downplaying atrocities committed by the British and their allies. Emperor Wilhelm II was forced to abdicate and flee to neutral Holland. His cousin, King George V, who had really started the war by declaring war on Germany on August 4, 1914, accused Wilhelm II of being "the greatest criminal in history." This must be the best example of the "kettle calling the pot black." Though Wilhelm's crimes against humanity were far less than those committed by President

Obama and many other American presidents he would have been prosecuted for such crimes had Holland not refused to extradite him.

Proof that the First World War was a war initiated by the British to preserve its imperial hegemony is found in the fact that so much of the war was outside Europe and in the Western held colonies in Africa, the Middle East and Asia. British India alone supplied 1.3 million soldiers and workers to help the British defeat Germany. Both the Indians and Arabs were foolish to think that the British would grant them their independence if they helped Britain to defeat Germany. While India did succeed in getting its independence after the Second World War the Arabs continue to be fooled by the West even today. Having long since abandoned its propaganda that Germany was the devil the West has resorted to a new propaganda tool, *terrorism.* The West replaced Adolf Hitler with Osama Bin Laden to continue its theft of the land, the oil and the other resources of Arab lands. The West also continues to blame Hitler for Israel's theft of Palestinian land and Israel's supreme right to commit the worst crimes imaginable against Palestinians, Arabs and Iranians. Israel has unquestioned support by the civilized West, including Canada. In fact, Canada's prime minister, Steven Harper, is the most ardent and outspoken supporter of Israeli atrocities. But like the United States, Canada would never give up some of the land it stole from the First Nations for Israeli settlements or an independent state of Israel in Canada. Why the Palestinians have to pay for the crimes of Hitler against the Jews is never asked by a subservient, docile and ignorant Western media?

The defeat of Germany in the First World War ensured British imperial hegemony and increased her colonial possessions by transferring many German colonies to Britain. All of the German colonies were stolen but some went to France, Italy, Portugal, Belgium, Japan, Australia, South Africa and New Zealand. Since Australia and New Zealand were colonies of Britain the theft of the German colonies in the Pacific by Australia and New Zealand was really a theft by Britain. Likewise the theft of German South-West Africa by South Africa was really a theft by Britain since South Africa was a British colony. Britain gained most in Africa, confirming our view that the First World War was a war over which Western power would steal the most colonies. The First World

War returned Britain and France to their nineteenth century positions of being the two dominant Western European and colonial powers. But together they would have to fight another war with Germany for European and imperial hegemony. The Second World War would not be as great for Britain and France as the First World War had been. Britain and France would defeat Germany for a second time and maintain their dominant Western European status. But imperial hegemony would be lost to new empires such as the American and Russian empires.

The Second World War for *Imperial Hegemony* and the Surrender of Western European "Leadership" of the World to the American Empire

The British and French had waged war on Germany to destroy Germany's challenge to their respective flaunting of imperial superiority. British and French culture was supposedly superior to all others. Their brash pomposity and bragging had no bounds or limits. They were chosen by God to rule the world and civilize all others. Even to mildly suggest otherwise was a sign of your stupidity and inferior upbringing. All others were born of a lower **caste** or, worse still, **race.** Britain and France had fought many wars for three centuries to steal the imperial hegemony from Portugal, Spain and Holland. Together they had fought each other for first and second place. Neither was willing to see Germany steal either first or second place status. Having won the first war against Germany they were determined to punish Germany severely both for having the audacity to challenge them and to destroy Germany to the point that it could never recover sufficiently to challenge them ever again. How dare a "primitive" race like the Germans think they could ever challenge much less defeat, the far superior British and French races? The Germans had to be taught a civilized lesson by the conquering British and French.

First, all of the colonies of Germany had to be stolen by Britain, France and others so that Germany could never claim to be even a puny empire. Second, some German territory in continental Europe also had to be restolen by France so that France would reclaim its historical status of leading Western European power on the continent. This included the Alsace-Lorraine region lost to Prussia in 1870. To further ensure French dominance, Germany also lost territory to Poland, Belgium, Demark and Czechoslovakia. East Prussia was separated from the rest of Germany by the transfer of German territory, including the city of Danzig, to Poland. At the time 95 percent of the population of Danzig was German. Third, Germany was forced to significantly destroy and permanently reduce the size of its military. Finally, Germany was required to pay such a huge reparation amount to permanently weaken its economy. These punitive peace terms were denounced by the world's leading economist, *John Maynard Keynes,* who was British. Germany was plagued by hyperinflation partly as a result of the punitive peace terms.

Britain and France had made **two** serious mistakes in launching their pompous war against Germany. While they had punished and severely degraded the German economy, military and territory in Europe and overseas, they had benefitted far less from the war than the American Empire. While the British and French economies had been severely weakened by the immense resources shifted from useful production to armaments and fighting, the Americans supplied munitions and other exports to Europe, both during the war and after the war. This was a big boost to the American economy. A bigger American economy meant a bigger sustainable American Empire. Smaller British and French economies meant smaller sustainable empires. Furthermore the Americans began to lend and invest heavily in rebuilding the German economy. The second mistake was to ask the colonies to help them fight Germany. The colonial people in both the British and French colonies participated mostly to increase their bargaining power to become independent countries. In time, Britain and France lost more territory than Germany as a result of the colonial independence movements inspired by the participation of the British and French colonial peoples in defeating Germany.

Germans are no less warmongering than the British or French. The Germans had been humiliated by their military defeat, punitive peace terms and the insistence of Britain and France that Germany had been solely responsible for the war. The last was a blatant lie. The war was caused far more by Britain and France than by Germany. Britain and France had far more to lose if Germany's political, economic and military rise was not stopped by war. Germany's punitive peace terms imposed by Britain and France were compounded by the economic disaster of the *Great Depression.* The economies of all three countries, Germany, Britain and France, were devastated by the Great Depression. High unemployment rates and lost output caused significant declines in incomes while the stock market crash of 1929 ruined the wealthy. In Germany the unemployment rate peaked at 30 percent of the labor force. The Americans, also hit by the Great Depression, were unable to continue their loans and investment in Germany and demanded repayment of earlier loans. Germans turned to Adolf Hitler and the Nazis to solve their severe economic problems.

The *Nationalist Socialist German Workers' Party* was founded in 1920. It had begun the year before as the German **Workers'** Party. Many countries in Europe had been struggling to embrace **communism** and socialism to reduce income and wealth inequalities produced by the industrial revolution. In October 1918, Germany had experienced a revolution similar to that of the Russian revolution of 1917. Socialism was extremely popular with many Germans and the establishment feared a **communist** government similar to that in Russia. In Munich the revolution forced the king of Bavaria to flee the city. At that time Munich was the capital city of the Kingdom of Bavaria. Vladimir Lenin had lived in Munich and in February of 1919 the Soviet-style *Bavarian Soviet Republic* was established. Communism did not succeed in Germany but Munich became the city in which Hitler and the National **Socialists** initially flourished. It was the city in which the Nazi Party staged the coup to overthrow the German government in 1923. The Nazi Party was an effort to combine the **socialist** ideals with nationalism. The **racist** roots of the Nazi Party were definitely not unique. All of the countries in the West embraced **racism.** The worst example was the United States, born out of both African and First Nations slavery, and deep seated **racism** against all nonwhite races. Both Canada and the United States maintained a white majority only by using extremely **racist** immigration policies. Racism directed against Jews was also very common in all of the Western countries.

The Nazi opposition to **communism** was also not unique in the West. The United States was the leading Western country opposed to communism. The United States had stolen First Nations lands by disputing the notion of *communal property rights.* The First Nations in North America did not embrace private property rights. By promoting the sanctity of private property over communal property both Canada and the United States justified their theft of First Nations lands and resources. Communism was born in the West with the writings of Karl Marx. All of the countries in the West worked toward greater income equality to discourage their poor from embracing communism. They allowed labor unions, as well as a growing public sector, as alternatives to communism, in reducing income and wealth inequality. They also used their excellent propaganda skills to demonize communism. The state used their immense legal and policing powers to threaten, intimidate and punish severely, any who dared to embrace communism. They invaded Russia to defeat the communists by military force. They refused to trade, invest or engage in economic and financial exchanges with countries which embraced communism. The Nazi Party, therefore, had much in common, both in terms of their strong racist and anti-Semitic views, as well as their strong anti-Communist views, with all of the Western countries. It's important that we stress that from the beginning because our explanation for the Second World War, like our explanation for the First World War, is **not** Hitler or Nazism, but Germany's challenge to Britain and France for **imperial hegemony.**

A second distorted fact is the reason given for the alliance between Germany and Italy. This alliance, like the Second World War, had absolutely nothing to do with **Fascism** or **Nazism.** It was not Fascism and Nazism which drew Hitler and Mussolini to each other. It was the imperial greed of Britain and France which pushed these two leaders to join each other in the scramble for empire. Italy had very little to show for switching its alliance from Germany to Britain and France during the First World War. British and French greed had left little of the spoils of the First World War for Italy. Mussolini was well aware of that. When Hitler had shown his interest in unifying Germany and Austria it was Mussolini who had supported those in Austria who wanted an independent Austria. Only when it was crystal clear to Mussolini that British and French greed would keep not only Germany from acquiring a colonial empire, but also Italy out of Africa, did Mussolini see the obvious need for an alliance of Italy and Germany against British and

French greed. I have no reason to support any empire but to fall for the standard Western propaganda that Britain and America fought the Nazis and Fascists to save mankind rather than for their own selfish imperial hegemony, is to be more naïve than a kindergarten child.

Adolf Hitler became the leader of the Nazi party on July 26, 1921, replacing the founding leader, Anton Drexler. Hitler had joined the German Workers' Party, the precursor of the Nazi Party, on September 12, 1919. After leaving the German army in March 1920, Hitler worked full time for the Nazi Party. The Treaty of Versailles ending the First World War was extremely unpopular in Germany, and justifiably so. Hitler was a decorated veteran of that war and spoke out passionately in public against the peace treaty. His vitriolic public speeches attracted many to the Nazi Party. Hitler was arrested and imprisoned after he led a failed coup, the *Beer Hall Putsch,* against the German government. He was later pardoned by the Bavarian Supreme Court and released on December 20, 1924. But he was ordered by the state not to speak publicly. In prison he wrote the first volume of the two volumes of *Mein Kampf.* These were published in 1925 and 1926. In the book, Hitler urged the German people to oppose the punitive Versailles peace treaty and restore nationalist pride in their country. After Hitler's attempted coup, the German government banned the Nazi Party. This ban was lifted after Hitler agreed to the Nazi Party engaging in **democratic** elections only.

As the German economy improved between 1924 and 1928, the democratic support for the Nazi Party declined from thirty-two seats in the Reichstag to twelve seats. The Great Depression was therefore the miracle which led to the **democratic** election of the Nazi Party as Germany's ruling political party. Its seats in the Reichstag increased from 12 in 1928 to 288 in 1933. In 1928 the Nazi Party secured a mere 2.6 percent of the votes. Two years later it had risen to second place with over 18 percent of the votes and 107 seats in the Reichstag. The western demonization of the Nazi party is another prime example of the very **selective,** limited and restrictive nature of western democracy. When a political party liked by the west is democratically elected the West will glorify its democratic system. But if that same democratic system elects a political party disliked by the west the West will find a way to demonize that party. In the case of the **Nazi party** it used Nazism. In the case of **Hamas** it used terrorism. In the case of the **Muslim Brotherhood** it used Islamic extremism.

In1932 Hitler contested the presidential elections. The election was won by von Hindenburg but Hitler got 35 percent of the votes. As a result of Hitler's popularity, Hindenburg appointed Hitler as chancellor. In addition, two other strong Nazi Party members, Hermann Goring and Wilhelm Frick, were appointed as ministers. In the next general election of March 6, 1933, the Nazi Party increased its share of the votes to 44 percent from 35 percent in the year before. Hindenburg died on August 2, 1934. Hitler took the title of *Fuhrer,* merging the powers of president and chancellor. As head of state, Hitler became the supreme commander of the armed forces. Germany was imitating the United States where the position of *commander in chief* is far more significant for a dedicated warmonger, like the American Empire. See "The Washington Syndrome" in my *Rise and Fall of the American Empire,* chapter 4. Despite all of the hand wringing and denials by Western historians, Hitler came to power in Germany in a way not much different from the process whereby George Washington came to power in the United States. Germany and Hitler are demonized only because Germany lost the Second World War. Washington, Roosevelt, and the United States are revered because the United States won the Second World War. In my view the dropping of nuclear bombs on Hiroshima and Nagasaki by the United States is no less evil than gassing Jews in concentration camps. One of the key premises of my books is that the West deems as civilized only nations and empires able to win wars. The United States emerged as the civilized nation after the Second World War because it had the more civilized military weapon, nuclear bombs. It continues to be civilized today because it has unmanned drones and the capacity to bomb at will every country "back to the stone age" as it did to Iraq and threatened to do to Pakistan during its invasion of Afghanistan and Iraq.

Hitler's expansion of Germany into adjacent areas was far less than what the United States did after its independence from Britain. The United States expanded all across the continent stealing every piece of land populated by the First Nations. It then conquered more First Nations lands in Mexico. American invasions of First Nations lands were no less brutal or barbaric than Hitler's conquests in Europe. Of course, it is somewhat easier for the West to demonize the "naked red savage" than the white race in Poland, Denmark, Norway, Holland, Belgium, Luxembourg, or France. But if Hitler's actions were criminal, while those of the United States were not, simply because Hitler invaded and conquered lands populated by "whites," rather than lands populated by "reds," as the United States had done, then this is simply another evidence of white **racism.** The same can be said about the use of slave labor. Hitler used slave labor during the Second World War just as the Americans had used slave labor until their civil war. But American slaves were mostly **blacks,** with a minority of **reds.** Hitler used whites as slaves.

Under Hitler's leadership, unemployment in Germany fell from a high of six million in 1932 to one million in 1936. As the new chancellor, Hitler introduced both an easy money policy and an expansionary fiscal policy to increase spending and reduce the unemployment rate. Hitler began a reindustrialization of Germany modeled on the mass production of consumer durable goods in the United States. Middle-class German consumers would buy the same consumer durables as their American counterparts and this would both improve their standard of living while creating new jobs in industry. Next he focused on a car cheap enough for the German middle class consumer as Henry Ford had done in the United States. This was the famous *Volkswagen Beetle.* Hitler announced in 1933 that he wanted a "People's Car" produced cheaply for the average German consumer. When it could not be done by private enterprise he created a state-owned factory to build it.

Unfortunately, the outbreak of the Second World War made it necessary to switch production from cars to military vehicles. Hitler also rebuilt the infrastructure of the German economy which had been destroyed by World War I, punitive peace terms, and the Great Depression. Hitler was ready to return Germany to its pre–World War I position in Europe. This implied scrapping the terms of the Versailles treaty and recapturing lands lost both on the continent of Europe and its colonies outside Europe. It also meant a massive rearmament program. Such a program not only rearmed Germany but created jobs for the millions unemployed by the Great Depression. Britain and France would be willing to wage another war against Germany to prevent Germany from returning to its pre–World War I status. It was Germany's rise as a new European power that had so threatened the Anglo-French domination of the world, which had caused the First World War. Britain viewed these wars with Germany in the same light as its earlier wars with France, Holland, and Spain. Had the United States not emerged as the new world power after the Second World War, Britain would surely have engaged Germany in as many wars as it had engaged France and Holland.

The sad reality was that the Western European states fought each other for imperial hegemony since Portugal became the first worldwide colonial power. There was absolutely no reason for this to end if the United States had not become so big that it was simply no contest between this imposing giant and any one of the earlier Western European empires. Furthermore, since the American Empire stole the entire world outside Western Europe, there were no colonies left for the Western European empires to fight over. But Britain, France and Germany never expected the Second World War to change anything. Since Portugal became the first colonial power, Portugal, Spain, Holland, France, Britain and Germany, had fought more than a hundred wars among themselves. They had no reason to expect that this would end. The Second World War, as far as Britain and France were concerned, was simply, "business as usual." One side would win and there would be a peace treaty to rest up and prepare for the other war. The only certainty, at the time, was that one war would always be followed by another, and another. A war to end all wars is a dumb myth. The Second World War ended the wars among the Western European states not because it was intended to do that but because of the unexpected rise of the American Empire to such a humungous size that any challenge of the American Empire by one of the previously powerful Western European empires would be the equivalent of a dwarf challenging a giant.

German Territorial Expansion under Hitler

Western historians have blamed Adolf Hitler's conquests in Austria, Czechoslovakia and Poland for causing the Second World War. No such blame has ever been levied against the United States, despite its territorial expansion across a whole continent and into the Pacific. Hitler's territorial expansion, by comparison to those of the United States, was puny. See my *American Invasions: Canada to Afghanistan.* Nor have Western historians chastised Britain or France, in the same manner that they chastised Germany and Adolf Hitler, for their theft of most of Asia and Africa. Was this yet another example of blatant racism based on the fact that the people of Africa and Asia were not white?

It seems natural to me that Hitler would begin his territorial expansion of Germany with **German** Austria. Germany and **German** Austria had a long symbiotic relationship not unlike the Southern and Northern states of the United States. The Republic of **German-Austria** was created in late 1918 after the collapse of the Austro-Hungarian Empire during World War I. The term "German-Austria" had been used by Austrian Germans living in the Austro-Hungarian Empire. The Allies had defeated the Austro-Hungarian Empire and German Austrians wanted an independent state of their own. They created a provisional National Assembly in October 1918 and elected Karl Renner as chancellor. The Austro-Hungarian union had been terminated by the creation of the Democratic Republic of Hungary and the resignation of Emperor Charles I of Austria. Article 2 of the provisional constitution of the Republic of **German Austria** implied a union with Germany. This union which the German people wanted was prevented by the Allies. Yet these same Allies have glorified a union between the Southern and Northern states of the United States imposed by military force against the wishes of the Americans of the Southern Confederate States. President Lincoln is glorified worldwide as the savior of a union kept together only by military force and a brutal civil war. Hitler had the far greater moral right to unify Germany with Austria based on the expressed wishes of the German people of Austria in 1918, compared to Lincoln, who had to use military force to keep the Southern Americans in a union which they opposed.

Germans in Austria and Germany never gave up on their desire to be unified and this was yet another sore point among Germans with regard to the 1919 Treaty of Versailles. An example of this is the **German Workers' Party.** The original German Worker's Party was created in Austria, not Germany. As the name suggests it was made up of workers and trade unionists. While its origins date back to the German National Workers' League of 1893, its new name, German Workers' Party, dates back to 1903. The name was changed again in 1918 to the *German National Socialist Party,* DNSAP. As I pointed out above it was not until 1919 that the German Workers' Party was created in Germany. Like its earlier Austrian counterpart it too changed its name to the *National Socialist German Workers' Party,* NSDAP, in 1920. Most members of the Austrian DNSAP supported the German NSDAP led by Adolf Hitler. The West did not like Adolf Hitler but the Germans in both Austria and Germany liked him. Hitler's unification of Austria with Germany in 1938 was supported by a greater percent of Austrians than Lincoln's unification of the United States in 1865 was supported by Americans in the Southern states. When the West speaks of democracy and the right to self-determination it speaks with a forked tongue. *Allende* in Chile, *Hamas* in Palestine and the *Muslim Brotherhood* in Egypt are just a few examples of democratically elected governments opposed by the West just as the right to self-determination by the German people was denied by the West. The West has always, and will always, overthrow a democracy and impose a dictatorship if that suits its purpose.

The strong desire of Austrians to unify Austria with Germany began long before Adolf Hitler. What came to be called the "German Question" was a discussion over the best way of unifying Germans in Austria and in the German states beginning with the War of the Austrian Succession of 1740–1748. The many movements toward unification through the post-Napoleonic *German Confederation, Austro-Prussian War* and the creation of the *German Empire* in 1871, was terminated unilaterally by the Allies with the 1919 Treaty of Versailles. It was a termination imposed by the superior military force of the Allies. It had absolutely nothing to do with self-determination or democracy. Its primary purpose was to maintain the imperial hegemony of Britain and France. This imposed military separation of Austria and Germany led to the creation of the First Republic of Austria and the Greater German People's Party in 1920. The Greater German People's Party supported unification with Germany. Many of its members switched to the German National Socialist Party, DNSAP, beginning in the 1930s. The DNSAP continued to push for unification with Germany.

Another political party, the *Social Democratic Workers' Party of Austria,* **SDAPO,** also pushed for unification with Germany. Like the National Socialists, DNSAP, the Social Democrats, SDAPO, represented the lower income working class. Like the *Communist Party of Austria,* **KPO,** the SDAPO was pro-Marxist. The KPO was founded in 1918, only a year after the Russian revolution. It was less popular than the SDAPO and DNSAP and did not support unification with Germany. The other political party opposed to unification with Germany was the *Christian Social Party.* The Christian Social Party was both conservative and Catholic. It opposed unification with Germany on religious grounds since it was Catholic and Germany was largely Protestant. An interesting development in Austria during the 1930s was what came to be called **Austrofascism.** This was a move by the Christian Social Party to imitate Italian fascism and court the support of Benito Mussolini in opposing unification with Germany. In May 1932 *Engelbert Dollfuss* of the Christian Social Party became chancellor of Austria. He managed to establish a fascist dictatorship in Austria modeled on that of Mussolini in Italy. In August 1933 Mussolini issued a guarantee of Austrian independence. The banning of other political parties in Austria by Dollfuss led to a brief civil war in Austria in 1934. Dollfuss was assassinated in July 1934 but his dictatorship was continued under his successor, *Kurt von Schuschnigg.*

Prelude to Hitler's Invasion of Austria in 1938

Hitler became the chancellor of Germany on January 30, 1933, during the height of the Great Depression. His NSDAP party was **democratically** elected by the German people. The economy matters to voters and the government of the Weimar Republic had failed to deal with the massive unemployment problem. The unemployment rate exceeded 30 percent of the work force when Hitler took over the government. The Weimar Republic governed Germany after the First World War. It was a democratic government with an elected National Assembly located in the German city of Weimar in the state of Thuringia. After the communist-style revolutions in 1918 and 1919 the city of Weimar was chosen by the democratic government as a more peaceful and safer city compared with Munich or Berlin. The governing structure of the Weimar Republic was considered to be one of the most democratic of its time. Its president was elected by the people every seven years. Every German citizen over the age of twenty had the right to vote. The president appointed the chancellor, who was the prime minister or leader of the government. The members of the *Reichstag* were elected by the people every four years. The less powerful second chamber of parliament was made up of representatives from the seventeen states in Germany.

Proportional representation led to as many as forty parties securing seats in the Reichstag. Coalition governments were the norm. In the 1920 elections the three parties with the most seats were the SPD, *Social Democratic Party,* with 103; the USPD, *Independent Social Democratic Party,* with 83; and the DNVP, *National People's Party,* with 71. The total seats were 459. The SPD continued to win the majority of seats in the Reichstag in the elections of 1924 and 1928. It was the most popular of the many left leaning socialist parties in Germany. Most of the chancellors had come from the SPD or a coalition which included the SPD. The DNVP moved up to second place in the 1924 and 1928 elections. It was the primary opposition party in the Reichstag. The Weimar Republic struggled to govern Germany both because of the heavy burdens imposed on Germany by the peace treaty and because of one of the worst examples of hyperinflation in history. But by 1924 Germany was on the mend and had had five years of relative economic prosperity when it was hit by the Great Depression. It was the Great Depression which led German voters to turn to Hitler's *National Socialist* Party. His party increased its popular vote for seats in the *Reichstag* to 19 percent in the 1930 elections. Given the large number of parties contesting the elections, 19 percent was huge. Only the SPD received a larger percent of the popular vote. The SPD secured 143 of the 577 seats while NSDAP got 107 of the seats. The third largest party with 77 seats was the KPD, *Communist Party of Germany.* The KPD had improved from 4 seats in 1920 to 45 in 1924 to 54 in 1928.

In the July 31, 1932, elections Hitler's NSDAP got the majority of seats in the Reichstag. For the first time the SPD fell to second place with 133 seats compared to 230 seats for the NSDAP. The KPD continued to hold third place with 89 seats. The short-lived government led by Chancellor Franz von Papen dissolved the Reichstag after losing a vote of no confidence and called for new elections in the fall of 1932. The NSDAP continued its dominance in the Reichstag by winning 196 of the 584 seats in the November 6, 1932, elections. The SPD continued to be in second place with 121 seats and the KPD improved its third place position with one hundred seats. Kurt von Schleicher became the new chancellor on December 3, 1932, replacing von Papen, who now supported Hitler for chancellor, since Hitler's party had won the most seats in both of the elections in 1932. Kurt von Schleicher was forced to resign on January 28, 1933. Hitler's lobby for the chancellorship was backed not only by von Papen but also by the leader of the conservative DNVP party, *Alfred Hugenberg.* The DNVP party had supported the chancellorship of von Papen. But it had fallen from second place in the Reichstag in 1928 to fifth place in the November 1932 elections, winning only 52 seats. Without some kind of coalition with the NSDAP it had no hope of participating in the government of Germany.

Hitler agreed to Hugenberg's demand to be minister of Economics and Agriculture in his cabinet. Franz von Papen was given the vice chancellorship post. In the elections of March 5, 1933, the NSDAP increased its seats from 196 to 288. With the DNVP maintaining its 52 seats the NSDAP/DNVP coalition had a majority of 340 seats out of a total of 647. Hugenberg and von Papen supported the *Enabling Act* of March 23, which ended the Weimar Republic and replaced it with the *Third Reich.* The vote in the Reichstag in favor of the Enabling Act was 444. It got more than the required two-thirds majority as only ninety-four deputies voted against. The Enabling Act allowed the government to pass legislation without the approval of the Reichstag. Three months later Germany became a one-party state as all political parties except the NSDAP were banned. Like the United States and other Western countries, Hitler blamed the **communists** for justifying his crackdown on freedom. The West had felt threatened by communism since Karl Marx had published *das Kapital* in 1867. Communism was the scapegoat for American invasions across the globe. Hitler's invasions pale by comparison to those of the American Empire. But while Britain and the West were quite happy to have Hitler crack down on the communists,

Britain feared Germany's challenge to its imperial hegemony. The West cared little about Jews or communists. It made war on Hitler not because of what Hitler did to the Jews or the communists but because a Germany led by Hitler was a threat to British dominance of the world. The evidence of this is clear to any objective analyst.

Whether the world was ruled by Britain or France or Germany or the United States made little difference to the colonies populated by **nonwhites** in the Third World. But it mattered to Britain. Britain declared war on Germany to keep its imperial hegemony. The key difference between Britain and Hitler's Germany is what makes President Obama different from President George W. Bush. President Obama is a *Natural Born Liar,* much like the British are *Natural Born Liars.* Hitler and George W. Bush cannot lie nearly as well. The West likes those who are **hypocrites** and lie about the true intentions of their actions. Be mean, nasty, brutish, racist, anti-Semitic, dictatorial, warmongering and immoral but use the well-honed Western propaganda machine to make the world think you are the opposite. Hitler and Bush refused to play the part of the hypocrite. They were vilified not because of what they did, since every Western leader has done exactly the same, but because they refused to lie about what they did. As early as 1933 Germany was seen as a threat to the imperial hegemony of Britain and France. At the *London Economic Conference* of June 1933, Hitler's minister of Economics, Hugenberg, put forth the idea that Germany would conquer colonies in Eastern Europe and Africa as part of its program to end the Great Depression in Germany. Britain and France naturally disagreed.

In 1933 Germany was far too weak economically and militarily to challenge either Britain or France. Hitler was forced to disavow the statements of his Minster of Economics at the London Conference, related to Germany's intention of acquiring colonies. Hugenberg resigned from Hitler's cabinet on June 27, 1933, and was replaced as minister of Economics by *Kurt Schmitt.* Hitler's priority was the German economy and the Great Depression. He had continued the appointment of *Hjalmar Schacht* as president of the German Central Bank, the Reichsbank. Schacht had implemented an easy money policy of low interest rates to dig the German economy out of the Great Depression. Schacht also subscribed to the Keynesian macroeconomic model of increasing government spending and budget deficits to create jobs for the unemployed. In the United States, President Roosevelt had created the "New Deal" based on the ideas of Keynes. In August 1934 Hitler replaced Schmitt with Schacht as minister of Economics. Schacht introduced the "New Plan" to get the German economy out of the Great Depression. He began a massive construction program which created more than a million new jobs in the construction industry. Public Works combined with military expenditures reduced unemployment and ended the Great Depression in Germany. On March 7, 1936, Hitler sent his troops to reoccupy the demilitarized zone in the Rhineland, and in July of that same year, he began sending military aid to help General Franco in the Spanish Civil War. The German auto industry also began to boom and created more jobs. Hitler supported rising real incomes for the working class in Germany. He wanted them to have all of the household appliances which the American working class had. This enabled the working class to have the income needed to buy the new consumer durable goods while creating even more jobs in manufacturing.

Hitler's Invasion of Austria, Czechoslovakia, and Poland: 1938–1939

While we do not agree that Hitler's invasions of Austria, Czechoslovakia and Poland was the cause of World War II it's necessary to cover the invasions briefly. It was March of 1938 when Germany annexed Austria. The German army entered Austria on March 12, 1938. Since the annexation was popular with the majority of Austrians there was no military opposition. In fact, the German troops were publicly welcomed by the people. Hitler was born in Austria and returned to his birthplace that same day. He was welcomed by the Austrians. He spent three days on a public "meet and greet" tour of Austria. Hitler was somewhat surprised at how popular he was with the Austrian people. It was the exact opposite of Lincoln's annexation of the Southern states which had seceded from the United States. Lincoln was hated by most of the Americans in the South. Yet, the West vilifies Hitler for annexing Austria but adores Lincoln for his brutal invasion and conquest of the American South. This example of Western hypocrisy has little to do with the personalities or morality of Hitler and Lincoln. Both were men without principles or morality. But Hitler was vilified because the British controlled the media and the unification of Germany and Austria threatened British global thefts of land and resources from defenseless people. Hitler wanted to steal like the British and French had done. In the case of Lincoln the American Empire controlled the media and a unified United States would be a far more powerful colonizing thief than two independent countries. In fact, the Southern States were far less imperialist than the Northern States.

The addition of Austria into the Third Reich helped Germany's redevelopment of its economy and military by adding agricultural land, iron ore and other raw materials, foreign reserves and potential soldiers. But Hitler was no less greedy than the British or French and wanted more territory for Germany just as the British and French had insatiable appetites for overseas colonies. Hitler's next annexation for his planned eastern expansion of Germany was Czechoslovakia. As in Austria, many Germans lived in the *Sudetenland* region of Czechoslovakia. The allies had created the new state of Czechoslovakia after World War I and ignored the rights of the 3 million Germans residing there. Germans had lived in the region since the thirteenth century, far longer than Americans had lived in Texas before demanding secession from Mexico. In addition, the percent of Americans living in Texas in 1845 when the United States added Texas as its twenty-eighth state, was less than the percent of Germans living in the Sudetenland when Hitler added it to Germany. Yet U.S. president *Woodrow Wilson* had supported the creation of an independent state of Czechoslovakia as another punitive measure against the German people for Germany losing the First World War. In addition, the United States invaded and defeated Mexico on the battlefield to colonize Texas. Not so with Germany. Like Austria, the Germans in Sudetenland formed their own Nationalist Party, the *Sudeten German Party, SdP,* under the leadership of *Konrad Henlein.*

By 1935 the SdP had become the second largest party in Czechoslovakia. The Germans fully supported unification of Sudetenland with Germany and they were the majority population living there. Henlein met Hitler in Berlin on March 28, 1938, to discuss unification. They were supporting the principle of *self-determination* and it was difficult for Britain and France to argue against their case. As a result Hitler was able to negotiate the Munich Agreement with Britain and France on September 29, 1938. The influential *Time Magazine* declared Hitler "Man of the Year" for 1938. Sudetenland became part of Germany. It provided valuable additional resources, especially iron and steel, to aid Germany's economic and military advancement. Once again there had been no need for a military conflict because the transfer of Sudetenland to Germany was as popular with the people of Sudetenland as the transfer of Austria had been. In both cases the majority of the population were Germans. The Munich Agreement had been brokered by the British prime minister *Neville Chamberlain.* He has been vilified by Western historians for "appeasing" Hitler. At the same time Sir Winston Churchill, who replaced Chamberlain as British prime minister in May 1940, has been hailed as Britain's most important statesman. This view is yet another piece of evidence that the West always favors war over peace. Chamberlin foolishly believed Western hypocrisy about its desire for peace. Churchill was a dedicated **warmonger.** That is the only reason he has been admired and Chamberlin vilified.

Wars are extremely popular with the electorate in every Western country. Chamberlain was forced to resign because he led a group of British politicians still pursuing peace. Churchill replaced him because Churchill vehemently opposed any and all peace proposals. Churchill became Britain's greatest wartime prime minister because he enjoyed warmongering more than anything else. He was the quintessential warmonger. Those historians who coined the term "Appeasement" as a result of Chamberlain's failure in preventing World War II have no understanding of the addiction of the West to warmongering. As we have pointed out above there is always the need for a period of rest, recuperation, and rearmament after every major war. Prior to World War II the Western nations were simply resting, recuperating, and rearming after World War I. It was simply a matter of time until the next war. World War II did not take place because the Germans chose Adolf Hitler as their Fuhrer or because of the rise of the Nazi Party in Germany. It took place because incessant warmongering has been, and continues to be, the normal state of affairs in the so-called civilized West.

Hitler did not stop adding territory to Germany after adding the Sudetenland. Why should he? The British, French or Americans would not have stopped. The Americans did not stop adding First Nations lands after they got their independence from Britain. The British did not stop colonizing after their conquests in the New World. The French did not stop after their many conquests in Asia and Africa. All Western leaders conquered, colonized, invaded, subjugated and committed countless crimes against humanity. Why should Germany be any different? Hitler knew this and so did Mussolini. Hitler and Mussolini were as Western and civilized as British, American and French leaders. To be Western and civilized you had to invade, conquer and colonize. Even today the American Empire can justify a global war on "terrorism" because a few Americans were killed on September 11, 2001. All other leaders must follow like sheep or be demonized like the leader of North Korea. This massive global killing led by the West today is the exact opposite of civilized behavior. Hitler's madness pales by comparison. A few people manage to fly some planes into two American skyscrapers and the world goes insane.

The reason for the insanity is not the attack on the Twin towers but the long standing behavior of Western leaders since the Portuguese began to colonize Africa in the fifteenth century. Hitler and Mussolini were not exceptions to Western leadership. They were the very essence of the character, behavior, and morality of **every** Western leader since the fifteenth century. Hitler was simply following in the footsteps of the Americans, British and French when he decided that Poland was a militarily feasible addition to the German Empire. Why should the German invasion and colonization of Poland be any more of a crime against humanity than the theft of First Nations lands by the Americans and Canadians or the colonization of Asia and Africa by the British and French? In my view they are equally criminal. But the West also had a long history of fighting each other ever since the Portuguese competed with the Spanish. France and Britain felt that Germany was taking too much of the imperial spoils. If Hitler took Poland he had to be stopped from taking more. After all there was only one world, and if the Germans got more the British and French would get less. Hitler was well aware that Western leaders always justified their warmongering. He therefore argued that Germany had a legitimate concern about Poland's discrimination against ethnic Germans in Poland and Poland's policy of forced assimilation. In 1934 Hitler had signed the German-Polish Non-Aggression Pact in an attempt to reason with Poland for better treatment of Germans in Poland.

One of the many punitive actions imposed on Germany for losing World War I was taking away the City of Danzig and splitting Germany from East Prussia by what has been called the "Polish Corridor." The primary beneficiary of territory lost by Germany because of World War I was Poland. Poland had received most of West Prussia and Posen, an area of almost twenty-one thousand square miles and over 4 million people. Hitler rightly wanted some of that territory back. Danzig was a port city with a majority German population. Hitler campaigned for the return of Danzig and the "Polish Corridor" to Germany. Hitler used the same argument for annexing the German-majority Free City of Danzig in Poland, as he had used for annexing Austria and the Sudetenland. That argument was that the people of Danzig favored unification with Germany and Hitler complained that Poland was violating their sovereignty and right to self-determination. When Poland refused to negotiate with Hitler, Germany invaded Poland on September 1, 1939.

Britain and France now had the excuse they needed to begin another war against Germany. They had rested up and rearmed sufficiently since the end of World War I. It was time to feed their addiction to warmongering. They declared war on Germany two days after the German invasion of Poland. Hitler was no more of a warmonger than the leaders of Britain and France. The Second World War was never a war for freedom or a war to end wars or any other of that propaganda hogwash. It was a continuation of wars by Western European powers for colonies begun by Portugal and Spain, and continued by Holland, France and Britain. It's no coincidence that one piece of Western propaganda at the Nuremburg Trials was that Germany had allied with Japan to divide the world between them. After all, Portugal and Spain had done just that with the 1494 *Treaty of Tordesillas.* Nothing has changed since that treaty. In 1494 Western historians would have identified Portugal and Spain as the two most civilized countries. In the Second World War these same Western historians would have identified Britain, France, Germany,

Japan, and the United States as the most civilized countries. It supports our contention that to be deemed civilized by the West you must be a dedicated warmonger. The more wars you win the more civilized you are. Wars are games played by civilized people who care little for the death and destruction they inflict on the innocent and helpless. If anything, the modern technology associated with unmanned drones, fighter jets and WMDs has made wars much more of a **game** for military and political leaders, the military industrial complex, and soldiers and their families, to better feed their addiction today compared with 1494.

World War II Began *Not* with Hitler but with Western Imperialism in the Horn of Africa

The West was hell bent on invading and colonizing all of Africa much as it had done in all of the New World. Its colonization of the countries in the Horn of Africa is yet another piece of evidence that the Second World had absolutely nothing to do with freedom and everything to do with five centuries of Western imperialism and warmongering. In just one country in the Horn of Africa, there was **British** Somaliland, **French** Somaliland and **Italian** Somaliland. What more proof does anyone need? Today the West, now led by the American Empire, continues to invade, bomb, humiliate, destroy and impoverish, the people eking out a miserable living in the Horn of Africa. President Obama now uses unmanned drones to continue the killing of innocent people begun by the Portuguese, Dutch, French, British and Italians in this piece of Africa jutting out into the Arabian Sea. The West cannot blame any of this on Adolf Hitler, much as they have tried to. Western warmongering is a disease and an addiction. It invents excuses to feed its addiction and insatiable appetite. How ridiculous to think that people in this poverty stricken region can ever have the military capability to ever invade the West?

The British, French, Belgians and other Western Europeans had stolen most of Africa and the Italians wanted some of that booty. After the Italians had created the unified *Kingdom of Italy* in 1861, it felt militarily powerful enough to compete with Britain and France for thefts in Africa. Naturally, the British and French were far too greedy thieves not to resist a new competitor. The Italians began with *Eritrea,* one of the four countries in the Horn of Africa. Italians began with the strategic port city of Assab in 1869. Italians began to settle in Asmara and formally colonized Eritrea in 1890. As with all of the Western European imperialists, the Italian Catholic church helped the colonization process by converting the colonized Eritreans to their Christian God. By the beginning of World War II, there were about one hundred thousand Italian settlers in Eritrea. Italian colonization of Eritrea was taken as a threat to British and French thefts in Africa. Eritrea lay between the British colony of Sudan and the French colony of French Somaliland. There were regular military conflicts between the Italians and French in the areas bordering their respective colonies. The French had begun its colonization of French Somaliland in 1862. Formal French colonization took place between 1883 and 1894 when the permanent French administration of the colony was established in the city of *Djibouti.* French Somaliland is now the independent country of Djibouti in the Horn of Africa. It has a current population of about one million compared to Eritrea with a current population over five million.

British Somaliland was immediately south of the French colony. The British stole the land for this colony in 1888. Today it is part of Somalia, another independent country in the Horn of Africa with a current population of about ten million. Italian Somaliland was further south of British Somaliland. The Italians also stole the land in 1888 both to expand their African empire and to compete with the British and French. The ports in Italian Somaliland gave the Italians access both to the Gulf of Aden and to the Suez Canal. In 1960 British Somaliland in the north and Italian Somaliland in the south were united to become the independent country of the *Somali Republic,* with its capital in *Mogadishu,* the city which became infamous for *Black Hawk Down.* In 1993 a U.S. attempt to recolonize Somalia was defeated when the Somalis shot down the American Black Hawk helicopters. The Americans had to be rescued by the Pakistanis. President George W. Bush "repaid" the Pakistanis by threatening to bomb their country back to the Stone Age. Today President Obama is continuing "repayment" by bombing the Pakistanis with unmanned drones.

African countries, like Vietnam did, find themselves having to fight U.S. imperialism after defeating European imperialism. While the Second World War weakened the Western European empires sufficiently to enable their colonies to defeat them militarily and gain their independence, the powerful American Empire has allied itself with the weakened Western European empires to recolonize many of these ex-Western European colonies. That second fight for independence is on-going today in Africa, the Middle East, Asia and Latin America. So far, only the Vietnamese and China have been relatively successful in defeating the post–World War II Western imperialists. Even economically advanced countries like Japan and South Korea are semicolonized by the West. And countries like China and Vietnam often have to suck up to the West even when it's not in their interest to do so. The only leader tough enough to stand up to the constant bullying by the West has been Vladimir Putin of Russia. There has never been a bigger bully than the American Empire since the dawn of time.

The Italians wanted to expand outward from their base in Eritrea to colonize Ethiopia, the most populous country in the Horn of Africa. Its current population is close to 90 million. Initially, Italian attempts to conquer Ethiopia failed. Italy lost the first war against Ethiopia in 1895. But in 1911, Italy colonized Libya by defeating the Ottoman Empire. Italian settlers poured into Libya, especially the coastal regions close to the Mediterranean Sea, taking with them Catholic Christianity. In World War I, Italy was cheated by Britain and France with regard to sharing Africa. In a secret pact in London in 1915 Italy had been promised a share of German colonies in Africa. Until the rise of Mussolini, Italian leadership was too weak to shame Britain and France. But with Mussolini as prime minister, Italy decided to steal like Britain and France and challenge Ethiopia in a second war in 1935. This time Italy won and Ethiopia was added to the growing Italian Empire in Africa. King Victor Emmanuel III of Italy shamelessly took the title of emperor of Ethiopia. The British had set the precedent with emperor of India when Queen Victoria shamelessly took on the ridiculously pompous title of empress of India in 1876, and passed on the title of emperor of India to her son King Edward VII. In 1936 the Italian colonies of Eritrea, Italian Somaliland and Ethiopia were merged into *Italian East Africa.* Since Hitler needed Mussolini's support for his planned unification of Germany and Austria he supported Mussolini's conquest of Ethiopia and African colonization.

Once again we see Western imperialism at work in causing the Second World War. Mussolini had long opposed Germany's attempt to unify Austria and Germany. But Italy, like Germany, longed for a colonial empire. Italy found one in *Africa.* If Italy had no desire for a colonial empire in Africa, Mussolini would have continued his vocal and military support of Austrian independence, possibly averting World War II.

The Historical Roots of the Hitler-Mussolini Alliance

The World War II alliance between the two world leaders demonized by the West, Hitler and Mussolini, had nothing to do with dictatorship, democracy, Nazism, Fascism, or the personalities of Hitler and Mussolini. Italy and Germany needed an alliance against Britain and France to fight for colonies. That is the only explanation for the alliance. This alliance had its roots in the unification of Germany under Prussian leadership and the simultaneous struggle to unify Italy. During these simultaneous unifications, Italy and Germany had a common enemy in Austria. During the Austro-Prussian War of 1866 the Prussian chancellor, Otto von Bismarck, offered an alliance to Victor Emmanuel II, the king of the recently unified Kingdom of Italy, against Austria. This alliance enabled Italy to take Venice from Austria and add it to the Kingdom of Italy. During the subsequent Franco-Prussian War in 1870, Italy was able to add the Papal States to the Kingdom of Italy and claim Rome for its capital. When France refused to share the North African colony of Tunisia with Italy, Italy felt betrayed and was ever more convinced of its need for a formal alliance with Germany. This led to its Triple Alliance with Germany and Austria in 1882.

During World War I, Italy foolishly broke its long standing alliance with Germany to fight alongside Britain and France. It had been persuaded to join Britain and France against Germany with promises of colonies at a secret pact agreed to in London in 1915. Italy was promised German colonies in Africa and Asia as well as vast portions of territories in Europe controlled by the Ottoman Empire. When Germany was defeated, Britain and France gobbled up most of the spoils leaving Italy cheated and frustrated with the British and French. In particular, none of the German colonies went to Italy. This betrayal by Britain and France pushed Italy back into its earlier alliance with Germany and Austria. But Italy was plagued by weak leaders until *Benito Mussolini* came to power in 1922. Mussolini was no more evil than the leaders of Britain and France. He was disliked only because Britain and France could not push him around the way they had done with his predecessors. The West love weak leaders like Gorbachev because they can take advantage and easily bully them. They heap undeserved praise on them. They naturally hate strong leaders like Mussolini, Hitler, Stalin and Putin. They heap undeserved scorn on them.

Mussolini was the strong Italian leader who would regain for Italy its imperial prowess as the center of the Roman Empire. A new Italian Empire would control the Mediterranean and add territory in Europe and North Africa. One of Mussolini's first acts was to secure the *Dodecanese Islands* promised to Italy in the 1915 London pact. Mussolini secured this for Italy with the 1923 Treaty of Lausanne. Next, Mussolini was able to force Britain to hand over *Jubaland* to add to its African colony of Italian Somaliland after threatening British greed by invading the Greek island of Corfu. Mussolini then claimed some territory from France for Italy. This included Savoy, Corsica and Nice. Another failed promise for helping Britain and France defeating Germany was *Dalmatia* and territory in Eastern Europe. The secret 1915 London pact had guaranteed Dalmatia and Eastern European territory going to Italy for helping Britain and France. Mussolini was about to make good on those promises. He was simply settling a few scores with Britain and France for Italy having been cheated by them out of the spoils of World War I. Nevertheless, Britain and France still hung on to the lion's share of those spoils. Those who blame Italy's territorial claims under Mussolini for starting World War II are clearly biased. It was the continued greed of Britain and France which led Mussolini to join forces with Hitler and prevent the two biggest thieves, Britain and France, from taking all of the booty. Mussolini knew instinctively that prior to the American Empire, there was no bigger thief than the British. That is why the British people hated him so much. He, more than anyone else, knew the sad truth about British greed.

Mussolini had made overtures to Germany for an alliance against France since the 1920s. Initially, Mussolini had a dilemma allying with

Hitler because the pre–World War I Triple Alliance had included Austria. At first Mussolini supported Austrian independence from Germany. This made it impossible for him to have an alliance with Hitler since Hitler supported a union of Austria and Germany. When the Austrian independence movement was led by *Engelbert Dollfuss* it was Mussolini who underwrote Dollfus's leadership. Dollfuss became chancellor of Austria in 1932 and imitated Italian Fascism with *Austrofascism*. In August 1933 Mussolini issued an Italian guarantee of Austrian independence. But Mussolini was forced to choose between his campaign for an Italian Empire, denied to Italy by the greed of Britain and France, and Austrian independence. In the end he chose an Italian Empire. Since Britain and France would never have allowed Italy to compete with them in their worldwide theft of colonies, Mussolini had to ally with Hitler. In July of 1934, Dollfuss was assassinated by the Austrian Nazi party which Dollfuss had banned the year before. Mussolini was very angry but understood that Britain and France were united in denying both Italy and Germany any share in their imperial spoils.

Mussolini had also long favored an alliance with Germany against France. France had regained its long time leadership of continental Europe after Germany had been defeated in the First World War. Mussolini was very much aware that the only way of increasing Italian influence in Europe was to weaken that of France. He had made efforts to divide France and Britain but had not been as successful as he had hoped. On the other side, Hitler had long favored an alliance between Germany and Italy. When Hitler became chancellor, in January 1933, he sent a personal message of admiration to Mussolini and expressed his desire for a possible alliance. He also assured Mussolini that he had no interest in pursuing Germany's claim to South Tyrol, a land claim which Italy had feared. Hitler and Mussolini met personally in Venice on June 14, 1934. At the time Mussolini was still opposed to Hitler's plan to unify Germany and Austria. Mussolini only began to distance himself from supporting Austrian independence when he made the choice that colonizing Ethiopia and expanding African colonization was more important. He began the second *Italo-Ethiopian War* of 1935–1936 against Emperor Haile Selassie of Ethiopia after assurance of support from Hitler. Hitler's support was crucial since Britain and France were naturally opposed. Britain and France were well aware that stealing African land for their own imperial expansion was militarily easier than stealing African colonies from another Western European power such as Italy or Germany.

An Italian-German alliance would make it easier for Italy to get its overseas empire and for Germany to expand its territory on the European continent by colonizing Austria. Italy would also use this alliance to further its interest in colonizing *Albania.* During World War I Italy had invaded Albania but had retreated in 1920. With Mussolini providing the strong leadership Italy had lacked, Albania was a very likely target for Italian imperial expansion. Once Hitler had colonized Austria and Czechoslovakia, Mussolini felt the pressure to get his prize from the partnership. He invaded and conquered Albania in April 1939 a month after Hitler had invaded Czechoslovakia. In addition to cooperating on their respective imperial ambitions the Italian-German alliance would be a formidable rival for both Britain and France. It was unlikely that Italy would make the same mistake twice and be fooled by Britain and France in any secret deals against Germany as had occurred with the 1915 London pact.

While Hitler and Mussolini were feeling each other out an opportunity arose for a third country alliance with Spain. Spain had been very supportive of the French regime prior to its civil war. Both Mussolini and Hitler seized on the opportunity presented by the Spanish Civil War to aid the rebels and overthrow a pro-French, Spanish government. Mussolini had begun aiding the Spanish rebels in 1926. Once the Spanish Civil War began in July 1936, Mussolini and Hitler sent military support. Their military support to *General Francisco Franco* played a crucial role in securing victory for the rebels much like the role played by France in aiding the rebels and Washington in the American War for independence from Britain. The Spanish Civil War not only brought Spain into the Hitler-Mussolini orbit but simultaneously destroyed the possibility of Italy allying with Britain since Britain opposed the nationalist rebels in Spain. It was somewhat ironic that Britain allied with the Soviet Union in supporting the procommunist Republicans against the nationalists and the Christian church.

Hitler and Mussolini developed a useful working relationship during the Spanish Civil War, with Mussolini doing more of the heavy lifting and Hitler playing the subordinate role. During the three years of the Spanish Civil War, Hitler bonded well with Mussolini. The involvement of Italy and Germany in the Spanish Civil War provided valuable training for their subsequent prosecution of the Second World War which began shortly after the conclusion of the Spanish Civil War. The success of the rebels was a boost to Italy and Germany against Britain and France. Italy had scored a double military success with its conquest of Ethiopia and successful support of the victors in the Spanish Civil War. In like manner, Hitler had scored a double military victory with his conquest of Austria in 1938 and successful support of the victors in the Spanish Civil War. By 1939 three Western European leaders, Mussolini, Hitler and Franco, had each scored significant military victories and were on the same side. At the beginning of the 1930s Germany was still largely constrained by the straight jacket imposed on it by the Treaty of Versailles and Italy seemed doomed to be without an empire. By the end of the 1930s the world seemed to be in fear of the "three Amigos," Hitler, Mussolini and Franco. Britain and France had subjugated Germany, Austria and Italy with the First World War. By the end of the Spanish Civil War in April 1939, Germany, Austria and Italy were back and stronger than ever. Britain and France would prove to be far less successful in World War II than they had been in World War I.

Germany, Italy, and Japan: Tripartite Pact of the Axis Powers

Japan had longed to join the elite Western club formed by Britain and France. Russia had also longed for membership in this pompously superior body. It's the equivalent today of Eastern European countries and Turkey groveling for membership in the pompously superior EU. But Britain and France were more inclined to admit the Americans than the Japanese and Russians. Japan had hoped that its alliance with Britain, beginning in 1902, its naval defeat of Russia in 1905, and its crucial assistance to the allies in defeating Germany in World War I would have boosted its chance of membership. But the Americans opposed Japanese membership for two important reasons. First, the American Empire wanted all of the Pacific and Far East. Japan was its major competitor. Second, the Americans were fiercely **racist.** President Wilson had strongly opposed treating Japan as an equal in the League of Nations because the Japanese people were not **white.** The British had supported Wilson's openly racist views despite its hypocritical claims to racial equality in its multi-racial empire. Hitler, on the other hand, went out of his way to stress that he never thought of the Japanese as an inferior race and promoted them to the status of "honorary Aryans." Of course, Western writers proudly broadcast their hypocrisy by being totally silent on the extreme **racist** views of both President Woodrow Wilson and Britain's most celebrated **racist** statesman, Sir Winston Churchill, while loudly beating the drums of the racist views of Adolf Hitler. American immigration laws were also very anti-Japanese because of American **racism.** See my *Rise and Fall of the American Empire,* chapters 7 and 8.

Britain had to choose between Japan and the United States. It chose the United States as it had always done since the United States was its colony. Even today Britain treats the United States as its number one ally even though it's now the junior partner. With Britain choosing the United States over Japan, Japan had no other choice than forming an alliance with Germany. Somewhat ironically, Germany's interest in an alliance with Japan was to deter the United States from supporting Britain in a war with Germany. Hitler, like Western historians, erroneously believed U.S. propaganda of not having imperial motives. In reality, the United States dearly sought an excuse for a war against Japan to pursue its dream of being the dominant Pacific/Asian power. Hitler made two mistakes which lost him the war. The first was to misunderstand American determination to be a dominant imperial power. The second was to expand his continental conquest into Russia. Hitler had a good chance of defeating Britain and France without an alliance with Japan. But he had no chance whatsoever of defeating both the United States and Russia, even with an alliance with Japan. His alliance with Japan, far from deterring the United States from coming to the aid of Britain, provided the much needed excuse for the United States to enter the war. His attack on Russia was simply the madness which possesses every great military genius from Alexander the Great to Napoleon. They always cross a bridge too far.

Germany's relationship with Japan dates back to the "unequal treaties" imposed on Japan by the United States and Western European states. In 1854 the United States had forced Japan to accept the *Convention of Kanagawa.* Prussia forced a similar agreement on Japan in 1861. Japan benefitted from its alliance with Britain during the First World War by sharing the German colonies. While Britain was torn by having to choose between the United States or Japan, as its ally in World War II, Hitler was torn by having to choose between China and Japan. Japan had invaded Manchuria in September 1931 starting a conflict with China. Just as Britain chose the United States over Japan, Hitler chose Japan over China. By default the United States and Britain chose China over Japan. Germany concluded an alliance with Japan, the *Anti-Comintern Pact,* on November 25, 1936. At the time this alliance was directed mostly against the Soviet Union. But Japan was also able to get Hitler to renounce future claims to the German colonies in the Pacific which Japan had taken as a result of Germany's defeat in World War I. In addition, Germany recognized Japanese colonization of *Manchukuo* in China. In July 1937 the Japanese captured China's capital, *Beijing.* This marked the beginning of its invasion of all of China. China's major cities, *Shanghai* and *Nanking,* fell to the Japanese by December of 1937.

Japan's defeat of Russia in 1905 had moved it closer to great power status. In July 1938 Japan invaded the Soviet Union but without much success. Japan's 1936 alliance with Germany was sufficient compensation for losing its alliance with Britain. The British had paid a high price for its alliance with the United States. Britain had endangered all of its colonies in Asia, including Australia and New Zealand, by pushing Japan into an alliance with Germany. At the *Imperial Conference* in London, June 20 to August 5, 1921, the prime ministers of Australia and New Zealand pleaded with Britain to renew its alliance with Japan. But Britain terminated the alliance in 1923 because of American pressure backed by **Canadian** support for the Americans.

Italy joined the Anti-Comintern Pact in November 6, 1937. At the time Italy was still hoping to get an alliance with Britain and British support for Italian colonization of Tunisia. Italy had protested French colonization of Tunisia in 1881 because of significant numbers of Italian settlers, traders, professionals and businesses in Tunisia. But Britain had backed France over Italy in return for French support for British colonization of Cyprus. With Italy's renewed push by Mussolini for an Italian Empire which included North Africa and Albania, Italy returned to the question of Italian colonization of Tunisia. Italian immigrants had continued to pour into Tunisia after it had been colonized by France. Many were now poor peasants from Sicily and Sardinia looking for a better life in Tunisia. The Italian population in Tunisia had grown to over 105,000 matching the Italian population in the Italian colony of Libya. It far exceeded the French population. But they were discriminated against by the French regime and some left. Those remaining supported the new push by Mussolini for Italian colonization. Other Italians supported Mussolini because they wanted to migrate to Tunisia if it became an Italian colony. In the 1930s more Italians wanted to immigrate to North Africa than to the United States. Under French rule it was almost impossible for them to steal Tunisian land since the French had stolen most of it. Tunisia was also of strategic importance for Italian control of the Mediterranean.

But the British continued to support the French colonization of Tunisia. Just as Britain pushed Japan into an alliance with Germany by favoring the United States over Japan the British pushed Mussolini into a military alliance with Hitler by favoring France over Italy. The military alliance between Hitler and Mussolini was signed on May 22, 1939, and called the *Pact of Steel.* Somewhat ironically, the London Conference of 1915 had lured Italy into an alliance with Britain and France with the promise to Italy of the German colonies in Africa. Now it was Germany led by Hitler which was luring Italy into an alliance with the promise to help Italy steal African colonies from Britain and France. Hitler's next step toward his intended challenge of British hegemony was combining his alliances with Italy and Japan and adding others. On September 27, 1940, Germany signed the *Tripartite Pact* with Italy and Japan. The other countries which allied with Germany during the Second World War included many of the countries in Eastern Europe such as Hungary, Romania, Slovakia, Bulgaria, Yugoslavia, and Croatia. These alliances were consistent with Germany pursuing the goal of challenging France for the position of the dominant continental power in Europe. Britain had wisely made a clear choice of colonial hegemony over continental hegemony. But France had foolishly pursued both and in the end could not achieve either. Britain was the stronger colonial power and Germany was poised to become the stronger continental power.

Hungary's prime minister, *Gyula Gombos,* sought an alliance with Italy after he was elected in 1932. Gombos met with Mussolini in Rome on November 10, 1932. At the time Mussolini still supported Austrian independence and thought in terms of an alliance with both Hungary and Austria. When Hitler became chancellor in 1933, Gombos was the first leader to pay Hitler a diplomatic visit. Hitler, like Mussolini, had advocated an alliance between Germany and Italy since the 1920s. Gombos now advocated an alliance between Hungary, Germany and Italy. He needed the help of Germany and Italy to regain territory which the Allies had taken away from Hungary because of World War I. Hitler and Mussolini clearly identified Hungary as an additional ally since the First Vienna Award of November 2, 1938. In that award Hitler and Mussolini sanctioned the annexation of parts of Czechoslovakia by Hungary. It was territory which Hungary had lost with the 1920 *Treaty of Trianon* dictated without negotiation by the Allies on the Kingdom of Hungary. Hungary, like Germany, had been punished by the Allies for losing the First World War. With the dissolution of the Austro-Hungarian Empire in 1918 the Kingdom of Hungary was deprived of 72 percent of its territory and 64 percent of its population by the victorious Allies. Over 3 million ethnic Hungarians were forced out of their native Hungary. So much for the allied propaganda of self-determination! Czechoslovakia was one of three beneficiaries of the loss of Hungarian territory and population. Hungarians living in *Slovakia* became an ethnic minority in Czechoslovakia when the Allies made Slovakia a part of the new state of Czechoslovakia. The First Vienna Award forced Czechoslovakia to return Slovakia to Hungary. The Allied created state of Czechoslovakia had been weakened by its loss of the Sudetenland to Germany and further weakened by its loss of Slovakia and Ukrainian territory to Hungary.

One of the other beneficiaries of Hungarian territory lost by the Allied dictated Treaty of Trianon was the Kingdom of Romania. With the transfer of Transylvania and other territory to Romania by the Allies, Romania more than doubled its geographical area. Ethnic Hungarians were forced out of their native Hungary into Romania. Romania discriminated against both ethnic Hungarians and ethnic Germans who had previously lived in Transylvania. In the Second Vienna Award of August 30, 1940, Hitler and Mussolini forced Romania to return Northern Transylvania to Hungary. Given the assistance of Germany and Italy in regaining parts of its motherland forcibly deprived of by the Allies because of World War I, **Hungary** signed on to the Tripartite Pact on November 20, 1940.

Hitler and Mussolini forced Romania to return Bulgarian territory transferred to it by the Allies with the 1920 Treaty of Trianon. Hitler also promised Bulgaria that it would regain territory lost to Serbia and Greece by the Treaty of Trianon. **Bulgaria** signed the Tripartite Pact on March 1, 1941. With the loss of territory transferred to Hungary and Bulgaria, a weakened **Romania** also signed the Tripartite Pact on November 23, 1940. **Slovakia** was created from the disintegrating Allied state of Czechoslovakia on March 14, 1939. It too signed the Tripartite Pack on November 24, 1940. Yugoslavia, like Czechoslovakia, had been created out of the dissolved Austro-Hungarian Empire in 1918. It was an experiment at combining ethnic Croats with ethnic Serbs. The Independent State of Croatia was carved out of Yugoslavia on April 10, 1939. **Yugoslavia** signed the Tripartite Agreement on March 25, 1941, and **Croatia** signed the Tripartite Pact on June 15, 1941.

Russian Defeat of Germany and U.S. Defeat of Japan

World War II changed the world in one significant way. Western European states had dominated the world beginning with the Portuguese Empire in the fifteenth century. After World War II the world was dominated by the American Empire. The primary cause of World War II was the German challenge to British hegemony. In the end Britain became somewhat irrelevant and it was Russia which defeated Germany. Russia emerged from World War II more powerful than both Britain and Germany. This was an immense achievement for Josef Stalin. Stalin had achieved more for the Russian people than any of its famous Czars. The only Russian leader coming close to what Stalin achieved for Russia is Vladimir Putin. The best measure of the success of a non-Western leader is the extent to which the West vilifies him. After teaching their children to refer to Stalin as Uncle Joe when Stalin helped the West defeat Hitler the West vilified Stalin as soon as Stalin began to compete with the West for colonies. In like manner if Putin had been foolish enough to have helped the West colonize Iran, Syria, Libya, North Korea and Ukraine he would have become Uncle Vladimir to the children of the Western imperialists and warmongers.

Russia had competed for great power acceptance by Britain and France for centuries. During the centuries of rule by the Czars, Russia was never able to get acceptance as an equal by Britain or France. Under a centrally planned Communist leader, it surpassed both Britain and France and became the principal rival to the American Empire for world domination. This brought about another change in the world. Up until World War II, the Western European Empires fought each other for continental leadership in Europe and for worldwide colonies. The American Empire used massive amounts of propaganda to convince the world that the competition between the United States and Russia was one of democracy versus communism. This was a total lie but the United States used excessive fear mongering to silence all those who dared to say otherwise. The U.S./Russian competition was a continuation of the old competition for worldwide colonies. But the United States felt the need to be hypocritical and pretend it had no imperial aspirations. It did fool many people because of its extensive and effective propaganda machine. But it very likely fooled a larger percent of Americans than non-Americans. A larger percent of non-Americans pretended to believe the U.S. propaganda out of fear of U.S. reprisals, which were brutal and unforgiving.

When Britain and France declared war on Germany on September 3, 1939, Hitler and Stalin were allies. Had this alliance not been broken by Hitler it's very likely that Britain would have lost the Second World War. In 1926 Germany and Russia had signed a neutrality and nonaggression pact, *Treaty of Berlin*. It was renewed in 1931 and 1933. This military treaty was complemented with trade agreements which increased trade between the two countries. The Soviet Union had been fighting a war with the West and capitalism since its communist revolution in 1917. An alliance between Hitler and Stalin made logical sense since British leadership of the West was both anti-Soviet and anti-German. Germany needed raw materials from the Soviets and Stalin needed both German industrial capital and technology and an assurance that Hitler would not expand his continental empire into Russia. The Hitler-Stalin alliance began with negotiations on a trade agreement. This led to the *German-Soviet Commercial Agreement* of August 19, 1939. This was followed by the *Molotov-Ribbentrop* military agreement of August 23, 1939, and a trade pact in February 1940. That military pact between Russia and Germany guaranteed that Stalin would not aid Britain and France in a war with Germany. It also guaranteed that Hitler could expand his territorial gains into Poland without fear of a war with Russia. After colonizing Austria and Czechoslovakia, Hitler wanted Western Poland. But there were Soviet troops in Poland. A pact with Stalin would guarantee Russia's neutrality.

For Stalin, not only would the military alliance guarantee noninvasion of Russia by Germany, Russia could gobble up what was left of Poland after the German invasion and create a buffer state between Russia and any Western continental advance against the Soviet Republics. Russia had suffered territorial loss just like Germany as a result of the First World War. Both countries found a common cause in the punitive Treaty of Versailles. Those territorial losses included losses in the allied created independent state of Poland. By 1939 "independent" Poland was up for colonization by the great powers of Europe. With Britain and France busy expanding their worldwide colonial empires, especially in Africa, Poland was up for grabs by Germany and Russia. It was safer for these two great powers to share Poland and use that opportunity to cooperate in order to cement their alliance against Britain and France rather than fight each other for all of Poland. Russia invaded on September 17, 1939, and Poland was divided up on October 6, 1939. The German and Russian invasions of West and East Poland, respectively, did not cause the Second World War. It was simply time for another war among nations addicted to centuries of incessant warmongering. Britain and France had rested sufficiently after the end of the First World War in 1918. It was time to feed the ever hungry war machine.

It came as no surprise that the alliance agreed to by Stalin and Hitler had other territorial conquests besides Poland. There were many other European states which had been made independent of Germany and Russia by the allied victory in World War I. These states included Finland, Romania, Estonia, Lithuania and Latvia. These territories would also be divided up by Russia and Germany. After invading Poland, the Russians invaded Finland, Romania and the Baltic states of Estonia, Latvia and Lithuania. Germany invaded Denmark and Norway in the north, west into France, Belgium, Holland and Luxembourg, as well as territory in Eastern and Southern Europe, including Greece and Yugoslavia. Italy also invaded France in June 1940. In addition, Italy captured the English colony of British Somaliland in Africa. By early 1941, Germany, Russia and Italy had conquered most of continental Europe. The war was going well for Hitler, Stalin and Mussolini. Hitler had shown great wisdom in choosing his European alliances up to this point. As I explained above his choice of an Asian alliance with Japan was questionable and totally unnecessary. His Japanese alliance would bring him into conflict with the emerging world's superpower of the United States. That was difficult enough. But his decision to turn on his Russian ally was pure madness. His invasion of Russia was as disastrous as that of Napoleon. Weakened by that foolish blunder, Hitler had to face the wrath of the American Empire because he had allied with the Japanese Empire.

Hitler's Disastrous and Unnecessary Invasion of Russia Begins His Defeat

Hitler had first indicated his desire to conquer the Soviet Union in 1925 when he wrote *Mien Kampf.* But Hitler was wise to recognize later that the enemy was Britain not the Soviet Union. Hence his subsequent alliance with Stalin. Hitler's decision to turn on his friend has no logical explanation. But warmongers and invaders have never been rational leaders or generals. Their military victories seem to convince them that they are gods rather than mortals. Military victories lead them to believe that no conquest is impossible. They lose sight of reality and goals. They invade and conquer because they become driven by a madness which only death can relieve. All conquering invaders have succumbed to this fate. It was January of 1941, when Hitler, Stalin and Mussolini had become the all-conquering heroes of the world, that Hitler signed a border and commercial agreement with his friend Stalin. But a month earlier Hitler had authorized the invasion of the Soviet Union. *Directive 21* issued on December 20, 1940, stated, "The German Armed Forces must be prepared, even before the conclusion of the war against England, *to crush Soviet Russia in a rapid campaign* (Case Barbarossa)."

Hitler had clearly lost sight of his goal of a German Empire based on continental domination of Europe and worldwide colonies to match those of Britain and France. He had become like Napoleon, Caesar, Genghis Khan, Alexander the Great and all those who had perished from the same madness inflicted on them by their previous conquests and their military genius. He had become delusional because of his quick victories in the East, North, West and South. Conquest of the Soviet Union served no purpose even if he could have achieved the impossible. Russia had never been fully accepted by the West and Russian territory would not have turned Germany into the dominant world power. It was still viewed in the West as a vast backward behemoth. To many, the communist revolution had made it even more backward than when it was ruled by the Czars. Governing such a vast expanse of territory would have been impossible. It would have drained all of the resources needed to govern a worldwide empire and continental Europe. Germany needed to defeat Britain, not Russia, to become the world's superpower. As it turned out Hitler's invasion failed miserably. He mounted an invasion force of 4 million men, 750,000 horses, and 600,000 vehicles. Most of this massive invasion force perished. The result was to so weaken his military capability that he was no longer able to defeat Britain.

Hitler's Alliance with Japan Created the American Superpower: The Pacific War between the American and Japanese Empires

Adding insult to injury Hitler's unwise alliance with Japan, after he had made an enemy of Stalin, unleashed on him the wrath of the world's emerging superpower, the United States. Hitler would have had a difficult time defeating Britain after he had made an enemy of Stalin. Defeating Britain when he faced off against both the Soviet Union and the United States was impossible for a military God much less a mere mortal. Somewhat ironically, Hitler's unintentional drag of the American Empire into the affairs of Western Europe enabled the United States to rule the world but also caused it to overextend its reach. As we have explained, every empire declines because it overextends its reach. The American Empire ruled the world after the Second World War as long as Asia was poor. What we have called the *global shift* to the emerging economies, most of which are in Asia, will reduce the relative size of the U.S. economy making it impossible for it to continue to rule the world. President Obama's decision to "rebalance" or "pivot" its military forces to Asia will simply return the United States to its position before World War II when it "isolated" its empire to the New World and the Asia Pacific. The stated goal of President Obama is to have 60 percent of American forces in Asia by 2020. This was announced by the U.S. Defense secretary on June 2, 2012, at the *Shangri-La Dialogue* in Singapore. With the remaining 40 percent it can hold on to the New World of the Americas and the Caribbean. It cannot hold on to the entire globe.

The United States had dreams of empire even before it had become an independent nation-state. But it did not crave that empire in Europe. Western historians have deliberately or foolishly made two mistakes about the United States. The first is to believe its propaganda that it never wanted to be an empire. The second mistake was to speak of U.S. "isolationism." The United States was clever enough to know that its imperial aspirations must be westward from its colonial beginning and not eastward. Its sensible pursuit of empire in the New World and across the Pacific to Asia meant ignoring Europe. Historians foolishly called this "American isolationism." The United States has never been isolationist. While it fought for its independence from Britain it invaded Canada. In the next century it conquered all of the First Nations lands across the continent and used the *Monroe Doctrine* to call the imperial shots in the New World with the blessing of Great Britain, its former imperial master. At the same time it expanded across the Pacific colonizing many islands and facing off against Japan for imperial hegemony in Asia. All of this is covered in my *American Invasions.*

With so much on its plate it had no time or incentive to meddle in the five century old fight among the European states for Western-European hegemony. This was not isolationism but wisdom. Western

Europe was overcrowded with Portugal, Spain, Holland, France, Britain and Germany. While they were fighting each other for Western European dominance, the United States was carving out a much larger empire in the New World and Asia Pacific. Had the Germans not allied with Japan it's very doubtful if the United States would ever have been drawn into the European quagmire. Western Europeans had waged numerous wars against each other since the Portuguese had begun their voyages along the west coast of Africa in the early fifteenth century. Columbus had discovered a whole New World and the Americans had taken all of it from the Western Europeans. That was far more than the United States could ever have conquered in Western Europe had it joined the squabble after its independence instead of expanding westward across the First Nations lands. The Western Europeans had also colonized Asia and Africa. But an "upstart" Asian power, *Japan,* had kept parts of Asia. By taking on this Asian power, Japan, the United States was once again showing sound judgment. Competing in Asia with any one of the Western European powers which had gone there before, and all of them had, would have drawn it into the overcrowded Western European theatre. By taking on Japan it could have a far larger Asia-Pacific Empire to add to its already massive empire in the New World. This was **not** isolationism. It was smart imperial domination.

American imperial challenge to Japan began in 1791 when the American Empire sent two ships which arrived in Japan on May 6, 1791. At the time Japan had made it very clear to the West that it had absolutely no desire to trade or have voluntary relations with the West apart from its limited relationship with Holland via the single port of Nagasaki. See my *American Invasions,* chapter 3. The American decision to send ships under these circumstances was clearly aggressive and imperial. As I have explained before trade is a voluntary agreement by two or more trading partners. If you have made it very clear that you have no desire to sell your car then someone insisting on getting your car is intent on stealing it not trading for it. Likewise, the United States had to be on a colonizing mission **not** a trading mission when it sent ships to Japan in 1791. The American flag was planted on the Japanese island of *Kii Oshima* by the American captains, John Kendrick and William Douglas. This marked the beginning of U.S. colonization of Japan which continues to this day. There is no such thing as a friendly American flag. It's an explicit act of war, conquest, intimidation and bullying. The American Empire, like the Roman Empire before, cannot have friends. When you control, bully and dominate every inch of the globe an "American friend" becomes an oxymoron. Of course, in 1791 the United States was far too weak militarily to conquer Japan. But that is irrelevant. When Columbus arrived in the New World in 1492 Spain did not immediately colonize all of the New World. But it signaled its intention to do so. This is exactly the same with the first U.S. expedition to reach Japan in 1791. Just as the West never ceased in its military efforts to conquer and colonize all of the New World after 1492 the United States never ceased in its efforts to conquer and colonize all of Japan after 1791.

By the outbreak of World War II the United States had colonized a string of strategic islands in the Pacific. These included Hawaii, the Philippines, Midway, Guam, Wake and Samoa. See our *American Invasions,* chapter 5. The United States had sent a signal of its intent to challenge Japan for hegemony by pressuring the British to end its alliance with Japan. When Japan invaded China in 1937 the United States sent military aid to China to oppose Japan's colonization of China. As with Cuba and the Philippines before, and Korea and Vietnam after, the U.S. goal was to colonize China itself. In 1939 the United States ended its trade treaty with Japan and began to place an embargo on its oil, iron, steel and other exports to Japan. It joined other Western countries in freezing Japanese overseas assets. Japan saw this as an implicit declaration of war by the American Empire. Japan responded by attacking the American fleet anchored in the American *uncolony* of Hawaii. It was the response the United States had hoped for as it gave the United States the excuse it needed to declare all-out war on the Japanese Empire. As usual the United States never liked being viewed as an imperial power. It likes to be seen as the power which intervenes on behalf of those colonized by some other power. In Cuba and the Philippines that other power was Spain. In the Pacific and China that other power was Japan. The United States had the propaganda it needed to hide its colonial intentions in China, Japan, and the Asia Pacific. The ever vigilant and wide-awake "Sleeping Giant" and ever intervening "isolationist" was able to pretend that it was awakened by the call to protect the weak. This was just another case of the white man's burden being used to steal the land and resources of those colonized by the West.

War between the empires of Japan and the United States was inevitable. The Japanese bombing of the stolen American *uncolony* of Hawaii was as good an excuse for the American Empire to use to justify feeding its addiction to warmongering as any of the other frivolous and self-serving excuses it used before and after World War II. So began what has been rightly called the *Pacific War.* Some historians date the beginning of the Pacific War between the American and Japanese Empire with the Japanese invasion of Manchuria on September 19, 1931. That date has much merit given our claim that the United States wanted to colonize China as much as Japan wanted China as its colony. In fact, the United States wanted to colonize both China and Japan. It failed to colonize China only because of Mao Zedong. But it did succeed in colonizing Japan along with South Korea and Taiwan. The American Empire defeated the Japanese Empire by using nuclear weapons. Many in the West preach the evil of nuclear weapons. Yet it is the West which exonerated the American Empire for using nuclear bombs twice in Hiroshima and Nagasaki and it was the Japanese, not the Americans, who were charged with crimes against humanity. This is simply another of countless examples of Western hypocrisy and propaganda in claiming concerns for war crimes or crimes against humanity. They use such propaganda to hold others to account not themselves. They gain by both shielding themselves from such charges while punishing their victims and those they defeat in wars.

CHAPTER 9

The Bad, the Ugly, and the Uglier American Empire

The United States did not set out to become the world's superpower. It did set out to be a global empire rivaling the Western European empires. But its focus was westward from the Caribbean to the Asia Pacific not eastward into Europe. It was the Second World War which made it the world's superpower by default. The Western European empires had fought each other for five centuries and were so weakened by these incessant wars that they became puny compared to the United States, in both economic and military capability. Second, the United States had acquired the atomic bomb and showed its desire to use it by bombing Hiroshima and Nagasaki. Third, air power had replaced sea power as the decisive weapon for colonization. The end of sea power as the decisive military weapon ended the possibility of a world ruled by maritime powers such as Britain, France, Holland, Portugal and Spain. The American Empire had fought long and hard, using superior propaganda, deceit and lies, to become an empire which could rival Britain and France. The Second World War had handed it global superpower status on a silver platter.

The post–World War II American Empire quickly developed a new imperial doctrine which can be summed up as: "If you are not with us, you are against us." The Western European empires had never envisaged permanent alliances with other empires to become a single Global Super Empire. But the United States did just that after the Second World War. It made it very clear to states such as Britain, France, Germany, Italy, Spain, Canada, Australia, Japan, South Korea, Taiwan, the Philippines and many others that it would tolerate no dissent, discussion or disagreements with its single minded pursuit of global domination. The United States used a modified carrot and stick approach to get countries on board. This modified approach was small carrots with very big sticks. Countries which came on board were rewarded with small amounts of aid, mostly military aid. But their primary reward was access to free foreign capital inflows, global financial markets and international trade with the booming economies of the West. Those who refused or even wavered were severely punished. Cuba, Guyana, Chile, China, East Germany, North Korea and Iran are good examples of those punished severely. The United States would invade militarily and use its enormous economic, political, financial, media and propaganda clout to get boycotts and embargoes imposed by itself and all of the countries which had come on board. After World War II, the United States controlled the IMF, the World Bank, the UN, the world's reserve currency, the GATT/ WTO and global financial markets, and the global media.

Britain and its white ex-colonies such as Canada, Australia and New Zealand were the most willing participants of this U.S.-dominated club. They quickly prostituted themselves for the American dollar and willingly accepted the United States as their pimp. Asian member prostitutes of the American pimp included Japan, South Korea, Taiwan, Singapore and Hong Kong. France, led by *Charles de Gaulle,* attempted to resist the U.S. pressure by forming the six-member European Coal and Steel Community with West Germany, Italy, Belgium, Holland and Luxembourg. But Western Europe was as divided as ever and failed to integrate sufficiently to compete with the United States and its Anglo allies/prostitutes of the UK, Canada, Australia, and New Zealand together with their wannabe Asian-Anglo prostitutes of Japan, South Korea, Taiwan, Hong Kong, and Singapore. Without deep integration, the independent states of Western Europe were individually far too weak to ever threaten the American Empire and its growing list of allies. In the end Western Europe acquiesced to American pressure and formed a military alliance called NATO.

Western Europeans were somewhat war weary after five centuries of warmongering and NATO provided an excellent opportunity for the war weary Western Europeans to shift the financial cost of incessant warmongering to the eager Americans. The Americans could easily afford to pay for warmongering and still have the highest standard of living in the world. Its economy was large and growing by leaps and bounds. Its highly productive goods sector could afford a growing nonproductive military sector. American corporations were willing participants because of the profits from arms production for the American military as well as arms sales to the West. The United States became the world's largest arms buyer and arms exporter. American women signed up in droves to have military husbands and fathers to pay the bills. Young impoverished Americans were eager for a financially rewarding military career.

Abolition of the draft had little impact on the size of the U.S. military. For the first time, it seemed like an economy did not have to choose between the familiar "Guns versus Butter," but could have both. Furthermore, its unproductive military could be used to steal from those colonized. Saudi oil, Latin American bananas, and Hawaiian pineapples, are but a few examples of what was stolen from the American *uncolonies.* The Americans also perfected the doctrine of regime change previously used by the Western European empires. By installing a local puppet it ensured local support for its colonization. By giving its colony access to the markets, capital and resources of the West it enriched the local inhabitants of its colonies. The West boomed and the Third World suffered in poverty and silence.

This booming West, became what the West called the "International Community." The fact that this so-called international community left out two-thirds of the world's population was a blatant piece of propaganda that the Western media "presstitutes" were happy to ignore. Being poor or communist implied that you were not of this world according to Western propaganda. You may just have well been Martians. A blatant example of this is voting by the permanent members of the UN Security Council. Often the United States would propose a UN resolution to punish a country demanding **freedom.** The two U.S. prostitutes who are permanent members, Britain and France, will of course vote with their pimp, the United States. With three out of five votes, the media *presstitutes* would report that the UN resolution was supported by the *International Community* even though the combined population of China and Russia exceeded the combined population of the United States, Britain, and France.

While NATO began with twelve countries, the United States was by far the key financial and military player. The other eleven countries were the UK, France, Italy, Portugal, Canada, Holland, Belgium, Luxembourg, Iceland, Norway, and Denmark. But the American Empire wanted the whole world. Western Europe, the New World, and a large chunk of the Asia/Pacific region, was not enough. Those countries opposed to American domination attempted to form opposing groups as the French president General De Gaulle had tried to do in Western Europe. Two of these groups had some initial success in opposing American domination. The more successful of these two groups were countries which aligned with the Soviet Union and led by Russia. The other group, led by India, was called "nonaligned countries." We will begin with the Soviet Union group since it was the more successful.

Opposition to American Domination by Russia and Its Allies

Russia had two very powerful leaders who were largely responsible for their defiance of American domination. The first of these two leaders was *Josef Stalin.* The second is *Vladimir Putin.* When the West uses its most powerful propaganda to demonize a world leader that is the best guide to recognizing that leader as one who fights for freedom from Western/American bullying and intimidation. Josef Stalin rescued the West from defeat by Hitler. Yet he is as demonized as Hitler. The reason is that the British wanted to rule the world and Hitler stood in their way. So the British sucked up to Stalin and demonized Hitler. In like manner the Americans wanted to rule the world after the Brits and Stalin stood in their way. So the Americans demonized Stalin. In the process of doing so the Americans turned *Communism* from being the most worthwhile promise for advancing equality to the most reviled word. The **C** word had been embraced by most Western intellectuals as the best way to reduce the gross inequalities imposed on the postindustrial societies. But American propaganda sent Western intellectuals scurrying for cover from the dreaded **C** word after the American Empire unleashed its most vicious attacks on all those who would not openly denounce it as the greatest sin mankind could ever commit. To be a *Communist* under the rule of the American Empire was far worse than being a *Nazi,* a *Fascist,* or a *Dictator.* In fact there was nothing more evil than being a *Communist.*

The American Empire had found a very simple method for determining those for and against the United States. You were with the United States if you denounced communism as evil and prostituted yourself for the Yankee dollar. You were against the United States if you did not loudly and unequivocally denounce communism as evil. Silence was taken by the Americans to imply that you were communist. There was no middle ground. Freedom became a word to be shouted by the West from every media because there was so little freedom in practice. Western media "presstituted" itself to the Yankee dollar as much as many countries prostituted themselves to the same Yankee dollar. The less freedom you had the louder you were forced to shout that you were free. You were told that you were free because you were saved from the evil of communism. To have the freedom to choose communism was the clearest sign for the West that you were unfree. The evil of *Sodom* and *Gomorrah* pale by comparison to the evil of communism. Therefore, no one would freely choose communism. By the same token, freely choosing communism was a contradiction. This was the power of American propaganda and the brutal punishments imposed on all who dared to even wish for this evil kind of ungodly freedom. Western freedoms were really the freedoms you were brainwashed into believing you had, or scared into pretending you had, to avoid being punished. Punishments included military attacks, imprisonments, torture, executions and regime change. But they were more often economic. A country would be isolated from trade and finance, boycotted and impoverished. A person would be denied employment or career advancement. It was the old carrot and stick approach. The carrot was economic and income growth. The stick was military invasions and bombing of countries back to the Stone Age, regime change, and imprisonment and torture of individuals.

Western disdain for Russia did not begin, nor did it ever have anything to do with, its Communist revolution of 1917. It simply had to do with its geographical location outside Western Europe. Once the Roman Empire had fallen, the notion of cultural superiority had shifted to the people residing in Western Europe. Neither Russia nor Japan could ever understand this since they were both very proud of their cultural heritage. The reality, however, was that after the Western pope had divided the civilized world between Spain and Portugal in 1493, it was countries on the extreme of Western Europe, Holland, Britain and France, which had the navies to dominate the world. The dominant military power is deemed by Western historians as the most culturally civilized. Russia and Japan never understood that, and both tried desperately to be accepted as equals in the exclusive Western club. The United States, initially, was referred to derogatively by the Brits as a "puny" empire. However, by the Second World War, the Brits were sucking up to the "Yanks" to help them defeat the German threat to their dominance. By default the Yanks became the leader of this exclusive Western club after Britain, France and Germany had largely self-destructed. American culture was now implicitly the dominant culture, replacing British, French and other Western European cultures, simply because the U.S. air power was militarily superior to everyone else. The implicit and explicit identification of cultural superiority based on military superiority is as old as the Earth.

American culture was superior to British, French, German, Italian and Japanese simply because the Yanks had won the Second World War. The British, French, Germans, Italians and Japanese grudgingly accepted that reality. But the "poor" Russians did not understand that and asked why they should be treated as inferior. After all they had done as much, if not more than the Americans, to defeat the Germans in both the First and Second World Wars. Even more confusing to the Russians, the Americans, British and French no longer had to hate the Russians because of their historical cultural inferiority due to their geographical location outside Western Europe, but because they were now **communists.** The communist revolution in Russia had provided the Americans with a golden propaganda opportunity to demonize the Russians, not because of their long perceived backwardness due to Czarist rule, the Russian Orthodox Church or geographical location, but because they were communists. To be a communist was more evil than any other barbaric affliction. And the Americans could be explicit and open about this new Russian disease. It did not have to be politically correct anymore as the British, French, Austrians or Germans had been. For example, the West did not admit the Japanese to their exclusive club either but it was politically incorrect to say loudly and openly that it was due to the **race** of the Japanese people. But if Japan had a communist revolution the West could openly and loudly say the Japanese were evil because they were communists. The key point is that the West never hated the Russians because they were communists. They hated the Russians long before their communist revolution. But communism was a useful scapegoat because American propaganda had turned communism into such an evil affliction, worse than racism, sexism, Nazism, homophobia, religious extremism, fascism, imperialism, or addictive warmongering.

The Russians had no illusions about the extensive reach of American imperialism. By the time the United States first invaded Russia in 1918, it had already invaded China, Japan, the Philippines, Hawaii, Cuba and many other countries, large and small, across the globe. (See my *American Invasions*). Far from its ridiculous pretense of not having any imperial ambition, it was becoming the most expansive empire the world had ever experienced. The 1918–1920 U.S. invasion of Russia failed, but the United States is never one to let failure deter it from future colonization. As we saw in *American Invasions* the United States had invaded the same country many times. It's ironic that acquiring the atom bomb by the United States made the United States top dog in the imperial race by the Western countries, but the same weapon provided the deterrent to further U.S. invasion of the Soviet Union. As I said above Josef Stalin was the first brilliant Soviet leader. He knew that Russia had to get nuclear weapons to prevent the United States from doing to it what it had done to Japan.

While the United States was busy with its reconstruction plans for its Western allies following its nuking of Japan, the Russians had the needed breathing space to develop its nuclear deterrent. It was the Russian nuclear deterrent, and nothing else, which stopped the American Empire from invading, nuking and colonizing the entire globe. If you do not agree, ask yourself why an empire which began as a tiny strip of land on the Atlantic seaboard would invade and colonize across an entire continent and into the Pacific in Hawaii, the Philippines, Pacific islands, Japan, South Korea and Taiwan and then voluntarily stop there? Not a chance in hell! The Soviet Union, far from being the evil empire, was the savior for those who believed in freedom from American colonization. It was, and is, the American Empire which is the aggressor, invader, destroyer and colonizer. It has a way of hiding its evil nature with the best propaganda machine invented by mankind.

The Russians, like the allies and Germany, were investigating the feasibility of nuclear weapons during World War II. Stalin was aware of the research being done in the United States, Germany, and Britain. As a result, he began the Soviet nuclear program as early as 1942. The Americans had begun in 1939. (See my *Rise and Fall of the American Empire,* chapter 8). The United States had an important advantage over Russia because it was willingly supplied with uranium by its subservient ally/prostitute, Canada. The United States obtained additional supplies from the Belgian Congo which was then controlled by another of its ally/prostitute, Britain. The British and Canadian governments naturally cooperated fully with their U.S. pimp. The Russians had great difficulty acquiring uranium. As a result of its earlier start and ready access to supplies of uranium from Canada and the Congo, the United States tested its first nuclear device in 1945. Russia had its first test four years later in 1949.

Stalin was well aware of the imperialist ambition of the United States. However, when Hitler turned against him he had no choice but to ally with the United States against Germany. When Stalin was deliberately kept out of the loop by the United States and Britain during their discussions on nuking Japan, Stalin knew instinctively that the Americans and Brits were sending a clear message to him that their next nuclear target would be the Soviet Union. It was Britain's extremely **racist** wartime prime minister, Winston Churchill, who coined the term "Iron Curtain" to goad the Americans into continuing its warmongering to contain the Soviet Union. Stalin had no choice but to get allies to defend the Soviet Union against American/British imperialism. He found an obvious ally in *Mao Zedong.* The United States had hoped to colonize China and had found a puppet leader in *Chiang Kai-shek.* But Mao defeated Chiang on the battlefield, despite U.S. military aid to Chiang, and sent him packing to the island of Taiwan. The United States colonized Taiwan but not China.

When the United States invaded Korea, Mao came to the aid of the Koreans, and the United States threatened to nuke China. This was where the Russian nuclear deterrent was first tested. Stalin informed the Americans that he would use his nuclear weapons to defend China, and the United States backed off. They got South Korea but not North Korea or China. Another obvious ally in Asia was *Ho Chi Minh.* Vietnam was one of many examples of ex-Western European colonies which the United

States intended to colonize. The United States found many puppet Vietnamese leaders to help their colonization of Vietnam but was defeated by Vietnam's most popular leader, Ho Chi Minh, with the aid of Russia and China. (See my *Rise and Fall of the American Empire,* chapters 8, 9, and 10.)

Stalin had no difficulty in getting many of the Third World countries in Asia, Africa, Latin America and the Caribbean, to support his defense of American expansionism. Many of these Third World countries had been colonized by Portugal, Spain, Holland, France and Britain and were now being threatened by American colonization. Their only hope in avoiding American colonization was to seek help and protection from the Soviet Union. Given the massive propaganda machine of the West, the Americans turned the sequence of events on its head. Having threatened the Third World countries with colonization, when these countries sought help from Russia, the Americans used their control of the media to claim that it invaded not to colonize but to prevent the spread of that dreaded evil disease, Communism. Many of the Third World leaders were confused by the behavior of the West. Since they had studied at Western universities in Europe and the United States, they had learned about the ideals of a communist society being far more egalitarian than the unequal distribution of wealth under private property capitalism. They had been taught this by Western intellectuals and professors. What they did not know was that these Western intellectuals and professors could no longer teach such ideas during the invented Cold War. They were totally unaware that academic freedom in the West was simply propaganda.

There was no freedom of speech, press or academia in the West. The hidden agenda of the West was colonization of the world, but the explicit agenda was fighting Communism and the Cold War. When Third World leaders sought military protection from American colonization by asking Russia for help, they were doomed to be destroyed by American military invasion or economic, financial and trade embargoes. Impoverished by American military and economic policies, they would be forced to seek financial aid from Russia. This would fuel the American propaganda about their communist sins while simultaneously portray their poverty as being caused by their sinful use of such an ungodly governance of their people. It was a self-fulfilling prophesy. Now the Americans had no choice but to invade to save the people who did not deserve such abuse by their communist leaders. It was simply the white man's burden to make the ultimate sacrifice to save those less fortunate. That such ridiculous nonsense is still believed by so many is a testimony to the stupidity of the human race. In Canada, for example, Canadians finally concluded that forcing the First Nations to copy the white man's culture was a terrible mistake so they have now "grown intellectually" to forcing Afghans to copy the white man's culture. I still wonder how they graduated from kindergarten?

By the time Stalin died in 1953 he had made Russia and its allies a formidable force against American imperialism. The Russian economy had grown much faster than that of the United States. The Russians had put a man in space before the Americans. This *Soviet bloc* of countries across the globe prevented the United States from dominating the world. The West had gathered together most of the white rich countries which had preyed on the poor since the rise of the Portuguese Empire. It was still the more wealthy and militarily advanced. But it could not fool the entire world despite its massive propaganda machine. Stalin's legacy continued under his successor, *Nikita Khrushchev.* But when Khrushchev was forced out in 1964 it marked the beginning of weak leaders of Russia until *Vladimir Putin* became the president in 2000.

The United States took advantage of the weak leadership of Russia, its economic decline under these weak leaders, the conflict between Mao Zedong and the Russian leaders, and the disastrous economic policies of Mao, to wean more and more countries to the West, with promises of U.S. aid and threats of U.S. economic embargoes. By the time Putin took over the presidency of Russia, the Soviet Union had disintegrated, there was no Soviet bloc to keep the West in check and Russia was but a shadow of its great Stalin/Khrushchev's days. The United States had become the world's only superpower and invaded every corner of the globe. With the death of Communism it invented a new evil, *Terrorism.* By 2009 the membership of NATO had expanded to twenty-eight countries. A united Germany became a member of NATO in addition to other European countries, Spain, Albania, Bulgaria, Croatia, Estonia, Greece, Hungary, Latvia, Lithuania, Poland, Romania, Slovakia, Slovenia and the Czech Republic. Turkey, straddling both Europe and Asia is also a member. Today NATO threatens to add the Ukraine and move to destabilize Russia itself. If it fails, its failure will be due mostly to the supreme leadership of Vladimir Putin, a leader of conscience and talent, far surpassing any such qualities in any Western leader. Western leaders like Obama and Canada's Steven Harper are disgraces to the human race. No wonder the North Korean government called President Obama a "monkey in a tropical jungle," after he egged on the Sony Corporation to release the Western propaganda movie, *the Interview.*

Opposition to American Domination by the Nonaligned Movement

The Western world, dumfounded by its own propaganda about the white man's burden is sometimes at a loss to understand that no country likes being colonized. Of course there are some within every country who will benefit from doing the white man's bidding and cooperate with the colonization of their own people for their own selfish gains. Others are so intimidated by the military, economic, financial and brutally vicious punishments meted out to those who oppose that they pretend liking being colonized by the democratic, freedom-loving, civilized West. After five centuries of barbaric colonization, exploitation and theft of their lands and resources, the Second World War had presented these colonies with an opportunity to be free from the Western yoke. The two major colonial powers during the Second World War were Britain and France. Both had enticed their colonies to fight the Germans with the promise of freedom, much like Lincoln had promised freedom to American blacks to help him defeat the South. More importantly, the Second World War had weakened both Britain and France. Since no one volunteers to be colonized this weakened military state made it much more difficult to prevent most of the colonies from revolting. Much like the American colonies had done earlier. India, Britain's "Jewel in the Crown" would be one of the leaders of this worldwide revolt.

If any country knew the pain and suffering from Western colonization it was India. The West glorifies the nonviolence preaching of Mahatma Gandhi without understanding how Gandhi was only one among many

Indians who had suffered severely during centuries of resistance to British barbarity, racism, exploitation and theft of the resources and rich culture of India. As I said earlier the British had the audacity to crown Queen Victoria as empress of India. There could be no greater humiliation than that. A big country with centuries of history being imposed upon with an emperor from some island somewhere close to an alien continent most Indians had never heard of. The popular Indian saying, "Queen Victoria, very good **man,"** sums it all up. Fear of brutal reprisals by the British air of racial and cultural superiority led to a culture of the Indian expression of British "goodness" as a matter of course, with no meaning or significance of good or bad. Thank God that the vast majority of Indians had no knowledge of who the British were much less that they had ever been governed by them, the so-called *British raj*.

In previous chapters we have documented some of the earlier revolts by Indians against British colonization. These included the defense of India by the Nawab of Bengal, Tipu Sultan, the Mughal Empire and the Maratha Empire. India's struggle for independence continued through the nineteenth and twentieth centuries. Some of the more prominent uprisings were the sepoy mutiny of 1806 at Fort Vellore, the wars waged by the Sikhs in 1845 and 1848, the large scale sepoy rebellion of 1857 incited by the use of cow and pig fat in the cartridges of the British rifles given to the sepoys, the formation of the *Indian National Congress* in 1885, and the return of Gandhi to India in 1915. While the Indian National Congress was dominated by the Indian elite, Gandhi attracted the masses to the Indian independence movement. Even the British, despite their long history of brutality against their colonists, found it difficult, if not impossible, to slaughter millions of Indians.

During World War I the British made the same kinds of promises of independence to Indian leaders as it had made to Arab leaders to get their military support against Germany. India provided well over a million men for the British war against Germany. As with the Arabs, the British had absolutely no intention of keeping their promise of independence to India. Post World War I India was poorer and more exploited by the British than before the War. Attempts by the leaders of the Indian National Congress and Gandhi to hold the British to their World War I promises led the British to imprison them. The Indian Independence movement was leaderless. The Second World War provided the most important opportunity for Indian Independence. Having learned the hard way about British deceit, the Indian leaders demanded independence for India as a **precondition** for India's military support against Germany. Once again the British responded by imprisoning Gandhi and the leaders of the Indian National Congress. But unlike the First World War, the British emerged from World War II, far too weak to keep such a large country as India in bondage. It was the weakened post–World War II British economy which forced Britain to hand over independence to India in 1947.

While Britain and France had been weakened by World War II the American Empire had gained in strength. Despite its massive propaganda to the contrary the American Empire was determined to recolonize **any and all** of the British and French colonies which had successfully revolted. The American Empire imposed on these ex-colonies in Asia, Africa, Latin America and the Caribbean, the unwanted choice of American colonization or Soviet help against American imperialism. A few of these countries, India being the leading example, were sufficiently strong to resist the American pressures without explicit Soviet aid. These countries knew that the American pressure would not be easily resisted. With the American policy of small carrot and big stick, many of the millions of poor in these ex-colonies would choose the small carrot over the big stick. The American Empire had the military capability to bomb any country "back to the stone age" as President George W. Bush threatened to do to Pakistan during his invasion of Afghanistan. With the Americans nuking Japan the people knew that this was no idle threat.

The poor want basic food and shelter. They do not care much how they get that. The American Empire had the military, economic and financial power to impose lasting poverty on you. The people of Japan, South Korea, Taiwan, Hong Kong and Singapore followed the example of the white British colonies of Canada, Australia and New Zealand and voted for the small American carrot over its big stick. They prospered not because of the tiny amount of American aid but because they were not subjected to the powerful American trade, financial and economic embargoes. An ex-colony cannot develop without access to international trade and foreign investment. Every ex-colony which opposed American imperialism was black listed by the American Empire and forced into poverty, alleviated by Russian aid. Impoverished countries like North Korea, Cuba and Iran are still used today by the American Empire to feed its powerful propaganda machine. This propaganda implies that countries are poor not because of the evil embargoes imposed by the West, but because they are too stupid and sinful to accept the gracious and self-sacrificing help of the generous American people blessed by God to bear the white man's burden.

India felt it could help its own independence, and other ex-colonies dreaming of freedom from American imperialism, by speaking out against Western interference. One of the most important, gifted, and brilliant leaders, who had fought tirelessly for Indian Independence, was the Indian diplomat, *V. K. Krishna Menon.* His most important insight was never to be fooled by Western propaganda. As such he was privately awed by Western leaders and publicly reviled by them. When the Western media and Western leaders demonize you, as they have done more recently with leaders like Vladimir Putin, Mahmoud Ahmadinejad and Hugo Chavez, you know that these demonized leaders are telling the truth. When the West celebrates you like Nelson Mandela, the Dalai Lama and Archbishop Desmond Tutu, you know that these celebrated leaders have been co-opted and compromised by the West. Time Magazine depicted Menon on their cover as a snake charmer while President Eisenhower said he was a menace. Some Western leaders grudgingly referred to him as an "evil genius." But British intellectuals such as Bertrand Russell, Aneurin Bevan, and Harold Laski admired his talents.

Menon coined the term "nonaligned movement," during a speech to the UN in 1953. This clearly did not sit well with the implicit ideology of the American Empire that you are either for us or against us. No country had the right to reject the American vision of freedom which was a perfect copycat of the Roman Empire's vision of freedom. Rejecting American imposed freedom was tantamount to rejecting the divine will of God. Americans were the people chosen by God to dictate to the world what freedom is. To question was to disobey and incur the wrath of God. The American Empire had God's permission to determine the severity and brutality of your punishment. In Menon's case the British

Secret Service *MI5* spied on him, beginning in 1929, long before the American Empire replaced the British after World War II. As the world's hero *Edward Snowden* revealed in 2013, Western spying by agencies such as the NSA in the United States has increased rather than decreased, since the American Empire became the leader of the "unfree world."

India knew that it would be playing a very dangerous game by denying absolute allegiance to the American Empire and encouraging others to join this band of rebels. But the fact that every country in Africa, with two minor exceptions, is a member of the *nonaligned group,* despite the American threat and its powerful propaganda, is the most telling example of the innate desire of people to be **free.** Brilliant minds like Menon were convinced that the ex-colonies of Britain, France, Holland, Spain, and Portugal would never voluntarily choose to replace one imperial master with American imperialism. But the ex-colonies were poor after five centuries of theft of their resources by Western Europe. America, by contrast, was rich and powerful, handing out small carrots and wielding very big sticks. Furthermore, seeking any kind of aid from the Soviet Union, because you were embargoed by the West, would make the American Empire extremely angry and you would be punished even more severely. The American Empire would denounce you as a Communist and you would be placed on a black list worse than the devil could dream up.

Nevertheless, India was determined not to replace British colonization by American colonization. It forged ahead with its plans to form a loosely knit nonaligned group of nations that could support each other against the big bad American bully. India's first postindependence prime minister, *Jawaharlal Nehru,* was fully committed to Menon's nonaligned movement. As high commissioner to Britain, Menon was India's leading spokesperson on foreign relations and a very close friend and colleague of Nehru during India's struggle for independence from Britain. India was supported in this quest for a nonaligned group by some of the most prominent leaders of the postcolonial *Third World.* The term "Third World" was really a politically correct term to refer to the countries which had been impoverished by five centuries of Western colonization and theft of their lands and resources. The *Bandung Conference* of April 1955, hosted by the first president of the Republic of

Indonesia, *Sukarno,* marked the beginning of semiformal meetings by the nonaligned nations.

Indonesia, like India, had to struggle long and hard for independence from Dutch colonial rule. Unlike India, which played both sides during World War II, Sukarno fully supported the Japanese invasion of Indonesia as an opportunity to seize its independence. This did not sit well with the British and the Americans. But Sukarno was clever enough to declare Indonesia an independent state immediately after Japan had surrendered to the United States. With the American Empire's own propaganda that it was never an imperial power it was difficult for the United States to explicitly recolonize Indonesia. In addition, the United States had its hands full administering all of its many ill-gotten gains from its emergence as the new leader of the "unfree" world. Post–World War II Holland naturally reinvaded Indonesia with British military aid. After four years of war Holland reluctantly recognized the independence of Indonesia on December 27, 1949. Just as post World War II Britain was too weak to recolonize India and post–World War II France was too weak to recolonize Vietnam/Indo-China, post–World War II Holland was too weak to recolonize Indonesia.

India and Indonesia were joined by many of the ex-colonies of Britain and other Western European imperial powers in forming the nonaligned group. The founding five National Third World leaders were Nehru of India, Suharto of Indonesia, Gamal Nasser of Egypt, Josep Tito of Yugoslavia, and Kwame Nkrumah of Ghana. Some of the more prominent countries which participated in the Bandung Conference included India, China, Japan, Pakistan, Egypt, Iran, Iraq, Saudi Arabia, the Philippines, Turkey, Thailand, Afghanistan, Burma, Ceylon, Vietnam, Ghana and the host country, Indonesia. A total of thirty countries were represented. It was a very auspicious beginning for the promising leaders of what many saw optimistically as the beginning of a postcolonial world. Leaders of the Third World taking center stage were unheard of before. Names like *Zhou Enlai, Nkrumah, Suharto, Nehru, Menon, Nasser, Tito, Indira Gandhi, Ho Chi Minh, Norodom Sihanouk, Cheddi Jagan, Adam Clayton Powell Jr.,* and others who represented their countries would soon become household names across the globe. As more and more colonies claimed their independence their leaders became respected by the Western media as well as the domestic media.

As a young boy growing up in the British colony of British Guiana, I became aware of the names of a growing list of Third World leaders attending sessions of the UN, Commonwealth conferences, and may other international forums. Yugoslavia hosted the second meeting of the nonaligned states in 1961, and Egypt hosted the third meeting in 1964. The *sixties* may be remembered in the West for the Vietnam War, President Kennedy, Fidel Castro, Khrushchev, the Peace movement, the hippies, youth rebellion, university sit-ins, free love and the sexual revolution. But in the Third World it was a time of optimism and celebration of independence from Western imperialism and pride in the quality of its leaders. It was the best example of the domino effect where one colony after another claimed its independence, became a proud member of the UN and produced leaders recognized on the world stage as brilliant statesmen.

Unfortunately, the optimism of the late '50s and early '60s was followed by a downward spiral of economic decline, conflicts, poor leadership, petty squabbling, and increasing dependence on the West or the Soviet Union. It's as if by some strange coincidence that the year 1964 which saw the beginning of the decline of the Soviet Union, with the removal of Khrushchev, also marked the high point of leadership by the nonaligned nations of the Third World. Third World leaders had brought to the world a new type of leadership focusing on peace and cooperation rather than warmongering; trade and economic sharing rather than theft by colonization; social, cultural, racial and income equality rather than capitalist extremes based on private property and Western racial and cultural superiority. After 1964 the Third World leaders abandoned those ideals in favor of the same petty warmongering practices they had criticized Western leaders for possessing. Hope for change and a New World Order had gone out the window. The cherished UN had degenerated into a tool for continued Western imperialism and intervention in the domestic affairs of the Third World by the American Empire and its allies. Today the nonaligned group still exists and meets, but its role in the world has decreased rather than increased since the sixties. South Africa played host for the first time in 1998. Cuba played host for the second time in 2006 and Iran hosted the 2012 meeting.

The "Bad" of the American Empire: Democracy and the Democratization of Consumption by the United States and Its Allies

In documenting what we see as the Bad, Ugly and Uglier, of the American Empire, we begin with the Bad. Here we identify two important and related "bads."

1. **Overconsumption or overt materialism causing planetary degradation and inequalities**
2. **Destruction of true democracy**

Western democracy is materialistic and based on excessive and conspicuous consumption fueled by debt, gluttony and greed. Excessive price competition drives down prices paid by Western consumers leading to Western international corporations paying ridiculously low wages to labor in Third World countries and producing both agricultural and manufactured goods under conditions which are very unsafe for the workers. It has polluted the air and caused excessive waste products and planetary degradation. It has increased the numbers of fat or obese children. The global shift to the emerging economies of China, India, Latin America, Africa and other parts of Asia has led to massive pollution and traffic congestion in those countries which now produce most of the low wage manufactured goods for the spoilt western consumers. Until recently, **racist** immigration policies limited the movement of poor Third World people to the white West. The worship of private property and capitalism over the ideals of communism created growing wealth and income inequality.

I have made it abundantly clear that I have little respect for Western democracy as a political form of government. Political parties in the West must conform to certain norms shaped by the massive use of propaganda and control of the media and **buying** votes with promises of goodies. Worse still, leadership is dumbed down to the lowest common denominator as dictated by brain-dead daytime talk show hosts. However, an important factor in keeping voters happy is the mass production of consumer goods at market prices that the great majority of voters can afford. This began in the United States in the 1920s with what some economists have called the second industrial revolution. It was this availability of consumer goods more than any political ideology which won over Americans to their government and made Russian consumers so critical of their government. Stalin's Russia focused on the production of capital goods to boost its economic growth. This severely limited the production of consumer goods. When people across the globe say they want to go to America most do not know or care about the politics. They see better economic opportunity in America. People in China, for example, could easily see how much better off Asians were in Taiwan, Hong Kong, Japan, South Korea and Singapore.

In the 1920s Americans developed the complementary revolutions of mass production and mass consumption. It was what Hitler wanted so desperately to copy for the German people. Eventually this mass production combined with mass consumption was copied in every Western country, Britain, France, Canada, Germany, Australia, Japan, South Korea, etc. Entrepreneurs like Henry Ford did not plan to bring democracy to the American people but his Model T along with the mass production of consumer durables supported by installment payments did far more for the popularity of Western democracies than universal franchise. The car was the ultimate symbol of wealth and when car ownership was democratized the Americans had won the Cold War. This is why Hitler tried to democratize the Volkswagen and Tata Motors has more recently produced the "People's car" in India. It's ironic that the Western media speak compulsively and incessantly of the need for the Communist Party of China to protect its longevity by giving Chinese consumers economic growth but ignore the fact that it was economic growth in the West which sustained its **mock** democracy. The only difference of course, was that the West gave its citizens high incomes and economic growth by stealing from those it colonized. China's economic growth is fueled by the *global shift* we explain in our last chapter.

In the first part of chapter 8 of our *Rise and Fall of the American Empire* we explained how mass production and mass consumption was a unique American invention. The first industrial revolution pioneered by Britain had produced cheap manufactured goods, such as textiles, for both domestic consumption and exports. English workers in these factories worked long hours, in filthy and dangerous working environments, for very low wages. They were not much better off than those who were employed on the banana or coffee plantations in the Third World. It was the miserable working conditions of the factory workers in England, Germany and France, which generated interest in communism and socialism as ways to help this downtrodden class. Western European entrepreneurs had no vision of mass production combined with mass consumption by the workers who produced the industrial goods. This was a unique American invention copied by every other American ally fighting Communism. It was the McDonalds, KFC's and credit to buy cars and consumer durables which really won the Cold War and explain why there is now a growing list of countries from the Third World jumping on this band wagon. Is it not ironic that the Western media now point to China to support this same view that China's "Communist" government must produce mass consumption to prevent popular dissent? The best evidence of this is Vietnam. The American Empire lost its first major invasion after throwing its massive military advantage and propaganda into that disaster only to find out that it could have easily won over the Vietnamese people by establishing a chain of KFC's and McDonalds along with other symbols of American consumption.

The democratization of consumption by the West was not planned by its political process. When the United States took over the leadership of the "unfree" world after the Second World War, it was opposed only by the Soviet Union. The Communist Revolution of 1917 suggested a propaganda tool for the United States, which was to denounce Communism as evil and sinful. This form of government was contrasted with Western democracy as good and godly. The people would be allowed to vote freely for the candidates of two or three parties. But the political parties could not be too different from each other. In particular they could not be Communist or too socialist. Private property was sacred. In reality it was much like the one party Communist States except that there was the ritual of elections where each party would compete with the other by promising more "free" goods and services than the other almost identical party. These "free" goods and services would be paid for by the voters who were told that they were free by taking some of their income in the form of what was called taxes.

As an example of the parties being almost identical, if President George W. Bush invades Iraq and Afghanistan, President Obama has to do the same. President Obama may send a few more soldiers to Afghanistan and a few less to Iraq than President George W. Bush but there can be no significant difference in the total amount of warmongering. Likewise, in domestic policy. Both will have to portray Main Street as being more important than Wall Street but must implement policies which always favor Wall Street over Main Street. Income inequality will likely increase under both the Republicans and the Democrats. The poor will be told that their vote is important but will remain poor. Many will be given the opportunity to join the armed forces and fight for their country because that was the right thing to do. Since American and Canadian soldiers are sent to far off countries like Afghanistan and told that they are sent to "defend their respective countries," an idiotic implication would be that somehow Canada and the United States bubbles up territory across the globe much like the "China Syndrome." For those of you who did not see that Hollywood movie the China Syndrome refers to the fact that a nuclear leak in the United States can penetrate underground all the way to China. It's the same with U.S. and Canadian territory. Since they bubble up all the way to Afghanistan our "brave young soldiers" never go there to kill Afghans, as Prince Harry did, but only to defend Canada or defend the United States, as the case may be. They would never be allowed to question who or why they were told to kill, maim, and destroy and impoverish. Should they disobey and question, they would be deemed to be terrorists and sent to prison in Guantanamo because Guantanamo is not on American soil but Cuban territory—stolen by the American Empire simply because it has the military capability to steal whatever it wants and the propaganda machine to convince many that it was a good kind of stealing. Any bad is automatically converted to a good if done by Canada or the United States.

For example, the key point about the December 9, 2014, Senate Intelligence Committee Report on torture by the CIA is not the use of torture. The West has always used extreme forms of torture and will continue to do so. The key point of the Report is the fact that it was done outside the United States, like Guantanamo, and by private contractors. The United States had begun the practice of *Extraordinary Rendition* since the administration of President Bill Clinton. This policy of sending people, many of whom had committed no crime, to other countries to be tortured was done simply to make it more difficult to prosecute Americans. Guantanamo had become too well-known to the world as the prison where Americans practiced extreme torture. The Americans had to create what came to be called "black sites" around the world to be able to hone its powerful propaganda machine that it was against the use of torture. Once again, the Americans and its Western allies can speak out loudly against the use of torture so as to kill and prosecute Third World leaders suspected of using torture. At the same time it is free to use far more extreme forms of torture in these secret prisons. Using private contractors was a further precaution against American officials being prosecuted for war crimes.

The above was what the political process did. But without being fully aware, this highly propagandized political process of the good capitalists versus the bad Communists was underpinned more by accident than design by the entrepreneurial inventions of mass production, mass consumption and mass marketing. Spirituality went out the window without even being cognizant of that. The voters still went to church and celebrated Christian and Jewish holidays but these spiritual celebrations became more and more materialistic. Christmas and Easter became huge successful commercial events for Western businesses. Countries like India where spiritualism was emphasized were demonized by the West as poor and backward. Islamic countries were demonized as extremists and in time religious extremism was demonized as more evil than Communism. The Western entrepreneurs produced the goods and services at prices affordable to the majority of consumers aided by mass marketing and generous availability of credit. In cases where workers in Third World countries were paid ridiculously low wages and worked in insanitary and unsafe conditions the prices to the Western consumers were ridiculously low. Bananas and coffee are old examples. Clothing is a more recent example occurring after some Third World economies like China, India, Brazil and others graduated from Third World status to emerging economy status.

Voters in these so-called democracies were really bribed to support the political process which pitted the West against the Communists and now against Islam. Since these voters cared very little about the political process and far more about their materialistic needs and those of their families, protecting their jobs became paramount. The West won the war because of an environment which was far more conducive to entrepreneurship. It is extremely difficult for entrepreneurship to flourish either in a Planned economy, like the Soviet Union, or in highly religious societies, where spirituality trumps materialism or where workers have to disrupt work to pray five times every day, or women are **too respected** to perform certain kinds of work or tasks.

Bombarded by the ready availability of consumer goods, from cheap restaurants to cars to blue jeans and Hollywood movies, it is understandable why so many of the poor of the Third World wanted so desperately to emigrate to the West. In many cases these workers were poor, not because of the spirituality of their countries, but because the Western countries had colonized them and forced them to seek employment on the plantations of the lands stolen by the imperial power. Work on the banana and coffee plantations owned by the imperial powers paid very little. Today it's the garment factories in Bangladesh, for example. They wanted to migrate to the West not because of any deep understanding of democracy or freedom but because of economic opportunities and the ability to afford those consumer goods they knew of from the Hollywood movies they had seen. The problem, of course, was that only **whites** could migrate to the West, especially if you were poor and not highly educated.

Up until the *global shift,* which we explain in our last chapter, the West had a monopoly on the mass production of consumer goods at prices which the majority of consumers could afford. Those people in the Third World who did not subscribe to the notion that spirituality trumped poverty, were not allowed to migrate to the West to share in that bonanza of consumer goods. Nor were the people living in the

Communist countries, who cared little about the politics of Communism versus Capitalism, allowed to migrate to the West. Apart from the odd dissident artist who publicized his ignorant belief in the freedoms of the West, these people dreamed of migrating to America and the West for purely materialistic reasons. America was rich and they were poor. It's that simple. America and the West were rich both because of their military superiority which enabled them to colonize and steal as well as their materialistic societies and free enterprise economic systems which enabled entrepreneurship to flourish. The Protestant work ethic combined with private property and opportunities for entrepreneurship trumped all other motivations.

The ability of the average American consumer to afford a car and eat out was the good side of the democratization of consumption. At a time when most of the people of the Third World suffered from severe malnutrition the average American was well fed, housed, clothed and transported. Cheap supply of protein from beef and other meat products made the Americans the tallest people on the globe. But soon this cheap and ready abundance of consumer goods and food led to severe problems associated with obesity, gluttony, pollution and volumes of junk. Restaurants followed McDonalds and other fast food outlets with ridiculously cheap "supersize me" portions of food and carbonated drinks. Marketing and credit encouraged the consumption of new products which embodied new and fast changing technologies. High and rising consumption fueled more by debt than rising incomes became the mantra for economic growth, employment, and solutions for every ailment in the West. Despite the rising volume of junk and damage to the environment, every Western leader pleads with consumers to buy ever more of this junk, to be able to create ever more worthless jobs to get them reelected to office, or to compete with other countries driven by the same madness. While driving this engine of disaster, they simultaneously preach the virtues of recycling, much like those who feed their obesity with supersize portions, experiment with every new diet, exercise machine, and weight reduction program. As with warmongering, imperialism and military invasions, these Western leaders follow each other like sheep.

Every Western country today has a serious obesity problem, a serious waste disposal problem, and a serious debt problem. Its population is aging and will require expensive heath care and financial support during many years of retirement. Colonization is no longer profitable as the cost of military invasions now exceeds the value of what can be stolen. Classic examples of this are the latest American invasions of Iraq and Afghanistan. Increased taxation is extremely unpopular and impossible to implement in Western democracies where the vote has to be bought with policies that the majority of the electorate support. No Western country is addressing these problems. Instead they are exporting these same problems to the Third World countries by using the production of consumer goods as the most recent yardstick of human progress and civilized behavior. India's emphasis on spirituality, for example, has been abandoned and Muslim countries are urged to Westernize. Chinese consumers are encouraged to abandon the "primitive" bicycle for the Western status symbol of the car. Obesity has replaced malnourishment as the global disease.

A more positive change has been the significant increase in nonwhite immigration into the West. I see this as positive because it is one way of equalizing global incomes. It's bad enough that Canada, for example, stole so much land from the First Nations instead of sharing the abundance of land with them. Worse is that such a vast amount of land should be shared and enjoyed by so few of the world's teeming billions. One reason for this increase in nonwhite immigration into the West is the declining birthrates in Canada and across Western Europe. Another reason has been the improvement in white attitudes toward nonwhites. Overt racism, especially at the street level, has declined dramatically in the West. Whites today are far more tolerant and respectful of nonwhite immigrants. The numbers of nonwhites in Canada, for example, has grown significantly in the present century. It's still the case that the leadership positions in politics, business and education are dominated by whites. This is another example of bad democracy. Democratic racism is deemed acceptable by whites because it's to their advantage. When democracy produced governments which were "*Communist*" or not sufficiently pro-West, or more recently, governments such as the *Muslim Brotherhood* or *Hamas,* the West quickly disowned democracy. But when democracy serves to protect the historical racist benefits of whites the West embraces it wholeheartedly. In time nonwhites may become the majority in many Western countries and democracy could then be to their advantage as is the case today in South Africa. Of course, under President Mandela, blacks made very little economic or political progress even with democracy working in their favor in the elections. Mandela seemed more interested in the worldwide celebrations of his birthdays in every Western country than in promoting the economic advancement of his black voters.

The Ugly and Uglier American Empire: Major Crimes against Humanity Committed by the Civilized West: First Nations Genocide and Concentration Camps, African Slavery, Hiroshima/Nagasaki, Allende/Pinochet, Vietnam, Iraq/Afghanistan, Palestine/Gaza

The Term "Ugly American" was popularized by the 1963 Hollywood movie using that title and starring the iconic and truly **civilized** American, Marlon Brando. As I have said before Hollywood is often ahead of the times. We have deliberately entitled this chapter as the "Bad, Ugly and Uglier" to emphasize the very **Ugly,** implying far worse than **Bad or Ugly,** nature of American Imperialism. As we have said many times the United States manipulates the message by controlling the world's media and manages to convince the majority of Americans and a significant minority of non-Americans that its worldwide military invasions and colonizations are not imperialistic but a beneficent self-sacrifice by Americans to aid the poor and defenseless people of the Third World. I am of the minority view that these military invasions and colonizations are exactly the opposite in that they are not just bad but indeed very ugly, brutal, nasty, inhumane and barbaric. In this section we will identify a total of **four** separate facts of American history which justifies my claim that the United States is a **Very Ugly** American Empire which does not deserve to be referred to as civilized. It is indeed more barbaric than any other state or empire. These four facts, which we consider in more detail below, are the genocide committed against the First Nations and the theft of their land, resources and culture, the enslavement and racism against Africans, the military invasions and economic punishment imposed on states across the globe and the use of a massive propaganda machine and control of international institutions and media to portray itself as exactly the opposite of what it is.

Being bad is a sin against God. But being Ugly is being worse than the devil. It's worse because we know the devil is bad. But to be the devil and claim you are God is far worse. It's similar to the reason that I have said that President George W. Bush could never have been as evil as President Obama. President Bush never tried to hide the fact that he was evil. But President Obama is just as evil but claims to be good. Propaganda works. Why else would it be used? President Obama is more evil because his propaganda convinces many that he is good. This gives him a free ride with little criticism or blowback when he commits his evil deeds. He has even convinced the world that warmongering is good.

Many in the Western media had proudly proclaimed their dislike of George W. Bush, during his presidencies, because he was a warmonger. None has said that of Barack Obama even though he has invaded more countries and used more drones to kill than President Bush. Hell! Obama has even been awarded the Nobel Peace Prize for his warmongering. Since his presidency the world has become supportive of American warmongering and invasions, or at least silent about it. The fact is that the deliberate exportation of America's evil culture to the rest of the world under the guise of spreading democracy, freedom and civilized behavior is used to aid its military invasions and successful conquests and colonizations. Even the French have come onboard. That is the extent to which Obama has manipulated public opinion. Wield a bigger stick than Bush but be soft about it. For the relatively few who admired Bush, the outspoken warmonger, they now have to settle for Canada's prime minister, Steven Harper. Poor Steven does his best to imitate Bush but Canada does not have the clout. Unlike the venom spewed at Bush for his warmongering bravado, Harper is ignored except by the unimportant Canadian media.

The Western media admires a warmongering leader. But it hates one who boasts about it. You must pretend that your warmongering is only for the betterment of the world. Use the Second World War as your guide to becoming a beloved warmonger. Pretend there is an evil like Hitler that you need to squash like a bug to save humanity. The media will support your drones, your Gantanamos, your Abu Graibs, your extraordinary renditions to "black sites" outside the United States, and even the use of nuclear weapons. President Obama is the quintessential media loving warmonger. But boast about your warmongering desires and you become another media hating George W. Bush. The irony, of course, is that boasting warmongers like George W. Bush are our only hope. Western leaders are elected by people who, by and large, want all of their leaders to invade, conquer, colonize and steal from those who cannot defend their lands. Having a leader like George W. Bush, who boasts about achieving what the people elected him to do, draw the ire of the media and thereby limits his warmongering. With leaders like Barack Obama who are very skillful at pretending not to be warmongers, or even disliking warmongering, there are no limits to their warmongering and military invasions. Not only do they get a free ride they are egged on by the media to do more and more because the media foolishly believes that they are showing too much restraint because of their ability to hide their love of warmongering.

First Nations Genocide and Concentration Camps

Among the many heinous crimes against humanity committed by the American Empire and the West, the most important of these crimes, as measured by the large numbers of people affected, must be the crimes inflicted on the **indigenous peoples** who inhabited the New World and countries like Australia and New Zealand. Many of these people were killed off during the military invasions of the Western European Empires but others were imprisoned on "Reserves" much like Concentration Camps. Many are still imprisoned on these Reserves/Concentration Camps today. Canada and the United States constantly remind the world of the Jews killed in the Concentration camps but are silent on their continued genocide and human rights abuse of the First Nations whose lands they stole to become the States we know as Canada and the United States. They preach to the rest of the world but never to themselves and do their utmost to keep their voters ignorant of the First Nations still imprisoned on Reserves. Worse still, they deliberately educate their voters to think of First Nations as a drain on taxpayers and lazy dependents.

The reality is that the First Nations Reserves were created on the most useless lands not worth stealing so that the few surviving First Nations could be made docile, idle drunks and dependent on food and subsistence from their white captors. They would never have the opportunity to acquire the wherewithal to be able to fight those who had stolen their lands, their culture, their language, their dignity, their children, their religion, their self-respect and their manhood. After generations of this determined policy to make the First Nations dependent and docile, Canada and the United States teach this generation that the First Nations are poor drunks who pay no taxes but beg for ever more taxpayer assistance. A lot of the taxpayer dollars funding for the First Nations Reserves are mismanaged by governments who refuse to make the First Nations self-governing. A lot more is spent in legal costs fighting the First Nations in the courts. It was these white thieves who fed the First Nations alcohol to make it easier to steal their lands and now the children on the Reserves sniff gas because alcohol is too expensive. The world knows nothing about these continued human rights abuses because the West controls the world's media and propaganda machine. Instead we hear of the incessant preaching of Canada and the United States to countries like China which treat their ethnic minorities with far more dignity and self-respect.

One of the most amazing example of Western hypocrisy is its simultaneous condemnation of Hitler's genocide committed against the Jews, and its total silence of its own genocide committed against the First Nations of the United States, Canada, and the Aborigines in Australia. This genocide committed against First Nations, fully documented in my *American Invasions,* as well as the theft of their lands, resources, culture, languages, customs, children and sanity, is the most heinous crime committed by the West over a period of five centuries. The United States and Canada should be totally ashamed to accuse any country of any human rights abuses since their human rights abuses pale in comparison to those committed by Canada and the United States against the First Nations and continue to be committed to this day because no one speaks about it in the same way that Canada accuses others openly and disgustingly without shame. This is truly the Ugliest of the Bad, the Ugly and the Uglier.

The English and French came to North America looking for gold and a sea passage to Asia just as the Spanish and Portuguese had done before. They pretended to be traders when they initially encountered the First Nations. But as soon they were militarily strong enough they began to steal their lands and resources, to kill at will, to enslave, to commit acts of great barbarity and to convert to Christianity by combining their heinous crimes with the most subversive and demented pretense of being godly or religious. It was no wonder that the First Nations were so confused by the priests standing side by side with the thieves and killers. Of course some of the First Nations chose to take refuge in the church, if they had no way of escaping the brutality of the invaders, by pretending to believe in the evil Christian God. But the world cannot pretend that either Canada or the United States is a legitimate country any more than if the Europeans had committed the same level of genocide in South Africa or India and not returned those countries to their original inhabitants. Buying a stolen car can never make you the legitimate owner any more than newcomers buying stolen land in Canada or the United States can make them legitimate owners. Hitler committed crimes against the Jews but he did not steal Germany from them. The Jews killed by Hitler numbered 6 million. The First Nations killed by Canada and the United States numbered 10 million. Canada and the United States committed the same crimes and **Holocaust** against the First Nations as Hitler did against the Jews but also stole their countries and continue to bully the world into accepting these stolen countries as if they were their own. That is far more evil than what Hitler did but the world is silent on this matter and both of these evil countries are allowed to preach to others whose crimes are far less. The United States is even bold enough to call its Holocaust and Genocide of the First Nations **Manifest Destiny.**

What is even more quintessential American/Canadian about our comparison with Hitler's treatment of the Jews, is that unlike Germany which has acknowledged Hitler's crimes against the Jews, the United States and Canada still have the few survivors of its **holocaust** imprisoned on reserves. Before Canada and the United States can begin to make amends for their crimes against the First Nations it has to begin by acknowledging them as Germany has done. But both Canada and the United States pretend that there was no crime and continue to point fingers at others. Canada and the United States are large enough to share the lands with the First Nations. In the beginning the First Nations were willing to share but the thieves wanted them all. Today the First Nations still want to share but still the descendants of the thieves want it all. And still the world points fingers at Hitler or North Korea or Iran or China or Putin, but not at these two prime evildoers, Canada and the United States. The West has made the world an upside-down world, with justice turned on its head, and where its well-honed propaganda machine reigns supreme. People are rightfully confused.

After the Spanish had explored the western coast of North America, the French, English, Dutch, and Russians, made contacts with the First Nations on both the west and east coasts. It was not until the beginning of the seventeenth century that the English, Dutch and French, began to steal the lands of the First Nations on the Atlantic coast. Their weapons were superior to the bows and arrows and spears used by the First Nations. In addition, they carried diseases such as small pox and measles which they used widely to infect the First Nations who had no immunity to these diseases. Since the ten million First Nations were dispersed over a vast land area the Dutch, French and English invaders conquered and stole relatively small parcels of land along the Atlantic seaboard, running north from Newfoundland and south as far as Florida, which, at the time, had already been stolen from the First Nations by Spain. The few surviving First Nations escaped to the west. As the invaders brought more and more Western Europeans with bigger and bigger ships and guns they slaughtered and infected ever greater numbers of First Nations, enslaved some, converted some to Christianity, imprisoned some on reserves, and chased the others further west into the interior.

As I explained in my prequels, the Western Europeans faced an inevitable limit to their conquests and thefts of First Nations lands by the fact that they had to bring their guns, ammunition and supplies across the Atlantic Ocean at a time when sea transportation was not as fast or developed as it is today. Had the English, Dutch and French not enabled the creation of an independent United States of America in 1775, it's very likely that the First Nations would have kept all of North America. They would certainly have kept most of it and governed what they kept as the blacks in South Africa now do. The Western Europeans would have continued to steal relatively small parcels of land on both the Atlantic and Pacific coasts but with the bulk of North America still populated by First Nations, as India and South Africa were populated by Indians and Africans, respectively, the First Nations might have been able to reclaim those lands after the Second World War, as both the Indians and South Africans have done.

The newly created United States of America on stolen First Nations land marked the beginning of the end of the First Nations in all of North America. In my *American Invasions* I have documented fully how the tiny USA of 1775, expanded westward to steal every inch of First Nations land south of what we call Canada today, and north of what we call Mexico today. The many wars with the First Nations are also documented in my *American Invasions.* The theft of such a vast amount of land took more than a century of wars, but the USA was far more determined in its commitment to **exterminate** the First Nations than Germany was in its commitment to exterminate the Jews. As many an American general has proclaimed, "the only good Indian is a dead Indian, kill them all, women and children." As the USA expanded from its initial size in 1775, it gained in military and economic power with every new state it created with additional stolen land, while the First Nations became weaker militarily. Unlike the USA, which continued to be a single nation, even when it added stolen land far exceeding its original size, the First Nations were never a single nation. That was an additional weakness over and above the superior military of the USA and its continued use of biological warfare. The USA naturally expanded by first stealing lands adjacent to its original Atlantic base. But with the advent of canals and railways it was able to expand further and further inland. In the seventy-five years between 1775 and 1850 the USA had more than tripled its size by waging wars and stealing First Nations lands to add eighteen new states to its original thirteen states. Some of these states, such as Florida, Texas, and California, had been previously stolen from the First Nations by Spain and Mexico and were then stolen again from Spain and Mexico by the USA.

During this seventy-five-year period the USA had become so militarily powerful that it no longer stole only from the First Nations, but from those who had previously stolen from the First Nations, such as Spain, Holland, France, England and Mexico. When the Southern states threatened to break up this growing behemoth into two separate countries President Lincoln set about **killing his own people** in numbers that make future leaders like President Assad of Syria and Gaddafi of Libya, look like Mother Teresa. With any break-up of the USA put to rest by Lincoln's **brutal** war on the South, the USA continued its wars and thefts of First Nations lands, adding another nineteen states, including Alaska and Hawaii, by the beginning of the First World War. During the century and a half following the creation of the USA in 1775, the First Nations lost all of their lands in North America. Their loss of land in Mexico had begun much earlier with the invasion of Spain and the creation of the new country of Mexico. Like the United States later, the children of the Europeans who had initially stolen the land from the First Nations, rebelled against their parents and took the land for themselves. Canada was the last of the "Three Amigos" to steal what was left of North America from the First Nations and Inuit.

Under NAFTA today, the "Three Amigos" argue with each other over trade, investments, pipelines, border security, immigration and drugs. There is not even a casual reference to the First Nations they almost wiped out and whose lands, culture and resources they stole over the last five centuries. In like manner Quebec argues with English Canada about its rights to the lands in Quebec as if those lands in Quebec and English Canada had never been stolen from the First Nations. While the United States boasts of Manifest Destiny as their excuse for committing **genocide,** the Canadians portray their Nation as a bastion for human rights. Both of these unashamed **thieves** portrayed the First Nations as far less than animals, deserving the slaughter inflicted on them for the good of the human race. Canadians and Americans continue to portray themselves as the most civilized of the civilized West. Nothing could be further from the truth. Only their military weapons, use of germ warfare, greed and hypocrisy were, and are, civilized.

The Canadian Accomplice of the Ugly American

The Americans did not steal North America all by themselves. While the United States was the crucial and indispensable leader in enabling the theft of all of North America from the First Nations, Mexico and Canada were the junior accomplices in this act of **genocide.** The land stolen by Mexico was more densely populated than that stolen by the United States while the land stolen by Canada was less populated than that of the United States. Recent estimates suggest that there were about 20 million First Nations living in the lands stolen by Mexico, the USA and Canada. Half of them lived in the lands stolen by the USA and Canada, with about 2 million living in what is now Canada. Our primary contention is that without France and England aiding the creation of the new country of the United States, neither the territory of the current United States nor the territory of what is now Canada would have been stolen from the First Nations. The First Nations may still have lost the lands which became Mexico, but not the lands which became Canada and the United States. We now turn briefly to the Canadian theft and **genocide.**

Once the USA became a new country in 1775, it developed the military muscle as well as the propaganda and barbarity, with which to invade and conquer most of the New World. This included the First Nations lands which were stolen by Canada. Prior to the creation of the United States, many Western European Nations had fought the First Nations for their lands. These included the Norsemen, the Spanish, the Portuguese, the Dutch, the French, the British and the Swedes. But by the time the United States was created as a new independent country, the fight for First Nations lands in North America was among the Americans, British and Mexicans. With the British engaged elsewhere, fighting the French for world domination, the Americans had the upper hand since neither the First Nations nor the Mexicans had the same level of sophisticated military and propaganda, as well as the penchant for barbarity, which the Americans possessed. From the very beginning American invaders, traders, trappers, hunters, settlers, thieves, miners and missionaries saw the First Nation as a **Wild Indian** to be hunted and killed like game. They even coined the term "Tame Indian" to indicate that a First Nation had been "tamed" like any wild animal had been. You did not need to kill him now that he had been "tamed" just like you do not need to kill a wild animal that had been tamed not to bite or attack people.

In clearing the forest for settlements, plantations, farms and cities the First Nation had to be slaughtered like any other wild animal that stood in the way of "progress." First Nations were best killed off with guns or diseases but a few could be "tamed" by imprisoning them on reserves much like corralling wild horses to tame them. The children of the rich Western Europeans colluded, complained, rebelled, and invented propaganda to convince France and Britain to grant them independence. Once they had achieved that goal they set about exterminating the *Wild Indians* along with other wild animals such as the buffalo and bison to colonize and conquer all of the New World. But the English and Mexicans opposed them in the North American portion of the New World. While the First Nations also opposed the Americans, they were disunited. They had always been many *Nations,* and continued to operate in that fashion. When the British, French and Spanish competed with each other, the disunity of the First Nations was not as destructive since different First Nations could form alliances with different Western European powers. But with the unity of the ever larger American state, the disunity of the First Nations was suicidal. Many First Nation leaders attempted to unite the First Nations in an alliance with the English against the Americans. This was only partially successful. Many First Nations continued to fight each other or, worse still, allied with the Americans. With the First Nations disunited, the English engaged elsewhere, and the Mexicans still struggling for their independence from Spain, the Americans conquered the lands which became the fifty states of the USA. The Mexicans held on to about half of what Spain had originally stolen from the First Nations, and the English kept the lands which became Canada.

Our contention is that without the constant threat of the Americans to steal all of the Americas, the English may very well have stuck to their original intent of not stealing First Nations lands west of the Royal Proclamation line England had agreed to with the First Nations in October 1763. These were the lands west of the Appalachian Mountains. As we explained in our *Rise and Fall of the American Empire,* the English had formed a long lasting alliance with the six Nations of the Iroquois League, to defeat the French in North America. These First Nations were given the status of *British subjects* with the Treaty of Utrecht of

1713. The more important reason, of course, was that it would have been uneconomical for the English to first wage wars on the First Nations over such a vast area and then hold the land permanently by military force. Already the conquest of eight of the eleven English forts by the First Nations led by *Pontiac* had been the incentive for the English agreeing to the Proclamation line. As I have said before, the Western Europeans knew it's better to trade than colonize whenever the gains from trade exceed the military cost of stealing. The lucrative fur trade, for example, could be genuine trade rather than colonization under the guise of trade. England had been stretched to its limit in North America, by the lands it had stolen from the First Nations east of the Appalachian Mountains. It had to hold them both from the First Nations and the French. Its remaining military resources, and its powerful navy, were best used in other parts of the globe such as Asia and Africa. Peace with the First Nations meant that a few English soldiers, and a few scattered forts across Canada, would guarantee the safety of the lucrative fur trade to England. But the Americans would not leave well alone. They agitated for full independence and afterward showed such aggression in their conquests and colonization, that the English had no choice but to respond, if England wanted to maintain its credibility as the world's leading empire.

The United States signaled its intention of invading and colonizing Canada during its War of Independence by invading Canada in 1775. The French Empire colluded with the Americans hoping to regain some of the lands it had stolen from the First Nations which Britain had, in turn, stolen from the French. When this war ended, the British granted independence to the United States. As a result many Americans, the United Empire Loyalists, moved into First Nations lands in Canada. These new lands stolen from the First Nations were initially called *Upper Canada*. We know it today as Canada's most populous province of Ontario. The British welcomed this influx of new settlers into its colonies in Canada since they would overwhelm the smaller numbers of French settlers whose lands the English had stolen after the Seven Years' War. Of course, it was the lands which the French had initially stolen from the First Nations. In addition, the United Empire Loyalists would help to defend the English Canadian colonies from future U.S. invasions. Finally, these additional settlers would help England to continue to export supplies to its **slave** sugar plantations in the Caribbean from Canada, replacing the exports from the thirteen American colonies, now that these thirteen colonies in the United States had been lost to the new American Empire.

With the loss of the thirteen American colonies, England encouraged **white** immigrants into its colonies in Canada. The newly independent United States was attracting large numbers of European immigrants and England saw this as an American threat to its Canadian colonies. This English response to the newly created USA, dealt a double blow to the First Nations in North America. First, American independence ended English military protection of the First Nations lands west of the Appalachian Mountains, and the English response to the new American threat, of encouraging settlements over trade in its Canadian colonies, meant English theft of more First Nations lands in Canada. Whereas, prior to U.S. independence, the English had halted further colonization and theft of First Nations lands, in both what became the United States and Canada, it now **competed** with the United States in **stealing** more First Nations lands. The new American Empire had replaced the French Empire as the prime competitor of Britain for the theft of First Nations lands in North America. The British surrender of its stolen First Nations lands to the new American Empire had ended the military and political influence of Britain's First Nations ally, the *Six Nation Iroquois League.* This alliance had served the British well when the British were fighting the French. But the First Nations were no match for the new American juggernaut. The British switched its military strategy from one of copying the French, by forming an alliance with those First Nations not allied with the French, to one of copying the Americans, by encouraging European settlers to steal First Nations lands in Canada, just as the Americans were encouraging European settlers to steal First Nations lands in the United States. This is the key to understanding how American independence led to the theft of all of the First Nations in North America.

The British maintained an uneasy alliance with the First Nations until the second invasion of Canada by the United States in 1812. During that war, the First Nations played its final part as an ally of the British. Their last great military leader, *Tecumseh,* was killed in battle and after this war the First Nations were never militarily powerful enough either to resist the Americans or the British. At the time of the 1812–1814 War, the American population was 7 million while the English/French population in Canada was less than a million. With so many First Nations killed off by wars and European diseases it was clear to the British that their alliance with a dwindling number of First Nations could never match the massive growth of the American/European population. Encouraging Europeans to move to its colonies in Canada, and **steal** the First Nations lands in Canada, was clearly a superior military strategy after the 1812–1814 War. This war had put the final nail in the coffin for the First Nations in North America. If the British did not colonize Canada the Americans would have. This does not justify the Canadian denial that Canada was founded on lands stolen from the First Nations. Canada's recognition of its theft could lead to a genuine sharing of this huge piece of real estate with those from whom it has been stolen. But Canada continues to deny its First Nations, their own state, separate from the Canadian state. While the world today rightly clamors for a two-state solution to the Palestine/Israeli conflict, no equivalent solution has been offered to the First Nations of Canada.

On the Pacific coast the Spanish and Russians had given up their competition with the English and Americans. But once again it was the American threat to the English which led to the theft and hasty colonization of the First Nations lands in what we now know as Canada's Western province of British Columbia. As in other parts of the United States, it was the discovery of gold in British Columbia, which led to the stampede of Americans into British Columbia and the resulting fear of the British that the Americans would colonize British Columbia, if they did not beat them to it. The influx of European Americans into the lands of the First Nations on the West coast, also infected the First Nations with the same European diseases, such as small pox, to which they had no immunity. The British were able to beat the Americans by using the resources of its powerful trading company, the *Hudson Bay Company, HBC*. The HBC had moved across the entire width of Canada from Montreal to the Pacific coast, to expand its fur trade with the First Nations. As with the lands in Upper Canada, it was the American threat which was the impetus for English colonization and theft of the First Nations lands across all of Canada.

Canada imitated the American policy of killing off the First Nations by wars and diseases and imprisoning and **taming** the remainder on reserves. Reserves were typically set up on land of little economic value to the European thieves and intended to make the First Nations dependent on the state, like prisoners, so that they would never have the will or the means to resist the thieves by force. New European settlers reduced the hunting and fishing opportunities for the surviving First Nations. Like the buffalo in the United States, the bison disappeared in Canada. With their lands and resources stolen, the First Nations were herded like sheep into Reserves and became dependent on handouts from the Canadian government. Canada also implemented a barbaric policy of forcing the children of First Nations to live in what was called *Residential schools* where Christian priests would torture and sexually abuse the children as part of some kind of primitive religious ritual of exterminating "Indian" culture and language from future generations of First Nations. Other First Nations cultural practices such as the potlatch were made illegal. With no pride, independence, self-worth, language, culture or religion, the First Nations on the Reserves killed time by getting drunk. Today their children get high by sniffing gas. They continue to live in squalor without decent schools, running water, heat, housing and health care. Like the United States, the Canadian policy after the 1812–1814 War, was one of combining extermination, **genocide,** with forced assimilation, **cultural genocide.** With the overwhelming military advantage of the Canadian governments, the remaining First Nations fight Canada in the courts, occasionally blockading roads, and rallying with Canadians who oppose the Canadian government's policies of destroying natural habitats, polluting the environment with its insatiable search for oil and gas, pipelines and dangerous rail transportation, and promotion of economic growth over environmental protection.

The 2013 *Idle No More* movement and rallies were favorably supported by many Canadians. The Canadian government formally apologized to the First Nations in 2008 for the disastrous Residential schools, but shows no sign of discontinuing its fight in the courts over land claims, or ever granting full Nation status to the First Nations.

Instead, Canada continues to spread propaganda about mistreatment of ethnic minorities around the globe to take the spotlight off its own continuing history of **genocide** and **holocaust.** This kind of hypocrisy suggests to me that Canada is more likely to create two states with English and French rather than with Canada and First Nations. While the French have every right to a state of their own, they came to Quebec long after the First Nations. Therefore, the First Nations have a much higher moral claim to their own state compared with either the French or the English.

Slavery and Racism in the United States and Canada

Our second indictment of what we see as the **Very Ugly** in the **Uglier American** is its enslavement of the **black** race, and to a much lesser extent the **red** race, for economic, political, and military advantage, and to support its illegitimate claims to stolen territory, based on racial superiority and being civilized. This second indictment of what is **Very Ugly** is not totally unrelated to our foremost indictment of what is **Very Ugly** about the American Empire. The American Empire had stolen so much land from the First Nations that it could not develop the stolen land by bringing **whites** from Europe. Not wanting to contaminate its "lily-white image" of what it called its freedom-loving republic, where all men are created equal, with Asian or African immigrants, it imported **black slaves** from Africa. As we explained in our first chapter, when America proclaims its democratic roots with Greece, and republican roots with Rome, we see only its connection with **slavery and empire.** In addition to the enslavement of Africans, estimates suggest that the British sold into slavery as many as fifty thousand First Nations, living in what is now part of the United States. Some readers may foolishly think that the American enslavement of blacks is passé. Nothing could be further from the truth.

The USA and Canada were created as models of states with entrenched freedoms for all. But from their inception they used propaganda and hypocrisy, and continue with that same hypocrisy and propaganda to send young men to Afghanistan, Iraq, Vietnam, Syria, Libya, Ukraine, Palestine, Yemen, Somalia, etc., to kill, maim, and destroy the lives of millions of innocent people, by claiming that these young men are defending their country and defending freedoms. In reality these young men are not defending **anything.** You do not defend your country unless it's invaded by an aggressor and you defend it in your **homeland** not thousands of miles away in some unknown mountains. These young men such as Prince Harry, armed with his killer copter, are sent to **kill innocent people,** not to defend anything. The probability of an Afghan invading Canada, the United States, or Britain by **flying carpet and a slingshot** is zero. It's therefore important that you understand the roots of this hypocrisy and propaganda. Those roots are to be found in the genocide of the First Nations and the theft of their lands, combined with the importation and enslavement of Africans, while preaching the same propaganda of creating freedom for all, as they do today when they invade and destroy the lives of so many.

The pretend freedom-loving republic was governed by men who were **slave owners.** The much lauded American constitution legalized the most primitive and barbaric institution, **slavery.** It also enshrined the most barbaric and inhumane of all trade, the **slave trade.** In fact, when Britain finally abolished the Atlantic slave trade in 1807, the United States created its own internal slave trade rightly called the new **Middle Passage.** The Roman Empire enslaved those who rebelled against Rome and were captured in battle. The Americans bought Africans caught and transported in chains, under the most barbaric conditions imaginable, across the Atlantic and down the Mississippi River. When Britain abolished slavery in all of its colonies in 1833, the United States continued its barbaric institution of **slavery.** President Lincoln's much ballyhooed "Gettysburg Address" that "Four score and seven years ago our fathers brought forth on this continent, a new nation, conceived in Liberty, and dedicated to the proposition that all men are created equal" is such **unadulterated nonsense** that it is a classic example of how the West uses its so-called freedom of the press to lie and promote its powerful propaganda machine. If indeed, a new nation had been conceived four score and seven years ago dedicated to the proposition that "all men are created equal," why would Lincoln have needed to wage a barbaric civil war on the Southern states, **and kill so many of his own people,** to end slavery? Why would this new nation elect a prominent

slave owner, George Washington, to be its first president? Why would this new nation continue to elect **slave owners** as its future presidents? Why would this new nation **expand** its use of slavery by adding cotton plantations on stolen First Nations lands after it had been created? Why would it increase its slave population to **four million** after it had been created? Why would the blacks, who were mostly slaves, increase as a percent of the total U.S. population to 19 percent in 1810 after this so-called freedom-loving republic had been created? Having convincingly piled the horse manure ever higher and deeper in his Gettysburg Address, President Lincoln must have been most surprised that Harvard University did not award him an honorary Ph.D. for his lies.

Why would the British be able to entice American blacks to join its army and fight this new nation by promising freedom to the blacks, as Lord Dunmore did in 1775, and the British did again in the War of 1812–1814? Why would American blacks escape all the way to Canada on the very dangerous "Underground railroad" if this new nation had been created by the proposition that all men are created equal? Why would American blacks escape all the way to the Spanish colony in Florida, if this new nation had been conceived by the proposition that all men are equal? Why would this new nation invade and colonize parts of Mexico to practice slavery, when the Mexican government had abolished slavery? Why would American blacks be whipped, beaten, hung, killed, murdered, burnt, mutilated, shackled, branded, raped, punished severely for failing to pick assigned unrealistic quotas of cotton, and generally brutalized, without access to the courts, if they were equal in this new nation? Why would it be illegal to teach them to read or write? Why would you need slave codes? Why would you need to return American blacks, born in the new nation, to colonies such as Liberia in Africa? Why would Britain be forced to pay compensation to American slave owners, for freeing American blacks during the War of 1812–1814? Why would American blacks, who had converted to Christianity, be forced to sit in the back rows when they attend your Christian church? Why would your new nation pass a primitive and brutal new **Fugitive Slave Act** in 1850, when so many nations you deem to be less civilized than you, had long abolished slavery?

The reality was not that a new nation had been conceived on the proposition that all men were created equal, but that President Lincoln had learned lessons from the British, during the wars in 1775–1783 and 1812–1814, which he was willing to use to win the Civil War and end the **killing of his own people.** Without enticing the blacks with the promise of their freedom, as the British had done in 1775–1783 and 1812–1814, he may very well have lost the Southern states permanently from the Union. This was intolerable to Lincoln, not because he was against the barbaric institution of slavery, or because he was a civilized human being, but because he wanted a powerful American Empire, which could one day rule the world. For this imperial dream, Lincoln was willing to **kill many more of his own people,** than Gaddafi or Bashar Al-Assad were accused of doing by President Obama. Such a powerful empire would be impossible if he had agreed to the two-state solution which the Southern states wanted. This new nation created with lies and propaganda had grown into an economic powerhouse, both because it had the military muscle to **steal** the lands of the First Nations, and the barbarity to grow tobacco, cotton and sugar with **African slaves** on the stolen land. This combination of two evils, **genocide** against the First Nations, and barbaric transportation and enslavement of innocent peaceful Africans, was certainly worse than the crimes committed by Adolf Hitler. If the cost of keeping the American Empire united, prosperous, and ever expanding was the abolition of slavery, then so be it. The new leaders would have to get by with laws which would discriminate against blacks, and limit their freedoms in other ways, rather than through enslavement. The bottom line was that Lincoln could not contribute to the United States becoming the new global empire, without abolishing slavery. While Lincoln was a dedicated proslavery president he was far more pro-imperial than proslavery.

Lincoln, like Washington and all those who became American presidents before him, wanted to imitate the Roman Empire in all its glory including powerful leaders having far more slaves than commoners. The number of slaves owned was an important yardstick to measure how civilized the leaders of this modern day Roman Empire was. It was unthinkable to Lincoln, and previous American presidents, that the leaders of the new Roman Empire would not be allowed to have their slaves to do their manual chores and wait on them hand and foot. But in civil wars, you do dastardly deeds such as **killing your own people.** If that is deemed to be for the good of the empire, then surely the freeing of slaves can also be viewed as another necessary evil for the survival of the empire. The key difference between the Roman Empire and the American Empire was the sophistication of the propaganda of the American Empire. Instead of convincing the gullible Western media that his freeing the slaves was a necessary evil, to save the empire, Lincoln convinced it that freeing slaves was the civilized act of a civilized empire. The British parliament, led by William Wilberforce, had fought a long and difficult battle to convince the civilized Western Europeans, that the African slave trade, and the continued enslavement of Africans, were acts of **barbarity.** Lincoln saw the opportunity to use this modern view of empire to convince the gullible Western media, that he was freeing the slaves in America, not to preserve the American Empire, but to modernize the American Empire to be in line with the Western European empires. The American Empire dearly wanted to be accepted by the exclusive club of Western European empires as an equal.

In 1865, the United States was not yet leader of the unfree world. Had it been, it would surely have convinced the Western Europeans that slavery was civilized, instead of the Western Europeans convincing it that slavery was barbaric. The Greeks and Romans convinced the world that slavery was civilized. Since the American Empire became the undisputed leader of the unfree world, it has convinced the world that acts of barbarity, when committed by the American Empire, are civilized. The American Empire convinced the Western Europeans and Canadians that nuking Hiroshima and Nagasaki was civilized. It has convinced them that demonizing communism is civilized. It has convinced them that torture in Guantanamo and Abu Ghraib are civilized. It has taught them that spying on every world leader is civilized. It has taught them that using unmanned drones to kill people across the globe is civilized. It has taught them to justify murder, invasions and the killing of women and children by declaring it a civilized war on terrorism. It has taught them that military invasions of Muslim countries are civilized because fighting Islamists is the new crusade.

Did Lincoln Kill His Own People, like Gaddafi and Assad?

This latest propaganda tool is so offensive to anyone with even a pea brain that we feel obliged to be somewhat repetitive. With the Western **invasions** of Libya and Syria, a new propaganda tool was invented by the West. Leaders like Muammar Gaddafi and Bashar Al-Assad were demonized as the worst possible monsters because they "killed their own people." The public is so **stupid** that they really believe that in civil wars, leaders never kill their own people—only these two "monsters" have committed this heinous crime. The implication is that during the American Civil War, Lincoln was careful to kill only **aliens,** who had somehow descended from **Mars,** and joined the armed forces of the Southern rebels, because an American icon like President Lincoln, would never "kill his own people" like "devils" such as Gaddafi and Assad. We feel obliged to compare how the **devils,** Gaddafi and Assad, "killed their own people" during the Western **imperialist** and Western **puppet UN**-instigated civil wars, in Libya and Syria, but the **iconic** Lincoln succeeded in **not** "killing his own people," during the American Civil War, one that was **not instigated** by the then powerful British and French empires. We covered the U.S. Civil War in chapter 6 of our *Rise and Fall of the American Empire* and in chapter 4 of our *American Invasions.* During our extensive research for those prequels, we found no evidence to support the implicit assumption of the West, that President Lincoln only killed **alien Martians,** and never "his own people." In fact we found voluminous evidence that he did indeed kill many of his own people, far more than the devils Gaddafi and Assad killed. In the light of that persistent and very vocal implicit Western denial that Lincoln "killed his own people," we need at least a summary review of the evidence.

Lincoln was forced to end slavery in the United States, to win his bloody Civil War, where he killed so many of his own people. But forcing the Southern states to remain in his imperial union, would have meant long-term resistance, much like colonies resist their masters. It was not surprising to me that one of the friends of those Lincoln had killed to further American imperialism, succeeded in killing him. Resistance by colonial people, is never terrorism, but resistance to those who use terror because of their civilized military. President Lincoln was the **terrorist**, not John Wilkes Booth, the person who shot him.

For blacks, freed from slavery, the most important form of resistance from the colonized South was denial of postslavery rights. The South was well aware that Lincoln had freed the slaves only to win the Civil War. They knew that Lincoln was no less of a **racist** than they were. They would never condone what the North had done, simply to colonize them and turn them into semislaves. They made every effort to keep the ex-slaves in conditions of semislavery on the plantations, and elsewhere in the Southern states. They created the *Ku Klux Klan* to terrorize the ex-slaves into submission and acceptance of the deprivation of their rights as free men and women. While the Northern states may have been less repressive, they also practiced an **extreme** form of racial segregation, to maintain the inferior economic, educational and political status, of the blacks. Blacks today are still largely second class citizens in the United States. It was not until 2009, that the U.S. Senate passed a resolution apologizing for slavery, but even then, offered no financial compensation. We will see in our next chapter that black leaders have given up on their attempts to make the United States a more freedom-loving and less warmongering republic and have instead joined the white leaders in suppressing freedoms and engaging in worldwide warmongering, invasions, and regime change, in Afghanistan, Iraq, Libya, Syria, Yemen, Egypt, Ukraine, and elsewhere. Historical black leaders such as W. E. B. Du Bois, Malcolm X, and Muhammad Ali must surely be very disappointed.

American Invasions and Regime Change

Our third indictment of what we see as the **Very Ugly** in the **Uglier American** is its numerous military invasions of countries across the globe and imposing regime change on these countries. This was the key topic of one of our prequels, *American Invasions: Canada to Afghanistan.* American military invasions began with the invasion of Canada in 1775 and has never let up. There has not been a single year in the short history of the American Empire where it did not invade a country. Military invasions are a continuous and integral part of its everyday existence. Unlike the

Western European Empires which took some time out from their many wars and invasions to rest, recuperate and rebuild their war chests, the American Empire has never needed such respites, having new wars and military invasions overlapping continuously with old wars and military invasions. In this regard it was very much like the Roman Empire. Wars and military invasions are integral parts of its nature much like working, eating and sleeping. An American soldier is indoctrinated to think and act like a Roman soldier. He is defending the world against those who would dare to rebel against the Divine authority of the American Empire. The world needs American control, guidance, stability, materialism, culture, make believe freedoms and propaganda. Those who rebel are terrorists, communists, Islamists, extremists, un-American fools and trouble makers. They must be exterminated and taught to behave in a civilized subservient manner, mostly for their own good, but also for the good of others, especially the wise, all knowing and all powerful, American leaders.

Since the United States does not have the manpower to govern every nook and cranny of the world, it needs to impose local leaders who understand and obey the wishes of the American Empire. An important goal of military invasions is to change any local leader who is unsuitable to the American Empire, and replace him with a local leader who is willing and able to carry out the wishes of the American Empire, and put down rebellions with brute force. The new leader is rewarded with inclusion of his country in the world economy. The Americans often benefit financially from this arrangement. With few American administrators and soldiers the puppet local leader provides most of the military needed to suppress rebellions. The local economy flourishes because of its access to global trade, foreign investment and access to the world financial markets for cheap loans. Rising incomes provide tax revenues sufficient to do the bidding of the American Empire as well as line the pockets of the puppet leaders. The people share in the economic affluence long denied to them by previous American embargoes. American businesses earn profits by setting up branch plants or selling exports of American produce. Military bases create jobs for Americans. American movies, music, culture, McDonalds, Starbucks, KFCs, hotels, etc., are sold to another American *uncolony.*

All you have to do is compare South Korea with North Korea. The affluence of South Korea is not a drain on the American taxpayer, unlike Cuba, which was a drain on the Soviet taxpayer. Cuba was subsidized by the Soviet Union. No such subsidy is required by countries invaded by the American Empire. Once its leader has been replaced by a subservient local puppet its economy grows and becomes rich enough to pay for the military needed to suppress dissenters and engage in Western-style propaganda. The South Korean economy flourishes. Military opposition to regime change like North Korea brings with it pariah status in the world. Every country must disengage with North Korea or feel the wrath of the American Empire. Denial of access to world trade, foreign investment and the cheap loans from the world financial centers, impoverishes the country until it succumbs to regime change. An important deterrent to military invasion by the American Empire is nuclear weapons. The impoverished country is often convinced to give up its nuclear program for some relief from punitive sanctions. Once that is accepted the American Empire will invade and change its regime. Libya is the most recent example of this. The West punished Gaddafi until he agreed to discontinue his nuclear program. Once he had signed that death warrant they overthrew him.

Regime change has been used by all of the Western European empires and by the American Empire before President George W. Bush. But it's since the presidency of George W. Bush that **regime change** has become the explicit policy for American military invasions. The fact that regime change of the government of any Nation is contradictory to the Western proclaimed policy of **self-determination** has never been mentioned by the complicit Western media. It's as if Western Double Standards is the accepted norm for Western behavior and pronouncements. Speaking with a "forked tongue" is an embedded Western trait, part of their DNA.

In the case of Afghanistan, regime change was needed because the Taliban was deemed a terrorist government. In the case of Iraq, regime change was needed because Saddam Hussein possessed WMDs. In the case of Libya and Syria, regime change was needed because Gaddafi and Bashar Al-Assad "killed their own people" instead of other people. In the case of Yemen and Egypt, regime change was needed because the people demonstrated in the streets. When people demonstrate in the streets of a country which is not part of the Western alliance it is the duty of the American Empire to invade and change the regime to make that country another *uncolony* of the American Empire. In the case of Egypt a second regime change was needed because the people foolishly elected a **Democratic government, the Muslim Brotherhood.** Democracies led by Allende in Chile, Dr. Cheddi Jagan in Guyana, Hamas in Gaza are a few of the more well-publicized **Democratic governments** previously regime-changed by the American Empire. Some voters do not know that Western democracy means the obligation to elect governments which are pro-American. Canadian voters are well aware of that obligation and practice it without much questioning.

The leaders of Cuba, Libya, Iran and North Korea are under tremendous stress from their people because of the poverty imposed by Western sanctions. The Western media is unrelenting in its feeding of misinformation. The people of Cuba, North Korea, Libya and Iran are told by the Western media that their terrible plight is the result of their stupid, insane and mad-dog leaders. If only the people would rise up and depose such mad leaders who govern them by treachery and dictatorship the world would welcome them into the international community. The sad truth is that these impoverished economies will blossom after an American imposed regime change. But they blossom not because their leaders were mad men but because their leaders refused to prostitute their countries for the Yankee dollar. Western control of international institutions such as the UN, the World Bank, the WTO, the IMF, international finance, is so tight that no country can escape poverty even with the smartest leaders, if sanctions are imposed. American imperialism is backed not only by superior military weapons, but control of these institutions and the world's media and propaganda machine. In our last chapter we will see how the global shift to the emerging economies is likely to weaken that stranglehold.

Since we have documented the many invasions of the American Empire up to Afghanistan in our prequel, *American Invasions: 1775 to 2010,* we will simply update here what has occurred since 2010. Since 2010 the American Empire has invaded Libya and Syria, while continuing its invasion in Iraq, Afghanistan and Yemen. In *American*

Invasions we ended with the American Invasion of Yemen since that was the last American Invasion at that time. The explicit target of that invasion was *Al Qaeda in Yemen,* and the broader target of *Al Qaeda in the Arabian Peninsula.* That American Invasion, far from curbing Muslim resistance to Christian military invasions, and indiscriminate bombing and destruction of Muslim countries, only served to widen the area of the geographical resistance to Western imperialism, across a vast swath of territory spreading outward from Palestine, Lebanon, Iraq, Syria, Libya, Somalia, Yemen, Tunisia, Egypt, North Africa, Sudan, Ethiopia, Afghanistan, Pakistan, Iran, Nigeria, and Mali.

Unable to contain this disaster, President Obama has begun to threaten China with his so-called pivot to Asia. We will return to these examples of regime change under President Obama, in our next chapter. This chapter has turned out to be longer than I had anticipated. Despite my best efforts to summarize and focus on the worst crimes committed by the American Empire and its allies, these crimes are so many that this chapter has simply expanded. I will end the chapter by briefly summarizing the crimes involved with the nuking of the Japanese civilians in Nagasaki and Hiroshima, the theft of the lands and resources of the Palestinians and the bombing of Gaza back to the Stone Age, the removal of the democratic government elected by the people of Chile and imposing the Pinochet dictatorship, the invasion of Vietnam and the use of tautology. I have covered some of these topics in greater detail before but they have to be included again here to complete my list of the worst crimes committed by the Ugly American and their accomplices.

Use of Nuclear Bombs: Hiroshima/Nagasaki

American nuking of two major cities populated mostly by civilians must be the worst war crime ever committed. We will never know for sure the extent of war crimes committed by leaders defined by the West as dictators. These leaders include Adolf Hitler, Josef Stalin, Saddam Hussein, Muammar Gaddafi and Bashar al-Assad. The reason we will never know is that the West exaggerates their crimes for propaganda purposes while the accused make efforts to hide their crimes because of fear of prosecution by the West. The American Empire uses a different tactic. It uses its **war crimes** as propaganda for defending freedoms, upholding the law, doing God's work, spreading democracy, fighting communism, fighting terrorism, fighting Islamic extremism, and generally telling the world that America is **above the law.** This is the only reason that the American Empire has never been held to account for committing the worst war crime in history.

When the American Empire nuked Hiroshima and Nagasaki the civilian population was close to 600,000. The population of Hiroshima at the time the nuclear bomb was dropped by the cowardly American pilot and his cowardly accomplices has been estimated to be close to 350,000. The population of Nagasaki at the time the cowardly American pilots dropped the nuclear bomb has been estimated to be close to 250,000. Over the years since 1945 the cowardice of American pilots has increased as their aircrafts have become impossible targets for the poorly defended civilians they drop their massive bombs on. In the latest war declared on ISIS the Americans and Western allies such as Canada have now entrenched that cowardly behavior by refusing to put any boots on the ground. In the war against ISIS the West will provide the aircrafts, the bombs and the weapons, but the boots on the ground are to be supplied by the people of the Middle East who are less cowardly than Americans. The other reason for the lack of criminal charges against the American Empire is that only American lives matter. The 3,000 Americans killed on September 11 are worth far more than the 600,000 Japanese or millions of Muslims killed in the Middle East by the bombs dropped by the cowardly American pilots and President Obama's unmanned drones.

The Americans had long demonized the **yellow** race as inferior and subhuman. President Truman had called the Japanese people a **beast.** It was not difficult to indoctrinate Americans to hate the Japanese people by demonizing them as subhuman. Americans had been "educated" to view the First Nation as the **Naked Savage** because his skin was red. Americans had been "educated" to view Africans as subhuman because they were black and enslaved. Having committed genocide on the reds and enslaved the blacks it was the turn of the yellow race to be exterminated by the "racially superior" Americans. Prior to the use of the nuclear bombs the American Empire had firebombed Tokyo and other Japanese cities. This was itself a **war crime.** In a single firebombing, the Americans had killed 125,000 Japanese, the great majority being civilians. Deliberately targeting civilians is a war crime. Think of how Americans would react if 125,000 were killed on September 11 instead of 3,000 and that this was only one of many such attacks on the lands stolen by the American Empire from the First Nations.

It should be clear to any objective historian that the war crimes committed by the American Empire were as great if not greater than those committed by Germany or Japan. Had the Americans lost the war, the same number of American leaders would have been tried for war crimes, as German leaders were? Bombing civilians with the intention of shortening the duration of a war is a war crime. Bombing civilians because you think they belong to an inferior race is a war crime. Bombing civilians because you think your enemy is committing war crimes is a war crime. Bombing civilians to terrorize and instill fear in the people who are your enemy is a war crime. Bombing holy sites and infrastructure such as the Buddhist temples, hospitals, schools and homes of the people of Japan is a war crime. The use of nuclear bombs is not only a war crime but a crime against humanity.

It should also be clear to any objective historian that the American use of nuclear bombs had nothing to do with winning the Second World War or ending wars. It had to do with simple possession. The American Empire had used every military weapon it had developed before developing the atomic bomb. It had used every one of its military weapons against the enemy regardless of questions of morality or criminal behavior. It used the first atomic bomb as soon as it was ready for use. It did not wait even one day to question the morality of its use. It dropped a second atomic bomb as soon as it was ready for use and delivery. It did not wait a single day to discuss the morality of using it. Had the American Empire developed an atomic bomb with one hundred times the destructive force of the bomb it dropped on Hiroshima it would have used it. The American Empire continues to behave in this manner to this day. It does not use nuclear bombs anymore for one reason only, and that is, the Russian nuclear deterrent. But it develops and uses bigger and bigger non-nuclear bombs and drops them indiscriminately on any country which does not have a nuclear deterrent. The United States was created as an illegal state on stolen First Nations land and has always behaved as a **rogue state** above the law. It will continue to do so unless checked by another powerful state such as the Soviet Union during the cold war.

Palestine and Gaza

In Palestine the American Empire is continuing to do to the Palestinians what it has done to the First Nations across the lands which we now know as the USA. In my *American Invasions* I documented how the USA expanded from the relatively small land area stolen from the British across the American continent. The British had stolen that relatively small land area from the First Nations. From that relatively small land area the USA engaged in wars which killed off most of the original owners of the much larger land area to the west and imprisoned the few survivors on reservations. In like manner, the British stole a relatively small land area in Palestine to create a home for the Jews. I have written extensively of how the Jews have been persecuted and discriminated against throughout history.

In creating its worldwide empire the British saw an opportunity to use the Jews to further its imperial ambition. In my *Rise and Fall of the American Empire* I documented how the Jews were used by the British to help the British defeat their imperial rival, Germany, in return for a Jewish homeland in Palestine. When Britain and Germany both self-destructed as great powers because of the Second World War the American Empire took over the world. In Palestine it took over the control of Israeli theft of Palestinian lands. Israel became its imperial base for colonization of the Middle East. It armed Israel with the most civilized military weapons, including nuclear weapons. Using its powerful propaganda and control of the world's economic, financial, media, trade, reserve currency and the UN, the American Empire prevented any other country in the Middle East from acquiring nuclear weapons and the most civilized weaponry. While publicly preaching to Israel to restrain its genocide against the Palestinian people it supplies more and more arms and military aid to Israel to enable Israel to steal more and more lands and resources from the Palestinians and to imprison the surviving Palestinians in two **concentration camps,** Gaza and the West Bank.

Unlike the reservations created on the American continent for the First Nations, the American armed Israeli air force sharpens its military preparedness by periodically dropping massive bombs on the Palestinian refugees living in the two concentration camps. The most recent example of these periodic Israeli atrocities committed with these bombing exercises was July, 2014. Israel called it "Operation Protective Edge." The French Foreign minister, *Laurent Fabius,* referred to it as "carnage in Gaza." The bombing spree of the American armed Israeli air force killed some two thousand more of the surviving Palestinians in the Gaza concentration camp, mostly women and children. Another ten thousand were wounded, mostly women and children. Destruction of homes, schools, mosques and infrastructure was over $5 billion.

In the United States and Canada, the First Nations had been mostly killed off before the few survivors were imprisoned on the reserves. In Palestine, while many Palestinians were killed off by the United States and Israel and many more emigrated out of Palestine after their lands and resources were stolen, a relatively larger percentage remained. With relatively high birthrates their numbers did not decline in the same way as the numbers of First Nations in the United States and Canada had. This is why the genocide continues with these periodic bombing exercises supported by both Canada and the United States. Until the Palestinians can be "tamed" the way Canada and the United States "tamed" the **Wild Indian,** the American supplied bombs of the Israeli air force will keep sharpening their pilot skills by committing genocide on the Palestinian women and children.

The plan of the American Empire was to use Israel as its base for imperial expansion in the Middle East. While it has succeeded in stealing more territory in Palestine, its ultimate goal of colonizing the entire Middle East and North Africa, as the Romans, British and French did, shows little sign of succeeding. It has lost wars in Iraq, Afghanistan, Libya, Somali and elsewhere. Its cowardly use of bombing without boots on the ground to avoid being killed by the enemy brings limited results. Likewise with unmanned drones. Being too **cowardly** to fight like the Romans, or even the British and French, the American Empire will have to invent robots if it is to have any chance of colonizing the entire Middle East and North Africa. In the meantime it vents its frustrations by supplying more and more advanced civilized bombs to the Israeli air force. The Palestinians are trapped target practice. The world looks on and cheers on the American Empire by saying how civilized, democratic, freedom loving, and godly it is.

American Atrocities in Vietnam, Cambodia, and Laos

We have documented in great detail the American invasion of Vietnam during the two decades, 1955–1975, in our prequels, *Rise and Fall of the American Empire* and *American Invasions.* Here we address the invasion briefly as one more dastardly crime against humanity by the Ugly American Empire. The American invasion of territory which had previously been colonized by France and referred to as *French Indochina,* was one of many examples of the American Empire attempting to colonize areas of the globe which had been previously colonized by the Western European empires of Portugal, Spain, Holland, France, Britain, Germany and Italy. Unlike the Western European empires which used the propaganda that they were on a mission to convert the heathens to Christianity and carry the white man's burden, the propaganda of the American Empire was fighting communism. To those being colonized it mattered not who the imperial power was nor the propaganda used. All the colonists saw was their lands and resources being stolen by military force, their religion and customs denigrated, their women raped and molested, their children killed, maimed and brutalized, their lives ruined and their freedoms denied. They fought the invaders but their weapons were primitive while the invaders had civilized weapons.

The American Empire dropped countless bombs, used biological and germ warfare, massacred civilians, tortured those captured, and generally committed atrocities without any restraint. According to the lead American commander, General Westmoreland, the implicit strategy of the American Empire was to kill off or wound as many of the Vietnamese people as needed to win the war. It was the same strategy used against the First Nations. Kill everyone you can, men, women and children, until the survivors surrender. Impose a local dictator as puppet ruler and station your military permanently by building military bases with the most civilized military facilities. Boast to the world that you have defeated the communists. Steal and rape the resources to pay the bills and feed your addiction to warmongering.

The Vietnamese people resisted American colonization and paid dearly in lives lost and property damaged. It has been estimated that over **three million** people in Vietnam, Laos and Cambodia lost their lives fighting for true freedom not the make believe freedoms of the West. Today, children and adults continue to be killed from the bombs dropped by the American Empire which did not explode on impact. The financial damage to property and infrastructure has been estimated to exceed $60 billion. Vietnamese who colluded with the American Empire became refugees fleeing to Hong Kong, China and the West. It was the beginning of the creation of the massive refugee problem where the UN estimates that these Western wars have created upward of 60 million refugees. The Syrian refugees today hire criminals who dump them within reach of the Italian coastguard. The West prosecutes the wars which create the refugees but refuses to admit them legally into their countries. The poor countries such as Pakistan, Lebanon, Jordan and Turkey are forced to take the refugees created by Canada, the United States, and Western Europe. But no matter how difficult the West makes it for the refugees they create to come to their countries, the refugees will find a way to come and pay them back for the crimes they committed in their home countries.

American Removal of Democrat Allende and Installation of Dictator Pinochet

American overthrow of the Allende government of Chile on **September 11, 1973,** provides the quintessential example of why the American Empire preaches the virtues of democracy but secretly fears it. Democracy is America's worst nightmare, and the leaders of the American Empire are fully aware of this. Despite its powerful propaganda machine the American Empire knows that its propaganda fools only a minority of the people of its many *uncolonies.* Whether it's Chile or Saudi Arabia or Egypt or Palestine, give the voters democracy and they will always elect a government which is anti-American. The reason is simple. No people like being colonized. Give them the freedom to choose and they will always vote against the imperial power. So it was in Chile.

Since the American Empire is fully aware that democratic elections will always lead to an anti-American government, the American Empire uses its vast spy network, bribes, threats, propaganda, media, allies and terrorism, to prevent true democratic elections. But sometimes it fails as it did in Cuba, North Korea, Zimbabwe, Guyana and Chile. After it fails it will either instigate a military coup, as it did in Chile, or impoverish the state as it did in Cuba, North Korea and Zimbabwe, or replace the democratically elected leader with a more pro-American opposition party leader, as it did in Guyana. When Allende was elected in Chile, the Nixon administration was determined to impoverish Chile had **Henry Kissinger** failed to instigate a successful military coup. But the military coup was successful and the seventeen-year reign of Dictator Pinochet began.

Obscene Use of Tautology: America Is Good Because Americans Are Good. Israel Is Good Because Israelis Are Good. Canada Is Good Because Canadians Are Good. North Korea Is Bad Because North Koreans Are Bad. Iran Is Bad Because Iranians Are Bad. Venezuela Is Bad Because Venezuelans Are Bad.

We end our nonexhaustive list of atrocities committed by the ugly American Empire by pointing to the obscene tautological justification used by the United States and its subservient allies to determine important questions such as rights to nuclear weapons, access to international institutions, imposition of embargoes, definitions of terrorists, limits on freedoms, types of education, human development, economic development, basic human rights and dignity, as a sure sign that people are not being educated but subjected to propaganda, denied freedom of expression, denied free thinking, denied choice of behavior, and generally making them subservient robots subject to the whims of talk show hosts, shepherds driving sheep, and herders driving cattle.

Should anyone dare express an independent opinion he/she is ostracized by society, threatened with loss of job and career opportunities, threatened with arrest and imprisonment, threatened with harassment, blackmail, and grossly unfair judicial trials pretending to be impartial, and generally isolated as a social outcast branded with mental disorder. Even if the critic shows overwhelming proof of wrongful deeds by those with power, society backs the perpetrators of the crime, rather than the victim. Using a simple example, someone stoned as punishment for a crime in Iran would be portrayed by the Canadian media as proof of Iran being bad. The same act in Canada would be portrayed by the Canadian media as proof that the person stoned was a vile terrorist deserving of a much worse punishment such as torture in Guantanamo. But Canada is too civilized a country to steal Cuban land to have its own Guantanamo. If the Americans were to oblige by imprisoning and torture him/her in Guantanamo, as they did with Omar Khadr, it would be just fine with Canada.

This double standard and Western arrogance permeates every aspect of Western society, from the pope to the peasants. It's now ingrained in everyone's DNA, with few exceptions like Edward Snowden, Julian Assange, and Seymour Hersh. The reality is that every country has similar proportions of good, very good, bad and very bad people. What differs across countries is power. The United States holds the most power and uses its power indiscriminately to determine good versus evil. No country dares to challenge it. But those who bow down to the American dictates of good versus evil, like Canada, piggy-backs on the American indiscriminate use of their power. Only the global shift to emerging economies beginning with the rise of China, will ever diminish this Western arrogance honed, cultivated and cherished since Portugal began its enslavement of Africans in the middle of the fifteenth century.

CHAPTER 10

The Disaster That Was Obama

Blacks, liberals, and doves should not feel guilty over the disastrous failures of their president, *Barack Hussein Obama.* He is **not** black, he is **not** a liberal and far from being a dove, he is a dedicated and determined **warmonger.** His greatest quality is his innate ability to **deceive.** I am not easily fooled by Western leaders, but the night I saw on TV the election of Obama to the U.S. presidency, I had great difficulty holding back tears of joy. If he could fool me I totally understand why he was able, and continues to be able, to fool so many.

In 2007 candidate Barack Obama ran on a campaign of hope and promise for a new America and a New World Order. Many in both the United States and around the world were angry at the seemingly unnecessary level of warmongering by the United States under the presidency of George W. Bush. The claim by President Bush that he had invaded Iraq because of undeniable evidence of the possession by Saddam Hussein of WMDs turned out to be false. Many believed that President Bush had deliberately misled both the United States and the world because he had a personal desire to remove Saddam Hussein because Saddam had threatened to kill his father, President H. W. Bush. He found overwhelming support for his invasion of Iraq from the *Neo-cons,* a powerful group of Americans who had an agenda to use the demise of the Soviet Union to get the United States to increase immensely its domination of the world. See my *Rise and Fall of the American Empire,* chapter 10. The Neo-cons convinced George W. that conquering Iraq would be an easy slam-dunk, since Iraq had been decimated by a decade of relentless bombing by the United States and her "prostitute," Britain. His easy military conquest of Iraq would boost his popularity as commander in chief and enable him to get popular support to invade and conquer Iran and North Korea. Britain would continue to make believe that "Britannia still ruled the waves." George W. would achieve what General MacArthur had failed to do in the Korean War, which was American colonization of all of Korea instead of only half of it. By conquering Iran he would be able to do what the Crusades had failed to do, and that was the Western conquest of the Middle East.

Countries love warmongering and no country loves warmongering more than the United States. But only successful warmongering is popular with voters. When President George W. failed to conquer Iraq, much less Iran and North Korea, his popularity plummeted. People began to question the need for such warmongering. It provided the opportunity for a "Dove." Enter Candidate Obama. His essential credential was the fact that he had **not** voted for the invasion of Iraq. This is what gave him the edge over Candidate Hillary Clinton. Clinton had been the anointed Democratic candidate because of the popularity of her husband, President Bill Clinton, and because of the women's vote. Candidate Obama had the black vote but that was no winner against the women's vote and the popularity of President Bill Clinton. Obama's Ace was not voting for the Iraqi invasion. Hillary had voted for the Iraqi invasion.

While the "Dove" characteristic was Obama's Ace over Hillary, Obama also peddled his "Main Street" and "Change and Hope" personas, over "Wall Street" and "Establishment" personas. He would be for the poor and disenfranchised rather than the fat cats and Washington elites. His combination of hope, change, nonestablishment, anti-Wall Street, and peace maker, galvanized the young, the blacks, the other minorities, the poor, the downtrodden the tech savvy, the peace movements, the liberals, the anti-imperialists, and the naïve. He was the second coming of Kennedy and the hope of the sixties generation. He brought tears of joy to so many, including me, when he won the presidency. It was to be the "Dawn of Aquarius." In the history of mankind no one promised so much and delivered so little. He turned out to be the quintessential American propagandist, liar and addicted **warmonger.** President Obama brought shame to the Nobel Peace Prize, disappointed the masses, enjoyed golfing with the privileged Wall Street fat cats and, together with his wife Michelle, emulated the image of a lily-white family in Camelot, imprinted in the minds of Americans by Jacqueline Kennedy. We begin our assessment of his disasters with his primary deceit and failure which was his pretense to be a peacemaker while wholeheartedly waging more wars than any previous American president. This was quite an achievement given that the American Empire has conducted more military invasions than any other empire in history, despite its much shorter history as an empire. See our *American Invasions.* **Obama's warmongering** made George W's warmongering pale by comparison.

In this chapter we explore why we go against popular opinion that Obama is **black** or the first **black president,** using that opportunity to address the complex issue of **race** in America. We provide facts to support our view that President Obama favored Wall Street over Main Street. We look at his many failed promises of addressing poverty, dealing with America's growing debt, closing Guantanamo, providing a solution for immigration, and harmonizing relations with the world outside America's "prostitutes," Britain, Canada, Australia, Germany, France, Japan, South Korea, Italy, Spain, Georgia, Taiwan, Ireland, and Poland. But first we continue our topic of American Invasions, Global Warmongering, and Regime Change under President Obama.

Barack Obama as Warmonger-in-Chief: Afghanistan, Iraq, Pakistan, Yemen, Sudan, Libya, Syria, Egypt, Palestine, ISIS

Candidate Obama had ran on a platform to end the war in Iraq but expand America's war in Afghanistan. It was a popular platform because many more Americans had supported the American invasion of Afghanistan than the American invasion of Iraq. Even Candidate Hillary Clinton has acknowledged that she made a mistake in voting for the U.S. invasion of Iraq. It was therefore expected that President Obama would withdraw U.S. forces from Iraq and send more U.S. forces to Afghanistan. What was **not** expected was a **net increase** in warmongering. Candidate Obama had not only spoken out against the U.S. invasion of Iraq but had preached that *wars were never the solution.* He would replace wars and military invasions with dialogue. Many of us, yearning for peace over wars, foolishly believed him.

Obama's Quagmire of Afghanistan, Iraq, and Pakistan and Failure of His High-Tech Unmanned Drones Solution

Anyone looking objectively at the mess created by President Obama in the region which includes Afghanistan, Iraq, Pakistan and Syria, must conclude that the United States was governed by a moronic warmonger, supported by brain-dead Western leaders in Canada, Britain, France, Germany and Australia. The United States has a long history of making enemies of their friends going back to Josef Stalin and earlier. In like manner the quagmire created by President Obama goes back to the United States, turning on American-backed leaders in Afghanistan, Pakistan, Iraq, Libya, Egypt, and Syria. This began after the bombing of two U.S. embassies in Tanzania and Kenya on August 7, 1998. Osama bin Laden metamorphosed from America's most revered **freedom fighter** to most wanted **terrorist.** American controlled media in Canada, Britain and across the globe, could finally exhibit their "freedom of the press," and chastise bin Laden at will. The so-called Western Free Press would have to wait longer before they received permission from the White House to openly chastise Saddam Hussein of Iraq, Moammar Gaddafi of Libya, Hosni Mubarak of Egypt and Bashar al-Assad of Syria.

As we explained in *American Invasions, pages 286–290,* Osama bin Laden, the Mujahideen, the Taliban, Saudi Arabia, and Pakistan were anointed by the West as the "good guys" in America's war against the evil Soviet Empire. Once Osama bin Laden discovered that the evil empire was not the Soviet Empire, but the American Empire, America and its Western prostitutes had to change their propaganda. Osama bin Laden could not be bought, controlled or killed by the American Empire, the Saudis or Pakistan. The American Empire switched sides in Afghanistan from supporting the Taliban against the Northern Alliance, to supporting the Northern Alliance against the Taliban. This confused America's two other allies, Saudi Arabia and Pakistan. Their support continued because of threats from the American Empire, but was never as committed as when the Americans helped the Taliban fight the Northern Alliance. Another noteworthy metamorphosis of the Taliban, based on Canadian and other Western views of their stand on **women's rights,** was that before the fall of the Soviet Empire the Taliban, as Western allies, implicitly protected women's rights, but after the U.S. invasion of 2001, Canadians felt that it was their moral duty to support the U.S. invasion, because the Taliban did not respect women's rights. Switching opinion on such important matters, when told to do so by the leader of the unfree world, is proof of the vibrancy of Canadian democracy.

President Obama further angered his Pakistani ally by expanding his use of unmanned drones in Pakistani territory and by invading Pakistan to capture Osama bin Laden. President Obama's first drone attack in Pakistan, just three days after moving into the White House, initially reported killing ten enemy fighters. The reality was that his proclaimed precision targeted drone strike had killed nine civilians and seriously injured the tenth. A second drone attack later that same third day of his presidency killed several other Pakistani civilians. President Obama had begun his presidency by dismissing civilian murders as "collateral damage," much like his predecessors, and Israel. Murders by powerful Western states are always collateral damage. Anyone fooled by Candidate Obama into thinking he would restrain America's casual use of its civilized WMDs to kill, maim and destroy at will, was rudely awakened to reality. The response of the American media to this murder of nine Pakistanis by their commander in chief was that American military aid to the Pakistani military should be withheld until the Pakistani military was more helpful in killing more Pakistanis. President Obama should not have to do it alone. By implication American military aid to Pakistan meant committing the Pakistani government to "kill their own people," on behalf of America. "Killing your own people," is not evil if it's the civilized American Empire that commands you to do it, just as nuking innocent civilians in Hiroshima and Nagasaki is not evil, if it's the civilized American Empire that drops the nukes.

President Obama has made unmanned drone strikes in Pakistan and Yemen his key military weapon in his so-called War on Terror, for one and only one reason. He is as dedicated to warmongering as every American president. After the military failures of George W. Bush, the American public was tired of American casualties of war. Sure they had no sympathy for the thousands killed by their civilized armed forces, but they mourned publicly and privately, their relatively few deaths and injuries. Obama could have easily ridden this wave of public support for ending the wars in both Iraq and Afghanistan. But being addicted to warmongering, and needing to feed America's addiction to this disease, he found a new weapon to be able to continue the killing while minimizing, even further than George W., American casualties. President Obama knows that the American public care very little about the deaths of Pakistani or Yemeni civilians. To Americans these people are all enemies of "America's way of life." If the *precision* drones kill innocent women and children it's the fault of the terrorists for hiding among civilians. They should come out in the open and wear a bright tag saying "cowardly terrorist" so that President Obama can use his *precision* drones to target them *precisely* and *precisely* kill only them.

President Obama failed to understand that the full scale American invasions of both Afghanistan and Iraq by President George W. Bush, irretrievably linked America's newly created enemies in Afghanistan, Pakistan and Iraq. Fulfilling his election promise to simultaneously end America's war in Iraq, while stepping up the war in Afghanistan, was well-nigh impossible. But angering Pakistan with his killer drones over Pakistani air space and opening up three new fronts in Yemen, Libya and Syria, doomed him to utter disaster. American invasion of Afghanistan begat George W's dissensions in Pakistan and Saudi Arabia. His invasion of Iraq brought al-Qaeda and bin Laden's Mujahedeen from Afghanistan to Iraq, forever linking those two invasions. Yemen became the haven for al-Qaeda in the Arabian Peninsula, while Obama's instigated civil wars in Libya and Syria begat ISIS. The Muslims had helped the American Empire to defeat the Soviet Empire, but have since recognized that the greater threat to Islam was the Christian West. President Obama foolishly underestimated the Muslim threat to American imperialism in the Middle East, Afghanistan, Pakistan and North Africa.

President George W. Bush had failed in his plan to invade Iraq as a stepping stone to conquering what he called the "axis of evil," Iraq, Iran and North Korea. In like manner President Obama failed in his goal to conquer Afghanistan, Yemen, Libya and Syria. We documented President Obama's invasion of Yemen in *American Invasions, pages 296–298.* As in Pakistan, President Obama's weapon of choice for killing Yeminis was his unmanned drones. He was determined not only to be a bigger warmonger than George W., but one who was more popular with the

American public, by using a weapon which would minimize American casualties more than George W. had done. He had been awarded the Nobel Peace Prize **after** opening his new front in Yemen in America's "War on terrorism."

We now address President Obama's failed interventions in Tunisia, Egypt, Libya and Syria, to show how President Obama responds to every failed war and invasion, by digging the American Empire into an ever-expanding quagmire of wars, invasions, regime changes, and confusion for America's allies. He manages to take the spotlight off every crisis he creates by adding a new crisis. This inevitably links the ever-increasing crises into one giant mess. Since American presidents are great at creating problems, but useless at solving them, there is no hope that Obama's successor will pull back America from the brink. The rest of the world will be forced to grow up and not look to American leadership.

The Jasmine Revolutions and More American Invasions and Regime Changes by the American Empire under President Obama

Let me remind you once again that the only goal of the West is to maintain its political, economic and military colonization of the world. The two World Wars reduced the colonizing powers of Britain and France while increasing those of the United States, Canada, and Australia. This was simply a continuation of the transition of Western colonizing powers from Portugal to Spain to Holland to France to Britain to Germany. For those colonized, the **Third World,** there was no difference as to which Western power was the dominant colonizer. In addition to passing on the baton from one Western power to another, the West continuously adapted the methods used as the world evolved. For example, when colonies rebelled against political control there was greater use of economic and financial controls. When colonies developed better armies to fight for independence more use was made of naval and air forces by the imperial powers. When one puppet dictator became too unpopular or threatened his colonial master he was replaced by another puppet dictator. The *Arab Spring* which began with the Jasmine

Revolution in Tunisia is simply another example of the West needing to adapt its colonizing techniques.

For those who are naïve or downright stupid we need to remind you that the West has zero interest in democracy. The West wants puppet regimes that will help them commit crimes against humanity. Your government can be absolutely controlled by a mad monk such as Rasputin, or a vicious dictator like Pinochet, it will never bother the West as long as it's a puppet of the West. As we have explained many times before, the West overthrew democratic governments in Chile and Guyana because they tried to be independent of the West. Their governments were branded as communists. More recently the democratic governments under Hamas in Palestine and the Muslim Brotherhood in Egypt, were branded as terrorists and Muslim extremists, respectively. Whether it's the older Tiananmen protests, or the Jasmine revolutions, or the more recent protests in Hong Kong, these protestors have no idea how vicious the West can be if you do not do their bidding. The West has the military power and will to regime change you and bomb you back to the Stone Age, as well as the economic and financial power and will to impoverish you.

The Arabs had foolishly helped the West defeat the Ottoman Empire thinking that they would not be colonized by the West. The Arab Spring is a continuation of the long struggle for independence from the West. The fact that those who rebel against their local rulers seek help from the West is just another example of the power of Western propaganda. Just as Arabs who aided the West during the First and Second World Wars were duped into thinking that the West would grant them independence, those who seek Western help to depose their autocratic rulers fail to understand that those autocratic rulers were empowered by military, economic, financial, propaganda, and media support, from the West. The West will always be ready to assist you in replacing one pro-Western government with another pro-Western government. It matters little to the West whether the pro-Western government is democratic, barbaric, incompetent, delusional, dictatorial, fundamentalist, tyrannical or wise, so long as it serves the interests of its Western imperial master.

We saw earlier that the two World Wars had severely weakened the Western European imperial powers forcing many of them, Britain, France, Italy, Germany, to grant greater political independence to their colonies. But there was a new sheriff in town, the American Empire, more powerful than all of the Western European empires combined. It was as determined as the Western European empires had been, to maintain and enhance Western imperialism. But this same empire had denounced the Western European imperialism and claimed never to be a colonizer. It would simply steal all of the lands of the First Nations, including some previously stolen by Mexico, and claim that it was simply the largest and most powerful state in the world. It could enslave millions of Africans to work the stolen land but still preach freedom and equality for all. Next it would invent a Cold War against Communism and wage incessant wars against any who would not denounce its self-invented evil of Communism. When the Soviet Union disintegrated, it invented a new evil, *terrorism,* to continue to justify its many wars, invasions and regime changes. Having made a total mess in Afghanistan and Iraq, it would now move to pile the mess higher and deeper in Pakistan, Yemen, Tunisia, Egypt, Libya and Syria.

The American Empire became the most powerful empire in history, not only because it had stolen so much land and resources from the First Nations and enslaved Africans, but by co-opting those who willingly or unwillingly did its bidding. The Anglo nations of Britain, Canada, Australia and New Zealand, were the easiest to co-opt. Next were the nation-states of Western Europe; France, Italy, Spain, Portugal and Germany, followed by Asian countries such as Japan, South Korea, Taiwan, Hong Kong and Singapore. In many cases these countries were co-opted by carrots rather than sticks. The carrots were access to the WTO, capital and financial markets, military and economic aid. But the big stick of military invasion, regime change, and economic sanctions was always threatened for noncompliance.

The ex-colonies of the Third World, not only those in the Middle East, faced the stark choice of continued political semicolonial status or impoverishing their people who had fought long and hard to rid themselves of the Western imperial yoke. American media and propaganda developed new ways of broadcasting this continued Western colonization as simply a continuation of the *white man's burden and Christian duty.* Now it was the American people who had emigrated from

Europe to populate the **stolen** First Nations lands that would carry most of the burden and willingly serve their Christian God.

Regime Change in Tunisia

Five Muslim countries, *Tunisia, Egypt, Libya, Yemen and Syria,* were singled out by the West for regime change partly as a result of the Jasmine revolutions and Arab Spring. These were all countries which had been colonized by the West, and had been given a degree of independence because of the weakening of the Western European empires by the two World Wars. Since the Jasmine revolutions began in Tunisia in January 2011, we begin with the regime change in Tunisia, even though President Obama had been pursuing regime change in Yemen earlier. Tunisia, like so many parts of the Third World, had been colonized by the West. It became a **French** colony in 1881. As with other Western colonies, the West had no intention of ever granting Tunisia full political, economic, military, cultural, religious or financial independence. But in Tunisia, as in every other Western colony, the West used its powerful propaganda to convince many that it had granted independence but maintained its colonial connection only to help Tunisians follow the path of the West for their own good. After all, only the West knows what is best for everyone. You follow the paths of countries like Canada, Australia, Hong Kong, Taiwan, South Korea, etc., and you will receive the blessings of wealth, Christianity, excessive consumption and materialism. You reject Western wisdom and you become as **poor** and as "stupid and retarded" as North Koreans and Zimbabweans.

The fact that the Tunisian revolution caught the West, especially the United States, by surprise, is of no consequence since the West has the media and resources to quickly react to such incidents. When you continue to colonize a country you are fully aware that there will be resistance, rebellions, revolts, demonstrations, protests and complaints. You are fully prepared to squelch any such actions and you have the resources to do so. Many have attempted to explain why this particular revolt became so widespread. The lightening rod was the self-immolation by the street fruit vendor, *Mohamed Bouazizi,* on December 17, 2010, as a protest against the confiscation of his fruit by a local inspector. Bouazizi, like blacks in the United States, had been harassed by the police for years. The unemployment rate in the town in Tunisia where Bouazizi lived was as high as many U.S. cities where poor blacks live, 30 percent. But many self-immolations across the globe have taken place without starting a revolution. The only other exception was Buddhist monk, *Quang Duc,* in Vietnam on June 11, 1963. See *Rise and Fall of the American Empire,* page 418.

Bouazizi's tragic death has an eerie resemblance to the more recent death of the American black, *Eric Garner.* Garner, like Bouazizi, had been harassed for years by police for the simple reason that he was poor but very determined to make a living to support himself and his family. This is a great example to educate American blacks as to why they should be more like Muhammad Ali, and far less like President Obama, and reject forcibly, American invasions and colonizations which impoverish American blacks and so many more blacks in Africa and other people like Bouazizi, throughout the Third World.

Eric Garner was killed in New York by an American policeman on July 17, 2014. He had a wife and six children to support. He also had three grandchildren. Bouazizi supported his mother and younger siblings because his father had died when he was three years old. Garner's alleged crime was selling cigarettes on the street to support his family. Bouazizi's alleged crime was selling fruits and vegetables on the street to support his family. When Bouazizi's cart and produce were confiscated by the Tunisian police in the morning of December 17, 2010, he went to the governor's office in his home state of Sidi Bouzid, to complain. The governor refused to see him even after he threatened self-immolation. He returned outside the governor's office with gasoline and set himself on fire.

The vastly different responses by the presidents of Tunisia and the United States to these two rather similar tragedies are very instructive as to how the West uses propaganda rather than concern. When Bouazizi was transferred to a specialized Burn and Trauma hospital because of his severe burns, he was visited by the president of Tunisia, Ben Ali. The president promised to send him to France for better medical treatment but unfortunately Bouazizi died before that could be done. Public protests erupted after his death. These protests forced the president of Tunisia to flee Tunisia with his family to Saudi Arabia. The tragedy led to the removal of a president who had served Tunisia for twenty-three years. The main streets in Sidi Bouzid, his birthplace, and in Tunis, capital of Tunisia, were renamed Boulevard Mohamed Bouazizi.

When American policeman Daniel Pantaleo killed Eric Garner he was brought before a grand jury but acquitted. When American blacks complained about the acquittal to President Obama his response to the killing of Eric Garner was simply that it was an "American problem." Was President Obama implying that his job was to fix problems in Tunisia and other parts of the globe, and lesser U.S. governments should deal with American problems?

There are numerous reasons for the Arab Spring. But the two dominant reasons are the single-minded determination of the West to continue to colonize and dominate these countries and the equally determined efforts of the colonized people to resist Western imperialism. Much of the confusion springs from the divergent means of both the colonizing methods and the resistance methods. The Western colonizing efforts include surveillance, spying, intelligence gathering, military force, military aid, military bases, regime changes, economic aid, economic sanctions, financial aid, financial sanctions, divide-and-rule tactics, Christianizing missions, propaganda, and misinformation. On the other side of the equation the resistance efforts include peaceful demonstrations, use of primitive weapons, appeals to religious resistance, appeals for democratic rule, use of social media and emigration to the West. Further confusing the explanations is the dichotomy between those who believe the Western propaganda and those who understand the lies. Western propaganda deliberately intensifies dissentions by demonizing those who oppose Western colonization as extremists, radicalized and terrorists, while heaping praise on those who are misled. The educated are demonized by the West, while the naïve are called "educated."

The Italians, English and French were competing to colonize Tunisia during the nineteenth century. The West saw an opportunity to gobble up the lands of the sick and declining Ottoman Empire. The French had the advantage because they had already colonized neighboring Algeria. Under the Ottoman Empire the *bey of Tunisia* exercised a great degree of independence from the Ottoman sultan. His mistake was to borrow heavily from the West. Today, it's the American Empire which is borrowing from the East, China. Western creditors supported the French colonization because France agreed to repay Tunisia's Western debts. The British grudgingly supported France over the Italians. French citizens and French businesses received preferential treatment over Tunisians after Tunisia became a French colony. The primary Tunisian resource stolen by France was phosphates used for fertilizer. However, deposits of iron, zinc, lead and copper, were also stolen in smaller quantities. As usual these colonial thefts provided lucrative employment opportunities for French nationals. Tunisia was also used as a market for French exports of manufactured goods, destroying the local higher-cost manual, nonmechanized, producers. Finally, much of the agricultural land was stolen from the Tunisian tribal owners and handed over to French immigrants and French businesses. Large numbers of French migrated to Tunisia during French rule.

Unlike many other Arab countries, Tunisia was not anti-Ottoman, since it had been given a great degree of independence by the Ottoman Empire. Compared with the French and Italians relatively few Ottoman Turks migrated to settle in Tunisia. Western colonization by France was therefore a step backward. As a result, Tunisians greatly resented Western colonization and never ceased to fight for their independence. This independence struggle gathered steam during the twentieth century. As in all of the French and British colonies, Tunisians were called upon by France to fight the Germans in the two World Wars. This served to encourage the independence movements. While generous American economic aid helped the British and French recover their economies sufficiently after World War II, to continue their military control over their colonies, it was impossible to put back the independence genie in the bottle. Under the leadership of *Habib Bourguiba,* the Tunisian nationalist political party, *Le Destour,* founded in 1920, continued to fight for Tunisian independence through the UN and the Arab League. In 1950, Bourguiba traveled to Paris to speak directly with the French government about Tunisian independence. Armed resistance to French colonization increased as well.

At the time the French were also under armed rebellions in neighboring Algeria and Morocco as well as in Indo-China. Unable to control such widespread rebellions in so many of its colonies the French granted independence to Tunisia in 1956. Tunisia became an independent republic of over 10 million people on March 20, 1956, and Bourguiba became its first president. A majority of Europeans returned to Europe after Tunisia's independence, since they could no longer maintain their privileged status above Tunisians.

Independent Tunisia, like all of the Arab countries, had to deal with a fundamental problem. As we have explained before, Islam does not recognize a separation of religion and state. But during the Western colonizations many of the inhabitants, especially the young, had heard of the Western separation of religion and state. They want the same. As we have suggested, this notion of separation of religion and state in the West, is more propaganda than reality, but that is of no consequence since those in the Muslim ex-colonies who prefer the separation of religion and state, firmly believe the Western propaganda about religious freedoms and all the other lies about freedom of speech, democracy, etc. As we have correctly pointed out, no Muslim or Communist would ever be allowed to be a candidate for the American presidency, much less become president. As a result of one of the many legacies of Western colonization, the postindependence governments in all of the Muslim countries have to straddle a fine line between those who want a return to the Islamic rule which existed before Western colonization, and those who have been brainwashed into thinking that all things Western are indeed civilized. The West naturally exploits this legacy of its colonization, to continue to divide and dominate these ex-colonies.

President Bourguiba was generally pro-Western, suppressing what the West propagandized as Islamic fundamentalism. This pro-Western stance meant that there was access to Western markets and Western finance. It was good for the economy. But it meant an autocratic style, since those who had fought long and hard for independence from the West, would be opposed to this economic colonization. Such opposition had to be quashed. While this was necessary to prevent economic and financial sanctions by the West, the Western media was not always supportive. Often the Western media is itself extremely naïve and more willing to critique abuses in non-Western countries than the same abuses in the West. They act as if they are blind to the fact that it's the West which forces the non-Western leaders to be autocratic. For example, the Western media would speak openly of the Israeli prime minister Benjamin Netanyahu, ordering the assassination of the Hamas leader Khaled Mashal, or President Obama ordering the assassination of Osama bin Laden, as if it's normal, legal, ethical, moral, and just. But woe betides even the smallest suspicion that President Putin was remotely involved in ordering the assassination of the most heinous Russian criminal or Western spy. This kind of double standard has been so common during the entire period of what is erroneously called "freedom of the press" by the West, that Western reporters are no longer even conscious of their biases.

General *Ben Ali* took advantage of Bourguiba's ill health to organize what some called a "medical coup d'état. With the help of **Italy,** Ben Ali replaced Bourguiba as president of Tunisia on November 7, 1987. Ben Ali, like his predecessor, attempted to rule liberally. But that is impossible when you need access to Western markets and finance for economic reasons, but fear opposition from those who see you as not sufficiently independent. Like President Bourguiba before him, President Ben Ali became increasingly autocratic and used a firm hand against the opposition. The West, unfortunately, leaves you no middle ground. To prevent their harsh economic and financial sanctions you have to do their bidding. Yet their media criticize you for dealing harshly with those who oppose your pro-Western policies. It would have been a miracle if Ben Ali had not fallen from grace with his people, just as Bourguiba had fallen. The West push democracy on you but when the people democratically elect an anti-Western leader, such as Allende, Morsi, or Jagan, the West punishes you with powerful economic and financial sanctions, which impoverish your people. President Zine El Abidine Ben Ali was overthrown in 2011 by naïve Tunisians brainwashed by Western propaganda.

Dictators are tolerated by the West until they become too unpopular. The cycle of one repressive dictator replacing another is the normal outcome. The West will never leave these ex-colonies to truly govern themselves, make their own choices with regard to religion and the role of the state, make their own mistakes and find their own solutions. Western interventions in Iraq and Afghanistan are excellent examples of the total mess created by such interventions. Yet the West insist that only it knows how to solve the mess without even acknowledging that it alone was responsible for creating the mess in the first place.

The Jasmine revolutions caught the eye of Britain and France before President Obama. Obama had his hands full dealing with the mess in Iraq, Afghanistan, Pakistan and Yemen. France and Britain had a long simmering grudge against the United States for making them the junior partners in crime after the Second World War. Prior to WWII, it was the United States that was the junior partner. The Jasmine revolution presented an opportunity for them to act before the United States. France, the original colonial power, struck first. On February 4, 2011, just one month after the death of Bouazizi on January 4, 2011, the mayor of Paris, Bertrand Delanoe, decided that a square in Paris would be named in his honor, Place Mohamed Bouazizi. But the British were not about to let the French beat them a second time in the race to colonize Tunisia.

It was not surprising that it was the British Foreign secretary, *William Hague,* who was the first Western politician to visit Tunisia on February 8, 2011. While the mayor of Paris was busy unveiling Place Bouazizi in France's capital city on February 8, 2011, Hague was meeting Tunisian interim prime minister Mohamed Ghannouchi that same day in Tunisia. The newly elected Tunisian Foreign minister, *Rafik Abdessalem,* returned the favor by meeting Hague in London on March 28, 2012. As usual, the British media reported on increased British aid to Tunisia for education and culture, as if the British knew anything about either education or culture. British tourists continue to go to Tunisia to stay in five star hotels to be served by locals who are paid such low wages that they depend on tips which serve only to maintain the five centuries of British master-slave relations in British colonies.

What is most amusing is that these rich British tourists are so uneducated and lacking in cultural sensibilities that they think that Tunisians welcome their visits because of their tourist pounds. They would actually believe that a Tunisian waiter who says "thank you Massa" for a tip, really relish his servile status. No wonder those who survived the **defense of freedom and equality** by the armed rebel at the prestigious **Imperial** Marhaba Hotel in the relatively exclusive coastal resort city of *Sousse,* asked foolishly, Why? **Every** Western media reported this tragedy but there was no equivalent report by **any** Western media of the far greater numbers killed that same day, by bombs dropped from Western military jets and unmanned drones, and bombs dropped from the military jets of puppet governments of the West, such as Saudi Arabia, Iraq, Gulf states, and Egypt under the military rule of General el-Sisi. No wonder the only educated and culturally sensitive Englishman, *Russell Brand,* called the minute of silence and official day of mourning ordered on July 3, 2015, by British prime minister, David Cameron, **"Bullshit."**

The people of Tunisia rebelled against the recolonization of their country by Britain and the West. Among the first actions of the new Tunisian Resistance Movement was sending **freedom fighters** to Iraq and Syria to work cooperatively with ISIS to overthrow the New Western *Crusaders.* Tunisians soon became the largest group of foreign fighters to join ISIS. But the Resistance Movement also struck at home. The latest weapon used by the Western imperial powers was rich tourists. The Resistance Movement first struck on March 18, 2015. It targeted the Bardo National Museum in Tunisia's capital, Tunis. Tunis is one of the primary tourist destinations in Tunisia. By the standards of the **thousands** killed and injured by the bombs of the Western jets and those of their puppets, and the **millions** of refugees created by their destruction of property, the Tunisian freedom fighters killed and injured less than a hundred. The reason, of course, is that it's the West and their puppets who have the civilized weaponry and the freedom fighters who have the primitive weaponry.

The freedom fighters struck again on June 26, 2015. This time they targeted Tunisia's primary tourist destination, *Sousse,* Tunisia's third largest city. Its location along the Mediterranean Sea provides the golden sand beaches, while the five star hotels, night clubs, casinos and restaurants cater to the rich and famous. It attracts well over a million visitors annually. Most of the tourists are rich Western Europeans from the imperial powers of Britain, France, Italy and Germany. These were the imperial powers which had competed for Tunisia before France had won the prize. They never gave up on their colonization but changed their tactics over the centuries. In like manner, the Tunisian people never gave up their resistance and rebellion. Prior to the successful attack on June 26, 2015, the freedom fighters had made two earlier unsuccessful attempts in October 2013. Once again the numbers killed and injured were far fewer than those killed by the so-called Coalition bombing. The primitive weapons of the freedom fighters were no match for the civilized weapons of the West and their puppets. But the freedom fighters could take courage from the fact that most of those killed were from the primary recolonizer, **Britain.**

As to be expected, Britain's prime minister, David Cameron, used the tragedy of the killing of his people in Tunisia to make the case for increased warmongering. It should not be forgotten that the Americans inherited their warmongering DNA from their British forefathers during the time when Britain stole the lands of the First Nations to create the thirteen colonies which rebelled against Britain to create the USA. It should not be forgotten either that the British had called the American Empire a "puny" empire when Britannia ruled the waves. With the Arab Spring, David Cameron saw his opportunity to steal some thunder from the declining American Empire. As Russel Brand put it, at least he can increase the sale of weapons to fortify his war chest.

Regime Change in Egypt

We have previously dealt with Western colonization of Egypt. As with Tunisia, the French and English competed for Egypt. This time the British won and even the great Napoleon was unable to steal it from the British. The first Arab country to come under the spell of the Tunisian revolution was Egypt. Unlike Tunisia, Egypt's initial postcolonial history was much more anti-Western. In particular, Egypt's second president, Gamal Nasser, was one of the foremost leaders against continued meddling of the West in the domestic affairs of its ex-colonies. He was one of the founders and leaders of the *Non-Aligned Movement—NAM,* we summarized earlier. Nasser became an anti-colonial political activist at a very young age leading a student demonstration against British rule when he was only seventeen years old. He was shot by the police but survived. Two other demonstrators were killed. In a previous demonstration, Nasser had been arrested and spent a night in the British colonial prison. These demonstrations succeeded in getting the 1923 Egyptian constitution restored after it had been annulled ten years earlier. Nasser opposed the

1936 Anglo-Egyptian Treaty which gave the British the right to maintain military bases in Egypt. The excuse given by the British was that its troops were needed to protect the Suez Canal. Nasser felt that King Farouk of Egypt had made a bad deal with the British. His political activism proved to be an obstacle in getting admission to the Royal Military Academy but with persistence he was admitted in 1937. He fought the Israelis during the 1948 Arab-Israeli War.

Nasser was one of the leaders of a military coup against the Egyptian monarchy. King Farouk was seen to be too lenient against the British. He was overthrown on July 23, 1952, and Egypt became a republic. Nasser supported his superior officer, General Naguib, as the first president of the republic. He led the delegation which negotiated the British withdrawal from the Suez Canal. The British agreed to withdraw its troops from Egypt in October 1954. At the *Bandung Conference,* April 18–24, 1955, Nasser had supported the fight by Algeria, Tunisia and Morocco, for independence from France. The Bandung Conference was the second large scale meeting by postcolonial Asian and African states to cooperate with each other to fight recolonization by both the West and the Soviet Union. Conference delegates treated Nasser as the leader for all of the Arab states. China played an important role as well. The Conference led ultimately to the foundation of the NAM.

The withdrawal of British troops from Egypt was completed in June 1956. This was seen as full independence by Egyptian nationalists led by Nasser. Nasser had become the second president of the Egyptian Republic in January 1955. Unfortunately, no ex-colony is ever fully independent of its Western masters. When the West used its control of financial markets to blackmail Egypt, Egypt turned to the Soviet Union. This provided the excuse for invasion of Egypt by Britain, France, and Israel. Fortunately for Nasser, the United States was still in the process of establishing itself as the new leader of the West. It refused to aid an invasion led by the old Western leaders, Britain and France. The American threat worked. Henceforth the British became the primary "poodle" of every American president. The British "poodle" automatically brought with it the Canadian and Australian "poodles". The Americans had cleverly succeeded in getting a three for one deal by boycotting the British invasion of Egypt. Like little dogs they would typically bark louder than the big dog, their American master.

The American decision to fight the British and French for Western leadership proved to be only a minor setback for the West. Nasser and Egypt may have gloated over the Western disunity but the American decision proved to be the downfall of both the Third World and the Soviet Union. Prior to American leadership of the West, there had been the long-lasting implicit acceptance of a balance of power among several *great powers.* The Americans killed that long standing custom. It was the only *power* and you either supported it without question or received the most severe punishment. There were no more alliances. You towed the American line or suffered its wrath. All of the old great powers of Europe—Britain, France, Italy, Germany, Austria, Spain, Holland, and Portugal—fell in line. New states such as Canada, Australia, South Korea, Taiwan, and Singapore followed suit. Japan gave up its right to reemerge as a great power and kowtowed to the Americans. The Third World steered a dangerous course between the West and the Soviet Union. The West lost China and North Korea, but both were dirt-poor.

Egypt, led by Nasser as its second president, and supported by the Soviet Union, put up a brave fight against the West and its well-armed *uncolony,* Israel. But it was simply a matter of time before the unquestioned American led West would bring Egypt to its knees. Initially, the Americans attempted to bribe Nasser to sever his ties with the Soviet Union. When that failed they resorted to the old divide-and-rule tactic. Egypt had led the foundation of the *Arab League* in 1945. In opposition to it the West founded the *Baghdad Pact* in 1955. The Arab League initially included the countries of Egypt, Iraq, Jordan, Saudi Arabia, Syria and Yemen. The Baghdad Pact was led by Britain and initially included the countries of Pakistan, Turkey, Iran and Iraq in addition to Britain. This ploy by the West ensured that Muslims would never unite against the West and their countries would forever be subject states to be manipulated, bombed, demeaned and fought over, with their oil and other resources stolen and their population turned into refugees living in the most inhumane conditions in camps and shelters. If the First Nations of the New World thought they had it bad after the United States and Canada stole their lands just look at the hellish living conditions of the 60 million Muslim refugees created by the West and begging for aid in the UN make shift shelters in Jordan, Lebanon, Turkey, Pakistan and elsewhere today.

The Non-Aligned Movement, *NAM,* founded by Nasser and the leaders of India, Indonesia and Yugoslavia in 1961, was no match for Western imperialists. Nevertheless, Nasser's appointment as president of NAM in 1964 showed the movement's continued confidence in his anti-colonial stance. Nasser continued to press for greater independence from the West for both Arab and non-Arab Third World countries. Nasser's demise began with his loss of the1967 war with Israel. This military defeat made it crystal clear to Arabs that the West had planted the colony of Israel in their midst, not simply to help Jews, but also to facilitate its continued occupation of Arab lands and theft of Arab oil. Nasser's successor, Anwar Sadat, surrendered Egypt's leadership of opposing Western imperialism in the Middle East, and made peace with Israel. His pro-Western policies continued under his successor, Hosni Mubarak.

The Jasmine revolution arrived in Egypt on January 25, 2011. By that time the more commonly used term was *Arab Spring.* It was hailed by the brain-dead Western media as a democratic movement against the dictatorship of Hosni Mubarak. The Western media openly preaches that democratic means pro-Western and warmongering against those who are not. By their preaching it's impossible for any anti-Western government to be democratic. Moreover, if such governments do not invade and bomb countries as part of Obama's coalition they cannot be democratic. The United States and its media were initially confused when the Arab Spring arrived in Egypt. Mubarak was one of America's most reliable SOB dictators, supported by millions of dollars of military aid. He was definitely pro-Western and very supportive of the U.S.-backed atrocities committed by Israel on the Palestinian people. However, President Obama saw his opportunity to promote America's propaganda that it was pro-Democratic while replacing Mubarak with another pro-Western puppet leader in Egypt. He was supportive of regime change if the new regime was sufficiently pro-American. America has never had any qualms in dumping any of their imposed puppet dictators if politically expedient. Unfortunately, the Egyptian people voted for a government led by the **Muslim Brotherhood,** a Muslim group not supportive of Western colonization of Muslim lands.

Among those who are easily fooled by Western propaganda was the Egyptian politician *Mohammed ElBaradei.* ElBaradei had spent many years as director general of the International Atomic Energy Agency. During his term he tried to convince the United States that Saddam Hussein had no WMDs, that nuclear armed Israel was the cause of instability in the Middle East, that Iran did not pose a nuclear threat to Israel, and that the United States should pressure their puppet Egyptian leader, Hosni Mubarak, to reopen Egypt's border with Gaza for humanitarian reasons. Despite his failures on every one of these arguments, he never ceased to believe that the United States had good intentions. It was therefore not surprising that he would seize the opportunity of the Arab Spring to attempt to lead a democratic Egypt that would foster a better relationship with the United States based on respect and equality. It never amazes me how such "educated" people can be so easily fooled. To lead such an Egyptian government he returned to Egypt on January 27, 2011, and joined the protests in Tahir Square.

While many of the protestors supported ElBaradei as a possible democratic ruler to replace the "autocrat" Mubarak, he was opposed by those who had long supported the Muslim Brotherhood, a party banned by Mubarak. Like ElBaradei, the Muslim Brotherhood had embraced the protestors in Tahir Square on January 27, 2011. The next day the Egyptian government arrested one of the leaders of the Muslim Brotherhood, *Mohamed Morsi.* It was reported that ElBaradei was also arrested that same day. When interviewed by Al Jazeera on January 29, 2011, ElBaradei denied having been arrested. That same day Morsi escaped from prison. President Mubarak was forced to resign on February 11, 2011. Elections were held in June 2012, and Mohamed Morsi won 51.7 percent of the vote compared to his rival, Ahmed Shafik, who got the other 48.3 percent. Morsi began his presidency on June 30, 2012.

The Muslim Brotherhood was not the new Egyptian government expected by President Obama. We can only imagine the machinations, bribes and threats of the CIA and the White House during and before the elections. But those machinations had failed to stop the people's choice. It was a repeat of Allende in Chile in 1973. When covert actions fail, the

United States resort to military intervention. The democratic government led by Morsi was quickly ousted by President Obama with the help of the Egyptian military funded by American taxpayers. Obama's equivalent of General Pinochet in Chile was **Abdul Fatah el-Sisi.** The coup d'état took place on July 3, 2013, barely a year after Morsi took office. Protests erupted across Egypt but a military government has the weapons to crush protests. Backed by the world's most powerful military, the Egyptian military had nothing to fear. The military crackdown on demonstrators and those suspected of supporting the Muslim Brotherhood was merciless. The *Rabaa massacre* alone killed 638 civilians. The Egyptian judiciary was co-opted by the U.S.-backed Egyptian military. It sentenced President Morsi and over five hundred members of the Muslim Brotherhood to death, and many thousands to imprisonment.

Resistance goes underground and resort to guerilla tactics when confronted by civilized weaponry. Many Egyptians, like Iranians, support American intervention because they understand the financial power of the United States to embargo and impoverish them. Political freedom is not worth the economic cost to them. Egypt had long faced an insurgency in the Sinai Peninsula led by the local Bedouin population. The terrain is harsh and tribal, resembling the tribal areas of North-west Pakistan where the Pashtun tribes resist intrusion by the central government. Just as the U.S. invasion of Afghanistan forced the Taliban into these Pakistani tribal areas the U.S.-backed military coup in Egypt has forced the Muslim Brotherhood into the Sinai. It's ironic that the Morsi government had stepped up military operations against the Bedouin tribes in the Sinai in August 2012. A year later it was the military government, which had ousted Morsi that was hunting the Muslim Brotherhood in the Sinai. The mess created by President Obama in Libya and Syria has only served to provide more arms and fighters for the resistance.

Regime Change in Libya

After Egypt, Libya was the next victim of what the West called the Jasmine revolution. Western backed protests began on February 15, 2011. Unlike Tunisia and Egypt the West decided not to wait to see if the government would resign. It decided on a preemptive military invasion, using its puppet UN institution and its puppet secretary general, *Ban Ki-Moon,* to sanction its regime change by military force in Libya. The UN passed Resolution 1973 on March 17, 2011. As in Tunisia and Egypt, the two foremost Western European empires prior to the American Empire, Britain and France, took the lead with the United States to begin bombing Libya back to the Stone Age.

Libya, like Tunisia, was an **Islamic** country ruled by the Ottoman Empire until it was colonized by **Italy** in 1911. Italian colonization was resisted by the Muslim population and Italy used the same brutality and genocide against the locals as Canada and the United States have used against the First Nations. Many Italians migrated from Italy to Libya to settle the lands stolen from the Libyan people as the Europeans had done in Canada and the United States. The British and French fought the Italians and Germans for Libya during the Second World War. As a result of the defeat of Italy the British and French stole Libya from Italy. But the Libyans opposed the British and French as much as they had opposed the Italians. Weakened by the Second World War, France and Britain were forced to grant independence to Libya in 1951. The Jasmine Revolution of 2011 presented them with a second opportunity to steal Libya from her people.

As with all of the colonies in the Third World, the Western Europeans, and the now powerful American Empire, never granted any colony full political or economic independence. After Libya discovered an abundant supply of oil in 1959 it was even more of a target for continued Western colonization. As usual, when Libya refused to accept Western colonization the Americans attempted to assassinate its leader, Muammar Gaddafi. But the American airstrike on April 15, 1986, failed to kill Gaddafi. Their so-called **precision bombing** missed Gaddafi but killed a child, in addition to many other civilians. The infant girl, Hanna, had recently been adopted by Gaddafi. The American "precision bombing" was so "precise" that in addition to striking several civilian areas in Tripoli, it just narrowly missed the French embassy. Was that an intentional miss or a message to France because the French had refused the Americans permission to fly over French airspace? Such "collateral damage" is never referred to as war crimes because they are committed by God's chosen empire, the American Empire. As usual, liberals in the United States were critical of the bombing but only because the war crime had been committed by a Republican president, Ronald Reagan. Had it been committed by a Democratic president like President Obama he would surely have deserved the Nobel Peace Prize for such a dastardly act. After all, the world had been convinced by American propaganda that Gaddafi was the devil and that America was simply doing its **Christian** duty.

The Jasmine Revolution provided another opportunity for the American Empire to remove the Libyan leader, Gaddafi. As I have said before the Americans are never deterred by their failures. On this occasion the regime change was led by France. France had been forced to give up its colonies in North Africa, Algeria, Morocco and Tunisia. The Jasmine Revolution had provided an opportunity for it to recolonize Tunisia. But the British had beaten France to their planned recolonization of Tunisia. Now France saw an opportunity to re-steal Libya from her people as it had done with Britain during the Second World War, after the defeat of Italy. It was the first country to recognize a new regime in Libya on March 10, 2011. Its military jets were the first to enter Libyan airspace on March 19, 2011.

But Libyan resistance to recolonization by the West was fiercer in Libya than it had been in Tunisia. France would not have it as easy in Libya as the British in Tunisia. France has limited boots to put on the ground. Any chance of military victory over the people of Libya required use of the civilized military advantage which the West has, **aerial bombardment.** As part of the propaganda to get the UN resolution to sanctify what the West calls "coalition bombing," the West developed a new propaganda term, "killing his own people." Naked savage, guerilla, Communist, terrorist, jihadist, Islamist and fundamentalist were no longer sufficiently negative branding. "Killing his own people," was the latest ungodly term invented by the West to galvanize the Christian Crusaders of the godly West to bomb the heathens back to the Stone Age by using B-2 stealth bombers, each carrying sixteen two-thousand-pound bombs.

It is natural for any state to oppose its overthrow and this is precisely what the Libyan government did. But in bringing the rebels to justice the West turned this on its head by saying that Gaddafi was "killing his own people." While the rebels were backed by the West and supplied with arms, the West was reluctant to put many of its men in harm's way. It leads and provides civilized weaponry but locals must supply most of the boots on the ground. As a result there were very limited opportunities for the Libyan state to kill Americans or French or British even though the rebellion against the Libyan state was led by the French, British and Americans. The Western leaders used local puppets as their primary boots on the ground but supplied the weapons and the bombs. Adding insult to injury when the Libyans did kill four Americans at the American consulate, including Ambassador Christopher Stevens, on September 11, 2012, the Americans seemed surprised. Did the Americans not know that they were sending a message that killing was sanctioned by their Christian God as long as you did not "kill your own people"?

If the goal of the American Empire was to create as dysfunctional a state in Libya as they had created in Afghanistan and Iraq it succeeded in spades. The Libyan government was overthrown by the West on August 23, 2011. As many as thirty thousand Libyans lost their lives, including many women and children. Many more Libyans were injured. Even more Libyans were deprived of their homes and livelihood. Libyans became refugees in the UN camps across the Middle East. Many poor workers across Asia lost their jobs and were forced to return to dire poverty. But no lessons were learned. Like Afghanistan and Iraq the American Empire failed to colonize Libya and steal its oil and land. As in Iraq after the U.S. invasion of 2003, a second civil war erupted in Libya. The Libyan people struck a blow against the invaders when they carried out a successful attack on the American consulate in Benghazi on September 11, 2012.

The West has always depended on local puppets to support both their military conquests and securing and holding those conquests. The reason is quite simple. The population of the imperial powers is miniscule compared to the population conquered. What has changed in the twenty-first century is that the great majority of the people living in the imperial powers have little interest in participating actively in either the military conquests or the plum colonial administrative jobs. Where once a Brit or Scot would literally kill to get the opportunity to join the British East India Company and serve in India even with no chance of ever becoming a "Clive of India" or a Warren Hastings, few Yanks or

Brits or Frenchies today give a rat's ass for such jobs. They are too happy working at home with excellent employment, promotion and income prospects. Invasions, conquests and colonizations today by Western governments are the obsessions of a much smaller group of imperialists led by the David Camerons, Stephen Harpers, Barack Obamas, Francois Hollandes, Angela Merkels, and their military industrial complexes. They are provided with boots on the ground by relatively few young men, mostly young black men in the case of the United States, who are attracted by some foolish notion of serving their country, lack of employment and educational opportunities, desire to kick ass with guns and killer copters like the one given to Prince Harry, retards and psychopaths. They are not the ambitious young men drawn from the old Western European aristocratic families who were relatively well educated and saw great opportunities combined with adventure in seeking their fortunes and fame by serving their ever-expanding colonial empires when opportunities at home were scarce and reserved for the more senior members of the families.

This change in the availability of personnel from the Western imperial powers in holding captured territory in Afghanistan, Iraq, Tunisia, Egypt and Libya is the key reason why all of these imperial conquests eroded into civil wars and chaos. Regional powers were forced to intervene in the vacuum created by the instability. Those regional powers allied with the West such as Saudi Arabia, the Gulf States, Israel and the new military government in Egypt, were encouraged by the West to intervene on their behalf. Others such as Iran and ISIS intervened to assist those fighting the West and their local allies. Such local regional interventions combined with the civil wars to make the mess created by the West, an even much bigger mess, piled higher and deeper, a Ph.D. of a mess.

In the case of Libya the primary regional interveners were the new U.S.-backed military regime in Egypt and the United Arab Emirates, UAE. The Americans, British, French and Italians had killed Gaddafi to enable a new regime in Libya. But like the killing of Saddam Hussein by the Americans in Iraq, the killing of Gaddafi increased rather than reduced opposition to Western meddling in these countries. The Americans had learned the hard way that responding to the opposition which emerged after their killing of Saddam Hussein in Iraq was very costly and they had no appetite for dealing with the wrath of the opposition in Libya which emerged after their killing of Gaddafi. Without the United States, the French, British, and Italians, in 2012, are *paper tigers.*

Many Muslims were angered by the American military backed overthrow of the **democratically** elected government in Egypt simply because it was led by Muslims, the Muslim Brotherhood. Had the West not removed Gaddafi in Libya the Libyans would have had little to no opportunity of doing anything about the crime committed in Egypt by the West against all Muslims. But the failed state created by the West in Libya provided ample opportunity for Muslims to retaliate for the crime committed by the West in Egypt. Many of the members of the Muslim Brotherhood, in particular, found refuge in Libya. Since the Western backed military government led by General el-Sisi could not get the Americans, British, French, Canadians and Italians to start a new round of bombing in Libya he had to do it himself. President Obama had rather reluctantly agreed to the **second** round of Western bombing in Libya in 2011, *Operation Odyssey Dawn,* out of fear that the British, French and Italians would go it alone and he would seem to be a militarily weak leader of the civilized West. The United States had carried out its first round of bombing in Libya in 1986, *Operation El Dorado Canyon.* President Obama was in no mood to lead a **third** round of bombing in Libya, having by then added Syria and Iraq, to the never ending list of countries he had to bomb back to the Stone Age. In addition, political activist, *Ralph Nader,* had called for Obama to be impeached and tried as a war criminal for bombing the people of Libya. Documentary film maker, *Michael Moore,* asked Obama to return his Nobel Peace Prize. Rather surprisingly, it was mostly Republicans, not Democrats, who called out Obama as a warmonger for bombing the women and children of Libya and destroying the livelihoods of so many Libyans and poor foreign workers. President Obama had to be contented with only drone surveillance over Libya.

With the United States and its major mad-bomber allies, Britain, France, Australia and Canada, too busy bombing Syria and Iraq back to the Stone Age, Egypt took the lead in the third "coalition bombing" of Libya. With help from the UAE, General el-Sisi sent his military jets to begin a third round of "coalition bombing" of the people of Libya on August 17, 2014. It's very likely that the United States covertly provided intelligence to Egypt on the best military targets to hit. A perfect example of how the West ranks warmongering far higher than helping their poor and destitute is illustrated by Egypt's response to the February 2015 beheading of twenty-one poor and destitute Egyptians by ISIS in Libya. ISIS, like the Muslim Brotherhood, found the failed state created by President Obama in Libya, extremely strategic for opposing Western imperialism. Western leaders like David Cameron and Barack Obama have always found money for warmongering while cutting back on welfare by citing fiscal restraint. Their man in Egypt, General el-Sisi, naturally took a page from their book.

Many of the poor people of the world had found employment in Libya during the forty-two-year rule of Gaddafi. These included the poorest from Egypt. In Egypt, *Coptic Christians* would be the equivalent of poor blacks in America. The small Egyptian farming village of *el-Aour* in the Nile valley would be the equivalent of a black ghetto in the United States. Despite the rise of ISIS in Libya, after President Obama created the failed state, thirteen Coptic Christians living in el-Aour were so poor that they risked their lives to go to Libya to find work, fully knowing that ISIS was beheading Christians. When they were among the twenty-one Egyptian Christians caught and beheaded by ISIS, the Egyptian government found money to fly military jets with expensive bombs to drop on the people of Libya instead of using that money to help the remaining poor Coptic Christians in el-Aour. Egyptian jets bombed Libya on February 16, 2015, killing sixty-four. General el-Sisi was cheered on by every Western leader. He sent in ground troops two days later.

General el-Sisi, like the Barack Obamas, David Camerons, Francoise Hollandes and Stephen Harpers of the West, spend most of their waking hours hunting for politically acceptable excuses to feed their addiction to warmongering. General el-Sisi not only used the tragedy of Egypt's poor and destitute to bomb and invade Libya but to call on Obama and Canadian prime minister Steven Harper to broaden the targets of their military jets to include Libya. At the time the United States and Canada were bombing Syria and Iraq. How the dropping of expensive bombs in Libya helped the poor of Egypt—or of Britain, Canada, and the United States—is a mystery to me. But that is what General el-Sisi and his Western supporters claimed. France came out the winner in all of this. France sold over $6 billion worth of military jets to General el-Sisi to help the poor of Egypt by destroying their opportunities for jobs in Libya. The Defense minister of France, Jean-Yves Le Drian, was quick to claim that the new arms sale to Egypt was justified by the beheading of the Coptic Christians. That's the logic of Western civilization.

Regime Change in Syria and the Creation of ISIS

The last of the countries in the Middle East to be affected by the Jasmine Revolution was Syria. It was the last country not because President Obama had seen the error of his ways but because he had gone a bridge too far. His invasion of Syria and attempted regime change was the final disaster which gave birth to **ISIS.** The birth of ISIS meant diverting his warmongering to fighting ISIS rather than finding more regimes to change. President Obama saw his colonization of Syria as a stepping stone to Western recolonization of Iran. Ever since the Western puppet leader of Iran, the Shah, *Mohammad Reza Pahlavi,* had been removed by the Iranian Revolution of February 11, 1979, the West had used economic sanctions to recolonize Iran. The Jasmine Revolution provided the opportunity for a military solution. The new strategy of the West for regime change was to instigate a civil war and then condemn the expected response of the state by using its new propaganda that the leader of the state, in this case, *Bashar al-Assad,* was "killing his own people." It's okay to kill other people but not your own?

What the West did not expect was Russia blocking the use of a UN resolution to sanction the massive bombing operation needed to win the civil war. UN resolution 1973 had been passed by the UN to sanction the bombing of Libya because Russia and China had abstained. The United States had used B-2 stealth bombers, each dropping sixteen two-thousand-pound bombs on their targets. As I have said before the United States has no qualms about bombing a country back to the Stone Age simply because it has the civilized military capacity to do so. Canada under Steven Harper has been only too willing to join in this willful killing of women and children, destruction of livelihoods and adding to the millions of destitute refugees.

But the West had no such luck with its ploy to get a similar UN resolution to bomb Syria back to the Stone Age. Russian leader, **Vladimir Putin,** was fed up with the incessant warmongering by the West and had the courage and ability to stall the Western invasions. He knew that the American Empire had become too weak after its disasters in Afghanistan and Iraq to act unilaterally against Syria, even with British and Canadian help. Blocking a UN resolution would likely stall the Americans and their allies. Many American allies, including Canada, often insist on the Americans using the UN as a puppet to convince their gullible electorate that the war and invasion had been sanctified by what they falsely call the "international community," meaning the rich **white** countries. As a result, the Syrian rebels armed by the West, kept the civil war going but have yet to execute the regime change planned by the West. What the long civil war has done is add to the massive refugee crisis, add to the deaths and destruction, add to the political and economic instability, and add to the chaos and confusion, with no obvious goal. Syria has become the trench warfare of World War I. By 2015, half a million Syrians had been killed and some 12 million refugees created. Adding insult to injury the West blamed those who were defending their country from Western invasion, for these crimes.

In the meantime, the Western created instability in Syria has led to the emergence of *ISIS*. American failures in Afghanistan, Iraq, Libya, Egypt and Syria has led to a new movement which sees an opportunity in uniting these failures by creating a new, large and expanding Islamic state reminiscent of the days before the Western crusades. ISIS is breaking down the old Sunni/Shia conflict which the West had so long exploited. With ISIS, Sunnis are fighting other Sunnis. The Middle East has become an impossible quagmire for the West. The only beneficiaries are the warmongers and the arms dealers. In the meantime the massive numbers of refugees created shows no signs of abating.

ISIS had control of at least a third of the state of Syria by 2014, despite American and Canadian bombing. ISIS began its take-over of Syrian territory on September 18, 2013, when it captured the small town of *Azaz* on the border between Iraq and Syria. Somewhat ironic, the

United States and Canada had failed to get a UN resolution to bomb Bashar al-Assad but when their idiotic warmongering created ISIS they began bombing ISIS in Syria, thereby helping Bashar al-Assad. Prior to their creation of ISIS, Bashar al-Assad was a monster killing his own people. Their creation of ISIS made Assad their new Uncle Joe, much like Josef Stalin during World War II. U.S. bombing in Syria began on July 4, 2014, in an effort to rescue hostages, including Americans James Foley and Joel Sotloff. President Obama sent his unmanned drones into Syria on August 26, 2014. What is called "Coalition bombing" began targeting Syria on September 22, 2014. Canada first bombed Syria on April 8, 2015. Other members of this "Coalition" included Britain, Jordan, Saudi Arabia, Qatar, Bahrain, UAE, Turkey and Iran.

Of even greater significance than the creation of ISIS is the opportunity the Western military failures provided to Russia's capable leader, Vladimir Putin, to reassert Russia's historic presence in the Middle East. On September 30, 2015, Russian jets began bombing the Western backed rebels in Syria. Russia was invited to do so by Syria's legitimate government led by Bashar al-Assad. President Obama's response was not surprising. Russia will end up in a quagmire in Syria. Obama should know since he has been singlehandedly responsible for creating quagmires for the U.S. military in Afghanistan, Iraq, and Syria. With absolutely no leadership qualities whatsoever, president Obama can only pray that Putin will fail, as miserably as he has done.

Iraq Update

American and Canadian bombing of ISIS began in Iraq before Syria. The Americans first bombed Iraq because it had urged Iraq to invade Iran. When Saddam Hussein demanded financial help for the cost of this invasion the Americans hinted that it would be okay for Saddam to invade Kuwait and steal their oil as compensation. When Saudi Arabia objected, the Americans bombed Baghdad. That began in 1991. America continued to bomb Iraq for a quarter of a century, twenty-five long years. The excuse for this dastardly act by the United States and its allies, including Canada and Britain, kept changing. First it was Saddam's invasion of Kuwait, even though it was the United States that had told him with a "wink-wink nod-nod" that he should take the oil of Kuwait in lieu of U.S. payment for his invasion of Iran on behalf of the American Empire. Second, the bombing was to impose a no-fly zone to protect the Kurds even though it was the United States that had sold Saddam the chemical weapons he had used on the Kurds. The **third** excuse used was that Saddam had WMDs which should be destroyed since only the United States and its favored allies should have the right to possess WMDs. When this proved to be totally fabricated by the United States a **fourth** excuse was quickly found. Saddam was a dictator and Iraq needs a democracy. Never mind the fact that the United States owned this dictator when it asked him to invade Iran on their behalf. After the Americans killed Saddam they needed a fifth reason to continue the bombing. The **fifth** reason was that the American invasion of Afghanistan had pushed out some members of al-Qaeda from Afghanistan to Iraq. Never mind that members of al-Qaeda were called **freedom fighters** by President Reagan when they were allies of the United States against the Soviet Empire in Afghanistan. The **sixth** reason now is ISIS.

The American Empire began its bombing of ISIS in Iraq on August 8, 2014. Canada joined in this latest excuse for American bombing of the people of Iraq, on November 2, 2014. Other countries which contributed to this "Coalition bombing" in Iraq included Britain, Australia, Holland, France and Jordan. The only logical explanation for bombing the same country for over twenty-five years is addiction to warmongering. There is a direct correlation between the increase in funds for warmongering and the decrease in funds for reducing poverty. The poor in the United States, many of whom are blacks, are trapped by this American addiction to warmongering. They foolishly support it because they fear that cuts in the misnamed "defense" budget will reduce employment opportunities in the armed forces and make destitute the many communities in the United States, dependent on the spending by the families supported by those employed by the armed forces. Just as President Obama's Nobel Peace Prize is truly a *Warmongering* Prize, the U.S. defense budget is truly an *offence* budget. These warmongering leaders of the West not only deprive their poor of help by diverting funds to warmongering, they destroy the livelihoods of millions of very poor people in the Third

World, with their megaton bombs dropped from the heavens by mindless pilots pretending to be playing video games. These pilots are not heroes but demented killers. They drop deadly bombs on defenseless women and children.

Yemen Update

It was President Obama who was mostly responsible for the current failed state of Yemen. While it is true that many of President Reagan's *freedom fighters* found their way to Yemen after they had helped the American Empire to defeat the Soviet Empire, it was President Obama's mistake of putting too much faith in the military capabilities of his unmanned drones which ramped up America's warmongering in Yemen. President Reagan's *freedom fighters* were magically transformed by the power of Western propaganda into President George W. Bush's *al-Qaeda in Yemen* when George W. wanted a new excuse to feed America's addiction to warmongering after the C word, *communism,* had lost some of its propaganda power because of the disintegration of the Soviet Union. But George W. was much more focused on his warmongering in Afghanistan, Iraq and Pakistan than in Yemen.

President Obama withdrew American forces from Iraq to support his message that the invasion of Iraq by George W. was a military blunder. As a result he needed to find new countries to invade. Deploying many of the forces withdrawn from Iraq to Afghanistan was not sufficient. More importantly, Afghanistan was one of George W.'s original targets. President Obama wanted his name on a more original target. Yemen was an obvious alternative to Iraq and Afghanistan. It had already been engulfed by a very bloody American instigated civil war and moving toward failed state status. The Yemeni government was forced by both the United States and its ally, Saudi Arabia, to wage a war on its own people. "Killing your own people" is not a crime if the West tells you to do so. President Obama supplied the military weapons, intelligence, drone attacks and training.

The Jasmine Revolution had reached Yemen in January 2011. Protests forced the resignation of President *Ali Abdullah Saleh* and the election of President *Mansur Al-Hadi* on February 21, 2012. It is one of the poorest countries in the world. President Obama would not have to commit too much of America's stretched military resources to push it over the edge. Just as George W. had picked his invasion of Iraq as an easy target because of a decade of incessant bombing by the United States and Britain, and President Johnston had picked Vietnam as an easy target after half a decade of war with France, Yemen was President Obama's easy original target for his warmongering mention in history. As it turned out, none of these wars proved to be winnable, much less easy targets, for America's very advanced or civilized military. As I have explained many times before, the hallmark of what the West calls civilized is the advanced state of its military. To kill **many** with high tech drones and jets dropping megaton bombs is civilized. Nuking Hiroshima and Nagasaki to kill so many was very civilized. A suicide bomber killing a **few** is not civilized.

On January 22, 2015, *Houthi* rebels overthrew the American and Saudi backed government led by President Hadi. The Houthis are not affiliated with the al-Qaeda rebels. In fact, they were fighting both al-Qaeda and the Western backed governments of Saleh and Hadi. The Houthis had been fighting the Western and Saudi backed government of Yemen since 2004. The Houthis had supported those who had protested against the presidency of Saleh during the Jasmine Revolution. As in Libya and Syria there are multiple groups involved in the American instigated civil wars. In September 2014 the Houthis scored a significant defeat of the U.S.-and-Saudi-supported army of the Hadi presidency. They took control of Yemen's capital, Sana'a. Hadi fled to the old capital of Yemen, Aden, on February 21, 2015, claiming to be the legitimate president. The Houthis attacked and defeated his forces on the outskirts of Aden and forced him to flee to Saudi Arabia on March 25, 2015.

The response of President Obama to the mess he created in Yemen was similar to his response to the mess he created in Libya. Get a local puppet to do the heavy lifting. In the case of Libya that local puppet was the Egyptian military government of el-Sisi. In Yemen it was the Kingdom of Saudi Arabia, ruled by the Saudi family. The Saudi government began to bomb Yemen in lieu of the American Empire on March 25, 2015. The United States provided the intelligence. Saudi Arabia was assisted in the bombing campaigns by eight other Muslim states, Jordan, UAE, Bahrain, Kuwait, Morocco, Sudan, Qatar, and

Egypt. This coalition led by Saudi Arabia also imposed a blockade which prevented imports of food, water, and medicine into Yemen. Another humanitarian crisis and many more thousands of refugees were created in Yemen by the West. Almost half a million people were forced to flee or be evacuated by their home countries. As in Libya many of the poor from countries such as Somalia, Pakistan, Philippines, Malaysia, India, and China had found employment in Yemen. The West was determined to turn Yemen into another Libya. The attitude seems to be that if you cannot colonize a country, kill its inhabitants, and bomb it back to the Stone Age so that survivors have no hope of making a living. The West had done that to the original inhabitants in the New World and Australia. It was now committing the same genocide in the Middle East. The U.S.-supported coalition bombing has killed many civilians by indiscriminate bombing of densely populated areas and by bombing hospitals and schools. The bombing has violated international laws. As usual, the Saudis were accused of committing war crimes but will never be prosecuted unless the United States gives the green light to do so. And, as usual, the United States itself, will never be prosecuted for war crimes since it is above the law.

Who Is *Black* in America? And the Relevance of the Nonwhiting of the *White* West

In the Conclusion of *American Invasions* I made a brief reference to the color change spreading across the population of the Western countries, which dominated the world in the last five centuries. In these last two chapters I will address this change and speculate on the impact it will likely have on the decline and fall of the West. I will also address the related question I raised in the Conclusion of *American Invasions* as to the truth of the popular claim that President Obama was a **black** president instead of a **mixed-race** president?

As I write in 2015, America is embroiled over the question of race and racism. As I have argued in my prequels a country cannot resolve its problems without first acknowledging them. America continues to invade and invent wars because it has never acknowledged its addiction to warmongering. Likewise it continues to be **racist** because it has never acknowledged its racist origins. A warmongering elite who owned slaves can never create a freedom-loving republic. Anyone who thinks that is an idiot. To address both its addiction to warmongering and racism it must begin by admitting these wrongs. Acknowledge your theft of First Nations lands through military invasions. Acknowledge that you enslaved both First Nations and Africans. Acknowledge the fact that instead of creating a freedom loving republic you created a replica of the Roman Empire ruled by a white elite and bent on colonization of the nonwhite world. Acknowledge the fact that your bloody civil war was never fought to end slavery or racism but to secure your imperial ambitions and expand your conquest and theft of the lands and resources of nonwhites. Acknowledge that during that bloody Civil War, you killed far more of your own people than Gaddafi and Bashar al-Assad.

Black Americans can never expect equality of treatment if they join white Americans, in committing the same crimes globally. The American Empire is a monster both at home and overseas. Black Americans can never expect justice at home if they join white Americans in committing crimes overseas. Justice cannot be selective or manipulated. Jews cannot want public outcry for the holocaust while they kill Palestinians. In the past many black leaders, such as Muhammad Ali, recognized America's overseas crimes and refused to be a party to it. However, increasingly, black Americans and black American leaders have foolishly emulated white Americans thinking this would increase their equality. By acting, thinking, and committing international crimes like white Americans, black Americans pretend that they are equal. But equality cannot be built on a false premise just like creating a freedom loving republic cannot be built on a false premise. This transition from black leaders using the idea of *justice for all* to fight for racial equality, to black leaders **condoning and committing** the same crimes as white Americans, to fight for their racial equality in America, grew exponentially under the two terms of President Obama.

Under President Obama many of the new faces in the media projecting American power, American bullying, and American propaganda, during his two terms have been "black" faces. Far from President Obama reversing the disastrous foreign policy of his predecessor, George W. Bush, he has expanded exponentially the use of "black" American leaders to commit international crimes which in the past were reserved for white American leaders. George W. had begun this transition with Colin Powell and Condoleezza Rice.

In response to the killing of nine black Americans on June 17, 2015, by Dylann Roof, in the Emanuel African Episcopal Church in Charleston, South Carolina, President Obama belatedly and reluctantly joined the conversation on race in America. During his entire first term he had consistently refused to recognize, much less address, America's race problem. His excuse was that he was not a president for black Americans but the president of all Americans. He could just as easily have said, if he were honest, that his concerns were not those of black Americans or poor Americans, but of the fat cats of Wall Street and excuses for warmongering.

The reality is that until very recently, President Obama had little to no idea as to what being black meant. His mother was **white**, and he had been brought up by his **white** grandparents with no contact with his black father. His white mother separated from his black father a few **days** after his birth. It was a full decade later that his father would visit him just once in Hawaii in 1971. He never saw his father again. He would have consciously or unconsciously suppressed any connection to his father both because of his father's blackness and his father's Muslim religion. Every child in America knows that there is neither racial nor religious equality in the United States.

Young Barack chose to separate from his mother, who had remarried a **nonwhite** man, to live with his **white** grandparents in **Hawaii,** just before that one and only visit of his father. That choice would have further insulated him from the typical racism experienced by blacks in America. First, both of his grandparents were white. Second, Hawaii, stolen by the United States from the Hawaiian people, did not have anywhere near the white racism against blacks typical of large American cities. Third, his black father was never to be seen by anyone much less with Young Barack. People did not have any opportunity to link him with a black father. Finally, Young Barack was half white, mixed-race, **not** black. His color was more similar to the original Hawaiian owners, whose lands and resources had been stolen by white Americans, than to American blacks.

Obama's father had two serious strikes against him, his color, and his religion. It's extremely naïve to think that young Barack would not have heeded the advice of his white grandparents to bury any memory of his father since those two strikes against his father would have jeopardized any chance of Young Barack succeeding in America. As a result he became both **white** and **Christian.** As President Obama, he went to great lengths to deny both his black and Muslim roots. The fact that he is singlehandedly responsible for the creation of the first Islamic caliphate, ISIS, since the Crusades, must surely haunt him.

Obama was hailed as the first black president by the media and the public but he had little experience with living as a black American. He had to be educated during his presidency as to what being black meant and about the fact that America was still a racist country. By the time of the church shooting in Charleston on June 17, 2015, there had been many black protests related to blacks being killed by white policemen under questionable circumstances. President Obama's "black" attorney general, Eric Holder, had been forced to conduct federal investigations. President Obama was dragged into the race debate kicking and screaming.

It's Time for America to Replace the *N*-Word with the *M*-Word

In responding to the June 17 shooting in Charleston, President Obama used the dreaded *N*-word on public television. My contention is that America's confusion about race and racism has more to do with its refusal to use what I will call the *M*-word, than the *N*-word. I have invented the "M" word to refer to **mixed-race.** Questions about race and racism in America have their roots in Western European colonization. As in America, Western European empires brought whites, blacks, browns, and yellows to join reds or other blacks in the lands they colonized. This began a mixing of the races. In most of these colonies the custom which emerged was to find an acceptable term such as **mixed-race** or **coloreds** for the increasing populations of mixed-race inhabitants. South Africa and the Caribbean are good examples. Sometimes a derogatory term becomes the norm, unfortunately. In Latin America many terms were used depending on which two races mixed. But in America no such term was created. Instead the mixed-race population was misleadingly called **blacks.**

Today this is one of the root causes of America's continued confusion about race and racism and its search for solutions. This is exemplified by many "blacks" passing or trying to pass as whites and less frequently, some whites trying to pass as blacks. Whites and blacks alike show little sympathy for these understandably confused people. Think how horribly the American media and public treated Michael Jackson just because they perceived him as trying to pass as white even though there is no evidence that he did. That reinforces my view that Americans, blacks and whites, are confused about race and racism. Being confused makes solutions even more difficult to find.

In June 2015 a Civil Rights activist and NAACP leader, *Rachel Dolezal,* was "outed" by her parents for passing for black when she was white. Popular CNN mixed-race broadcaster, *Don Lemmon,* scorned her comment that she had been treated more fairly by the white establishment because of her "fair skin." What Dolezal said is the reality in the United States. Don Lemmon was either ignorant or deliberately hiding the truth to protect his own relatively privileged position. If he had any understanding or sympathy for the truth he would have made a gesture to explain the complexity of what it means to be black in America. Many Americans have some small percent of black, First Nation, or Asian blood. No one has ever asked the question as to what is the minimum percent of nonwhite blood you need to have to be switched over by American society from white to black? For all we know, one or both of Rachel's parents may have some small percent of nonwhite blood, but it was small enough to give them the option to pass for white, and that was what they chose.

Their daughter, Rachel, may have decided to choose not to pass for white, since she had four adopted **nonwhite** siblings and found more in common with blacks than with whites as evidenced by her desire to work for the NAACP and as a Civil Rights activist. While growing up with her four adopted nonwhite siblings, she may have bonded more with the mixed-race African-American community than with the white community. The problem is **not** Rachel Dolezal, but America's confusion of blacks with mixed-race, and the conscious or unconscious determination of the Don Lemons, Barack Obamas, and Michelle Obamas, to protect the privilege of their second-class status while working to move up to first-class status rather than helping third-class blacks get equality of opportunity.

A more recent example of America's confusion about race is the charge that a prominent leader of the *Black Lives Matter* movement, *Shaun King,* also lied about his race. While supposedly claiming to be black the charge is that he is white. Apparently King claimed that his mother was white but his father was black, just like President Obama. In this case the term, *biracial* is being bandied about. That is closer to my preferred term, mixed-race, rather than black. One of the many charges is that King lied about his race in order to qualify for a scholarship from Oprah Winfrey at Morehouse College, a historically black institution in Atlanta. The website *Brietbart* is claiming that it has a copy of King's birth certificate stating that his father is white, not black. Once again, what percent of nonwhite blood makes an American black?

Let us imagine going back to the very beginning of the creation of America's mixed-race population to understand why **blacks** are different from those of **mixed-race.** Imagine a white plantation owner having sex with an attractive young black slave or First Nation captive. She gives birth to a child. It's extremely naïve to think that this mixed-race child will experience the same degree of racism and disadvantages experienced by black slaves or First Nations captives. He or She will have far more privileges and education and employment opportunities than black slaves or First Nations. The degree of these extra privileges will depend crucially on whether the child was brought up by the white father or the black or First Nation mother.

Now imagine this mixed-race child growing up with privileges compared to black slaves and First Nations. He or she marries a white person. They get an offspring who is now only 25 percent black or First Nation. That child moves to a large cosmopolitan city where he or she can pass as white. Choosing to pass as white because of the privileges and opportunities would mean burying your black or First Nations roots.

Fast forward to the present. Mixed-race children born in America three centuries ago have had three centuries to build on those privileges and opportunities as well as denying their black or First Nations roots. Take a good look at the successful "blacks" you see on your TV or computer screens as politicians, broadcasters, leaders of the black community, priests, etc. Count how many are mixed-race compared to how many are black. Look at how many "blacks" President Obama appointed in his administration and see how many are truly black rather than mixed-race. Alternatively, think of a relatively privileged mixed-race person like Barack Obama marrying another relatively privileged mixed-race person like Michelle Obama and working in unison to enhance and to combine and protect those privileges. Barack Obama and Michelle Obama were able to secure admission to the prestigious Harvard Law School. How many young black men from America's many ghettoes would see the inside of any American College or University unless they sold their souls to the every hungry American military? How many black men in America's many ghettoes look like Barack Obama? How many black women in America's many ghettoes look like Michelle Obama? How many black children in America's many ghettoes look like Malia or Sasha Obama?

Growing up in the English colony of Guyana I have first-hand experience of the Imperial power gradually co-opting the mixed-race population as they hand over power to them and exclude the reds, blacks, browns, and yellows. In the United States the English turned over power to the children of the white colonizers. Relatively few would have been of mixed-race at that time. But as America and other English ex-colonies were shamed into reducing the excesses of white racism, they found a way to co-opt the nonwhites, and it was far easier to co-opt the mixed-race population since they also had centuries of privileges and opportunities that they wanted to protect just like the whites.

In America, bringing the mixed-race population into positions of power was much more easily hidden by the whites since they claimed to be sharing power with blacks. In reality, what was being done was creating another tier in the totem pole. The privileged whites can hold on to their first-class status by creating a willing second-class tier consisting mostly of mixed-race but camouflaged as blacks. This second-class tier always had privileges compared to the third-class blacks and was generally willing to protect the first-class tier to keep their second-class status. It appeared as if blacks were getting greater equality and opportunities but it was simply the creation of another tier where the whites generally kept their first-class status, the mixed-race were mostly co-opted in exchange for the protection of their second-class status and the others remained third-class. Some even remained or fell into fourth-class status, the very poor and the blacks in the ghettoes. As one comedian put it, the essence of the American dream is that you have to be asleep to dream. The increasing numbers of Americans staying or falling into fourth-class status confirms the fact that they keep the American dream alive because they are still asleep.

Born in Guyana myself, after immigrating to the province of BC in Canada, I learned that the first governor of BC, **James Douglas,** was also born in Guyana. What is hardly known is the fact that Douglas' mother was a mixed-race person. I had to do some independent research in the literature on racism to find this out. Douglas had the right percent of white in his skin color to pass for white. This is what he chose to do. The reason is obvious. He would never have been appointed to the position of governor of the English colony of British Columbia had it been public knowledge that he was **black** by the definition of black in America. It is therefore very likely that Obama was **not** the first black president in America using America's definition of black. Many blacks in America have chosen to pass as whites because of the privileges and opportunities automatically claimed by whites compared to the discrimination against blacks by those with the economic, political, social, cultural and religious power.

In 2015 black America is at an important crossroad. Leaders of the black community in America are **not** black. They are mixed-race. They have a privileged position to protect. Most of them take the view that half a cake is better than no cake. They know full well that fighting for racial equality will jeopardize their privileged second-class position. The few mixed-race leaders who speak out against racism are chastised for attacking their very own "black president." They are ostracized as much as Jewish leaders who speak out against Israel's terrible mistreatment of the Palestinians. Just as President Barack Obama has made warmongering acceptable to the Nobel Peace Prize committee and to liberals everywhere so too has his election as the first "black" president set back the clock on progress toward equality for blacks. As an example, while youth unemployment in the United States is high for all young workers at 15 percent, it's double that rate for young blacks. This is one reason why so many young blacks join the armed forces or turn to crime. Barack Obama has been a disaster both for the Peace movement and racial equality for blacks in America. In fact, there is another connection between his warmongering and racial disconnect. As I have said above he has co-opted blacks in America to fight his invented war on terror by giving the mixed-race leaders of the American blacks high profile political appointments.

Fixing Immigration: Obama: Deporter-in-chief, Economist, 2014

The large influx of **Hispanics,** and to a lesser extent, **Asians,** has further complicated America's racial divide and threat to its historic white supremacy. As with every **white** ex-English colony such as Canada, Australia and New Zealand, the United States rode its pretense of democracy and non–South Africa style apartheid by severely restricting nonwhite immigrants. But that is under threat today in both Canada and the United States. In Canada the threat comes mostly from the recent influx of Asian immigrants. In the United States the threat comes mostly from the recent influx of Hispanic immigrants. In our final chapter we will return to this issue of the mixing of the races in the Western countries, including the United States. It would be natural to expect that whites—and in the case of the United States, the mixed-race blacks as well—would seek to maintain their privileged position by fomenting dissentions and divisions among the nonwhites. This would be just another application of the age-old divide-and-rule tactic.

Among the many ills facing America that the "Audacity of Hope" Candidate Obama had promised to fix was **immigration.** Unlike Western Europe, which is struggling to deal with an immigration problem caused by their complicity in the many American invasions in Afghanistan, Iraq, Libya, Syria and North Africa, the U.S. immigration problem is the result of their much earlier invasion and conquest of Mexico. The common thread of these immigration problems in Western Europe and America is not simply that both have their roots in American warmongering but also in Western imperialism. Many of the immigrants crossing the Mediterranean into Italy and Greece, on their way to other countries in Western Europe, are from ex-colonies of the Western European empires. Likewise the immigrants coming into the United States are from Mexico and other Latin American countries, ex-*un-colonies* of the United States. The West had invaded, colonized and occupied much of the world beginning with Portugal in 1450. The colonized people had been robbed of their livelihoods and impoverished. By sheer determination they have trickled into the countries of their colonial masters despite the best efforts of their colonial masters to keep them out. While it's just a trickle, the numbers of the colonized peoples vastly outnumber the peoples of the imperial powers. For example, the recent warmongering of the West created 60 million refugees. Those who trickle into Western Europe would be far less than **a few** million, but to the people living in the countries of the imperial masters a few thousand is too many.

In the case of the United States the numbers are far more. Unlike the immigrants into Western Europe who are blocked by the dangerous water of the Mediterranean Sea, the Mexicans and other Latin Americans cross only land borders, far easier to penetrate, even with walls, fences and "shoot to-kill" armed guards and vigilantes. Americans bemoan this influx of Latinos and like the Western European voters, require their government to take action to stop it. But as usual neither Western Europeans nor Americans elect leaders who have the capacity to solve their problems. Voters get promises from every newly elected leader. You buy votes in Western democracies with promises not solutions. In this regard Candidate Obama was no different. But people were more hopeful because he came across in the campaign as smarter. Once again we were fooled by his brilliant rhetoric. He is as incapable of solving the immigration problem as he is incapable of ending wars, increasing racial equality, reducing poverty, or closing Guantanamo.

A headline in the Economist Magazine, February 2014, "Barack Obama, deporter-in-chief," caught my attention. Was he fixing America's immigration problem by deporting the immigrants? According to the Economist Magazine, America under President Obama was deporting "illegal" immigrants at a rate **nine times** the rate two decades earlier. The article also pointed out that Obama had deported far more than George W. So much for Candidate Obama favoring Main Street over Wall Street!

Despite Obama's determined efforts to deport the poor, the hungry, the desperate, the downtrodden, the family members and children of poor Americans, the **nonwhite,** he has failed in his efforts to stem the net influx of nonwhites into the lily-white Camelot he had imagined for himself, Michelle, Malia, and Sasha. The color of America is browning. Today the American Hispanic population exceeds blacks, 17.5 percent of America's total population compared to 13.5 percent for blacks. Add another 9 percent for Asians, First Nations and mixed-race, and America's nonwhite population is close to 40 percent.

President Obama has spent billions of dollars to prevent immigrants entering the United States and on deporting immigrants. But the world is populated by a far larger number of nonwhites compared to whites. Had the whites stayed home instead of colonizing the nonwhite people they would have kept their countries white. The twenty-first century is pay-back for six centuries of whites leaving their homes to colonize and steal the wealth of the nonwhites. Civilized weapons enabled the theft of the lands and resources of the nonwhites by the whites. So far the whites are at a loss to invent a weapon to keep the nonwhites from invading and occupying their lands in Europe and the lands the whites stole from the original inhabitants in the United States, Canada, Mexico, Australia, and New Zealand.

In the case of the large influx of Hispanics into the United States, there is the added fact that America stole First Nations lands in California, Texas, Florida, Arizona, and New Mexico, previously stolen by the Spanish Empire and inherited by Mexico. These are the states where the great majority of Hispanics have immigrated to in order to reclaim their stolen land. California has the largest number of Hispanics, some 15 million. Texas has 10 million, Florida has 4.5 million, Arizona has 2 million, and New Mexico has one million. Many American employers, large and small, welcome the influx of these Hispanic immigrants since they are a source of cheap labor. American consumers benefit from the low prices for consumer goods using the cheap labor. It reduces imports from China which many Americans applaud.

Income and Wealth Inequality: Occupy Wall Street: Barack Obama as Debt-Monger-in Chief and as

Money-Printer-in-Chief: Budget Deficits, Trade Deficits, China, Future of the U.S. Dollar as the World's Reserve Currency, and America's Growing Foreign Debt

In this final section we address several other failed promises of Candidate Obama and also show how these American problems are linked. We begin with Candidate Obama's promise to help those Americans with low incomes and zero or negative wealth by favoring Main Street over Wall Street. His failure to keep this promise is part of his failure to reduce racial discrimination against blacks since blacks are among the poorest in America. Once again black celebrities on TV, in the movies, in music and in sports, provide a totally misleading picture of black income. Like black politicians and leaders of the "black" communities they are often mixed-race rather than black and represent a tiny percent of those blacks who are not mixed-race and live mostly in the black ghettoes. Obama's failure to prevent increasing income and wealth inequality, much less reduce it, is also linked to many of America's other problems identified during his campaign for the presidency and in our heading above.

Income inequality produced under **Capitalism** was the primary incentive for the work of Marx and Engels which ultimately made the West so fearful of **Communism** that it transformed its free enterprise economic system into mixed economic systems. These mixed economies reduced income inequality by legalizing trade unions, imposing progressive income taxes, increased transfer payments such as welfare to the poor, and expanding their public sectors where price is not set by the market. More recently, however, the United States and many other Western states have regressed. The power of unions has been reduced and union membership, as a percent of the labor force has fallen. Income inequality has increased instead of falling both because income inequality created by the free enterprise private sector has increased while the redistribution effects of government policies have been reduced. In the United States and many other Western states, the drain on tax revenues from increased **warmongering** has further reduced programs which help the poor. Fighting the invented "War on Terror" takes precedence over fighting the "War on Poverty." Canada's prime minister, Steven Harper, and Britain's prime minister, David Cameron, are the strongest and most vocal proponents of this view.

The "War on Poverty" is as old as imperialism and religion. Pope Francis is only the latest of a long line of religious leaders who have spoken out against increased poverty. In 2015 Pope Francis visited Latin America so that the millions of poor who inhabit that region can pay homage to him. They did not disappoint. They came out in the millions to greet him. But the prayers of the pope did not help the poor any more than the centuries of prayers by every religious sect. What it did was to prompt Vancouver's mayor, Gregor Robertson, to divert taxpayer money from the homeless in Vancouver to pay for a flight to the Vatican. Robertson needed justification for a taxpayer funded holiday to Rome. He determined that a visit to the pope would provide him with sage advice on fulfilling his election promise to end homelessness in the Canadian city of Vancouver. In the United States, President Reagan ramped up America's long "War on Drugs." As a result of this war, thousands of young blacks in America's many "inner" cities were harassed, mistreated, and incarcerated. Many were fathers. Black children grew up without fathers. Blacks who had served their years in prison returned to their poor neighborhoods with a criminal record. This made it difficult to find employers willing to hire them. This increased the already high unemployment rate, forcing them to return to dealing drugs. The war created a vicious cycle of poverty. As an example, the American city of Los Angeles has fifty thousand homeless inhabitants in 2016, making it America's homeless capital city. America's "War on Drugs" failed to reduce, much less end, use of illegal drugs by Americans. All it did was increase the millions of poor in the United States. In the post-Reagan years it has also created millions of poor in Mexico after the United States cajoled the Mexican government into helping it fight America's "War on Drugs."

Just as General el-Sisi could have helped the poor of Egypt by giving them the money he spent on bombing Libya, the pope could have helped the poor of Latin America by giving them the money he spent to pay for his visit, and Robertson could have helped the poor by giving them the money he spent to pay for his trip to the Vatican. In like manner, the American and Mexican governments could have helped the poor by giving them the money they paid for the "War on Drugs." These are only a few examples to show how the actions of Western leaders—from the pope to presidents and prime ministers, to city mayors like Robertson—betray their loud proclamations of wanting to help the poor. These examples support our claim that the unspoken goal of the West is to create even more millions of poor by bombing their countries back to the Stone Age, inventing excuses for wars, and creating millions of refugees and homeless city dwellers.

Some of the following statistics for the United States will indicate both the high degree of income inequality and its **increase,** not decrease, as promised by Candidate Obama. It was this increase in income inequality under the "Audacity of Hope" president which inspired the "Occupy Wall Street" movement. As expected, that movement inspired lots of rhetoric from the silver tongued "talk is Cheap" Obama but absolutely no action. Another round of golf with his Wall Street buddies was sufficient to ease his conscience. Michelle probably bought some more clothing to display her knowledge of the latest fashion. She likes the media commenting on how fashion savvy she is.

President Obama came to power when the United States suffered its worst economic recession since the Great Depression of the 1930s. The years 2007–2008 were dubbed the Great Recession. The incomes of all Americans fell. Some 9 million Americans lost their jobs and about one and a half million lost their homes. President Obama oversaw the economic recovery beginning in 2009. It was during this recovery that income inequality in the United States worsened the most. Some will defend President Obama by pointing out that income inequality in the United States had been increasing since 1980. My response is that many supported Candidate Obama precisely because he campaigned to reverse this trend with his slogan of Main Street over Wall Street. It's not simply shocking but utterly disgraceful that in **2013** the top **one-tenth** of one percent of households living in the self-proclaimed "leader of the free world" country and the self-proclaimed greatest democratic republic, created by **slave owners** like George Washington, received **10** percent of the economy's total income. In that same year, when President Obama was already into the second term of his presidency of unfulfilled promises, the top **one percent** of American households received **20** percent of the total income of the American economy. The flip side of that coin was that half of the American people were poor or low income.

While income inequality is a problem in every country the United States ranks worse than most developed economies. Since 2009, when the self-professed Main Street president took over the management of the U.S. economy, the share of total income received by the top one percent of American households increased from 13.3 percent to 14.6 percent by 2011. In the following year the income of this privileged one percent rose by **20 percent** while the income of the other 99 percent increased only **one percent.** This top one percent took 95 percent of total income growth in the United States during Obama's first term leaving just 5 percent for the remaining 99 percent. During Obama's first term the inflation adjusted income of this top one percent grew by almost 32 percent while the inflation adjusted income of the other 99 percent grew **less than half of one percent,** almost zero. By the end of Obama's first term the share of total income received by the richest **ten percent** of Americans **exceeded** half of America's total income. Imagine 90 percent of Americans surviving on less than the income received by only10 percent, during the first term of a president they voted for because he promised to reduce income inequality by changing America's preferential treatment of Wall Street over Main Street.

Wealth Inequality in the United States Is Worse than Income Inequality

It's unfortunate that the public, the media, and most writers, use wealth and income interchangeably. That is totally **incorrect.** A household's economic wellbeing depends both on its annual income and its accumulated wealth or assets. Its annual income can be from work, interest, dividends, rental property or capital gains from sale of assets. But its wealth is the value of its net worth, assets less debt, accumulated from inheritance and net savings. Assets include residential and commercial real estate, stocks and bonds, treasury bills and other money market instruments, bank deposits, gold and other precious metals, mineral deposits and oil and natural gas ownership, cars and other vehicles. While the poor in the United States typically have some income, no matter how small, many have negative net worth or wealth. This is because the poor have few, if any assets, perhaps an old car, but have some debt. Most of this debt will be from credit cards or payday loans. This is one reason why wealth in the United States, as in most countries, is more unequally distributed than income. The most widely accepted measure of both income and wealth inequality is the *Gini coefficient.* The value of this coefficient varies from zero to one. The closer this coefficient is to one the higher is inequality. In the United States the Gini coefficient for income is about **0.53** while it is about **0.85** for wealth. Both wealth and income inequality in the United States exceed that of many developed countries.

But there are many other reasons for the greater degree of wealth inequality than income inequality. One key reason is inheritance. Most wealthy households pass on some of their wealth to their children. The poor have no wealth to pass on to their children and some will pass on some of their outstanding debt or negative wealth. A second key reason is that the wealthy can afford to take risks with investments in real estate, the stock market, bonds and small businesses. These investments typically provide relatively high average real returns, including capital gains. The poor have no wealth to invest but middle income households will have some savings which they would typically put into secured bank deposits with negative real returns. The returns are negative because the nominal interest rate on the bank deposit is often less than the inflation rate. The U.S. low-interest rate policy of the last two decades has worsened the discrepancy between returns on investment by the wealthy compared to returns on savings by the lower middle class. Another reason for higher wealth inequality compared with income inequality is that wealth is accumulated over the lifetime of the household and over several generations. Income is for the current year only.

There is an important connection between wealth inequality and income inequality. While the poor get income only from employment or welfare the high income earners get income from labor, capital, land, and entrepreneurship, including annual net capital gains. Despite this connection it's important to discuss both income and wealth inequality separately to fully understand the plight of the poor in America. Their low income often means getting into debt. In the case of emergencies such as illness, unemployment, natural disasters, pension loss caused by the 2007–2008 financial crisis or disability, they have no net wealth to fall back on or to cushion the devastation of such misfortunes. Furthermore, they are likely to dig themselves into a deeper hole of a mountain of debt caused not only by borrowing but borrowing at much higher interest rates than wealthy or high income borrowers. The reason is that the lenders demand compensation for taking higher risks associated with lending to the poor. Children and blacks suffer the most from these calamities. While **one in three** white American households inherited substantial wealth only **one in ten** black households inherited substantial wealth. The children of the wealthy have access to the best universities. They get an advantage both from inherited wealth and higher education.

The wealthy class in every society wields enormous economic, financial, political and legal power. This is even truer in the United States, where the wealthy fund the expensive political campaigns and political lobby groups. The United States was an aristocracy before and after its birth as an independent country. That aristocratic hold on political power has not been eroded by its pretend democracy. The poor may have the vote but little else. Both parties are funded by and protect the rich and powerful. The only shift in power in the United States has been from the slave owning Southern aristocrats to the Northern capitalists and imperialists. In America today the wealthiest one percent owns 40 percent of the total wealth in the United States. This wealthiest one percent also owns more wealth than the lowest 90 percent. This is the one percent of Americans who call the shots both at home and in foreign policy. They can afford to spend billions on civilized weapons to invade, kill, and destroy, across the globe. They have the power to punish dissenters in every corner of the globe, impoverish them, or bomb their countries back to the Stone Age, which they do with great relish and enthusiasm. They have an almost endless supply of poor blacks to put boots on the ground where they cannot coerce enough of the local poor to kill their own, for the mighty Yankee dollar.

The Occupy Wall Street Movement

The *Occupy Wall Street* movement was a direct result of President Obama's failure to deal with the problem of rising inequalities in America. Income and wealth inequality, for example, had been increasing for four decades prior to the election of President Obama. The movement's slogan of **99** percent comes from the fact that the percent of total U.S. income going to the top one percent of American households had been increasing since the 1970s. In business courses students are taught that every change or crisis brings both challenges and opportunities. That is true of the financial crisis of 2007 which President Obama inherited. However, instead of looking for opportunities presented by this financial meltdown, President Obama looked at it only as a challenge and used it to find excuses for not dealing with inequalities. In particular, instead of using his own team of economic and financial advisors to bring to justice those responsible for the mismanagement and greed which caused the crisis, he sacked his team of advisors and hired the very experts who had caused the crisis to work under him to fix the crisis. In other words, instead of punishing them he rewarded them with plum jobs.

A second missed opportunity by President Obama was his use of American tax dollars, printing of money and Government debt to bail out Wall Street instead of Main Street. Two key sectors at risk because of the crisis were mortgage lenders, investment bankers and insurance corporations, such as commercial banks, Fannie Mae and Freddie Mac, AIG and Lehman Brothers, in the financial sector; and car producers such as GM in the real sector, of the economy. Imagine if President Obama had used public funds to provide interest free loans or even gifts to those at risk of losing their homes or small businesses? They would have kept their homes and small businesses and paid their mortgages to prevent the mortgage lenders from needing bailout money. Likewise interest free loans or gifts could have been made to the poor and lower middle class to buy American cars. This would have redistributed income and saved the money used to bailout GM and other American car makers. Rather than using the opportunity presented by the 2007 financial crisis to save the banks and car makers while simultaneously satisfying his mandate to reduce inequalities President Obama deliberately used the financial crisis as an excuse to increase inequalities by favoring Wall Street over Main Street.

The Occupy Wall Street movement was inspired by the **Jasmine revolutions** in Egypt and Tunisia; the protest of American consumerism represented by the **Adbusters** group in Canada; the **labor unions**; the **Anonymous** Internet hackers; **Green Peace**; the **Black Lives Matter** group; those protesting **budget cuts** in the United States, England, Spain, and other EU countries; **artists**; **anarchists**; **Marxists**; **techies**; **social media activists**; those protesting **corruption and greed**; and those protesting against **capitalism,** in particular the reversal of the post–World War II decline in the share of total income going to labor relative to capital and the related increased political influence, greed, and corruption of corporate America and Wall Street.

It's not surprising to me that the movement fizzled out. Western democracies are good at propaganda and fear mongering. This prevents any real change by society. Voters are told that they have unlimited freedoms, political power and that the people of the non-Western democracies envy their lifestyle. Their governments must spend billions on warmongering rather than reducing poverty and inequalities to protect their envied lifestyle. Unfortunately, the great majority of voters living in these Western democracies believe these lies. Opposition to these lies rest with a tiny intelligent minority which has never garnered more than one percent support in the six centuries that the West conquered the world. President Obama may be a liar but he knows that the majority of American voters are on his side. Those who are vocal supporters of movements for change such as the Occupy Wall Street movement are eventually branded as traitors, un-American, anarchists, communists or even terrorists. It's not surprising to learn that the FBI and the U.S. Department of Homeland Security used its **Joint Terrorism Task Force** to survey and spy on the organizers.

America's Staggering Growth in Debt and Money Supply under President Obama

In addition to the much deserved titles of warmonger-in-chief and deporter-in-chief, President Obama can be labeled as *Debt-monger-in-Chief* and *Money-Printer-in-Chief* since he added more government debt and increased the U.S. money supply more than any other American president. Had he added this debt or printed money to help the poor and move from favoring Wall Street over Main Street it could have been excused as implied by his election promise! But President Obama created this debt and printed money to pay for his other two titles as warmonger-in-chief and deporter-in-chief as well as bailing out Wall Street. While the cost of bailing out Wall Street and deporting immigrants has contributed to America's debt problem under President Obama, the primary cause of America's debt is its invented "War on Terror."

At the end of President Bill Clinton's two terms, America's federal government's debt was $US 5.8 trillion. This was a 32 percent increase from the debt left at the end of President H. W. Bush's term. President George W. Bush added significantly to this debt to wage America's invented War on Terror. George W. added $US 5.85 trillion, doubling the federal debt left by President Clinton. Not to be outdone, President Obama added **$US 8 trillion.** It's difficult to comprehend the magnitude of any country's debt problem without context. In the past, debt was incurred by rich countries such as the United States, only to fight wars. Poor countries incurred debt to provide the basic government services because most of the population was too poor to pay taxes and the few rich did their best to evade taxes.

But many rich countries today incur debt to buy the votes of the electorate in democracies. While most of the rich countries like Greece, Ireland, Puerto Rico, Cyprus, Iceland, Spain and Italy, incurred this debt to pay for social services the United States incurred its debt to pay for its addiction to warmongering. In either case the democratic system is an abject failure. The West has created a political system which is rife with corruption and dishonest politicians. All of the politicians running for public office promise the moon **and** tax cuts. That is impossible but voters are too ignorant and easily manipulated. In the West leadership is sorely lacking. Politicians seek advice from day time talk show hosts as voters have been dumbed down to that level of thinking. What Civilization needs is **Leadership,** Freedom, Justice, and Education, not Western Dumbed-Down and Vote-Buying Democracy and Propaganda! It's our view that Western democracy has been a total failure in advancing the human spirit, granting real freedoms, ending warmongering and colonizations or balancing the desire for materialism with the needs of the environment, equitable income distribution and justice. It has not even dispelled the myths surrounding religious beliefs such as virgin births, walking on water, miracles and ascending of physical bodies to some heavenly space above.

What is even more unbelievable is that its gloried democracy would be so uneducated that it would not see fit to the question why the richest country in the world cannot find a leader who can balance its budget? Why is it that the United States cannot live within its means and is forced to borrow from the poorer countries, like China? It's the equivalent of the richest person in the world borrowing to fund his/her annual expenditures! I can understand why Americans are so uneducated not to ask why America has engaged in more warmongering that any other country in history since warmongering is innate in the DNA of most Americans. But America was not always the world's largest borrower. In fact, when America was much poorer it was the world's largest lender. How could America have grown so much richer and simultaneously accumulated the largest public and private debt of any country in history without those who vote in this acclaimed bastion of democracy and freedom not being educated enough to ask why?

America's federal debt has ballooned out of all proportion under the presidencies of George W. Bush and Barack Obama and yet it's barely on the radar of those who vote. The typical American voter seemed rather angry at those members of the Republican and Tea parties who worked tirelessly to shine a light on this gynormous problem. Governments need to balance their annual budgets by controlling total expenditures to total tax revenues imposed on their electorate. However, most governments incur annual deficits which accumulate with interest to create the public debt. In the century and a quarter between 1789 and 1913, annual budget deficits by the federal government of the United States were so small that the public debt had accumulated to only **$US 3 billion.** This federal debt increased significantly during the U.S. Civil war and the First and Second World Wars. Nevertheless, at the end of the Second World War it had accumulated to a manageable **$US 259 billion.**

While the U.S. federal debt increased after World War II its debt as a percent of its annual GDP fell because the growth in nominal GDP outpaced the growth in the debt. This was before Western politicians realized how easy it was to buy votes with wild promises of all kinds of goodies at no cost to taxpayers. Politicians in every democracy learned that taxes are unpopular with voters but public services are very popular. They could buy votes by creating budget deficits or printing money. The year 1974 was the critical year for the United States, Canada, and many Western countries to follow each other in creating a mountain of debt to buy votes in democracies. As annual deficits became ever bigger, despite the printing of money to help pay for public services, the federal debt in the United States and many rich countries grew faster than nominal GDP, that is, real GDP plus inflation. The printing of money to help pay for public services increased the inflation rate but the debt still grew more than inflation plus economic growth. This ballooning of deficits and debt began to concern some voters and politicians in some democracies, including Canada and the United States, and they began to scale back.

In the United States, President Jimmy Carter added $US 299 billion to the federal debt but reduced the federal-debt-to-GDP ratio. At the end of Carter's presidency the U.S. federal debt was still below the trillion dollar mark at **$US 998 billion.** It's ironic that the next U.S. president, Ronald Reagan, won the presidency by campaigning on a program of austerity because of the growing concern over rising deficits and debt but reversed President Carter's achievement. Under President Reagan $US 1.86 trillion was added to the federal debt. This more than doubled the federal debt and clearly increased the federal-debt-to-GDP ratio. To comprehend the enormity of what President Reagan had done, you need to recognize that he had added more federal debt during his **eight years** in office than all of the presidents combined before him. Of course prices were higher, so the inflation adjusted increase was somewhat less. But the enormity of adding more debt in eight years compared to how much was accumulated over more than **two centuries** should never have gone unnoticed by American voters, had they not been totally brain-dead. It was President Reagan, more than any other president, who sent the message to future American presidents that there was no limit to how much debt American voters would tolerate. Voters in Western-style democracies were never really smart enough to question how all the goodies they voted for would be paid for without tax increases. Just look at Greece, the birthplace of this beloved Western-style democracy.

No president took more advantage of this ignorance of voters in democracies than President Obama. He fought the Republican and Tea parties tooth and nail against imposing any debt ceiling and he won that battle hands down. President Obama's victory over the very determined efforts of the Republican and Tea parties efforts to impose a debt ceiling only serves to support my thesis that he expanded the wars of George W. into Afghanistan, Pakistan, Yemen, Libya and Syria, not because of any pressure from the Republican Party but because of his own dedication to warmongering. Likewise he did nothing for blacks and the poor because his sympathies were with Wall Street not Main Street.

Not to be outdone by President Reagan, President H. W. Bush added another $1.6 trillion to America's federal debt in just four years. Since President Reagan, America's foreign debt had to be measured in trillions instead of billions. President Bill Clinton eased up somewhat on his predecessor's staggering increase. He added a mere $US 1.4 trillion over eight years, even bringing down the federal-debt-to-GDP ratio somewhat. George W. continued his father's legacy of outdoing his predecessors in increasing America's federal debt. George W.'s excuse was his invented War on Terror. Despite Candidate Obama's rejection of George W.'s War on Terror, once in office he did everything not simply to imitate George W. but to outdo him. He captured and killed Osama bin Laden, kept Guantanamo open, expanded the War on Terror and increased the federal debt by more. By the end of his second term America's federal debt had skyrocketed to a staggering **$US 20 trillion.** Within **eight years** President Obama had accumulated almost as much federal debt as was accumulated by the United States over the previous **220 years.** How could that have gone largely unnoticed had voters been educated at a level higher than kindergarten?

Our focus so far has been on America's federal debt. But government debt is also incurred by state and local governments. In many ways this is more serious since they cannot print money. One American city, **Detroit,** was forced to declare bankruptcy. Both California and Puerto Rico have serious debt problems which could lead to bankruptcy. Another immense debt problem that the federal government has been kicking down the years is the unfunded liabilities for **Social Security, Medicare and Medicaid**. These unfunded liabilities have been estimated at a staggering **$US 50 trillion** far exceeding the combined public debt of the federal, state and local governments. President Obama has totally ignored this gynormous problem. Like so many "leaders" of Western democracies he leaves such problems to future "leaders."

Adding to America's debt woes is the enormous increase in private debt incurred by American households addicted to the use of credit cards to buy junk which pollute and degrade the environment. In the past the savings rate of rich countries was very high compared to poor countries. Now it's the opposite. The savings rate in the United States is close to zero. In many poor countries today the savings rate is much higher. The key reason is less access to credit cards. Had private savings in the United States been high, it would have partially compensated for the negative savings of its governments. As it is, America is forced to borrow from poorer countries and print lots and lots of money.

An even greater concern for American taxpayers is the high probability that interest rates will increase in the future. So far the Fed has managed to keep nominal interest rates so low that the cost of servicing this massive debt is zero or even negative. That is unlikely to be continued indefinitely. Once real interest rates become positive and increase over time, servicing this huge debt will exceed the huge cost of America's addiction to warmongering. Of course, it's the poor and black Americans who will suffer the most as welfare programs are reduced to minimize the budget deficits.

Monetizing the Federal Debt

The power to print money has been abused since the beginning of time, at least, since the end of the use of pure commodity money. Ever since rulers were able to create money by using alloys in the gold and silver coins they minted they have created money to pay their bills. When paper money was invented this abuse of the power to create money increased exponentially. The American rulers have abused this power more than any other country in history. It has been able to do that because the American dollar became the world's de facto **reserve currency** after the British Empire self-destructed during World War II. The United States has also used its economic, political, military, financial and media control clout to force many countries to use only the $US to buy or sell many commodities such as oil.

Most countries print some money to pay for public services because taxes are politically unpopular. Canada, for example, prints money to pay for about 15 percent of services provided by its federal government. One reason that a country like Canada or the United States can never become bankrupt is that it is free to print as much money as is needed to pay its bills. Unfortunately for Greece it cannot do that because it gave up the right to use its own currency when it joined the Eurocurrency group. Likewise, the city of Detroit could not print its own currency to prevent bankruptcy. Neither can California or Puerto Rico.

Of course, printing lots of money to pay all of your bills will create massive inflation and that is not popular with voters either. Most governments will pay their bills by combining taxes, printing money and borrowing. Printing money, if not abused, not only reduces taxes directly but reduces taxes indirectly by reducing the interest cost of borrowing by keeping interest rates relatively low. The financial meltdown in the United States in 2007 was caused partly by the Fed printing too much money and keeping interest rates artificially low for a very long period.

Large and rising deficits added fiscal stimulus to the monetary stimulus overheating the U.S. economy. Add to that the fact that most of the budget deficits financed wars rather than the production of consumer goods, guns over butter, total spending increased far more than consumable output. Once this financial crisis impacted the real economy causing the severe 2008 economic recession, President Obama determined that the solution to a crisis caused by too much money, budget deficits and warmongering, was to print even more money, increase the budget deficits and start more wars. His argument was that the real economy was in such a deep recession that it needed both fiscal and monetary stimulus as well as more warmongering. Invoking the name of the great economist, John Maynard Keynes, to support his idiotic solution to the *Great Recession* must surely have made Keynes roll over in his grave.

The Fed, like the Bank of Canada, manages the sale of new bonds and treasury bills issued by the federal government to pay for annual expenditures in excess of tax revenues. Most of the new securities are sold in what is called the **Open Market** but some are bought by the Central Bank with newly printed dollars. This represents the portion of the federal debt which is monetized. The newly printed dollars are deposited into the banks which use it as required reserves to increase bank money (bank deposits) by a multiple of the dollars printed. For example if the Fed prints $1 million and the required reserve is 5 percent, bank money will rise by $20 million. In addition, if the Fed wants to implement an **easy money policy** to lower interest rates it would buy back securities previously sold. This would increase the reserves of the banks and lower the interest rate as banks increase loans and the money supply. Lower interest rate will stimulate the economy as businesses and consumers, as well as state and local governments, increase spending. Businesses respond to increased spending by increasing output and employment.

As a result of the 2007 financial meltdown the Fed was co-opted by President Obama and lost whatever independence it had. Typically Central Banks like the Fed and the Bank of Canada are not federal government departments in order to safeguard against the federal government using them to print money to pay their bills because taxes are politically unpopular. They try to act independent of politics. But the Great Recession caused by the financial mismanagement of the U.S. economy was deemed to be a national emergency by President Obama and the Fed was co-opted to fix the problem in ways determined by the White House. President Obama had already used his power to ease **fiscal policy** with massive bailouts. These bailouts had begun under his predecessor, George W. Bush. This was the infamous **TARP** or **Troubled Asset Relief Program,** devised by George W.'s Treasury secretary, **Henry Paulson.** Under TARP the United States would bail out the banks, AIG, Fannie Mae, and Freddie Mac to the tune of $US 700 billion, by purchasing their toxic mortgage-backed securities. This would be done not by printing money but by increasing an already humongous annual budget deficit for 2008. Many opposed this bailout of Wall Street and rich investment bankers. Those who take excessive risks for the low probability of high returns should be penalized by the market and the rich should never be bailed out by taxpayers, most of whom are poorer than those who took these excessive risks. But President Obama supported the program since he was a closet supporter of the rich and Wall Street over Main Street. After initial rejection of TARP by the U.S. House of Representatives on September 29, 2008, the *Emergency Economic Stabilization Act* was passed on October 3, 2008.

On taking office, President Obama felt that this easing of fiscal policy would not be sufficient to get the economy out of such a deep recession. He was convinced by those who had overseen the financial meltdown that the economy needed massive monetary stimulus in addition to this massive fiscal stimulus. The Fed injected additional excess reserves into the banks in the traditional way by buying short term treasury bills. By March 2009, the Fed had committed a massive $US 7.8 trillion to prevent further collapse of the U.S. financial system, dwarfing the $US 700 billion TARP fiscal stimulus. But the traditional easy money policy was inadequate to provide sufficient monetary stimulus to the U.S. economy. Injecting excess reserves into the banks by buying short term treasury bills was unlikely to get banks to lend, both because of the high risk of loan defaults and the low returns on loans because interest rates were so low. In fact, the banks had made lots of unsafe loans because of their greed and irresponsible management which had helped to cause the crash of 2007. Despite the many taxpayer and Fed bailouts the banks were still holding massive amounts of toxic assets. The last thing the banks wanted to do was increase their loans since the recession had made it impossible for businesses to make profits and for consumers to have secured employment income.

Economists were well aware that an easy money policy was totally ineffective when interest rates were very low, the so-called **Liquidity trap.** But the Fed gave it their best shot. The inability of the Fed to force banks to lend, the "cannot push on a string" analogy, was not the only concern of President Obama. While he had pushed the Fed to pump excess reserves into the banks to reduce unemployment by increasing spending, President Obama also feared an even greater financial meltdown caused not only by the toxic assets held by banks but also the toxic assets held by the two U.S. primary mortgage lenders, **Fanny Mae and Freddie Mac.** Mac and Mae are two federal government-sponsored enterprises, **GSEs,** much like the state-owned enterprises, **SOEs,** in China, which the leaders of the *unfree* world, and Canada, love to bash as evidence of the dreaded contagious disease feared by the West, **Communism.** The toxic assets held by Mac and Mae were worthless mortgaged-backed securities. Finally, President Obama was given an economics lesson in supply and demand and the **crowding-out effect.** He was told that interest rates are determined by the supply and demand for credit. His massive increase in borrowing would push up the interest rate, which would reduce investment and consumption thereby preventing the recovery intended by the easing of fiscal policy, the so-called crowding-out effect, where increased public spending reduces or crowds out private spending.

These were the three problems which inspired a rather innovative monetary policy called **Quantitative Easing, QE.** QE would address simultaneously the problem of toxic assets held by American banks, the problem of toxic assets held by two SOEs, sorry, noncommunist GSEs, Mac and Mae, and the crowding-out effect of the massive expansionary fiscal policy of President Obama. With QE the Fed would purchase both the toxic assets and longer term federal bonds. Purchase of the toxic assets would make the banks and Freddie Mac and Fannie Mae more solvent while purchase of the federal debt would prevent interest rates from rising. By having the Fed fund the massive borrowing of the federal government with QE the crowding out effect is prevented. In effect, QE was monetizing the debt as well as purchasing toxic debt from the banks and Freddie Mac and Fannie Mae. **QE1** began in December 2008 when the Fed decided to purchase up to $US 600 billion of government bonds and mortgage-backed securities. These combined monetary stimulus programs **tripled** the assets held by the Fed from $US 750 billion before the financial crash to $US 2.1 trillion by June 2010. **QE2** began in November 2010 when the Fed announced that it will purchase another $US 600 billion of toxic mortgage-backed securities and federal debt. **QE3** began in September 2012 when the Fed announced increased monthly purchases of these securities. This continued until January 2014 when the Fed began to reduce monthly purchases. By October 2014 the Fed had accumulated total assets of $US 4.5 trillion. The Fed has announced its intention to phase out QE when the U.S. economic recovery is strong enough to permit that.

The monetary stimulus injected by the Fed to respond to the 2007 financial meltdown has increased the toxic assets and federal government securities to a staggering $US 5 trillion, **six times** its prerecession purchases. Like the massive federal debt, monetary stimulus, including Quantitative Easing, is a short-term band aid solution to fundamental long-run problems which President Obama had no interest in tackling. It's short-term gain, for long-term **pain.** He was only too happy to kick the can down the road to secure election for a second term. The Fed's purchase of federal government bonds did succeed in keeping U.S. interest rates artificially low. This helped the mild economic recovery to continue. Rising interest rates would have reduced GDP and increased unemployment. But it's the same dilemma faced by Greece in 2015. Greece had accumulated a mountain of debt to pay for "free" public services. When that became unsustainable the creditors imposed austerity measures. But austerity prevents any recovery and reduces the ability to repay debt. The problem is that if the borrower is not "punished," no lessons are learned and the borrower will likely continue to kick the can down the road. That is the concern of the Republican and Tea parties to President Obama's solution. The Great Recession in the United States in 2007/08 was caused primarily by too much easing of both fiscal and monetary policies. If you prevent this recession from worsening by further easing both monetary and fiscal policies what guarantee is there that you will ever balance your budget or let interest rates be determined by market forces? The answer in these vote-buying democracies such as the United States is **none.** President Obama chose the popular way out. Greece wants to do the same but its creditors want blood. In general, creditors are as much to blame for a debt crisis as borrowers. Creditors make high risk loans and should suffer the consequences of defaults by borrowers. In the Greek crisis the creditors were pretending that only the Greek people had behaved irresponsibly and therefore only they should be punished. By voting **no** in the July 2015 referendum the Greek people resoundingly told the creditors of their negligence.

President Obama's monetary easing like his fiscal easing bailed out the rich and powerful, increased the price of stocks held by the rich, while lowering interest rates for the pensioners and low income savers. Like the fiscal policy he could have used monetary easing to support Main Street over Wall Street. Instead of buying the toxic assets of the banks and mortgage lenders and funding the federal debt for waging wars he could have given the printed money to low and lower middle income households. Recall that the toxic assets were bought by the government well below market prices so most of it was a gift to the irresponsible lenders. It rewarded those most responsible for the crash. An equivalent gift to the poor and lower middle class would have saved their houses and the housing sector while increasing overall spending, output and employment in the economy. Most importantly, it would have reversed America's increasing income and wealth inequalities which Candidate Obama had promised to do.

Budget Deficits, Trade Deficits, and the China/U.S. Relationship

We address the above concerns often mentioned in the media by explaining how they are connected, which journalists are incapable of doing. The impression you get from CNN, CBC and the BBC, is that China is flooding the United States with cheap manufactured goods because China's very bad Communist government is artificially keeping the Yuan too low. Why this is bad, since consumers love it, is never really explained except that it may cost American workers their jobs by creating trade deficits. It may also make China more powerful which is bad because only Western countries are good and all others are bad especially those with Communist governments. The reality is far more complex.

China and the United States have had an intense love/hate relationship since President Nixon visited China in 1972 and signaled to the West that it was now okay with the leader of the *unfree* world to do business with China. That visit by Nixon was prompted by the desire of the United States to court China away from the Soviet Union. China responded favorably because its economy was in shambles. After the fall of the Soviet Union the need to continue the relationship shifted from the fight against the Communist Soviet Union to economic growth. In 1972 China needed the United States to boost its economic growth. After the fall of the Soviet Union it was the United States that needed China to boost growth in the United States. The global shift which occurred after the fall of the Soviet Union increased economic growth in China to a record 10 percent annually while reducing that of the United States to a measly 2 percent. That had transformed China to the second largest economy after the United States with both needing each other to sustain high economic growth. The low income growth in the United States required cheap imports from China to boost the real incomes of Americans. China needed the U.S. market to sell its manufactured goods which were the primary engine of its economic growth.

During this global shift the Soviet Union had departed from Afghanistan only to be replaced by the American Empire in 2001. This is ironic because the Americans had courted both China and the Taliban to fight the Soviets. After 2001 the American Empire invaded Afghanistan to fight the Taliban. As the American invasion expanded from Afghanistan to Pakistan, Iraq, Yemen, Libya and Syria, the United States needed to find new foreign lenders in addition to Japan, the UK, oil exporters and Caribbean bankers. This is where the two most powerful emerging economies, China and Brazil became useful. The United States began borrowing so much from China and Brazil that it exceeded its borrowing from Japan and the UK, even though its borrowing from Japan continued to rise. After 2001 the American budget deficits and federal debt increased exponentially with its total federal debt quadrupling during the sixteen years of George W. Bush and Barack Obama. Since half of this growing debt had to be funded by foreigners this capital inflow showed up as annual surpluses in its capital account. This increased the demand for the $US on the foreign exchange market. Foreign lenders can only lend to the United States by buying $US. As the $US rose American exports fell while imports rose. This caused the ever-increasing trade deficit. The U.S. budget deficits caused by its endless warmongering caused its growing trade deficit with China and other countries.

As to the fear of Americans losing jobs because of the trade deficit with China, that is also complicated. When the United States pays for imports with exports, jobs lost because of imports are fully offset by higher paying jobs in the export sector. With the trade deficit exports do not fully pay for imports and some jobs are lost. However, if unemployment depresses real wages then unemployed workers will find jobs. Real wages have fallen or not increased much in the United States since 2001. But the price of consumer goods has fallen because of cheap imports from China. This has been a net gain to American workers. In addition, the increase in warmongering has increased employment in this mostly nonproductive sector creating incomes for the soldiers, their families and the communities where they live with their families.

Future of the U.S. Dollar as the World's Reserve Currency and America's Growing Foreign Debt

With the destruction of Britain and Germany during WW II the United States was powerful enough to force the world to accept the $US as the world's reserve currency despite objections from prominent economists such as Lord Keynes. Under the Bretton Woods system established in 1944, the $US was freely exchangeable for gold at $35 per ounce. U.S. trade deficits resulting from its disastrous invasion of Vietnam forced the United States to float the dollar against the price of gold. But the $US retained its status as the world's leading reserve currency. This placed the United States with the responsibility of restraining its foreign debt. During the period when the United States was the world's leading creditor nation there was no risk to countries holding dollar reserves. However, the significant increase in the foreign debt of the United States and the switch from the United States being the largest creditor nation to the largest debtor nation has worried many countries, including China, the largest single foreign lender to the United States. The total U.S. federal debt held by foreigners is now close to $US 7 trillion. With the low-interest-rate policy pursued by the Fed the nominal interest rate is very low causing the real interest rate received by the lenders to be negative. Many lenders are worried that interest rates will rise in the future and cause them significant capital loss.

Many countries also worry about the United States abusing its privileged position of having its currency as the dominant currency for foreign trade and investment. Banks in foreign countries should not be subject to U.S. laws but are often fined by the United States for violating U.S. laws because of the threat by the United States of denying them the use of the $US for foreign transactions. The printing of paper money by the United States for the use of countries other than the United States is also seen by many as an unfair windfall to Americans. Another unfair advantage is that Americans can borrow and pay for imports more cheaply since they do not need to exchange their currency as all other countries have to. Many commodities such as oil are priced in $US, which makes it difficult and expensive for producers to sell in their own currency or that of the importing country. We will return to this topic in the next chapter when we discuss the relative rise of China and its desire to make its currency, the Yuan, an alternative to the $US as the world's reserve currency.

CHAPTER 11

The Global Shift: The Rise of BRICS and the Transformation of Third World Economies to Emerging Economies

The fall of the West is largely due to the relative increase in wealth in the East over the last half century. Military power must be supported by wealth. The wealth of the West grew relative to the East for six centuries beginning in the fifteenth century. This was largely due to the accidental rediscovery of the New World by Columbus. In like manner it was the accidental worldwide influence of the *Maquiladoras Program of 1965* between the United States and Mexico that explains the resurgence of the East. Another similarity is that the accidental discovery of the New World was not significant for the rise of the West until the American Empire became much more than the "puny" empire the British called it. In like manner the accidental global shift from the West created by the birth of the Maquiladoras was not significant in the resurgence of the East until the twenty-first-century rise of China. There has never been an effort by the West to share power with the East. This most recent rise of the West since the fifteenth century is no exception. When an economic power refuses to share power and its economic power declines relative to the emerging power, that combination causes it to lose much more power than if it had shown some willingness to share power. That is the key premise of my book.

In this chapter, I will explain the accidental increase in the relative economic power of the East during the last half century. Many writers have called this *Globalization.* I would like to give it a slightly different name, *global shift.* The reason for this is that Globalization dates back to the beginning of time, long before the Maquiladoras. Using the same terminology is one reason why these writers miss the key difference between traditional globalization dating back to ancient times and the new globalization of the last half century. Two other commonly used names for what we call global shift, *outsourcing* and *foreign investment,* are equally misleading. Traditional outsourcing refers to a company purchasing some intermediate product, which it was previously producing itself, from another company. Today's outsourcing caused by the global shift is different in two important ways. First, it's the same company starting another plant or factory in an emerging economy, not purchasing from another company. Second, it's not an intermediate product but the same final product.

Likewise traditional foreign direct investment went into countries to produce the same product for the consumers of the **rich host** countries. Popular examples are coca cola and McDonalds. The most famous example of this traditional foreign direct investment is the branch plant economy of Canada created by American companies setting up factories in Canada, to get around high Canadian tariffs, to sell cars and consumer durables to rich Canadians. The foreign direct investment created by the global shift sets up factories in **low income** emerging economies to take advantage of cheap labor to produce consumer goods for the **home** countries. The goods are transported back to the home countries in container ships to be sold to the high income consumers in the home countries. Before I can explain this global shift I need to provide a historical overview of the old or traditional globalization so that readers can fully appreciate how the global shift of the last half century has been critically different from what took place before.

A Historical Overview of Globalization before the Global Shift of the Last Half Century

Globalization is simply a term for international trade, capital flows and labor flows among politically "independent" countries. Such international exchange of goods, ideas, labor and capital, is ancient. When such exchanges are voluntary we will call them **trade.** When they are enforced by military means we will call them **imperialism.** While both have occurred simultaneously it's extremely important to make this distinction. The key reason is that **free** trade is mutually beneficial to both trading partners. That is why both countries voluntarily engage in it. It is not a zero sum game. Imperialism benefits the imperial power at the expense of the weaker military power. That is why it requires military coercion. It is a zero sum game.

One of the great mistakes committed by many political writers and economists with political agendas is their confusion of the **evil** of imperialism, with capitalism, free markets, globalization, international trade and foreign investment. There is not a single example of any country developing without international trade, foreign investment and free markets. This is how the UK, Western European states, United States, Canada, Australia, Germany, Japan, South Korea, Taiwan, Singapore, Hong Kong, developed earlier, and countries like China, India, Brazil, Indonesia, Malaya, Thailand, and Vietnam are developing today. The West traded whenever it did not have the military power to colonize. Trade benefits both trading partners. It matters not whether its commodity trade or trade of manufactured goods.

Colonization is theft by military force. If **free** trade was as bad as imperialism, as these writers imply, why would the West ever use military force to colonize. Colonization implies that the imperial power **steal** from the colonies. The imperial power gains but the colony loses. **Free** trade is voluntary and must be a win-win for both sides. This reality has been the foundation of economic theory for centuries. If those who **rightly** condemn imperialism also condemn capitalism, **free** markets or globalization they are dooming ex-colonies to the same poverty they suffered from colonial theft of their lands and resources. Their good intentions not only let imperialism off the hook but prolong the poverty and misery of the long exploited Third World. It does not matter what name they give it: **commodity trade, dependency theory, neo-liberal economics, globalization, capitalism, free markets.** The only **bad** is imperialism, not any of those other terms invented by these writers who have absolutely no understanding of the proven benefits of **free** trade and voluntary exchange.

Having said that, it's not easy for countries, long subject to political and economic colonization by the West, to switch from **colonial exploitation** to **free** trade relationships. This is in fact quite a challenge especially when the imperial power often pretends it is trading when in fact it is colonizing. But this is no excuse to condemn both as being equally bad since they are true opposites, imperialism being totally bad and **free** trade being totally good. No colony has ever benefitted from being colonized. But in like manner, no ex-colony has developed without **free** trade. Cuba and North Korea are examples of independence without **free** international trade, imposed on them by the United States and its allies. Canada, Australia, the United States, Taiwan, Hong Kong, Singapore, Brazil are examples of ex-colonies embracing **free** trade.

It's unfortunate that **free** trade and voluntary exchange has always suffered from attempts by some to rob and steal rather than trade or exchange freely. Even when sellers and buyers congregated in the only village market to barter they had to be on the look-out for thieves and robbers and for those who pretended to trade but used their superior military, political, economic or financial powers to coerce concessions from the weak. As the development of relatively primitive transportation infrastructure, such as dirt roads, enabled trade and exchange further outside the local village so too did the opportunities for the robbers, thieves and "pretend" traders. Genuine traders were forced to spend heavily on security, protection and bribes. Corruption, thievery, robbery and piracy grew in tandem with **free** trade. For this reason there has never been truly "free" trade.

Imperialism is simply the worst example of removing any element of trade and replacing it with total coercion and theft. Colonization not only steals the lands and all of the resources but replaces the government and steals the language, culture, religion and political rights of the original inhabitants. The imperial power engages in ethnic and cultural genocide and enslavement of the original owners. That is what Canada and the United States did to the First Nations. Another extreme example of **misuse** of what economists like David Ricardo meant by free trade is the many references to the buying and selling of slaves as the slave "trade." Slavery implies coercion and the use of brutal force by the enslaver. This is the opposite of **free** trade. What has been misleadingly called the slave "trade" is as **evil** as imperialism.

Free trade, like any form of entrepreneurship, has inherent financial risks. But the determination and increasing skills and weapons of the thieves, robbers, pirates, and, most importantly, the "pretend" traders, **imperialists, and slavers** added tremendously to the total financial and security risks. Nevertheless, the enormous benefits of specialization required trade expansion. As a result **free** trade and exchange expanded out of the local villages to cities and towns and over greater and greater distances. Traders are risk takers who are willing to take enormous risks for the relatively small probability of enormous riches.

It was natural for trade to begin with the exchange of agricultural produce. But it soon expanded to high value commodities which were not perishable and could be relatively cheaply transported over greater and greater distances. These commodities included salt, spices, silk, ivory, gold and silver. These were some of the products demanded by the wealthy which made the security risks inherent in early trade worth taking by the trade entrepreneurs. It's not unlike those who today supply the lucrative American demand for illegal drugs. Dirt roads were complemented by canals and other forms of water transportation. Transportation through deserts was made by camel caravans. Then came the famous Silk Road linking the West to China. The Vikings opened up trade between the West and Russia leading to the creation of the Hanseatic League.

Capital flows tend to follow trade flows. Trade needs to be financed. Bankers are willing to get on board supplying loans to trade entrepreneurs and trading companies. People flows follow the traders and merchants to enhance the opportunities for trade or as religious fanatics spreading their religious beliefs further afield or as adventurers and tourists. In time there are labor flows where labor seeks employment opportunities in distant lands. International exchange involves trade flows, capital flows and labor flows. Economic development and growth requires all three flows. Despite the proven economic benefits of all three flows all three are highly restricted by independent nation-states for political reasons. Despite these restrictions and the security risks we have explained earlier, trade entrepreneurs, lenders and borrowers, and labor push the boundaries and increase these flows. Two of the most obvious current examples of this pushing of the boundaries are the sale of illegal drugs to Americans we referred to earlier and the many workers making their way into the EU and the United States despite their strict immigration laws.

As economists like David Ricardo have proven, free trade based on the theory of comparative advantage, is mutually beneficial to both trading partners. It replaces lower wage jobs with higher paid jobs without creating or adding to natural unemployment in either economy. It increases the GDP and living standards of both economies. Capital flows enable savings and entrepreneurial talents to flow from developed economies to developing economies. Direct foreign investment creates much needed and profitable infrastructures in developing economies and new businesses that create demand for labor, which increases employment and wages. It is crucial for developing economies to shift from a largely primary products economy to an industrial economy. Without this shift, labor in developing economies are doomed to low paying jobs in the agricultural sector. As population grows these jobs become more scarce and low wage. Those who pick bananas or coffee for large multinationals to sell dirt cheap to Western consumers will never get out of this centuries old poverty trap without the expansion of a domestic industrial sector which provides them with alternative employment opportunities. As the industrial sector expands and draws labor to it, multinationals will be forced to pay farm workers higher wages and Western consumers will be forced to pay higher prices for commodities.

This is why countries like Canada and Australia, with relatively low worker/land ratios have benefitted from the commodity trade while Latin American and Caribbean countries with relatively high worker/land ratios have not. With higher natural population growth combined with smaller land area compared to Canada and Australia, Latin America will never escape the poverty trap without foreign investment developing its infrastructure and industrial base. Portfolio investments to governments have often been mismanaged creating *sovereign* debt crises in many developing countries but more recently in rich countries like Iceland, Ireland, Greece and Cyprus. This is unfortunate as it could provide much needed funds for developing infrastructure if wisely used. This would complement the inflows of direct investment.

People flows also add to the development and growth of economies. Tourism is a very large and significant contribution to every country's GDP. Labor flows out of low wage economies puts upward pressure on wages in these relatively poor countries. At the same time it enhances the supply of both skilled and unskilled labor to developed economies eliminating labor bottlenecks in its development and growth. It puts downward pressure on rising nominal wage rates and inflation making consumer goods more affordable. It enables the flow of ideas, entrepreneurship, cultures, art, languages, food, talents, athletics, medical knowledge, science, mathematics and technologies across countries.

Expansion of World Trade from Specialized Products for the Wealthy, to Primary Products, to Industrial Goods, to Services

As we saw above profitable trade attracted daring and brave entrepreneurs willing to risk life and limb to bring the spices, silks and precious metals to wealthy consumers. While this type of trade began with Eastern countries like India trading with China it expanded outward further and further westward to reach the Mediterranean and beyond to the countries of Western Europe. It was helped by new discoveries of sources of salt, ivory, gold, lumber, silver, tin, copper, bronze and iron; Arab traders with their camel caravans, the Roman Empire, the Vikings, the Mongolian Empire, the Venetian merchants, the Hanseatic League, Marco Polo and his father and uncle, canals, the Nile, the Mediterranean Sea, the Indus, the Yellow River, the Tigris and Euphrates, improved boat building technology, explorers and adventurers.

The next great leap in the growth of trade is inseparably tied to Western imperialism. While trade has never been separate from imperialism, the birth of the Western European empires of Portugal, Spain, Holland, France and Britain, after the fourteenth century, made it impossible to separate trade from colonization. The primary goal by these countries was **colonization.** Trade was a by-product. As I said before these countries would only engage in **free** trade if they lacked the military power to colonize. The great expansion of trade in primary products such as spices, silver, furs, lumber, wheat, rubber, sugar, tin, bananas, pineapples, tea and coffee took place within the context of Western European states competing with each other for colonies as their primary objective. It was deemed to be far more profitable for the imperial power to spend resources on military weapons to fight both the original inhabitants and the competing Western European empires to **steal** rather than to engage in free trade. That, I believe, was not only **evil** but a long-term mistake. It may have provided quick short term gains but as we see today the cost of American warmongering far outweighs what it is able to steal. The British first recognized that when they let the thirteen American colonies take their independence. It was a one-time recognition. Britain today still spends vast amounts on its military adventures in the Middle East and North Africa attempting to colonize and steal rather than trade. The only countries that made permanent long-term gains from this theft of lands and resources during the five centuries of Western European imperialism were not the Western European states of Britain, France, Germany, Italy, Spain, Holland, and Portugal but the United States, Canada, Australia, New Zealand, Mexico, Brazil, and other countries of Latin America and the Caribbean.

Industrialization was the next great boost to international trade, capital and labor flows. It was the same Western European states which dominated the *age of imperialism* which were the countries to first industrialize, beginning with Britain. Industrialization gave a big boost to imperialism. First, it enabled the production of advanced civilized weapons which were used to kill and slaughter the people whose lands and resources were to be stolen. Unlike **free** trade, colonization is naturally resisted by the people whose lands, resources, culture, language and religion the imperial power is intent on stealing. They have to be brutally slaughtered by the very civilized imperial powers since they have the civilized weapons. The old and feeble, with a few young bucks, are imprisoned on reserves if necessary. Children are forced to live in residential schools to be abused by priests and have their culture beaten out of them. All of this is propagandized as the white man's burden. The heathens must be primitive since their weapons are primitive and the color of their skin less white.

Second, colonies provided both the raw materials to feed the industrialization in the imperial states and markets for the cheap industrial goods such as textiles. Third, capital found new profitable investment opportunities in the building of infrastructure to facilitate imperial control of the colonies and transportation of the primary products and cheap manufactures. Colonies needed roads, ports, railways, telecommunications, hospitals and research facilities. Finally, people flows increased because of new opportunities for religious fanatics, administrators, supervisors, emigrants, experts, tourists, adventurers and explorers.

So it was that international exchange or traditional globalization expanded from high value products for the rich to primary products to industrial goods to services. As population increased much more rapidly in the colonies compared to the imperial states in Western Europe, both because of lower birthrates and emigration from the imperial states to the colonies, wages rose much more in the imperial states and remained low in the colonies except for a small minority of whites. Theft of the lands and resources of the colonial inhabitants was combined with cheap colonial labor to provide high wages and low prices for the workers in the imperial states. Of course, many colonies used **slave labor** because that was even cheaper than the pittance paid to indigenous farm workers. Use of slave labor also supported the propaganda that the white man was far superior. The more slaves you owned the more civilized you were. This is why the United States was founded by civilized slave owners like George Washington who created a freedom-loving republic where all men were equal. Blacks and First Nations were not men.

As the imperial states industrialized they became wealthy because of industrialization, theft from colonization and low wages paid to farm workers in the colonies. The citizens of the rich countries demanded more and more industrial goods in addition to primary products. The prices of industrial goods rose relative to primary products. The rise of the chemical industry created synthetic substitutes for many raw materials such as rubber. Beet sugar replaced cane sugar. Synthetic fibers replaced cotton and silk. This rise in the price of industrial goods relative to primary products widened the wealth gap between the industrialized countries and the nonindustrial Third World. The value of trade in manufactures grew much faster than the value of trade in primary products. The value of trade among the rich industrialized countries soon exceeded the value of trade between the rich imperial states and their colonies and ex-colonies. By the time the global shift began in the 1970s the value of international trade between the countries within the wealthy West far exceeded the value of international trade between the countries in the wealthy West and the rest of the world.

Plagued by the devastation caused by five centuries of Western imperialism, lack of industrialization, low prices for primary products, exclusion from **Western** institutions such as the WTO, IMF, World Bank, UN, capital and financial markets, continued military invasions and civilized bombing with megaton bombs by military jets and drones, political interference, Western instigated civil wars, Western imposed dictators, rapid population growth, famine and diseases, it seemed as if the Third World was forever doomed to poverty and despair. The Western countries restricted immigration from the low wage countries to their high wage economies. But the accidental global shift beginning with the Maquiladoras and President Nixon's visit to China changed everything. Just as the voyages of da Gama and Columbus changed everything for the West in their favor, the global shift will change everything for the West against them. It will not be against their economic development or prosperity but against their political and military control.

Western imperialism has never been all about economic prosperity. They could have achieved that with **free** trade. But the West, like all of the conquerors of the past, wanted most of all, military domination, political dominance, religious dominance, cultural dominance, racial dominance, media dominance, propaganda dominance and submissive behavior by those conquered. The West wanted to feel **superior** and make others feel **inferior.** The West wanted the right to **preach** to others. Their Jesus was the true God because he was of virgin birth, walked on water and ascended to heaven after being crucified. The people of the Third World must be made to **fear** the might of the West. They must be made to believe that they are inferior, primitive and backward. Their customs, religions, dress codes, beliefs, languages, arts, entertainments and thinking are backward and uncivilized. To be civilized in the West does not mean acceptance of equality, but only some tolerance for such "backward thinking." The West changes the way they preach but they never stop preaching much like they never stop colonizing, stealing, invading and destroying.

The Global Shift to the Emerging Economies

What we are calling the global shift began in Mexico along the U.S.-Mexico border, moved south into Latin America, to China after President Nixon's visit, to India, Vietnam, Indonesia, Malaya and other parts of Asia and into Africa. As far as I am aware no author has attempted to analyze comprehensively the significance of this global shift to the relative decline of continued Western domination of the world. Combined with the recent vast immigration of **nonwhites** into the lands that the whites had stolen from the original inhabitants, during its six centuries of colonization, as well as **nonwhites** moving in larger numbers from the ex-colonies of the Western European states into those states, this global shift is leading to a relative decline in the domination of nonwhites by whites. As the white Christian West continues its disastrous policy of unbridled warmongering, invasions, and forced regime changes, its opportunity to cooperate with the emerging economies and govern its increasingly diverse racial domestic voters will face very difficult leadership challenges. If it is unwilling to acknowledge its many sins of the past, it will be unable to improve its behavior.

Birth of the Global Shift with the Maquiladoras Program of 1965

In 1965 the world was divided between rich countries populated by the few and poor countries populated by the many. The teeming billions of poor were prevented from immigrating into the rich countries by strict immigration rules. Two important changes after 1965 were moving the factories producing the industrial goods from the rich countries to the poor countries, and the determined efforts by the poor to migrate to the rich countries as refugees or "illegal migrants." Here we begin with the building of factories in the poor countries by companies in the rich countries, specifically to take advantage of low wage workers. In the past such branch plants had been done to expand markets. The key difference after 1965 was that the branch plants produced manufactured goods for the consumers in the rich countries where the parent company was located. Cheap labor and cheap transportation cost were the essential requirements **not** market expansion. This was a totally new phenomenon, unheard of before. Western imperialism had colonized for six centuries either to steal raw materials or to expand markets for their industrial produce. They had developed infrastructure in the colonies either to govern effectively or to transport produce or manufactured imports to the ports. That was about to change without the West fully understanding the political implication of this economically motivated change.

In 1965, the United States negotiated with Mexico, the *Border Industrialization Program.* This rather innocent arrangement between two countries sharing a two-thousand-mile geographical border was the origin of what we call the global shift, which will reverse the Western domination of the world begun by the voyages of Columbus and da Gama. In this program the factories were built not in the rich United States but in poor Mexico. The raw materials used in the factories did not flow from poor Mexico to the rich United States but in the opposite direction. It was a reversal of six centuries of Western colonization. Of course, it made prefect economic sense. But imperialism is never just about economics. It's mostly about political control. At the time the political implication of this tiny program could never have been imagined just as no one could have ever imagined that the unexpected rediscovery of America by Columbus, looking for the spices of Asia, could have ever created the world's most powerful empire in the United States. Just as thirteen tiny ex-English colonies along the Atlantic seaboard colonized a continent before colonizing the world, so too will a tiny program between the United States and Mexico change the world.

The obvious economic benefit of American corporations located along the width of the U.S. border with Mexico constructing branch plants on the Mexican side of the border was to take advantage of cheaper Mexican workers barred from immigrating into the United States. When American corporations created branch plants in Canada it was to circumvent Canadian tariffs imposed on imports of manufactured goods from the United States. The Border Industrialization or *Maquiladoras Program* circumvented U.S. immigration laws. It was an export-led industrialization program for Mexico instead of the old import-substitution Canadian program. Raw materials flowed into Mexico duty free from the United States and the manufactured goods, produced or assembled with the raw materials and parts, with cheap Mexican labor, flowed back to the United States under preferential tariffs. The Mexican factory was typically fully owned by the U.S. parent corporation.

There was another common factor. Canada had always been looked at by the United States for potential military conquest and colonization. It shared the same language and similar history and culture. As I said before the West will trade if colonization is not an option. In the case of Mexico, the 11 million inhabitants of the so-called *Borderlands* on both sides of the border shared a common language, Spanish, and history and culture. Prior to the U.S. invasion and conquest of the Borderlands on the U.S. side of the border it had been part of Mexico. These commonalities of language, history and culture complemented the economics of cheap labor in the creation of the Mexican Maquiladoras as much as they complemented the economics of market expansion in the case of the earlier Canadian branch plant economy. On the Mexican side of the Borderlands, where the Maquiladoras originated, there are some five thousand factories employing over one and a half million Mexican workers. The program effectively transformed a wide narrow stretch of Mexican territory with a population of 5 million into an industrial zone.

As this initial program showed how American corporations could reduce costs by locating factories where labor was cheap and plentiful these branch plants expanded further south into Mexico and further south into Latin America. The industrialization of Mexico and Latin America attracted more foreign investment, the development of infrastructure and domestic markets for some of the output. Cheap labor employed in the branch plants had the income to create domestic demand. As wages rose, domestic demand increased and the program simply fed on itself. As Mexico increased its economic development it was brought into the U.S.-Canada FTA as an equal partner in 1994, creating the North American Free Trade Agreement, NAFTA. This further enhanced the role of Mexico in providing leadership for the economic transformation of all of Latin America. Today, over half of Mexico's exports to the United States still come from the Maquiladoras. Rather ironically, it was the imitation of the Maquiladoras type branch plants by Western corporations in Asia which simultaneously created our global shift and limited the gains in Mexico and Latin America. We now turn to that imitation.

The Awakening of a New Sleeping Giant: China

It was not the Japanese bombing of the Hawaiian territory of Pearl Harbor that awoke the Sleeping Giant, which subsequently became the American Empire, but with the courting of the United States by Britain to help it defeat its most recent competitor for imperial hegemony, Germany. Even in 1939 Britain still thought of the American Empire as a "puny" empire, worthwhile as an ally in its war against Germany, but certainly no potential rival for imperial hegemony. In like manner, when the American Empire decided to court China in its cold war against the Soviet Union, it never imagined that poverty stricken China could ever challenge it for imperial hegemony. But that is what the global shift has done. We have argued that the West could never have achieved its total dominance of the world without the accidental birth of the American Empire. Sure enough, the British, French, Germans and Italians were powerful relative to Russia, Turkey, China and India. But without the overwhelming might of the American Empire the West would have faced strong competition. In like manner, the twenty-first-century global shift to the many emerging economies would make them very powerful compared to their plight during the seventeenth to the twentieth centuries. But without China they would face intense competition from the West for political and military equality of treatment. In 1978 China's GDP measured at market exchange rates was a measly $US 217 billion. By 2014 it had increased to a staggering $US 10,361 billion.

In the past the Soviet Union had presented a serious challenge to Western domination but self-destructed after Khrushchev. Japan could have led a new challenge but decided to become a subservient ally of the West. So far China shows no sign of following the path of Japan but more the path of the Soviet Union. However, it has learned lessons both from the damage it dealt to itself during its self-isolation before the twentieth century, and the "Iron Curtain" isolation of the Soviet Bloc countries enforced by America's demonization of Communism. Its current leadership is treading a fine line between subservience to the

American Empire and angering the American Empire. By showing some degree of subservience to American hegemony the United States allows China to engage with the international community. For the time being China will avoid actions which will lead the United States to stop the West from trading and investing in China as that would prevent China from growing and surpassing the United States. In the meantime the Chinese economy grows at a rate three times that of the U.S. economy shrinking the gap in GDP. In 2016 China's GDP measured by market exchange rates is still somewhat lower than the United States. But if GDP is measured using purchasing power parity, *ppp*, China's GDP is larger than the United States. Most projections suggest that the Chinese economy will overtake the U.S. economy by **2021** even if we use the market exchange rates to measure the GDP of both countries. However, the average Chinese citizen would still be much poorer than the average American since China's population is four times that of the United States. In terms of military comparison the United States outspends China on offensive military weapons but China has the advantage for putting boots on the ground.

Somewhat ironically, despite the much lower GDP per capita of China compared to the United States, it is the United States that is borrowing heavily from China. The primary reason for this is the American addiction to warmongering. Many have correctly pointed out that American invasions were motivated by America's military ability and desire to steal the lands and resources of the many countries it has invaded since its birth. What no one has yet asserted before me is the more important reason for these invasions. That overriding reason is its addiction to warmongering. American invasions since its invasion of Vietnam have had a far higher military cost than the value of what was stolen. Yet America continues to invade ever more and more countries. This can only be explained by a severe addiction. Americans invade and kill simply because they have the power to do so and no one can hold them to account. They are truly above the law. But these invasions are costly, forcing them to borrow heavily from other countries. Prior to the global shift the United States borrowed from Japan, Caribbean bankers, oil producing nations, the UK, Taiwan, Switzerland, Hong Kong, Luxembourg, and Belgium. It continues to borrow from these sources but its increased warmongering requires additional lenders. Since the global shift it has added China, Brazil and India to its growing list of lenders. China has become the single largest lender to the United States with Japan a close second.

Before the global shift rescued the Chinese economy, China had experienced a century of economic, political and military decline. Even before the West isolated China because of its choice of a Communist government in 1949, it had suffered humiliating treatment from all of the great powers; Britain, France, Russia, Japan, and the United States. I covered these humiliations in my *Rise and Fall of the American Empire.* The 1949 revolution overthrew the foreign humiliations and sent the American puppet, General *Chiang Kai-shek,* packing to Taiwan. Under the leadership of Mao Zedong, China embraced the Centrally Planned Economic System which had been successful in Russia under Josef Stalin. The Americans used its powerful propaganda machine to demonize Communism as evil and built an imaginary Iron Curtain to isolate all countries which were Communist states.

With an ever growing list of countries refusing to cow tow to American propaganda it seemed for a while that the West was losing the battle for world dominance. But Russia was plagued by weak leaders after Nikita Khrushchev and Mao's Cultural Revolution was an economic disaster. However, the American Empire was still fearful of the Soviet Union and its military capabilities. President Nixon decided to exploit the ideological split between Beijing and Moscow by warming up to China. China grabbed the opportunity because of the economic suffering of its people. But neither the Americans nor the Chinese understood that this rapprochement would mark the beginning of a global shift from West to East. The Americans simply saw it as a strategic move against the Russians in its Cold War. The Chinese simply saw it as a way to prevent starvation for its teeming millions.

To understand why the rapprochement between the United States and China was an important first step is to recognize that when the United States isolates a country all others must follow the American lead or face their own isolation from the international community. This is important to understand because it was not American entrepreneurs who first took advantage of the rapprochement with China. It was the

American allies closest to China, Japan, Taiwan and South Korea, as well as the ex-English colony of Hong Kong and ex-Portuguese colony of Macau. The Americans and Western Europeans followed their Asian allies. In 1979 China facilitated the influx of foreign investments by creating four *free trade areas, SEZs* (special economic zones), in southern China close to Taiwan and Hong Kong. Three of these were close to Hong Kong, which was returned to China in 1997. These were *Shenzhen, Shantou and Zhuhai.* The fourth SEZ, *Xiamen,* was across the strait from Taiwan. Once the process born with the Mexican Maquiladoras took roots in Southern China it moved further North into China and then into the rest of Asia much like the Mexican Maquiladoras moving south into Mexico from the Borderlands, and then into all of Latin America and the Caribbean.

In 1984–1988 China created the first fourteen *national economic and technological development zones, ETDZs,* to further encourage the inflow of foreign investment. By 2015 China had established a total of fifty-four ETDZs. While most of them were located in the largest coastal port cities, twenty-two had been created inland. What had begun in the Pearl River delta area in Guangdong and the Southern coast had moved north to Shanghai and further inland. Complementing the SEZs and ETDZs were fifty-four *high-tech industrial development zones, HIDZs,* established both inland and in coastal regions. This policy of encouraging foreign investment by providing special concessions led to one of the most rapid rates of industrialization in history. As early as 1985 China had moved 17 percent of its labor force into its booming industrial sector to produce 46 percent of its GDP. Meanwhile, 63 percent of its labor force remained in agriculture producing only 33 percent of its GDP. International trade was 20 percent of GDP. Its primary export was textiles, and Japan was its primary trading partner. GDP grew at a staggering 9 percent annually and continued at this rate after 1985. China was transforming from a tiny part of the global economy in the 1970s to challenging the largest economy, the United States, for first place. By every measure this was miraculous. And it was all the result of the accidental insight provided to Western entrepreneurs by the Maquiladoras that the way to get around restrictive immigration laws which severely limit the influx of cheap Asian labor is to take the manufacturing plants to countries in

Asia willing to open their economies to the foreign entrepreneurs and encourage their teeming millions to move from subsistence farming to the port cities. China was leading by example. It became the second largest recipient of foreign direct investment after the United States.

As with the five centuries of Western colonization, the coastal areas were the initial locations for the Western factories since they were the most accessible to the ships needed to transport the finished manufactured goods to the Western consumers hungry for cheap manufactures. The rise of *Containerization* as a cheap form of transporting the manufactured goods to the West was a necessary complement to the process. Estimates suggest that the use of containers has reduced shipping cost to **one-twentieth** the traditional cost based on crews of twenty-one longshoremen packing cargoes into a ship. Today eight of the twelve largest container ports are in China, including Hong Kong. By contrast the largest container port in the United States is ranked number 18. This global shift is unstoppable because Western entrepreneurs compete with each other to take advantage of cheap labor to lower prices for Western consumers. Just as American land owners in Latin America producing bananas with cheap labor cannot unilaterally raise prices for bananas in the United States to pay their farm labor higher wages, Western manufacturers can no longer afford not to use this new form of "outsourcing" to lower their costs to stay competitive with other manufacturers. Despite the low wages and dangerous working conditions combined with the massive pollution of the environment, this global shift has taken millions out of poverty and evened the playing field between the West and the Third World. No longer can the West think in terms of poverty and backwardness when they think of China and India. These two countries that dominated the world economy up to the seventeenth century were once again seen as competitive giants on the global scene.

Every country initially industrialized by using cheap labor working long hours in dangerous working conditions and polluting the environment by using coal as energy and concentrating on heavy industry. Britain was the classic example. But these countries eventually underwent a second industrial revolution by shifting to light industry using electric power. Some of the increased income was then used to clean up the environment. It's ridiculous to expect China or other emerging economies to do better than Britain when the global competition today is far greater than when Britain industrialized. It's even more ridiculous to expect the emerging economies to pay for the damage to the global environment, *global warming,* when most of the goods produced are for Western consumers. It's also ridiculous for the West to measure pollution by total units rather than per capita units. A long time ago the economist, Arthur Pigou, suggested that the solution for the external cost of pollution is a tax equal to that cost. If all of the economies in the world were to impose such a Pigovian tax we would solve this problem. However, Western leaders never look for solutions only propaganda to gain a competitive edge.

In 2016 China was the world's largest exporter in international trade. Half of these exports are produced by foreign firms located in China. The United States was its largest export market followed by Hong Kong, Japan and South Korea. China was also the world's largest exporter of steel. Since exports pay for imports China was also the world's largest importer. Its primary import partner was South Korea followed by Japan, Taiwan, the United States, Australia, and Germany. China is Australia's largest trading partner. China is increasingly viewed by the world as the rising superpower while the United States is increasingly viewed as the declining superpower. As the West increasingly views both China and Russia as threats to its global hegemony, China has increased trade with Russia. Today Russia is China's eighth largest trading partner and China is Russia's fourth largest trading partner. The *Shanghai Cooperation Organization, SCO,* is increasingly viewed as a rival to NATO. This organization was founded in 2001 and is made up of China, Russia and four Central Asian countries, *Kazakhstan*, *Kyrgyzstan*, *Tajikistan*, and *Uzbekistan*. India and Pakistan have been approved by the SCO for membership and are expected to be admitted as full members in 2016.

Prior to the Second World War, Japan had beaten the United States, Britain, France, and Russia to emerge as the dominant empire in the Asia-Pacific region. Japan's defeat during the Second World War made the United States the dominant imperial power in the Asia-Pacific region. Today China is the dominant power in Asia and is determined to hold that position against threats from the United States, Japan, South Korea,

Taiwan, India, the Philippines, or any other rival. President Obama's so-called pivot to Asia, far from instilling fear into China, will only serve to galvanize China into stepping up its determination to flex its own military muscle. China's past humiliation by the West will never be allowed to happen again under China's current leaders. In addition to modernizing its armed forces and forging an alliance with Russia it is working hard to reduce its dependence on the $US as a reserve currency. Its first move in that regard was to use the Western accepted financial center in Hong Kong. In 2004 banks in Hong Kong began to accept deposits in the Yuan, RMB. Depositors could get debit and credit cards in the Yuan and remit funds to other countries from their Yuan accounts. In 2013 Yuan deposits in Hong Kong banks accounted for 12 percent of total bank deposits. In December 2008 China began currency swaps with other countries to by-pass the $US. These countries now number 25 and include the EU, the UK, Canada, Australia, South Korea, Singapore, Brazil, Argentina, New Zealand, Iceland, Indonesia, Malaysia, Thailand, Russia, Hungary, Qatar, Pakistan, Nepal, Suriname, Mongolia, Kazakhstan, Uzbekistan, Turkey, Ukraine, Albania, Sri Lanka, and Belarus. The next move in promoting the Yuan as a global currency began with the creation of offshore RMB clearing banks. Once again this began with Hong Kong in December 2013 but quickly added new centers in the UK, Australia, Canada, Germany, France, South Korea, Malaysia, Thailand, Macau, Taiwan, Singapore, Chile, Qatar and Luxembourg. As a result of these moves by China, 20 percent of its global trade today is done with its own currency, the Yuan.

In 2006 the share of the world's GDP produced by China and India combined was only 6.8 percent. At that time the United States produced 28.6 percent of the world's GDP, Japan produced 10.7 percent and Germany produced 6.5 percent. These are based on market exchange rates at the time. Using the ppp measure the share of China and India would be much higher. For example, China's GDP in 2006 based on exchanges rates was $US 2,730 billion but $7,328 billion using ppp. However, despite the rapid growth of both China and India caused by the global shift, in 2006 the West still dominated. China's total GDP, measured by exchange rates, lagged behind Britain, France and Italy.

India was even further behind. A decade later the ranking had changed dramatically in favor of both China and India.

China had moved up to second place to the United States, using market exchange rates, ousting Japan. It was by far the largest economy in Asia. Using the ppp measure China's output exceeded that of the United States in 2014. Using the ppp measure China's GDP was $17, 632 billion in 2014 compared to the exchange rate value of $US10, 361 billion. The ppp measure is explained in my *Rise and Fall of the American Empire,* pages 479–480. India's GDP is predicted to overtake the United States by 2043 using market exchange rates. In 2014 China was also the world's largest producer of manufactured goods. While China dominates in manufacturing, India dominates in the production of services. As early as 2009, China had overtaken both Japan and the United States to become the world's largest producer of vehicles. In 2011 China produced 45 percent of the world's output of steel.

Rise of the BRICS: Brazil, Russia, China, India, and South Africa

Rather than review the effect of the global shift on each of the emerging economies as we did with China we will save time by looking at the five most powerful emerging economies as a group. These five countries are commonly referred to as the BRICS or the new G5 (group of five). In 2016 this group accounted for almost a quarter of the world's GDP, using market exchange rates, more than a quarter of the world's land area and almost half of the world's population. They are seen as a potential threat to the original G5, the five largest Western economies, the United States, Germany, Japan, Britain, and France. While the GDP of the Western G5 in 2016 was twice that of the BRICS, using market exchange rates, the GDP of these two groups of five countries was roughly equal if we use the ppp measure. In addition, the population of the BRICS far exceeds that of the Western G5. Goldman Sachs has predicted that by 2030 the GDP of the BRICS will equal that of the Western G5 even if market exchange rates are used.

Among the goals of the BRICS is the creation of a new reserve currency to replace the $US, voting reforms to give more voting power to the BRICS in the IMF and World Bank, the creation of a New Development Bank, NDB, and adding new members such as India to the UN Security Council. The NDB will focus on loans for environment-friendly infrastructure projects. It began making loans in 2016. It was founded by the five member BRICS countries with each contributing an equal amount of capital and each having an equal say in its governance. Its head office is located in the financial district in Shanghai, China. The NDB hopes to attract new members in the future. The BRICS acronym was coined in 2001 by Jim O'Neill of Goldman Sachs and has come into widespread use as a result of the global shift of wealth from the original Western G5 to the emerging economies.

In 2010 China replaced Japan as the world's second largest economy and in 2012 Brazil replaced Britain as the world's sixth largest economy. Using the ppp measure instead of market exchange rates China is now ranked the largest economy in the world and India is ranked the third largest economy in the world. Using market exchange rates, Goldman Sachs has predicted that by 2030 China will surpass the United States and India will be ranked third. At that time the GDP of the five BRICS countries will equal that of the five largest Western economies, the original G5, even if we use market exchange rates. This prediction assumes that in the next fifteen years the rate of growth of GDP in the five BRICS countries continues to exceed significantly that of the rate of growth of GDP in the Western G5 countries. No one can be sure of that. There are already signs of growth slowing in Brazil, Russia, and China.

Emerging Economies, G20, and the Asian Century

The global shift is not limited to the BRICS. The most common term used to identify all of the economies which have benefitted from the global shift is *emerging economies.* As we explained earlier the origin of the global shift was the Maquiladoras of Mexico. Mexico has been and continues to be one of the primary beneficiaries of the global shift. A further boost was given to Mexico when it was added to the FTA between Canada and the United States, creating one of the largest free trade areas, NAFTA. When NAFTA was created, Canada's GDP far exceeded that of Mexico, about twice as much, using market exchange rates. By 2016 Mexico's GDP at market exchange rates was about the same as Canada's. Goldman Sachs prediction is that by 2030 Mexico's GDP at market exchange rates would be one and a half times that of Canada. Furthermore, Goldman Sachs has predicted that by 2050 Mexico will become the fifth largest economy in the world after China, the United States, India, and Brazil, even using market exchange rates. But the global shift was not limited to Mexico but moved southward into all of Latin America and the Caribbean. Argentina, Colombia, Peru, Chile and Venezuela are other Latin American economies, in addition to Mexico and Brazil, which have been significantly affected by the global shift in this region of the world.

In recognition of this global shift a new group of wealthy countries was created in 1999, the G20, to replace the G8. The G8 was created by expanding the membership of the original Western G5 countries to include Italy, Russia and Canada. The G20 includes the five BRICS countries which in 2014 had the same total GDP as the original Western G5, if the ppp measure is used. Other countries in the G20 are Argentina, Australia, Indonesia, South Korea, Mexico, Saudi Arabia, and Turkey. The EU is the twentieth member.

While the global shift had its origin in Latin America it is Asia which has become the key player leading many to predict that the twenty-first century will be the *Asian Century.* Prior to the global shift, Asia had the largest share of the global population. But Asian countries were among the poorest because of the low per capita GDP, compared to the West. What the global shift achieved was to increase GDP per capita significantly while maintaining population dominance. If we use the ppp measure, Asia's per capita GDP is predicted to be equal to that of the West by 2050. Among the countries contributing to the rise of Asia, besides China and India, are Indonesia, Malaysia, Vietnam, Thailand, Pakistan, Bangladesh and the Philippines. Of course, Japan, South Korea and Taiwan are also large Asian economies but part of the Western alliance. They will very likely shift allegiance to Asia as the stick wielded by the United States weakens.

Many African countries have also benefitted from the global shift in addition to South Africa. The leading African countries include Nigeria, Egypt and Algeria. Other countries not previously mentioned include

Iran, UAE, Iraq and Kazakhstan. Many of the emerging economies are included in the **top 50** largest economies in the world for 2014. The emerging economies in this top 50 list, in order of size, as measured by market exchange rates for GDP, are China, India, Russia, Brazil, Mexico, Indonesia, Turkey, Iran, Saudi Arabia, Argentina, Thailand, South Africa, Pakistan, Egypt, Colombia, Malaysia, Nigeria, Philippines, Venezuela, Vietnam, Peru, Chile, Bangladesh, Algeria, UAE, Iraq, and Kazakhstan. As we can see from this, more than half of the largest economies in the world in 2014 were emerging economies created by the global shift. Prior to this a total of twenty Western economies produced most of the world's GDP. These twenty Western countries were the USA, Japan, Germany, Britain, France, Italy, Spain, Canada, Australia, South Korea, Holland, Austria, Switzerland, Sweden, Belgium, Singapore, Norway, Israel, Portugal, and Greece. The rise of the West began with the Portuguese conquest of Ceuta on the West African coast in 1415. Western dominance has lasted for six centuries to 2015. The global shift is less than half a century old but the twenty largest emerging economies in 2015 are comparable in size to the twenty largest Western economies, after less than half a century. That is truly revolutionary.

The Browning of the *White* West

We return here to this topic we began to address in the previous chapter. In the previous chapter our primary focus was the browning of America caused by the increasing numbers of mixed-race births leading to the confusion as to who is black in America. The browning of the white West is caused by many other factors in addition to mixed-race births. First, in the case of countries such as the United States, Canada, and Australia, the whites who stole the lands of the original owners killed off many of those owners but not all of them. These original owners, First Nations and Aborigines, are not white. Second, blacks were imported as slaves into the United States and Canada. Other blacks immigrated into many Western countries. African countries were colonized by Portugal, Britain and France. Some blacks migrated directly from these colonies to Britain, France and other Western European countries and to Canada and the United States. Others went from the Caribbean where their forefathers had been taken as slaves by Britain, Holland and France. Third, America and Canada brought Chinese to build the railroads. Britain and France colonized many countries in Asia. Many Asians went directly from these colonies to Britain, France and other parts of Western Europe. Others went from British and French colonies in the Caribbean and across the globe where their forefathers had been brought as indentured servants to work for the Western imperial powers. Canada, America and Australia are also attracting large numbers of Asian immigrants. Fourth, the United States is attracting large numbers of Hispanics as cheap labor or Mexicans whose lands had been stolen by the United States when the United States invaded and conquered half of Mexico. Finally, the Western invasions of Afghanistan, Iraq, Libya, Syria and North Africa created 60 million refugees and many are migrating to Western Europe.

It's impossible to get accurate estimates of the percent of nonwhites currently living in Western Europe, the United States, Canada, and Australia. But the percent is large and growing. It's growing both because of new immigrants and mixed-race births. The question we are addressing here is how this rapidly increasing percent of nonwhites in the West, defined by its long history of white superiority, white racism, white invasions of nonwhite countries, white colonization of nonwhite countries, white domination of global institutions—such as the media, the UN, the WTO, the World Bank, the IMF, the reserve currencies, the financial markets, Christianity, and the perception of good versus evil—will contribute to the global shift from West to East? These nonwhite immigrants bring with them new religions, cultures, and customs. They have ties to the nonwhite countries being invaded, bombed, destroyed, denounced, terrorized, belittled, lied about by the public, the media, and the politicians.

The most obvious way in which this new reality of the browning of the white West is affecting the West today is the increasing threat of what the West calls **"home-grown terrorism."** The West is careful to denounce these people as **jihadists, radicalized, extremists, misguided youths, idiots, fanatics, Islamists, retards, disenfranchised, insane, etc.** The West dares not encourage even the slightest suggestion that these people are fighting the injustices of the West being inflicted on their home-lands and the lands of their forefathers. As usual the West clamps down on freedom of speech and freedom of the media. No one dares suggest or hint that these people have even the slightest justification for their actions. On the contrary, the public and the media must be encouraged to both denounce such actions severely and loudly while simultaneously praise publicly and loudly the bombing and the killing of the innocents in the home-lands of these people as fighting terrorism. The more these so-called lone wolfs defend the rights of their homelands the more extreme is the call of the public, the media, and the politicians for bigger bombs, more frequent bombing, more destruction, more refugees, more legal restrictions on freedoms, and more wasted dollars on the military, propaganda, and surveillance. It's a vicious circle that is spinning wildly out of control with not a single Western leader from the far left to the far right with the balls to even try to rein it in. That is how demented Western leadership has become.

The Western European countries face a unique challenge with its new immigrants from the countries being bombed and devastated by America's war on terrorism. They are Muslims, mostly. Another of the Western propaganda we have unraveled in our books is the false notion that there is a separation of church and state in the West. Nothing can be further from the truth. Ever since the Roman Empire embraced Christianity the West has been a group of **Christian** nation-states. In the beginning these Christian states were extremely intolerant of other religions especially Jews and Muslims. Spain was the leading state which used the dreaded *Spanish Inquisition* to torture non-Christians. But all of them had their equivalents of the Spanish Inquisition. When Spain conquered Grenada it wiped out all traces of its Muslim roots. After the birth of Protestant Christianity, thanks to the determination of Henry VIII to have seven wives and a son to inherit his throne, England became the leading Protestant Christian state along with Holland. This led to the United States, Canada, and Australia also becoming Protestant Christian states. Protestants were more concerned with materialism than religion. This enabled a greater degree of religious tolerance in Protestant Christian states than was the case with the Catholic Christian states. Making money and getting rich was more important than religious affiliations.

Over time it became fashionable in the West to preach religious tolerance. This did not mean a separation of church and state or religious equality. It simply provided another tool for the West to denounce nonwhites for their supposed religious intolerance. Never mind the fact that prior to the rise of the West, Muslims were much more tolerant of Jews and other religions than Christians. Up until the planting of Israel on Palestinian land the West continued their long history of intolerance of Jews. Germany was simply an extreme example, much like Spain was the earlier extreme example of religious intolerance. The need for an American uncolony in the Muslim lands changed the behavior of the West to Jews. But it simultaneously increased Western intolerance of Muslims. The Western propaganda was that Israel was a much needed home for Jews because of the holocaust and Muslims were showing religious intolerance by not supporting this homeland for Jews. It would have been un-Western to point out that America and Canada had stolen so much land from the First Nations that each of them could have easily created ten Israels on their stolen lands. But the true purpose of the creation of Israel by the West, not by the Jews, was to reclaim the lands lost during the Crusades. The Jews were happy because they were handed a homeland on a silver platter by the Americans and defended by a military funded by the American taxpayer. The West was happy because it had a new propaganda to reconquer the Middle East.

With the ever-increasing intolerance of Muslims by the West after the creation of Israel how will Western Europe, the birthplace of this intolerance, deal with the influx of refugees who are primarily Muslims? Somewhat ironically the Anglo states of Britain, Canada, and the United States, mostly responsible for the creation of the 60 million refugees, are taking only a miniscule fraction of these refugees. Poorer countries like Greece and Italy, far less responsible for the crisis, are bearing the brunt of the influx. It's a matter of access rather than policy. Canada will likely take a few thousand after years of haggling, shaming and complaining. Typically Canada is the loudest in terms of what it will do but the last to actually do anything. By pretending loudly what it plans to do it procrastinates until others have done it. It then pats itself on the back as if it had done something. The reality is that Canada is insulated by distance. It can afford to bomb and destroy these countries to satisfy its innate urge to kill and maim those who are defenseless knowing full well that very few of the refugees it creates will ever reach the shores of Canada. Prime Minister Steven Harper's response to the refugee crisis has been consistent. More bombs and bigger bombs against ISIS. One Canadian reporter hinted at the truth when he said that bringing twenty thousand Muslims into Canada was not smart politics. President Obama has been silent on the issue of helping the refugees. The United States, like Canada and Australia, is also largely unreachable by the refugees. It can afford to step up the bombing without consequences. Britain, the fourth **mad Anglo bomber** creating the refugee problem, has spent millions to **prevent** the refugees from crossing the English Channel into Britain from France. To these countries killing Muslims today has all of the hallmarks of killing First Nations or Aborigines in the past. Just like the old saying, "the only good Indian is a dead Indian, the unspoken saying today in many countries in the West, especially Harper's Canada, is "the only good Muslim is a dead Muslim."

At first these Muslim refugees will simply be happy to be taken in by countries such as Germany. But over time it's difficult to expect that they will not oppose the continued destruction of their homelands by the West. Some will believe the Western propaganda of fighting terrorism. But others will see it as the continuation of the religious war between Muslims and Christians. I do not believe in religion but most people do. Most of the wars fought throughout history had a religious component to them. Religion has been a force for both good and evil throughout history. Like racism it is childish but potent. The West renewed the war between Islam and Christianity when it planted Israel in the Middle East on stolen land. As usual it will blame the Muslims for renewing the war. But that is precisely why it will never end. If the voters in the West are convinced by propaganda that the war is caused by Muslim fanatics they will continue to support it. Since that is **false** the Muslims will continue to oppose it. The West has the civilized weaponry but the Muslims have Allah. Heaven help us all since the warmongers will prevail.

While the percent of nonwhites in the West has increased significantly, nonwhites have not yet penetrated the top echelons of the white establishment in industry, government or the professions. One rather ironic result of the global shift is the reversal of the brain drain from East to West. Prior to the recent influx of nonwhites into the West there was a trickle of the most highly qualified nonwhites into the West. This boosted the fortunes of the West while impoverishing further the nonwhite countries of origin. With increasing opportunities in the nonwhite countries, provided by the global shift, many of the highly qualified nonwhites, and some whites, are moving from the West to the East. This has the double effect of boosting the global shift by aiding the emerging economies with highly educated and trained workers while doing the opposite in the West. Its impact on the browning of the West is that a smaller percent of nonwhites will be highly educated compared to previously. This will further delay the nonwhites move-up into the higher echelons of power in the West and reinforce the ghettoizing of nonwhite immigrants and youths in the West, feeding dissolution with the West, and yearning for their homelands. They are more likely to be critical of continued bombing and destruction of their homelands.

As we have seen in the previous chapter, blacks in America, led by affluent mixed-race Americans such as President Obama, have mostly fallen in line with white American warmongers and given up on their previous rebellion against such invasions, as exemplified by Muhammad Ali. It will be interesting to see whether the white establishment in the West will be able to co-opt the majority of nonwhites to their cause. There is no doubt that many nonwhites have already been co-opted and that many more will. It's not just propaganda that enables this but fear. Western societies are vicious in how it ostracizes those who do not openly and unabashedly praise their pretend freedoms and pretend democracies just as the United States is vicious in punishing the likes of North Korea, Cuba and Iran. As it is, a nonwhite person is heavily discriminated against in employment, education, politics, management, promotion, the media, the arts, etc. When whites are heavily chastised for speaking out about injustices committed by their countries or of warmongering and invasions imagine how nonwhites will fare? Think of whites such as Julian Assange, Edward Snowden, or Bradley Manning. Nonwhites have to be twice as careful as whites in even seeming to be critical of their Western country, even if they are third or fourth generations. Color has a nasty habit of being permanent and visible.

The question then is not whether many will be co-opted but whether the majority will be? This is an important question for the future of the West. White leaders have made zero change in their atrocious behaviors for six centuries. They will never change those behaviors if they continue to lead. But if the majority of nonwhites are not co-opted to that cause there is some small hope for change in the future. If nonwhites begin to challenge the perverse propaganda that war is good and peace is bad, that justice is more important than the law, that insane inequalities are insane, that freedoms trump privilege, expediency, religion, and surveillance; that countries like Canada, the United States, and Australia stole the lands of the First Nations by military force and enslaved Africans to enrich these lands; that Western democracy is a vote-buying farce; that people have an inherent right to be different and have independent objective views, that countries have an inherent right to be different and have independence and sovereignty; that free trade is both moral and beneficial while colonization is theft and immoral; that the truth matters; then we will see change and human progress. To be civilized is to be free without civilized weapons of mass destruction. Civilization should not be measured by the power of your military weapons as it has always been throughout history.

President Obama's Moves to Improve Relations with Cuba and Iran

The recent diplomatic moves by President Obama to reopen the American Embassy in Havana and to sign a nuclear deal with Iran must be seen by many of President Obama's die-hard supporters as vindication of their faith in him to do the right thing. For seven years these die-hard supports had to manufacture excuses for his many failures. Now at last they could celebrate two achievements. If only he would close Guantanamo before he leaves office their prayers would be answered. The reality is that Obama is first and foremost a politician and his "Audacity of Hope" was his gift to get to the highest office with his "Camelot" family. Today America needs Cuba and Iran more than they need America. Let us deal with Cuba first. While Obama was warmongering in the Middle East the global shift enabled Latin America to grow up to the point that it can now assert its independence from the once powerful

United States. The Monroe doctrine is dying. Every Latin American country insists that the United States must engage with Cuba if America wants to continue to do business and engage with Latin America. At the Fifth Summit of the Americas in 2009 President Obama was forced to signal his intension of engaging the United States with Cuba. The United States can no longer threaten Latin America with its invasions, CIA and propaganda. Its hands are full containing China, Putin and ISIS. It needs its Latin American backyard and especially its Cuban playground. In addition there was pressure from the UN and Pope Francis to end the suffering of the Cuban people caused by the U.S.-imposed embargo. As I have pointed out before a U.S. embargo must be followed by the entire world or face the all-powerful American wrath. Cuba was also listed by the United States as a sponsor of state terrorism and a member of those countries referred to by American leaders as the "Axis of evil." In 2006 President George W. Bush created a task force to catch and punish much more severely any violators of the U.S. embargo while mounting a much more aggressive propaganda program against Cuba. Violators of the embargo were threatened with imprisonment for ten years.

In the past Cuban Americans lobbied hard for the United States to maintain its embargo and punish their homeland for the removal of their privileges by the Castro government. Prior to the revolution, these Cuban Americans had served as puppets for the United States and received privileges for that support. Cuba was one of the uncolonies of the American Empire. Maintaining an uncolony requires local puppets. During the presidencies of General Fulgencio Batista, the Cuban economy was totally dominated by American corporations, and corruption and crime were rampant. When America's notorious crime bosses were prosecuted in the United States, they found safe sanctuary in Havana. But Batista was a close friend and ally of the United States, courted by every U.S. president. As U.S. ambassador Earl T. Smith put it, Batista was an SOB, but he was our SOB. When the local Cuban puppets chose to flee to the United States rather than surrender those privileges, they hoped to overthrow the Castro government by having the United States impoverish their homeland. Since the United States is a vote-buying democracy, political leaders could not ignore the Cuban American vote, especially in Florida.

The younger generation of Cuban Americans do not understand this grudge by their parents and now clamor for normalized relations with the homeland of their parents. They want to help rather than hurt that homeland. They want to visit freely and reunite with families and friends. Once again the vote-buying American democracy cannot ignore these young voters. President Obama received more than half the Cuban American vote in 2008. For these many reasons President Obama decided to start the lengthy process of normalizing relations with Cuba in December 2014, a full six years after taking office. Since 2006 Fidel Castro's brother, Raul Castro, has replaced Fidel as the Cuban president. In 2012 Raul announced that Cuba was willing to engage in talks with the United States. Obama shook hands with Raul at the state memorial service for Nelson Mandela in December 2013. U.S. travel restrictions on Americans to Cuba were eased following negotiations mediated by Pope Francis at the Vatican in 2014. In May 2015 Cuba was taken off the U.S. list of countries sponsoring state terrorism. Formal diplomatic relations were resumed in July 2015. On August 14, 2015, the U.S. embassy in Havana was reopened and the U.S. flag hoisted. But the United States will continue to operate its infamous prison in Guantanamo where it can torture prisoners held without charges or trials by insisting it's not American soil.

While Cuba was the big headache for the United States during its invented Cold War with the Soviet Union as a means to dominate the world, today it's Iran. Cuba was its big headache then because the United States feared all of Latin America and the Caribbean imitating Cuba. The many countries of this region had fought hard for independence from Spain, Britain, France and Portugal. The last thing they wanted was American colonization. Despite the massive American propaganda about the evils of Communism, poor people in ex-colonies knew that they had a far greater chance of removal from poverty if the land and resources returned to them from the Western thieves were more equally shared under Communism than privately owned by a few under Capitalism. When the United States insisted on colonizing them they turned to the Soviet Union for help from the U.S. monstrosity. But the United States turned the table on them by fooling the world that it was invading and colonizing these countries to save the world from the evil of

Communism. Western intellectuals who had preached the moral virtues of Communism over the inequalities of Capitalism went into hiding fearing imprisonment and torture by the powerful United States. In the Western pretend democracy no one dared create a Communist Party. Members would be immediately imprisoned. Being a Communist was the best known unwritten crime in the West. All of that changed with the defeat of the Soviet Union by the American Empire. The United States had to invent another evil and that came to be known as **terrorism.** The hot-bed of this newly invented evil is not Latin America and the Caribbean but the Middle East and the equivalent of Cuba is Iran.

Initially Western colonization of Iran had to do more with stealing its oil rather than fighting Communism or terrorism. But it was the British not the Americans who was stealing Iran's oil. In fact, just as Cuba encouraged the United States to help it gain independence from Spain the Iranians initially encouraged the United States to help it gain independence from Britain. The British refused to share Iran's oil wealth with the Iranian people much as it had refused to share the First Nations lands it stole with the First Nations of the New World. It was an Englishman, William Knox d'Arcy, who negotiated the initial concession with the Shah of Iran in 1901 to drill for oil. When oil was found in 1908 the *Anglo-Persian Oil Company, APOC,* was created the following year. When Britain decided to phase out the use of coal in favor of oil to modernize its powerful navy, Iranian oil became strategically important to maintaining its empire. As usual, empires prefer to steal rather than trade, simply because it has the military power to steal. Naturally the Iranian people felt cheated by the D'Arcy concession which gave only 16 percent of the oil profits to Iran. Attempts by Iran to renegotiate a better deal for Iran failed. Adding insult to injury oil price collapsed during the Great Depression of the 1930s further reducing oil revenues to Iran. When the Shah complained he was removed by the British and replaced by his son who the British saw as an easier puppet to do business with.

U.S.-Iranian relations during the early post–World War II years were as friendly as that of U.S.-Cuba relations. During the long rule of Shah Mohammad Reza Pahlavi from 1941 to 1979 the United States was Iran's foremost political, economic and military ally. The Pahlavi family had ruled Iran since 1925 but it was the British who had forced the abdication of the senior Pahlavi in favor of his son in 1941. Shah Reza junior made frequent visits to Washington to confer with U.S. presidents from Truman to Eisenhower to Kennedy to Nixon to Carter. But like Cuba the increased domination of Iran by the United States eroded Iran's independence and the Shah was increasingly viewed by Iranians as a U.S. puppet dictator like Batista in Cuba. In the post–World War II period the Americans had replaced the British and French as the dominant military power in the Middle East.

In 1951 the Iranian people found a democratically elected prime minister, *Mohammad Mosaddegh,* who was not willing to be a puppet of either the British or the Americans. This is good news for democracy but not for the economy. As we have said many times before, the West can bomb you back to the Stone Age or impoverish you with economic embargoes. Mosaddegh was a seasoned Iranian politician who had begun his political career opposing the Anglo-Persian Agreement of 1919. That was the unratified agreement, which basically gave away the Iranian oil to the British by confirming the drilling rights of APOC as well as reinstating British semicolonial rule of Iran. Prior to this agreement Britain had competed with Russia for colonial control of Iran. The 1919 agreement made Iran the British buffer semicolonial state between the now Communist state of Russia and the British jewel of the Crown, India. By 1951 Iranians were fed up with the British both because of their colonial aspirations and their continued theft of Iranian oil. Mosaddegh led a movement to nationalize APOC which the Iranian parliament supported. The Western puppet Shah attempted to replace Mosaddegh but failed. Enter the American propaganda about the evils of Communism. If the Shah was pro-Western then Mosaddegh must be a Communist. How else can you explain a politician who could ever dislike American freedoms to conquer, kill and invade at will? The West had every right to steal Iran's oil if only to prevent the Communists from getting it.

The Americans launched "Operation Ajax" to help the British overthrow the **democratic** government of Iran and continue to steal Iran's oil. The British had already enforced a military blockade to prevent Iran from selling its oil. This was intended to impoverish the Iranian people into submission to Western imperialism. But without American support the British would not have succeeded. They were no longer the world's superpower. Britain's **racist** prime minister, Winston Churchill, was able to convince the American president, Dwight Eisenhower, that Iran's **democratically** elected secular leader, Mosaddegh, was a threat to the West in its Cold War with the Soviet Union. That was not difficult to do since any leader who was not vehemently pro-American was a Communist spy for the Soviet Union, by definition. The American CIA went to work on Iran with a vengeance shortly after Eisenhower's election to the American presidency. Eisenhower's secretary of state, *John Foster Dulles,* became a world-famous Western leader by drafting plans for the overthrow of the **democratic** government of Iran. It was a bit surprising that Dulles did not receive the Nobel "War" Prize for being the savior of Western civilization. In addition to overthrowing the Iranian **democracy**, he aided the French **warmongering** in Vietnam, another reason for the Nobel Committee to have awarded him the "war" prize they awarded to President Obama and other American **warmongers** like Henry Kissinger and Teddy Roosevelt. Dulles referred to Communism as "godless terrorism." Since his brother, Allen Dulles, was the head of the CIA it was easy for John Foster to get the CIA to do its dirty propaganda work in Iran and organize the coup to overthrow Mosaddegh. His brother allocated $US 1 million for the removal of Mosaddegh, and John Foster sent Kermit "the Frog" Roosevelt to Tehran to oversee the coup. Kermit Roosevelt was the grandson of Nobel Laureate, **warmongering** Teddy Roosevelt. John Foster Dulles's success was rewarded by *Time Magazine* as Man of the Year, but not by the Nobel Committee. How sad?

Among the weapons used by the CIA was a mink coat given to the Shah's sister as a bribe. Apparently, the Shah's sister, Ashraf Pahlavi, was a popular political troublemaker who could influence her brother to agree to the crime being committed by the United States and Britain. Even puppets fear future prosecutions with good cause. Once they help the West to get what the West wants they are always abandoned by the West. Look at what President George H. Bush did to one of their own SOB dictators, **Saddam Hussein,** after he failed to successfully conquer Iran for the American Empire. A more recent example is that in 2015, the Canadian government announced its intention to prosecute the Syrian who tortured their citizen Maher Arar in Syria, even though it was the Canadian government which conspired with the Americans to deport him to Syria in 2002 to be tortured, as one of many instances of extraordinary renditions by the United States under President George W. Bush. Of course, no one, besides the Americans, would ever dare to prosecute the Canadian government for their complicity in the torture.

The mink coat bribe to the sister of the Shah and the U.S. threat to proceed unilaterally helped to bring the Shah on side as coconspirator in the American military coup to topple yet another **democratic** government. The Shah feared being left out in the cold since the United States is always able to find another local puppet to replace their prior local puppet. After safely escaping to Rome the Shah issued a decree to replace the prime minister, democratically elected by the Iranian people, with an American puppet, **General** Fazlollah Zahedi. Military coups need military men not civilians. The Shah's support provided the propaganda for the United States to claim legitimacy. General Fazlollah Zahedi personally led the tanks to the home of the **democratically** elected prime minister and arrested him on August 20, 1953. With Mosaddegh safely behind bars the Shah returned from hiding in Rome two days later. Mosaddegh was kept under house arrest until his death in 1967. The United States provided the military support to the Shah to rule Iran as a U.S.-backed military dictatorship. Twenty years later Henry Kissinger applied the same Kermit "the frog" Roosevelt's Iranian model in Chile, to overthrow the **democratically** elected Allende, and replace him with the Pinochet military dictatorship. Unlike Dulles, Kissinger did receive the Nobel "war" prize for his efforts. This overthrow of **democracy** by the United States in Iran enabled the continued theft of Iranian oil by the British. How can Iranians ever forgive the Americans and British for such a crime? Of course the British and Americans will never be punished for such crimes because they are "above the law." The typical convoluted logic of Western civilization demonizes the victim, Iran, not the criminals, Britain and the United States.

Imperialists never learn that colonized peoples will not fully surrender their freedoms. They retreat in the face of overwhelming military force only to find new ways to fight. So it was with Iran. Iranians had experienced many years of Western influence which had developed their economy and made them aware of western values and traditions. Many Iranians were receptive to westernization but not to Western colonization. Iranians had voted for Mosaddegh because he was seen as their leader in a secular **democracy** and one strong enough to resist British imperialism. Alongside this long history of westernization was strong resistance by some to this secularization and straying from traditions and faith. The insistence by Britain to steal Iran's oil and the military and intelligence aid provided to the British by the United States, using the ridiculous excuse of fighting Communism, was the catalyst for Iranians to support the overthrow of Western imperial powers by the religious traditionalists led by the popular *Ayatollah Khomeini.*

I will never understand why religion has the power to garner such mass support for revolutions. But I am fully aware of its immense power to persuade the poor, the hungry, the angry, the disillusioned, the clergy, the rich, the army, the leaders, the educated, the betrayed, the weak and the powerful alike. This is what the exiled Ayatollah harnessed against the militarily powerful American *Satan* to banish their puppet, the Shah, and take back Iran for the Iranian people. That was 1979. It was followed by the Iranian "hostage crisis." A military rescue of the hostages failed. The United States began a policy of isolating Iran to impoverish it. It ended diplomatic relations on April 7, 1980. Military intervention had failed so it resorted to its secondary weapon, economic embargo. It was using the same weapon President Kennedy initiated against Cuba after America's failed "Bay of Pigs" military invasion of Cuba. As I said before the Americans bomb you back to the Stone Age or impoverish you if you indicate even the slightest sign that you are not totally in love with their warmongering ways.

President Reagan never gave up on a military solution to Iran's desire to be independent of the United States and Britain. Rather than having the United States invade he would use Saddam Hussein to do his dirty deed. He removed Iraq from the American list of states sponsoring terrorism and supplied Saddam with arms including chemical and biological weapons. But like his predecessors he failed to understand the determination of people to resist colonization. Despite direct involvement of the American military in 1988 when the United States launched *Operation Praying Mantis* against Iran, the largest U.S. naval operation since WWII, the U.S.-inspired Iraq-Iran war ended in a stalemate and a financially bankrupted Saddam Hussein. When Saddam was given the green light by the United States to invade Kuwait and steal its oil in lieu of promised payment by the United States for the cost of war with Iran the Saudis complained. President George H. Bush saw it expedient to do the usual American betrayal of old allies. Saddam had served his purpose and was no longer useful to the United States. The Saudis were still extremely important to the United States. Attacking Saddam in Kuwait would both get rid of an embarrassing old ally and enhance America's relation with the now powerful Saudis. Iraq was weak and had failed to destroy Iran. The Saudis could now be used against Iran by exploiting an age-old religious dispute. Just like the Catholic/Protestant split in Christianity there is a Sunni/Shia split in Islam. Just as Britain led the Protestants against Catholic France and Spain the Saudis lead the Sunnis against Iran's leadership of the Shias.

Typical of its hypocrisy, the United States expressed its regret both for overthrowing Mosaddegh and instigating the Iraq-Iran war while continuing its policy of isolating Iran, supporting Israel and destroying the Middle East. That regret was voiced by President Clinton's secretary of state, Madeleine Albright, in 2000. It was the typical meaningless face-saving gestures made by American Democrats. In fact, Iran-U.S. trade was returning after the end of the Iraq-Iran war in 1988. It was President Clinton who imposed a total embargo on all trade with Iran in 1995. Economic sanctions against Iran imposed by President Clinton were never lifted and continued under his successors, Republican Bush and Democratic Obama.

As I have said many times before, the planting of Israel in the Middle East had very little to do with the creation of a home for persecuted Jews but mostly to do with reclaiming the entire Middle-East for Christianity. While the Soviet Union was a superpower it restrained the United States from overt military invasions. That restraint fell apart when Gorbachev foolishly believed the lies of the West. The West has never been against walls like the Berlin Wall because it's a wall. If it were it would not help Israel build a wall on Palestinian land. Today the United States is building a wall on its border with Mexico. EU states such as Hungary are busy building several walls to keep out refugees fleeing Western bombing of their countries. The West was against the Berlin Wall only because it helped the Soviets contain Western expansion eastward. But Gorbachev was a fool and brought about the collapse of the only deterrent the Middle East had against Western invasions. Rather belatedly, President Putin is fighting an uphill battle to restore that deterrent.

I have explained in my previous books how 9/11 gave the dedicated American warmongers the perfect excuse for invading and reconquering the Middle East. It began with the invasion of Afghanistan in 2001 but stalled after the failed invasion of Iraq in 2003. Prior to this failed invasion of Iraq, President George W. Bush had identified on January 29, 2002, the three countries for immediate regime change through unilateral military invasions by the United States. The three countries he called the "Axis of Evil" were Iraq, Iran and North Korea. As a result of his failure in Iraq his planned invasions never got to Iran much less conquer the entire Middle East as initially intended by him and his PNAC ideologues. *See Rise and Fall of the American Empire,* chapter 10. But the United States is never one to give up. The George W. Bush administration ignored evidence provided by UN inspectors that Iraq had no WMDs and invaded. In 2015 the Republicans are again ignoring the evidence of UN inspectors with regard to Iran's nuclear program to provide an excuse to invade Iran. The Democrats are somewhat more cautious. Can the United States benefit more from using Iran as it had done with Saddam Hussein before Iraq had self-destructed from eight years of U.S.-instigated war with Iran? In the lead up to the first U.S. war against Saddam Hussein the Western media never mentioned Saddam's prior role as America's SOB dictator. All it did was demonize Saddam. Likewise in 2015 the Western media made no mention of American wrongs against Iran. All it did was demonize Iran.

The United States began accusing Iran of building a nuclear bomb in 1973 in preparation for its planned invasion after its expected successful invasion of Iraq. Recall that the excuse it had used for invading Iraq was that Iraq had WMDs and only the United States has the civilized authority to determine who is allowed to possess WMDs. It does not matter if the country has WMDs or not. As we know Iraq did not possess WMDs and the United States knew that. What matters is only that the United States has accused the country of possessing WMDs. Once the United States makes the accusation the Western media will do the rest rather willingly since they are presstitutes. Despite its failed invasion of Iraq, in 2005, the United States warned the head of the "International" Atomic Energy Agency, Mohamed ElBaradei, to "toughen his stance" against Iran, in other words, fabricate lies about Iran's phantom nuclear program, or lose his job. As I have said before, what the Western media calls "International" means Western. Since 2003 Iran has lived with the fear of a military invasion by the United States similar to its invasions of Afghanistan and Iraq. Iran made numerous efforts to discuss the issue with the United States. The United States naturally rejected the overtures by Iran since it was bent on finding an excuse for military invasion. What saved Iran from invasion was America's failed invasions in Afghanistan and Iraq. Iran was never removed from the American agenda to invade only delayed in the hopes that its attempts at conquests in Afghanistan and Iraq would improve. That is still the hope of Republicans in 2015 despite more military failures in Libya, Syria and Yemen. In the meantime the CIA continues to conduct covert operations in Iran to undermine the government and find larger numbers of American puppets among the Iranian population. As the economic embargo impoverishes more and more Iranians, it's easier to find puppets who simply want to feed their families.

President Obama is desperate to improve on his legacy of failures. He has failed in Afghanistan, Iraq, Libya, Syria, Ukraine and Yemen. He sees absolutely no chance of a successful military invasion of Iran. Rather than adding one more failure to his very long list of failures he is hoping that Iran could be used to minimize his other failures. A deal with Iran will get Iranian help to fight ISIS in both Iraq and Syria. In addition, it will bring Iran, Russia and Bashar al-Assad on the same side with the United States in Syria. In 2015 Syria has become the most obvious failure of President Obama because of the growing millions of refugees. Obama's wars had already created 60 million refugees. What is different in 2015 is that a few of the refugees are forcing their way into Western Europe. Western Europe had no complaints with the 60 million refugees when they stayed in the Middle East. The purpose of the military invasions by the United States and its allies is to destroy the will of the Muslim inhabitants to resist reconquest by the Christians. By killing them, injuring them, destroying their homes, destroying their livelihoods, turning them into refugees and generally impoverishing and demoralizing them the West is using the same methods it used against the First Nations and original inhabitants in the New World, Australia and New Zealand. It's genocide on a massive scale.

But in 2015 a small fraction of the impoverished are finding their way to Western Europe. So far they number less than **two percent** of the 60 million created by the West, but to the West two percent is still too much. Canada, for example, has spent at least **five years** to agree on whether to take ten thousand. If it does eventually take the promised ten thousand, it will spend much to ensure that the ten thousand are the most educated and most pro-Western in their outlook. One Conservative candidate in Canada's 2015 general election, *Joe Daniel,* has already openly voiced what his boss, Steven Harper was implying. During the elections Harper repeated incessantly that Canadian security trumped humanitarian concerns but this Conservative candidate was not shy in expanding on the standard convoluted logic of Western civilization. "The refugee crisis was some type of conspiracy to plant Muslims in Europe and he did not want to see that in Canada." His convoluted logical explanation of the creation of 60 million refugees by the genocidal bombing by Canada and the West was that these refugees had mysteriously forced the hand of the West to bomb their countries so that they would become refugees and stream into Europe to "plant Muslims in Europe." Give the man a prize for graduating from kindergarten. Many of his voters have not. Another Conservative candidate, *Dianne Watts,* said that "the violence inflicted on the people of Syria and Iraq cannot go unanswered." Her solution for this crime was not to stop the violence inflicted by Canadian bombers but to warn Canadians to fear "jihadi terrorists" and support the increased bombing proposed by her boss, Steven Harper. Implicitly, her solution to the violence inflicted on the people of Syria and Iraq was to inflict more violence on them. Another great example of the convoluted logic of Western civilization.

As a result of a few of the 60 million refugees finding their way into Europe, President Obama has been pressured by his Western European allies to find some kind of peaceful resolution to the civil war he created in Syria. Colonizing the Middle East is an admirable crusading act for all Christians but if it brings the Muslims we are trying to destroy into our homelands the cost far exceeds the conquest. The two decades of incessant Western bombing with their civilized jets had not succeeded in destroying Muslim resistance. The West's foremost ally in the Middle East, *Saudi Arabia,* had stepped up to the plate by bombing Yemen back to the Stone Age, but that had failed to stop ISIS. Another Western ally, *Egypt,* had created its own internal mess by forcing the Muslim Brotherhood to combine forces with al-Qaeda. A peaceful resolution, albeit a temporary one, was the only way to halt the imminent flow of refugees into Europe until a more robust military solution is invented. If such a temporary peaceful solution can only be achieved by sucking up to Iran rather than continuing to demonize Iran, so be it. Use the powerful Western propaganda machine and the subservient Western media to transform Iran from the devil to the savior. Iran desperately wants relief from Western sanctions. The West knows that Iran could never be a threat to Israel since it was the West that fabricated that myth.

So it was that President Obama would get the opportunity of leaving a legacy where he had made peace with two of America's arch enemies, Cuba and Iran. He would finally be able to justify his Nobel Peace Prize and argue that it was not a war prize. He wins and his Western European allies win. Iran elected a new president, Hassan Rouhani, in 2013. This made it easier for the Western propaganda machine since the West had not yet demonized him the way it had demonized the former president, Mahmoud Ahmadinejad. The Iranian constitution did not allow Ahmadinejad to run again since he had served the permitted two terms but the West could easily suggest to its gullible electorate that he had been ousted by the people of Iran and replaced by a lesser devil. The West had already accused Ahmadinejad of stealing the 2009 election much like the Democrats had accused George W. Bush of stealing both the 2000 and 2004 elections. Moreover, President Obama could argue that rapprochement with Iran was based on reaching a nuclear deal with Iran rather than stopping the flow of refugees the West had created and dealing with the *Islamophobia* he and other Western leaders had stirred up.

Prior to the planting of Israel in the Middle East by the West as an instrument to help its recolonization of the Middle East the West had stirred up anti-Semitic hatred against Jews. This deep seated discrimination of Jews by the West is well documented. After creating the state of Israel the West has moved toward reducing anti-Semitism but has so far failed. At the present time it has more to gain from promoting Islamophobia than condemning it. But its pretense at civilized behavior prevent most, but not all, of its leaders from openly and explicitly promoting hatred of Muslims. Some leaders like Canada's Steven Harper openly promote hatred of Muslims under the guise of protecting women from having to wear the Niqab. President Obama finds himself on the horns of a dilemma. He wants a temporary peace with Iran to stop the flow of refugees to Western Europe from the countries he and his allies have bombed back to the Stone Age, Afghanistan, Iraq, Syria, Libya, and Yemen. But he cannot be seen as against Islamophobia since that's the lynchpin of his warmongering foreign policy. It's no longer sufficient to wage wars and invasions to fight Communism. He must be firm in his conviction that the threat to the United States is not Communism but Islam to justify his addiction to warmongering and military invasions. That is the reason for framing his rapprochement with Iran within the context of nuclear disarmament. But that is also easier said than done given the prior American propaganda that UN inspectors could not be trusted. They could not be trusted to verify lack of WMDs in Iraq and cannot be trusted to tell the truth about Iran's nuclear program. In reality, UN inspectors could not be threatened or bribed into telling lies since **falsifying** what the inspections find is the only reason the United States permit its puppet, the UN, to inspect.

Caught between a rock and a hard place on Iran, President Obama has determined that fighting the U.S. propaganda that Iran and UN inspectors could not be trusted was less of a challenge than fighting the U.S. propaganda that Islam is the greatest threat to American security. Together with his allies, Britain, France, Germany and the EU, he concluded a nuclear deal with Iran in July 2015. China and Russia naturally supported the deal since they have always trusted Iran and opposed Western invasions in the Middle East. China and Russia see this as a win for them as well as Iran and Syria. They rightly see it as the relative decline in Western hegemony resulting from the global shift in economic power from the West to the East. Despite decades of Western support for Israel, Egypt and Saudi Arabia; Iran and Syria could not be conquered or destroyed. Without the conquest or destruction of Iran and

Syria the Western goal of recolonizing the Middle East since its defeat of the Ottoman Empire during World War I, has stalled once again. George W. Bush failed, despite the lack of Russian objections, because he could not conquer Iraq. President Obama failed because Vladimir Putin restored Russia's historic protection of Iran and Syria from Western warmongering.

Saudi and Israeli Objections

It should be clear that I do not subscribe to the view that any American president, including President Obama, is smart. It should therefore not be surprising to anyone that President Obama would repeat the mistake of President George H. Bush with regard to prior consultation with America's second most important ally in the Middle East after Israel, Saudi Arabia, before acting. George H. had given the green light to Saddam Hussein to invade Kuwait without prior consultation with Saudi Arabia. As a result George H. was forced to begin the First Gulf War to oust Saddam from Kuwait. That war began the gradual erosion of Iraqi support for U.S. colonization in the Middle East. The United States kept Israel and Saudi Arabia as allies but lost Iraq. By default the loss of her third most important ally in the region increased the influence of Iran.

The United States exploited the Shia/Sunni split in Islam to pit Saudi Arabia against Iran in its fight to colonize the Middle East. The United States also provided the military and economic support for Israel to aid its colonization of the Middle East. This pitted Islam against Judaism. The Christian wars against Islam co-opted the support of Judaism by creating the Jewish state on Palestinian land. The West knows the power of religion and used both the Jews and the Sunni Muslims to aid its colonizing mission. But this policy of pitting both the Jews and Sunni Muslims against Iran has so far failed to destroy Iran. Russian intervention and the flow of Muslim refugees to America's allies in Western Europe has forced President Obama to rethink America's long war with Iran. This does not sit well with America's two foremost allies, Israel and Saudi Arabia.

With the failure of both President George W. Bush and President Obama to invade and destroy Iran the United States is now faced with having to work cooperatively with Iran to deal with attacks from ISIS. The turning point for the West came when Russia refused to sanction the destruction of Syria in the same manner in which the West had destroyed Libya. Russian intervention prevented a UN resolution to destroy Syria, and Russian bombing aided the Assad regime against the Western-supported rebels. President Obama's decision to switch his warmongering from regime change in Syria to fighting ISIS has further strengthened the influence of Iran in the region. This has angered America's two remaining allies in the Middle East, Israel and Saudi Arabia. The nuclear deal agreed to by President Obama in April 2015 further angered both Israel and Saudi Arabia. Relief from economic and financial sanctions will increase the economic growth of Iran relative to Saudi Arabia and Israel.

Saudi Arabia has been flexing its muscle in the region to signal its anger with the United States and President Obama. It invaded Yemen but was unable to colonize it. On January 2, 2016, Saudi Arabia executed a popular Shia religious leader, *Nimr Baqir al-Nimr.* Protests erupted across the region and the Saudi embassy in Iran was attacked. In response to the attack on the Saudi embassy, Saudi Arabia broke off diplomatic relations with Iran. Several Sunni-Muslim states broke off diplomatic relations with Iran in support of Saudi Arabia.

BIBLIOGRAPHY AND REFERENCES

In addition to the books listed below, I have used the Internet extensively to check my facts. Anyone using references from the web knows that one article provides references to other articles. It would be too time consuming to list here every article I used as fact checks. The reader can easily google the topic to check my facts. The following is a small sample only. The interpretation of these facts is entirely my own.

1. Armstrong, Karen: *Holy War: The Crusades and Their Impact on Today's World*, Anchor Books, New York, 2001
2. Baker, Simon: *Ancient Rome: The Rise and Fall of an Empire*, BBC Books, London, 2006
3. Bard, Mitchell G.: *The Complete Idiot's Guide to the Middle East*, third edition, Alpha Books, New York, 2005
4. Bloom, Jonathan and Blair, Sheila: *Islam: The Empire of Faith*, BBC Worldwide Ltd., London, 2001
5. Boatswain, Tim and Nicolson, Colin: *A Traveller's History of Greece*, second edition, Windrush Press, London, 2003
6. Boatwright, Mart T., Gargola, Daniel J. and Talbert, Richard J. A. : *The Romans: From Village to Empire*, Oxford University Press, New York, 2004
7. Camp, John and Fisher, Elizabeth: *The World of the Ancient Greeks*, Thames & Hudson Ltd., London, 2002
8. Chua, Amy: *Day of Empire: How Hyperpowers Rise to Global Dominance and Why They Fall*, Doubleday, New York, 2007
9. David, Ron: *Arabs & Israel for Beginners*, Writers and Readers Inc., USA, 2001
10. en.wikipedia.org/wiki/Slavery in ancient Greece
11. en.wikipedia.org/wiki/Peloponnesian War
12. en.wikipedia.org/wiki/Alexander the Great
13. en.wikipedia.org/wiki/Military of ancient Rome
14. en.wikipedia.org/wiki/Constantine the Great
15. en.wikipedia.org/wiki/Islam
16. en.wikipedia.org/wiki/Byzantine Empire

17. en.wikipedia.org/wiki/Sassanid Empire
18. en.wikipedia.org/wiki/Saudi Arabia
19. en.wikipedia.org/wiki/Persian Gulf
20. en.wikipedia.org/wiki/Battle of Yarmouk
21. en.wikipedia.org/wiki/Gregorian mission
22. en.wikipedia.org/wiki/History of the Papacy
23. en.wikipedia.org/wiki/Dome of the Rock
24. en.wikipedia.org/wiki/Maccabees
25. en.wikipedia.org/wiki/Carolingian Empire
26. en.wikipedia.org/wiki/Franks
27. en.wikipedia.org/wiki/Battle of Tours
28. en.wikipedia.org/wiki/Third Crusade
29. en.wikipedia.org/wiki/Anglo-Dutch Wars
30. en.wikipedia.org/wiki/War in Afghanistan (2001–present)
31. en.wikipedia.org/.../1998 United States embassy bombings
32. en.wikipedia.org/?title = Barack Obama
33. en.wikipedia.org/wiki/Michelle Obama
34. en.wikipedia.org/wiki/Egyptian Revolution of 2011
35. en.wikipedia.org/wiki/Illegal immigration to the United States
36. en.wikipedia.org/wiki/Occupy Wall Street
37. en.wikipedia.org/.../Wealth inequality in the United States
38. en.wikipedia.org/wiki/Syrian Civil War
39. en.wikipedia.org/wiki/Military intervention against ISIL
40. en.wikipedia.org/wiki/Yemeni Civil War (2015)
41. en.wikipedia.org/wiki/Al-Qaeda insurgency in Yemen
42. Ferguson, Niall: *Civilization: Is the West History?* TV documentary, Knowledge Network, Burnaby BC, Canada, 2011
43. Ferguson, Niall: *Empire: The Rise and Demise of the British World Order and the Lessons for Global Power*, Basic Books, New York, 2003
44. Glubb, John Bagot: *The Lost Centuries: From the Muslim Empires to the Renaissance of Europe: 1145–1453*, Hodder and Stoughton, London, 1967
45. Goldschmidt Jr., Arthur and Davidson, Lawrence: *A Concise History of the Middle East*, eighth edition, Westview Press, Boulder, Colorado, 2006

46. Gombrich, E. H.: *A Little History of the World*, Translated by Caroline Mustill, Yale University Press, New Haven and London, 2005
47. Gott, Richard: *Britain's Empire: Resistance, Repression and Revolt*, verso, London, 2011
48. Grant, Michael: *The Founders of the Western World: A History of Greece and Rome*, Macmillan Publishing Company, New York, 1991
49. Heurtley, W. A., Crawley, C. W. and Woodhouse, C. M.: *A Short History of Greece: From Early Times to 1964*, Cambridge University Press, London, 1965
50. Hindley, Geoffrey: *The Crusades: Islam and Christianity in the Struggle for Supremacy*, Carroll & Graf Publishers, New York, 2003
51. Hourani, Albert: *A History of the Arab Peoples*, Harvard University Press, Cambridge, 2002
52. Jeffers, H. Paul: *The Complete Idiot's Guide to Jerusalem*, Alpha Books, New York, 2004
53. Kamen, Henry: *Empire: How Spain Became a World Power: 1492–1763*, Harper Collins Publishers, New York, 2003
54. Kerrigan, Michael: *Ancient Greece and the Mediterranean*, BBC Worldwide Ltd., London, 2001
55. Lang, Sean: *European History for Dummies*, John Wiley & Sons, England, 2006
56. Lewis, Bernard: *What Went Wrong? Western Impact and Middle Eastern Response*, Oxford University Press, New York, 2002
57. Lye, Keith: *World Fact Book*, second edition, Firefly books, Canada, 2006
58. Mackey, Sandra: *The Iranians: Persia, Islam and the Soul of a Nation*, Penguin Books, New York, 1996
59. Mansfield, Peter: *A History of the Middle East*, Viking, London, 1991
60. Morgan, Giles: *Byzantium: Capital of an Ancient Empire*, Pocket Essentials, Harpenden, Herts, 2007
61. National Geographic: *Essential Visual History of the World*, Washington DC, 2007

62. Palmer, R. R. and Colton, Joel: *A History of the Modern World*, Fourth edition, Alfred A. Knopf, Inc. New York, 1971
63. Paris, Erna: *The End of Days: A Story of Tolerance, Tyranny, and the Expulsion of Jews from Spain*, Lester Publishing, Toronto, 1995
64. Read, Jan: *The Moors in Spain and Portugal*, Rowman and Littlefield, New Jersey, 1974
65. Roberts, J. M.: *The New Penguin History of the World*, Fifth edition, Penguin Books, London, 2007
66. Roberts, J. M.: *The Penguin History of Europe*, Penguin Books, London, 1997
67. Robinson, Francis, editor: *The Cambridge Illustrated History of the Islamic World*, Cambridge University Press, London, 1996
68. Schaeffer, Francis A.: *How Should We Then Live? The Rise and Decline of Western Thought and Culture*, Crossway Books, Westchester, Illinois, 1985
69. Spengler, Oswald: *The Decline of the West*, Abridged edition, Vintage Books, New York, 1962
70. Time Life's Lost Civilizations: *Rome: The Ultimate Empire*, Time Life Video & Television, Alexandria, VA 22314, 1995
71. Tragert, Joseph: *The Complete Idiot's Guide to Understanding Iraq*, Second edition, Alpha Books, New York, 2004
72. Wells, H. G.: *A Short History of the World*, Penguin Books, Penguin Classics, London, 2006
73. www.economist.com/.../21595902-expelling-record-numbers-immigrants-costly-way-make-america-less-dynamic-barack-obama
74. www.washingtonpost.com/.../forget-what-youre-hearing-the-civil-war-in-yemen-is-not-a-sectarian-conflict/
75. www.cfr.org/yemen/al-qaeda-arabian-peninsula-aqap/p9369

INDEX

C

L

M

N

O

P

R

S

T

Printed in the United States
By Bookmasters